Pengui

Law and Society

General Editors: O. Kahn-Freund and
K. W. Wedderburn

Law in a Changing Society
Second edition

Wolfgang Friedmann

Law in a Changing Society
Second edition

Wolfgang Friedmann

Penguin Books

To May

Penguin Books Ltd, Harmondsworth,
Middlesex, England
Penguin Books Inc., 7110 Ambassador Road,
Baltimore, Md 21207, U.S.A.
Penguin Books Australia Ltd,
Ringwood, Victoria, Australia

First published by Stevens & Sons 1959
Abridged edition published by Penguin Books 1964
Second edition published by Stevens & Sons
and Penguin Books 1972
Copyright © Stevens & Sons, 1959, 1964, 1972

Made and printed in Great Britain by
Richard Clay (The Chaucer Press) Ltd, Bungay, Suffolk
Set in Monotype Times Roman

Contents

Editorial Foreword

Professor Wolfgang Friedmann is a pioneer in the venture to which we hope this series can make a contribution: indeed without the lifelong work of such an author Law and Society as a series might never have been born. This book is a thoroughly revised second edition of a work first published in 1959 which, as Professor Friedmann explains, was itself based on his *Law and Social Change in Contemporary Britain* published twenty years ago in 1951. In his Foreword to that book Lord Denning remarked that its great merit was 'that it shows us the pattern of legal development against its social background: and thus enables us to know what we are about'. Since then this influential work has become a first reader for all those students, lawyers or even judges, who have been led to inquire into the relationship of law and society.

The present volume maintains, even expands, the enormous canvas of scholarship and knowledge on which Professor Friedmann paints his picture. If it often concentrates upon English and North American sources, elsewhere it reaches out to Commonwealth, Continental, Soviet and other foreign systems and, last but certainly not least, to the problems of the international community of nations where the role of 'law' is at once still so uncertain, and so important. The author brings to this massive sweep of material his own personal selection and interpretation.

It is seen through one man's eyes, but they are the eyes of a man with a background of training and research in a wide variety of legal systems and who has devoted years of his life to the quest for the elusive interrelation of these legal systems and their surrounding social fabric.

'The basic theme of the present book – the dual function of the legal order as a reactor to, and increasingly as initiator of, social change –

has remained unaltered', Professor Friedmann writes. The theme is as pertinent now as it was when the author began his long career. And what he has to say remains in this new edition the essential starting point for all inquiring readers.

O.K.M.F.
K.W.W.

Preface to Second Edition

The first edition of the present book – itself a greatly enlarged version of an earlier book entitled *Law and Social Change in Contemporary Britain* (1951) – was published in 1959. The abridged Pelican edition was published in 1964.

The intervening decade has seen many important legal changes in many fields. The basic theme of the present book – i.e. the dual function of the legal order as a reacter to, and increasingly as initiator of, social change – has remained unaltered. Hence, the first chapter is the only one that has not undergone any substantial change except for a new section on civil disobedience and legal change. For the rest, the book has been largely re-written, although the changes in some of the chapters have been more fundamental than in others.

In some areas, such as family law, the last decade has brought fundamental changes in many countries, with respect to divorce, abortion, the status of illegitimate children, matrimonial property, and other matters. The very function and ambit of criminal law and criminal sanction has been put in question by recent developments in social psychology and genetic engineering. The substitution of insurance for tort liability, particularly in the field of motor car accidents, has become a problem of increasing urgency. The growing mechanization, and the centralization of power, both at the government and the corporate level, has made a re-examination of the relation between public power and the individual a matter of urgent necessity. The role of international law and organization in international society has more and more become a question on which the ordered survival of mankind will depend. And any student of the relation of law and society must reflect on the changing function of law in the increasingly interdependent society of the 1970s, as one of a number of interreacting components in a complex web of systems analysis, social planning and decision-making.

In an attempt to respond to these and other developments in the interrelation of law and society, the present edition contains two entirely new chapters: chapter 8, which examines the alternatives of economic competition, public regulation and public enterprise; and a concluding chapter, which examines the changing role of law in the society of the seventies.

Chapters 5, 6 and 7 are entirely rewritten versions of chapters dealing with the same subject in the previous edition. Chapters 9 and 10 of the former edition have been combined into one new chapter on 'corporate power, the law, the individual and the state,' which has also been largely rewritten.

In the Public Law section, it is mainly chapter 12: 'The Problem of Administrative Remedies and Procedures' that has been rewritten, in view of the new challenges posed by the threat to environment, and the increasing adoption of the Ombudsman institution, as an attempt to reestablish direct contact between public power and the individual.

The section on 'Law between Nations' reflects the many developments in international law, and even more the many unsolved challenges to our generation by the growing chasm between the needs of an increasingly interdependent world, and the anachronism of a world of 'sovereign' states, which still fail to cooperate in matters of common survival.

The major revision in the chapter on 'Courts and the Evolution of the Law' consists in a survey of the 'Warren Court' period in the United States, and the somewhat more fitful law-making ventures of the House of Lords.

Revisions in the chapters on 'Contract and Property' reflect the growing concern, especially in American law, with the protection of the consumer, and the growing use of public law restrictions on the rights of property, caused by slum conditions and the rapid deterioration of the environment. The need for a drastic strengthening of public law controls over private enterprise and property – as a matter of survival rather than of ideology – is a persistent theme throughout the book.

Apart from bringing statutory and judicial developments up to date, the comparative base of the book has been greatly widened.

While English and American law supply the bulk of materials used, significant developments in different systems, both of the common law and the civil law world, have been noted, without any attempt at exhaustiveness.

I am deeply conscious of the great difficulty of the task attempted here. The field is immense, and even the most comprehensive approach must remain fragmentary. Nor does the law stand still: references have been included, for example, to the English Industrial Relations Act of 1971, but the tone of my discussion of law and the labour systems rests inevitably on the wealth of case law decided before that Act received the Royal Assent (and he would be a rash author anyway who assumed that a new Act rendered previous case law obsolete). Finally, while I am painfully conscious of the inadequacy of my knowledge in many of the subjects surveyed in this book, a symposium could not be a substitute for a book that must reflect one man's approach and philosophy.

Every reader will find something missing. A partial explanation is that a number of matters that would be pertinent to the present book have been fully discussed in the most recent edition of my *Legal Theory* (5th edn, 1967). Among these is a chapter on 'Science and Legal Theory', which would otherwise have been included in the present book. Since I want to avoid unnecessary duplication, I must refer readers to *Legal Theory* for some of the theoretical foundations of contemporary legal science.

Acknowledgements

I am greatly indebted to my research assistant, Michael Kaprelian, J.D. for the great care with which he has checked on statutory and judicial developments as well as recent writings in the many fields and countries covered by this book. His help has been indispensable.

I am also indebted to my administrative assistant, Miss Dorothy Kane, B.A. for her help in preparing the manuscript for publication.

My Columbia University colleagues, William L. Cary, Walter Gellhorn and Albert J. Rosenthal have read individual chapters and made helpful criticisms and suggestions.

Professor Otto Kahn-Freund of Oxford University has read all the parts concerned with collective bargaining, labour relations and family law and has made many detailed comments and criticisms which have been invaluable to me. This is only the most recent of innumerable occasions on which I have benefited from the scholarship, insight and generosity of a friend who decades ago made me aware of the social function of law. My debt to this eminent scholar and teacher is great indeed.

I am grateful to Penguin and Stevens & Sons for their collaboration in producing this volume.

Part One
Instruments of Legal Change

Chapter 1
The Interactions of Legal and Social Change

Savigny and Bentham

The controversy between those who believe that law should essentially follow, not lead, and that it should do so slowly, in response to clearly formulated social sentiment – and those who believe that the law should be a determined agent in the creation of new norms, is one of the recurrent themes of the history of legal thought. It is tellingly illustrated by the conflicting approaches of Savigny and Bentham.[1]

For Savigny, a bitter opponent of the rationalizing and law-making tendencies spurred by the French Revolution, law was 'found', not 'made'. Only when popular custom, in part articulated by lawyers, had fully evolved, could and should the legislature take action. Savigny particularly deprecated the trend towards the codification of law, inaugurated by the Napoleonic Codes, and spreading rapidly over the civilized world.

By contrast, Bentham, a fervent believer in the efficacy of rationally constructed reforming laws, devoted a great part of his life to the drafting of codes for a large number of countries, from Czarist Russia to the newly emergent republics of Latin America. While most of these efforts were not immediately successful, notably in his own country, whether in the field of civil law, criminal law, evidence or poverty law, his philosophy became increasingly influential as the nineteenth century progressed. It was Bentham's philosophy, and that of his disciples, which turned the British Parliament – and similar institutions in other countries – into active legislative instruments, effecting social reforms, partly in response to, and partly in stimulation of, felt social needs.[2] It is essentially the judge-made law that,

1. For a more detailed account of their theories see Friedmann (1967, pp. 209–13 on Savigny, pp. 312–20 on Bentham).
2. The evolution is brilliantly analysed in Dicey (1914).

in the countries of the common-law world, has still in large measure resisted legislative – as distinct from judicial – reform although even in the traditional fields of the common law, legislative activity is steadily increasing. In most other fields – of which electoral reform, social welfare legislation in the broadest sense, tax law and the reform of the machinery of justice are examples – the Bentham philosophy triumphed in the practice of states, as the urbanization and industrialization of nineteenth-century Western society proceeded, and long before the political and social cataclysms of the twentieth century posed a series of new challenges with which this book is essentially concerned.

Ehrlich

Savigny's theory is today a matter of history, too much out of tune with the basic condition of modern society to be a matter of serious discussion. But the far more subtle and realistic theory proposed a century later by the Austrian jurist Eugen Ehrlich, forms a convenient starting point for the reflections offered in this chapter.[3]

The similarity of Ehrlich's to Savigny's approach lies in his emphasis on the 'living law of people', based on social behaviour rather than the compulsive norm of the state. Norms observed by the people, whether in matters of religious habits, family life, or commercial relations, are law, even if they are never recognized or formulated by the norm of the state.[4] For Ehrlich, the main sphere of the compulsive state norm is in the fields specifically connected with the purposes of the state, i.e. military organization, taxation and police administration. While he admits that the sphere of essential state activities, and, therefore, of the norms created for their protection, has expanded in our time, it still remains for him an ancillary part of the law, and one he separates from the 'living law' of the community.

It is this basic differentiation between a main body of the law,

3. Ehrlich's principal work (1912) has been translated and published in English (1936).
4. It should be noted that Ehrlich's approach was strongly influenced by his study of the social, and especially of the family, habits of numerous nations and races combined at the time of the Austro-Hungarian Empire.

which develops from the social life of the 'people', living as nations, church congregations, business communities or families, and a limited sphere of 'state norms', created for purposes of organization and protection, that has lost its validity and meaning in the increasingly industrialized and articulate society of our time. Today, the legislature is everywhere heavily at work, flanked by a multiplicity of administrative agencies on the one side and a variety of judicial institutions on the other side. It actively moulds and regulates the scope of business enterprise as well as the property relations of families and even breeding habits. Hire-purchase legislation strongly affects purchasing habits, while zoning and town planning legislation has a decisive influence on the pattern of land ownership and other property rights. A highly urbanized and mechanized society, in which great numbers of peoples live close together and are ever more dependent upon each other's actions and the supply of necessities outside their own sphere of control, has led to an increasingly active and creative role of the conscious law-making instrumentalities of the state.

The Interplay of State Action and Public Opinion

It is only certain organic theories of state – which found their climax in the Hegelian philosophy of law and state, carried to ultimate frenzy in the Fascist theories of twentieth-century Germany and Italy – that have turned the state into an abstract and mystical entity, moving and acting with a mind and soul of its own. The state is indeed the organized power of the community, equipped with a steadily increasing armoury of instruments of action, and, as such, it is opposed to the unorganized groundswell of public opinion. The power of those who control the machinery of the state has been multiplied manifold, absolutely and relatively, by the development of the modern legislative and administrative machinery as well as the growing concentration of physical and technical power, and the means of communication. But it is still the *people*, groups and individuals, who control the machinery. They are, themselves, to a greater or lesser extent, the representatives of the social forces which, in turn, they seek to mould and control through the instrumentalities of the state. At the one extreme, a ruthless individual or a small group, holding in their hands a concentrated power which the modern Fascist and Communist systems have demonstrated, may seek to impose their will, in the form of laws, regulations and police action, on an apathetic or cowed community. At the other extreme, prevalent in primitive communities, but increasingly infrequent in our time – a government may be essentially representative, taking the minimum of action, when required by overwhelming pressure to do so. But whether we are concerned with the abolition of secret police powers, the creation of legal remedies against administrative action, the enactment of an anti-trust law, or the introduction of new divorce grounds, there is always some interrelation between the state machinery which produces these changes, and the social opinion of the community in which they are intended to operate. The kind of interrelation that obtains in any given situation is essentially determined by two factors: (a) the type of political system that controls legal action; (b) the type of social interest which is the object of the legal regulation in question.

Constitutional Patterns and Legal Change

Modern dictatorship resembles older forms of absolutism in its hostility to any form of separation of powers, and in the concentration of as many functions of government in as few hands as possible. It is distinguished from older forms of absolutism by the sophistication and refinement of the legislative, administrative and judicial techniques, developed in intermediate centuries. A system of government that controls, directly or through faithful henchmen, the machinery and all levels of executive power subject to no judicial supervision, and that, through a combination of political appointments, insecurity of tenure and direct instructions, also controls the administration of justice, has an apparently unlimited power to make whatever laws the ruling junta deems necessary. As such a government has, among its many other powers, complete power over all forms of education and the media of communication, it may, in due course, be able to mould and condition the minds of the people which it controls to such an extent that they will meekly, or even enthusiastically, accept whatever laws the masters impose upon them – either by direct decree or by using the trappings of a pseudo-democractic legislative process. Twelve years of Nazi government in

Germany showed the length to which such a process, ruthlessly and fanatically pursued, may go.

More significant, perhaps, is a study of the interrelation of law and social change in the Soviet Union (Hazard, 1953; 1969; Guins, 1954). For the Soviet system has now been in operation for well over fifty years, long enough to refashion the entire political, economic and legal system of the country as well as the education and growth of an entire generation. The Soviet legal revolution has gone much further than the Nazi legal revolution. Unlike the latter, it has not confined itself to the constitutional structure and the system of political power, but basically changed the conditions of production and commercial transactions and, with it, the structure of legal ownership and contract. It has also effected basic changes in family relationships, by approximating the making and dissolution of marriages to the conclusion and discharge of contracts, by creating complete equality between men and women, by drastically improving the status of the illegitimate child, and by the legalization of abortion (Hazard, 1953, pp. 245–73; 1969). Like the Nazi system, the Soviet system has entirely subordinated the rights of the individual and of groups to the state, using for that purpose the para-legal powers of a powerful secret police, with its own quasi-criminal procedure, the political pressures of the ubiquitous Communist Party, and mass detention and deportation without trial.

But the survival and consolidation of the Communist regime in the Soviet Union is in large measure due to its positive achievements. Whereas the Nazi Government despised education and educated people and, during its short regime, largely lived on the intellectual achievements of former generations of Germans, the Soviet Government strove successfully to turn a backward into an educated nation, albeit to the exclusion of free thought in political matters. The result of this process is, it seems, that the Government can no longer impose the most ruthless forms of civil oppression upon a new and better educated generation. This would seem to explain the drastic curtailment of the once almost unlimited powers of the MVD and several other reforms in the judicial process, although they do not basically affect the concentration of legal and political power in the hands of the Government.

Equally significant is the fact that after more than fifty years of

Soviet law, despite many basic differences between the Soviet and other legal systems, no basically new concepts or legal relationships have developed. The machinery of justice operates in forms and procedures comparable to those of other systems, although, of course, not in the independence cherished by democratic forms of government. Groups within the state, such as churches or trade unions, survive, the former tolerated despite the basic hostility of the Marxist philosophy and the official doctrine of the Soviet State to any organized religion; the latter an essential part of the State, but with very limited functions and without the essential autonomy that is part of the liberal concept of freedom of association. Marriage survives as a monogamous institution, and although it is in theory a much less strict union than, for example, the American marriage, comparison of the practice of marriage in both countries would make this assertion very doubtful (see p. 238). Contracts continue to be concluded and enforced, although the most important contracts are those between government-owned corporations, which operate the main branches of industry and commerce. Private property exists and is recognized, although on a much more limited scale than in non-Socialist countries. Tort actions prosper and are dealt with very much as in other industrialized countries. The social insurance system is closely comparable to that of Great Britain or the Scandinavian countries.

A totalitarian government can, indeed, use its monopoly of the law-making and executive powers for the re-shaping of law, in disregard of the democratic processes of opinion, to a far greater extent than other systems, but it is limited by the need to secure at least the acquiescence and, where it produces an educated minority, the willing acceptance of its law. It is, on the other hand, limited by the permanence of certain categories of social relationships, dictated by the conditions of human life and society rather than by a specific political ideology.

In a democracy, the interplay between social opinion and the law-moulding activities of the state is a more obvious and articulate one. Public opinion on vital social issues constantly expresses itself not only through the elected representatives in the legislative assemblies, but through public discussion in press, radio, public lectures, pressure groups and, on a more sophisticated level, through scientific and professional associations, universities and a multitude of other channels.

Because of this constant interaction between the articulation of public opinion and the legislative process, the tension between the legal and the social norm can seldom be too great. It is not possible in a democratic system to impose a law on an utterly hostile community.[5] But, a strong social ground swell sooner or later compels legal action. Between these two extremes, there is a great variety of the patterns of challenge and response. On the one hand, the law may at length, and tardily, respond to an irresistible tide of social habit or opinion. Such is the case with the gradual enlargement of divorce grounds in the great majority of non-Catholic western countries – either through the addition of new divorce grounds (cruelty, incompatibility, etc.) or the judicial extension of existing grounds for divorce or annulment. The extension of legitimate divorce is a response to the increasing freedom of movement of the married woman in modern western society, a loosening of religious ties and social taboos, and the development of social habits which lead to the dissolution of a vastly increased number of marriages, with or without the sanction of law. Here the alternative for the legislator is to permit an increasing gap between legal theory and social practice to develop, or to respond to an overwhelming change in the social facts of life (see ch. 7). Again, suicide which is still in theory a crime in the common-law jurisdictions, has in fact ceased to be so, not through an act of the legislator, but through an all but universal practice of regarding suicide *ipso facto* as committed 'while of unsound mind'.

On the other hand, a determined and courageous individual or small minority group may initiate and pursue a legal change, in the face of governmental or parliamentary lethargy, and an indifferent public opinion. Such legislation as now exists in many countries for the preservation of forests or wild life, or the conservation of other vital resources, has been the belated result of the determined efforts of small groups of men who saw beyond the immediate interests not

5. As has been demonstrated by the history of Prohibition in the USA, or the indifferent success of various English statutes over the last century, invalidating betting transactions, in fighting the deeply ingrained national passion for betting.

only of vested interests but of the ordinary legislator and government executive. A much needed liberalization of the English divorce law effected in 1937 was the result of the almost single-handed efforts of an individual Member of Parliament, A. P. Herbert. But while the determination of far-sighted individuals is often an indispensable factor, it cannot become effective in a democracy unless there is a minimum of acceptance by public opinion. When President Franklin Roosevelt carried through the legal revolution in American labour relations, symbolized by the National Labour Relations Act, he enjoyed the unusual combination of a brilliant political mind and a large Congressional majority – although the opposition of a majority of the Supreme Court judges retarded the process for a while. But he could not have carried through the change unless far-reaching changes in industrial organization, on the side both of employers and labour, had made the acceptance of collective bargaining as the essential instrument of negotiation a vital necessity, and unless the convulsions of the great depression of the early thirties had greatly weakened both the power of the employers and the ideological strength of extreme economic individualism. Town planning legislation in England, and zoning legislation in the United States, has been the belated, and far from sufficient, response to the social and aesthetic chaos created by generations of unplanned speculative building and urban development. But the pioneering efforts of what was originally a small group of town planners and sociologists would not have come to fruition until the point had been reached when even the ordinary citizen and the average national and local legislator had at last been impressed with the immediate urgency of the conditions which it was sought to remedy. In recent years, the Indian Constitution of 1949 has abolished both the polygamous marriage and the caste system, in the face of age-old social and religious custom. How far this legal revolution will be successful, is still a matter of some uncertainty. That it has even been attempted is, in itself, a sign of the greatly increased power of modern state action as against old social custom. But not even the prestige of a Nehru, or the predominance of the Congress Party in organized political life in India, could have attempted such far-reaching reforms, unless the impact of Western ideas had effected a far-reaching change in educated public opinion.

Similar problems arise in the transformation of long-standing and, until recently, unalterable personal status laws in the Muslim world. The sacrosanctity of the Sharī'a – the canon law of Islam – derived partly from its predominantly theological origin[6] and partly from the static character of overwhelmingly rural, nomadic and autocratically governed societies. But while the hold of Islamic religion remains as strong as ever, the majority of Islamic States are in a process of rapid economic and social change, leading to increasing commercialization and industrialization. The first and major legal impact has been in the field of civil and commercial law, where a majority of Islamic States have introduced codes based on the leading western (particularly French) systems or a blend of Sharī'a and western principles (Anderson, 1956, p. 43). But more recently, the effect of this transformation and the closer contact with other systems has increasingly affected family law and, in particular, the 'miserable lot of Muslim wives' (p. 45). Egypt, Iraq, Jordan, Lebanon, Pakistan and the Sudan have at least begun to introduce reforms which give some rights to the wife. Here, as in India, legislative action could not have been attempted unless social changes, such as urbanization, and intellectual influences (from western ideas absorbed by the younger educated generation) had prepared the soil. The transformation of personal status law is, however, likely to be far slower and more difficult than the introduction of western-modelled modern principles of obligation and commercial transactions.

Examples have already been given of the response of the law to social change not through legislation, but through judicial reinterpretations.[7] When the Supreme Court of the United States, in 1954,[8] after a series of preparatory judgements, upset the interpretation of the Fourteenth Amendment of the equality of races, given nearly half a century earlier, it partly responded to, and partly led, public opinion. It certainly could not have made the attempt – how successfully, is still an open question – unless the intervening period

6. The Qur'ān (the Revelation of God) and the Sunna (the Practice of the Prophet) (Vesey-Fitzgerald, 'Nature and sources of the Shari'a', in Khadduri and Liebesney, 1955, pp. 85, 87).
7. See further on the role of the courts in response of law to social change, ch. 2.
8. *Brown* v. *Board of Education*, 347 US 483 (1954).

had brought a great change in the economic and educational status of the American Negro, and a corresponding evolution in the attitude of responsible individuals and important social groups, such as the armed forces, churches, universities and at least part of organized labour.

State Powers and the Control of Personal Liberties and Economic Rights

The rights of business and labour to organize, concentrate and monopolize, social security legislation of all kinds, matters of education and of the political and civic status of religious and racial groups within the state, all these are matters of such general impact on the life of the community that they call sooner or later for legislative, administrative or, in some cases, judicial action. By contrast, the so-called 'lawyers' law' is generally concerned with matters of more technical and limited import. They are essentially within the sphere of the traditional common law, regulated by a gradually evolving judge-made law in the common-law jurisdictions, and the civil codes in most other jurisdictions. In this sphere, there is a more strictly defined interplay of social change, legal evolution by judicial interpretation, and legislative action, which varies from country to country and from time to time. Professional groups and the technical training of the lawyer play a predominant role, and it is in this field that the courts are still largely expected to carry on the process of legal evolution in response to social change, although, as we shall see, they have often failed to rise to the challenge. In matters of contract, tort, definition of property rights, form and validity of wills, matrimonial rights and the like, the interaction between law and social change, while often of considerable social and economic importance, is predominantly a matter of give and take between relatively small and highly trained professional groups on the one side, and the courts or, in certain cases, the legislature, on the other side. In this field are such matters as the erosion of the contributory negligence rule evolved by the common law, the recognition of comparative negligence in England and a number of American jurisdictions, and the consequent apportionment of damages in proportion to the respective fault of the parties; liability of occupiers of land to various categories of visitors, formal validity of wills made abroad, or changes in the rule against perpetuities. These matters are generally the jealously guarded preserve of the trained lawyer, and they have a subordinate place in the attention of the legislative bodies which are preoccupied with matters of more obvious and popular concern to the community at large. But while the necessary corollary should be the adaptation of the law by an interplay of social pressure and judicial response, the courts have often been handicapped, notably in the common-law jurisdictions, by their adherence to precedent and a frequent disinclination to take note of changes in public opinion (see p. 47). After the English House of Lords had resolutely refused to effect the necessary simplification and rationalization of the liability of occupiers of land to visitors, despite the fluid state of the precedents and a great deal of professional writing on the subject, it was necessary to appoint a Royal Commission and, subsequently, to enact legislation to reform this branch of the law. The same was true some years earlier of the law of comparative negligence, which, in the United States, still varies from state to state. In some fields, the courts are unable to effect the necessary reform of the common law not only because of long tradition, but because the interests of governments are too closely involved. The British Crown Proceedings Act of 1947 and, less extensively, the American Federal Tort Claims Act of 1946 have abolished most of the archaic and socially untenable rule of immunity of governments from suit in contract and tort, but in the majority of the American jurisdictions the rule survives, wholly or in part (see p. 415). While the courts with few exceptions feel unable to abolish it, state legislatures and governments seldom feel impelled to take action. In the field of family law, some relations are capable of judicial adjustments; others are too fundamental to respond to any legislative change. Generally, legislative reform has been necessary to effect the adjustment of the property rights of the married woman to her drastically changed position in the modern Western world. Sometimes, a matter of what is normally 'lawyers' law' becomes entangled with state policy in a different field. One of the most fundamental differences between the civil and the common law is that between the various systems of community property – embodied, in one form or another, in all contemporary civil codes – and the system of separation of property enshrined in the common law. But some of the western and southern jurisdictions in the United States have community-property systems based on former French or Spanish affiliations. When some years ago, these states applied the community-property system to income-tax law by enabling husbands and wives to split their total joint income for income-tax purposes, a number of common-law jurisdictions proceeded to introduce community property solely for the purpose of legislating corresponding tax concessions. When the Federal Tax Law made the joint income-tax return universal, they speedily reverted to their traditional common-law system. Again, there are certain branches of family law in which only legislation can create a new status. The adoption and legitimation of children responds to a widely felt need, and it is overwhelmingly approved by contemporary public opinion. It is only legislative action which can create the status of an adopted or legitimated child, for such a status requires a specific regulation of the respective rights and duties, as between the various parties concerned, and administrative machinery, which cannot be effected by judicial adaptation (see p. 73).

The Various Patterns of Democracy and Legal Change

The contemporary Constitutions of France, Great Britain, India, West Germany and the United States can all be characterized as democratic, but such are the differences in their constitutional structure that the interchange between social opinion and the legislative process is greatly affected. In the parliamentary system developed by Great Britain, and adopted by the major members of the British Commonwealth, a two-party pattern prevails. The government formed by the victorious party almost invariably controls a safe majority for a number of years, and is therefore usually able to push through important legislative measures. Cabinet leadership and government initiative are decisive, in relation to the law-making role of the private Member of Parliament, who is only occasionally able to put through a major legislative measure, with a mixture of luck and dogged persistence.

The importance of government leadership and predominance in the legislative process is further enhanced where a parliamentary system of the type just described goes together with the overwhelming – and more than temporary – predominance of one party. This has, until recently, been the case in contemporary India, where the Congress Party – now seriously challenged – under Nehru's leadership controlled the Legislature as well as the Executive, though not the Judiciary.

Where, as in the French Fourth Republic or in the Weimar Republic, the parliamentary regime is built upon a plurality of parties – some representing sectional interests rather than national political movements – none of which is able to govern singly, so that governments are formed by shifting and unstable coalitions of a number of parties, the scales are more heavily weighted against the translation of new social developments into legislative reform. For such reforms demand positive action, and the difficulty of obtaining agreement among coalition partners, usually united only in a 'mariage de convenance' and deeply divided over major issues, means, in effect, a veto power of any one of the partners. Thus, French Socialists and Popular Republicans have found themselves usually united over questions of international policy and social reform, but deeply divided over questions of educational policy. On the other hand, Left and Right are sharply divided over questions of foreign and colonial policy. There are deep conflicts between the various parties over questions of tax policy and social services. The result is more often than not a maximum of debate and a minimum of legislative action.

It should, however, be pointed out that the unofficial veto power of minority groups obtains in all democracies, to a greater or lesser extent, and that it need not necessarily find organized expression in any one political party. In terms of legal and social reform, democracy means implementation of the will of the majority only with very severe restrictions. Thus a well organized and influential minority can delay changes to which it objects strongly almost indefinitely, even though a majority of the people might favour it. There is, for example, a widespread movement for the establishment of public birth-control and family advice centres, as one means of reducing the countless thousands of illegal abortions performed annually in all industrialized countries where abortion is not legalized or put under public guidance. In many of the American states, e.g. in the State of New York, Catholic opposition to any form of official sanction of birth-control for many years made the establishment of such centres difficult, even though a majority of the people might favour them. As long as we are concerned with criminal sanctions, e.g. for suicide, infanticide, abortion in cases of extreme necessity, such as imminent danger to health or rape (see p. 264), it is somewhat easier to effect a tacit legal change by abstention from prosecution, by verdicts of acquittal, or by a permanent judicial fiction such as that of the state of 'unsound mind', invariably presumed nowadays in the case of suicide. This, however, affords no relief where positive action is required, for example, by the establishment of birth-control clinics, or a change in the legal status of illegitimate children or abortion. But where the social pressure for legal change becomes too strong, eventually legal reform by stealth, i.e. by changes in interpretation, legal fictions and the like, will no longer suffice. Thus, in the late 1960s, the pressure for legislative reform of the abortion laws, both in Britain and the United States, became too strong to be ignored by the legislators. A number of American states have adopted the recommendations of the American Model Penal Code, which proposes a considerable liberalization of the presently prevailing laws, in cases of rape, incest or the prospect of mental defectiveness. The British Abortion Law of 1967 adopts these recommendations but goes further in permitting abortion in circumstances which may be described as 'social indication', i.e. consideration of family circumstances. And some of the American states – including the state of New York in 1970 – have gone even further by making abortion a matter of consent between the woman and her doctor. The reasons for this remarkable swing of legislative opinion – after decades of stubborn resistance to much more modest reforms – are multiple, but two probably outweigh all others: one is the general trend towards individual freedom of decision, in personal matters, in a pluralistic society. The other is an increasing – and worldwide – apprehension of the dangers of further uncontrolled population growth. Whatever the reasons, the explosion of legislative reforms in the field of abortion is a remarkable illustration of the way in which changes in moral values and social thinking first modify the administration and interpretation of the law, but eventually force a more systematic, i.e. legislative, change.

Legal change in federal systems

Many obstacles to the translation of social into legal change are offered by federal constitutions. A federal system is predicated on a balance of power. Although there are significant differences between various federal states, the preponderant effect of the system of balances is to reduce the power of government and, with it, the power of positive action.

While each federal structure has its particular composite of checks and counter-checks, many of them based on historical and local characteristics, three major factors, each tending to retard legislative action and response to new social needs, are built into the federal system as such:

First, the distribution of powers between federation and states. As recent history has shown, it does not make much difference whether the federation or the states have the residuary legislative power. In Australia, it is the Commonwealth, in Canada it is the Provinces which have enumerated legislative powers. Yet, the constitutionality of the so-called Canadian New Deal legislation of the early thirties was invalidated by the Privy Council, then the highest constitutional tribunal for Canada, by a narrow interpretation of the power of the Dominion to legislate for 'peace, order and good government' in the light of the provincial powers to legislate for 'property and civil rights'.[9] On the other hand, the Australian High Court limited the apparently unambiguous power of the Commonwealth to legislate in respect to banking by extending the meaning of another clause of the Constitution, guaranteeing the free flow of trade, so as to turn it into a protection of individual freedom to trade, as an implied constitutional prohibition of the nationalization of banking.[10] During the decade following the initiation of the 'New Deal' in the United States, a considerable proportion of the social-service legislation, in regard to collective bargaining, protection of children and women, minimum standards, etc., was effected and judicially upheld by means of the Inter-state Commerce Clause. The

9. See, for a survey, the O'Connor Report, Ottawa, 1939, Annex I, pp. 18–52.

10. *Bank of New South Wales* v. *Commonwealth* (1948) 16 *C.L.R.* 1; (1949) 79 *Crim. L. Rev.* 497.

power of the Federation in matters of inter-state commerce was read so as to include compliance with certain social standards.[11]

Generally, however, the distribution of powers between the federation and the states acts as a brake. As there is almost invariably an interlocking of various subject-matters, which are seldom united either in federal or state hands, it is often possible, as we have just seen, to emphasize either the one or the other aspect. In cases of serious doubt, necessary legislation will not be initiated. Even the approval by a constitutional organ specially designed to safeguard the interest of the states, such as the United States Senate or the German *Bundesrat*, will not bring about a change which any one of the states may challenge as being an infringement of its reserve. Thus, the states of the 'deep South', today, claim, in effect, that any legislative or judicial federal power in regard to the constitutionally guaranteed equality of races is implicitly limited by the State power in regard to education.

The second major built-in brake lies in the separation of functions between the three branches of government. In the typical modern federation, such as the United States, Australia, Canada, India and West Germany (but not Switzerland), the principal restraining function is exercised by the Supreme Court of the country, which passes the final verdict on the constitutionality of both federal and state legislation. The immense influence which the exercise of this power can have on the social structure of a country is illustrated by the effective postponement of social-security legislation in the United States, through the interpretation given by the Supreme Court for many decades to both federal and state acts enacting compulsory social standards as being an unconstitutional violation of the 'due process' clauses; a parallel, of shorter duration, is the invalidation of the social-security legislation of Canada, until an amendment of the British North America Act was passed. Given the general pattern of distribution of functions between federal and state governments, the court can decisively influence the national pattern of social welfare, transport and communications, trade and business, education, and many other vital fields.

The power of the court – acting negatively, through the striking

11. *US* v. *Darby*, 312 U.S. 100 (1941).

down of legislation, not positively through the stimulus to new legislation – is greatly increased where a constitution embodies a 'bill of rights' (Freund, 1949, p. 9). This is the case, notably in the Constitution of the United States, and the post-war Constitutions of West Germany and India, but not in the Federal Constitution of Australia. Canada, in 1960, enacted a bill of rights that does not have the formal status of a 'higher' constitutional law but which has been interpreted by the Supreme Court as overriding inconsistent legislation (see p. 59). The basic freedoms usually enshrined in such bills of rights – of worship, speech, association, movement, property and trade – and the equalities guaranteed in regard to race, sex, religion, are inevitably of such sweeping and general character that the role of interpreter comes close to that of the legislator. The judicial function merges with the policy-making function. This is hardly a matter of choice for the court, but of necessity. A court which, as in *Plessy* v. *Ferguson*,[12] interprets the constitution as guaranteeing 'separate but equal', but not integrated, facilities of education for whites and Negroes is as much a policy-maker as a court which interprets the constitution as guaranteeing complete equality in every respect, including the integration of schools.[13] The constitution is the basic law of the country, designed to endure for a long time, and notoriously difficult to amend. If, as is claimed by some, the interpretation of the court should strictly accord with the intentions of the makers of the constitution at the time of its enactment, this would mean, for example, that a clause such as the Inter-state Commerce Clause has the same meaning in the 1970s as in the pre-industrial eighteenth century.

As we have seen, the British parliamentary pattern, as it prevails in the Federations of Australia and Canada, shows a high degree of conformity between the executive and legislature. By contrast, the United States Constitution imposes a further vital check on the adaptation of law to social change by the rigid separation of the executive and legislature. Even in the not too frequent cases of coincidence of Presidential and Congressional control, executive initiative meets with a multitude of obstacles in the legislature. In the

12. 163 U.S. SS7 (1897).
13. *Brown* v. *Board of Education*, 347 U.S. 483 (1954).

American system of government, these checks operate, first, through a multitude of legislative committees, often controlled by a majority hostile to the executive; and, secondly, through the duplication of the legislative process in the two Houses of Congress, where one of them, the Senate, incorporates the federal element. The federal element is, in some federations, notably the United States, further reinforced by the weighting of votes and influence in favour of the smaller states.[14] In the United States Senate, each of the fifty states is represented by two Senators. Although, in due course, the progressive industrialization and urbanization of the country may diminish the gap between the outlook of the highly industrialized, densely populated major states on the one part, and the smaller, rural states on the other part, it is still significant. The social problems, for example, of Vermont or Nebraska, are not the same as those of New York or California. But the influence of the smaller states – which will usually, though not invariably, feel far less impelled than the larger industrialized states to enact legislation in response to social demands coming from urbanized and industrialized regions – will, in the Senate, be disproportionately large. It is usually only in times of major emergencies – war, major economic depressions or natural catastrophes of nation-wide proportions – that these divergent pulls can be overcome, as, for example, in the early years of the New Deal. Normally, the factors of conservatism and inertia will retard or impede positive action, e.g. in the field of economic aid for foreign countries, the reorganization of the armed services, or the extension of federal aid to schools and other educational institutions.

14. Only the Australian Constitution appears to imitate the US Constitution by composing the Senate of sixty members, ten from each of the six states. This has on more than one occasion resulted in political stalemates. Of the newer Federal Constitutions, the West German *Grundgesetz* of 1949 compromises between equality and proportionality by giving each of the ten *Länder* in the Upper Chamber, the *Bundesrat*, a minimum of three votes, with one additional vote for any *Land* with more than two million, and a second additional vote for any *Land* with more than six million, inhabitants. Under the Indian Constitution of 1949–51, the Council of States, which represents the federal element, has twelve members, nominated by the President from the fields of literature, science, art, and social service – a small concession to the 'corporative' idea – and the remaining number – at present exceeding 200, but not yet up to the constitutional maximum of 238 (art. 81) – fixed in proportion to the population of the different states (Fourth Schedule).

Revolution, Civil Disobedience and Legal Change

The continuity of a legal order, including its processes of legal change, has, throughout the history of civilization, been liable to disruption by revolutionary upheavals. These may come from within or from without. Although the overthrow of a legal order may occur peacefully, major revolutions have usually been marked by violence. The French Revolution of 1789, and the Bolshevik Revolution of 1917, totally and violently destroyed the existing constitutional and legal structure. Eventually a new constitutional and legal order dominated by radically different principles was substituted. There is no legal continuity between the old and the new order. The post-war German and Japanese constitutions are the products of a revolution imposed from without by virtue of the legal authority assumed by the victorious enemies of the Nazi regime. If an attempted revolution fails, its leaders are traitors under the norms of the existing legal system. If it is successful, it is accepted – by acquiescence within the community, and by *de facto* or *de jure* recognition of the new regime by other governments in international legal relations. The German jurist, Georg Jellinek, in a famous phrase, has called this process '*die normative Kraft des Faktischen*'.

In the last decade, and most notably in the United States, a more limited and specialized type of resistance to the existing legal order – commonly described as 'civil disobedience' – has become an important social phenomenon, and the subject of widespread discussion. Civil disobedience has been sparked by two developments which have dominated the American scene during the last decade: the continuing and increasingly militant fight of the black community for social and economic as well as legal equality with the white citizens of the United States; and the widespread resistance to the American involvement in the Vietnam War.

A few years after the Supreme Court decision in the school desegregation case[15] had spelled out the principle of equality between black and white under the Constitution, southern Negroes, under the leadership of the late Martin Luther King, assisted by white sympathizers, began to obstruct the numerous laws and practices of southern states prescribing segregated transport, catering and other social

15. *Brown* v. *Board of Education*, 347 U.S. 483 (1954).

facilities for blacks and whites. They marched and demonstrated, demanded to be transported under conditions of equality with their white fellow citizens, and to be served in segregated restaurants. Many of these actions were prima facie illegal because they were contrary to existing state laws and regulations. However, some were later upheld by Federal Court decisions, which declared the relevant laws to be unconstitutional. The principles for which the protestors had fought through acts of disobedience were eventually embodied in new federal legislation, notably the Civil Rights Acts of 1964 and 1965.

It is doubtful whether this type of action can be described as 'disobedience'. It can be so characterized only by those who believe that there is a duty of obedience to the – local or state – law that is prima facie binding, until legal appeal procedures may establish their unconstitutionality and thus retroactively legitimate what appeared to be illegal behaviour.

The better view would appear to be, however, that a citizen who challenges the legality of a law or ordinance may support his belief not only by initiating legal action but by refusing to obey laws that he believes to be illegal – at the risk of being proved wrong. Whether he has acted legally or illegally remains uncertain until the highest court has ruled.[16] The US Constitution is not a kind of future higher law that comes into existence only when the decision of the highest court is rendered; it is always there, and he who defies an incompatible local or state law acts in accordance with a superior legal norm that in retrospect is shown to have existed all the time, though it is

16. This appears to accord substantially with the view of Archibald Cox, a former Solicitor-General of the United States who, in an article published in 1968 ('Civil rights, the constitution and the courts', 40 *New York State Bar Journal* 161–7) maintains that those who conscientiously believe that what they are doing involves the exercise of a legal right, which the courts will eventually affirm by declaring the contrary law unconstitutional, are morally justified in disobeying the law in question. From these Cox distinguishes 'those who violate a plainly valid law knowing that their conduct is illegal'. A similar view is that of Graham Hughes ('Civil disobedience and the political question doctrine', 43 *New York University L. Rev.* 1, 17 (1968)) who justifies non-violent disobedience where the defendant had a legitimate doubt about the constitutionality of the law in question and had no way short of disobedience by which to obtain a legitimation of the validity of the law.

often articulated only by a decision on a question not previously decided.[17]

The various expressions of resistance to legal commands connected with the Vietnam hostilities are in a different category. Such actions as the burning of draft cards or the refusal to accept induction under the Selective Service Act are deliberate acts of defiance of positive law. Usually it is not the legality of the relevant legislation or order, but its morality, that is challenged. Nor is it easy any longer to legitimate refusal of service in the Vietnam War on the ground that, no war having been declared, the US military involvement is unconstitutional, or that obedience to orders given to US soldiers, in a war in violation of international law that many jurists of repute (Falk, 1968; 1969; Taylor, 1970) hold to be incompatible with the Nuremberg principles would involve them in illegal behaviour. The US Supreme Court has twice denied a petition for a writ of certiorari in cases where a petitioner appealed a conviction for refusal to report for induction. At least impliedly, therefore, the majority of the Court confirmed the view of lower courts that the legality of the war was a 'political' and therefore non-justiciable matter.[18]

What then distinguishes 'civil disobedience' from other acts of violation of positive law on the one hand, and from revolution on the other? The most comprehensive definition of the characteristics of civil disobedience is that given by an eminent theologian:

Civil disobedience is (1) a non-violent, (2) public violation (3) of a specific law or set of laws, or of a policy of government having the effect of law, (4) which expresses a sense of justice in a civil society of cooperation among equals and (5) which is generally undertaken in the name of a presumed higher authority than the law in question (6) as a last resort (7) for the purpose of changing the law and (8) with the intention of accepting the penalty which the prevailing law imposes (Adams, 1970, p. 294).

Some of these criteria, such as the requirement of non-violence, will not be universally accepted; others are characterizations rather

17. That the Supreme Court – and other courts – sometimes reverse themselves, is part of the uncertainties inherent in all legal interpretation. It is not a specific problem of disobedience.
18. See *Mitchell* v. *US*, 386 U.S. 972 (1966); *Mora* v. *McNamara*, 389 U.S. 934 (1967).

than definitions. Professor Adams's eight criteria include, however, at least three that are essential to assess the role of civil disobedience in the context of legal change. First, it is indeed characteristic of acts of civil disobedience that they do not normally aim at the overthrow of the entire legal order but oppose 'a specific law or set of laws'. The borderlines between acts of specific disobedience and acts of a more generally revolutionary character are, however, fluid (Jones, 1969, p. 93). A refusal to accept induction into the armed services so widespread as to make the operation of the military system impossible would shake the roots of the legal order. So would a general refusal to pay taxes, in protest against the continuation of the war. Nevertheless, it remains true that civil disobedience is, in the great majority of cases, a specific act of resistance directed against specific laws or administrative actions, rather than an attempt to destroy the entire constitutional structure. It is equally true that, as distinct from a murder, a rape or a burglary, the disobedience is generally motivated by a moral conviction that conflicts with the law in force and is designed to change the law so as to make it morally acceptable.

Where the protestor is willing to accept the penalty imposed by the law for disobedience, e.g. imprisonment or dishonourable discharge from the service, or dismissal from employment, he does in fact act within the existing legal structure. His intention is to draw attention to the injustice of the legal order by the moral indignation that he hopes will attend his conviction. He may also hope that his example will be followed so widely that disobedience may become so widespread as to compel a change in the law in order to avoid a total breakdown of the legal order. To some extent, and in some cases, these objects of civil disobedience have been attained. Thus the trial and conviction – reversed in some cases on appeal – of such well-known public personalities as Dr Spock and Dr Coffin undoubtedly underlined, for wide sections of the public, a discrepancy between legal prescription and moral conscience.

For the lawyer the greatest difficulty lies in the definition of the 'presumed higher authority', i.e. of the moral purpose that will distinguish civil disobedience for a higher cause from other violations of the law. In a totalitarian society, concepts of morality that differ from the official philosophy, as expressed in the law, are not tolerated.

In a liberal and pluralistic society – the only one in which 'civil disobedience' can have any place – there are many diverging and antithetic concepts of morality. And although in the days of Thomas Aquinas – when the secular authority of the state was not yet firmly established – it was possible to maintain that certain state laws were not valid if they offended against the 'higher' law of nature as embodied in the authority of the Church, this is no longer argued by the champions of the natural law philosophy.[19] In the Nuremberg and Tokyo trials of German and Japanese war criminals, there were indeed hints that individuals had legal duties higher than those of obedience to the positive law of their sovereign. But essentially the Nuremberg Tribunal, and the other courts that derived their jurisdiction from the Nuremberg Charter, based themselves on the binding force of the positive law imposed upon Germany by virtue of the Allied Military Government.

The Nuremberg Tribunals are not German courts. They are not enforcing German law. The charges are not based on violation by the defendants of German law. On the contrary, the jurisdiction of this Tribunal rests on international authority. It enforces the law as declared by the IMT Charter and C.C. Law 10, and within the limitations on the power conferred, it enforces international law as superior in authority to any German statute or decree. It is true, as defendants contend, that German courts under the Third Reich were required to follow German law (i.e. the expressed will of Hitler) even when it was contrary to international law. But no such limitation can be applied to this Tribunal. Here we have the paramount substantive law, plus a Tribunal authorized and required to apply it notwithstanding the inconsistent provisions of German local law.[20]

Subsequent history has made it abundantly clear that, at least in the present phase of international law, no sovereign state, including those that sat in judgement at Nuremberg and Tokyo, will accept the commands of a higher law as superior to those of the national legal order.

It is not therefore possible to justify disobedience to law in the name

19. Modern Church doctrine condemns objectionable state laws (such as divorce laws) as immoral but does not command its followers to disobey them (Friedmann, 1967, pp. 388–91).

20. 'The Justice Case' (Case 3) 954 ff, 984, *Trials of War Criminals before the Nuremberg Military Tribunals*, vol. 3 (1951).

of law. What is possible – and indeed necessary at a time of deep social tensions and dissatisfaction with the foundations of society, and of the legal order that supports it – is the articulation of the considerations that may make civil disobedience morally acceptable, not only in the eyes of the individual but of major segments of society. These may sometimes be powerful enough to induce a change in the law. Among the studies recently undertaken in this direction are those of Ronald Dworkin (1968, 1970) and of Kent Greenawalt (1970; see also Fortas, 1968; Wasserstrom[21]). Both writers admit that there is a delicate and complex balance of interests, and that obedience to law is itself one of the major social values to be considered. Dworkin – whose line of reasoning is far from easy to follow – takes as his point of departure that the American Constitution displays a strong respect for individual rights. He deduces from this premise that in certain situations citizens have a 'right' to break the law, in the sense that 'the Government would do wrong to stop him by arresting him, prosecuting him. . . .' It must dispense with the claim that citizens never have a right to break its law, and it must not define citizens' rights so that these are cut off for supposed reasons of the general good. The essay concludes with a kind of natural law argument: 'The Government will not reestablish respect for law without giving the law some claim to respect. It cannot do that if it neglects the one feature that distinguishes law from order to brutality.'

This does not seem to take us much further, for the simple reason that the question of the proper balancing of values, and in particular the question when the interest in the maintenance of the fabric of society outweighs the right of the individual protestor, cannot be absolutely answered. The same ambiguity is implicit in the formulation of a more radical writer (Zinn, 1968), who defines disobedience as 'the deliberate violation of law for a vital social purpose'. Even in a relatively homogeneous society different groups and people differ deeply on the relative priority of social purposes. They do so even more in a highly pluralistic and heterogeneous society like that of the United States. Greenawalt, who accepts the criterion of 'probable contribution to the social good', more constructively outlines some of the principal interests at stake. The first factor is

21. 'The obligation to obey the law', 10 *University of California, Los Angeles L. Rev.* 780 (1963).

'damage to the interests of others'. There must be some proportionality between the degree of injury caused to others and the good accomplished by the act of disobedience. Second, there is the element already referred to, i.e. 'the reason for disobedience'. The stronger the moral indignation caused by the law that the offender disobeys, the stronger the likelihood of approbation and eventual change of the unjust law. This, however, is true only in societies where dissent is permitted. Greenawalt rightly mentions the example of those who, contrary to the law, assisted Jews to escape from Nazi Germany. But this, of course, was not a morality permitted by the law of Germany at the time. It was accepted, within Germany, by the resistors – a small minority – and outside Germany by those who, after the defeat of the Nazi regime, could transform their moral indignation into the new positive law. In the United States at this time resistance to the military draft provides divided reactions. A majority of the nation probably regards not only the duty to obey the laws of the country, but also the moral justification of military service as superior to the moral considerations that impel resistance to the draft. But, unlike in Nazi Germany or other totalitarian systems, debate on the merits of the Vietnam War, and of the US role in it, is permissible. The very fact that there is an orderly process of discussion and that 'citizens can affect policies by open discussion and peaceful petition' is a factor to be weighed in balancing deliberate violation of the law against attempts to alter it by peaceful methods of change. The correlation between the availability of orderly methods of legal change and the right to civil disobedience is stressed more strongly by Wasserstrom,[22] who asserts that '. . . a person is never justified in disobeying the law as long as there exist alternative, "peaceful" procedures by which to bring about the amendment of repeal of undesirable or repressive laws'.

Civil disobedience has, at least in some countries, become a powerful instrument of legal change. Where public conviction of the moral rightness of the existing legal system is shaky or divided, it can promote or accelerate overdue legal change. There is a definite causal connection between the protest actions of the early 1960s and the civil rights legislation of 1964 and 1965. Disobedience or evasion of

22. 'The obligation to obey the law', 10 *University of California, Los Angeles L. Rev.*, 797–8 (1963).

the draft has at least had a marginal effect upon the beginning of the disengagement of the United States from that war, which has deeply shaken the confidence of large sections of the nation in the moral posture of their country. But it is not possible to develop a consistent *legal* theory of change by disobedience to law. There are situations in which defiance of a law that no longer has strong moral support in public opinion will lead to legal change without developing into a general revolution. But where the legal order is so generally corrupted or weakened that if it is widely defied civil disobedience is nothing but the prelude to revolution.

Conclusions

We have seen that in a democratic system of state organization there is a great variety of interactions between social evolution and legal change. The stimulus may come from a variety of sources, some of which have been briefly surveyed. There may be the slowly growing pressure of changed patterns and norms of social life, creating an increasing gap between the facts of life and the law, to which the latter must eventually respond. There may be the sudden imperious demand of a national emergency, for a redistribution of natural resources or a new standard of social justice. There may be a far-sighted initiative of a small group of individuals, slowly moulding official opinion until the time is ripe for action. There may be a technical injustice or inconsistency of the law demanding correction. There may be new scientific developments calling for new forms of legal evidence (such as acceptance of blood-group tests for the negative proof of paternity).

The law responds in various ways, too. The speed and manner of its response is usually proportionate to the degree of social pressure. It is also influenced by the constitutional structure. But circumstances and personalities may hasten or retard the response. In the sphere of 'political law' or where a new status is created, legislative action is required. In other fields, there is a give and take between legislative and judicial remedial action, in part determined by the subject-matter but in part by the changing and diverse attitudes of legislators and judges.

Chapter 2
The Courts and the Evolution of the Law

Every legal order, federal or unitary, whether of civilian or common-law background, faces the problem of the role of the courts in the evolution of law.

This problem has become increasingly articulate and complex in the present century. Until the turn of the century the opinion prevailed in theory and practice that there was a clear-cut division between the spheres of the legislator and the judiciary. It was the function of the former to make the laws, and of the latter to apply them. Perhaps this simple doctrine, propounded by the analytical jurisprudence of both English and Continental provenance, would have been less categorical if it had had a closer acquaintance with, and understanding of, the role of the Supreme Court in the United States. However, despite the natural-law flavour of many of the decisions of that latter Court, it seemed, itself, predominantly convinced of the absence of any intention on its part to interpret the Constitution according to any but self-evident principles of construction.

It is difficult to say whether it was primarily the increasing challenge of new social problems, or a gradual revolution in thinking, or – as the present author would be inclined to think – an interaction of these factors, that, towards the turn of the century, led writers and, subsequently, courts in the leading countries of the Western world to challenge the assumptions so easily held during the nineteenth century.

When the French jurist, Gény, in a work first published in 1899,[1] looked back on nearly a century of legal developments under the Code Civil, he found that the courts had transformed the Code through creative interpretation in many vital respects. French courts

1. *Méthode d'interprétation et sources de droit privé positif*, Paris.

have, for example, adapted the delict provisions of the Code Civil (articles 1382–6) to the new realities of industrial accidents, of railway traffic, motor cars and aeroplanes. The results of such thought were apparent in the German Civil Code of 1900, whose general clauses have enabled the German courts to cope with such tremendous upheavals as the great inflation following the First World War or to develop a comprehensive law of unfair competition.[2] Even more clearly, the Swiss Civil Code of 1907 directs the judge to decide as if he were a legislator when he finds a gap in the law, guided by 'approved legal doctrine and judicial tradition'. A more recent version of the same idea is article 3 of the Italian Civil Code of 1942, which directs the court, in cases that remain doubtful after the exhaustion of normal methods of construction, to decide 'according to the general principles of the jurisprudential organization of the state'.

From very different premises, English and American jurists came to conclusions not very different from those of the Continental jurists and legislators. Dicey, in his *Law and Public Opinion in England during the Nineteenth Century*, analysed the transition from the liberal premises of Benthamite philosophy to the increasing importance of active social-service legislation, and the beginnings of the collectivist society which is now in full blossom.

In the United States, over half a century ago, Roscoe Pound started to examine law and legal problems from the point of view of conflicting interests and values. The examination, not only of problems of constitutional law, but of common law, labour law, criminal law and other fields, led Pound, and the many jurists who developed and modified his approach, to see law predominantly as an instrument of social engineering in which conflicting pulls of political philosophy, economic interests, ethical values, constantly struggle for recognition against a background of history, tradition, and legal technique. Mr Justice Cardozo formulated the result of a life time of reflection and practical experience in the following terms:

logic and history, and custom, and utility, and the accepted standards of right conduct, are the forces which singly or in combination shape the

2. In both cases, judicial creativeness was later supplemented by legislative action.

progress of the law. Which of these forces shall dominate in any case, must depend largely upon the comparative importance or value of the social interests that will be thereby promoted or impaired. One of the most fundamental social interests is that law shall be uniform and impartial. There must be nothing in its action that savours of prejudice or even arbitrary whim or fitfulness. Therefore in the main there shall be adherence to precedent. There shall be symmetrical development, consistently with history or custom when history or custom has been the motive force, or the chief one, in giving shape to existing rules, and with logic or philosophy when the motive power has been theirs. But symmetrical development may be bought at too high a price. Uniformity ceases to be a good when it becomes uniformity of oppression. The social interest served by symmetry or certainty must then be balanced against the social interest served by equity and fairness or other elements of social welfare. These may enjoin upon the judge the duty of drawing the line at another angle, of staking the path along new courses, of marking a new point of departure from which others who come after him will set out upon their journey.

If you ask how he is to know when one interest outweighs another, I can only answer that he must get his knowledge just as the legislator gets it, from experience and study and reflection; in brief, from life itself. Here, indeed, is the point of contact between the legislator's work and his (1921, pp. 112–13).

Even before the First World War the growing pressure of new industrial and technical developments, of new social and political philosophies, had led jurists of many countries, independently of each other, to think about law in new terms: to see it primarily as an instrument of social evolution. Legal logic and techniques came to be seen as elements, but by no means the sole, or even the predominant factor, in the unending race between law and new social problems.

Precedent and Social Change in the Common Law

Since the First World War the tempo of social change has accelerated beyond all imagination. With it, the challenge to the law has become more powerful and urgent. We have seen that many years ago, leading jurists and judges concurred that it was not only the right but the duty of the judge to take note of fundamental changes in public opinion. Indeed, it is almost certain that the common law would no longer exist if great judges had not from time to time accepted the challenge and boldly laid down new principles to meet new social problems. The decisions which reflect such judicial revolutions are relatively few in number, but they stand out as landmarks. Every one of them symbolizes a new social epoch and has laid the foundations on which hundreds of elaborations or routine decisions can be built up. A few examples may suffice to illustrate this point.

When Blackburn J. formulated the rule in *Rylands* v. *Fletcher*,[3] he began to adapt the principles of tort liability to the era of expanding industrial enterprise in a once predominantly agricultural society.[4] The technique by which that great judge accomplished this feat was the collection, synthesis and remoulding of several instances of liability which, in Dean Wigmore's language,

wandered about, unhoused and unshepherded, except for a casual attention, in the pathless fields of jurisprudence, until they were met by the master-mind of Mr Justice Blackburn who guided them to the safe fold where they have since rested. In a sentence epochal in its consequences this judge coordinated them all in their true category.[5]

Another judgement of Blackburn J.[6] laid the foundations for the principle of legal liability of public authorities, now of outstanding importance in the age of government enterprise.

The twentieth-century counterpart of the rule in *Rylands* v. *Fletcher*,[7] the juridical creation of a direct action by a user or consumer against the manufacturer of a faulty product, is technically simply an abandonment of the principle that *A*, if contractually liable to *B*, cannot simultaneously be liable in tort for the same action or omission to *C*. But sociologically, it means the judicial recognition of the age of mass manufacture and standardized products, an age in which the economic position of the retailer is vitally changed. In the field of contract, the development of the doctrine of frustration was stimulated by the upheavals of the First and Second World Wars. The doctrine has, in English and American law, not yet assumed the

3. (1868) L.R. 3 H.L. 330.
4. This is brought out in Professor Bohlen's classical essay on the rule (1926).
5. 'Responsibility for Tortious acts', 7 *Harvard L. Rev.*, 441, 454 (1894).
6. *Mersey Docks Trustees* v. *Gibbs* [1866] L.R. 1 H.L. 93.
7. *McPherson* v. *Buick*, 217 N.Y. 382, 111 N.E. 1050 (1916); *Donoghue* v. *Stevenson* [1932] A.C. 562.

same significance as on the Continent, mainly because the social and economic upheavals have not been as great. The main impetus was given to it by the requisitioning of the British Merchant Navy in the First World War, an event of basic economic importance in a maritime nation. It was the shattering inflation following the First World War which led the German courts to develop the doctrine of frustration of contract from certain general clauses in the German Civil Code. It became an instrument for the judicial adjustment of obligations which had become grossly unjust as a result of drastic currency devaluation. This doctrine has had great influence on other Continental systems such as French, Swiss and Greek law. That its significance in English law has also increased is shown by some recent decisions of the Court of Appeal.[8] While the doctrine of frustration is accepted in American law, its practical impact has been small, because the economy of the United States has not so far been basically shaken by wars or inflations. The two most interesting decisions on the subject were characteristically provoked by a priority system for automobiles established during the Second World War,[9] and a severe shortage of certain materials caused by the Korean War.[10] In neither case was the disturbance of the contract situation found drastic enough to justify exoneration of the party affected.

The principle of *stare decisis* has set certain limits to judicial law-making which are apparent in the fate of the doctrine of common employment. Invented at a time when judges thought in terms of patriarchal households and small-scale business,[11] it has long been found utterly unsuited to the facts of modern industrial employment. In a number of decisions, the House of Lords whittled down the doctrine, but was unable to abolish it (Friedmann, 1967, pp. 465–6). This was eventually accomplished by the legislator through the Law Reform (Personal Injuries) Act 1948.

Another area in which the courts have played an important role in the adjustment of law to new social realities is the field of

8. *Parkinson* v. *Commissioners of Works* [1949] 2 K.B. 632; *British Movietonews* v. *London Cinemas* [1951] 1 K.B. 190. The latter decision was reversed by the House of Lords [1952] A.C. 166.

9. *Lloyds* v. *Murphy*, 25 Cal. 2d 48, 153 P. 2d 47 (1944).

10. *Peerless Cash Co.* v. *Weymouth Gardens Inc.*, 215 F. 2d 362 (1st Cir. 1954).

11. *Priestley* v. *Fowler* [1837] 3 M. & W. 1.

matrimonial relations. Here, English courts have, in recent years, introduced certain ideas of community property into the settlement of property issues between husband and wife (see p. 273).

It was largely in reaction, both to the post-war housing shortage and to the widespread desertion of war-time brides that the Court of Appeal, in *Bendall* v. *McWhirter*[12] granted the deserted wife the right to continued occupation of her matrimonial home in which she had no legal ownership, as against the husband's trustee in bankruptcy. This decision was overruled by the House of Lords in 1965.[13] But the Court of Appeal's initiative in providing for the wife a kind of 'homestead' right, as it is embodied in many American and Canadian statutes, inspired the recommendation of the Royal Commission on Marriage and Divorce in 1956, which in turn was implemented in the Matrimonial Homes Act 1967.

Yet the majority of the British and Commonwealth judges still take the view that there is a difference, not only of degree, but of kind, between the making of the law – which is the legislator's field – and the application of the law, which is the judge's domain. This view was put in blunt terms by Lord Jowitt L.C. on the occasion of the Seventh Legal Convention of the Law Council of Australia.[14]

Please do not get yourself into the frame of mind of entrusting to the judges the working out of a whole new set of principles which does accord with the requirements of modern conditions. Leave that to the legislature, and leave us to confine ourselves to trying to find out what the law is.

These observations were occasioned by the discussion of a learned paper by Mr Justice Fullagar of the High Court of Australia, dealing with the problem of 'Liability for representations at common law', a problem recently underlined by the decision of the English Court of Appeal in *Candler* v. *Crane, Christmas & Co.*[15]

Some years later, the House of Lords itself refuted Lord Jowitt's thesis, by reversing unanimously, in *Hedley Byrne* v. *Heller*,[16] the

12. [1952] 2 Q.B. 466.
13. *National Provincial Bank* v. *Ainsworth* [1965] A.C. 1175.
14. (1951) 25 *Australian L.J.* p. 296.
15. [1951] 2 K.B. 164.
16. [1964] A.C. 465.

principle of the *Candler* case. So great was the law reforming zeal of the House of Lords in 1965 that it chose a case in which it would not have been strictly necessary to discuss the merits of *Candler*. The action – brought against a bank for negligent information on the financial solidity of a client – was dismissed on the ground that the defendant had excluded liability for his information. The House nevertheless took this opportunity to lay down, in a number of elaborate statements from the Bench, the principle of legal responsibility for negligently made statements causing financial damage, at least where there is a 'special relationship'. This change in judicial philosophy – certainly made in part in response to widespread criticism of *Candler*, and the corresponding American decision in *Ultramares* v. *Touche*[17] reflects the fact that, in an increasingly interdependent society, consumers of all kinds need protection. Although it is very difficult to define the 'special relationship' that constitutes a duty, with precision,[18] extension of the consumer's protection, from the manufacture of standard products to the professional purveyor of information, and the corresponding extension of the types of damage that qualify for reparation, is logical. But whatever one may think of the merits of *Hedley Byrne*, it is clearly incompatible with Lord Jowitt's thesis of the division of functions between legislators and judiciary.[19]

In 1969, Lord Reid expressed a view on the law-making function of courts, which differs significantly from that expressed eighteen years earlier by Lord Jowitt. He observed that courts certainly had an important function in the adaptation of law to new circumstances, but that they could not assume the function of Parliament in matters of 'general policy'.[20]

The history of the common law has been a constant give and take between consolidation and progress, between the legal technicians and the creative jurists. In the past, the tempo of social change was very much less rapid than it is today, and it cannot be assumed that the

17. 225 N.Y. 170 (1931). *Ultramares* has not yet been reversed in the United States.

18. See further p. 162.

19. For a discussion of the complexities of the delimitation of functions see pp. 34, 382.

20. *Pettit* v. *Pettit* [1969] 2 All E.R. 385, 390. See, for a discussion of this decision, p. 274.

'lawyer's law' will always remain a prerogative of the professional lawyer, a backwater removed from urgent social and political problems. What could once be regarded as more or less technical 'lawyers' law', may today be a matter of urgent economic and social policy. There is no more telling illustration of this shift than the recent transfer of the whole field of restrictive trade practices from the common-law domain – where it had rested, in England, for centuries – to a statutory regulation which entrusts the administration of this vital sphere of national economic policy to a mixture of administrative commissions, governmental authorities and, more recently, a special tribunal composed of a majority of non-lawyers instead of the law courts (see p. 300).

Those who oppose the notion that law courts should take an active part in the adaptation of law to social problems usually argue that to do so would sacrifice certainty, the primary virtue of the law, to utility. If adhesion to legal technique and the exclusion of value-judgements had achieved certainty, the contention would have force. Certainty is one of the paramount objectives of law. It is usually achieved in the thousands of routine decisions which quantitatively make up the bulk of the law. But in the relatively small number of leading cases which give direction to hundreds of others, stability and certainty have seldom been either aimed at or achieved. The distinction between *ratio decidendi* and *obiter dictum*, the differentiation of cases on facts, the reliance on one or the other judgement in a decision by a higher court, and many other factors give a choice vastly wider than is apparent on the surface. The divergences outlined in the cases mentioned earlier cannot be accounted for by technical arguments or legal logic. These are indispensable but highly flexible instruments of legal reasoning. They are the servants, not the masters. When they are built up into the position of masters, it is by choice, not by necessity.[21]

21. For an analysis of this whole process, see, among many others, Stone (1946, p. 171). On the difficulties of discovering the *ratio decidendi* and the consequent opportunities of choice between different solutions, see Paton and Sawer (1947), 63 *L.Q.Rev.*, p. 461; on the problem in general, see Friedmann (1967), chs. 31, 32. See also the controversy between Montrose and Simpson in (1957) 20 *Mod.L.Rev.* 124, 413; (1958) 21 *Mod.L.Rev.* 155; Goodhart (1959) 22 *Mod.L.Rev.* 117.

Nor is the inevitability of the creative function of the courts in the interpretation of the law challenged by the leading modern representatives of analytical jurisprudence. The Vienna School, led by Merkl and Kelsen, has long recognized, in its *Stufentheorie*, that the judicial function, while far more circumscribed in the freedom to create law than the legislature, nevertheless involves the making of law in the process of applying the norm to individual facts. However, the Vienna School refuses to indicate the principles by which this creative judicial process should be guided, since this is held to be outside the task of a 'pure legal science'. Similarly a contemporary English jurist, who has concentrated on the elucidation of the meaning of legal concepts, has this to say

There must be a core of settled meaning, but there will be, as well, a penumbra of debatable cases in which words are neither obviously applicable nor obviously ruled out. . . .

. . . instead of saying that the recurrence of penumbral questions shows us that legal rules are essentially incomplete, and that, when they fail to determine decisions, judges must legislate and so exercise a creative choice between alternatives, we shall say that the social policies which guide the judges' choice are in a sense there for them to discover; the judges are only 'drawing out' of the rule what, if it is properly understood, is 'latent' within it.[22]

Once it is admitted that there is an area of uncertainty in the interpretation of (common-law or statutory) concepts, the question whether the solution to a doubtful situation is found by drawing out 'a latent meaning', or by a creative interpretation, becomes a verbal dispute.[23] No serious student of the problem has ever disputed that certain terms, such as 'bankruptcy' or 'vehicle' have a greater area of settled interpretation than others, such as 'freedom of speech' or 'clear and present danger'. The freedom, and the agony, of choice does, indeed, greatly differ from case to case. This increases the urgency of our task to formulate rational guiding lines whether or

22. H. L. A. Hart, 'Positivism and the separation of law and morals', 71 *Harvard L.Rev.* 593 (1958), pp. 607–8 and 612.
23. Professor Fuller, in 'Positivism and fidelity to law: a reply to Professor Hart', 71 *Harvard L. Rev.*, 630, 661–9 (1958), has rightly disputed the validity of the distinction between a 'core' and a 'penumbra' of meaning.

not this is defined as part of the process of finding the law as it is, or an infusion of the law as it ought to be.[24]

The analysis of recent trends in the common law thus underlines the theoretical observations made earlier in this chapter. The Swiss and Italian Civil Codes, the conclusions reached by Gény in France, by Holmes, Stone or Cardozo in America, by Lord Wright or Lord Denning in England, express the same thought in different ways. In his application of precedent, as in the interpretation of statutes, the judge must take note of major shifts in public opinion and social policy, of developments sufficiently fundamental to be accepted by the consensus of public opinion and to be expressed by the general trend in legislative policy. The theoretical formulation of such an approach must always remain somewhat vague, for the ways in which changes in public opinion express themselves in a democratic society are many and it is not an easy task for a court to fix the borderline between accepted evolutions in public opinion, on the one hand, and personal philosophy or prejudice, on the other.

It is, however, not difficult to illustrate by concrete examples the distinction between personal idiosyncrasy and the incorporation of new social policies in the administration of the law.[25] Any court of a contemporary industrialized country must, for example, recognize collective bargaining and labour organization as a legitimate and

24. See the controversy between Hart and Fuller, and the admission by Hart that 'the interpretations stigmatized as automatic have resulted from the conviction that it is fairer in a criminal statute to take a meaning which would jump to the mind of the ordinary man at the cost even of defeating other values, and this itself is a social policy (though possibly a bad one); or much more frequently, what is stigmatized as "mechanical" and "automatic" is a determined choice made indeed in the light of a social aim but a conservative social aim', Hart, 71 *Harvard L. Rev.* 611 (1958).

25. See the observations by Judge Traynor, on 'Courts and Lawmaking' in Paulsen (1959): 'Although the judge's predilections may play a part in setting the initial direction he takes towards the creative solution, there is little danger of their determining the solution itself, however much it bears the stamp of his individual workmanship. Our great creative judges have been men of outstanding skill, adept at discounting their own predilections and careful to discount them with conscientious severity. The disinterestedness of the creative decision is further assured by the judge's arduous articulation of the reasons that compel the formulation of an original solution and by the full disclosure in his opinion of all aspects of the problem and of the data pertinent to its solution.'

commonly accepted instrument of social action. One result is the shrinking of the tort of conspiracy. What was, fifty years ago, regarded as personal malice, is now juridically recognized as a legitimate weapon in the economic struggle between organized social groups.[26] The Supreme Court of the United States, as late as 1936[27] regarded a minimum wage act as an unconstitutional interference with the freedom of property. Today such a denial would not be seriously contemplated. As one problem is solved, a new one opens up. Trade unions are no longer outlaws, or underdogs, but powerful and often monopolistic organizations. Today, the problem of the closed shop shows the clash between two equally accepted legal principles: the right to bargain collectively and the freedom of the individual to choose his place of work and his associations.

The reaction of public opinion against the power of trade unions, to paralyse certain key sectors of public life, such as transport, was reflected in the decision of the House of Lords in *Rookes* v. *Barnard*.[28] The House of Lords held two fellow employees and the union organizer liable in damages to the plaintiff, an employee of the BOAC, who had been dismissed – without breach of contract – under a threat uttered by the defendants acting on behalf of the union that, without the plaintiff's dismissal there would be a strike – in breach of a 'no strike' agreement. Although all the judgements were couched in analytical language, it was obvious that the various constructions – notably the unearthing of an all but forgotten tort of 'intimidation', as distinct from conspiracy – and the virtual dismantling of the key provisions of the Trade Disputes Act of 1906, were thin disguises for a policy reversal, a deliberate attempt to restrict the power of trade unions to disrupt vital services.[29]

Again, contemporary British and American courts must base their decisions on the principle of the equality of races, religions and sexes. Practical expressions of this trend are the recent decisions of the United States Supreme Court prohibiting discrimination against

26. *Crofter Handwoven Harris Tweed Co.* v. *Veitch* [1942] A.C. 435.
27. *Morehead* v. *Tipaldo*, 298 U.S. 587 (1936).
28. [1964] A.C. 1129. See further on this decision, pp. 356–8.
29. The principles of this decision were reversed by the Trade Disputes Act 1965 which together with the Trade Disputes Act 1906, was repealed by the Industrial Relations Act 1971.

Negroes,[30] or the award of damages by an English court for violation of a common-law right[31] to a coloured person who had been refused admittance to a public hotel. A corresponding evolution in the field of public law is the increasing rejection of crown privileges in the field of civil liabilities, privileges which are incompatible both with the rule of law in a democracy and the growing role of government in commercial and industrial enterprise.

Statutory Interpretation and the Conflict of Values

The clash of values and interests, the conflict between different judicial approaches, is no less marked in the interpretation of statutes than is in the common law. The controversy between the 'literal' and 'liberal' theories of statutory interpretation corresponds closely to that between the adherents of a static and a dynamic interpretation. The former regard the interpretation of a statute as essentially an exercise in grammar, based on a strict distinction between the legislative and the interpretative function. The latter regard it as a process of purposeful collaboration based on an understanding of the legislative purpose, for which the rules of *Heydon's Case* (1584) or Plowden's celebrated note on *Eyston* v. *Studd* (see Friedmann, 1967, pp. 452–61) can still serve as a guide:

And in order to form a right judgement when the letter of a statute is restrained, and when enlarged, by equity, it is a good way, when you peruse a statute, to suppose that the law-maker is present, and that you have asked him the question you want to know touching the equity; then you must give yourself such an answer as you imagine he would have done, if he had been present . . . . And if the law-maker would have followed the equity, notwithstanding the words of the law . . . you may safely do the like.

To illustrate the problem by a few recent cases in different fields: In a Canadian case,[32] the fortuitous profits of private trading clashed with the claim of government – a non-Socialist government – to redistribute profits caused by governmental price regulation in the

30. e.g. *Smith* v. *Allwright* (1944) 321 U.S. 649; *Shelley* v. *Kraemer* (1948) 334 U.S. 1; and in particular, *Brown* v. *Board of Education of Topeka*, 349 U.S. (1954) p. 294; and see p. 64.
31. *Constantine* v. *Imperial Hotels Ltd* [1944] K.B. 693.
32. *Canadian Wheat Board* v. *Nolar* et al. [1951] S.C.R. 81; [1951] D.L.R. 466.

interest of the community. This conflict was barely hidden by a grammatical controversy about the meaning of a clause in the National Emergency Transitional Powers Act. The English Court of Appeal,[33] some years ago, had to decide whether ministerial powers under a new Town and Country Planning Act superseded the terms of an agreement between a local authority and a private company concerning the development of an estate, a decision which plainly hung on the evaluation of the relation between old contractual ties and new legislative powers.

The Appeal Court of Wisconsin was faced with a choice between two conflicting statutory provisions – one authorizing the receivability of blood-group tests in evidence to determine the parentage of a child, the other burdening a party asserting the illegitimacy of a child born in wedlock with 'proof beyond all reasonable doubt' – when a mother, who had had intercourse with her husband eight months before delivery, swore that he was the father, while blood tests excluded all possibility of his fatherhood.[34] The decision depended on a balancing of the respective weight of two conflicting legislative directives, not on a logical choice.

An excellent illustration of the clash of social philosophies – concealed behind different interpretations of a statutory term, is the decision of the US Supreme Court in *US* v. *Republic Steel Corporation*.[35] The Court split five to four on the question whether the term 'obstruction', as used in the Rivers and Harbours Act of 1890, prohibited the defendant from unloading industrial deposits in a navigable river, with the result that the depth of the channel was reduced. The majority interpreted 'obstruction' as not limited to some kind of structure, although enumeration of objectionable activities – in Section 10 of the Act – is confined to structures and buildings. The majority construed the act as expressing the broad purpose of securing navigation and commerce in a vital waterway. Today it would no doubt add the concern with pollution as an overriding policy objective of the Act. But the minority regarded this approach as 'reading into the statute things that are actually not there', and as an attempt by the judiciary to fill deficiencies in a

33. *Ransom & Luck* v. *Surbiton* [1949] Ch. 180.
34. *Prochnow* v. *Prochnow*, 274 Wis. 491 (1957).
35. 362 U.S. 482 (1960).

statute which should properly be remedied by Congress. Both majority and minority supported themselves by numerous precedents.

Most important of all, the interpretation of constitutions constantly brings up conflicts of social principles. This conflict may appear in the interpretation of the 'property and civil rights' clause in the British North America Act, of the 'due process' clauses of the American Constitution, or of the 'freedom of trade, commerce and intercourse' clause in the Australian Constitution; the basic social problems which appear in different legal forms are essentially the same.

Can we – as is so often contended – dismiss these social issues from our legal conscience by adhering to a 'strict' or 'technical' interpretation of statutes? This problem divides itself into two. First, is it correct to speak of statutes as a genus for purposes of interpretation? Do the same rules of interpretation apply to a written constitution and to a bankruptcy Act, a taxation Act or a criminal statute? Second, if one set of rules is to be applied to all statutes, are they sufficiently clear and certain to eliminate conflicting interpretations?

In an earlier analysis,[36] I have suggested that statutes are by no means all of one kind and that both judicial practice and principle indicate important differences between the rules of interpretation appropriate to different types of statutes. An eminently political and general document, such as a constitution, is not and cannot be treated in the same way as a statute concerned with the registration of land or with criminal procedure. Lord Jowitt, Lord Wright, Lord Greene, Mr Justice Dixon and Mr Justice Frankfurter are among the eminent judges whose views were quoted for confirmation of such a differentiation.[37]

36. (1948) 26 *Canadian Bar Rev.* 1277; for an incisive criticism of the literal approach to statutory interpretation, see also Willis, 'Statute interpretation in a nutshell' (1938) *Canadian Bar Rev.* 1.

37. Sir C. K. Allen (1967, p. 528) objects that: 'It is to be feared, however, that any such attempted classification would merely add a series of ambiguous adjectives to the existing difficulties of interpretation. Categories of this kind, and others which might easily be suggested, could not possibly be precise and would overlap at many points.' It cannot be denied that a precise delimitation of different categories of statutes is difficult. This is, however, a difficulty of any principle of interpretation. None can be more than a general guide to the understanding of the specific problem at hand. Support for the approach suggested here has come from

This approach has now received powerful confirmation in a decision of the Canadian Supreme Court, of fundamental jurisprudential importance. The Canadian Bill of Rights of 1960[38] – technically an ordinary statute – proclaims, *inter alia* that

1. It is hereby recognized and declared that in Canada there have existed and shall continue to exist without discrimination by reason of race, national origin, colour, religion or sex, the following human rights and fundamental freedoms, namely, . . .
(b) the right of the individual to equality before the law and the protection of the law; . . .
2. Every law of Canada shall, unless it is expressly declared by an Act of the Parliament of Canada that it shall operate notwithstanding the *Canadian Bill of Rights*, be so construed and applied as not to abrogate, abridge or infringe or to authorize the abrogation, abridgement or infringement of any of the rights of freedoms herein recognized and declared. . . .

The Indian Act of 1952, applicable to the Northwest Territories, imposed penalties on Indians found intoxicated off a reserve, far more severe than those applicable to other Canadians. By a majority of six to three the Court held in a case decided in 1970[39] that the Bill of Rights superseded any provision of any Canadian law inconsistent with it. In criticizing the view of another judge that section (1) of the Bill of Rights should be regarded merely as a canon of construction for the interpretation of legislation existing when it was enacted, Ritchie, J., observed:

This proposition appears to me to strike at the very foundations of the *Bill of Rights* and to convert it from its apparent character as a statutory declaration of the fundamental human rights and freedoms which it recognizes, into being little more than a rule for the construction of federal statutes. . . .

---

an American jurist: 'The unresolved conflict between the opposing approaches stems from the false assumption that all statues are alike. All statutes are not alike, and, in fact, are not treated similarly. Yet judicial standards of construction and rationale of interpretation purport to apply a single approach to all statutes. What is required is an acknowledged pluralistic treatment. The close application approach is appropriate to one kind of statute, and the creative elaboration approach to another kind of statute. There are intermediate variations suitable to statutes of intermediate kinds' (Breitel, 1959).
38. Stat. Can. 1960, Ch. 44.
39. *Regina* v. *Drybones*, 9 D.L.R. (3rd) 473 (1970).

I think that section 1(b) means at least that no individual or group of individuals is to be treated more harshly than another under that law, and I am therefore of opinion that an individual is denied equality before the law if it is made an offence punishable at law, on account of his race, for him to do something which his fellow Canadians are free to do without having committed any offence or having been made subject to any penalty.

The present case discloses laws of Canada which abrogate, abridge and infringe the right of an individual Indian to equality before the law and in my opinion if those laws are to be applied in accordance with the express language used by Parliament in section 2 of the *Bill of Rights*, then section 94(b) of the *Indian Act* must be declared to be inoperative.[40]

In other words, the Bill of Rights is not like any other statute. It is one embodying fundamental principles of public policy, which modifies and, where necessary supersedes, statutes incompatible with it – even though it is not, like the US Constitution, a 'higher law', formally superior to ordinary statutes. The Bill of Rights may, of course, itself be superseded by another ordinary statute. But this does not derogate from the fact that it has the substantive weight of a constitutional document, that there are 'statutes and statutes'.

But even if it were assumed that there are uniform rules of interpretation for all types of statutes, the further question remains whether these rules are so clear, so technical and so unpolitical in their character as to avoid any conflict of values. Technical rules are to a large extent self-contradictory, and in decisions of fundamental importance the issue has seldom turned on them. The House of Lords – generally more attached to 'strict' or 'technical' interpretations of statutes and precedents than any other high court of the common-law world – has not hesitated to depart from literal interpretation or established canons of construction when the problem at issue appeared sufficiently important to justify it.

In *Roberts* v. *Hopwood*,[41] a London Borough Council had fixed a minimum wage of £4 a week for all its employees, male and female. This, one should have thought, it had a clear power to do, under a statute which empowered local authorities to allow such wages 'as [they] may think fit'. Yet the House of Lords added the word 'reasonably' to this phrase, and then proceeded to quash the action of the

40. *Regina* v. *Drybones* at 481, 484, 485.
41. [1925] A.C. 578.

council as unreasonable (see further pp. 393–4). On the other hand, in *Liversidge* v. *Anderson*,[42] the House was concerned with the interpretation of Defence Regulation 18B, which gave the Home Secretary certain powers of detention, where he had 'reasonable cause to believe' certain persons to be of hostile associations. This formulation had been adopted, after a parliamentary debate, in order to provide some check on the Home Secretary's discretion. But the majority, anxious this time to help the executive in a time of great emergency, refused to examine whether the Home Secretary had, in fact, had reasonable cause. In effect, 'where . . . he *thinks* he has reasonable cause to believe' was substituted for 'had reasonable cause', a construction which Lord Atkin had little difficulty in showing was contrary to all precedent and to the usual canons of interpretation. In a post-war decision,[43] the Privy Council confirmed Lord Atkin's view when, in a clause virtually identical with 18B, it affirmed the right of judicial scrutiny as to whether an administrative authority had, in fact, acted reasonably, and all but dissented from *Liversidge* v. *Anderson*.

Social Change and the Interpretation of Constitutions

The belief that the Privy Council and the Commonwealth courts have avoided the political problems and tensions of the United States Supreme Court by interpreting the relevant constitutions as 'statutes' is untenable.

The interpretation of the British North America Act, especially by the Privy Council, has been as fraught with political meaning as that of the American Constitution by the Supreme Court of the United States, and as far reaching in its social consequences (see p. 33). And this approach has not ensured certainty either of principle or of precedent. The decisions on such matters as the Dominion's residuary power, the treaty-making power, and the regulation of trade and commerce are neither more consistent nor more certain than those of any other political or social character.

Where the power of government is divided between a federation and its member states, advocacy of planning or *laissez-faire* alone cannot resolve the conflict; for the further constitutional question

42. [1942] A.C. 206.
43. *Nakkuda Ali* v. *Jayaratne* (1950), 66 T.L.R. (pt 2), 214.

arises whether, in a federation, there is an inviolable minimum of state powers which a federation cannot infringe by an expansive interpretation of taxing power, interstate commerce, and of other powers to which modern social conditions give a meaning vastly different from the one it had at the time of the Founding Fathers. Moreover, judges in a free society will often deliberately check their own preferences because they regard even the appearance of a biased decision as more harmful than a result which they personally disapprove.[44] Even when the issue of principle is clear, the question remains, how the exercise of a specific power should be classified. The discussion of principles can lead to a clarification of issues. It cannot eliminate the responsibility of decision in a given issue.

The much attacked judgements of the United States Supreme Court, whether unanimous or divided, reflect and interpret a real world, a world of conflict and tensions, of uncertainties and divided opinions. They do not pretend that the application of the general formulas of the Constitution to the complexities of a concrete problem is a simple task. True to the tradition of Holmes, Brandeis, Cardozo, Stone and Frankfurter, the Court no longer confuses – as it once did – the duty to be as impartial and detached as the conflicts of human minds permit with the illusion that political problems are not political problems, an illusion to which British courts are so often prone.

The New Deal period served as the main catalyst for the Court's thinking. For a few years, the conservative majority of the Court prevailed in its stubborn adherence to its well-entrenched due-process philosophy, invalidating the main pieces of the new edifice of social legislation. The reappraisal came when the dissident minority, for which Justice Stone had become the principal spokesman in succession to Justice Holmes, was converted into a majority, through the accession of Chief Justice Hughes and Justice Roberts. In a

44. The High Court of Australia, in March 1951, by a majority of six to one, invalidated the Government Act outlawing the Australian Communist Party. None of the judges representing the majority could be suspected of any sympathy for the Communist Party and some of them quite probably approved the political objectives of the Act (Beasley, 'Australia's Communist Party Dissolution Act' (1951) 29 *Canadian Bar Rev.* 490).

famous trilogy of decisions in 1937[45] the Court upheld the collective-bargaining principle of the new labour legislation, the new social-security legislation and a minimum-wage statute. It not only abandoned the attitude, which it had maintained for so long, that such regulatory interferences on the part of the elected legislature constituted a violation of 'due process', which it had elevated from a procedural safeguard into a natural-law principal of *laissez faire*. What is more important, it came to adopt the attitude of restraint long advocated in regard to measures of social and economic reform by Holmes, Stone and others, that the Court could not substitute itself as a non-elected legislator for the will of the elected legislator, except in cases of manifest violation of the Constitution.[46] Through all the subsequent vicissitudes and controversies, the Court has generally maintained this attitude of respect for the expressed will of the legislator. It has not, however, been able to escape other and no less bitter ideological battles. The intensity of the 'cold war', and the often hysterical accusations levelled in the less responsible press and in congressional committees against persons and organizations alleged to be subversive, have forced the Court to draw a line between the legitimate concerns of national security and the irreducible minimum safeguards of individual liberty in a Constitutional democracy.

The issue of equal protection, regardless of race or colour – an issue over which the Civil War was fought and which is enshrined in the Bill of Rights (article XV) of the United States Constitution –

45. *West Coast Hotel* v. *Parrish*, 300 U.S. 379 (1937), holding valid a minimum wage statute; *N. L. R. B.* v. *Jones & Laughlin Steel Corp.*, 301 U.S. 1 (1937), sustaining the National Labour Relations Act; and *Steward Machine Co.* v. *Davis*, 301 U.S. 548 (1937), sustaining the Social Security Act.

46. See, in elaboration of Holmes's celebrated dictum that 'the Fourteenth Amendment does not enact Mr Herbert Spencer's Social Statistics', *Lochner* v. *New York* (1904) 198 U.S. 45, Justice Stone's dissenting opinion in *Morehead* v. *Tipaldo* 298 U.S. 587 (1936), which invalidated a New York Minimum Wages Act: 'It is not for the courts to resolve whether the remedy by wage regulation is as efficacious as many believe, or is better than some other, or is better even than the blind operation of uncontrolled economic forces. The legislature must be free to choose unless the government is to be rendered impotent. The Fourteenth Amendment has no more embedded in the Constitution our preference for some particular set of economic beliefs than it has adopted, in the name of liberty, the system of theology which we may happen to approve' (p. 636).

has been another vital matter in which the Supreme Court has been compelled to reappraise the hierachy of values explicit or implicit in the Constitution. Here the Court has gradually reversed the priority of constitutional values by according to government and legislature the right to experiment in social affairs, and, on the other hand, affirming far more strongly than at any previous time the substantive meaning of racial equality. Proceeding from the condemnation of discriminatory practices and laws in elections, including primaries, to the condemnation of separate university facilities for whites and Negroes, the Court finally, in 1954,[47] condemned the system of separate public schools for whites and Negroes, prevalent in the South, and with it, specifically overruled its own previous 'equal but separate facilities' doctrine of *Plessy* v. *Ferguson.*[48]

Normally, controversies about the proper canons of interpretation of a constitution remain a matter of essentially professional concern. But when they touch vital political and social questions they may have far deeper repercussions. The prolonged refusal of the Supreme Court, during the early phase of the New Deal reforms, to recognize the constitutionality of some of its most important statutory measures led President Roosevelt to his – fortunately unsuccessful – attempt to alter the law governing the composition of the Court, so as to be able to fill the newly arising vacancies with nominees of his choice. The crisis was eventually solved by the above-mentioned change in the attitude of the Court. A succession of decisions, which have re-interpreted various aspects of the Constitution, in such matters as the constitutionality of 'separate but equal' facilities for the education of whites and Negroes (see p. 70) or the relation of federal to state power, in criminal prosecutions,[49] or the constitutionality of various state statutes dealing with 'subversive activities', as being

47. *Brown* v. *Board of Education*, 347 U.S. 483 (1954), 349 U.S. 294 (1955); *Cooper* v. *Aaron* 358 U.S. 1 (1958).

48. 163 U.S. 537 (1897). The Court softened the effect of the decision by leaving its implementation to the supervision of the US District courts. Their power to approve schemes which would bring about integration in gradual stages 'with all deliberate speed' has not prevented widespread obstruction.

49. Under which Federal Statutes, e.g. in matters of sedition or regulation of labour relations, 'pre-empt' the field, and thus invalidate or suspend incompatible state legislation. See, in particular, *Pennsylvania* v. *Nelson*, 350 U.S. 497 (1956).

improper interferences with the constitutionally protected liberties of the citizen,[50] or the limits put to Congressional investigation by the First Amendment,[51] have led to a nation-wide discussion, both in professional and non-professional circles, of the proper function of the Court in the interpretation of the Constitution. Not surprisingly, a dispassionate approach to the infinitely complex problem of balance in constitutional interpretation has, in the great majority of cases, given way to partisanship for or against the particular decisions involved. Some of those who, before the Court's change of posture in 1937, condemned judicial obstruction of legislative reforms as an improper infusion of reactionary political beliefs into the arbitral function of a Constitutional Court, now see in the Court a vital bulwark of basic liberties against popular hysterias and administrative or legislative pressures. On the other hand, many of those who, in the mid-1930s, regarded the Supreme Court's sweeping interpretation of the due process clauses, and the consequent invalidation of the New Deal legislation, as the only solid bulwark of a 'government under laws' against the arbitrary will of legislators, consider the Court's present emphasis on constitutional liberties as an intolerable interference with the will of the legislator. Lawyers as well as laymen have again advanced the proposition that the Court must stick to the interpretation of the Constitution as it can be deduced from the actual or presumed intention of the Founding Fathers.[52] This patently absurd proposition can best be answered in the words of the late Judge Learned Hand:

Not only is it true that, 'if by the statement that what the Constitution meant at the time of its adoption is what it means today it is intended to say that the great clauses of the Constitution must be confined to the interpretation which the framers with the conditions and outlook of their time, would have placed upon them, the statement carries its own refutation', but it is also impossible to fabricate how the 'Framers' would have

50. *Sweezy* v. *New Hampshire*, 354 U.S. 234 (1957).

51. *Watkins* v. *US*, 354 U.S. 178 (1957); but see *Barenblatt* v. *US*, 79 S.Ct. 1081 (1959) where the court restored to Congress some of the freedom of investigation which it had appeared to restrict severely in *Watkins*.

52. See, among many others, a statement by Chief Judge Felton of the Court of Appeals of Georgia – issued by the Georgia Commission on Education: 'When is a Supreme Court Decision the Law of the Land?'

answered the problems that arise in a modern society had they been reared in the civilization that has produced those problems. We should indeed have to be sorcerers to conjure up how they would have responded (1958, p. 34).

Far more serious is the revival of the time-worn thesis that the Court should 'apply', but not 'make', the law, that it should not intrude into the field of policy-making; for this found the qualified approval of the Conference of Chief Justices held in August 1958. In a resolution adopted by thirty-eight votes against eight dissenters, the Conference resolved, *inter alia*:

That this Conference, while recognizing that the application of constitutional rules to changed conditions must be sufficiently flexible as to make such rules adaptable to altered conditions, believes that a fundamental purpose of having a written constitution is to promote the certainty and stability of the provisions of law set forth in such a constitution.

That this Conference hereby respectfully urges that the Supreme Court of the United States, in exercising the great powers confided to it for the determination of questions as to the allocation and extent of national and state powers, respectively, and as to the validity under the federal Constitution of the exercise of powers reserved to the states, exercise one of the greatest of all judicial powers – the power of judicial self-restraint – by recognizing and giving effect to the difference between that which, on the one hand, the Constitution may prescribe or permit, and that which, on the other, a majority of the Supreme Court, as from time to time constituted, may deem desirable or undesirable, to the end that our system of federalism may continue to function with and through the preservation of local self-government.[53]

Neither the Conference nor any responsible critic advocates that the Supreme Court of the United States should adopt the strict doctrine of *stare decisis*, abandoned in 1966 by House of Lords, which does not interpret a federal constitution.[54] In the elaborate Report accompanying the resolution,[55] one looks in vain for any guidance on the distinction between application of law and policy-

53. Resolution of the Conference of Chief Justices Pasadena, California, August 1958, reproduced at *Harvard L. Record*, 28 October 1958, p. 1.

54. Statement of the Lord Chancellor, 26 July 1966, reproduced in 82 *Law Q. Rev.*, 442 (1966).

55. See *Harvard L. Record*, 28 October 1958, p. 1.

making, other than a criticism of specific decisions and a general admonition to caution.

The vagueness and, indeed, emptiness of the attempted distinction between interpretations, alleged to apply existing law, and those alleged to make policy, was pointed out by one of the dissenters, the Chief Justice of New Jersey (Weintraub C.J.):

The Constitution does not offer a literal, definitive answer to the awesome problems which confront the Court. One may read the commerce clause, the due-process clause, the equal-protection clause, a thousand times and still not detect the slightest clue to the proper decision. The answer must be found elsewhere. The constitutional framework, as we all know, is a mere skeleton expression of governmental power and individual rights. The actual contours of those powers and rights must be determined in the context of changing conditions, by a process which is more than a mere mechanical application of a constitutional phrase to a set of facts.[56]

We have already stressed in a different context that, in a constantly changing society, in which, for example, the status, education and the public estimation of the Negro component of the American people have greatly changed as compared with the end of the last century, a decision to preserve 'separate but equal' facilities is as much a policy decision as one aiming at gradual integration. At most, it can be conceded that a change of interpretation should, as far as possible, be confined to matters of major and fundamental importance, and rest on the greatest possible consensus of judicial opinion. This was, indeed, the case in the desegregation decisions (see note 47) which were given by a unanimous Court.

In a federal constitutional system, any attempt to cut off the courts from the power to reflect major evolutions in public policy, would possibly be more fatal even than in unitary systems, where legislative change is easier. Ultimately, the proper balance between the conflicting values of stability and change can only be struck by judicial tact rather than abstract principle. To quote Judge Learned Hand again:

No doubt it is inevitable, however circumscribed his duty may be, that the personal proclivities of an interpreter will to some extent interject themselves into the meaning he imputes to a text, but in very much the greater

56. ibid., at p. 7.

part of a judge's duties he is charged with freeing himself as far as he can from all personal preferences, and that becomes difficult in proportion as these are strong. The degree to which he will secure compliance with his commands depends in large measure upon how far the community believes him to be the mouthpiece of public will, conceived as the resultant of many conflicting strains that have come, at least provisionally, to a consensus (1958, p. 71).

That this prescription will leave many cases of divided courts, as well as of bitter political attacks upon judicial decisions, is an inevitable reflection of the strains and stresses of a changing society. Any attempt to solve this problem by restricting the Court to a static, i.e. conservative, interpretation,[57] will not solve the problem of the judicial process, while it is likely to dam up one of the constitutional outlets for gradual legal evolution. As another distinguished American lawyer has said in a survey of the policy-making powers of the Supreme Court:

The difficulty in modification of the Constitution makes the Supreme Court a very powerful body in shaping the course of our civilization. In dealing with the constitutional guarantees of human dignity, it often has the application of the national conscience in its keeping. It is a sort of diplomatic priesthood.[58]

But we are still left with the question what principles are to guide the umpire in the agonizing choice between values, inevitable in a constitution that seeks to regulate the principles of life in a vast and constantly changing society – and that not over years or decades, but over centuries.

Does the sway of the battle leave us with anything more than the resigned acceptance of changing political tides and pressures, of individual preferences dictated by the conflicting beliefs of individual judges and resulting in shifting and accidental majority decisions?

The difficulty is illustrated by the attempt to articulate the choice values in the so-called 'preferred freedoms' doctrine.

The proposition that certain freedoms in the United States Constitution, i.e. those guaranteeing the basic personal liberties, might be

57. Perhaps on the model of the *Dred Scott* case, which is universally held to have been a major contributing cause to the American Civil War of the 1860s.
58. Ribble, 'Policy Making Powers of the Supreme Court and the Position of the Individual', 14 *Washington and Lee L. Rev.* 167, 184–5 (1957).

more fundamental than any concerned with changing processes of economic and social organization, was first tentatively mooted by the late Chief Justice Stone:[59]

Regulatory legislation affecting ordinary commercial transaction is not to be pronounced unconstitutional unless in the light of the facts made known or generally assumed it is of such a character as to preclude the assumption that it rests upon some rational basis within the knowledge and experience of the legislators. There may be narrower scope for operations of the presumption of constitutionality when legislation appears on its face to be within a specific prohibition of the Constitution, such as those of the first Ten Amendments, which are deemed equally specific when held to be embraced within the Fourteenth.

This approach has been supported by Justices Black and Douglas and, in effect, though perhaps not in words, by Chief Justice Warren in a number of decisions or dissents where the inviolability of freedom of speech and expression was asserted against the encroachments of national-security legislation or of other legislative efforts.[60] On the other hand, a judge as strongly in the tradition of Holmes and Stone as Justice Frankfurter has criticized the doctrine as being incompatible with the need for self-restraint by a non-elected court.[61] While acknowledging that 'those liberties of the individual which history has attested as the indispensable conditions of an open . . . society' have greater weight than liberties deriving from 'shifting economic arrangements' – which acknowledges a hierarchy of constitutional

59. *US* v. *Carolene Products Company*, 304 U.S. 144, 152 (1938). A similar approach is inherent in the observation by Cardozo J. (in *Palko* v. *Connecticut*, 302 U.S. 319, 327 (1937) that freedom of thought and speech is 'the matrix, the indispensable condition, of nearly every other form of freedom'.

60. The tension between freedom of publication and national security was dramatically illustrated in *New York Times* v. *United States* (403 U.S. 713 (1971)). The *New York Times* had obtained copies of a highly confidential government document concerning the history of US involvement in the Vietnam War by improper disclosure. The majority of the court, led by Black J., held that the First Amendment unconditionally prohibited the abridgement of 'the freedom of speech, or of the press', and that no considerations of national security empowered the Executive to restrain publication. But three judges, including the Chief Justice, dissented. In the judgement of Harlan J., the court was probably over-stepping the boundaries of judicial restraint in matters of national security, which were primarily the responsibility of the Executive.

61. *A. F. of L.* v. *American Sash and Door Co.*, 335 U.S. 538, 555 (1949).

values, Frankfurter regarded any 'preferred freedom' philosophy as a dangerous over-simplification of a complex process of legislative experimentation.[62]

The doctrine has been unconditionally criticized by Judge Learned Hand in the following words:

I cannot help thinking that it would have seemed a strange anomaly to those who penned the words in the Fifth to learn that they constituted severer restrictions as to liberty than property, especially now that liberty not only includes freedom from personal restraint, but enough economic security to allow its possessor the enjoyment of a satisfactory life. I can see no more persuasive reason for supposing that a legislature is *a priori* less qualified to choose between 'personal' than between economic values; and there have been strong protests, to me unanswerable, that there is no constitutional basis for asserting a larger measure of judicial supervision over the first than over the second (1958, pp. 50–51).

The problems outlined in the foregoing pages have been intensified by the almost unprecedented activism of the 'Warren Court' (1954 to 1969), when Chief Justice Earl Warren presided over a court, whose guiding philosophy has been, in the words of a commentator, the 'egalitarian society'.[63] The majority of the court, during that period, was inspired by the goal of translating the very general – and in many cases, dormant – provisions of the American Constitution concerning equality and the rights of the individual, in a liberal and pluralistic society, into social reality. The attempt to impose equality by judicial fiat, through the abolition of school segregation proclaimed in *Brown* v. *Board of Education*[64] led the courts as well as legislators and administrators – toward an increasing measure of constraint, to be imposed and enforced by public authority, inevitably at the expense of individual freedom of choice. In his Holmes Lectures of 1959, Professor Wechsler (1961) pointed out that the invocation of the Bill of Rights and of the Fourteenth Amendment does not solve the dilemma, since there may be a conflict, for example, between freedom of association and contract on the one hand, and racial non-discrimination on the other hand. As Professor Bickel has

62. *Kovacs* v. *Cooper*, 336 U.S. 77, 95 (1949).
63. Kurland, 'Foreword: Equal in origin and equal in title to the legislative and executive branches of the government', 78 *Harvard L. Rev.*, 143 (1964).
64. 347 U.S. 483 (1954).

pointed out in a recent analysis (1970, ch. 4), the attempt to implement the principle of *Brown* v. *Board of Education* has led the Supreme Court, and the subordinate courts, to more and more interference with local autonomy, as illustrated by the controversial ordering of 'compulsory bussing'. In order to enforce a better balance of races in public schools, more particularly in order to eliminate, or at least dilute, the *de facto* inequality and separation between predominantly white and predominantly black schools, many state and local authorities have been ordered to provide compulsory public transport from neighbourhood schools to other schools.[65] A number of Southern states and local authorities have countered this policy, by subsidizing private schools – in effect a way of reconstituting segregated schools. This in turn has been countered by a ruling of the Internal Revenue (July 1970) that such schools would no longer be tax exempt. In the wake of the new black militancy, many communities have recently demanded segregated black schools of higher quality. These new segregationist tendencies are clearly contrary to the philosophy of *Brown* v. *Board of Education*, but the question has been put (Bickel, 1970, p. 188) whether such demands are necessarily contrary to the Constitution. They express the pluralistic, decentralizing, multi-racial aspects of American society, as against the centralizing tendencies, which would have to be greatly strengthened in order to implement racial integration.

The difficulties of the egalitarian philosophy of the Supreme Court have been no less evident in the sequel to the 'one man, one vote' principle proclaimed in 1962.[66] In these decisions the Court laid down that state legislative districts must be approximately equal. Quite apart from the dissent of those who, like Justice Frankfurter, felt that this was an improper intrusion of the Court into the sphere of the legislature, rational distinctions between acceptable and un-

65. Despite the conservative trend of the Supreme Court under the leadership of Chief Justice Burger, the Court in *Swan* v. *Charlotte-Mecklenburg Board of Education*, 28 L. Ed. 2d 554 (1971), unanimously held that an order requiring the bussing of students for the purposes of achieving racial balance within a school system was within the power of the Federal Courts to remedy a violation of the 'equal protection' guarantee of the Constitution.

66. See *Baker* v. *Carr*, 369 U.S. 186 (1962); *Reynolds* v. *Sims*, 377 U.S. 533 (1964).

acceptable legislature reforms designed to redraw election boundaries, have proved very difficult.

The dilemma produced by the heroic efforts of the Warren Court to imprint a new social policy and a new moral philosophy upon a Constitution nearly two hundred years old, raises two, interrelated, questions:

First, has the Supreme Court, during the Warren era, strayed from judicial neutrality and self-restraint into policy-making, in a manner which has undermined its function and dragged it into the arena of political controversy?

Second, are there inherent limits to the change of society by judicial fiat, limits not imposed by any duty of self-restraint or 'neutrality', but by the nature of the judicial, as compared with the legislative and the administrative function?

A return to a more restrained and principled approach has been postulated by several distinguished American constitutional lawyers. Thus, the late Professor Henry M. Hart has written that judicial supremacy is justifiable only if it is 'a voice of reason, charged with the creative function of discerning impersonal and durable principles'.[67] Professor Herbert Wechsler has defined a principled decision as one that rests 'with respect to every step that is involved in reaching judgement on analysis and reasons quite transcending the immediate result that is achieved' (1961, ch. 5). A decade later, Professor Bickel has criticized the Warren Court's frequent refusal to submit to the discipline of the analytically tenable distinction and he has insisted that reason in the judicial process, and analytical coherence and principled judgement, despite conscious lapses, constitute 'an unmistakable thread in the fabric of our law' (1970, p. 81).

But 'principled neutrality' has its limits. As this chapter should have amply demonstrated, it cannot possibly mean the abandonment of a choice of values. Professor Wechsler concedes that, in the interpretation of the Bill of Rights and of the Fourteenth Amendment – as indeed in the construction of statutes and the interpretations of precedents – a value choice is inevitable. And Professor Bickel's own solution is not free from ambiguities. On the one hand

67. H. M. Hart Jr, 'Foreword: the time charts of the justices', 73 *Harvard L. Rev.* 84, 99 (1959).

he stresses that 'society . . . values the capacity of the judges to draw its attention to issues of the largest principles that may have gone unheeded in the welter of the pragmatic doings. *Brown* v. *Board of Education*, and other education cases, as also the reapportionment decisions, fulfilled this role of the court' (Bickel, 1970, p. 177). On the other hand he suggests – somewhat inconsistently – that

in dealing with problems of great magnitude and pervasive ramifications, problems with complex roots and unpredictably multiplying offshoots – in dealing with such problems, the society is best allowed to develop its own strains out of its tradition; it moves forward most effectively, perhaps, in empirical fashion, deploying its full tradition, in all its contradictions, . . . as it retreats and advances, shifts and responds in accordance with experience, and with pressures brought to bear by the political process (Bickel, 1970, p. 175).

Without strong guidance by the Warren Court, if left 'to develop its own strands out of its tradition', American society would hardly have moved towards the, admittedly uneven, yet dramatic change in the structure of society and the relation of the races which has occurred. The Court rightly articulated, and by its articulation greatly accelerated, some basic changes in the public philosophy – which we have attempted to rationalize in the first chapter. Its critics are unquestionably right in suggesting that the Warren Court has often, in its desire to move society forward, engaged in distinctions that are not susceptible to rationalization and analytical principle. But it would be highly dangerous to return from the occasional confusions of the Warren Court to the downright hostility to social change which has characterized earlier periods of the Court – with disastrous consequences to American society. 'Strict constructionism' generally means looking to the past, and that is certainly no less policymaking than looking to the present or to the future.

The deeper problem of the Warren Court era is the second one: that of the limits of the judicial function in promoting social change. Clearly, the Supreme Court has involved itself in increasing difficulties in seeking to prescribe or to invalidate specific forms of school or voting districting, or various methods of school administration, public transport and other administrative aspects of public education.

The reason is that, as I have suggested elsewhere,[68] '[c]ourts can and indeed are called upon to adjust rights and liabilities in accordance with changing canons of public policy. But because they develop the law on a case by case basis they cannot as can the legislature, undertake the establishment of a new legal institution.' Chief Justice Traynor agrees 'that there are many such problems whose resolution entails extensive study or detailed regulation or substantial administration that a court cannot appropriately or effectively undertake.[69]

It is entirely appropriate for a lower court to reinterpret the meaning of gifts to 'children' in a will, so as to include illegitimate children, in accordance with changing social values. It is equally proper for a court that has to interpret a generally worded constitution to re-define the meaning of 'equality' and other general concepts. The Warren Court was conscious of the difficulties of the implementation of such a broad principle when it delegated the supervision of the implementation of *Brown* v. *Board of Education* to the federal district courts. But this too has proved fragile, because the courts cannot properly undertake detailed regulation and administration. The court, in such situations acts as a pace maker. It can and should inspire legislators and administrators to translate general principles into 'detailed regulation or substantial administration'.

So we come back to our earlier theme: the need for a constant interplay between legislators, administrators and courts, in the articulation and implementation of social change. What would be fatal and illusory, would be any attempt to return to the nineteenth-century myth of a judiciary that simply interprets statutes or precedents, in accordance with legal logic, but need not concern itself with the deeper struggles and agonies of society.

Judicial Law-Making and the Criminal Law

The approach to judicial creativeness in the field both of common-law development and statutory interpretation needs considerable

68. See Friedmann, 'Legal philosophy and judicial lawmaking,' 61 *Colum. L. Rev.* 841 (1960), reprinted in *Essays on Jurisprudence from the Columbia Law Review*, 101, 119 (1963).

69. Traynor, 'La rude vita, la dolce giustizia; or hard cases can make good law' 29 *University of Chicago L. Rev.* 223 (1962).

modification in the application of criminal law. Private law – whether common-law developed or statutory – is essentially concerned with an adjustment of economic relations, with the shifting of a financial burden or liability from one party to another. Criminal law, on the other hand, lays down on behalf of the community at large a set of sanctions against the individual offender, ranging from monetary fines to long terms of deprivation of liberty and, in extreme cases, capital punishment. This is a far more serious matter than the adjustment of financial losses, and the application of sanctions must therefore be surrounded with stricter safeguards against the extension of sanctions to the detriment of the individual.

This general proposition is embodied in the maxim *nullum crimen sine lege*. This maxim is a cherished pillar of individual freedom, often embodied in a bill of constitutional rights. It means that an offender should not be punished for any action, without a clear and definite legal basis. This excludes in particular the retroactive effect of a penal statute. The basis of this maxim is the concept of individual guilt as the foundation of ciminal law. An offender should be punished only for an action for which he can be held morally responsible, because he is aware of its illegality. The application of this maxim divides itself into two parts: the construction of penal statutes, and the interpretation of common-law offences, the latter a problem essentially confined to the common-law jurisdictions where the criminal law is not, or not fully, codified. In both respects, it is subject to substantial qualifications.

In the first place, the maxim assumes that the protection of the individual is generally, in the hierachy of values, superior to the interest of the community in preventing or punishing a certain socially objectionable conduct. This, however, is dependent on the scope and purposes of criminal law, which have in many contemporary systems been either substantially modified or widened. In the form that is most objectionable to a liberal system of values, the power to punish is widened by statutory authorization of judicial extension of offences, in accordance with the predominant policy of the state. This is the real meaning of the notorious clause introduced into the German criminal law by an Act of 1935 (under the Nazi regime), under which: 'Any person who commits an act which the law declares to be punishable or which is deserving of penalty according to the fundamental conceptions of a penal law and sound popular feeling, shall be punished. . . .' Similarly, the RSFSR Penal Code of 1926 provides that 'a crime is any socially dangerous act or commission which threatens the foundations of the Soviet political structure and that system of law which has been established by the Workers and Peasants Government for the period of transition to a Communist structure'.[70] Such clauses, introduced into totalitarian systems where the essential independence of the judiciary from the policy-making bodies has been curtailed or abolished, are a thinly disguised invitation (which, in such systems, means a command sanctioned by a variety of harsh penalties) to the judge to pervert the Code, or to interpret it in line with current political directives.

The practical significance of these spectacular and dangerous clauses is not nearly as great as appears on the surface, for in totalitarian systems many other means exist to undermine or destroy the legal protection of the individual. Important crimes are taken away from the jurisdiction of the ordinary courts and subjected to special political tribunals, while a special police, controlled not by the judiciary, but only by the political authorities, exercises para-legal powers of punishment, altogether outside the sphere of the criminal law proper, as, e.g. the South African law that permits detention for ninety days without trial.

In the common-law sphere, many of these offences were, like the

70. This is supplemented by another provision permitting analogous punishment 'in accordance with those articles of the criminal code which deal with crimes most closely approximating, in gravity, and in kind, to the crimes actually committed. . . .' It should be added, however, that many Soviet jurists have for a number of years been critical of such provisions and have maintained that their practical significance was always limited, while the incorporation of the provision in the Penal Code gave an excuse to the enemies of the Soviet Union to attack its principles of administration of justice. The new 'basis', as published in 1958, incorporating the general principles for new criminal codes to be adopted by the Soviet Republic seems to abolish the analogy principle by saying that 'no one may be held criminally responsible and be subjected to punishment except for acts constituting a crime provided by the criminal law'. Another article of the new basis says that 'criminal punishment may be applied only by court sentence in accordance with law'. For some years the trend in Soviet legal thinking was in favour of the 'legality' principle. But 'crimes against the state' can, like the formula of 'clear and present danger', be easily expanded to curtail any form of dissent (Hazard, 1969, p. 473).

rest of the common law, originally judge-made and judge-developed (e.g. homicide, rape, larceny, arson). The Court of Star Chamber played a prominent part in the creation of new offences. But it was the Court of King's Bench which, in 1616, declared that

to this court belongs authority, not only to correct errors in judicial proceedings, but other errors and misdemeanours extra-judicial, tending to the breach of peace, or oppression of the subjects, or to the raising of faction, controversy, debate or to any manner of misgovernment; so that no wrong

or injury, either public or private, can be done, but that it shall be reformed or punished in due course of law.[71]

As late as 1774, Lord Mansfield, for many years Lord Chief Justice of England, declared that:

Whatever is *contra bonos mores et decorum*, the principles of our law prohibit, and the King's court, as the general censor and guardian of the public manners, is bound to restrain and punish.[72]

Gradually, as the principle of legality increased, together with the body of statutorily defined offences, the pace of further development of common-law crimes slackened. How objectionable it had become to predominant opinion in the course of the nineteenth century, is shown by the dictum of one of the most famous of English criminal lawyers, Stephen L.J., in a case, deciding whether the burning of a corpse could be declared a criminal offence, without statutory basis:

The great leading rule of criminal law is that nothing is a crime unless it is plainly forbidden by law. This rule is no doubt subject to exceptions, but they are rare, narrow, and to be admitted with the greatest reluctance, and only upon the strongest reasons.

Because it had become more or less accepted that courts would not invent new offences, an English decision of 1933 stirred up deep opposition. In *R.* v. *Manley*,[73] the Court of Criminal Appeal declared that a false allegation of robbery made to the police and causing them to make unnecessary investigations was a public mischief, and therefore a criminal misdemeanour. More objectionable than the judgement as such was the statement by Lord Hewart

71. *Bagg* (1616), 11 Co. Rep. at 98a, 77 E.R. at 1277.
72. *Jones* v. *Randall* (1774), Lofft 383, 98 E.R. 706.
73. [1933] 1 K.B. 529.

C.J.: 'We think that the law remains as it was stated to be by Lawrence J. in *R.* v. *Higgins*:[74] 'All offences of a public nature, that is, all such acts or attempts as tend to the prejudice of the community, are indictable.'

Protests against this sweeping statement, which, in view of the vague and ubiquitous meaning of the phrase 'acts or attempts as tend to the prejudice of the community' lends itself to gross abuse, were so universal (see Williams, 1961, p. 606) that it seemed highly unlikely that this decision would form the basis of a new wave of judicial crime-making. It is representative of contemporary thinking on this problem that the new Canadian criminal code of 1954 has specifically excluded common-law crimes (section 8), while creating a new statutory offence covering the *Manley* situation (section 120).

However, the judicial power to create new offences, by means of a sweeping interpretation of an allegedly surviving common-law offence called 'conspiracy to corrupt public morals' was revived by the House of Lords in the much discussed decision of *Shaw* v. *Director of Public Prosecutions*.[75] In this case the appellant had published a magazine called *Ladies Directory* which contained the names, addresses and other particulars of prostitutes, with the object of assisting prostitutes to ply their trade. For this the appellant received fees from the prostitutes concerned and he also derived profit from the magazine.

Against the vigorous dissent of Lord Reid, the House specifically held that an offence of conspiracy to corrupt public morals existed at common law and that conduct calculated and intended to corrupt public morals – such as the appellant's conduct – constituted an indictable offence of this character.

After protesting that he was no advocate of the right of the judges to create new criminal offences, Lord Simonds observed as follows:

The fallacy in the argument that was addressed to us lay in the attempt to exclude from the scope of general words acts well calculated to corrupt public morals just because they had not been committed or had not been brought to the notice of the court before. It is not thus that the common law has developed. We are, perhaps, more accustomed to hear this matter discussed on the question whether such and such a transaction is contrary

74. 2 East 5.
75. [1962] A.C. 220.

to public policy. At once the controversy arises. On the one hand it is said that it is not possible in the twentieth century for the court to create a new head of public policy, on the other it is said that this is but a new example of a well-established head. In the sphere of criminal law, I entertain no doubt that there remains in the courts of law a residual poser to enforce the supreme and fundamental purpose of the law, to conserve not only the safety and order but also the moral welfare of the state, and that it is their duty to guard it against attacks which may be the more insidious because they are novel and unprepared for.

The opposite approach to the creation of new criminal offences by contemporary courts was expressed by Lord Reid. He drew a distinction between the possible extension of tort liability, e.g. through the widening of the categories of negligence, and the creation of new criminal offences by the courts.

Every argument against creating new offences by an individual appears to me to be equally valid against creating new offences by a combination of individuals . . . Even if there is still a vestigial power of this kind, it ought not, in my view, to be used unless there appears to be general agreement that the offence to which it is applied ought to be criminal if committed by an individual. Notoriously there are wide differences of opinion today how far the law ought to punish immoral acts which are not done in the face of the public. Some think that the law already goes too far, some that it does not go far enough. Parliament is the proper place, and I am firmly of opinion the only proper place, to settle that.

The observations made earlier in this section, on the respective functions of law courts in the evolution of civil and criminal law, can leave little doubt as to the present writer's view on the respective merits of the majority opinion, and of Lord Reid's dissenting judgement. The House of Lords, which has so often refused to adjust the fields of the common law that are concerned with the balance of economic and social rights and obligations – and none more emphatically than Lord Simonds[76] – affirms such a power in sweeping terms,

76. See his statements in *Jacobs* v. *LCC* [1950] A.C. 361, at p. 361: 'to determine what the law is, not what it ought to be, is the present task'; or, in *Scruttons* v. *Midland Silicones* [1962] 2 W.L.R. 186, at p. 191: 'to me heterodoxy, or, as some might say, heresy, is not the more attractive because it is dignified by the name of reform'. See generally Dworkin '*Stare decisis* in the House of Lords' 25 *Mod. L. Rev.* 163 (1962).

in the very field in which democratic and liberal conceptions of justice are said to differ from totalitarian concepts of justice, by refusing to extend criminal offences by analogy, and thus to make them, in effect, retroactive. Indeed, one critic (Hart, 1963, p. 12) has rightly pointed out that the nearest counterpart to the doctrine of the House of Lords enunciated in *Shaw's* case is to be found in the above-mentioned German statute of 1935. For reasons discussed in the preceding two chapters, it is in the field of the civil aspects of the common law that the courts have a vital function in the continuous evolution of the law, whereas it is in the field of criminal law that the legislature must now be taken to have the exclusive power to formulate new offences. Moral indignation does not make good legal theory.

While this more blatant form of creation of new crimes by the judges in development of the common law will probably remain exceptional, a far more complex problem arises in the case of certain common-law crimes, notably those of conspiracy and sedition, which are so sweeping that they are subject to many divergent interpretations, in the light of changing political and social conditions.[77] But apart from these relatively few, though potentially dangerous, offences, which, in the American jurisdictions, have been defined by statute, there remains the more complex problem of the application of a precedent to a new situation. The main significance of this problem, has, however, in modern times, shifted from the pure common-law interpretation to the judicial interpretation of penal statutes.

While the great majority of the older offences are now defined by statute, whether in the form of a codification or not,[78] new offences are created by statute all the time, especially in the fields of public communications, transport and welfare standards. In all of these, the

77. See, e.g. the recent revival of the common law public order crime of riotous assembly in *Reg.* v. *Caird* (*The Times*, 20 August 1970). Moreover it may well be argued that a totalitarian regime with a subservient judiciary could use the crime of sedition for the complete suppression of liberties and opposition, without any new drastic legislation.

78. In the civilian sphere, codifications of criminal law appear to be universal. In the common-law sphere, the state of the English criminal law, in which most offences are defined by statute, but not codified, contrasts with the Canadian Criminal Code of 1954.

problem of 'strict' or 'liberal' interpretation arises. Even if we accept as still valid the maxim, *nullum crimen sine lege*, this is no answer to the question whether a given penal statute should be construed narrowly or liberally. It is a policy choice in either case. To construe a statute narrowly is simply to assume on the part of the legislator one purpose rather than another. Thus, no basic value of democracy or liberty is involved in the construction of the expression 'self-propelled vehicle' in a penal statute as excluding rather than including an aeroplane.[79] Is it required by the democratic canon of values to make a notorious child kidnapper's conviction for murder 'turn on whether the window in the nursery was open or shut, with the law until comparatively recently unsettled if the window were partly open'?[80] Is it an essential application of *nullum crimen sine lege* to hold that the statute punishing larceny of 'cows' does not include heifers?[81]

It is, of course, a *petitio principii* to say that the maxim *nullum crimen sine lege* demands a 'strict' construction of a penal statute, i.e. a construction which, in the face of two or more alternatives and, in terms of logic or grammatical construction, equally admissible interpretations, must choose the one that narrows the scope of the criminal offence. For the tacit assumption, the 'inarticulate premiss', of such contention is that, whenever a statute contains a penal sanction, the intent of the legislator and the general principles applicable to the interpretation of statutory language do not apply. The effect of such a widely held view – which was attacked strongly by Dean Pound over sixty years ago,[82] has been to produce, in the United States, a number of specific abrogations of the common-law

79. As held by the Supreme Court of the United States in *McBoyle* v. *US*, 283 U.S. 25 (1931), *per* Holmes, J.

80. Livingston Hall, 'Strict or liberal construction of penal statutes', 48 *Harvard L. Rev.*, 748, 760 (1935).

81. So held in the English cases as quoted in Livingston Hall, p. 760; *contra* a Californian decision of 1874.

82. In 'Common law and legislation' 21 *Harvard L. Rev.* 383, 407 (1908): 'The public cannot be relied upon permanently to tolerate judicial obstruction or nullification of the social policies to which more and more it is compelled to be committed.' See also Waite (1934, p. 16), bitterly criticizing the widespread judicial policy 'to utilize casuistic plausibility or any dubiety of the situation for the benefit of the accused rather than for the immediate safety of society'.

rule, either in special statutes or through the adoption of a general liberal construction rule for statutes. Thus a number of states have adopted the suggestion of the Field Draft Penal Code, originally prepared for New York in 1864, that all penal statutes 'are to be construed according to the fair import of their terms, with a view to effect their objects and to promote justice'. Other states have abolished the distinction between the construction of civil and penal statutes, and substituted for all statutes a general direction 'to carry out the intention of the legislature' (see Livingston Hall, *ibid.*, p. 752, Appendix p. 771).

The Model Penal Code of 1962 (Section 1.02(3)) adopts a formulation similar to the Field Code:

The provisions of the Code shall be construed according to the fair import of their terms but when the language is susceptible of differing constructions it shall be interpreted to further the general purposes stated in this section and the special purposes of the particular provision involved. The discretionary powers conferred by the Code shall be exercised in accordance with the criteria stated in the Code and, in so far as such criteria are not decisive, to further the general purposes stated in this section.

Clearly, the crux of the problem lies in the generality of the term 'penal statute', and in the continued application to modern conditions of a principle developed under entirely different circumstances. While the older common-law offences survive, a vast variety of new offences has been added, essentially as one of many ways in which the modern Welfare State must ensure the maintenance of social standards required by the community. Just as modern penal statutes and judicial constructions have, for a large proportion of these offences, accepted the principles of strict liability (see p. 202), so we shall have to differentiate in the construction of penal statutes. There is certainly no justification for throwing out the strict construction principle, lock, stock and barrel, in so far as it serves the reasonable protection of citizens from arbitrary punishment. In cases of grave offences, where the construction of a statute is in reasonable doubt, not only should the accused be given the benefit of the doubt, but the principle of strict *stare decisis*, generally adhered to by the English courts, should be mitigated. In the same spirit, it would seem reasonable to acquit a defendant who has committed an offence in reliance on a decision, e.g. on the invalidity of a statute which is subsequently overruled. An American court has held in such a case that the overruling decision can only have prospective effect for future cases.[83] Here, the ratio of Taylor's case applies even more strongly. The defendant should not be penalized for reliance on an official declaration, even if it is later departed from.

The confusion prevailing in this field extends to the wider domain of an honest mistake of law as a defence to a criminal offence (Williams, 1961, ch. 8). While there has been an increasing departure from the rigidity of the 'strict construction' principle for penal statutes, it is very difficult to formulate an alternative principle. Here, as in other fields of law, it is a matter of reasonable balance between the conflicting interests of the community in fighting certain social evils or maintaining certain social standards, and in protecting the individual from punishment for acts where it is unreasonable to expect punishment. This is not identical with the principle of fault, for as we shall see later, many statutes of an essentially public-welfare character with a predominant interest in maintenance of standards have led to the partial discarding of the fault principle. Neither is a solution possible on the lines that the courts should avoid all but strictly grammatical construction of a statute, for this is patently impossible and contrary to universal judicial principles and experience.[84]

The following guiding principles would be in accord with the general approach to judicial interpretation as portrayed in this chapter:

1. It is beyond the province of the courts to create basically new offences. These are properly the province of the legislator.

2. Where a court is faced with conflicting interpretations of the language of a statute, either of which is compatible with reasonable canons of construction, it must balance the legislative purpose of the statute, in the light of the object matter and the policies at stake, with the principle that a person should not be convicted of an offence which he can reasonably regard as a non-criminal action.[85]

83. *State* v. *Longiro*, 109 Miss, 125, 67, So. 902 (1915).

84. For an example of analogical extension of a statute, no doubt under the influence of war-time emotions, see the famous case of *William Joyce* [1946] A.C. 347, where the statutory law of treason was applied to an alien – although he was not on British soil at the time and had declared the intention of renouncing British nationality – on the sole ground that he still possessed a British passport.

85. This would seem to be close to the approach of Professor Livingston Hall in

Such an approach does not separate the modern criminal law, with its variety of purposes and policies, from the rest of the law in an artificial and socially unjustifiable manner, while it preserves the sound substance of the principle that in a free society the citizen should not be punished for acts that he cannot reasonably construe as criminal.

Judicial Law-Making in International Law

Although, as we have seen, even the highly organized legislative machinery of the modern state demands an active and constructive participation of the courts in the evolution of the law, the scope of such judicial law-making should, at first sight, be far greater in international law. Contemporary international society is still loosely organized; it lacks legislative and executive organs with power to make decisions, other than by consent of the member states. Substantive international law is still a collection of fragments rather than an integrated system of rules governing the conduct of nations in their mutual relations. The highest judicial organ of contemporary international society, the International Court of Justice is, in article 38 of its statute, directed to apply to its decisions of disputes, next to international conventions and international custom, 'the general principles of law recognized by civilized nations', and 'judicial decisions and the teachings of the most highly qualified publicists of the various nations, as subsidiary means for the determination of rules of law'.

The field for judicial development of the law is, therefore, wide and open, and the challenge presented to the Court by its own statute to create new law while deciding cases, seemingly irresistible. However, the same causes which account for the relative weakness and in-

---

the above quoted article (note 79), in which he suggests that: 'A penal statute may be construed strictly where such construction is necessary (1) to make the words of the statute not misleading to persons acting in good faith and honestly attempting to comply with all provisions of law regulating their conduct; or (2) to prevent the imposition of a penalty which is so disproportionate to other penalties imposed by law or which is so clearly inappropriate in view of changed social or economic conditions in the state that it is reasonable to believe that the legislature did not intend such a result.'

completeness of contemporary international law also restrain the highest international court as well as other international judicial organs, in the exercise of such a creative function. International law is still based upon the principle of state sovereignty, and international obligations derive from the consent of the states to restrict their freedom of action by certain specified commitments. Thus the principle of consent still controls the interpretation of legal obligations in international law, and this strongly restrains the International Court in its attempt to develop international law through judicial decisions. For any creative interpretation is likely to be resented by the party against whom judgement is given, as an encroachment on the principle of sovereignty and the limited character of the obligation by virtue of which the Court is called to give a decision. This is apt to be the case, whether the decision is given under a specific agreement between two States to submit a dispute to the Court, or under the so-called 'optional clause' by which a large number of states have agreed to submit certain types of legal disputes generally to the jurisdiction of the Court.[86]

The precarious position in which an international judicial organ finds itself in a society still dominated by (an increasing number of) sovereign states and national conflicts of interest, therefore drastically curtails the scope of judicial law-making in international law, even though the necessity for such creativeness is urgent, and the field immense.[87] The inevitable dependence of the effectiveness of legal institutions on the degree of social cohesion in the society which they serve and represent, is demonstrated. The composition of the Court itself reflects to a large extent the divergent national interests that impede its creative function. Yet, the role of the Court in the evolu-

86. The extent of the reservations attached by most states to this general commitment under the optional clause has assumed such proportions that Judge Lauterpacht, in a separate opinion delivered in the *Case of Norwegian Loans* [1957], I.C.J. Rep. 9, 55 *et seq.* regarded reservations that leave freedom to decide whether a particular dispute is justiciable or not to the party concerned (and by virtue of the principle of reciprocity, correspondingly reduce the extent of the obligation of the other party) as nullifying the acceptance altogether.

87. For a searching analysis of the function of the International Court of Justice in the development of international law, see Sir Hersch Lauterpacht (1958, in particular Pt 5, dealing with the 'Court and state sovereignty'), see also Schwarzenberger (vol. 1, 1957), an analysis of the practice of international courts.

tion of international law is far from being purely passive or negative. The very creation of such an institution – now fifty years old – represents, for all its limitations, an advance in the social cohesiveness of the family of nations, a small step from a society to a community of nations. The number of cases in which the International Court has felt able and willing to push international law forward boldly, either by way of a judgement or an advisory opinion, is small but important. Outstanding, in this writer's opinion, is the Advisory Opinion in which the International Court, by a strong majority, bestowed full international legal personality upon the United Nations as a condition of its capacity to demand reparation for injury suffered by one of its servants (Count Bernadotte). In going beyond the wording of article 104 of the UN Charter, which cautiously refrained from declaring such international legal personality, the Court firmly established the advance from a system of international law in which states are the sole subjects, to one in which international organizations, without being super states, live and function as personalities in their own right.[88] Hardly less important for the advance of international organization is a subsequent Advisory Opinion,[89] where the Court, again by a substantial majority, held that the General Assembly of the United Nations, once having created an independent tribunal with power to make final awards in the determination of disputes between the United Nations and its employees, was not free to overrule or disregard its awards simply because it had been the creator of the tribunal. This Opinion powerfully advances the principle of judicial integrity and independence in international organization, while it indirectly also strengthens the status of the individual as against both states and the international organizations of which they are members. In another field, the Court, this time in a judgement on a dispute between two states,[90] made an important contribution to the highly controversial and fluid problem of the limits of territorial waters, by holding that economic conditions as well as historical tradition and geographical peculiari-

88. *Reparation for Injuries suffered in the Service of the United Nations* [1949] I.C.J. Rep. 174.
89. *Effect of Awards of Compensation made by the UN Administrative Tribunal* [1951] I.C.J. Rep. 116, 47.
90. *Fisheries Case (United Kingdom* v. *Norway)* [1951] I.C.J. Rep. 116.

ties, justified the delimitation of Norwegian territorial waters by a series of straight base lines connecting points on the islands off the coast, instead of the base line following the actual low-water mark and not exceeding four miles from the shore at any point.

In a recent judgement[91] the Court confirmed the status of the continental shelf as a general principle of customary law and laid down certain – though far from uncontroversial – principles on the equitable apportionment of the shelf between neighbouring states, one of which has a strongly indented coastline.

In the development of general principles of law recognized among 'civilized nations', the Court has generally been extremely cautious (Lauterpacht, 1958; Schwarzenberger, 1957; Cheng, 1953). In this field, it seems that more important judicial advances will continue to come from special international tribunals, or from arbitration tribunals established by economic development agreements between governments and foreign investors. Such institutions as the mixed Arbitral Tribunals created between the Allied States and Germany after the First World War, or the General Claims Commission established by the United States and Mexico have made important contributions to the principles of restitution and reparation for injuries suffered by nationals of one state at the hands of another (see p. 486).

It is a corollary to the close interdependence of social cohesion and legal development that much of the development of international law through judicial law-making is likely to continue to come from the judicial institutions of more closely knit communities of states, such as the Court of Justice of the European Economic Community. The European Court of Human Rights, empowered to pass on claims raised by individuals and groups against their own states, has so far decided only a few cases, which have passed the screening of the European Commission – a quasi-judicial body. This is so far a symbolic rather than an incisive attempt to subject sovereign states to minimum standards of justice – though its very existence has, on several occasions, led member states to modify their measures against which complaints had been raised.

While the judicial development of international law is thus inevitably lagging very seriously behind the necessities of contemporary

91. *The North Sea Continental Shelf Cases* [1969] I.C.J. Rep. 3.

society, it is likely to function, together with the increasingly numerous international conventions between states, as an important agent in the gradual transition from international anarchy to international law.

Judicial Dilemmas in Modern Democratic Society

In modern democratic society, the judge must steer his way between the Scylla of subservience to government and the Charybdis of remoteness from constantly changing social pressures and economic needs. There is little need to point out the dangers of complete political subservience which the judiciary has experienced under both Fascism and Communism. The administration of law under these systems becomes a predominantly political function and an instrument of government policy. Under Fascism and Communism certain spheres of social and commercial law are left relatively intact because the government does not consider them as sufficiently important to interfere, or regards it as desirable that citizens should enjoy some security of rights in spheres not directly touching government policy.

In democracies, on the other hand, the illusion is still widespread, despite the warnings of many jurists, that the judge can ignore the social and political issues on which he is asked to adjudicate. It was Lord Justice Scrutton, one of the most conservative as well as one of the most learned of English judges, who warned in the following terms against confusion of prejudices with objectivity:

the habits you are trained in, the people with whom you mix, lead to your having a certain class of ideas of such a nature that, when you have to deal with other ideas, you do not give as sound and accurate judgements as you would wish. . . . It is very difficult sometimes to be sure that you have put yourself into a thoroughly impartial position between two disputants, one of your own class and one not of your class.[92]

Part of the illusion still current among many lawyers is an antiquated conception of the separation of powers. In its absolute and rigid formulation, the doctrine of the separation of powers has never been a correct reflection of politics (see p. 382). The independence of the judiciary from both executive and legislature remains a cornerstone of democratic government, but it cannot be absolute. The

92. (1922) 1 *Cambridge L.J.* 1, p. 8.

notion of 'quasi-judicial' has been extended by a judiciary anxious to maintain some control over the executive, through the prerogative writs.[93] When law courts have felt doubtful about the wisdom of bringing too many ministerial actions under judicial control, they have tended to narrow down the concept of quasi-judicial functions.[94] On the other hand, the English law courts have proceeded to widen drastically the scope of judicial review of the decisions of 'domestic tribunals'.[95]

Certainly the problem of the proper scope of judicial control of the executive or of social groups, such as professional associations or trade unions, cannot be solved by categorical absolutes. It is futile to demand the abolition of government regulation in the kind of society in which we live. Discretion, and even arbitrariness, is no monopoly of the executive. Offenders as well as prison administrators are keenly enough aware of the vast discrepancies in the scale of punishment inflicted upon motor-car owners for speeding offences, or for crimes committed under the influence of alcohol.

It is now increasingly recognized by contemporary jurists that cooperation rather than separation, in a constant interchange of give and take between legislature, executive and judiciary, reflects the reality of the legal process.

The statute lays down a principle which must be applied in cases and circumstances not yet in being. Obviously, while it is difficult enough to determine the rule for transactions which have arisen, it is all the more difficult to do the same for transactions that have yet to occur. Hence, a legislature must speculate more perilously as to how future cases will arise and what contingencies they will involve.

Because perfect generalization for the future is impossible, no generalization is complete. Aware of this impossibility, legislatures often do no

93. A high-water mark is the decision of the Court of Appeal in *R.* v. *Electricity Commissioners* [1924] 1 K.B. 171. In *Ridge* v. *Baldwin* [1964] A.C. 60 (1963) where the House of Lords annulled the dismissal of a chief constable, the judgements emphasized the violations of the principles of 'natural justice' rather than 'quasi-judicial' functions as the basis of judicial review.

94. cf. in particular *Franklin* v. *Minister of Town and Country Planning* [1948] A.C. 87; *Robinson* v. *Minister of Town and Country Planning* [1947] K.B. 702.

95. *Lee* v. *Showmen's Guild* [1952] 2 Q.B. 329; *Bonsor* v. *Musicians' Union* [1956] A.C. 104. On this see now the Industrial Relations Act 1971, Part IV.

more than purport to lay down the most general statements of law, intending that the courts and other law-applying agencies shall creatively adapt the general principle to specific cases. Thus, every time a statute uses rule of reason, or a standard of fairness without specification, there is conscious and deliberate delegation of this responsibility to the courts (Breitel, 1959).

The task of the modern judge is increasingly complex. Hardly any major decision can be made without a careful evaluation of the conflicting values and interests of which some examples have been given in the preceding pages. Totalitarian government eliminates much of the conflict by dictating what should be done.

The lot of the democratic judge is heavier and nobler. He cannot escape the burden of individual responsibility, and the great, as distinct from the competent, judges have, I submit, been those who have shouldered that burden and made their decisions as articulate a reflection of the conflicts before them as possible. They do not dismiss the techniques of law, but they are aware that by themselves they provide no solution to the social conflicts of which the law is an inevitable reflection.

The law must aspire at certainty, at justice, at progressiveness, but these objectives are constantly in conflict with each other. What the great judges and jurists have taught is not infallible knowledge, or a certain answer to all legal problems, but an awareness of the problems of contemporary society and an acceptance of the burden of decision which no amount of technical legal knowledge can take from us.

Part Two
Social Change and Legal Institutions

Chapter 3
Changing Concepts of Property

The Key Position of Property in Modern Industrial Society

That property and its distribution occupies a central – and in the view of many a decisive – position in modern industrial society is a view shared by legal and political philosophers from the extreme right to the extreme left. The right to property as an inalienable, 'natural' right of the citizen, immune from interference by government or other individuals, becomes a central element in the legal philosophy of Locke, of the Founding Fathers, of the '*Déclaration des Droits de l'Homme*', while it permeates the interpretation of the United States Constitution, and the Neo-Scholastic political and legal philosophy of the Catholic Church.[1] Land ownership had, of course, played a dominant role in feudal society. But it was *tenure* of land, based on the hierarchical order of feudalism that characterized the role of property in medieval feudal society. The detachment of the right of property as such accompanies the rise of modern Western commercial and industrial society.

At the other end of the scale, Marxist analysis clearly regards property as the key to the control of modern industrial society. The capitalist, by virtue of his ownership of the means of production, effectively controls society. He exercises the powers of command which ought to be vested in the community. Hence, Marxist theory demands a transfer of the ownership and the means of production to the community, which, in the initial stages, exercises its control through a dictatorship of the proletariat and the coercive power of the state, until the latter 'withers away'. This key function of property

1. In the medieval scholastic philosophy of St Thomas Aquinas, and even centuries later of Suarez, the right of property was not proclaimed as a 'natural' law, but as a matter of social utility and convenience. See further on this subject, Friedmann (1967, pp. 110–11).

and the establishment of a social order remains, almost without qualification, part of modern Soviet philosophy. It still maintains that, with the transfer of ownership in substantially all means of industrial and agricultural production to the community, the problem of social justice has been substantially solved in Soviet society.[2] Ideologically and politically, the property philosophy of the American Constitution and the Catholic Church is bitterly opposed to that of modern communism, and of all forms of Marxist interpretation of history. But they share the heritage of modern Western political philosophy: the controlling significance of property in the social order. In that, they differ from earlier phases of occidental civilization as well as from other civilizations.

Different Concepts of Property

In its political and sociological – and, indeed, in its popular – sense 'property' is clearly not confined to ownership in 'things' (*Sachen*). It comprises not only the realty and personalty – or, more precisely, immovable and movable objects – but also patents,[3] copyrights, shares, claims. In this respect, Anglo-American conceptions of property are closely in line with the sociological and popular meaning, whereas civilian concepts of property still labour under an artificial analytical division inherited from Roman jurisprudence, and out of step with the reality of modern industrial society. The French Civil Code of 1804, the German Civil Code of 1900, the Swiss Civil Code of 1907 and the Italian Civil Code of 1942 – but also the Soviet Civil Code of 1923 – agree in confining ownership, in a legal sense, to 'things', movable and immovable. There cannot be, technically speaking, an ownership of mortgages or of copyrights. There has even been much elaborate and futile discussion of the question whether such a commodity as electricity can be classified as a '*Sache*' and, therefore, be the object of ownership.

The common law is mercifully free of these distinctions which artificially divide things that economically and sociologically belong

2. For a presentation to that effect, see Pashkov, *Transactions of the Third World Sociological Congress*, Amsterdam, 1956, f. 213.

3. In the words of the U.S. Patent Code 35 U.S.C. §261 (1964), a patent has 'the attributes of personal property'.

together. In this field, at least, the empirical development of the common law, its aversion to theoretical definitions of legal concepts, its preference for thinking in terms of legal relationships, of powers and liabilities, rights and obligations, types of action rather than of abstract concepts, has proved an advantage. 'The English lawyer does not find it incongruous to say that the claim for the repayment of a loan, a mortgage on another man's land, or a share in a limited company, belongs to a person's "property" ' (Kahn-Freund, 1949, p. 19). Property, as the same learned author says, is 'a bundle of powers'. Similarly, an American writer has defined property as a 'bundle of rights' by which one claimant is enabled to exclude others, and therefore property is not limited to corporeal things (Hording, 1958, p. 81). Not only is Anglo-American law untroubled by conceptual limitations of ownership; it also knows degrees of ownership. This may, perhaps, be attributed to two characteristic features of Anglo-American legal development: on the one hand, the evolution of the trust concept has attuned the common-law mind to the division of property between different parties, each endowed with certain parts of the property right which, in the classical Continental definition of article 544 of the French Civil Code is '*le droit de jouir et de disposer des choses de la manière la plus absolue.* . . .' The trustee and, to a certain degree, the settlor, has the power to dispose; the beneficiary has the right to enjoy. On the other hand, the predominance of land law in the formative era of the common law, and its impregnation with a feudal concept, under which only various degrees of estate are held, while the residue – and theoretically the only full right of property – is vested in the Crown, has resulted in the establishment of various 'estates' in land rather than full ownership. While some contemporary jurists (Cheshire, 1967, p. 27) regard the survival of the theoretical ownership by the Crown of all land as a mere fiction to be disregarded,[4] and therefore describe the fee simple as full

4. The Land Commission Act 1967, ch. 1 (since repealed), provides for a special form of disposition of land by the Land Commission: the 'crownhold' disposition. The disposition is made subject to covenants restricting the development of the land as may be necessary to retain to the Crown any element of value attributable to the prospect of the development of the land. Such value is gained by the Crown by imposition of a 'betterment levy' upon realization of the development value. For a summary of the act, see Garner, 'Land Commission Act 1967', 30 *Mod. L. Rev.* 303 (1967).

ownership, others[5] strongly criticize such a conception as unhistorical and contrary to the spirit of English law, and maintain that in English law there are only various forms of 'estate' in land, ranging from the near-absolute fee simple to limited tenancies with correspondingly more or less far-reaching degrees of protection of possession in relation to others. A similar, though not identical, conception underlies the formulation in the American Restatement of the Law of Property of 1936, which defines an estate as 'ownership measured in terms of duration'. Whether or not there is, theoretically, a full ownership in land in the common law, does not greatly affect the social realities of modern land tenure. It is probably less important than the fact that common law conceives of the substratum as well as the dimensions of property in terms of function rather than of definition.

The artificiality of a definition of property which confines it to the complete control over a 'thing', has been modified to some extent by giving 'similar' or 'quasi-proprietary' rights, such as copyrights or patents, the same legal protection as property, for instance, in the law of torts.[6]

But it is not only the development of the physical sciences and the increasing importance of sources of energy, such as electricity or nuclear power, which makes the romanistic distinctions between 'things' and 'non-things' archaic. The economic significance of intangible property rights such as patents, copyrights, shares or options has revealed the dogmatic aridity of the civilian definition of property; even more important is the increasing realization that in modern industrial and commercial society, property is not an exclusive relation of dominance, exercised by one person, physical or corporate, over the thing or even a number of 'quasi-things', but that it is rather a collective description for a complex of powers, functions, expectations, liabilities, which may be apportioned between different parties to a legal transaction. The most significant expression of this trend is, perhaps, the modern French concept of

5. e.g. Hargreaves in 19 *Mod. L. Rev.* (1956), p. 14.
6. cf. Art. 823 of the German Civil Code, and the voluminous jurisprudence defining the meaning of a '*Sonstiges Recht*', the violation of which engenders tort liability in the same way as the violation of the right of property.

'*propriété commerciale*' (Morin, *Le sens et l'evolution contemporaine du droit de propiété*' (*Etudes Ripert*, vol. 2, p. 7); Ripert, 1955, section 86). Under modern French legislation, both businessmen and farmers, who rent their premises and land respectively, enjoy certain rights as against the owner, which are generally described as '*propriété commerciale*'. The essence of this right is a claim of the occupier against the owner for renewal of the lease, except in certain strictly defined circumstances. The owner is to that extent deprived of his legal power to dispose of his property, in favour of the lessee's right to the continuity of his enterprise. In the words of Ripert:

The businessman has over the immovable property a right which permits him the utilization of the asset for his benefit, a right which he can oppose to the owner of the land as to any third party (pp. 215–16).

In Ripert's view, the fact that this right is derived from a contract has disguised the property-like character of this right. But another jurist has, perhaps, more accurately observed that the right of the *commerçant* over the land on which he conducts his business has not the character of a property right. It is rather a concomitant of the legal protection given him for his other assets, his '*fonds de commerce*'. The owner can refuse renewal against proper compensation (Bastian, 1950, p. 76). Whatever the analytical solution may be, here, as in the English trust, the powers and rights once concentrated in the owner of the land are now divided between owner and user. Unlike the common-law trust, civilian systems cannot dissect property into its various components, but they have transferred certain functions of property from the owner to others, responding to new economic needs and social policies. Legislation protecting tenant farmers as against the owners is known in many countries, in France[7] as in the United Kingdom[8] and elsewhere. The scarcity of housing may demand a quasi-property protection of the tenant, such as is provided by the English Rent Act 1968; the national needs of food production may demand the strengthening of the right of the tenant farmer against the absentee owner. Such social pressures

7. *Statut du Fermage; loi du 1 septembre 1948.*
8. Agricultural Act 1947 (c. 48), and Agricultural Holdings Act 1948 (c. 63).

produce an evolution in the concept of property. The romanistic definition remains at best a point of departure, of decreasing significance in the modern social context. The necessary correspondence between changes in the function and the concept of property is brought out in the analysis of a contemporary Danish jurist (Kruse, 1950, p. 435). Kruse considers the right of property in contemporary society as 'the driving force in the economy of the community, of its widely diffused economic mechanism, of the production, distribution and credit of society, with their numerous carefully enumerated sections' (p. 436). In such a society, a 'division of labour' takes place in the 'internal economy of the property'. Rights of use, easements, rent-charges, mortgages and claims arise through a division of the right of property. These 'partial' rights of property must be included in the definition of property not only because they form part of its total function, but also because they are protected against expropriation by others, and because the holder enjoys the same powers over them as over the complete right of property.[9]

Thus, slowly, modern Continental law is arriving at a more elastic and functional concept of property, similar to that of the common law. This development clearly makes the notion of property more adaptable to the constantly changing demands that modern society makes upon it.

The function of property in modern industrial society is a problem which transcends the historical and conceptual differences between civilian and common-law thinking. The comparative study of this problem will therefore be facilitated by the evolution that has narrowed the gap between Continental and common-law analysis. One important consequence of this is the possibility of developing property concepts in international law acceptable to all civilized nations. Much attention has recently been devoted to the scope of protection of property interests in international law. There is at least no conceptual obstacle to the recognition of economic interests such as concessions, licences and contractual promises of various kinds as being included in 'property' for purposes of international legal regulation (see p. 490).

9. From a sociological point of view, Renner, half a century ago, pursued a similar line of thought when he spoke of the 'Konnexinstitut' of property, as drawing off more and more of the substance of the property function (see p. 100).

Property Law and the Evolution of Industrial Society

Whether in the restricted definition that dominates Continental civil codes, or in the wider meaning traditionally given to property in the common law, property denotes the most complete form of control that the law permits. The definitions of the various civil codes from the French to the Soviet code, agree on this point, although all these codes make, with varying emphasis, the obvious reservation that this absolute control operates within the limits of the law. The impact of this reservation varies, of course, in accordance with the prevailing social philosophy and economic conditions, a fact which has enabled the definition of the French civil code to survive through radical changes in the *actual*, as distinct from the *theoretical*, role of property in society (see p. 97). While the more modern German and Swiss civil codes exclusively emphasize the power of the owner to *dispose* of the object of property, the older French civil code, more comprehensively and accurately, underlines the two aspects of property: '*la propriété est le droit de jouir et de disposer des choses. . . .*' It is indeed this dual aspect of property: the power to enjoy and the power to control – which any contemporary analysis of the function of property in society must take as its point of departure. For it is the increasing divorce of these two, once normally united, aspects of property which is the most characteristic feature of modern evolutions of property. Correspondingly, the legal restrictions on the rights of property are different in impact and social significance, according to whether they seek to restrain the power to enjoy or the power to control.

In a primitive and essentially self-supporting society, property coincides broadly with the sphere of work of an individual – at least if we include with the head of the household his family. 'Property, . . . the central institution of private law, fulfilled, in the system of simple commodity production, the functions of providing an order of goods and, in part, an order of power' (Kahn-Freund, 1949, n. 4, p. 26). In a broadly accurate simplification, the owner of a farm or a workshop in such a society owns the land, the stock, the tools, which he needs to live or to produce in exchange for certain elementary commodities. Hired labour or trade in commodities are generally ancillary rather than essential complements of property. Power and enjoyment of property and the capacity to work are not too far apart from each other.

Although even pre-industrial society shows an increasing tension and separation between these different functions of property, the decisive break comes with the industrial age. In the earlier phase of industrial society, the power aspect of property becomes immensely extended. The ownership of physical assets enables the early capitalist entrepreneur to multiply not only his power over things – factories, commodities or products – but also over men. The power to make contracts, to hire and fire, becomes, perhaps, the most important function of property. In the earlier days of industrialism, before trade unions were legitimate and powerful, this power enabled the owner of industrial assets to become, in Renner's analysis, a 'commander'. He exercises, by arrogation or toleration, a quasi-public authority over people and social relationships that ought to belong to public authority only, and in the theory of democracy, to a public authority responsible to the people as a whole. There are industrial empires, parallel to autocratic political empires, although domination is disguised by the theoretical equality of contract under the civil law, an equality as little concerned with the differences of economic power between the parties as the law that, in Anatole France's famous phrase, in majestic impartiality permits rich and poor alike to sleep out on embankments.

Renner's analysis stops at a point where ownership is still the exclusive key to control in modern capitalistic society. It is true that the means of exercising this control has become diversified through the 'Konnexinstitut', such as the power to rent, to hire and fire, and other complementary institutions to which we have referred earlier (see p. 98). But legal ownership still remains, as in earlier Marxist analysis, the key to economic power. The owner keeps the title to the surplus value. He surrenders only the use of his property, 'an item in which he never was interested'.

This analysis neglects the decisive and dominant function which the modern large-scale corporate enterprise is exercising in contemporary capitalism (under private capitalism as well as state ownership). In the present century, corporate enterprise has taken control of all the major fields of industrial and business operations, and the structure of corporate enterprise itself has drastically changed in the process. The development of the modern corporation is characterized by an increasing divorce of ownership and control, a phenomenon analysed by a now classic American treatise published a few years after Renner published the last edition of his work (Berle and Means, 1968).

Renner saw capitalist ownership as an octopus whose numerous tentacles – contracts of service, loan, hire or instalment purchase, etc. – enveloped more and more victims. But in the overwhelmingly important field of corporate enterprise, the nominal owner, that is the shareholder, is becoming more and more powerless. He turns into a mere recipient of dividends, often barely distinguishable from the bond or debenture holder. In the analysis of Berle and Means, control has been wrested from the shareholder owner by five different devices: firstly, control through almost complete ownership; secondly, majority control; thirdly, control through a legal device without majority ownership; fourthly, minority control; fifthly, management control. Of these, only the last four are of major sociological importance. Some of the forms of control, especially those achieved through a voting trust, are peculiar to Anglo-American law, although the delegation of votes to banks or other agents can achieve very similar results in Continental company law. But, on the whole, the devices which vest control either in a minority directed by interests outside the company itself, or in the management, at the expense of scattered and passive shareholders, are the same in Continental and Anglo-American law, for the social and economic factors which account for this transformation are similar: the increase in the vastness and complexity of modern industry in most fields, the dispersal of shares among multitudes of small shareholders whose joint influence does not compare with that of a single compact minority interest, and the increasing importance of the managerial as against the financial element, owing to the technical and administrative complexities of modern large-scale enterprise.

Among the devices for separation of ownership and control discussed by Berle and Means, two seem particularly significant. A group of entrepreneurs – industrial or financial – may build up a pyramid of corporations. They need the ownership of a majority or near-majority of shares, at most at the top of the pyramid, preferably in a holding company. The holding company acquires a controlling interest in a series of operating or other holding companies, each of which acquires a controlling influence in the company next below in the pyramid. By this device, the original group of entrepreneurs can acquire a decisive or even monopoly control over an entire industry.[10] Ownership and control are even more completely divorced where the management of a vast and complex corporate enterprise can either govern undisturbed because of the dispersal of shareholdings among multitudes of small owners, or because it can, if necessary, stir up the majority of shareholders in order to fight the dominant minority.

The powers formerly necessarily attendant on property have now largely passed to those who, without necessarily being owners, can control and direct a variety of owners of shares or assets in an enterprise, whether this be the result of diffusion of ownership, of apathy, of skilful manipulation, of the centralization of know-how and administrative control in the hands of management, or a combination of all these factors.

Public Restraints on the Rights of Property

Although many of the major powers flowing from property rights have now passed from the property owner to others, notably the managers of corporations, such power still *derives* from property. While the social demand to restrain the power of the 'over-mighty subject' is no longer necessarily directed against the legal owner of such property, the need for social restraint on private property is as urgent as it has ever been. In accordance with the analysis given earlier, we shall survey the various moves which have, over a century, led to an increasing range as well as a growing intensity of public restraints on property from two aspects: restraints on the *enjoyment* of property designed to mitigate the privileges which it confers in the enjoyment of the things that life has to offer; and restraints on the private *power* to use the control of industrial property as a 'delegated power of command', as a means of a quasi-governmental private control over the major assets of a nation.

10. Berle and Means give as an example the Brothers van Sweringen. In 1930, an investment of less than $20,000,000 was able to control eight Class I railroads, with combined assets of over two billion dollars.

The distinction between these two aspects of property rights is both legally and sociologically important. It is possible for a legislator to concentrate on one or the other aspect. Social welfare and socialism (or even state supervision of private industry) are not the same. Indeed, modern capitalism as applied, for example, in the United States, has a multitude of legal restraints on private property designed as alternatives to socialism. Social obligations have often become the price to be paid for continued private control over the productive assets of the nation. On the other hand, a legal restraint on property may, and often does, affect both the enforcement and the power aspects of property. Thus, legislation against the abuse of patents is directed against the dangers of excessive financial benefits as much as the dangers of a stranglehold over industrial development. Progressive taxation primarily aims at mitigating the inequalities in the access to commodities flowing from unequal accumulations of property. But driven to extremes, it may affect the conduct of industry and business as such.

Restrictions on the use and enjoyment of private property

Abuse of rights. In recent years, comparative lawyers have devoted attention to the problem of abuse of rights. They have contrasted the attitude of modern Continental civil codes with that of English law, still dominated by a decision of the House of Lords of 1895.[11] Continental legal systems such as the French, German and Swiss, make the abuse of property rights a good defence where the predominant objective of the exercise of a property right has been chicanery, or the intent to do injury to another party.[12] English law still basically adheres to the principle that a person can do with his property what he likes, except for specific statutory restrictions. Some isolated decisions in nuisance cases have, however, given preference to the plaintiff's reasonable economic interests against the defendant's unsocial use of his private-property right.[13] This approach has been

11. *Bradford Corporation* v. *Pickles* [1895] A.C. 597.
12. For detailed discussion, cf. Gutteridge, 5 *Cambridge L.J.*, pp. 22–45.
13. Notably *Hollywood Silver Fox Farm* v. *Emmett* [1936] 2 K.B. 468, where the defendant was restrained from firing his gun repeatedly in order to interfere with the plaintiff's breeding of silver foxes.

carried somewhat further in American law. It is now settled in the great majority of jurisdictions that, where a defendant erects a fence for the sole purpose of shutting off the plaintiff's view – as distinct from putting up such a structure for a useful purpose, even if a malicious motive has played a part in the action – he may be restrained from doing so (Prosser, 1964, pp. 618–19). Again, there is abundant authority for holding that a drilling of a well, not in order to procure water on the defendant's premises, but to cut off the plaintiff's underground water, is unlawful (Prosser, 1964, p. 619). But where – as was the case in *Bradford* v. *Pickles* – a landowner digs a hole in his ground so as to abstract water from a neighbouring property, in order to raise the purchasing price of his property wanted by a local authority, it may be doubted whether, at least in a primarily private-property-oriented legal system, there is not a legitimate, though ruthlessly pursued, economic objective.[14]

The practical significance of the whole doctrine is very much smaller than its theoretical interest. In the practice of American, French, German or Swiss courts, it means little more than that the very unusual kind of landowner who creates obstacles out of spite for his neighbour, or who prefers to leave a piece of land unused rather than grant a right of passage, may be restrained by the courts.[15] Continental courts have understandably refrained from developing the principle into a more fundamental social doctrine by which the use of property is subject to the needs of the community. It is in this wider sense that the principle of *abus de droit* has sometimes been used to justify (together with the principle of unjust enrichment) the *propriété commerciale*, i.e. the right of a lessee to demand continuation of his

14. Professor Gutteridge in 5 *Cambridge L.J.*, pp. 22 et seq., felt certain that the German court would restrain such an action. For some criticism of this view, see 21 *Canadian Bar Rev.*, 374 (1943).

15. It is not often that the fantastic situation arises which occupied the Dutch courts some years ago. A determined engineer, feuding with his neighbour, a lawyer, erected a mock water-tower at a place where it obstructed his neighbour's view of the sea. When enjoined to refrain, the ingenious engineer converted the mock water-tower into an effective water supply. He was restrained none the less because the Hooge Raad, in a decision of 13 March 1936, held that he could equally well have erected this water-tower on a different part of his property where it did not obstruct the neighbour's view. (This account is based on oral information given to the author by a Dutch lawyer.)

lease from the owner of the premises. But here the principle loses all legal precision and becomes a moral precept rather than a juristic concept (Bastian, 1950, n. 11, p. 87).

Again, the 'abuse of rights' stands for a completely different social philosophy of property as applied in article 1 of the Soviet civil code, which withholds protection from private rights 'exercised in contradiction to their social and economic purpose'.[16]

Property in socialized economies

In socialized systems, the function – and to some extent, the concept – of property differs fundamentally from that of the systems in which property is the foundation of private enterprise. The transfer of the major means of production into the hands of the state, and the direction by a central economic plan, removes property as an instrument of power from private ownership. It is therefore a logical consequence that state enterprises hold the assets which they administer in 'trust' rather than in full ownership. Even as owners they would be subject to the direction of the government regarding its use and disposition. The 1965 reforms on public enterprises in the USSR have considerably widened the powers of the managers of state enterprises with regard to the assets under their control, but this is a matter of management decentralization and accountability rather than any basic change in the property concept. While the transfer of not only theoretical ownership but of the basic power of direction and control into the hands of the state is common to all of the communist countries, it is somewhat different in Yugoslavia, which, since 1953, has developed a very distinctive ideology of 'workers' enterprise'. State ownership and state-directed power over the enterprises has been minimized, and control over the individual enterprises been conferred upon the workers – who comprise all employees, from the manager to the most lowly manual labourer. These communities of workers hold the assets of the enterprise in 'social trust', i.e. they do not own it in the sense of the Western concept of property. Despite numerous discussions, Yugoslavia has not so far defined property in the gradual revision of its legal system. What is emerging, is a concept intermediate between the state owner-

16. s. 1, Civil Code of the R.S.F.S.R.: see Gsovski (1948, vol. 1, pp. 314–38).

ship of the communist world, and the private ownership of the western world. One might describe it as collectivized ownership affected with a social trust.

In contrast to the abolition of private property in productive enterprises, private ownership in personal assets, i.e. the enjoyment function of property, has been preserved, and, since the early days of the Soviet Revolution, even strengthened in the communist systems. The USSR Constitution of 1936 (Article 10) laid down that '[t]he personal property right of citizens in their incomes and savings from work, in their dwelling houses and subsidiary home enterprises, in articles of domestic economy and use and articles of personal use and convenience, as well as the right of citizens to inherit personal property, is protected by law'[33] (Hazard, Shapiro and Maggs, 1969, p. 167.)

This permission to own personal property, outside the sphere of economic production, has led to considerable inequalities of wealth in the Soviet Union, a development strongly rejected by the much more puritan version of communism adopted by Mao-Tse-Tung's China. Successful writers, composers and scientists, in many cases derive large incomes from their royalties. These inequalities – which are rejected by Chinese communism and would have been generally repugnant to early socialists – are somewhat more magnified by the surprising legalization of inheritance in the law of the Soviet Union and other communist states. A convincing explanation for the preservation and restoration of the right to inheritance – a form of unearned income that would appear to be repugnant to the socialist principle: 'from each according to his work, to each according to his need' is given by Professor Hazard in the following observation:

In an inheritance pattern tending both to stimulate production and to hold the family together through property transmission was useful. In short, there was no good reason to alter inheritance law radically, and good reason to preserve it (1969, p. 242).

An Australian student of Soviet law has observed that 'no one reading the provisions of Soviet codes would be tempted to say that there is a socialist law as opposed to a capitalist one'.[17]

17. Tay, 'The law of inheritance and the new Russian Civil Code of 1964' 17 *Int. & Comp. L.Q.* (1968), at p. 472.

It is somewhat easier to reconcile the reaffirmation of patent and copyright in the Soviet law. For these are the rewards of creative intellect and artistic imagination, which communist societies value highly for the sake of technological progress and general education – although the conformism of communist ideology puts, of course, severe restraints on liberty of expression. On the other hand professors whose works are officially accepted, as textbooks or in some other way, enjoy a large assured market.

To sum up the attitudes of contemporary communist systems towards property, we may say that they underline the distinction between the power and enjoyment aspects of property. The former is the preserve of the state, the latter is permitted in private hands. Although certain limits are set to the accumulation of private wealth, the legal concept of private property in socialist systems is not significantly different from that of non-socialist systems. The owner of a private house, of a motor car, of domestic animals or of a workshop, pursues his private claims and is subject to legal responsibilities very much like his counterpart in capitalistic societies. It is the ambit rather than the nature of private property that is different.

Statutory restraints on the use of property

An increasing array of statutory duties affects the freedom of property of landowners, factory owners, employers, retailers, public utilities, in a multitude of ways.

Restraints on producers and employers. There are provisions for the safety of machinery or mines, for sanitation and drainage, for the purity of foods and water. They enjoy the sanctions of criminal and civil law; statutory penalties for these 'public welfare' offences[18] do not normally require a *mens rea*. The protection of civil law is often a twofold one: the extension of the obligations of the manufacturer towards the consumer[19] has greatly widened the scope of protection of the public against deficient products. English courts have also

18. On 'public welfare' offences see p. 202. For recent studies of the problems involved in prosecuting 'public welfare' offences, see Smith and Pearson, 'The value of strict liability' [1969] *Crim. L. Rev.* 5; Dickens, 'Discretion in local authority prosecutions' [1970] *Crim. L. Rev.* 618.

19. Following *Donoghue* v. *Stevenson* [1932] A.C. 562.

increasingly awarded damages to individuals for the breach of statutory duties as such, for example, to a third party injured in a car which, contrary to statute, had no third-party insurance,[20] or to a ratepayer poisoned by impure water supplied by a local authority.[21] In the United States the position is complex because of the large number of jurisdictions and the infinite variety of statutes (Prosser, 1964, p. 181). Many statutes have been construed as only imposing a public duty (e.g. most statutes providing for compulsory licensing). But many private claims have been granted (e.g. to employees against the employers for violation of a statutory obligation to fence dangerous machinery, or to children injured by the failure of a railway to comply with a fencing statute) (Prosser, 1964, pp. 195–6).

Official acts and regulations increasingly not only forbid but also prescribe. Economic emergencies have greatly accentuated this development. The state lays down utility standards for a wide range of consumers' products; or it allocates scarce raw materials or foreign currencies according to priorities. The most powerful and dangerous of state powers, the right of direction of labour, has so far been sparingly used in democratic systems, except in war, for freedom to choose one's occupation is a far more elementary aspect of human freedom than liberty to do with one's material property as he likes. But a grave economic crisis which makes a nation dependent on its essential resources always increases the pressure for compulsory direction or freezing of certain forms of labour, such as coal mining or agriculture, which, in normal times, tend to lose more labour than they attract.

Restraints on the ownership and use of land. Defence needs, economic emergencies and the need for conservation and the best possible utilization of existing land and mineral resources have been the principal causes of far-reaching public interferences with the private uses of land. They have led to powers of dispossession and, in certain cases, even to legislative restrictions on the amount of land that can be privately owned by any single individual. The emphasis and intensity of these restrictions on private land-ownership vary from country to country. They are conditioned by the need for the avail-

20. *Monk* v. *Warbey* [1935] 1 K.B. 75.
21. *Read* v. *Croydon Corporation* [1938] 4 All E.R. 631.

able national resources, by the degree of economic emergency which natural conditions or human-made catastrophes such as war impose; they are, of course, also influenced by the distribution of power between different social groups within the country. What is common to all these developments, especially in the last decade, is a growing awareness of the prior claims of the *utilization* of land, as against its mere status. As a French jurist has expressed it: '*l'humanité a pris conscience de ce que la propriété qui est seulement matière ne fructifie que par le travail de l'homme*' (Savatier, 1952).

It is not surprising that, in France, where the political power of the small farmer is greater and better organized than in any other Western country, the protection of the rights of the tenant farmer has taken pride of place. We have previously mentioned the *propriété commerciale*, a short and not altogether accurate description of the rights enjoyed by the small businessman – another powerful political force in France – against the owner, on the premises of which he conducts his business. The rights of the tenant farmer (*fermiers et métayers*) go further. Under legislation which has developed over the years and which was consolidated – after the war – in 1945 and 1946,[22] the tenant farmer is virtually irremovable from the land which he farms, at the termination of the lease. The duration of the lease and the rent are fixed by law. After the statutory duration of nine years, the lease can be indefinitely renewed at the option of the lessee. Nor can the owner of the land terminate the lease against the payment of an indemnity. He can reoccupy the land only if he wants to cultivate it personally, or through his children. Furthermore, the tenant farmer has a right of pre-emption whenever the owner wishes to sell the land. While the parties may abrogate from the terms of the law in certain details, they cannot abrogate by contract the essential principles of the law which, in the French legal terminology, is *d'ordre public*.

In Great Britain, where the social power and economic influence of the farmer do not compare with that of his counterpart in France, war emergencies, food shortages and an increased need to rely on native produce have nevertheless strengthened the legal position of the farmer and superimposed a public power of dispossession over the private rights of parties. Under the British Agriculture Act of

22. *Ordinances du 17 Octobre 1945*, Law of 13 April 1946, *sur le statut des Baux Ruraux*.

1947, the Minister of Agriculture has the power, where necessary in the 'interest of the national supply of food or other agricultural products', to specify, e.g. the crops to be raised, the land to be used and appropriate methods of good estate management and husbandry.[23] Coupled with this are statutory standard terms for agricultural tenancies.[24] This restriction of the rights of private property expresses the recognition of agricultural land as a national asset, which private owners and tenants must use to the advantage of the community. This type of legislation shows a new technique: positive administrative action; it displaces private terms of contract, instead of negative administrative measures (clearance orders) as used by the Housing Acts.

Another type of public interference with the private use of land is illustrated by the powers of the Minister under the Town and Country Planning Acts 1962–1968. Under this legislation, basic planning control rests with local planning authorities, who can withhold permission for private development of land in the interest of town and country planning, subject to confirmation by the competent Minister when appeals are taken. In a case where, under a previous Act, a local authority and private landowners had agreed on private development of the land, and laid out certain moneys toward this purpose, the Minister was confirmed by the Court of Appeal in the withholding of his permission for further development under the new Act. The statutory power was held to be a limiting factor in any private agreements previously entered into.[25]

Yet another aspect of the shift of emphasis from private to public uses of land is illustrated by the New Towns Act 1965, the major piece of legislation incorporating a planned policy of decentralization, and an attempt to draw a small portion at least of the population of the major British cities into smaller communities in outer surrounding belts. Under the Act, which replaces an earlier act of 1946, public corporations called New Town Development Corporations have powers to expropriate private land after certain hearings of an administrative and quasi-judicial character.

The United States has hitherto been only slightly affected by the

23. Agricultural Act 1947 (c. 48), s. 95.
24. For details see Agricultural Holdings Act 1948 (c. 63), s. 5, Sch. 1.
25. *Ransom & Luck Ltd* v. *Surbiton Borough Council* [1949] 1 Ch. 180.

disorders of wars and economic upheavals, which have shaken all of Europe, with the exception of a few smaller neutral countries. Moreover, it is a country of abundant resources, vast spaces, and its history and political philosophy is permeated by distrust of state interference in property and economic enterprise. Yet, even American land law has witnessed a remarkable evolution (Williams, 1956, p. 196). Both legislation and court decisions have, since the great depression of the early 1930s, substantially restricted the rights of creditors against land which served as security for debts.[26] More gradually, the courts have developed concepts of good husbandry and increased the concept of waste by owners of possessory interests in land, reflecting changing patterns of land utilization. The increasing urbanization of living, reducing the percentage of rural population from 60·3 per cent in 1900 to 30·1 per cent in 1960, has accounted for a steady increase in public regulation of urban land-users, mainly through zoning legislation.[27] By a wider interpretation of the 'police power' inherent in both federal and state governments, the courts have generally upheld official attempts to regulate land use by laying down minimum sizes and minimum floor space for homes.[28] The great majority of states now also have enabling legislation authorizing various local and county authorities to regulate subdivision practices. Through such control, subdividers may be required to provide adequate road networks and public utilities, space for parks, playgrounds and schools as a condition of acquiring lots. Conservation legislation in many states now seeks to prohibit the waste of natural resources, such as natural gas, thus restricting the right of the landowner to do with his property what he likes. Perhaps the most remarkable illustration of the extent to which natural and social conditions may modify the prevailing ideology is the legislation prevailing in certain western areas of the United States, which are chronically short of water. Here, no owner is permitted to possess or control more than a certain area of

26. See *Suring State Bank* v. *Giese*, 210 Wis. 489, 246 N.W. 556 (1933).

27. Every one of the states now has zoning enabling legislation, and at least 90 per cent of the cities with a population exceeding 10,000 now regulate through zoning ordinances such matters as the use of urban land (Williams, 1956, p. 198).

28. See *Lyon's Head Lake Inc.* v. *Township of Wayne*, 10 N.J. 165, 89 A. 2d. 693 (1952), appeal dismissed, 344 U.S. 919 (1953).

land if he wishes to qualify for water supply from public irrigation projects.[29]

Housing controls and social justice

During the last decade, there has been, in the United States, a dramatic change in the acceptance of public controls over the uses of property, designed to ensure social justice. Of the many aspects of this historic change in the relation of public power and private property, two of the most important may be briefly mentioned here.

One is the use of all three arms of government, i.e. the legislative, administrative and judicial branches, for the implementation of the constitutional prohibitions against racial discrimination. The other is the use of various legal devices to protect the poor tenant against abuses or exploitation by the landlords, i.e. the owners of the property which they rent.

In *Hunter* v. *Erickson*[30] the Supreme Court of the United States held that the City of Akron, Ohio had denied a Negro citizen the equal protection of its laws by amending the City Charter so as to prevent the City Council from implementing any ordinance dealing with racial, religious or ancestral discrimination in housing without the approval of the majority of the voters of Akron. This amendment had been used by a real-estate agent to prevent the complainant from looking at houses for possible purchase, whose owners had specified their wish not to sell to Negroes.

The Civil Rights Act of 1964 provided that 'all citizens of the United States shall have the same right, in every state and territory, as is enjoyed by white citizens thereof to inherit, purchase, lease, sell, hold and convey real and personal property'. Building on this legislation, the Civil Rights Act of 1968 specifically declares unlawful a variety of devices discriminating in the sale or rental of housing on the ground of race, colour, religion or national origin. In *Jones* v. *Mayer Co.*,[31] the Supreme Court affirmed the constitutionality of

29. Act of 17 June, 1902, §,5, 32 Stat. 389, as amended, 43 U.S.C. §431. See the discussion at *Report of the President's Water Resources Policy Commission: Water Resource Law* (1950), vol. 3, pp. 217–37.

30. 393 U.S. 385 (1969).

31. 392 U.S. 409 (1968).

the non-discrimination provisions of the 1964 Act, read in conjunction with an earlier statute of 1866 and held that it invalidated *all* racial discrimination, private as well as public, in the sale or rental of property, as a valid exercise of the power of Congress to enforce the Thirteenth Amendment.

The various attempts made in recent years by a number of municipal housing laws, and supported at least in part by the federal courts, to protect tenants against eviction and to legitimate refusals to pay rent in the case of serious violations of minimum standards of housing by landlords, are of even greater jurisprudential interest.[32]

A number of modern municipal housing laws seek to impose minimum housing standards. The efficacy of these laws depends, however, on their enforcement. One approach – used in recent years by several state statutes – authorizes welfare departments to make rental payments for their welfare clients directly to the landlord. They also empower the welfare agency to withhold the rent where the premises are found to be in serious violation of the housing laws. At the same time, in such cases the landlord is denied the customary remedy for non-payment of rent, i.e. the right to evict the tenant. In New York, a social welfare law providing rent abatement for welfare tenants who live in buildings 'dangerous, hazardous or detrimental to life or health' was declared constitutional by the Appeal Court of the State of New York.[33]

The most remarkable translation of spontaneous collective action, originally in breach of the law, into a legitimate remedy, is a New York law of 1965, which entitles 'one-third or more of the tenants occupying a multiple dwelling' to bring an action against the landlord where there exists in the building lack of heat, water, light, electricity or other serious deficiencies. If the landlord does not undertake the repairs, all the tenants in the building are ordered to pay into the Court the rents due, and the Court is authorized to appoint an administrator of the property.

There have been several recent judgements against eviction notices where the landlord had failed to remedy serious violations of sanitary codes and other statutory housing standards. In one of the best

32. The relevant statutes and decisions are surveyed and commented on by Plager, *New Approaches in the Law of Property* (1970), Pts 1 and 2.
33. *Farrell* v. *Drew*, 19 N.Y. 2nd 486, 227 N.E. 2nd 824 (1967).

known of these judgements[34] the Court of Appeals for the District of Washington remanded an eviction case to the Court of General Sessions for a new trial, with a specific direction that the plaintiff would be permitted to prove to a jury that her landlord, who sought to evict her, had harboured a retaliatory intent. The forthright observations of Judge Skelly Wright deserve citation:

In trying to effect the will of Congress and as a court of equity we have the responsibility to consider the social context in which our decisions will have operational effect. In light of the appalling condition and shortage of housing in Washington, the expense of moving, the inequality of bargaining power between tenant and landlord, and the social and economic importance of assuring at least minimum standards in housing conditions, we do not hesitate to declare that retaliatory eviction cannot be tolerated. There can be no doubt that the slum dweller, even though his home be marred by housing code violations, will pause long before he complains of them if he fears eviction as a consequence. Hence an eviction under the circumstances of this case would not only punish appellant for making a complaint which she had a constitutional right to make, a result which we would not impute to the will of Congress simply on the basis of an essentially procedural enactment, but also would stand as a warning to others that they dare not be so bold, a result which, from the authorization of the housing code, we think Congress affirmatively sought to avoid.

These statutory, administrative and judicial developments indicate the magnitude of the revolution in legal thinking on the sacrosanctity of property produced by a growing urban crisis and the miseries of slum dwelling. But important though they are, they can touch only the fringes of the major social problem. The law can support, accelerate, and, in some cases, initiate a struggle against discrimination, or the exploitation of the poor by unscrupulous property owners. But major changes can only come about by the basic reordering of social priorities, i.e. a comprehensive planning process, which of necessity involves a massive redistribution of wealth, through taxation and other legislative devices.

Taxation and credit control as a means of redistribution of property
Taxation is one of the most important weapons by which the state can mitigate the two objectionable aspects of unrestricted private

34. *Edwards* v. *Habib*, 397 F. 2nd. 687 (D.C. Cir. 1968).

property: firstly, the inequalities of wealth, and secondly, the power to use property for private profit, and without regard to community purposes. In popular consciousness the first aim still predominates. By graded taxation and surtax on high incomes, gross inequalities of wealth are evened out more easily than by the equalization of incomes or the abolition of private property. But the second aspect of taxation policy is becoming increasingly more important. On the one hand, taxation is a cheap means by which the state finances its costly social service schemes. Under the British National Health Service Act 1946, medical services are free for all, or subject only to minor charges. The cost of medical services is no longer met by millions of contributions of varying magnitude from private pockets, but out of public revenue. This means that income and property taxes largely pay for the medical services of the poorer classes. To the extent that the state contributes to the cost of national insurance the same applies.

On the other hand, differential taxes and customs duties form part of national economic planning. The import of non-essential goods is penalized by higher duties. A purchase tax is put on luxury goods, which are earmarked for export instead of home consumption. Some countries, Sweden for example, finance their comprehensive health and social services by state-controlled high prices for alcoholic drinks, which are sold through a state-supervised monopoly. The law of taxation is gradually revolutionizing private as well as public law. The incidence of taxation will be one of the main considerations determining the lawyer's advice on the form of a settlement or a will, or the formation of a subsidiary company. The rise of the incorporated charitable foundation is largely a result of the incidence of taxation on large estates (see ch. 9).

Public control of financial credit is another means by which the state curtails privately financed capital. Low interest rates may limit the income from private credit and other banking transactions, but by far the more important aspect of official credit restrictions is the curtailment of the power of private capital to influence the national economy through the expansion or restriction of credits. Agricultural banks in Germany and other Continental countries have, through their mortgaging policy, greatly influenced the structure of the national economy (Kahn-Freund, 1949, p. 186). The raising or lowering of discount rates is the paramount means of control by government banks over credit policy, and thereby, the expansion or contraction of the economy.

Curbing the Power of Property

It is not surprising that the many different devices by which the contemporary property owner is checked and restrained by the law in his *droit de jouir et de disposer des choses* are of an essentially restrictive and regulatory character. The *abus de droit* as a defence to an action, the compulsory licensing by administrative order or judicial decision of a misused or non-used patent, the numerous duties imposed by statute upon factory owners, employers and others, the restrictions on the use and disposition of land, these and many other legal innovations attempt varying degrees of restraint and redistribution of property, with the object of distributing the benefits of property over wider sections of the community.

By contrast, the more serious countermoves against the *power* aspects of property in modern industrial society have been of an essentially *institutional* character. These new institutional developments represent either organized countervailing power, matching and curbing the formerly unrestrained power of the property owner in early industrial society, or they provide new institutions as a substitute for private property.

The power aspects of property in contemporary industrial society result overwhelmingly from the concentration of industrial assets. It is as owner and controller of industrial assets that, in Renner's terminology, the industrial owner becomes a 'commander'. But in the twentieth century, the industrial property owner is hardly ever in form – and very seldom in substance – a physical individual. The owner and controller of industrial assets is the corporation. And it is with the impact of corporate ownership and corporate power that modern legal and social countertrends are overwhelmingly concerned.

We have seen that the power to contract is in industrial society a most vital aspect of property. It is, therefore, the countervailing influence of trade-union organization and the institution of collective bargaining which constitute by far the most important restraint on the power of the industrial property owner to command the services of people through his control over industrial assets. We will deal with this aspect of restraint of the power of property in connexion with the evolution of the contract (see ch. 4).

As all these devices and developments are overwhelmingly the result of the growth of *corporate* property and power, we shall deal with them under this aspect in a later chapter.

Decline and Rebirth of the Right of Property

Surveying the many restraints which new public policies have imposed upon the untrammelled use of property rights, both in private and public law, many – and most articulately the upholders of a conservative philosophy of property – have decried the passing of property. This philosophy, articulated in the earlier, and now discarded, interpretations of the 'due process' clauses by the United States Supreme Court, sees property menaced or even destroyed by statutory welfare obligations, curbs on the employers' freedom in labour contracts, taxation, zoning or conservation legislation, not to speak of powers of expropriation in the public interest. It is certainly true that the right of property, in its traditional limitation to the more or less unlimited use and enjoyment of things, such as land, industrial assets, and quasi-corporeal rights, such as patents, has been severely curbed. But it is at this point that the redefinition of the concept of property, outlined earlier in this chapter, shows its philosophical and social significance. Thus, as has always been inherent in the common-law concept of property, and as is increasingly recognized in the civilian legal systems, property is not confined to the control of 'things', but extended to the whole field of legitimate economic interests and expectations. The protection of property rights today is spread over the community as a whole, where it has, in the past, essentially benefited the very limited class of owners of land and commercial property. The effect of the law was to give excessive protection – often at the expense of the essential necessities and liberties of the rest of the community – to the owners of large estates and industrial assets. Today, the balance is being restored, by a wider conception of property. Gradually, new social and economic philosophies are influencing the legal concepts. For the vast majority of people, the most essential economic interest is the right to use one's labour and skill, and to be protected in the exercise of these capacities.

The big landowner or the industrial entrepreneur is unquestionably today far more restricted in the free use of his property than in earlier times. But from the standpoint of the average person, who disposes of limited physical assets and mainly depends for his own and his family's livelihood on the ability to work, on fair conditions of trade, and on the enjoyment of minimum standards of living, it is truer to say that 'the notion that private property is an essential condition of human freedom is still accepted. We are perhaps giving the idea a greater practical effect than did our predecessors' (Hording, 1958, p. 106).

Chapter 4
The Changing Function
of Contract

The social function of contract in the formative era of modern industrial and capitalist society may be summed up in four elements: freedom of movement; insurance against calculated economic risks; freedom of will; and equality between parties. These four elements are closely linked, and to some extent, overlapping, but each has a distinct meaning. The problems of legal adjustment and interpretation, however, which they have posed in a rapidly changing society, are not of the same order. The first two of our four elements are essentially formal in character, the latter two also express political and social ideologies. The difficulty of bridging the gap between the formal and substantive aspects of both freedom and equality is evident in the pathetic contrast between the law of contract as it is taught in most textbooks, and modern contract as it functions in society.

The Corner-Stones of Contract in the 'Classical' Era
Freedom of movement

For a developing industrial society contract supplied the legal instrument which enabled men and goods to move freely. It is this aspect of contract above all which is expressed by Maine's theory that progressive societies have developed from status to contract. As against a legal status determined by ties and conditions outside personal decisions, contract allows the individual to change his country or employment. In the American Civil War, the contest between status and contract stood behind the ideological struggle between slavery and personal freedom. The static rural and patriarchal society of the South wanted a hierarchical immobility. The slave, as part of the estate, was at the bottom of the social scale, although, as the future showed, his economic and social lot was often better than under the mobile and free economic society which the industrialized and commercialized North wanted and achieved. Freedom to hire and fire, and the unrestricted mobility of labour, were essential to this society, which regarded economic bargaining value as the main standard by which the demand for labour was regulated.

The evolution from status to contract, from immobility to mobility, gradually pervaded all spheres of life, beyond the fields of commercial and labour contracts. It invaded family relations, and the law of succession. It became the basis of club and union membership. Gradually it penetrated even into the law of land tenure, sale and succession. In the English property legislation of 1925, the right of free disposal over land, including the power to disentail, was finally recognized.[1] In some respects, this movement from status to contract still continues, especially in so far as the modern state gradually abandons its ancient legal privileges, as the price to be paid for the vastly increased functions of modern government. The British Crown Proceedings Act of 1947, and corresponding legislation in the Commonwealth,[2] abolishes petition of right as the form of proceedings between subject and Crown, as well as the immunity of the Crown from liability in tort, based on the feudal and absolute status of the Sovereign. It introduces instead ordinary actions in contract, tort and property, as between subject and Crown.[3]

But this aspect of contract is increasingly overshadowed by a return to a new kind of immobility resulting from the profound changes produced by the social welfare responsibilities of the modern state, by group organization and collective bargaining in industry and commerce, and, last but not least, the state of industrial mobilization into which international strife has forced western states since the outbreak of the First World War.

1. By-products of the former immobility and non-commercial characterization of land ownership remained, e.g. in the rule in *Cavalier* v. *Pope* [1906] A.C. 428, under which the landlord was exempt from liability to his tenant for dangers existing on the premises. But see now Occupiers' Liability Act 1957, c. 31, s. 4 (1).
2. e.g. West Australian Crown Proceedings Act 1947.
3. See further on the relations of government and governed, p. 398.

Insurance against calculated economic risks

The economic correlate of common-law contract in its formative phase is a free enterprise society, in which the economic rewards for enterprise or speculation are restricted only within very wide limits, if at all. The functioning of such an economic system depends on the guarantee of the law that enterprise or speculation, in so far as it implies contracts for labour, goods or shares, will be protected by the award of damages or specific performance. At this stage, we need not discuss the various theories of contract, especially the controversy between those who see the essence of contract in the legitimate expectation of its performance, and those who see it in the guarantee against loss by damages.[4] On either assumption, the sanctions of contract enable the hirer of services, the manufacturer of goods, the speculator in land or the purchaser of shares, to engage in calculated economic risks. This part of contract has been comparatively free from difficulties of ideology or adaptation to social change. It is a significant application of the Aristotelean principle of distributive justice, which demands the equal treatment of those equal before the law. It assumes that parties entering into a contract are equal before the law, and therefore entitled to the same remedies for breach of contract. It need not enter into the problem of social or economic equality between the rich and poor, capitalists and workers, groups and individuals. The courts have been mainly concerned with working out the comparatively technical, or to some extent logical, problems of possession, of remoteness of damage, and of 'positive' and 'negative' interest. Occasionally, social and economic problems intrude. The *Liesbosch* case[5] arose in tort, but might equally have arisen in contract. The owners of a dredger, under contract to a third party to complete special work in a given time, were put to much greater expense in fulfilling this contract because they were too poor to buy a substitute for the dredger sunk by the negligence of the defendants. Was this poverty too remote a consequence to be taken into consideration? The House of Lords held that it was, and assumed that, for the purposes

4. For a survey of the different theories, cf. Paton (1951, s. 80); Cohen (1933, pp. 69–111); Pound (1957, ch. 6).
5. *Liesbosch Dredger* v. *Edison S. S.* [1933] A.C. 449.

of the law of damages, poverty is a misfortune for which the law cannot take responsibility. A similar philosophy was adopted by the English courts during the few years when 'expectation of happiness' played an exciting though slightly fantastic role in English law.[6] As Lord Simon put it, in *Benham*'s case, 'Lawyers and judges may . . . join hands with moralists and philosophers and declare that the degree of happiness to be attained by a human being does not depend on wealth or status.' But on the whole, the problem of sanctions for breach of contract, while vital to its function in modern industrial society, has remained relatively technical.

Freedom of will

In one sense, freedom of will is only another way of expressing the essential mobility of contractual obligation. But freedom of contract has acquired a wider and more problematic significance, because of its philosophical and political connotation. Freedom of will goes both to the making and to the terms of contract. It means that a servant, an agricultural or an industrial worker, must be free to change his employer and his job. It means, on the other hand, that an employer can hire and fire at will, according to economic motives or personal dislikes, or for other reasons for which he is not generally accountable to anybody but himself. It means that a landowner can give notice to quit to a farmer-tenant whether his husbandry is good or not, and whether the land will go to waste or not. Freedom to make or unmake a contract also implies that a person cannot tie himself indefinitely to another. In other words, contract must not become a disguised form of status. This issue has not often come before the courts, but in *Horwood* v. *Millar's Timber and Trading Co.*,[7] the Court of Appeal held a contract illegal by which a man had, without any limitation of time, assigned his salary to a money-lender, contracted with him never to terminate his employment

6. Between the decisions of the House of Lords in *Rose* v. *Ford* [1937] A.C. 826 and *Benham* v. *Gambling* [1941] A.C. 157. In the latter case, the House reduced the amount of damages to be awarded for loss of expectation of happiness in respect of a child two and a half years old from £1200 to £200.
7. [1917] 1 K.B. 305.

without the moneylender's consent, never to obtain credit, move from his house, and in several other respects to restrict his personal movements.[8]

This freedom also applies to the terms of contract. The parties, it is assumed, are free to bargain out among themselves the conditions and terms of agreement. The classical theory of contract assumes the legal individual also to be a physical individual. The foundations of the theory were shattered when corporations increasingly displaced physical persons as legal individuals, and as parties to commercial and industrial contracts. Because the theory was that two or more individual persons freely bargained with each other, control over the terms of contract was limited to a few categories of illegality. The idea that the state on behalf of the community should intervene to dictate or alter terms of contracts in the public interest, is, on the whole, alien to the classical theory of common-law contract. It is true that contracts in restraint of trade are supposed to be void if they are 'unreasonable', and reasonableness is measured by the interests of the parties as well as the interests of the public. Yet, in the long series of cases in which English courts have dealt with contracts in restraint of trade, there is only one case[9] in which consideration of the public interest produced a decision different from that resulting from a consideration of the interests of the parties. It was used to deny the plaintiff a pension which the defendants had promised him, on condition that he would not compete against them in the wool trade. Although the plaintiff did not plead restraint, but

8. French law accords with English law in invalidating agreements that subject one party to the will of another (Planiol, *Traité élémentaire de droit civil*, II, § 43; III, §1123). But French law is much stricter than English law in the condemnation of contractual restrictions on freedom of marriage and religion. For a detailed comparison, see Lloyd (1953, p. 30). Any condition obliging a person to follow a particular religious belief would be counter to the secular and tolerant approach to religion which has dominated French law since the Revolution. While English and Canadian decisions have in the past tended to regard discriminatory covenants as a legitimate aspect of freedom of property and contract, such legislative developments as the Canadian Bill of Rights 1960, as interpreted in the *Drybones* case (p. 59), or the English Race Relations Act 1968 indicate a basic change in public policy. The US Supreme Court, more conscious of the issue of discrimination, has declared such covenants unenforceable (*Shelley* v. *Kraemer*, 334 U.S. 1 (1947)).

9. *Wyatt* v. *Kreglinger* [1933] 1 K.B. 793.

was anxious to comply and take the pension, the contract was held void as against the public interest.[10]

Equality

To some extent, the concepts of freedom and equality in contract are interchangeable. Lack of freedom to make or unmake a contract, or to bargain on its terms, also implies lack of equality. As long as we restrict both concepts to the limited meaning which the orthodox theory of contract gives them, one usually implies the other. In so far as a person is free from physical restraint or other direct compulsion to make and unmake a contract, he is also assumed to be in a position of equality. Because the law will impartially award damages or an injunction according to the same principles of corrective justice to the employer and to the employee, it is not generally concerned with the inequality resulting from the fact that one may be a corporation, controlling the entire oil or chemical industry of the country, and the other a worker on weekly wage and notice. And formal equality, to vote, to make contracts, to migrate, to marry, was regarded by early utilitarianism and democratic theory as automatically conducive to social liberty and equality.

The increasing gap between this theory and the reality of developing capitalist society, which led to the gradual reversal of the earlier Benthamite theory,[11] had its particular effect on the law of contract, the legal symbol *par excellence* of this society. It is the main purpose of this chapter to analyse the extent to which a mixture of legislative developments and judicial interpretations have bridged the growing gap between the early philosophy of contract and the reality of contemporary society. It will become apparent that the evolution of the law of contract in response to fundamental social changes has overwhelmingly occurred outside the court room. Unfortunately, cases still form the almost exclusive material for English textbooks.[12] By contrast, American students of the law of contract have become

10. For a criticism of this extremely questionable use of the notion of public interest, see (1933) 49 *L.Q.Rev.* 465–7.

11. This is brilliantly analysed in Dicey (1914).

12. The leading English textbook, Cheshire and Fifoot (1969), still makes only a passing and indirect reference to standardized contract (p. 121).

increasingly conscious of the importance of 'contracts of adhesion' and the inclusion of standard terms in the materials of contract law.[13]

It would not, however, be correct to infer that the courts have been entirely blind to the discrepancy between the formal postulates of freedom and equality in contract and the social reality. There are, of course, well into recent times, judges who continue to uphold the assumptions of the early nineteenth century, either believing that they are still a true reflection of society, or that the law should not attempt to take note of any social evolution.

Perhaps the most telling expression of this view is that of Justice Pitney in *Coppage* v. *Kansas*.[14] But the majority of judges have striven, in however haphazard a way, to mitigate at least some particularly blatant consequences of the early theory. If they have not achieved very much, this is to some extent due to judicial conservatism, but to a far greater extent, to the organic weakness of judicial-law reform. It is easy enough to detect inarticulate premises or prejudices, or ignorance of economic and social realities, in English and American case law. It is far more difficult to suggest an alternative. Vital developments of modern contract, especially in the sphere of collective bargaining, have largely proceeded outside the law courts. But even in so far as law courts can and wish to take into account the social implications of legal concepts, how far are they to go? Within the framework of the American Constitution, the Supreme Court has, since 1936, reversed the priority of values. It has, on the one hand, departed from the long line of decisions by which the court had interpreted the due-process clauses, so as to invalidate, for example, maximum hour legislation, or the legislative prohibition of

13. See e.g. Fuller (1947); Kessler and Sharp (1953); and the excellent symposium in 43 *Columbia L. Rev.* 565 (1943), in particular Hale 'Bargaining duress and economic liberty' (p. 605), and Kessler 'Contracts of adhesion' (p. 629).

14. 236 U.S. 1, 17 (1915) (see also Dodd, 43 *Columbia L. Rev.*, 667): 'It is impossible to uphold freedom of contract and the right of private property without at the same time recognizing as legitimate those inequalities of fortune that are the necessary result of the exercise of those rights . . . Indeed, a little reflection will show that whenever the right of private property and the right of free contract co-exist, each party, when contracting, is inevitably more or less influenced by the question whether he has much property or little or none: for the contract is made to the very end that each may gain something he needs or desires more urgently than that which he proposes to give in exchange.'

'yellow-dog' contracts. In this way, the court recognized that the main responsibility for translating the postulates of equality, freedom and other political values into legal reality, was normally the job of the legislator in which the court ought not to interfere except in extreme cases. On the other hand, the court has, in recent years, emphasized the provisions of the constitutions which guarantee political and social equality, regardless of race and religion. It has, to some extent, but by no means clearly or unanimously, adopted a 'preferred freedoms' philosophy, a hierarchy of values, in which basic personal freedoms are more immune from legislative interference than economic freedoms.[15] What Professor Corwin has described as a 'Constitutional Revolution Limited', is a judicial revolution made possible as well as limited by the political principles incorporated in a written constitution and accessible to judicial interpretation. Even so, the American courts can only play a minor part in the fundamental changes in the function of contract which are taking place all the time. The judicial function is far more limited in Britain, where the courts have no specific catalogue of political rights to interpret.

Equality between parties

Neither in the common law nor in any other developed system of law has there ever been absolute freedom of contract, or complete passivity in the face of patent inequality between the parties. It is largely as a result of the early constructive influence of equity that the protection of infants and of beneficiaries under trusts has been extended, that remedies against both innocent and fraudulent misrepresentation and undue influence have been developed, and that, generally, property rights of persons suffering legal disabilities such as married women or infants, have been protected against the encroachments of rapacious husbands or parents. But equity shows even more clearly the strict limitations of such judicial interference. Anyone who approaches the study of equity by looking at its twelve

15. See, among others, Schwartz, 'The changing role of the United States Supreme Court' (1950) 28 *Canadian Bar Rev*. 48; Mason (1955); Friedmann, 'Property, freedom, security and the Supreme Court of the United States' (1956) 19 *Mod. L. Rev*. 461; and see further, pp. 68–70.

maxims must beware of reading too much into such noble phrases as 'equality is equity', or 'equity will not suffer a wrong to be without remedy'. Their scope does not extend much beyond the adjustment of property rights, such as the rights between joint tenants, co-mortgagees, or co-sureties.

A much bolder attempt to apply the maxim that equality is equity to a modern contract between a government agency and one of the most powerful corporations in the country was made when the US Government sought to recover from the Bethlehem Steel Corporation vast profits claimed under wartime contracts made in 1918 between Bethlehem Steel and the US Steel Corporation.[16] Bethlehem Steel undertook to build a number of ships to meet the emergency caused by German submarine warfare. The Government claimed that the agreed profits averaging over 22 per cent of the computed cost were excessive, and, due to the exploitation by Bethlehem Steel of a wartime emergency, the Government was compelled to accept the terms of the country's leading shipbuilder. The majority of the US Supreme Court (deciding against a similar background during the Second World War) rejected this attempt to apply, as 'corrective justice', the principle of 'social solidarity' in wartime to a commercial contract, partly because it rejected the suggestion that the US Government was in a position of bargaining inferiority, partly because it held that it was for Congress, not for the Court, to determine the proper method of obtaining war supplies from the citizens. But Frankfurter J., in a powerful dissenting judgement, held that 'the Court should not permit Bethlehem Steel to recover these unconscionable profits and thereby make the Court the instrument of injustice'. Had the majority followed this view, the Court would have made itself the arbiter of 'just profit' and, to some extent, of the proper distribution of the social product (Kessler and Sharp, 1953, p. 274). From such a task – which has faced the United States courts more frequently and directly in the interpretation of the Sherman Anti-Trust Act (see p. 298) – it shrank. It thereby agreed with the great majority of judges in all countries with a developed legal system, who refuse to use the judicial function for measures of social or economic redistribution. In that interpretation, the maxim of equity retains a limited significance of technical, not social, adjustment.

16. *United States* v. *Bethlehem Steel Corporation*, 315 U.S. 289 (1942).

The prevailing attitude of the courts has been to protect freedom and equality of contract against physical coercion, inequality, or the use of 'unlawful' means. But what are unlawful means? In the *Crofter* case,[17] the House of Lords recognized that group pressure, applied for economic or social ends, as distinct from personal malice, and carried out by means not in themselves unlawful, was a legitimate weapon of modern economic and social conflict (Salmond, 1969, pp. 137–8). But more than twenty years later it retreated from this position by resurrecting the tort of intimidation.[18]

Common-law courts have thus gradually come to sanction judicially the restoration of a rough equality in the economic and social conflicts, by recognizing group pressure as legitimate. They have gone somewhat further in counteracting social or economic inequality in twentieth-century decisions on restraint of trade. Going back to the *Nordenfelt* case,[19] they have held that restrictive covenants are generally valid, if entered in consideration of the sale of a business goodwill. The parties in such situations are presumed to be generally equal in economic power. On the other hand, since *Mason's* case,[20] a covenant by which an employee engages himself not to use his skill and labour, has been held to be void, because the employee is presumed to be in a weaker bargaining position, and the restriction on his main or only capital, that is, labour and skill, is not to be encouraged. Here the courts have touched at least the fringe of that great and dominating problem, the gap between the formal equality of parties free to make contracts as they wish, and the actual inequality and lack of freedom caused by stark differences of economic bargaining power[21]. Yet it is obvious that the courts can only go a very limited distance along that road. The sphere of law which is not actually or potentially touched by the legislator is steadily shrinking. Over a century ago, English courts invented the doctrine of common employment. A century later, its abolition though favoured by the

17. *Crofter Harris Tweed Co.* v. *Veitch* [1942] A.C. 435.
18. *Rookes* v. *Barnard* [1964] A.C. 1129.
19. *Nordenfelt* v. *Maxim Nordenfelt Guns and Ammunition Co.* [1894] A.C. 535.
20. *Mason* v. *Provident Clothing Co.* [1913] A.C. 724.
21. Employees' covenants are generally valid if they prohibit the use of trade secrets acquired in the employment: cf. *Morris* v. *Saxelby* [1916] 1 A.C. 688. See also Cheshire and Fifoot (1969, pp. 347–51).

judiciary, had to be left to the legislator.[22] Judicial temperament, and beliefs, will make some courts go much farther than others in the reform of injustices through the discriminating use of precedent or the manifold other devices of judicial reform (Friedmann, 1967, chs. 32, 33).

The inevitable limitations of judicial reform in the field of major economic and social adjustments were underlined by the legislation immediately following the decision in the *Bethlehem Steel Corporation* case. Resulting from voluntary negotiations between various defence procurement agencies and private contractors for price adjustment by so-called 'renegotiation clauses', the United States enacted the Renegotiation Act of 1943. The basic conception of this Act was that wartime contracts for vital defence supplies, between the government on the one part, and private contractors on the other, could not be left to the free play of supply and demand or to the unchecked 'profit motive'. It provided for 'renegotiation' of certain categories of contracts, with special emphasis on excessive profits.

The Main Social Causes of the Transformation of Contract

Four major factors may be regarded as being mainly responsible for a transformation in the function and substance of contract, which is creating a widening gap between legal reality and the traditional textbook approach. The first is the widespread process of concentration in industry and business, corresponding to an increasing urbanization and standardization of life. Its legal result is the 'standard' contract, or 'contract of adhesion'.

The second factor is the increasing substitution of collective for individual bargaining in industrial society. Its legal product is the collective contract between management and labour, with a varying degree of state interference.

The third factor is the tremendous expansion of the welfare and social-service functions of the state in all common-law jurisdictions; its legal product is twofold: on the one hand, it has led to a multitude of statutory terms of contract, substituted for, or added to, the terms agreed between the parties; on the other hand, it has led to a vast

22. Law Reform (Personal Injuries) Act 1948, c. 41, s. 1.

increase of contracts where government departments or other public authorities are on one side, and a private party on the other. The effect of this on the law of contract, though as yet little explored, is profound.

All these developments affect the theory and practice of contract, but in different ways. The social-security ideology means emphasis on stability and a corresponding lack of mobility, especially in employment contracts. The standardization of contract greatly restricts the freedom of the weaker party, and is usually accompanied by inequality of bargaining power. Collective bargaining, on the other hand, has substantially restored equality of bargaining power between employers and employees, though increasingly at the cost of individual freedom, as the legal or practical compulsion to join employers' associations and trade unions progresses. The imposition of statutory duties in the interest of social justice largely sacrifices mobility for stability and security. The increasing participation of public authority in contract creates the wider and as yet generally unexplored problem of the dual function of the state, as a superior and as an equal.[23]

Lastly, the economic security aspect of contract, the elaboration of remedies for breach, is increasingly affected by the spread of such political, economic, and social upheavals as war, revolution or inflation. Its legal result is the doctrine of frustration of contract, with its consequent extension of legal excuses for the non-performance of contract.

Standardization of contract[24]

In extreme cases, a single corporation controlling an entire industry or business can impose its conditions upon an unorganized multitude of individual parties. In the vast majority of cases the firms operating in a particular industry or business are organized in an association, through which they formulate general conditions, which, by virtue of their membership, they are under an obligation to

23. On the public-law element in contract see p. 135.
24. See Prausnitz (1937); Llewellyn, 'What price contract?' 40 *Yale L.J.* 704 (1931); Book Review, 52 *Harvard L. Rev.* 700 (1939); Kessler, 'Contracts of adhesion', 43 *Columbia L. Rev.* 629 (1943).

incorporate in their individual transactions. Most contracts which govern our daily lives are of a standardized character. We travel under standard terms, by rail, ship, aeroplane or tramway. We make contracts for life or accident assurances under standardized conditions. We rent houses or rooms under similarly controlled terms; authors or broadcasters, whether dealing with public or private institutions, sign standard agreements; government departments regulate the conditions of purchases by standard conditions (see p. 403). In many ways, this standardization of contract terms simplifies business; indeed, it is an inevitable aspect of the mechanization of modern life. The working out of thousands of individual contract terms for substantially similar transactions would be as uneconomical as the use of antiquated machinery. It has even been suggested that 'By standardizing contracts, a law increases that real security which is a necessary basis of initiatives and tolerable risks' (Cohen, 1933, p. 106). At the same time, it is certain that the standardization of contracts affects both freedom and equality of bargaining, except where groups of approximately equal strength confront each other. This is seldom the case in the type of transaction mentioned earlier. Freedom is affected in so far as the individual has a purely fictitious alternative to accepting the terms presented to him. The traveller may have a choice between different airlines or shipping companies, but it will hardly ever be a choice between different terms. The same applies to those who wish to insure themselves, mortgage their houses, or buy goods on hire-purchase. A shipping company or a government department will not agree to individual modifications of terms where a standard voyage or purchase is in question. In a case which concerned the effect of conditions printed on the back of a railway pass, Scott L.J. spoke of a 'misuse of contract which makes the legislature tend to substitute status'.[25] The absence of such freedom is, however, important mainly because of the ensuing inequality of bargaining power. Standard terms invariably detract from common-law rights: by limiting or excluding liability;[26] by making the landlord the judge of whether the tenant has infringed certain terms of the tenancy agreement;[27] by making a government

25. *Henson* v. *L.N.E.R.* [1946] 1 All E.R. 653.
26. e.g. in the typical shipping or air-transport contract.
27. Frequent clause in Landlord and Tenant agreements.

department as contractor the sole judge of whether it is justified to terminate a contract because of altered circumstances.[28] Courts, or even the legislature, can do very little to alter this situation, which is inherent in modern conditions of life. It is difficult to see how it would be practicable for courts to 'enforce only those terms to which a reasonable offeree would have agreed if he had enjoyed equal bargaining power with the offeror'.[29] An alternative approach to the problem of standardized terms of contract imposed on all comers by a party of overwhelming economic power is that of deconcentration by legislation, as attempted by the American anti-trust legislation in civil or criminal law (see p. 306). But it is fair to say that, while a certain degree of competition may be restored or preserved by such legislation and jurisdiction, its effect on the standardization of terms as between industry and the customer is small.

Protection of the consumer

The legislator and the courts have been somewhat more active in countering another form of inequality, that resulting from the fact that one party draws up terms of contract as a result of experience, long consideration, and expert advice, while the other party has no more than a hasty opportunity to scrutinize the terms. In some cases, the legislator has attempted to counter this inequality, for example, in the English Hire-Purchase Act 1965, which makes the enforceability of a hire-purchase agreement dependent upon, e.g. the delivery to the hirer of a note which sets out the essential terms of the agreement, and contains a legible note of the hirer's rights in a form prescribed by the Act.[30] In addition the Hire Purchase (Advertisements) Act 1967, prescribes the information about the terms of credit that is to be included in the advertising of goods available on hire-purchase terms and the formula for the calculation of the interest rate.

28. *Standard Conditions of British Government Contracts for Store Purchases* (1947 edn.).

29. Note 'Contract clauses in fine print' 63 *Harvard L. Rev.* 504 (1950).

30. The Act requires that the contract be in writing, be signed by the hirer, and that the hirer be given a copy. The layout of the contract is prescribed by the Hire Purchase (Documents) (Legibility and Statutory Statements) Regulations 1965 (S.I. 1965, No. 1646).

In the United States, the last decade has been marked by a variety of attempts to protect the consumer against the more glaring abuses of small-print conditions and other aspects of standardized contract making. This is of particular importance in a society which is to an increasing extent built on credit transactions. Manufacturers, banks and other providers of necessary services – strengthened by elaborate techniques of advertising and salesmanship – have tended to magnify the natural inequality between them and the consumer of their products or services, by concealing the true terms of the transaction. Here again, it is the interplay of public opinion, judicial interpretations and legislative reforms that characterizes a growing movement to counter the predominance of the stronger party. In a landmark decision of 1960,[31] the Supreme Court of New Jersey entered judgement in favour of the buyer of a Plymouth car – and of his wife, who was not a party to the transaction but had been severely injured when using the car – against both the dealer and the manufacturer, in the following circumstances: the purchase order was a printed form, the end of which, in small and barely legible type, substituted an express warranty for all other express or implied warranties, including the implied warranty of merchantability. The substituted warranty, which *inter alia* compelled the purchaser to send in all defective parts of the automobile within a certain period to the manufacturer, was worthless, particularly in the case involved where, owing to a grave steering defect, the wife of the purchaser had been gravely injured and the car was a total loss. Here the Court substituted in effect the terms of the implied warranty for the fine print terms of a lesser express warranty.

Some recent decisions[32] have applied similar approaches to insurance policies, which are notoriously unintelligible, even to a careful reader. The policies purported to exclude coverage for certain accidents, in a manner which the courts found to be improper and unfair to the insured. In both cases, the policies, under the heading of 'comprehensive personal liability', contained in fine print in the later sections, certain exclusionary clauses which it seems highly unlikely that the ordinary insured would have so understood. . . .

31. *Henningsen* v. *Bloomfield Motors, Inc.*, 32 N.J. 358, 161 A. 2nd 69 (1960).
32. *Gray* v. *Zurich Insurance Co.*, 54 Cal. Rptr. 104, 419 P. 2nd 168 (1966); *Gerhardt* v. *Continental Insurance Co.*, 48 N.J. 291, 225 A. 2nd. 328 (1966).

on his or her own reading. . . . [N]owhere was there any straightforward and unconditional statement that the policy was not intended to protect the insured against the workman's compensation claim by a resident's employee injured at the insured's home.[33]

Although courts have long followed the basic precept that they would look to the words of the contract to find the meaning which the parties expected from them, they have also applied the doctrine of the adhesion contract to insurance policies, holding that in view of the disparate bargaining status of the parties we must ascertain that meaning of the contract which the insured would reasonably expect.[34]

A legislative implementation of the same way of thinking is the Truth in Lending Act of 1968,[35] This act covers consumer credit transactions, for which it lays down the various charges that must be included in the 'finance charge', the procedures to be used in calculating the annual percentage rate, and the information that must be disclosed at the various stages of a credit relationship. Various provisions deal with the administrative enforcement, with criminal liability for willing and knowing violations, and with civil liability for a failure to disclose any required information. In certain cases the borrower has also a right of rescinding the contract. One of the most useful aspects of the act has been to compel banks to disclose the true rate of interest for personal bank loans, 'privilege accounts' and the like, which had generally been misstated or concealed.

Such legislative reforms are useful, as far as they go, and they are tokens of a growing concern with the rights of the – generally unorganized – consumer, as against the enormously more powerful and organized institutions with which he has to deal. Increasing concern with the overwhelming power of industrial and business organizations have recently led, in the United States, to more systematic efforts to make the voice of the consumer heard, including demands for the appointment of representatives of the public to the boards of corporations.

Earlier legislation imposes an obligation upon the providers of vital utilities to make services available under certain statutory conditions, or regulates the minimum terms from which they cannot

33. *Gerhardt* v. *Continental Insurance Co.*, 48 N.J. at 299, 225 A. 2nd at 333.
34. *Gray* v. *Zurich Insurance Co.*, 54 Cal. Rptr. 419 at 107–8, 419 P. 2d, at 171–2.
35. 82 Stat. 146 (1968).

derogate in the provision of services. Thus the British Road Traffic Act 1960, and the British Transport Act 1962, prohibit the exclusion or limitation of liability in contracts for the conveyance of passengers on public-service vehicles.[36] American courts have developed similar principles without legislation. 'The law seems well settled that a common carrier, owing a duty to serve all proper persons who apply, cannot, when acting in its public capacity, validly exempt itself by contract from liability for negligence.'[37]

Similar stipulations by private contractors are discouraged, at least where the user is dependent on the contractor's services.

Moreover, American courts have developed a theory by which a party holding a practical monopoly of service is assumed to have incurred a duty to render public service, and cannot therefore arbitrarily refuse to contract. Yet 'the field of genuine compulsory contract has not, on the whole, transcended that of public utilities and compulsory insurance'.[38] It is this problem of squaring the *de facto* exercise of public functions with the private-law liberty of making or refusing to make a contract, with all its ensuing powers of discrimination and abuse, which has, in some countries, led to the demand for the socialization of public utilities and insurance.[39]

Public control over terms

The variety of impacts of public law on contract is almost infinite, but it may suffice to indicate four broad methods of public control over the terms of contract for our purposes:[40]

1. Public policy, through statutory or judicial prohibitions, may

36. For details of the rather complex legislation, see Kahn-Freund (1965, pp. 562–70).

37. *Fairfax Gas & Supply Co.* v. *Hadary*, 151 F. 2d 939, 940 (4th Cir. 1945).

38. Lenhoff, 'The scope of compulsory contract proper', 43 *Columbia L. Rev.* 595 (1943).

39. See, generally, on the major public enterprises in different countries, Friedmann and Garner (1970); Hanson (1955; pp. 338–42). Socialization, as such, is not, however, a sufficient safeguard against exploitation. Legislation may still be needed to protect the user against abuse of superior power (see, e.g. the British Transport Communication Passenger Charges Scheme 1954).

40. cf. for a slightly different classification Eastwood and Wortley [1938], *J.S.P.T.L.*, pp. 23–4.

declare contracts void, either wholly or in part, in so far as they offend against certain principles of social or economic equality. Reference has already been made to the line of cases which have invalidated restrictive covenants between employers and employees purporting to restrict the exercise of the employee's skill and labour. This is a relatively rare instance of judicial correction of an inequality of bargaining power. A statutory parallel may be seen in the Truck Acts prohibiting the payment of wages in goods instead of money (Cooper and Wood, 1966, p. 256). These Acts invalidate contracts by which an employer undertakes to pay any part of a workman's wages otherwise than in current coin, or lays down conditions as to the manner or place in which the workman had to spend his wages (e.g. by having to buy at the employer's store). Subject to certain exceptions laid down in the Act, the employer cannot make any deduction from wages in respect of meals or other benefits in kind.[41] The practical importance of these forms of legislative or judicial protection has, of course, been greatly diminished by the far-reaching restoration of equality of bargaining power through collective bargaining. They retain importance mainly in regard to unorganized employees.

2. Of greater practical importance are the many forms of compulsory terms incorporated in contracts for the enforcement of certain social policies. The most frequent way of incorporating social duties in contracts is by means of statutory duties, which come into existence as by-products of the master-and-servant relationship. Technically, the breach of such statutory duties will usually be sanctioned either by penalties or by actions for damages akin to tort actions. For example, the breach of a statutory duty to fence dangerous machinery, or provide minimum standards of sanitation, may result in an action for damage by the person injured through neglect of these provisions. Workmen's compensation legislation – now replaced in Britain by the comprehensive National Insurance (Industrial Injuries) Act – provides a statutory obligation, regardless of fault, for compensation in the case of accidents suffered in the course of employment. Sometimes, legislation of this type imposes statutory duties of a quasi-contractual type, added to a contract proper, for example, between landlord and tenant. A familiar

41. cf. *Pratt* v. *Cook* [1940] A.C. 437.

example in English social legislation is the Housing Act of 1936, by which lessors of houses below a certain rateable value incur a statutory warranty of 'fitness for human habitation'. The relation of this statutory provision to the contractual terms has been the subject of some judicial differences of opinion. All the judgements expressed strong doubt whether contractual conditions such as notice of defects should be imported into statutory terms added to the contract in the public interest.

Another type of compulsory term imposed upon private contracts is that resulting from minimum-wage legislation. Two kinds of minimum-wage legislation have gained importance in English law. The first type makes it compulsory for contracting parties in a number of industries to incorporate 'fair wages' standards, that is, to negotiate wages in accordance with recognized standards. These principles have been embodied in particular in a large number of Acts, which provide assistance to industries and public authorities, by way of grant, loan, subsidy, guarantee or licence.[42] This means that contracting parties are compelled to adopt minimum conditions determined by reference to standards outside their own volition and control. The second type of minimum-wages regulation directly imposes statutory minimum standards on a number of industries. Wage fixing is normally done through boards or councils, known as 'wage-regulating authorities', which make their orders after having heard the parties concerned. In substance, this is sometimes much like a process of collective bargaining, but in form it is a state act which, by means of a statutory order, imposes terms on the parties themselves. In Britain, this machinery is used in a few industries where collective organization is weak, notably in agriculture, catering[43] and in the retail trade.

3. Another way of imposing public law upon private agreements is the variation of certain terms of contract by public authority, that is, either automatically by statute, or more frequently, by ministerial

42. cf. *Industrial Relation Handbook* (1961, pp. 149–52); Kahn-Freund 'Legislation through adjudication: the legal aspect of fair wages clauses and recognized conditions' (1948) 11 *Mod. L. Rev.* 269, 429.

43. For details, see *Industrial Relations Handbook* (1961, ch. 10); Kahn-Freund, 'Minimum wage legislation in Great Britain', 97 *Pennsylvania L. Rev.*, 778, 784 (1949).

order. In so far as collective agreements are made automatically binding on individual contracts between employers and employees, the terms of the collective agreements are automatically substituted for those of the individual contract, to the extent that it derogates from the collective terms.[44] The English Agriculture Holdings Act 1948 provides an interesting example of a variation of contractual terms in the name of national agricultural policy. Section 10 empowers an arbitrator, either on the application of the landlord or the tenant, or otherwise, to vary a contract which provides for the maintenance of certain land as permanent pasture, by directing that certain parts of the land shall be treated as arable land. In this way the state ensures that the land is cultivated according to what appear to be paramount national interests, in preference to the agreement of the parties.

4. The various judicial and legislative efforts to correct the terms of standardized contracts in favour of the consumer can also be characterized as a form of public rectification of the terms of contract. Finally, the recent statutory and judicial interventions in the legal relations between landlord and tenant – which have been briefly described in the chapter on Property Law – bear on the law of contract. Restrictions on the rights of the property owner *vis-à-vis* the tenant are also public law restrictions on freedom of contract.

Public authorities as parties

The modifications of the traditional principles of contract discussed so far are familiar to all common-law countries. Moreover, it is their frequency and importance, rather than their existence, which is a

44. This situation prevails on Continental Europe (see Kahn-Freund, 1965, pp. 11–12 and the various case studies). With respect to Great Britain, Kahn-Freund observes that only in a few minor cases have collective agreements been given compulsory effect by statute. Generally, the terms of a collective agreement do have effect in that the terms are 'tacitly incorporated in the employment contract as implied terms', except in so far as they will be excluded by the express terms of the contract or by the custom of the trade (28–30), and Drake (1969, pp. 88–94). See also Kahn-Freund's observations on section 8 of the Terms and Conditions of Employment Act 1959, which provides some machinery to ensure observance of collective agreement terms in individual contracts (1968, p. 26).

fairly recent development. By far the most important modification of the law of contract, however, results from the increasing role played by the government, by local authorities and the growing number of incorporated public authorities as owners and managers of industry, as providers of public utilities, administrators of social services, or in some other capacity which requires the making of contracts. It is perhaps not surprising that this problem has as yet been so little explored in the common-law systems. It is a familiar problem in Continental systems, where the relations between public authority and the citizen have, for many decades, been the concern of the science of public law. The legal classification of conflicts between public authorities and the citizen is also indispensable for the allocation of a particular dispute, either to a civil court or an administrative tribunal. In the common-law systems, on the other hand, public law has crept in gradually and by stealth. As all common-law countries now have highly developed government machineries, social services, public utilities, and publicly owned industries, the significance of public law in these countries is steadily growing. But public law has to be developed mainly out of the categories of common law. The impact of public law on common law concepts, however, is of at least equal significance. It presents itself in two forms. First, government departments or other public authorities are employers, buy and sell goods or services, manage factories, grant loans, repair dykes or regulate watercourses, and exercise a multitude of other activities which bring them into legal contact with the citizen. On the other hand, public authorities contract with each other. The British Transport Commission must buy coal from the National Coal Board, and the National Coal Board uses nationalized railways. This theme will be developed further in a later chapter, assessing the growth and place of public law in the common-law world (see pp. 377–84).

So far as the conditions imposing social and economic policies are concerned, no bargaining takes place; the contract clauses embodying those policies are prescribed and printed in advance, becoming standard 'boiler-plate' in the contractual document.

To a large extent, accordingly, the Government contract is an instrument of a power relationship, and only vaguely resembles the consensual agreement extolled by Maine and relied upon by Adam Smith. The significant decision is that of the Government in setting the terms and conditions of the proposed agreement. . . .[45]

Contract in a socialized economy

To an increasing extent, government departments or incorporated authorities now deal with each other. The greater the sector of socialized industry, the more important is this type of transaction. Against a different legal background, it has become the predominant form of contract in the Soviet system, where all industry is nationalized. Through the establishment of the different industries as quasi-autonomous legal corporations, Soviet law has treated them as separate legal managerial and accounting units which are able to make contracts. But contracts between state-owned corporations working under an overall economic and political plan are obviously different in substance, if not in form, from the private-law contract of both common-law and the civil-law systems, which are based on the principle of individual ownership and free economic enterprise.

In modern Soviet jurisprudence, contract has been restored as the chief legal instrument in the relations between state enterprises. Earlier Soviet jurists who, under the leadership of Pashukanis, relegated all law, and contract in particular, to the scrapheap as an instrument of bourgeois society have been castigated as 'wreckers'. But the restitution of contract to a place of honour serves mainly the purpose of administrative decentralization, and of the accountancy of state enterprises to the political planners. 'The two – contracts and plans – bear a polar relation to each other.'[46]

In general, the Soviet Civil Law, which is in many ways modelled upon the modern civil codes of Continental Europe, applies to the transactions between state enterprises. Liability for breach of contract depends upon fault; the familiar rules of civil law regarding mistake, impossibility, unjust enrichment, illegality, are applied (Berman, 1963, pp. 130–44; Hazard, 1969, pp. 315–26). Special commercial

45. Arthur S. Miller, 'Government contracts and social control: a preliminary inquiry', 41 *Virginia L. Rev.* (1955), pp. 56–7; Friedmann (1951, p. 71), and Cohen (1933, pp. 102–11).

46. Berman, 'Commercial contracts in Soviet law', 35 *California L. Rev.* 191, 225 (1947); Berman (1963, pp. 141–4).

courts, the *Gosarbitrazh*, adjudicate on disputes between state enterprises. Though separate from the ordinary courts and closely linked with the administrative branch of government, these courts have been increasingly directed to apply law rather than general equity or policy principles.[47] Yet the interpretation and enforcement of contracts between Soviet enterprises – which are above all instruments of national planning – account for at least two distinctive features: first, in the decisions of the *Gosarbitrazh* administrative and penal sanctions are coupled with civil sanctions. Where the court regards a particular breach of contract as injurious to the national economy, it will report to the superior authorities.[48] Secondly, the ability to fulfil a contract is often influenced by policy and planning decisions outside of the control of the parties. This is perhaps only a difference of degree as compared with the present position in Britain or the United States, where the official allocation of raw materials, the prohibition of certain transactions, the imposition of price controls and other aspects of a semi-planned economy are familiar phenomena in times of war or economic emergencies. The Soviet commercial contract is of necessity part of an overall plan laid down by the superior authority.

Although the application of the law of contract to transactions between state enterprises has been specifically reaffirmed by the 1961 Fundamental Principles of Civil Law, and supported by the law governing the status of public enterprises of 1965, which has considerably reinforced their managerial autonomy and competitive status, basic differences between the function of contract in an essentially planned and centralized society, and the, more or less, market-directed societies of the Western world remain. The Fundamental Principles declare that civil rights and obligations arise from

47. See the Soviet authorities quoted by Berman (1963, pp. 124–8).
48. Thus, in a case reported by Berman, 35 *California L. Rev.* 230, a factory, operating under the paper machine construction trust, which was insufficiently equipped for the manufacture of pergament machines, had contracted to manufacture such a machine. It was rejected as faulty by the plaintiff, a Siberian paper factory of the People's Commissariat of Timber. Not only were the defendant factory and its superior administration held liable for the breach of contract, but the court also notified the People's Commissariat of General Machine Construction that no steps had been taken by the defendant administration to remedy the position (see also Berman, 1963, pp. 128, 166).

administrative acts and planning acts. As a German scholar has observed (Loeber, 1965, pp. 128, 141), no other legal system seems to have embodied such a principle. It means that a legal institution based upon the voluntary agreement of autonomous parties is controlled by compulsory norms of public law. As Professor Hazard points out (1969, p. 356), 'harmonizing the administrative obligation to contract with a policy fostering local initiative in negotiating contracts on a consensual basis is the task of state arbitration. . . .' This is done by way of a procedure that does not fit into the system of contract in unplanned societies, and which is called 'pre-contract' dispute (Berman, 1963, pp. 131–4). Since contract is the means by which essential supplies and services – and thus the whole economy – is kept in operation, disagreement on the terms of a contract will not be the end of the matter. In case of disagreement, therefore, the state arbitration boards will resolve the dispute by laying down terms which they consider fair and acceptable to the parties (Hazard, 1969).

Another difference between contracts in planned and unplanned economies is the different significance of specific performance. In the unplanned economy, damages are generally an adequate substitute for performance, and are, in effect, the predominant means of reparation. In a planned economy – which also means normally a scarcity economy – performance is an essential means of keeping the economy going. In the socialist economies, therefore, 'specific performance is the rule' (Hazard, 1969, p. 359). The same factor probably also accounts for the generally harsh interpretation of 'fault' by the arbitration tribunals in socialist economies. When, for example, a metallurgical factory, which was under contract to deliver certain quantities of cast iron, pleaded in excuse of its default that it had not received sufficient allocation orders from the regional economic council to which it was subordinate, the state arbitrator held it liable for the agreed penalty. A western critic (Loeber, 1965, p. 147) has commented that such a harsh decision is inevitable in a planned economy in order to avoid a flood of pleas of inability to supply. As Professor Hazard has observed (1969, p. 356) 'the contract, seen as establishing a civil law relationship rather than an administrative relationship, becomes an exercise in managerial initiative'.

In non-Socialist society, the penalty of miscalculation is a financial one, although the increasing intervention of government considerably cushions such effects of a *laissez-faire* economy, by guarantees, compensation clauses, and other means. In Soviet law the sanctions of contract are used as a whip. Damages will show up in the accounts of the enterprises concerned; penalties will bring it into bad odour; court reports to the superior authorities will expose the management to disciplinary measures. Even though the form and sanctions of contract are largely similar to those of non-Soviet law, its social function is different.

Where the predominant type of legal transaction is between public authorities, law becomes far more closely linked with and dependent upon state policy and planning. We may add to this category the increasingly important area of contracts where private firms supply public authorities with essential products. In the United States, where the huge defence procurement dominates a major sector of the economy, the suppliers of war materials are private contractors, and superficially they fit into the established categories of the private enterprise and private contract system. However, as Galbraith has pointed out in *The New Industrial State* (see p. 332), they fulfill in effect essential functions for the government, which will, if necessary, subsidize them and with which they are closely linked through the so-called 'techno-structure'.

The differences between the socialist and non-socialist systems of contracts are thus relative rather than absolute.

Economic upheavals

Before the First World War, physical or legal impossibility was the only means by which contract could be discharged, apart from breach of contract. The First World War produced the problem of frustration of contract, as a result of political, social or economic upheavals. A further impetus was given to the doctrine by the postwar inflation in Germany, which led to important judicial developments, especially to the doctrine of 'foundation of contract'. The French doctrine of *imprévision* in administrative contracts also had considerable influence. What emerged was a doctrine which, in civil, commercial and industrial relations, supplemented the strict categories of impossibility by 'frustration' of contract, where war, devaluation, major social unrest, or similar factors beyond the control of the parties had vitally affected the ability of one or both parties to perform. By now the doctrine of frustration is an established part of most civil-law and common-law jurisdictions.[49] This is mainly a reflection of the vicissitudes and uncertainties of a period of wars, international tensions, social revolution and economic upheavals. The law recognizes that these factors, due to national or international policies, go beyond reasonable calculations of economic risk, to safeguard which is the function of the law of contract. This is not the place to discuss in detail the extent to which the doctrine of frustration has now been incorporated in the law of contract of the Western systems, both in the common-law and the civil-law[50] systems. Frustration of contract is still predominantly a judicial doctrine, although it has been incorporated in a recent civil code.[51] A vital change of circumstances may lead sometimes to the complete discharge, and sometimes to the judicial modification of the terms of contract.[52] The doctrine of frustration has recently gained increased importance in English law. This is a natural consequence of the upheavals of war, inflation and any such social and legal changes as are produced by the nationalization of industries. Reference has already been made to the instances of statutory frustration, where the boards of nationalized industries are empowered to disclaim certain contracts and leases. In English law the doctrine owed its main expansion to the First and Second World Wars. But the courts stopped short of varying the terms of contracts, until the

49. cf. the comparative survey in *Journal of Comparative Legislation*, vol. 28, pp. 1–25 (Scots law, French law and German law); vol. 29, pp. 1–18 (American law and Soviet law); vol. 30, p. 55 (Swiss law). Also Zepos, 'Frustration of contract in comparative law and the new Greek Code of 1946' (1948) 11 *Mod. L. Rev.* 36–46; Smit, 'Frustration of contract', 58 *Columbia L. Rev.* 287 (1958).

50. For details, see the articles quoted in *J.C.L.* (n. 49).

51. Greek Civil Code, article 388, cf. Zepos, pp. 36, 42.

52. The latter is the normal effect of *imprévision* in French law; German courts have applied similar principles under section 242, German Civil Code; section 388 of the Greek Civil Code of 1946 specifically empowers the court to reduce the promisor's obligation, or decree the discharge of the contract, where because of a change due to extraordinary and unforeseen events the obligation has become excessively onerous.

Court of Appeal[53] followed some Continental models and boldly revised the terms of contract. A contract between the Commissioner of Works and a private firm had stipulated that the sum to be paid to the contractor 'should not be greater than the actual cost plus a net profit remuneration of £300,000'. The parties had contracted for about £5,000,000, but extra work ordered brought the total cost up to £6,683,000. The court awarded the contractors extra remuneration in proportion to the excess cost. In another case,[54] a contract for the supply of newsfilms made during the war was to continue until a Cinematograph Film Order, made in 1943, under the Defence Act 1939, was cancelled. When the Defence Act expired after the war, the order was continued under the Supplies and Services Act 1945. The Court of Appeal considered the circumstances which had led to the agreement and came to the conclusion that the order had been continued for reasons different from those leading to the original Cinematograph Film Order, and it discharged the defendants from further performance of the contract, despite its clear wording. Lord Justice Denning regarded this as more than a matter of construction.

In these frustration cases, as Lord Wright said, the court really exercises a qualifying power – a power to qualify the absolute, literal or wide terms of the contract – in order to do what is just and reasonable in the new situation, and it can now by statute make ancillary orders to that end. Until recently the court only exercised this power when there was a frustrating event, that is a supervening event which struck away the foundations of the contract. In the important decision of *Sir Lindsay Parkinson & Co., Ltd* v. *Commissioners of Works & Public Buildings* however this court exercised a like power when there was no frustrating event, but only an uncontemplated turn of events.[55]

But the House of Lords, in reversing the decision, went out of its way to repudiate the suggestion that courts had a broad qualifying power in regard to contracts. The decision in *Parkinson*'s case was

53. *Sir Lindsay Parkinson & Co. Ltd* v. *Commissioners of Works & Public Buildings* [1949] 2 K.B. 632.
54. *British Movietonews* v. *London & District Cinemas Ltd* [1950] 2 All E.R. 390.
55. [1950] 2 All E.R., p. 395.

reduced to one of construction, following from the language of the contract.

On the basis of a comprehensive comparative analysis, an American study[56] suggests the 'gap-filling doctrine' as a suitable rationalization:

Where circumstances occur, neither foreseen nor reasonably foreseeable at the time of the promise, it follows from application of the proper standard of interpretation that the promise may not reasonably be construed to express an intention to be found also in the unanticipated situation. Broad terms do not cover unforeseen contingencies. Since, therefore, in regard to the unforeseen circumstances, the contract shows a gap, supplementation with provisions ensuing from reasonableness is required.

Such a rationalization can, however, only serve as the framework within which courts, guided by the intensity of the upheaval, will supplement, modify, or supersede the intentions of the parties expressed at the time of the making of the contract. Despite such judicial emphasis on *pacta sunt servanda* and other traditional aspects of contract, the character of contract as a legal instrument of contemporary society is undergoing profound changes, in which elements of the old mingle with the new. The normal commercial contract – between individuals or corporate persons – can still be handled with the traditional categories and approaches. But whenever elements of public policy enter into the making of a contract, either through the status of one or both of the parties, or through the terms of the contract itself, the policy aspects of contract increase. In a private-enterprise economy, like that of the United States, war procurement is still largely handled through contracts between governmental authorities and private contractors. It is nevertheless an instrument of policy, and as the various Renegotiation Acts show, they are subject to considerations that do not apply to the normal commercial contract.

Collective bargaining

The increasing substitution of collective bargaining for individual contracts is a phenomenon common to all industrialized countries,

56. Smit, 'Frustration of contract', 58 *Columbia L. Rev.* 287 (1958).

and transcending the differences of legal systems. It is one of the most important features of a society in which effective power has shifted from the individual to various groups representing the collective interests of employers, workers, professions and – in a movement that is beginning to gather strength – consumers.

In industrial relations, collective bargaining has – except in certain fields, and for small-scale enterprises – essentially displaced the former master–servant relationship. But the question of the extent to which the law should regulate the collective bargaining processes, and the manner in which it should do so, remains controversial and a matter of fundamental divergences of approach, across the various systems of the common law and the civil law world. Nor is the difference of approaches simply a consequence of contrasting democratic and totalitarian philosophies to freedom of labour, and the relationship between the state, employers and the workers. While it is true that in totalitarian systems, such as those of Nazi Germany, Fascist Italy, or Franco's Spain – and, in a different context, in the Communist world – there is no free process of collective bargaining and the state has full control over the organization and conditions of labour and industrial relations, there are widely divergent concepts of 'industrial democracy', in non-totalitarian systems.

Among the Continental systems that have firmly integrated collective bargaining in the legal structure, and subjected it to sanctions are those of Germany and Sweden. Germany has, since 1927, had a special hierarchy of labour courts – which have the same status as other law courts – which deal with all sorts of disputes between employers and employees, as well as with the authoritative interpretation of collective agreements. In addition, the government has certain powers to make collective agreements binding upon an entire industry. Furthermore, the terms of collective agreements, apart from being binding between the parties, i.e. the employers and trade unions concerned, become 'normative' parts of the individual labour contracts that are affected by them. Deviations are void, and the terms of the collective agreement substituted for the invalid agreements.

The Swedish Collective Agreements Law of 1928 lays down that collective agreements entered into by an association are binding on its members and that employers and employees so bound may not, during the period of the validity of the agreement, engage in strikes, lockouts or other incompatible actions. Breach of these obligations entails liability for damages, including damages assessed on individual employees up to a certain limit.

Within the common-law world, there are striking differences between the highly industrialized states that share the common-law tradition. They show that, even in our increasingly standardized world, the differences of historical developments and social traditions still count.

Britain, the pioneer of the industrial revolution, also has the oldest history of labour conflict. The growth of trade unionism and collective bargaining are responses to the impotence and suppression of the individual worker in the early phases of the industrial revolution. But the development of collective bargaining has, until recently, predominantly occurred outside the purview of the law. Legislative action was needed to remove some of the more stringent obstacles to the legal recognition of trade unions, without which collective bargaining could not have been developed. To that extent, such pieces of legislation as the Trade Union Act of 1871 (with subsequent amendments) and the Conspiracy and Protection of Property Act 1875, which removed the stigma of criminal and civil conspiracy from trade unions, or the Trade Disputes Acts of 1906 and 1965 which provide legal immunities for those who commit certain torts in contemplation of furtherance of a trade dispute, have been an indispensable contribution of the law to the development of trade unionism and, therefore, of collective bargaining, in Britain. But the principles and techniques of collective agreements, as such, have predominantly developed outside the law. In a recent series of lectures Professor Kahn-Freund has pointed out (1968, p. 8) that collective bargaining and trade unionism were well established in Britain before workers (with the progressive abolition of property qualifications) obtained the right to vote, and could, therefore, exercise an influence on legislation.

[A]t the time when, owing to the extension of the parliamentary franchise, the unions would have been able to use political pressure power to secure the aid of the law toward their recognition by the employers as their bargaining partners or toward the enforcement of the minimum terms laid down in their agreements, they had already, through industrial action alone, secured a position in which they could, or thought they could, dispense with the aid of the law for these purposes.

Another commentator (Pelling, 1968) has added that in the nineteenth century the bulk of labour law was administered by county magistrates and that for trade unions, as for the individual worker, involvement with the law meant exposure to a hostile environment.

As a result, there has been, until recently, despite the tremendous growth of state intervention in other spheres of social life, very little legal regulation of collective bargaining. In the post-war period, the state began to intervene, mainly in weakly organized industries, through minimum-wage legislation (e.g. in the Agricultural Wages Act 1948). Moreover, the various nationalization acts enjoin the boards of the public corporations that manage the nationalized industries 'to enter into consultation with organizations, appearing to them to represent substantial proportions of the persons in the employment of the board', for the purpose of negotiating the terms and conditions of their employment. These are tokens of the indirect statutory recognition of collective bargaining.

During the last decade, these more or less marginal legislative contacts with the regulation of labour conditions and collective bargaining have given way to more direct forms of interference, and, in recent years, to a bitter public debate on the question whether the law should make collective agreements directly enforceable as contracts, possibly following the model of the Swedish law of 1928. The Terms and Conditions of Employment Act 1959 provides limited sanctioning for collective bargaining by enabling trade unions or employers organizations to secure adjudication by the Industrial Arbitration Board in cases where they think the employer is failing to observe terms and conditions of employment not less favourable than those established by agreement or award for a relevant sector of industry. Any award rendered by the Arbitration Board requiring the employer to observe the terms has the effect of an implied term of the contract of employment. The creation of industrial tribunals is a move towards a labour-court system as it exists, e.g. in Belgium, France and Germany. The Contract of Employment Act 1963, and the Redundancy Payments Act 1965, impose certain minimum conditions on contracts of employment. Under the former Act employees employed for at least thirteen weeks are entitled to a minimum notice of termination of their employment, varying according to the length of continuous service with an employer. Under the later Act employees dismissed, laid off, or kept on a short time by reason of redundancy are entitled to receive certain money payments. But all this leaves open the crucial question whether and in what manner the authority of the law should be put behind the enforcement of collective agreements. In an impressive chapter entitled 'The Enforcement of Collective Agreements'[57] the Donovan Commission stated its conviction that, in the current state of industrial-bargaining procedures in England, it would be misguided or at least premature to make collective agreements legally enforceable. The Commission based its argument not so much on section 4 of the Trade Union Act 1871,[58] which excluded direct enforceability of agreements between one trade union and another (which may include employers associations) before a court of law – since this provision would not have applied to the frequent agreements between an individual employer and a trade union – as on the 'intention' of the parties.

This lack of intention to make legally binding collective agreements, or, better perhaps, this intention and policy that collective bargaining and collective agreements should remain outside the law, is one of the characteristic features of our system of industrial relations which distinguishes it from other comparable systems. . . . [C]ollective bargaining is not in this country a series of easily distinguishable transactions comparable to the making of a number of contracts by two commerical firms. It is in fact a continuous process in which differences concerning the interpretation of an agreement merge imperceptibly into differences concerning claims to change its effect. Moreover, even at industry level, a great deal of collective bargaining takes place through standing bodies, such as joint industrial councils and national or regional negotiating boards, and the agreement appears as a 'resolution' or 'decision' of that body, variable at its will, and variable in particular in the light of such difficulties of interpretation as may arise. Such 'bargaining' does not fit into the categories of the law of contract (Para. 471).

57. *Report of the Royal Commission on Trade Unions and Employers' Associations, 1965–1968* (Cmnd 3623, 1968, ch. 8).
58. Now repealed by the Industrial Relations Act 1971.

The most telling argument of the Commission against direct legal sanctions of collective agreement (e.g. on the pattern of the Swedish Act) is that in Britain 95 per cent of all strikes in recent years have been unofficial strikes, which account for more than two-thirds of the days lost through work stoppages. Whereas official strikes in breach of official agreements are rare, unofficial strikes in breach of procedure agreements are 'common in a small number of important industries'.

The agreement breakers are not trade unions but groups of trade-union members. The high incidence of unofficial strikes – which, although usually of short individual duration, have done considerable collective harm to British production and export efforts – certainly cannot be met by legal sanctions against breaches of collective agreements. In the Commission's view the key problem is 'the inadequacy of our collective-bargaining system and especially the lack of clear, speedy, comprehensive and effective procedures for the settlement of grievances and other disputes, such as exist in other countries'. It is only when the system of industrial relations has improved that legal sanctions for the enforcement of agreed procedures are considered workable. Apart from 'grass-roots' efforts at the factory and company level for improved procedures, through joint production councils, grievance committees, and other devices, the most important of the Commission's recommendations on the official and nationwide level, the establishment of an Industrial Relations Commission, has since been implemented (see p. 364).

The Commission's view that parties to collective agreements did not intend to make them enforceable in law, was reinforced by the decision of Geoffrey Lane J. in *Ford Motor Company* v. *Amalgamated Union of Engineering and Foundry Workers.*[59] In 1955 the Ford Motor Company had negotiated an agreement with nineteen trade unions which provided that 'at each stage of the procedure set out in this Agreement, every attempt will be made to resolve issues raised, and that until such procedure has been carried through there shall be no stoppage of work or other unconstitutional action'. When, fourteen years later, the Ford Motor Company applied for an interlocutory injunction restraining two major industrial unions from calling an official strike contrary to the 1955 Agreement, the learned

59. [1969] 2 Q.B. 303.

judge dismissed the application, essentially on the ground that 'it will be clear that the climate of opinion was almost unanimous to the effect that no legally enforceable contract resulted from collective agreement. . . .'[60]

The Industrial Relations Act, of August 1971, differs sharply from the Donovan Commission by establishing a presumption in favour of the legal enforceability of collective agreements, which can be rebutted by a provision in the agreement that it is not intended to be legally enforceable. Breach of an enforceable agreement is an unfair industrial practice and actionable before the newly established Industrial Court (see p. 365).

Seeing the British evolution in a long-term perspective, there is no doubt that the 'hands off' approach of law to industrial relations, and particularly to collective bargaining, is in full retreat. The Prices and Incomes Board established in 1966 (which the present Government has abolished), represented an expression of official concern with the relation of prices and incomes of which labour wages are a vital component. In the United States, despite the profound traditional aversion to the official regulation of the economic process, President Nixon in August and October 1971 introduced an official prices and wages control policy and set up several agencies to implement it. Social pressures and economic necessity will ultimately prevail over historical traditions.

The growth of collective bargaining in the USA is of far more recent origin.[61] The lateness and the size of its growth, as well as its association with the New Deal legislation, have brought it far more within the purview of legal discussion and adjudication than in Britain. The National Labour Relations Act 1935, made it compulsory upon employers to bargain collectively with the chosen representatives of the employees. The National Labour Relations Board, established under the Act, and the courts deciding on appeal from that Board, have given hundreds of decisions trying to elucidate what type of action by the employer complies with the direction of

60. For a closely documented attack on the theory of this pronouncement, as well as on the judge's interpretation on actual practice, see Selwyn 'Collective agreements and the law' 32 *Mod. L. Rev.* 377 (1969), and the criticisms of Selwyn by Clark, 33 *Mod. L. Rev.* 47 (1970) and Wedderburn (1971, p. 175).

61. cf. Kahn-Freund, 6 *Mod. L. Rev.*, p. 118.

the Act. It is not necessary in our context to pursue that question.[62] The Labour Management Relations Act of 1947 made collective agreements specifically the subject of suits for enforcement in the Federal Court. This goes further than the 1971 British Act, under which collective agreements are still not directly enforceable unless the parties wish them to be. As regards the normative force of collective agreements on individual contracts of employment, the attitude of the courts is not unanimous.

Precedents can be found for almost any conceivable view: that collective agreements impose a mere moral obligation upon the parties;[63] that collective agreements create a usage, the incorporation of which into labour agreements is a question of fact;[64] that collective-bargaining agreements are void for want of consideration;[65] that collective agreements give both parties the full armoury of equitable remedies, especially injunctions and specific performance;[66] that the violation of a collective agreement is an unfair labour practice;[67] that individual employees may assert rights under collective agreements, either because the union has acted as their agent,[68] or as third-party beneficiaries.[69] On the whole, there has been a definite development towards full legal status and enforceability of collective agreements. They are increasingly given statutory recognition and protected by various private as well as public-law sanctions. The legal status of collective agreements was considerably strengthened when the Supreme Court in May 1970,[70] reversing a decision of 1962, held that federal district courts could enjoin strikes in violation of a no-strike clause, where the contract included an arbitration clause and the dispute was within that clause. The issuance of the injunction

62. cf. Cox and Dunlop, 63 *Harvard L. Rev.* (1950), 389–432.

63. See Teller, (1940), vol. 1, § 157.

64. See *Moody* v. *Model Window Glass Company*, 145 Ark. 197, 224 S.W. 436 (1920).

65. *Wilson* v. *Airline Coal Company*, 215 Iowa 855, 246 N.W. 753 (1933).

66. *Schlesinger* v. *Quinto*, 201 A.D. 487, 194 N.Y.S. 401 (1922).

67. *J. I. Case Company* v. *N. L. R. B.* 321 U.S. 332 (1944).

68. The practical difficulties of this theory are shown in *Shelley* v. *Portland Tug and Barge Company*, 76 P. 2d 477 (Oregon 1938).

69. See authorities quoted in Teller (1940), § 168, note 83. Further, *Leahy* v. *Smith*, 290 P. 2d 679 (1955) (action under collective agreement granted to non-union employee).

70. *Boy's Markets, Inc.* v. *Retail Clerk Union*, 398 U.S. 235 (1970).

was to be conditioned upon submission of the employer to arbitration and must be warranted under the ordinary principles of equity. Injunctive relief is in addition to a suit for damages under the Taft–Hartley Act of 1947. The public-law aspects are further underlined by the important role of the arbitrator, who, in United States and Canadian industrial labour practice, almost universally interprets disputes under the agreements, and whose creative role in the interpretation of comprehensive collective-labour agreements as living instruments of order, rather than as individual commercial contracts, has been stressed by authoritative commentators.[71]

In a leading case,[72] the Supreme Court, affirmed that arbitration of labour disputes under collective-bargaining agreements was 'part and parcel of the collective-bargaining process itself'. In the words of Douglas J. it was not, like normal commercial arbitration, a 'substitute for litigation' but a 'substitute for industrial strife'. The judgement expressed agreement with the views expressed by Cox and Shulman in characterizing the collective agreement as 'the common law of a particular industry or of a particular plant . . .', and as a 'system of industrial self-government' to govern a relationship that is unlike the usual contractual relationship. The purpose of labour arbitration was defined as 'the means of solving the unforeseeable by moulding a system of private law for all the problems which may arise and to provide for their solution in a way which will generally accord with the varying needs and desires of the parties'.

The view that a 'collective-bargaining agreement is not an ordinary contract', was confirmed by Harlan J. in *Wiley*'s case.[73]

The legal position in Canada is, as in many other fields, a blend between British and American legal developments. Similar to the position taken in the English decision, *Holland* v. *London Society of Compositors*,[74] is *Young* v. *Canadian Northern Railway*[75] a decision of the Judicial Committee on appeal from a Canadian court. In that

71. See, in particular, Shulman, 'Reason, contract and law in labour relations', 68 *Harvard L. Rev.* 999 (1955); Cox, 'Collective-bargaining agreements', 57 *Michigan L. Rev.* 1 (1958).

72. *United Steel Workers of America* v. *Warrior and Gulf Navigation Co.*, 363 U.S. 574 (1960).

73. *John Wiley & Sons, Inc.* v. *Livingston*, 376 U.S. 453 (1964).

74. (1929) 40 *Toronto L. Rev.* 440.

75. [1931] A.C. 83.

case, the plaintiff had sued a railway company for damages for wrongful dismissal, basing himself on a collective agreement between the Canadian Railway Board and a division of the American Federation of Labor. The Judicial Committee did not exclude that such an agreement might establish directly enforceable rights for an individual but held that, in this case, the collective agreement appeared

> to be intended merely to operate as an agreement between a body of employers and a labour organization. . . . If an employer refused to observe these rules, the effect would be, not an action by any employee, not even an action by the Union against the employer for specific performance or damages, but the calling of a strike until the grievance was remedied.

A number of later Canadian cases have also held that an individual workman cannot derive actionable rights from a collective agreement.[76] Subsequent Canadian legislation, both Federal and provincial, has put collective agreements on a statutory basis and given them definite legal effect, as between the parties to the agreement.[77]

A third type of collective bargaining is represented by Australia and New Zealand, where the machinery of collective bargaining entirely dominates labour conditions, but with a significant difference in that the terms of collective bargaining can be hardened, and thus be turned from group law into state law, by an award of the Commonwealth Industrial Court (Australia).[78] This may be either by a con-

---

76. e.g. *Aris* v. *Toronto, Hamilton and Buffalo Ry* [1933] O.R. 142; *Wright* v. *Calgary Herald* [1938] 1 *D. L. Rev.* 111.

77. cf. the Federal Industrial Relations and Disputes Investigation Act, 1952, and, among others, the Ontario Labour Relations Act 1950, R.S.O. 1960, ch. 202. Under the 1950 Ontario Act, for example, the sanctions for violation of a collective agreement consists in the right of either party to call for arbitration, in the power of the arbitrator to make awards which are sometimes tantamount to damages, and in the power of criminal prosecution for non-observance of the arbitrator's award.

78. The precise classification of the Australian and New Zealand systems is not easy. Recent developments in the Australian practice tend to reduce the collective bargaining element in industrial relations, and to emphasize increasingly the part of the Arbitration Court in laying down minimum terms for an entire industry or even all industries. The main share of the parties in that procedure lies in setting the machinery in motion (through application of a registered association of employers or employees). Once the conciliation and arbitration machinery has started to operate in a particular dispute, it is doubtful how far any

sent decree, or an award adjudicating between contesting points of view. Here the machinery of group bargaining is the basic factor, but the state machinery, in a capacity half-judicial, half-legislative, is superimposed upon it.

The vital significance of collective bargaining for the law of contract thus lies in its following aspects: first, it resembles a standard contract of business and industry in that standardized terms regulate the conditions of employment of millions of individuals. Secondly, it is a most important instance of a public-law function delegated, by the permissive or even imperative authority of the state, from government to social groups. Thirdly, the freedom of the individual to bargain on his terms of employment is inevitably curtailed by the prevalence of collective bargaining. It is even excluded where the 'closed shop' is recognized either legally or *de facto*. Fourthly, this lack of freedom is compensated by a substantial restoration of equality of bargaining power. It is not the individual employee who has regained equality, but the trade union negotiating on his behalf. Although the trade union is not, strictly speaking, the agent, it has, in effect, absorbed and consolidated the bargaining power formerly vested in the individual.

The future of the collective contract in the common-law jurisdictions is ultimately dependent on the degree to which group autonomy can survive in the planned society. In the completely planned state, as represented by Soviet Russia, the collective contract between management and labour survives, but it is overwhelmingly an instrument of planning and social solidarity, leaving only limited scope to complementary bargaining by individual plants or industries.[79] There are model collective contracts with all the emphasis on maximum production and labour discipline. Supplementary plant collective contracts mainly concentrate on social aspects, such as schools, nurseries, clinics and houses. In the Soviet state, manage-

---

right to collective action (e.g. by strike or lock-out) still remains. On this point, recent decisions are conflicting. For a brief survey of the general position, see Thomson, 'Voluntary collective agreements in Australia and New Zealand', 1 *University of Western Australia L. Rev.* 80–90. Further, *Industrial Regulation in Australia* (1947); Sykes, 'Labor arbitration in Australia', 13 *Amer. J. Comp. L.* 214 (1964).

79. See the Soviet sources quoted in Hazard and Weisberg (1950, p. 144).

ment and labour can represent conflicting interests only within very strict limits, in complete subordination to the state plan. These collective contracts do not create any legally enforceable obligations (Berman, 1963, pp. 357-8). By contrast, the individual rights of workers, in regard to wages, dismissal, holidays, are protected by an elaborate administrative and judicial procedure (Berman, 1963, pp. 359-62; Hazard and Weisberg, 1950, pp. 156-60, 164-74). This position is not far removed from that of Nazi labour law which merged all collective workers' organizations in a compulsory state labour front, but preserved the labour courts for the protection of individual rights. The modern totalitarian 'organic' state destroys the autonomy and freedom of its workers, but gives them security and protection in return. Anglo-American society is still far removed from such a state, but the ever-growing emphasis on defence and production, and the increasing responsibilities of government for the economic well-being of the people, are steadily increasing the public policy and planning elements and reducing the autonomy of groups.[80]

Contract and the Realization of Economic Expectations

The mixture of heterogeneous factors that make up the complex picture of modern contract and have turned it into something rather different from the chief commercial guarantee of a private enterprise society, is best illustrated by the problem of sanctions.

The controversy whether the primary sanction of contract is actual performance or a promise to make reparation for non-performance is of old standing. Oliver Wendell Holmes long ago proposed the view that 'the only universal consequence of a legally binding promise is that of the law making the promisor pay damages if the promised event does not come to pass' (1881, p. 301). This view has been widely criticized, mainly on the ground that the law does not leave the promisor the freedom to choose between performance and the payment of damages where he is able to perform.[81]

The history of the common law tends to support Holmes's view, in so far as the common-law sanction for breach of contract is

80. On contemporary developments in labour law, see ch. 9.
81. See, among others, Buckland, 8 *Cambridge L. J.* 247; Cohen, (1933, p. 100); Paton (1951, section 1, p. 359).

damages, whereas equity supplies the supplementary sanctions of specific performance and injunction, as additions or alternatives to the basic remedy of damages in meritorious situations. By contrast, the Civil Codes of the civilian systems regard performance as a primary, and damages as a secondary, remedy.[82] In practice, the difference is far less marked than in theory. Under both systems, the normal remedy for a breach of contract is pecuniary compensation, i.e. damages, whereas in appropriate situations where the individualized character of the transaction makes pecuniary compensation inadequate,[83] specific performance of injunction will, under both types of systems, take preference.

The proportion of public and private elements in a given contract determines the degree to which the traditional sanctions of contract apply. The normal commercial contract is still predominantly an insurance against economic risk. Its primary sanction is pecuniary compensation, including the loss of profits to be expected from the carrying out of the agreed transaction. In a minority of cases, it is specific performance.

But in a case like the *Bethlehem Steel* case (see p. 127), contract fulfils a substantially different function, although it is still cast largely in the traditional mould of an ordinary commercial contract. Mutual rights and obligations are fixed, times of delivery are specified, prices and profits are agreed, etc. But, at the same time, a contract of this type is a public transaction. In this case, the government and a powerful firm enter into a kind of partnership for the delivery of vitally needed commodities. It is this factor which induced a minority of the US Supreme Court to regard the Court as justified in a *post factum* adjustment of profits, in regarding, in other words, the contract to some extent as the discharge of a public duty. Even though the majority of the Court disagreed, and left this kind of adjustment to subsequent legislation, a transaction of this type still retains its public character. The participation of an administrative authority in

82. See for example, the German Civil Code, § 249. For a comparison of the Anglo-American and the Continental (French, German and Swiss) approach, see Szladits, 'The concept of specific performance in civil law', 4 *Amer. J. of Comp. Law* (1955), p. 208.

83. e.g. in the supply of a rare picture or the performance of an artist or the supply of a manuscript.

the adjustments of terms under the Renegotiation Act shows that this kind of transaction resembles the classical commercial contract in name rather than in substance.

Conclusions

It has not been possible, in this attempt at synthesizing the various changes in the structure and function of contract, to give more than a general picture of developments which require the most detailed study. It should, however, suffice to justify some general conclusions. First, it is clear that contract is becoming increasingly institutionalized. From being the instrument by which millions of individual parties bargain with each other, it has to a large extent become the way by which social and economic policies are expressed in legal form. This is another way of saying that public law now vitally affects and modifies the law of contract.

Secondly, in so far as the basic industries and economic commodities are now subject to standardized regulation by private insurance, transport or public utility undertakings, these exercise functions of public law. Because of the inability of the other party to bargain effectively on terms, such private enterprises exercise, by permission of the state, a quasi-legislative power. Where 'the sense of injustice' (Cahn, 1949) is strongly aroused, public law intervenes further, either by the imposition of statutory conditions, by the compulsory restoration of competition, by the 'renegotiation' of defence contracts, or, in the last resort, by the transfer of the industry or utility concerned into public ownership.

The exercise of public-law functions through nominally private-law groups is even more marked in the position of collective bargaining. By permitting or even directing the regulation of industrial conditions through collective contract, the state transfers a vital law-making function to the recognized organizations of employers and employees. Sometimes it formally strengthens this position by making the terms of representative collective agreements compulsory, sometimes it modifies them by state award.

In another way, collective bargaining narrows the gap between the mobility of contract and the stability of status. The paramount purpose of collective bargaining on an industry-wide or nation-wide scale is the stabilization of industrial conditions. The more successful the collective bargaining, the greater the approximation of the status of the employee to that of an official. Recently American collective agreements in industry have been preoccupied with the stabilization of conditions for a period varying from three to five years. A number of collective agreements between industrial giants and the most powerful labour unions – General Motors, Ford or United States Steel on the one hand, and the Automobile or Steel Workers' or Coalminers' Unions on the other hand – provide for rates of pay, with escalator clauses, holidays, seniority rights, pensions and grievance machinery, in return for no-strike promises. They go further than any previous agreement towards giving employees an assured status in exchange for a limited surrender of mobility.

Lastly, the increasing use of contract as an instrument of economic state policy, through the extension of government functions and the socialization of industries, makes contract largely the legal expression of economic and social policies. This weakens the degree to which contract can any longer fulfil the function of security against calculated risks. This is further emphasized by the development of the doctrine of frustration, which allows for the statutory or judicial consideration of circumstances beyond the control of the parties. To that extent, contract becomes the foundation for a broad adjustment of risks in which private agreement and public policy are mingled.

Chapter 5
Tort, Insurance and Social Responsibility

The law of tort or delict is concerned with the adjustment of risks, with the extent to which the manifold injuries to person and property caused by the contacts between people and things should be the subject of pecuniary compensation. As Oliver Wendell Holmes put it many years ago:

Be the exceptions more or less numerous, the general purpose of the law of torts is to secure a main indemnity against certain forms of harm to person, reputation or estate, at the hands of his neighbours, not because they are wrong, but because they are harms. . . . It is intended to reconcile the policy of letting accidents lie where they fall, and the reasonable freedom of others with the protection of the individual from injury. . . . As the law, on the one hand, allows certain harms to be inflicted irrespective of the moral condition of him who inflicts them, so, at the other extreme, it may on grounds of policy throw the absolute risk of certain transactions on the person engaging in them, irrespective of blameworthiness in any sense (1881, pp. 144–5).

It is obvious that this branch of the law must strongly reflect changing social conditions. The type and significance of risks incurred in social contact varies with the type of society in which we live. The principles of liability governing the readjustment are greatly influenced by changing moral and social ideas.

In the formative stage of the common law – and, indeed, of other legal systems – the law of torts is mainly concerned with the infringement of protected interests in land. Commerce and communications are ill-developed, towns and other close congregations of people are scarce and small, and the type of economic asset which predominates by far, in quantity and in legal esteem, is land. Consequently, the early law of tort is largely concerned with the protection of property in land. It is dominated by trespass to land, from which other actions upon the case branch out that are closely modelled upon trespass.

Urbanization, industrialization and, in particular, since the last century, the ever-growing development of fast-moving traffic, shift the emphasis gradually from injury to land and related interests to other and broader forms of property interests, and even more to reparation for personal injury. Although negligence has in recent years gone far to displace trespass or nuisance even as a remedy for injuries to property, it owes its main growth to the multiplication of personal injuries due to modern conditions of living. As emphasis shifted from definition by the kind of *interest* injured (as in the older torts) to the kind of *conduct* which engenders liability, negligence was obviously better fitted to become the modern tort action *par excellence*.[1]

The change in the type of interest with which the law is primarily concerned, and in the kind of injury that occurs most frequently, is accompanied by a struggle between conflicting theories of civil liability. There is not a single modern legal system in which principles of strict and fault liability are not closely intermingled, partly as a result of statutory intervention, and partly as a result of judicial law-making. A brief survey later in this chapter will attempt to analyse the conflicting trends and pulls as they appear to shape the contemporary common law in this field. In any attempt to bring some order into the mixture of conflicting ideas, theories and decisions, two major determining factors have to be borne in mind: delictual liability is firstly determined by a choice of moral philosophies which have deeply influenced the law. As some writers have pointed out,[2] the change from emphasis on liability for harmful acts regardless of fault, to liability for fault only – which dominated the eighteenth and the major part of the nineteenth century – is parallel to the movement from status to contract, and both affect the philosophy of the free will, symbol of the self-reliant individual who makes and unmakes his legal engagements freely and who bears responsibility for

1. See, for a concise survey of this shift, Seavey, '*Candler* v. *Crane*, *Christmas & Co.*', 67 *L.Q.Rev.* 466, 469 (1951).

2. See, e.g. Leflar, 'Negligence in name only', 27 *New York University L. Rev.* 564 (1952); Pound, 'The rule of the will in law', 68 *Harvard L. Rev.* 1 (1954).

his behaviour in society because he has a choice between good and evil. A great deal of this philosophy is still with us; indeed it could not be otherwise in any society that has not completely abandoned the ideal of individual responsibility for social conduct. But this philosophy has been increasingly countered by growing emphasis on the responsibility of the community for the accidents that befall the individual. And the growth of the new policy is due largely to the social transformation of modern Western society, a society in which more and more vicissitudes threaten a multitude of individuals whose liberty to avoid them shrinks steadily. The steady growth of the principle of social responsibility for injuries is not due to any cynical abandonment of the principle of individual responsibility but to the extent to which millions of individuals find themselves exposed to accidents arising in factories, on the roads, in aeroplanes or the threat of unemployment.

The advance of the idea of social responsibility against that of individual fault has not, however, entirely expressed itself in the substitution of strict liability, or even of insurance, for individual liability. It has, to a large extent, led to a gradual transformation of the idea of fault itself, in what one might call the objectivization of fault liability.

Judicial Widening of Tort Responsibility

A detailed analysis of the various ways in which the law courts – both of the common-law and of the civil-law world – have gradually widened the scope of social responsibility, in accordance with the changing character of industrial society, would go beyond the purposes of the present analysis.[3] The main lines of development may be briefly sketched out as follows:

1. The rule in *Rylands* v. *Fletcher*[4] was a relatively early indication of a trend towards the substitution of a liability not based on fault for the fault principle in certain situations. In Justice Blackburn's classical analysis, the control over certain types of property – in the case at hand a reservoir, from which water overflowed to neighbouring

3. For a more detailed survey (up to 1959) see the 1959 edition of this book.
4. (1868) L.R. 3 HL 330.

property – was held to impose upon the controller of such property the strict duty to avoid harm. The characterization of certain things as 'likely to do mischief if they escape', brought into the law the concept of things dangerous *per se* which has had a notable history in the subsequent development of the law of torts.[5] But the tempo of industrial development has made the concept of 'dangerous' things increasingly elusive. In 1929, an English jurist[6] listed any kind of chemical, hair dyes, electricity, motor cars, ginger beer, rusty wires, rocks and flagpoles as things that the court have held to be dangerous in certain circumstances. This may be compared with a list given by an American authority (Prosser, 1964, p. 662), which included coffee urns, cigarettes, hair combs, sewing machines, a bottle of perfume, a woman's dress, gasoline and electric stoves and a sofa bed.

Although the American Restatement on the law of torts, the Soviet Civil Code and other legislative formulations retain the concept of things dangerous *per se*, it has in effect been overtaken by the complexity of contemporary industrial society. This indeed is true of the rule in *Rylands* v. *Fletcher*, which today could almost certainly be dealt with as a case of negligence.

2. It is through the steady broadening of the concept of negligence that the most important expansion of social responsibility sanctionable through tort action has occurred. Major landmarks have been the American decision of *MacPherson* v. *Buick Motor Company*[7] and

5. A noteworthy adoption of the principle of increased liability for dangerous activities is that of the Soviet Civil Code of 1922 (Article 404), which has been maintained and expanded in the 1961 Fundamental Principles of Civil Law of the USSR, and in the new civil codes of the other European Communist States. The 1922 code stated that 'persons and enterprises whose activities present special danger to the persons around them, such as railroads, street carts, factories and mills, vendors of inflammable materials, keepers of wild animals, persons engaged in the erection of buildings and other structures, etc., are liable for injuries caused by the source of increased danger, unless they prove that the damage was caused as the result of *force majeure*, or as the result of a wilful act or gross negligence on the part of the injured party'. Subsequent court decisions included automobiles, and this was confirmed in the 1961 Fundamental Principles. See for a survey, Hazard (1969, pp. 391–7), and Gray (1965, pp. 180, 197).

6. Stallybrass, 'Dangerous things and the non-natural user of land' 3 *Cambridge L. J.* 326 (1929).

7. 217 N.Y. 382, 111 N.E. 1050 (1916).

the British decision in *Donoghue* v. *Stevenson*.[8] Both introduced, though in different formulations, the principle of responsibility of a manufacturer to the consumer of his product, for harmful defects of the product not attributable to an external cause. Through a variety of judicial shifts and constructions, this responsibility has gradually been widened so as to remove this type of 'negligence' increasingly from the traditional concept. Without going into details,[9] it may be said that the widening has occurred mainly in four directions: first, through the expansion of the term 'manufacturer' so as to include repairers and others; second, through the – already referred to – dilution of the concept of 'dangerous' things to a degree which makes it possible to say that today any object may be 'dangerous' in certain situations, i.e. if handled in a manner falling below a reasonable standard of care; third, through the use of *res ipsa loquitur*, which has, in effect, reversed the presumption of fault. The manufacturer or keeper of the thing is generally presumed to be responsible for the state of the product or operation emanating from his enterprise, unless he can prove intervention by an unconnected third party or *force majeure*; fourth, through the erosion of the former distinction between liability for the acts of a servant and nonliability for the acts of an independent contractor. This is in line with the increasing control that the manufacturer, and the controller of other operations and services, exercises in contemporary conditions over sub-contractors, retailers and others in the line that leads from the making of the product or the provision of a utility to the ultimate consumer or user.

At the same time, American and British courts have moved – though unevenly, and with significant exceptions – to abolish anachronistic immunities from tort liability, no longer justifiable in modern social conditions.[10] Among these anomalies are the historical

8. [1932] A.C. 562.

9. They will be found in any contemporary English or American treatise on the law of tort. See also Leflar, 'Negligence in name only', 27 *New York University L. Rev.* 564 (1952); Ehrenzweig (1951); Fleming, 'The role of negligence in modern tort law', 53 *Virginia L. Rev.* 815 (1967); Prakash Sinha, 'The problem of application of the fault principle to automobile accidents', 14 *Villanova L. Rev.* 386 (1969).

10. Among traditional immunities in England that are subject to change are the immunity of an owner of animals who lets them negligently stray out onto the

immunity of charitable hospitals in the United States from liability in negligence – unjustified in contemporary conditions, where the organization of charitable hospitals from that of other hospitals is indistinguishable;[11] and the derogation from the principle of vicarious liability of employers for the negligence of their employees, through the distinction between liability for administrative and clerical hospital staff, and non-liability for 'professional' personnel. Not only did this criterion lead to tortured distinctions (e.g. in the case of professionally trained nurses), but above all it went counter to the organization of modern medical institutions and was totally unjust from the standpoint of the patient. In Britain the distinction was – at least within the framework of the National Health Service – abolished by a decision of the Court of Appeal in 1954.[12] In the United States the situation still varies from one jurisdiction to another. A landmark in the abolition of the distinction is the decision of the New York Court of Appeals in *Bing* v. *Thunig*.[13] In the same direction, there have been the various moves to restrict or abolish the traditional immunities of public authorities from liability in negligence. In Britain and the Commonwealth, this is no longer a serious problem since, during the last few decades, the immunities of the Crown from liability in tort and contract have been abolished, and local authorities have, for more than a century, been classified as statutory authorities, clearly distinct from the legal status of the Crown. But in the United States, where, paradoxically, many of the common-law principles developed

highway and the immunity of the landowner who negligently injures trespasses. The immunity of the owner of animals has been narrowed by *Bativala* v. *West*, [1970] 1 Q.B. 716, 1 All E.R. 332 (1969), which held that a negligence standard would be applied where there were 'special circumstances', e.g. dangerous behaviour by the animal was foreseeable. The Law Commission has recommended the imposition of a negligence standard. Law Commission, Civil Liability for Animals (1968). The immunity of the landowner was upheld in *Commr. for Railways* v. *Quinlan*, [1964] A.C. 1054 (P.C.), reversing *Commr. for Railways* v. *Cordy*, 104 Commw. L.R. 274 (N.S.W. 1960); the landowner would be liable only for wilful acts or for acts done with reckless disregard of the presence of the trespasser.

11. See, e.g. the decision of the Supreme Court of New Jersey in *Collopy* v. *Newark Eye and Ear Infirmary*, 27 N.J. 29 (1958).

12. *Razzel* v. *Snowball*, [1954] 3 All E.R. 429.

13. 2 N.Y. 2nd 662, 163 N.Y. Supp. 2nd 3 (1958).

in a feudal England survive, this matter is far from settled. In a majority of the' state jurisdictions – and to a certain extent in the federal sphere – government immunities survive.[14] Moreover, local authorities in the United States are still considered as part of state government and therefore participate in its immunities. As in the case of hospitals, the legal immunity of local authorities – and of other types of public authorities – which nowadays carry out a multitude of functions that affect the citizen especially in the field of transport and other public utilities is a social anomaly, justified by no consideration of equity or justice.

Another important development of common-law duties of care designed to cope with social responsibilities in an industrial society, has been the gradual extension of the liability of employers towards employees. The courts have been concerned with this both through the development of common-law duties of care, and the interpretation of statutory duties. The formulation of a leading English decision[15] applies in essence to the United States (Prosser, 1964, p. 545). In this decision the House of Lords laid down a threefold common-law duty of the employer towards his employees: the provision of a competent staff of men; the provision of proper and safe appliances for their work; and a proper system of operation and efficient supervision. Here too, the tendency has been to interpret negligence in a sense that approximates strict liability.

Contrary to a widespread legend, according to which the courts of the civil-law countries are alleged to interpret codes and other statutes strictly, in contrast to the lawmaking ability of the common-law courts, civil-law courts have been no less active in the adaptation of code law to new conditions. The most celebrated example is the development, by the French courts, of a principle of strict liability for the keepers of motor cars, by an ingenious combination of two articles of the Code Civil. Article 1384 of the Code Civil imposes liability on a person 'not only for the damage he causes by his own

14. For a survey, see Leflar and Kantorowicz, 'Tort liability of the States' 29 *New York University L. Rev.* (1954), 1363. For more recent developments see Harper and James, *The Law of Torts*, 29.1–29.7 (1956, Supp. 1968); van Alstyne, 'Governmental liability: a decade of change' (1966) *University of Illinois L. Forum* 919; and see pp. 413–19.

15. *Wilsons & Clyde Coal Company Ltd* v. *English* [1938] A.C.57.

act, but also for that which is caused by . . . things that he has under his control'. The term 'things' was gradually construed to apply to motor vehicles, and the courts moved increasingly to impose strict liability on the motorist, where accidents are caused by him.[16] However, the transformation of a law through judicial lawmaking so as to adapt it to social change, while immensely important, has inevitably proved inadequate. This is due to a variety of factors: the chanciness of cases coming up for decision; the *ad hoc* character of judicial decisions; the vast differences of judicial philosophy – varying from jurisdiction to jurisdiction, from court to court and between the different judges – and altogether the increasing need for a specific regulation of the legal responsibilities, particularly of industrial enterprises and motorists towards employees and the public. This can be done effectively only by statutory and administrative regulation.

The Shift of Liability from Tort to Insurance

Preceding the now massive shift from individual tort liability to some system of private or social insurance – or a combination of both – is the earlier shift of civil liability from the immediate tortfeasor to a third party, who for a variety of reasons is considered to be better fitted to absorb the burden of compensation.

The first significant development in that direction was, quite a long time ago, the acceptance of the principle of vicarious liability of the master for the torts of his servant. Seen from the standpoint of the master, this appears as an example of strict liability. He is held responsible for a wrong which he has not himself committed but which is imputed to him. But seen from the standpoint of relationship between the injured and the wrongdoer, vicarious liability means a transfer of the primary responsibility from the immediate tortfeasor to a third party: the employer. The justification for this development is the power of control and direction exercised by the master over the servant. The enterprise rather than the individual cog in the wheel is seen as presenting certain risks to the community for which it must

16. For detailed surveys see, among many others, Esmein, 'Liability in French law for damages caused by motor vehicle accidents', 2 *Amer. J. Comp. L.* 156 (1953); von Mehren (1957); Keeton and O'Connell (1965, pp. 198–207).

assume responsibility. Such oddities as the now generally discarded 'fellow-servant' or 'common employment' rule only serve to under-line the significance of the shift from personal to enterprise liability.

But this shifting of the burden – of which vicarious liability was the first significant token – is now occurring on a vastly wider scale, mainly as a result of the progress of insurance. Tort liability is affected by the progress of private as well as of social insurance, though not in the same way.

Industrial Accident Insurance

In one field – that of industrial accidents – the principle of social insurance is now almost universally recognized, in common-law jurisdictions as well as in many other countries. The idea of work-men's compensation started out as an application of strict tort liability in substitution for fault liability.[17] The history of the relevant English legislation also confirms that the original purpose, first expressed in the Employers' Liability Act of 1880, was to lighten the injured workman's burden in proving the employer's negligence. This served at first to exclude the defence of common employment, but was soon found insufficient and superseded by a series of periodically amended Workmen's Compensation Acts. But the English Workmen's Compensation legislation still centred on the individual strict responsibility of the employer. The financial responsi-bility was his individual concern, against which he might or might not insure. Liability could be contested before the courts, which until the abrogation of the legislation led to a fantastic mass of contested cases; nor did the legislation abolish private actions in tort. The injured man was left with an election between the alternative

17. This is particularly clear where, as in France, workmen's compensation started as a judicial innovation, as an application of the principle of '*le risque créé*', which the French Cour de Cassation developed from the end of the nine-teenth to the middle of the present century in ever-widening spheres, especially the fields of industrial accidents and motor-car accidents. In the former, a statute of 1898 displaced the judge-made creation. In the latter, French law has so far failed to lead on from the principle of strict liability to that of insurance, except for the introduction of an Unsatisfied Judgement Fund for motor-car accidents. See on the whole development, Planiol et Ripert (1952, vol. 6, § § 476, 700).

remedies, a situation which in its turn led to much litigation and many social injustices, as well as administrative inconvenience. The national insurance legislation of 1946–9 substituted for the principle of individual compensation by the employer an overall system of national insurance, for industrial as well as other accidents. Apart from certain improvements in the definition of accidents coming under the Act, administration has been vested in the Ministry of National Insurance, i.e. it has become a matter of administrative rather than private law, and the appeal procedures do not involve the ordinary courts. Contributions are now jointly made by employers, workmen and the state. This legislation, which turned an important sector of individual responsibility for injuries into a matter of social insurance, also raised squarely the problem of the relation between tort and social insurance (see p. 180). Although British legislation did not take the ultimate step of abolishing tort liability, it could not avoid any longer an open legislative regulation of this relationship.

In Canada, following the model of the Ontario Workmen's Compensation Act of 1915, the insurance character of workmen's compensation became obvious much earlier, for here the common-law remedy was entirely abolished. A scale of statutory tariffs is administered by a public board under complete exclusion of the law courts, and there is no alternative common-law remedy. The accident fund is supplied by contributions made by the employers, in classes or groups of industries, and in the great majority of cases the employers are therefore collectively liable. Where an employer is individually liable, he may be required by the board to insure himself (e.g. the national railroad systems). Thus a group of the community assumes responsibility for a certain type of injuries caused as an incidence of modern industrial life. In the United States, the pattern is far more complex and less uniform. All American states, like French and German legislation,[18] preclude a common-law action supplementary to workmen's compensation and common-law action.[19] But in the United States, as elsewhere, the social insurance character of workmen's compensation is becoming increasingly evident.

18. See Riesenfeld, 'Contemporary trends in compensation for industrial accidents here and abroad' (1954) 42 *California L. Rev.* 531.
19. Riesenfeld, p. 559.

Workmen's compensation is not to be thought of as merely a way of disposing of a private quarrel between employer and employee about a personal injury; it is not a branch of strict liability in tort; it is not simply a substitute for common-law litigation between parties to a personal contest over private rights. Workmen's compensation is one segment or department in the overall pattern of income-insurance, which includes unemployment insurance, sickness and disability insurance, and old age and survivors' insurance.[20]

Some countries have, since the last world war, moved from industrial accident insurance to social insurance for all types of accidents. Sweden has a comprehensive system of social insurance, which includes full medical and health insurance, industrial injuries insurance, as well as accident insurance. Great Britain, in 1946, enacted a comprehensive national insurance scheme, of which the principal pillars were the National Insurance Act 1946; the National Insurance (Industrial Injuries) Act 1946; and the National Health Service Act 1946. These comprehensive social insurance schemes raised problems of the relation between tort and insurance, as well as problems of double compensation, which will be discussed later. What is beyond doubt is that, in the field of industrial accidents, the socialization of risks has proceeded earlier, and is internationally far more widespread than in the field of automobile accidents.

Automobile Accidents – Tort and Insurance

In its social importance, the incidence of injuries to the life, health and property of the public is certainly not inferior to that of industrial accidents. Both in public and in private transport, the motor vehicle has become the predominant carrier, as industrialization progresses. While the United States leads, by far, the other industrialized countries are rapidly catching up in the ratio of privately-owned motor vehicles to population, and in the rate of accidents.[21] Death or injury from a motor-car accident is certainly a much greater and regular hazard of daily life for the average citizen than an accident

20. Larson, 'Changing concepts in workmen's compensation', *N.A.C.C.A.L.J.* 23 (1954).
21. In the United States, the National Safety Council estimated that, in 1968, deaths from motor-car accidents numbered 55,200, injuries numbered 2,000,000.

in the course of work is for the employee. Why then has the resistance to the 'socialization' of risks in the field of automobile accidents been so much greater? Why is there, not only in the common-law countries, but also in many of the civil-law countries, a continued adherence to fault liability, i.e. negligence actions, as the basic remedy? Why is there widespread and even fanatical resistance, not only to publicly administered insurance schemes comparable to those prevalent in the industrial accidents field, but even – particularly in the United States – such strong resistance to compulsory *private* liability insurance that, at present, only three out of fifty American jurisdictions[22] have introduced it?

It is submitted that there are three major reasons for the differences in development:

First, there is a difference in the social situation. The early moves in the direction of the modern welfare state – dating well back to the nineteenth century – arose from the need to protect the exploited industrial worker and the poor. Workmen's compensation, now being enlarged in some states into a comprehensive system of industrial accident insurance – was an important move towards the protection of the worker against ruin and the crippling of his earning capacity through accidents. Old-age pensions and unemployment insurance also protect the weak and underprivileged sections of the community against the vicissitudes of life. By contrast, the automobile owner was, at least originally, generally a person of substance. Moreover, there is between him and the potential victim of an accident no link comparable to that of the employer–employee relationship.

Second, for the legal profession, the business arising from automobile accidents provides – particularly under a jury system – far and away the greatest single source of income, and accident cases constitute the overwhelming proportion of litigation. In the United States this pecuniary interest is stimulated by the permissibility and prevalent practice of contingency fees – which are prohibited in other countries.

Third, automobile insurance has become a major part of the business of private insurance companies – although in recent years, with the steep increase in accidents and costs, an increasingly un-

22. Massachusetts, New York and North Carolina.

profitable one. Paradoxically, the private insurance industry has been in the forefront of resistance – not to a socialized insurance scheme, which would be understandable – but to compulsory liability insurance, which would increase their business. Despite the fact that in most other industrialized countries compulsory liability insurance has long been accepted,[23] and that existing compulsory liability insurance schemes in the United States have not led to 'socialism', i.e. to state insurance schemes, the chief reasons for this resistance appears to be the fear of state insurance.

A compulsory form of insurance, which continues to be written through private insurance carriers, may stimulate public pressure for some form state insurance enterprise (Kline and Pearson, 1951).[24]

Ironically, it is perhaps the growing unprofitability of private motor-car insurance that may lessen resistance to some form of state participation or substitution. As in the case of the appeals for protective tariffs, import quotas or subsidies, the aid of the state is seldom refused, or even eagerly sought, when it is a question not of taking over profitable business but of shielding private enterprise from losses.

Some Reform Proposals – A Survey

While the above-mentioned factors have so far prevented the abolition – or even any far-reaching modification – of the traditional method of adjustment of injury by tort action in most countries, the pressure for legal reform of this field, which affects an ever-growing proportion of the population, is steadily growing. In this, essentially jurisprudential, analysis, it must suffice to indicate selectively the trend indicated by the most important types of reform proposals, both in the common-law and in the civil-law world. In the common-law world, the so-called Columbia Plan[25] 'has served as a point of departure for all subsequent attempts at comprehensive reform in

23. In Britain it was introduced in 1930.
24. For a full discussion of the criticisms of compulsory liability insurance, see Keeton and O'Connell (1965, pp. 91–102).
25. *Report by the Committee to Study Compensation for Automobile Accidents*, (Columbia University Council for Research in the Social Sciences, 1932).

this area' (Keeton and O'Connell, 1965, p. 133). Nearly forty years ago, the Columbia Plan proposed two basic and revolutionary changes. First, it suggested legislation that would 'impose on the owners of motor vehicles a limited liability, without regard to fault, for personal injuries or death caused by the operation of their motor vehicles'. This plain adoption of strict liability, in substitution for negligence, was, secondly, accompanied by a proposal for compulsory insurance. The compensation schedules proposed by the Columbia Report were based on schedules of workmen's compensation benefits as then used in New York and Massachusetts. Most importantly, the plan proposed such benefits as exclusive, entirely replacing the right to recover in common law, and to be administered by an administrative board. In all these respects the Columbia Plan was modelled upon workmen's compensation legislation – where, as we have seen, the principles of statutory instead of tort liability, and of administration by a public authority, have been generally accepted. Not surprisingly, the Columbia Plan provoked great opposition, and none of the many subsequent proposals has gone as far, particularly with regard to the total substitution of loss insurance for tort liability.[26] The act passed in 1946 by the Canadian Province of Saskatchewan does adopt the principle of loss insurance, in the form of a schedule of limited benefits comparable to workmen's compensation, and administered by the Saskatchewan Government Insurance Office. But the Saskatchewan Act allows a victim to obtain further damages by pursuing his common-law action in tort – a possibility of which ample use is made.

Of the various more important reform proposals put forward in the United States in the post-war period, those of Dean Leon Green (1958), Professor Ehrenzweig (1954) and Professors Morris and Paul [27] have essentially common features. They all favour minimum loss insurance without reference to fault, although some of them would admit tort action to a limited extent. The main rationale for this, partial or entire, transfer of automobile insurance from tort to

26. The New York State plan of 1970, under consideration by the Legislature, adopts, however, the main features of the Columbia Plan (see p. 176).

27. 'The financial impact of automobile accidents,' 110 *University of Pennsylvania L. Rev.* 913 (1962).

insurance has been cogently formulated by Dean Green. He sees the main social justification for such a transfer

In the massive and complicated network of negligence doctrines which by virtue of their administrative intransigence work to the advantage of the insurance carrier so that most of the victims of the highways are left outside the protection of the law altogether. With only a small percentage of the total traffic claims subject to the litigation process, the courts in the large centres are so congested as to defeat many meritorious cases. Insurers gain great advantage from this congestion while claimants suffer great losses. Liability insurance still falls far short of being either universal or adequate in amount, but even if it were both, the pattern of litigation is so forbidding as to deny many claimants access to the courts; hence they accept what is offered in settlement, or, if nothing is offered, decline to risk the hazards of litigating their claims (Green, 1958, p. 81).

It is not, however, essential to this idea of loss insurance that it should be administered by or on behalf of the government (as it is done under the Saskatchewan legislation). Alternative forms of administration, e.g. by the automobile insurers, by a joint autonomous body formed by those concerned, or by a public-trust fund, do not impair the idea of loss insurance.

The most recent – and the most fully documented – reform proposal is that of Professors Keeton and O'Connell (1965), whose principal features are: (a) a new form of compulsory automobile insurance (called basic protection insurance), which would compensate all persons injured in automobile accidents without regard to fault, up to a limit of $10,000 per person; and (b) exemption to all who have basic protection insurance, from tort liability, up to a certain limit.[28]

The only notable counterattack from academic quarters has come from Professors Blum and Kalven (1965). The authors dispute all the basic premises of the reform proposals. In the first place, Blum and Kalven do not regard fault in traffic cases as essentially different from other types of cases. Second, they deny that the system currently in operation so closely approximates a system of liability without fault that abandonment of fault liability would be a logical conclusion.

28. i.e. in those cases in which damages for pain and suffering would not exceed $5000 and other tort damages would not exceed the $10,000 limit of basic protection and coverage.

The authors see no adequate reason for placing additional burdens on the driver, who does not cause accidents in modern traffic conditions any more than the pedestrian. This is a rejection of the 'enterprise liability' concept mentioned earlier. Blum and Kalven suggest the adoption of traffic insurance as a new form of social security, i.e. as a government welfare programme.[29]

Finally, mention should be made of the conclusions reached by Professor Conard, in the light of a comprehensive study made by him and some colleagues (1964). Having shown in this study (generally referred to as 'The Michigan Survey') that both tort actions (55 per cent) and the victims' own loss insurance (38 per cent) and to a minor extent, social security payments, had made up the reparation paid for automobile accidents, Professor Conard concludes[30] 'that the way ahead is not for a single plan for automobile injuries; it is through keeping alive the plurality of existing programmes – from social security to tort damages – with some extensions, additions and correlations'.

The most important stimulus yet, in the United States, for a shift from tort to insurance comes from recent legislative moves in the States of New York and Massachusetts. The New York bill, unsuccessfully submitted by the Governor to the State Legislature in 1970, would abolish the fault principle for automobile accident victims and instead have all victims of such accidents compensated, without regard to fault, for all net economic losses sustained. The bill results from a comprehensive report, which concludes that the prevailing sustem of insurance, which maintains the fault principles, is ineffective, wasteful and vastly more expensive than the proposed reform.

In 1970 the state of Massachusetts passed a hotly disputed law that provides for:

1. A reduction of 15 per cent in premiums on all forms of automobile insurance coverage.

29. For a discussion and refutation of this approach see Keeton and O'Connell (1965, pp. 219–36); Calabresi, 'Fault, accident and the wonderful world of Blum and Kalven', 75 *Yale L.J.* 216 (1965).
30. 'The economic treatment of automobile injuries' 63 *Michigan L. Rev.* 279, at 326 (1964).

2. An obligation for insurers to renew all policies automatically regardless of the driver's record.

3. A compulsory no-fault plan, which would require insurance companies to pay the first $2000 of a policyholders claim for injury, including medical expenses, wages and out-of-pocket expenses, regardless of who was at fault. This would replace tort liability for all claims under $2000.

A report of the Insurers Commissioner for the State of New York, agrees that the long and complex tort actions cause high legal and administrative cost – estimated at 55 cents in every dollar paid in premiums.

A few of the major insurance companies of Massachusetts have refused to write insurance on these terms, largely under pressure from the legal profession. The result of any continued boycott will almost certainly be a state-sponsored insurance plan. This would hasten the direct involvement of the state that the private insurance business has sought to avoid.

Some Comparative Approaches

In all industrialized countries, regardless of their legal systems and traditions, the growing density of automobile traffic, with its attendant roll of accidents, has inevitably led to examinations of the question to what extent and in what form insurance should supplement or replace the traditional forms of tort liability. It is noteworthy that – except for the wider use of the concept of 'gross' or 'wilfull' negligence a concept derived from the Roman *culpa lata*, in non-common law systems[31] the problems and proposals essentially transcend the differences between the common-law and the civil-law systems.

The following institutional and procedural differences – mainly between the United States on the one hand, and the other industrialized countries on the other: should, however, be borne in mind:

1. Owing to the smaller scale, there is generally no specialized accident law bar, nor does any system outside the United States

31. See p. 188, for a demonstration that such concepts are neither unknown to, nor incompatible with, common law systems.

admit the contingency fee which provides a powerful stimulus for speculative actions.

2. Jury trial in civil cases – which plays a very important part in the psychology and scale of awards in the United States and Canada – is virtually unknown elsewhere.[32]

3. Court delays, while considerable in some countries, notably in France, are not generally comparable to those normal in the United States.

4. Comprehensive social insurance and security systems have been developed – e.g. in Britain and the major countries of the Commonwealth, in France, Germany and the Scandinavian countries – much earlier, and in greater scope, than in the United States.

5. While a majority of jurisdictions in the United States still adheres to the older principle of contributory negligence, i.e. the elimination of any responsibility of the defendant provided there is any negligence on the plaintiff's part – the civil-law systems, and since 1935, Britain, have adopted the principle of comparative negligence under which damages are apportioned according to the respective degrees of fault. This eliminates one of the greater injustices of the fault system as applied to traffic accidents in the United States, as it enables a broad apportionment of fault in the vast number of cases where the plaintiff is not entirely without fault, although that of the defendant predominates.

It is probably for a combination of these reasons that legal systems outside the United States – both of the common-law and the civil-law worlds – have not hitherto been under great pressure to abolish tort liability for traffic accidents.[33] Social insurance generally covers minimum needs; for motorists, compulsory liability insurance is the rule rather than the exception; litigation is both less costly and generally less tardy than in the United States. A number of countries, which do

32. In Great Britain jury trial in civil cases was, save for minor exceptions, abolished in 1932.

33. However, in two Commonwealth jurisdictions – New Zealand and British Columbia – Royal Commissions have recommended the replacement of the fault system by insurance systems. For summaries see 31 *Mod. L. Rev.* 544 (1968), 32 *Mod. L. Rev.* 547 (1969). In England, academic debate has increased. See Harris 'Compensation for accidents', 102 Solicitor's J. 729, 749, 765, 783 (1958); Street and Elliott (1968); Ison (1967).

not have compulsory liability insurance – these include the ten provinces of Canada, a number of American states and, since 1952, France – have adopted a limited system of risk pooling, by setting up unsatisfied judgement funds. These are administered by a special board, or sometimes a government department, to which automobile owners as well as the insurance companies contribute. This, of course, is not a displacement of tort liability, but rather an insurance that judgements will be satisfied.

All the common-law countries, and most of the civil-law countries, continue to adhere, in theory, to the fault principle, i.e. negligence. Under both systems, the negligence concept has gradually been widened so as to approximate strict liability. In France, as already noted, strict liability – conceptualized in private as in administrative law under the name of *le risque créé* – has been developed by the courts from Article 1384 of the Code Civil (see pp. 167–8). By contrast Germany, like some other European countries, has, since 1909, had a special statute, revised in 1952, which provides for strict liability for personal injury, as well as for limited property damage. However, a supplementary tort action is available to a victim who seeks to obtain fuller reimbursement. It is particularly interesting that the laws of the USSR, and of other socialist countries, which have comprehensive insurance systems, have retained the principle of fault liability. Strict liability is imposed only in the case of 'dangerous' activities – an exception which in the jurisprudence of contemporary common-law systems is barely distinguishable from fault liability.[34]

Among Continental legal critics, Professor Tunc – a French jurist – is foremost in demanding, like some of the American reform plans, that 'traffic accident victims now should receive their fulfilment in a statute that would entirely eliminate the principle of the law of torts and squarely place this compensation on the basis of the collective schemes already in existence'.[35]

34. See, for further details, Gray (1965); Hazard (1969); Barry, 'The motor car in Soviet criminal and civil law', 16 *Int. and Comp. L.Q.*, 56 (1967).
35. See Tunc, 'Current legal developments: France – tortius liability', 14 *Int. & Comp. L.Q.* 1041 (1965); see also the same writer's survey, 'Un Bilan Provisoire,' *Droit Social*, no. 2, Feb. 1967, pp. 71–89. Professor Tunc there argues for the setting up of an insurance fund within the framework of the Social Security Administration.

Tort and Insurance – Alternative Remedies and the Problem of Double Compensation

Any attempt to adjust insurance and tort liability, where the two methods of compensation arise from the same incident, must steer between the Scylla of double compensation for the victim, and the Charybdis of immunity for the tortfeasor. The victim ought to be compensated adequately – as far as monetary compensation can do it – for the injury suffered, but he should not make a profit out of the situation. On the other hand, the growing incidence of insurance – private or social – should not serve to let the individual tortfeasor off. The latter consideration is supported by divergent policy motivations. Some emphasize the moral element: tort is moral wrongdoing, and the wrongdoer should not be relieved of his burden because of the victim's insurance, or the beneficence of the modern welfare state. Others emphasize the deterrent character of tort-liability. Absolution from liability would increase carelessness, and with it the incidence of accidents.

It is only in recent years that the problem has received more than casual treatment. Where it had arisen before, notably in the field of industrial accidents, solutions differed and still do differ widely (see pp. 169–71).

Before we consider the relation of tort liability and insurance more systematically, in the light of the British study made on the subject and resulting in the Law Reform (Personal Injuries) Act of 1948, it should be pointed out that both the 'double compensation' argument, and the 'moral wrongdoing' argument, have a much narrower scope than would appear at first sight. In most cases the double benefits that an injured person may derive are not truly double compensation but compensation from what in the United States are called 'collateral sources'. In the field of social insurance some American courts regard the statutory benefit of workmen's compensation as properly mitigating damages others regard it as a collateral benefit not to be taken into account.[36] Practically all workmen's compensation laws have provided for subrogation or its equivalent (Harper and James, 1956, vol. 2, p. 1344, n. 7).

36. For a brief survey, and reference to the cases, see Note, 63 *Harvard L. Rev.* 333 (1949).

An Act of 1962[37] provides for the government's subrogation to a tort victim's right to recover against a third person the reasonable value of various hospital and medical services that the government has furnished the victim under authority or requirement provided by law.

In the field of private insurance, it is reasonably well settled that life or accident insurance are regarded as entirely separate transactions, creating separate interests, and not to be brought into mitigation of tort damages. On the other hand, fire and property insurance generally have subrogation clauses and thus exclude double recovery by the claimant (Harper and James, 1956, vol. 2, pp. 1350–52).

The 'moral wrongdoing' aspect has to be judged in the light of the foregoing discussion: the elimination of the moral element from the greater part of fault liability in tort. Both the alleged moral element in negligence liability and the argument that elimination or even reduction of tort liability in accident cases would increase the accident rate have been put forward time and again, often enough by those interested in the maintenance of a voluminous litigation in these fields, without either reflection on the nature of modern tort liability, or adequate statistical evidence. Neither the Saskatchewan experience nor American statistics appear to permit any conclusion that the degree of civil liability for the average negligence case has any relation one way or the other to carelessness and an increase in the accident rate.

The problem is thus somewhat less in dimension than might appear at first sight, but it remains of great importance. It is the advent of the comprehensive British National Insurance legislation after the Second World War which compelled a more systematic and thorough consideration of this problem. The relation between social insurance and tort liability was outlined in the Beveridge Report[38] partly implemented by the Law Reform (Personal Injuries) Act 1948.

The Act[39] adopted a compromise which some may regard as a model of Solomonic justice and others as a model of expediency. It contains the following clause:

37. 76 Stat. 593 (1962), 42 U.S.C. § 2651.
38. *Social Insurance and Allied Services Report by Sir William Beveridge* [1942] Cmd. no. 6404.
39. Law Reform (Personal Injuries) Act 1948.

In an action for damages for personal injuries (including any such action arising out of a contract), there shall in assessing those damages be taken into account, against any loss of earnings or profits which has accrued or probably will accrue to the injured person from the injuries, one half of the value of any rights which have accrued or probably will accrue to him therefrom in respect of industrial injury benefit, industrial disablement benefit, or sickness benefit for the five years beginning with the time when the cause of action accrued. . . . This subsection shall not be taken as requiring both the gross amount of the damages before taking into account the said rights and the net amount after taking them into account to be found separately (section 2(1)).

This compromise saves for the time being the law of tort and makes common-law actions still worth while. On the other hand it concedes to the insured, among whom employees are the most powerful group, that the new national insurance is an additional benefit for which the insured pays, partly in the form of an insurance contribution, and partly as a citizen of a nation which has decided through its Parliament that the wealthier sections should by taxation help to mitigate the inequalities of the social system. That for the time being leaves both sides reasonably satisfied.

By allowing a partial offsetting of benefits against damages, the insured is reminded that part of the social insurance benefits is provided for him by a benevolent state, and the danger of the odd case in which a relatively light injury would be compensated out of proportion to the damages suffered is reduced. The Act steers a middle line between two conflicting philosophies.

Professor Fleming James has investigated the broader problem of social insurance and tort liability in American law.[40] The learned author suggests that there are four alternative solutions to the problem of relation between social insurance and tort liability: (1) the abolition of one of the remedies, (2) compulsion for the claimant to elect one and forgo the other, (3) allowing the claimant to have accumulative benefits of two or several remedies, and (4) allowing the claimant to pursue all the available remedies but limiting his total recovery to the maximum amount he could recover from a single source.

40. James, 'Social insurance and tort liability', 27 *New York University L. Rev.* 552 (1952), restated in Harper and James (1956, §§ 25.19–25.23).

Professor James disapproves the total abolition of the tort remedy, as he does not wish to 'rip any more of the threads of individualism out of the social and economic fabric than we must in order to take adequate care of the basic human needs of all our people'. Next, the election of remedies is a familiar pattern in workmen's compensation law but it has been widely found by those who have studied the problem to be a wasteful and socially undesirable solution, especially because of the delays and uncertainties involved, and the danger that a lump sum recovery in damages may throw out the purpose of the social legislation. It is for these reasons that recent British legislation has abolished the election. Next the learned author turns to the more complex problem of cumulative remedies. Professor James has doubts about the prevalent judicial practice to allow double recovery in accident insurance cases, though he believes the harm of such practice to be small because the beneficiaries of accident policies usually are willing to settle their tort claims for less than they otherwise would (Harper and James, 1956, p. 556). But contrary to a widespread opinion, he believes that accident insurance provides a weak analogy for social insurance. Social-insurance schemes are not intended to provide windfalls. At least the philosophy of the American legislation, unlike recent British legislation, does not seek to redistribute the wealth beyond the point that indemnity or compensation calls for. Similarly, he suggests that private group schemes, such as Blue Cross insurance, should also be treated as providing indemnity or compensation rather than a windfall.

On the other hand, Professor James is sceptical of the argument that the tortfeasor should not be let off free. He supports the various studies made on the relation of fault liability to accident rates which do not suggest tort liability for negligence as relevant one way or another.

Finally, as to the problem of subrogation, Professor James points out the administrative inconveniences of the subrogation machinery, as well as the difficulties of finding a proper basis of redistribution of accident losses. Some social-insurance programmes are based on the principle that society should meet certain economic losses to individuals and distribute them widely by taxation; others distribute the loss among the beneficiaries. In the latter case subrogation makes sense, in the former less so. Where, for example, disability benefits are paid from a fund recruited by general taxation, there would seem to be little to be gained by making the motoring public group pay back to the government (i.e. the taxpayers) the amount of the social-insurance benefits which the latter has paid the claimants.

The problem to what extent insurance should take over the functions of tort law has been the subject of many studies in the Scandinavian countries.

The Danish Act on Contracts of Insurance of 1930 provides that the liability of a tortfeasor is not affected by the existence of life, health and accident insurance of the usual types, whereas it may be restricted in the case of fire insurance or other types of property insurance. But the important contribution to the general jurisprudence of the matter made by the Danish law is the authorization which it gives to the courts to exempt the tortfeasor from liability or to reduce the damages (a) if the liability is based on the defendant's negligence and the negligence was not gross or wanton, and (b) where the defendant was liable by virtue of the general rule of *respondeat superior*. Professor Ussing[41] cites a number of cases to illustrate how the Danish courts have used this discretion, broadly distinguishing between objectionable and less objectionable types of negligent conduct. Professor Ussing's conclusion is that only for some situations ought tort liability to be maintained in order to restrain tortious conduct but that, apart from this rather narrow field, it would be preferable to have compensation made by means of insurance. Such insurance against third-party risk should be compulsory for those who conduct ultra-hazardous activities and probably also for operators of motor vehicles and keepers of animals.

In the field of social insurance, Sweden in particular has gone to such lengths in providing overall insurance benefits in case of illness, disablement and accidents that a Swedish authority, Professor Ivar Strahl, has suggested that tort liability for harm to persons should in most cases be abolished.[42] Professor Hellner[43] shows that, despite the comprehensive nature of Swedish social insurance, in-

41. Ussing, 'The Scandinavian law of torts', 1 *Amer. J. Comp. L.* 359 (1952).
42. Ussing, p. 369.
43. 'Tort liability and liability insurance', 6 *Scandinavian Studies in Law* 129 (1962).

cluding accident and health insurance, tort actions based on traffic accidents remain 'among the most common of all civil-law suits in Sweden'. But benefits received under Sweden's general insurance lessen the liability of the tortfeasor, nor is there subrogation in favour of the insured. The injured person cannot claim against the tortfeasor for costs that have been met by insurance and public health services. According to a judgement of the Swedish Supreme Court of 1955, this applies even to those who cause injury intentionally or with gross negligence.

In a more recent study, Professor Hellner has given a more broadly based survey[44] of the various solutions attempted in the different Scandinavian countries for the problem of the relation between tort damage and insurance benefits. The alternatives are: (1) cumulative recovery, i.e. 'permitting the injured person to receive the special benefits in addition to the tort damages'; (2) deduction of the benefits obtained by way of tort damages, with subrogation allowed against the tortfeasor; (3) deduction of the benefits without allowing subrogation.

A fourth solution, which is found to some extent in Sweden and Norway, is to grant a discretion to the appropriate authority to reduce damages where other benefits are received.

As Professor Hellner points out, the deduction of benefits without subrogation is now the almost universal solution with regard to benefits obtained from social insurance. Professor Hellner leans in favour of extending this principle to the field of motor traffic accidents. He sees 'no decisive reason for maintaining a difference between social and private insurance in relation to damages for tort'. He points out, quite rightly, that many forms of so-called private insurance are hardly voluntary (e.g. employees' group insurance, which, in Scandinavia, as in the United States and other countries is often compulsory for the employee). On the other hand, some social insurance programmes are voluntary, and the same rules on deduction are applied to voluntary as to compulsory social insurance. 'Furthermore, social insurance and private insurance at present often appear in the light of competing institutions, offering the same main advantages but differing in minor matters.'

44. 'Damages for personal injury and the victim's private insurance', 18 *Amer. J. Comp. Law* 126 (1970).

An interesting method of assessing personal injuries – intermediate between public administration and private insurance – is presented by the personal injury boards in Sweden.[45] Most of the claims against liability insurers for personal injury and wrongful death are handled by two boards, briefly described as the Traffic Board and the Liability Board. The former is composed of four lawyers who are judges or former judges, and sixteen insurance-company officials who are mostly lawyers. The latter is composed of two judicial members and eight insurance experts, all of whom are appointed by the Association of Swedish Insurance Companies. Although the opinions of these boards are only consultative, and it is open to the claimant to sue the insurer in a court of law, the boards, by virtue of their composition and experience, enjoy great authority and are respected for their independence.

Finally, a legal system as different in social concept as the Soviet law has met with very similar problems of adjustment between social insurance and tort liability.

Article 404 of the Soviet Civil Code provides for strict liability as follows

persons and enterprises, whose activities present special danger to the persons around them, such as railroads, street cars, factories and mills, vendors of inflammable materials, keepers of wild animals, persons engaged in the erection of buildings and other structures, etc., are liable for injury caused by the source of increased danger, unless they prove that the damage was caused as the result of *force majeure*, or as the result of a wilful act or gross negligence on the part of the injured party.

Article 413 of the same Code bears directly on the relation of social insurance and tort liability:

A person or enterprise paying insurance premiums to protect an injured person under social insurance shall not be required to repair injury caused by the happening of the event against which the insurance has been purchased. . . . But if the injury is caused by the criminal act or failure to act of the management of the enterprise, the social-insurance agency which satisfies the injured person shall have the right to demand from the management of the enterprise an amount equal to the insurance benefits

45. Bengtsson, 'Personal injury boards in Sweden', 18 *Amer. J. Comp. Law* 108 (1970).

paid to the injured person (subrogation). . . . In such case, the injured person who has not received full reparation of his injury under social insurance has an additional claim against the entrepreneur.

This provision has been maintained by the Fundamental Principles of 1961, except that the protection of the enterprise paying the premium against suit by the insurance carrier for recovery of the benefits paid has been reduced. It is now given only if there is no fault at all on the part of the enterprise.[46] As Professor Hazard has pointed out, 'Tort law serves . . . as an instrument of policy in encouraging state economic administrators to give careful attention to the safety rules' (1953, p. 236). Most recently, a Roumanian jurist has spelled out this philosophy, in an article, which while directly concerned with contract, also applies to the tort sphere.

To neglect fault as a condition of the legal liability of socialist organizations would be equivalent to abandoning inducement efforts in the economic activity of the organization, since there would no longer be an incentive to work well if, regardless of the manner of working, unfavourable conditions beyond all control could entail liability. The introduction of fault into the legal responsibility of socialist organizations assures economic efficiency. Legal responsibility without fault is thus inconceivable.[47]

The, at first sight paradoxical, fact that it is the 'capitalist' countries that have tended to move away from the individual fault principle – characteristic of an individualist, *laissez-faire* economy – towards some form of insurance and collectivist liability, while the socialist countries maintain the fault principle, along with social insurance, is thus to be explained by the fact that in an economy not spurred by the profit motive, accountability is a principal instrument of control. The withdrawal of funds, which is implied in the payment of compensation, and the black mark incurred by an enterprise adjudged negligent, is essentially an instrument of administrative supervision in a planned economy.

46. Fundamental Principles, Article 91 (see Hazard, 1969, p. 389).
47. Trajan Ionasco, 'The fault requirement and the contract liability of socialist Organizations', 18 *Am. J. Comp. Law* 31, 33 (1970). This is not, however, uncontested. See, e.g. Laptev (1959, ch. 8, §4, ¶1) as cited by Ionasco, who maintains that liability without fault has the purpose of assuring unconditional execution of the tasks of the economic plan of the socialist enterprise.

Some Conclusions

No existing legal system, whether socialistically or capitalistically inclined, has so far shown any desire to abolish tort liability altogether until recently. On the other hand, systems as divergent as those of Denmark and the USSR have singled out criminal or gross negligence from that of negligence in general. It is submitted that the English Committee on alternative remedies was somewhat hasty in throwing out a similar suggestion as being incompatible with English law. The fact is that the concept of 'gross, criminal or wanton' negligence does play a considerable part in the common-law system. The importance of the concept of gross negligence in criminal law is well known. In *R.* v. *Bateman*,[48] this was defined as 'such disregard for the life and safety of others as to amount to a crime against the State and conduct deserving punishment'. In *Andrews* v. *DPP*,[49] Lord Atkin explained gross negligence in manslaughter in terms of recklessness. More recently the Irish Court of Criminal Appeal[50] distinguished negligence in manslaughter from tort negligence. In the former situation, 'a very high degree of negligence must be proved'.

Perhaps more apposite to the problem of civil liability is the adoption of the test of gross negligence in certain statutes, of which the 'guest statute' of Colorado is representative. Under this legislation a guest passenger in an automobile can recover damages from the driver who has caused an accident only where he can establish that 'such accident shall have been intentional on the part of such owner or operator or caused by his intoxication, or by negligence consisting of a wilful and wanton disregard of the rights of others'.[51]

It is not suggested that the delimitation of 'gross' or 'criminal' or 'wanton' negligence from other forms of negligence is conceptually satisfactory or practically simple. It may well be argued – and it has been argued – that there can only be either negligence or no negligence. This argument, however, does not dispose of the practical policy question. It is obvious that among the thousands of cases which come under the general heading of negligence, there is a limited number which call for prosecution because of the relatively

48. (1925) 19 Cr. App. R.8.
49. [1937] A.C. 576.
50. *People* v. *Dunleavy* [1948] Ir. R.95.
51. Colorado Revised Statutes, 13–9–1 (1963).

greater gravity of conduct. The same test can well be applied to tort actions. It is a matter of individual appreciation in the light of all the circumstances, and in this respect the distinction of gross negligence from other forms of negligence does not at all differ from such other judicial yardsticks as 'fair and reasonable' or the apportionment of guilt in comparative negligence.

The importance of this recent trend towards what Professor Ussing, in the above-quoted article, has aptly described as the effect of insurance on tort, namely, that it will bring about 'a certain broadening of tort liability', but at the same time 'a shrinking of the field of liability for tort', is that, after the dilution of the concept of fault in tort and the far-reaching inroad of insurance on tort liability, the admonitory function of tort is being reaffirmed in the more restricted sphere where it really has such a function. And this is a common rationale of the developments that have already taken place, among others in Scandinavia and in the Soviet Union, and as they are advocated by the American students of the subjects discussed earlier. The result would be that, for a very limited sphere, the law of tort would come closer again to criminal law in sanctioning immoral conduct, while for the vast number of accidents due to modern social conditions tort might either frankly become a matter of strict liability or be superseded by insurance.

It is difficult to attempt any general conclusions in a field so full of complexity. The following generalizations may, however, be attempted with some degree of confidence:

1. In those fields of tort which are socially most significant – traffic accidents, industrial accidents, responsibilities of employers, manufacturers, and other controllers of properties and enterprises – the fault principle has either been superseded by strict liability or lost its moral significance and become barely distinguishable from so-called strict liability.
2. Minimum compensation for the vicissitudes of modern life is a widely accepted principle, across borders and different legal systems. The need can be fulfilled either by (a) a comprehensive social insurance (United Kingdom, USSR, Sweden), (b) partial schemes of social insurance (Workmen's Compensation Statutes or the Saskatchewan automobile accident insurance legislation), or (c)

compulsory private insurance schemes, in particular, compulsory third-party liability.

As forecast by Holmes in his *Common Law*, published in 1881, it is conceivable that the state may at some time take over completely the field of compensation for injury and replace tort altogether. But no country, however advanced in its social-insurance schemes, has as yet gone this far, partly as a matter of compromise with the existing legal system and partly as a matter of deliberate social policy.

3. The double compensation on immunity for the tortfeasor is reduced by two factors: (a) many apparent cases of double compensation are really cases of collateral benefits where it is inequitable to offset insurance benefits against tort compensation; (b) partial or total relief for the tortfeasor is not as objectionable as it appears at first because (i) the tortfeasor may pay his share of compensation in some other capacity (as a motorist, a worker, an employer, or generally, as a taxpayer), and (ii) because the moral significance of fault liability, as pointed out above, has become restricted to very few situations.

4. The true admonitory function of tort liability could be restored – and this is a clearly apparent trend in many different legal systems – by restricting, in fields covered by social or private insurance, tort liability to cases of 'gross' or 'criminal' negligence. The consequence of such restriction would be a drastic reduction of negligence cases with all the resulting economy, and an approximation of fault liability in tort to fault liability in crime – the relationship that once existed but has been diluted by contemporary developments.

Chapter 6
Criminal Law in a Changing World

While the definition of a crime has aroused the usual spate of controversies connected with any attempt to define a legal concept (Williams, 1955 p. 107), the formulation of an eminent American authority may serve as a point of departure.

The purpose of the penal law is to express a formal social condemnation of forbidden conduct, buttressed by sanctions calculated to prevent it.[1]

Implicit in this formulation are three questions, to which different societies give very different answers:

First, what kind of conduct is 'forbidden'?

Second, what kind of 'formal social condemnation' is considered appropriate to prevent such conduct?

Third, what kind of sanctions are considered as best calculated to prevent officially outlawed conduct?

Fundamentalist and Utilitarian Approaches to the Function of Criminal Law

There are two conflicting approaches to the function of criminal law – a question that is at the bottom of much of the contemporary controversy about the uses of criminal law. At one end of the spectrum, there are what we may call the fundamentalists. To them the function of the criminal law is essentially that of the defender and protector of moral values. Generally, this approach goes together with the emphasis on guilt as the determining element of criminal behaviour, and with a retributive theory of punishment. It has, however, two aspects: one is the retribution, the revenge of society upon the criminal (and

1. Wechsler, 'The criteria of criminal responsibility', 22 *University of Chicago L. Rev.*, 374. (1955).

by implication, immoral) behaviour of the criminal. The other is the atonement, the expiation of the criminal for the sins which he has committed against society.

At the other end of the spectrum, the utilitarian approach sees criminal law and the criminal sanction essentially as one of a large number of devices by which society protects itself against injury done to it by certain kinds of behaviour. Its premise is that punishment, as an infliction of pain, is unjustifiable unless it can be shown that more good is likely to result from inflicting than from withholding it. The good that is thought to result from punishing criminals is a prevention or reduction of a greater evil, crime (Packer, 1968, p. 39). For this approach, guilt, i.e. the characterization of certain kinds of behaviour as evil, is not necessarily a precondition of punishment.[2] On the other hand, the use of the criminal sanction is, for this approach, not a necessary consequence of 'formal social condemnation of forbidden conduct'. It is a question of balancing the social advantages of the use of criminal law against the cost. The cost of using the apparatus of criminal law for trivial offences, or for conduct where the use of the criminal sanction is not likely to produce the deterrent effect which is one of the major purposes of punishment, either for the criminal himself or for others, may make alternative remedies preferable (Packer, 1968, p. 207). It follows that, depending on the utility criteria, remedies other than punishment may be socially preferable.

A classical statement of the fundamentalist (and retributive) view is that of the British nineteenth-century jurist Sir Fitzjames Stephen:

In short the infliction of punishment by law gives definite expression and solemn ratification and justification to the hatred which is excited by the commission of the offence and which constitutes the moral or popular, as distinct from the conscientious, sanction of that part of morality which is also sanctioned by the criminal law (1883, vol. 2, p. 80).

The contrary view was expressed by Bentham's greatest disciple, John Stuart Mill who, in his essay *On Liberty* said that 'the only purpose for which power can be rightfully exercised over any mem-

2. See further on the question of strict liability, especially with regard to public welfare offences, pp. 202–7.

ber of a civilized community, against his will, is to prevent harm to others' (ch. 1).

The controversy continues and has indeed been intensified by the greatly increased complexity of contemporary society, in which both the range of socially dangerous offences, and that of the possible responses to be made by society has vastly increased. The issue of the criminality of homosexual behaviour, as studied by the Wolfenden Committee, as well as the much debated decision of the House of Lords of 1961[3] formed the background for a debate between Lord Devlin and Professor H. L. A. Hart. In Shaw's case, the House of Lords had gone out of its way to add to the statutory convictions, a conviction for 'conspiracy to corrupt public morals'. This provoked a pamphlet by Professor Hart which expressed a combination of the utilitarian philosophy of John Stuart Mill, with affirmation of the faith of a modern liberal.

Recognition of individual liberty as a value involves, as a minimum, acceptance of the principle that the individual may do what he wants, even if others are distressed when they learn what it is that he does – unless, of course, there are other good grounds for forbidding it (Hart, 1963, p. 47).

Lord Devlin (1965, p. 1), while rejecting 'the platonic ideal . . . that the state exists to promote virtue among its citizens', said that any community could exist only if it had a certain 'sense of right and wrong', and that certain institutions – in the common-law legal process, the jury expressing the sense of justice of the ordinary man – had to represent the moral sense of the community. From that premise, it is possible to convict a person because his conduct, even if not harmful to the functioning of society, is offensive to the moral sense of the community.[4]

Lord Devlin's approach is close to the fundamentalist view, which emphasizes the outrage to the moral sense of the community as the basic rationale of the invocation of the criminal law; the utilitarians

3. *Shaw* v. *Director of Public Prosecutions*, [1962] A.C. 220.
4. For the discussion of a similar issue, i.e. the criminality of obscenity, see Henkin, 'Morals and the constitution: the sin of obscenity', 63 *Columbia L. Rev.* 391 (1963). See also Dworkin, 'Lord Devlin and the enforcement of morals', 75 *Yale L.J.* 986 (1966).

take 'public order' as the limiting factor. This explains the conflicting views on the criminality of homosexual behaviour carried out by consenting adult males in private.

It should, however, be borne in mind that 'public order' itself is not a static concept. In a theocratic or totalitarian society – the latter exemplified in its extreme form by Orwell's *1984* – the regulation of sexual practices, or freedom of discussion, even if held in private, may become very much a matter of 'public order'. Thoughts or private expressions of opinion may be 'ungood' in the framework of a totally controlled society. The much more limited concept of public order as it has been expressed by Mill, Hart and the Wolfenden Report, is acceptable only in the context of a liberal society, which allows the individual a maximum of physical, intellectual and spiritual freedom, and correspondingly limits the function of criminal law. The protection of juveniles, or the condemnation of public exposure, are among the minimum elements of public order as conceived in a liberal society. Where the line between permissible private conduct and the interest of the community in maintenance of public order is to be drawn, cannot be answered in absolute terms.

Social Values and the Ambit of Criminal Law

Obviously, the type of conduct that a particular society considers as sufficiently worthy of condemnation to prohibit it by criminal sanctions, is deeply influenced by the values governing that society. It therefore varies greatly, from one country to another, and from one period of history to another.

It may suffice here to illustrate the dependence of the scope of prohibited conduct on changing values and canons of social policy, by two examples: One is the area of economic crime, where the transition from a *laissez-faire* to a regulated and, in varying degrees, publicly controlled economy has led to the condemnation and criminality of actions which, in a system of economic individualism were legitimate and perhaps praiseworthy. The converse is the case in the area of sexual behaviour, where changing attitudes and social conditions have increasingly led to the abolition of criminality for actions that were formerly severely condemned and subject to criminal sanctions.

Economic Crimes against the Community

In a *laissez-faire* economy, the waste of property is, like its accumulation, a matter of private concern. The rape of the earth, through deforestation, overgrazing, waste of water, dust-bowl farming, is a matter for the individual owner, who is presumed to suffer the appropriate penalty through the diminution of his crops and financial returns. The same applies to the neglect or non-use of machinery, such as power plants, tractors, or of mineral resources, even if such abuse should lead to scarcity and the impoverishment of the community. Such a philosophy is no longer held, except by a diminishing band of passionate believers in the absolute sacrosanctity of property, immune from any official interference or regulation. A major cause of the change in the public philosophy has been the incidence of total war in the twentieth century. Scarcity of food has made the careful use of land a vital necessity, in blockaded countries, such as Germany in the First World War, or densely populated, entirely industrialized countries, dependent largely on sea supplies, like England in both world wars. This has meant at least a temporary change in legal values.[5] Similarly, waste or unauthorized use of precious resources becomes, in such situations, a criminal and social offence.

Outside the emergencies of war conditions, the growing recognition of the social function and use of property has led to more permanent changes in legal values.[6] The changed evaluation of the relation of property and individual has gone furthest in socialized legal systems. Following the constitutionally enshrined concept of 'public, socialist property as the sacred and inviolable foundation of the socialist system. . . .', in the Soviet Constitution[7] the destruction, the theft and the misuse of state-owned property – which embraces the bulk of the industrial, commercial and agricultural assets of the nation – is attended with criminal sanctions.[8] To a large degree,

5. See, e.g. the wartime agriculture legislation in England, consolidated in the Agriculture Act 1947.
6. See, for example, article 14 (2) of the West German Constitution of 1949: 'Property shall involve obligations. Its use shall also serve the common good.'
7. Article 131, Soviet Constitution of 1936.
8. See Chapter Two (Crimes Against Socialist Property) of the 1960 Criminal Code of the RSFSR, which imposes up to three years' imprisonment for, e.g. theft

penal sanctions in a socialized system must serve as a substitute for the regulatory effect of financial incentives, the 'profit motive'. But the philosophy of penalizing waste and misuse of public property has deeper roots. Where the national philosophy is the development of the national economy to the general benefit by the planned use of resources, the intentional or careless waste of national assets acquires basic importance.

The growing consciousness of the need to preserve vital assets for the community, and to protect it from the rapaciousness or neglect of the individual, goes far beyond socialized systems of the Soviet pattern. We have seen that, in some western parts of the United States, scarcity of water has produced restrictive legislation not only on the use of water, but even on the ownership of land (see p. 111). If, as many demographers and ecologists believe, the growth of the world's population will increasingly outstrip available resources, the conservation of agricultural, mineral and other natural assets will become an increasingly vital social and legal value, fortified by harsh criminal sanctions.

Meanwhile, the protection of vital resources and commodities has, in non-socialist societies, mainly developed through regulatory measures, attended with penal sanctions. Here, the most notable development has probably been in German law, the outcome of scarcity situations produced by two world wars, with intervening inflations, raw material, and currency shortages. Out of the multitude of statutes and decrees, controlling and regulating the supply of scarce commodities, and especially transactions in foreign exchange, has developed a whole body of *Wirtschaftsstrafrecht*. After the last world war, the Federal German Republic consolidated the concepts and offences gradually developed in a comprehensive *Wirtschafts-strafgesetz*.[9] The law distinguishes between a graver type of economic offence called *Straftat* and a lesser type, called *Ordnungswidrigkeit*.

(art. 89), swindling (art. 93) or negligent destruction or damaging (art. 99). The death penalty may be imposed for 'stealing state or social property on an especially large scale' (art. 93.1). The penalities for crimes against social property are more severe than similar offences against personal property. For an English text of the Code, see Berman (1966, and for discussion, see pp. 56–7, 136–7); Hazard (1969, pp. 461–2).

9. Of 26 July 1949, amended 25 March 1952 and 9 July 1954.

In the former category, is, above all, an action designed to 'retain, put aside, destroy or deliberately or negligently allow to perish, objects of vital need, where the actor knows or must, in the circumstances, be deemed to suppose that he thereby endangers the satisfaction of these needs'.[10] Other important offences in this category concern violations of rationing and price controls. The *Ordnungswidrigkeit* covers essentially violations of officially imposed supervisory duties in the conduct of an enterprise. There is also a category of *Zuwiderhandlungen* which may be either a *Straftat* or an *Ordnungswidrigkeit*. It is the former where the action 'violates the interest of the state in the conservation and integrity of the economic order as a whole or in individual branches'.

These concepts have been adopted in the West German Anti-trust Law (*Wettbewerbsgesetz*) of 1957, which regards an offence against the provisions directed to the elimination of various restrictive practices, monopolies and the like as an *Ordnungswidrigkeit*.

The most interesting aspect of this new classification of economic offences is its differentiation between what we might call the old-style type of criminal offence and the new type of administrative offence. The yardstick is both the gravity of the interest that has been injured, and the *mens rea* of the offender. There are new types of interest deserving of protection by the state and unknown to the older criminal law, but not all of these can be measured in terms of older concepts of criminal law.

Long before the development of these new concepts of economic crime in the Soviet Union, Germany and some other countries, following the economic dislocation of the present century, Canada (in its Criminal Code of 1889) and the United States (in its anti-trust legislation of 1890) had attempted to utilize the criminal law for another type of economic offence, which marks an equally significant, though differently based, departure from the traditional scope and purposes of the criminal law. By making it a misdemeanour to contract or engage in any combination or conspiracy in restraint of trade or commerce among the several States or with foreign nations, or to monopolize such trade or commerce, the Sherman Act of 1890 clearly recognized that it was the function of criminal law not only to protect private property against unlawful interference, but also to

10. Section 1 (author's translation).

protect the basic economic order of the nation, and the conditions of its existence, against unlawful interference by private subjects of the law. This was, indeed, a revolutionary departure from established concepts. It was, of course, based on an economic philosophy radically different from that later embodied in the Soviet Constitution, or even that of the German *Wirtschaftsstrafgesetz*. The interest to be protected was the maintenance of a competitive economy based on private enterprise. The state did not mean to become owner or entrepreneur, but it felt compelled to use its legislative, administrative and judicial machinery for the protection of the economic well-being of the community as a whole – as conceived by a liberal economic philosophy – and to defend it against powerful industrial and commercial interests. This is no less a revolution in legal thinking than the establishment of economic crimes in the Soviet law, despite the radical difference in the economic philosophies underlying American and Soviet law. United States anti-trust legislation, later supplemented by the establishment of the Federal Trade Commission, with powers largely parallel to those of the Department of Justice, envisages not only criminal action, but also a civil suit by the Department of Justice, either as an alternative or an addition to criminal action. Moreover, private litigants may bring the so-called triple-damage action, a procedure that has recently gained in popularity. The Federal Trade Commission, one of the major regulatory agencies that are essential to the American conception of government, has powers to issue 'cease and desist' orders for the enforcement of fair trade (including anti-trust offences), which may be sanctioned by a penalty. This, however, is a 'civil' penalty, what the Germans would call an *Ordnungsstrafe*, a means to enforce the authority of government, not a criminal sanction proper.

To this variety of proceedings must be added the possibility to terminate a pending suit by a 'consent decree' – a very frequently used procedure – and the many informal, behind-the-scenes negotiations by which, for example, the Department of Justice may give immunity to a contemplated action which might possibly violate the anti-trust laws.

The real effectiveness of legal sanctions depends, of course, above all, on the degree and methods of their practical implementation. In Canada, criminal sanctions comparable to those of the Sherman Act remained practically a dead letter until the reinvigoration of anti-trust enforcement after the Second World War.[11]

In the United States, a few years ago, criminal proceedings were instituted against a small number of middle senior executives of some major corporations, including the General Electric Company and Westinghouse, for violation of the anti-trust law provisions prohibiting price-fixing. The top executives of the corporations concerned were permitted to allege ignorance, while their subordinates served short sentences of imprisonment. Whether this kind of procedure actually served the end of justice, must remain a matter of doubt.[12] This use of the criminal sanction has remained exceptional.

On the whole, it must be concluded that, in so far as the anti-trust law has been effective in the restraint or elimination of monopolistic conditions, it has been due predominantly to administrative and civil measures, or just to the general sense of awareness caused by the existence of the legislation and the possibility of its interference with business operations. It is significant that the various recent anti-trust laws of other countries – with the limited exception of the German *Wettbewerbsgesetz* – have discarded the criminal sanction and relied on measures of publicity and administrative regulation rather than the deterrence of criminal offence (see pp. 297–303).

Environmental Pollution and the Criminal Law

An increasing use of the criminal sanction – often complementary to damages and administrative sanctions – is likely to result from the belated but traumatic recognition in the industrially developed nations that a massive pollution of the environment, through despoliation of land, water and the air, by industrial waste, chemicals, oil, the dumping of garbage, the indiscriminate use of pesticides and by many other means, threatens the very conditions of social survival.

11. On this, see Friedmann, 'Monopoly, reasonableness and public interests in the Canadian anti-combines law', 33 *Canadian Bar Rev.* 133 (1955); also Blair in Friedmann (ed.) (1956, p. 3).

12. See, for a full discussion, Walton and Cleveland (1964). One of the many private actions for treble damages, arising out of the price-fixing arrangements (*Philadelphia Electric Co.* v. *Westinghouse Electric Corp.* [1964] *Trad. Cas*, No. 71 123 (E.D. Pa. 1964)) resulted in damages of nearly twenty-nine million dollars.

Thus, an area, which until very recently, has remained outside legal regulation altogether – a concomitant of the profit-and-consumer-oriented society – is likely to become a major object of social condemnation buttressed by criminal sanctions. Already several countries have prohibited or severely restricted the use of DDT. The pollution of water and air through sulphur-laden oil and motor-car exhausts, the overheating of seas and rivers through thermal processes, the discharge of industrial solids into the rivers and lakes of North America and Western Europe, are rapidly becoming threats of such magnitude to the continued supply of the basic elements of life that the severest form of prohibition, i.e. criminal sanctions, in addition to monetary charges, damages and administrative injunctions, will become an absolute necessity.[13]

Sexual Permissiveness and the Criminal Law

In contrast to the increasing need for criminal sanctions to combat economic risks and social offences, notably the pollution of the environment, certain types of individual behaviour, once severely condemned by prevalent concepts of morality and public order, have become widely tolerated and more acceptable to society. This is notably so in the area of sexual behaviour, as shown by the spreading abolition of criminality of homosexual conduct between consenting adult males carried out in private, and the rapidly growing number of jurisdictions that have abolished, or greatly limited, the criminality of abortion.

The greater permissiveness towards homosexuality is essentially a

13. In April 1970, the USSR announced a comprehensive programme to curb industrial pollution sewage disposal and the contamination of water by a combination of administrative and criminal sanctions. These include the power to close down, or shut off the water supply, for offending enterprises, the payment of damages for harm caused by violations, and fines (*New York Times*, 28 April 1970). In May 1970, the US Federal Water Quality Administration issued an order by which any water dumped into Lake Michigan must be cooled to within one degree of the lake's temperature at that moment. About the same time, a federal indictment against the Chevron Oil Company for pollution of the ocean off the Gulf Coast due to leakage from inadequately secured wells was based on a provision of the Outer Continental Shelf Act of 1953, under which 'any person who knowingly or wilfully violates any rule or regulation prescribed by the Secretary [of the Interior]' is liable to a fine or imprisonment.

product of changed ideas of social morality.[14] In most western societies, homosexual conduct, if limited to adults and carried out in private, is no longer regarded as morally so blameworthy that it deserves the attention of the criminal law. In Britain, where a statute of 1967[15] abolished the criminality of this type of homosexual behaviour, the matter was fully discussed in the Report of the Wolfenden Committee, which recommended the abolition of the offence by a majority of twelve to one. Its philosophy is summed up in the following passage:

Unless a deliberate attempt is made by society acting through the agency of the law to equate this sphere of crime with that of sin, there must remain a realm of private morality and immorality which is, in brief and crude terms, not the law's business.[16]

Whereas the growing tolerance of male homosexualty is essentially the expression of a changing social morality, i.e. of changing ideas on the range of permissible individual behaviour in the field of sex, the rapidly spreading movement towards the abolition or modification of criminal sanctions for abortions is mainly a product of social change, i.e. of the growing need to permit a variety of ways to slow down or counter the world-wide growth of population – now perceived as one of the major dangers to the civilized survival of mankind. Combined with it is the realization of the fact – largely a product of the same social forces – that millions of illegal abortions have long made a mockery of the law, and that the growing pressure towards abortion will make the legal sanctions increasingly ineffective. Whereas, until very recently, the great majority of criminal laws in the western world legalized abortion only where the life (and, more dubiously, the health) of the mother were in danger (Williams,

14. On the distinction between ethics and social morality, see Strawson, 'Social morality and individual ideal', 37 *Philosophy* 1 (1961); and Friedmann (1967, p. 25).
15. Sexual Offences Act 1967, ch. 60.
16. *Report of the Committee on Homosexual Offences and Prostitution* (Cmnd 747, 1957), s. 61. The Model Penal Code of the American Law Institute, published in 1962, adopts a similar philosophy by omitting private homosexuality not involving force, imposition or corruption of the young from the offences listed in the Model Penal Code. This has not, however, been adopted as yet by the great majority of the states, which have jurisdiction in the criminal law.

1957, ch. 5), a rapidly growing number of laws now greatly widens the grounds of permissible abortions, or abolishes its criminality altogether.[17]

Criminal Law in the Welfare State – *Mens Rea* and the Public Welfare Offence

A whole new area of criminal law has developed out of the steadily increasing responsibilities of the modern state for the maintenance of certain crucial standards demanded by the proper functioning of a modern industrialized and urbanized society. These standards are embodied in a great variety of statutory regulations. They concern safety appliances and sanitary standards in factories and mines, minimum standards in housing accommodation, purity and minimum quality of foodstuffs, drugs and medical preparations offered to the public, compliance with statutory obligations, unemployment insurance and other forms of social security, registration of professional and trade qualifications, and a multitude of other matters which have become the accepted responsibility of a properly governed contemporary state. Almost invariably, the statutes provide sanctions for the fulfilment of such obligations, mainly in the form of fines. These fines are often imposed by administrative process in the first place, but subject to a trial, if contested by the defendant. In 1902, a German legal scholar, James Goldschmidt, characterized this whole area of criminal law as 'administrative penal law' (*Verwaltungsstrafrecht*). Much more recently, common lawyers have directed their attention to this type of criminal offence, and characterized the whole group as 'public-welfare offences'.[18]

This type of offence, while going under the general label of criminal law, is of an essentially different character from the criminal offences based on individual wrongdoing. Like all law, the conditions under which criminal liability is imposed depend upon a balance of values in a given society. Even the innocent killing of a man harms the society, but the law generally considers that a severe penalty for

17. See, for a detailed survey, pp. 263–8, and Ziff, 'Recent abortion law reforms', 60 *J. Crim. L.* 3 (1969).
18. See Sayre (1933) *Columbia L. Rev.* 71; Hall (1947, p. 281); Williams (1961, § 81); Schwenk, 'The administrative crime' (1943) 42 *Michigan L. Rev.* 51.

murder or manslaughter should not be imposed, except on proof of individual guilt. Public-welfare offences are, by contrast, essentially standardized. In the balance of values, it is generally considered more essential that violations of traffic rules or food laws should be strictly punished, in the interests of the public, rather than that the degree of individual guilt should be measured in each case. Moreover, a vast proportion of these offences are nowadays imputable to corporations rather than individuals in such areas as social-insurance obligations, safety and health standards, and the like. It is socially entirely desirable that the corporation, under whose name the business is conducted, should be the carrier of responsibility rather than the individual, although the person immediately responsible may, of course, be subject to a concurrent liability. Given the enormous number of offences falling under these categories, such as violations of traffic regulations, there is also the sheer practical difficulty involved in the limitless number of trials, in which individual guilt would have to be measured. On a balance of social interests, the widespread – though by no means universal – tendency of modern statutes to impose strict liability for violation of public-welfare laws is therefore justifiable. There should also be support for the principle proposed by the Model Penal Code of the American Law Institute (section 2.07 (2)), that: 'when absolute liability is imposed for the commission of an offence, a legislative purpose to impose liability on a corporation shall be assumed, unless the contrary plainly appears'.

Such a formulation leaves room for contrary interpretations where they must be reasonably inferred from the wording and spirit of a statute.[19] Attacks against the spread of the strict liability principle for this type of offence have often been based on the ground that the imposition of a relatively small fine, e.g. for the operation of dangerous machinery or the sale of injurious drugs, is in any case

19. See, e.g. the English Sale of Food (Weights and Measures) Act 1926, section 12 (2) which directs the discharge of a defendant, where he can prove 'that such deficiency was due to a bona fide mistake or accident, or other causes beyond his control, and in spite of all reasonable precautions being taken and due diligence exercised by the said defendant to prevent the occurrence of such deficiency, or was due to the action of some person over whom the defendant had no control . . .'

no adequate sanction (Hall, 1947, p. 331).[20] Such criticism seems to misconceive the essentially different character of the sanction imposed in these cases. The purpose is to impose certain standards of conduct in the interest of the community at large, and the maintenance of these standards would be seriously impaired if the individual defence of mistake or blamelessness were generally admitted. This was brought out clearly in a decision of the English Court of Criminal Appeal.[21]

A company whose business comprised the financing of hire-purchase transactions had innocently offended on seven occasions against a statutory order which, to safeguard the currency, had fixed minimum cash payment of 50 per cent for purchases of motor cars. The finance company had been deceived by the car dealer who had stated an inflated price and also falsely informed the finance company that the purchaser had already paid the required 50 per cent. Yet the finance company was convicted (though the nominal fine took account of its bona fides).

The court pointed out that

if Parliament enacts that a certain thing shall not be done it is not necessarily an excuse to say: 'I carry on my business in such a way that I may do this thing unwittingly and therefore should suffer no penalty if I transgress.' The answer in some cases is that the importance of not doing what is prohibited is such that the method of business must be rearranged so as to give the necessary knowledge.

The last-quoted sentence points to the real rationale of the apparent strictness of this type of offence.

The finance company was guiltless in the sense of the traditional criminal law. But it was not entirely blameless in the sense of managerial standards required by this type of public-welfare order. The fraud of the motor-car dealer was not beyond detection. This was not a case of *force majeure*. The finance company could easily

20. The opposite argument against strict liability, i.e. that the imposition of a fine on a shopkeeper or chemist for a statutory offence may have disastrous consequences, is put forward by Edwards (1955, p. 245).
21. *R.* v. *St Margaret's Trust Ltd* (1958) 2 All E.R. 289. For a recent judicial discussion of public-welfare offences see *Lin Chin Aik* v. *The Queen* [1963] A.C. 160, [1963] 1 All E.R. 223; *Sweet* v. *Parsley* [1969] 1 All E.R. 347.

have obtained verified statements, receipts, or affidavits on the relevant aspects of the transaction.

What is emerging in this type of public-welfare offence is a kind of 'negligence without fault' (see p. 165) as it has developed in the law of tort within the conceptual framework of fault liability. Its purpose is to compel business to apply stricter standards of inquiry and control to transactions which may endanger public security. This is a logical and sensible development, provided we recognize the importance of public interest in this type of contravention.

There is, however, a strong case for a clearer delimitation of this type of offence from a traditional and graver type of crime. We are, in fact, here dealing with what is essentially a branch of administrative rather than penal law, which should, consequently, be treated as part of the administrative rather than the penal process. Although the courts have sometimes wavered (Williams, 1961, ss. 76–81; Hall, 1947, p. 327; Edwards, 1955, p. 80), it is not correct in this writer's opinion to argue that 'the key to understanding the public-welfare offences, . . . is that they are designed to catch the wilful and the negligent; they are not intended to penalize those who were faultless' (Hall, 1947, p. 343).[22] The public approach to offences of this kind is, indeed, quite different. It makes a clear distinction between the moral impact of a conviction for fraud and conviction for a typical traffic or foodstuffs offence. This distinction is strongly supported by the most authoritative judicial pronouncement on this subject. In *Morissette* v. *US*,[23] the Supreme Court reversed the conviction for theft of one Morissette – who had collected, flattened and sold spent bomb casings, found on a bombing range, also used for deer hunting. The defendant maintained that he believed the casing to be abandoned, and that he did not intend to steal, but the Court of Appeals had confirmed the conviction on the ground that the relevant statute[24] provides that 'whoever embezzles, steals, purloins or knowingly converts' property of the United States, is guilty without proof of intent. The opinion of the Supreme Court, delivered by Jackson J., stressed the difference between public-welfare offences,

22. For a similar view see Henry M. Hart, 'The aims of the criminal law', 23 *Law and Contemporary Problems* (1958) p. 422.

23. 342 U.S. 246 (1952).

24. 18 U.S.C. § 641.

such as conviction under the Narcotic Drugs Act, for which intent is not required,[25] and the offences 'incorporated from the common law', where, in the absence of express statutory language to the contrary, the requirement of intent as evidence of the will to do evil must be presumed.

There is, on the other hand, great force in Hall's argument that specialized courts, investigatory boards and administrative tribunals should handle public-welfare offences rather than junior criminal courts (1947, p. 352). If this separation from ordinary criminal procedure were effected, the main criticism of such writers as Stallybrass, Sayre, Hall or Edwards, that the public-welfare offence undermines the principle of *mens rea*, would lose its force.

A notable attempt to distinguish the whole field of administrative penalties from that of criminal law is made in the Model Penal Code, prepared for the American Law Institute.[26]

It adds to the traditional categories of felony and misdemeanour – not only a 'petty misdemeanour' for minor crimes, but a new offence called 'violation', which is defined as follows:

An offence defined by this Code or by any other statute of this state constitutes a violation if it is so designated in this Code or in the law defining the offence or if no other sentence than a fine, or fine and forfeiture, or other civil penalty is authorized upon conviction or if it is defined by a statute other than this Code which now provides that the offence shall not constitute a crime. A violation does not constitute a crime and conviction of a violation shall not give rise to any disability or legal disadvantage based on conviction of a criminal offence (§ 104(5)).

The reasons for this innovation are stated in the following words of comment:

There is, however, need for a public sanction calculated to secure enforcement in situations where it would be impolitic or unjust to condemn the conduct involved as criminal. In our view, the proper way to satisfy that need is to use a category of non-criminal offence, for which the sentence authorized upon conviction does not exceed a fine or fine and forfeiture or other civil penalty, such, for example, as the cancellation or suspension of a licence. This plan, it is believed, will serve the legitimate needs of enforcement, without diluting the concept of crime or authorizing the abusive use

25. *US* v. *Behrmann*, 258 U.S. 250 (1922).
26. Proposed Official Draft, § 1.04 (1962).

of sanctions of imprisonment. It should, moreover, prove of great assistance in dealing with the problem of strict liability, a phenomenon of such pervasive scope in modern regulatory legislation. Abrogation of such liability may be impolitic but authorization of a sentence of imprisonment when the defendant, by hypothesis, has acted without fault seems wholly indefensible. Reducing strict liability offences to the grade of violations may, therefore, be the right solution (Comment to § 1.05 (now § 1.04), Tentative Draft No. 2 (1954), pp. 8–9).[27]

While the Model Penal Code does not go into procedural questions, it would be the logical corollary to its proposal to separate jurisdiction for 'civil' from that for 'criminal' offences.

Whatever the specific solution, we have to recognize that a whole new area of law has developed, as a concomitant to the social responsibilities of the modern state, an area to which the principles and procedures of traditional criminal law are only applicable to a very limited extent. That we have to accept an occasional injustice to the individual is part of the price we have to pay for living in a highly mechanized and closely settled kind of society, in which the health, safety, and well-being of each member of the community depends upon a vast number of other persons and institutions.

The Corporation and Criminal Liability

The fact that, today, the corporation is the predominant unit, and therefore the normal defendant, in actions of economic and social impact has a profound effect on this branch of the criminal law. A corporate body is, by the law, equated to a physical individual, but it is not an individual.[28] The characterization of the corporate body as a living organism is a symbolic gesture, even where it is not simply a disguise for the legitimation of omnipotence of the state over the individual. Except for the purely administrative or welfare offence – with which we have dealt in the preceding section – the criminal law appeals to the individual. It can direct itself to the corporate body only by a further process of imputation. Accordingly, the problem of

27. For suggestions of 'civil offences', see also Gausewitz, 12 *Wisconsin L. Rev.* 365 (1937) and Perkins 100 *University of Pennsylvania L. Rev.* 832 (1952).

28. Even in the more extreme versions of the organic theories of corporate personality (on which see Friedmann, 1967, pp. 556–72).

the criminal responsibility of corporations divides itself into several aspects:[29]

First, a clear distinction should be made between vicarious liability of the master for acts of the servant, and imputation of the actions of a person in the employment, or acting on behalf, of the corporation which are properly imputable to the latter. Imputed liability is not vicarious, but original, liability. The principle of vicarious responsibility has been developed in the law of tort, because it has seemed socially and economically necessary to hold the master – and that is in many cases a corporation – liable *vis-à-vis* third parties for acts committed within his sphere of operations. The master is held able to recover against his servant. The law of tort is, however, concerned with the economic adjustment of burdens and risks, and the principle of vicarious liability is applicable to the criminal law only in so far as the criminal law is approximated to the objectives of the law of tort, i.e. where the law is essentially concerned with the enforcement of certain objective standards of conduct, through the imposition of fines, rather than with the individual guilt of a person. This points to the area of strict responsibility which is largely, though not entirely, coextensive with the area of so-called public-welfare offences. For this reason, there has been justified criticism of an English decision[30] where a company was convicted of making false tax returns *with intent to deceive*, the managers of the company having embezzled the proceeds of sales of the company's stock and then made false returns in respect of purchase tax. Since the managers were acting in the course of their employment, vicarious liability in tort would have been entirely justified in this case, but hardly the criminal responsibility which the court imposed.

Secondly, the nature of criminal sanctions imposes certain obvious limitations on the categories of crimes which may be imputed to a corporation. Corporations cannot be executed or imprisoned. This would seem to exclude certain intensely personal offences, such as murder, rape and bigamy, and neither practice nor doctrine has hitherto extended the criminal responsibility of corporations to these

29. For recent illuminating discussions of various parts of this problem, see Williams (1961, para. 281); Welsh 'Criminal Liability of Corporations' (1946) 62 *L.Q.Rev.* 345; Michael and Wechsler (1956 Supp., pp. 159–62).

30. *Moore* v. *Bresler* (1944) 2 All E.R. 515; see Welsh, 62 *L.Q.Rev.* 345 (1946).

offences.[31] This leaves as a principal field of offences (other than public-welfare offences) crimes that arise out of economic dealings. Convictions for criminal offences that involve *mens rea* have, both in England and the United States, occurred mainly in the sphere of thefts, fraudulent dealings, and conspiracies (the latter relating for the most part to conspiracies to defraud or to acts in restraint of trade under the anti-trust laws).[32] Further limitations are indicated by the purpose of punishment. In the case of at least the larger corporations, statutory fines are seldom of a magnitude which would act as an effective deterrent through the suffering of serious financial injury. And the shareholders are usually too far removed, both financially and personally, to suffer effective personal detriment. A shareholder of General Motors does not feel personally affected by even a heavy fine imposed upon the corporation. Nor is he financially hit, since his participation is limited to his shareholding (Wechsler, in Michael and Wechsler, 1956, p. 159). The main effect and usefulness of a criminal conviction imposed upon a corporation cannot be seen either in any personal injury or, in most cases, in the financial detriment, but in the public opprobrium and stigma that attaches to a criminal conviction. Hence, it is particularly important to limit criminal convictions of corporations, for offences other than those which are essentially of an administrative character, to those offences that can properly and fairly expose the corporation to a moral opprobrium.

Third, the rejection of vicarious, as distinct from imputed, liability in the field of criminal law makes it necessary to define the type of relationship which makes it proper to impute the criminal action of an individual to the corporation. The basic criterion for this was laid down many years ago by Viscount Haldane L.C. in a classical passage:

The fault or privity (of the company within the meaning of a statute) is the fault or privity of somebody who is not merely a servant or agent for whom the company is liable upon the footing *respondeat superior*, but somebody

31. See Michael and Wechsler (1956 Supp., p. 161): 'no cases have been found in which a corporation was thought to be held criminally liable for such crimes as murder, treason, rape, or bigamy'.

32. See *I.C.R. Haulage Ltd* [1944] K.B. 551 (C.C.A.); *Moore* v. *Bresler* (1944) 2 All E.R. 515; Michael and Wechsler (1956 Supp., p. 161).

for whom the company is liable because his action is the very action of the company itself.[33]

What Lord Haldane has characterized in this way as the *alter ego* of the corporation is essentially described in the definition of the Model Penal Code suggested by the American Law Institute, by the term 'high managerial agent'. This is defined as

an officer of a corporation or an unincorporated association, or, in the case of a partnership, a partner, or any other agent of a corporation or association having duties of such responsibility that his conduct may fairly be assumed to represent the policy of the corporation or association (Proposed Official Draft, § 2.07 (4)(c) (1962)).

However precise the definition, a measure of discretion will always have to be left to the individual court in the decision whether a given high officer or group of officers or members of a corporation must, in any individual case, be deemed to have represented the corporation as such.

Special questions arise where the offending body is a government or a government-controlled corporation. Can a government be held capable of a criminal offence? If it is, can it be punished by a fine, which, in a sense, the government pays to itself?

These problems arose directly in an interesting Australian decision.[34]

Under the Australian Commonwealth Re-establishment and Employment Act 1945, employers are under a duty to reinstate persons who have completed a certain period of war service in their former employment. A further section provides that they shall not without reasonable cause terminate or vary such employment. Offenders are liable to a penalty of £100, to be imposed by a court of summary jurisdiction. Other sections of the Act provide, for certain other offences, imprisonment not exceeding six months, alternatively or in addition to a penalty. The whole Act is specifically declared binding upon the Crown.

The defendant, who was a manager of a Commonwealth munition factory, was prosecuted before a court of petty sessions in Victoria for unlawful termination of the plaintiff's employment. Conviction

33. *Lennard's Carrying Co. Ltd* v. *Asiatic Petroleum Co. Ltd* [1915], A.C., p. 713.
34. *Cain* v. *Doyle* 72 *Crim. L. Rev.* 409 (1946).

was possible only under section 5 of the Commonwealth Crimes Act, which provides that 'any person who procures or by any act of commission is in any way directly or indirectly knowingly concerned in or party to any offence against any law of the Commonwealth, shall be deemed to have committed that offence, and shall be punishable accordingly'.

The conviction of the manager, a servant, was dependent upon his being an accessory to an offence committed by the Crown. Although the High Court decided by a bare majority to confirm the order of the magistrate dismissing the information, the majority of the judges did not reject the possibility of the Crown being convicted for a criminal offence.

Only the Chief Justice (Latham C.J.) dismissed the idea that the Crown might commit a criminal offence as unacceptable in principle. His objections were, first, that the fundamental idea of the criminal law is a prosecution of offences against the King's peace; secondly, that the Crown itself would have to be a prosecutor in the case of serious offences; thirdly, that the Commonwealth would have to pay a fine to itself; and fourthly, that where imprisonment was at least an alternative penalty, the Crown could not be included as it could not be imprisoned. The other judges considered the criminal conviction of the Crown at least theoretically possible, though two of them formed a majority with the Chief Justice in rejecting the conviction in the particular case.

At a time when government departments and many independent corporations, directly or indirectly controlled by the government, assume an increasing variety of functions and responsibilities in the social and economic life of nations, the exemption of either government or government corporations from criminal liability generally is neither morally nor technically justified. As we have seen, the main purpose of a fine is not primarily to hurt the defendant financially.

It is to attach a stigma – pronounced by independent law courts – on the breach of legal obligations which have been imposed in the interest of the community. If a modern giant industrial concern is fined for a statutory offence, this does not normally hurt an individual. But an accumulation of such convictions will deservedly impair the standing and reputation of such a concern.

In the case of the British statutory public corporations formed in the process of nationalization of basic industries after the Second World War there is in fact no doubt that they are liable to be fined for statutory offences.

Moreover, private corporations have been quite frequently convicted of offences, for which imprisonment is provided, even though it cannot be inflicted on a corporation.[35]

Modern Science and the Responsibility of the Individual

We have so far outlined some of the impacts of the changing structures of contemporary society, on the ambit of criminal law, the purposes of punishment, and the partial displacement of *mens rea* by strict liability for certain types of offences of an essentially regulatory and administrative character. These are, as it were, changes from without.

It remains to examine some of the subtler but no less important changes brought about or adumbrated by contemporary scientific research into the structure of the human being. Modern psychology has explored the complex web of instincts and the area of the unconscious, and its impact on human behaviour. This has led to a reexamination of the causes of criminal behaviour, and the various degrees of mental abnormality. More recently, biological research – and more particularly modern genetics – has led to the discovery and isolation of man's genetic structure, which determines his character and behaviour. From this, we are about to pass to the next phase, described as 'genetic engineering'. This comprises various methods by which it may be possible to alter or determine the genetic structure of human beings, so as to eliminate or add certain characteristics. These developments may profoundly affect the traditional bases of moral and legal responsibility.

Modern Psychology, Control over Behaviour and the Criminal Law

In the approach to a generally condemned act, such as murder, rape or arson, the legal system may go from the one extreme of penalizing

35. The above criticism of *Cain's* case, made in more detail in *Law and Social Change in Contemporary Britain* (p. 102), has been endorsed by Williams (1961, § 282).

the act as such, without regard to subjective factors in the individual offender, to the other extreme of complete individualization, i.e. taking each individual as a composite of moral and intellectual faculties, genetic factors, social environment. Ultimately, this is a question of values, of the balancing between the interest in the safety and vigour of the community, and the consideration of the individual as a person. In no field has the conflict of these values been more dramatically, and often tragically, tested than in the treatment of insanity or mental deficiency. Persons thus afflicted are unquestionably a burden to society. And just as the Spartans killed by exposure weakling children so as not to impair the martial vigour of their state, so in recent times 'the suggestion has sometimes been made that the insane murderer should be punished equally with the sane, or that, although he ought not to be executed as a punishment, he should be painlessly exterminated as a measure of social hygiene'.[36] Such doctrines commended themselves to Nationalist Socialist Germany, which practised the extermination, confinement or sterilization of whole groups of people, considered as inferior, objectionable or useless, on a large scale. Overwhelmingly, the tradition of civilized nations, and of the criminal law, has been to take account of weaknesses of the individual as a defence against criminal prosecution, or at least in mitigation of punishment. But while some modern legal systems have gone a long way towards substituting alternative social sanctions for punishment, in the case of insane or mentally deficient persons as well as of juveniles, first offenders, and other special categories, none has held it possible to abolish the criminal law as a major and vital instrument of protection of society. Hence, the question remains at what point the borderline should be drawn, by what criteria criminal responsibility should be measured.

For more than a century, the basic test in the common-law jurisdictions has been supplied by the 'M'Naghten Rules', laid down by the House of Lords in the case of Daniel M'Naghten.[37] The essence of the directions given by the judges in that case to juries and for cases where the defence of insanity is raised is contained in the following passage:

36. Report of the Royal Commission on Capital Punishment, 1949–53, HMSO, Cmd 8932, hereafter cited as 'Report'.
37. (1843) 4 *St. Tr.* (N.S.) 847.

The jury ought to be told in all cases that every man is presumed to be sane, and to possess a sufficient degree of reason to be responsible for his crimes, until the contrary be proved to their satisfaction; and that, to establish a defence on the ground of insanity, it must be clearly proved that, at the time of the committing of the act, the party accused was labouring under such a defect of reason, from disease of the mind, as not to know the nature and quality of the act he was doing, or, if he did know it that he did not know he was doing what was wrong.

This test – adopted throughout the British Commonwealth and almost universally in the United States[38] – rests on the criterion of knowledge. It assumes that a person who intellectually apprehends the distinction between the right and wrong of a given conduct must be held criminally responsible. As such, it was soon attacked, above all by members of the medical profession, but also by some eminent lawyers (Stephen, 1883, vol. 2, p. 157), on the ground that 'insanity does not only, or primarily, affect the cognitive or intellectual faculties, but affects the whole personality of the patient, including both the will and the emotions' (Report, p. 80). As long ago as 1870, it was abandoned in the state of New Hampshire,[39] in favour of the test whether the accused 'had the capacity to entertain a criminal intent – whether, in point of fact, he did entertain such intent'. In the light of modern psychiatric developments, criminological science and changing conceptions of guilt, the criticism has assumed overwhelming proportions in recent years, both in England and the United States.[40] The gravamen of these criticisms can be summed up in the following formulation of an eminent American criminologist:

These tests proceed upon the following questionable assumptions of an outworn era in psychiatry: (1) that lack of knowledge of the 'nature or quality' of an act (assuming the meaning of such terms to be clear), or incapacity to know right from wrong, is the sole or even the most important symptom of mental disorder; (2) that such knowledge is the sole instigator and guide of conduct, or at least the most important element

38. See the survey in the Report, p. 105.

39. *State* v. *Pike*, 1870, 49 N.H. 399; *State* v. *Jones*, 1871, 50 N.H. 369.

40. For surveys, see Report, Sections 263 et seq., and, in regard to the law and practice in other countries, Section 298, 2307. See also the references in *Durham* v. *United States*, 214 F. 2d 862 (D.C.Cir. 1954), and further Michael and Wechsler (1956 Supp., pp. 187–209).

therein, and consequently should be the sole criterion of responsibility when insanity is involved; and (3) that the capacity of knowing right from wrong can be completely intact and functioning perfectly even though a defendant is otherwise demonstrably of disordered mind.[41]

In other words, a person must be seen in his entirety, and the faculty of reason, which is only one element in that personality, is not the sole determinant of his conduct.[42]

There is far less agreement on the alternative. It is almost universally conceded that some persons, who are perfectly capable of intellectually distinguishing between right and wrong, are yet driven to commit a criminal act by forces outside their control. This makes it improper to hold them criminally accountable in a legal system that bases criminal liability on personal responsibility. A widely accepted alternative, at least as a supplement to the M'Naghten Rules, has been the test of 'irresistible impulse'.[43] But a recent thorough investigation of the problem by a British Royal Commission, which, by a large majority, favoured the abolition or modification of the M'Naghten Rules, has described the concept of the 'irresistible impulse' as 'largely discredited' and as 'inherently inadequate and unsatisfactory'.

The real objection to the term 'irresistible impulse' is that it is too narrow, and carries an unfortunate and misleading implication that, where a crime is committed as a result of emotional disorder due to insanity, it must have been suddenly and impulsively committed after a sharp internal conflict. In many cases, such as those of melancholia, this is not true at all. The sufferer from this disease experiences a change of mood which alters the whole of his existence. He may believe, for instance, that a future of such degradation and misery awaits both him and his family that death for all is a less dreadful alternative. Even the thought that the acts he contemplates are murder and suicide pales into insignificance in contrast with what he otherwise expects. The criminal act, in such circumstances, may

41. Sheldon Glueck, 'Psychiatry and the criminal law', 12 *Mental Hygiene* 575, 580 (1928) as quoted in *Durham* v. *U.S.*, 214 F. 2d 862 (D.C.Cir. 1954).

42. *Durham* v. *U.S.*, 214 F. 2d 862 (D.C.Cir. 1954).

43. e.g. *Smith* v. *U.S.*, 36 F. 2d 548 (1929): 'In cases where insanity is interposed as a defence, and the facts are sufficient to call for the application of the rule of irresistible impulse, the jury should be so charged'. And see the various conflicting views of witnesses before the Royal Commission, Report, sections 264–70.

be the reverse of impulsive. It may be coolly and carefully prepared; yet it is still the act of a madman (Report, section 314).[44]

Instead, a powerful trend in modern psychiatric and legal opinion favours the adoption of a broader test, which correlates criminal liability with the capacity of the individual to control his conduct in conformity with the requirements of the law. Thus, a widely discussed decision of the United States Court of Appeals for the District of Columbia has formulated the rule 'that an accused is not criminally responsible if his unlawful act was the product of mental disease or mental defect'.[45] The majority report of the British Royal Commission suggests that:

the jury must be satisfied that at the time of committing the act, the accused, as a result of disease of the mind or mental deficiency, (a) did not know the nature and quality of the act or (b) did not know that it was wrong or (c) was incapable of preventing himself from committing it (Report, para. 317).

A smaller majority preferred to abolish the M'Naghten Rules altogether 'and leave the jury to determine whether at the time of the act the accused was suffering from disease of the mind or mental deficiency to such a degree that he ought not to be held responsible'.

The Model Penal Code, prepared by the American Law Institute, suggests the following formulation:

1. A person is not responsible for criminal conduct if at the time of such conduct as a result of mental disease or defect he lacks substantial capacity either to appreciate the criminality [wrongfulness] of his conduct or to conform his conduct to the requirements of law.
2. As used in this Article, the terms 'mental disease or defect' do not include an abnormality manifested only by repeated criminal or otherwise anti-social conduct.[46]

It should be noted that all these formulations not only supplement

44. This criticism was specially endorsed in *Durham* v. *U.S.* (see n. 40).

45. *Durham* v. *US*, 214 F. 2nd 862 (1954). This test has, however, been rejected in subsequent decisions of other US Appeal Courts, which felt bound by the 'right and wrong test' adopted by the *US Supreme Court* in *Davis* v. *U.S.*, 165 *U.S.* 373 (1897), but also doubted the correctness of the Durham test (e.g. *Sauer* v. *U.S.* (1957) 241 F. 2d 640; see also *Andersen* v. *U.S.*, 237 F. 2d 118 (1956)).

46. Proposed Official Draft, § 4.01 (1962). The Model Penal Code formulation has so far been adopted by eight states and by eight of the federal courts of appeals.

the purely intellectual appreciation of right and wrong of the M'Naghten Rules by a test of control over conduct as a guide for criminal responsibility, but that they also accept the findings of modern psychiatry in regard to mental 'disease' or 'deficiency', in addition to insanity. Mental deficiency generally connotes an 'intellectual defect, or defect of understanding, existing from birth or from an early age' (Report, p. 117). Mental abnormality is a more comprehensive concept, but it is mainly concerned with two categories of abnormal persons who are neither insane nor mentally deficient: epileptics and psychopaths. It is the latter category that forms probably the main preoccupation of modern psychiatrists, but is also the most difficult to define. It comprises a vast variety of persons who, for emotional reasons, stand, permanently or temporarily, to a greater or lesser extent apart from the 'normal' member of society.

The almost infinite variety of psychopathic disturbances,[47] and the still continuing and widening scope of psychiatric study of mental disturbances adds to the complexity of the problem. The M'Naghten Rules not only greatly oversimplify the problem of criminal responsibility by the 'right and wrong' test, but they also leave nothing between black and white, no intermediate stage between responsibility and irresponsibility (Report, appendix 9, p. 413). The doctrine of diminished responsibility was universally rejected in the law of England and in the common-law jurisdictions of the Commonwealth, until England accepted it for homicide in a recent statutory reform.[48] In the United States the position is somewhat obscure.[49] On the other

---

See *Blake* v. *United States*, 407 F. 2d 908, 913–16 (1969); Wechsler, 'Codification of criminal law in the United States: the Model Penal Code', 68 *Columbia L. Rev.* 1425, 1441–4 (1968). Professor Wechsler states that there is 'reason to believe that it may ultimately become the prevailing rule in the United States'.

47. See the ten types classified by Schneider as described in the Report, Section 396.

48. Homicide Act 1957, section 2. This was contrary to the recommendation of the Royal Commission. The defence of diminished responsibility has gradually but steadily replaced the insanity defence in murder cases (Walker, 1967, pp. 158–61).

49. In cases of homicide, some American jurisdictions have accepted mental abnormality as justifying a reduction from first degree to second degree murder, e.g. *People* v. *Moran*, 249 N.Y. 179, 163 N.E. 553 (1928), but a majority of the cases dealing with these questions have rejected the test. See the Brief for the United States in *Fischer* v. *U.S.*, 328 U.S. 463, 747 (1945).

hand, the law of Scotland, in regard to murder, and a number of Continental legal systems, have long accepted the doctrine of diminished responsibility as enabling the courts to mitigate the penalty. Perhaps, the most representative formulation is that of the Penal Code of Switzerland:

1. The administrative authority of the Canton will put into effect the judge's decision ordering detention, treatment or removal to hospital of offenders not responsible or only partially responsible for their actions.
2. The competent authority will order the termination of detention, treatment or confinement to hospital as soon as the reason for it no longer exists.

The judge will decide if and to what extent the sentence passed on an offender only partially responsible for his actions is then to be carried out (Article 17).

Clearly, the development in modern psychiatry which, between the fully normal and the fully abnormal person, recognizes an infinite variety of shades of disturbances lessening, to a varying degree, the emotional powers and capacities of self-control rather than intellectual discernment, calls for a corresponding elasticity in the legal approach to the problem of responsibility. But this very development makes it very difficult to devise precise legal formulas, by either statutory or judicial legislation. Any attempt to elaborate a series of new additional criteria, superimposed on the M'Naghten test, in correspondence with the many types and grades of mental disturbance, would lead to casuistry and a multitude of interpretations by different judges and juries. Hence, the above-quoted reform proposals of the British Royal Commission, of the American Model Penal Code, and others, suggest broad formulae correlating responsibility to control. It would seem not only logical but indispensable to extend this approach to the concept of 'diminished responsibility' as it has, by general consent, operated to general satisfaction in Scotland and in many Continental countries (where it is extended from murder to any criminal offence). In the evidence presented to the Royal Commission, preparatory to its Report, the British Medical Association suggested a reform to the effect that:

when a jury find that an accused person, at the time of committing the act, was labouring, as a result of disease of the mind, under a defect of reason or a disorder of emotion to such an extent as not to be fully accountable for his actions, they shall return a verdict of 'guilty with diminished responsibility' (Report, p. 93, section 264).

The introduction of such a flexible standard would add to the individualization of each case, in the light of the medical evidence presented, and the estimate given in the judge's direction and the jury's verdict. It is clear that any solution compatible with modern thinking will place a wide measure of discretion, and a great burden of responsibility, on the court, But it has hardly been different under the M'Naghten Rules, for the decision whether a person is capable of distinguishing between right and wrong is no less arduous and difficult a task for a court than the proposed more general tests of control and responsibility. It is, however, as we have seen, entirely out of tune with modern scientific and social thought. The modern formulations give greater scope and proper weight to expert evidence on matters which call for scientific scrutiny.

Because of the inherent difficulty of finding any test that will not leave a great measure of individual discretion in the hands of the court, a good many critics have suggested the abandonment of the M'Naghten Rules altogether, without the substitution of an alternative legal formula,[50] so that the jury would be left to determine in any individual case whether the accused ought to be held responsible or not. This is a realistic recognition of the fact that, under the guise of a directing formula, judges and juries have, in fact, given widely varying interpretations to the rule.[51]

50. e.g. a minority of the Royal Commission, Report, section 333, and Memorandum of Dissent at p. 285.
51. See the reply given by an eminent Scottish judge, Lord Cooper, when asked whether it was not desirable to have some yardstick to guide the jury: 'I do not think so, for this reason. . . . However much you charge a jury as to the M'Naghten Rules or any other test, the question they would put to themselves when they retire is – "Is this man mad or is he not?".' There was, in fact, considerable divergence of opinion among legal witnesses as to whether the M'Naghten Rules were, in practice, applied at all. The degree of elasticity left under the cover of a legal formula induced many of the most influential legal witnesses before the Royal Commission, such as the Lord Chief Justice of England and the Director of Public Prosecutions, to counsel against any alteration of the Rules at all (Report, section 268). However there is evidence to indicate that juries respond differently to different legal standards of criminal responsibility. For analysis of jury responses to M'Naghten and Durham Rules, and to the absence of instructions on criminal responsibility see Simon (1967, pp. 66–77).

These tests do not, of course, pretend to give anything but a broad guide for an individual decision of a court or, as the case may be, of an administrative authority. As the Report of the British Royal Commission observed wisely,

that a criterion of criminal responsibility is not necessarily to be rejected because it is imperfect and cannot be guaranteed to cover every case which it ought to cover. All legal definitions necessarily involve an element of abstraction and approximation, which may make their application difficult in marginal cases and may reasonably exclude cases which ought to be included; this is inevitable, since it is precisely the function of the law to draw clear lines for general guidance where there is no clear line in nature, and to deal with the difficulties and anomalies inherent in borderline cases by preserving a reasonable flexibility of interpretation (Report, section 325).

Modern legal theory has long recognized that general legal formulae could not or should not try to dispense with the individualizing application of justice to the case at hand. It is nevertheless of vital importance that the general directive should be in broad harmony with contemporary rather than outdated philosophy, morality and social thought.

Yet, a translation of modern medical insight into law, the acceptance of the complexity of the human being, the understanding of the many forces and emotions that struggle in the breast of a human being and produce an almost infinite scale of variations, from 'normality' to 'abnormality', in turn raises serious problems. '*Tout comprendre, c'est tout pardonner.*' Somewhere, society must draw the borderline and hold a person guilty of a crime, even though psychiatrists may regard the offender as a very disturbed human being, and philosophers may deny the 'free will' to choose between right and wrong. Many of those who would be held not responsible for their actions under the amended M'Naghten Rule are unquestionably individuals highly dangerous to society, usually with a long record of dangerous actions.[52] The alternative is inevitably between punishment and compulsory confinement to an institution for the care of mentally disturbed people. Where execution is ruled out, either because capital punishment has been abolished or is not applied, or because the defendant has been found 'guilty but insane', the choice is between the overcrowding of two sets of institutions, both of them

52. e.g. the accused in *Durham* v. *US* (note 44).

inadequate, quantitatively and qualitatively, in the great majority of modern states. Above all, it is still the overwhelming opinion of modern criminologists and sociologists that punishment for the criminal is an essential outlet in modern, as in earlier, societies (Flügel, 1945, p. 168; Reiwald, 1950). These needs of society might be threatened beyond danger point if the concept of 'mental defect' or 'mental disease' were stretched too far – if it were, for example, extended to the case of Mr Dallas O'Williams (*New Yorker*, 19 April 1958, p. 85), who, between 1932 and 1958, had been arrested more than a hundred times, convicted of eleven major crimes, ranging from assault to homicide. He had been judged criminally insane, but when committed to a mental institution, the psychiatrists were unable to find any evidence of mental disease or defect, other than propensity for crimes of violence. But if propensity for crime comes to be recognized as a mental disease as such, without any additional element indicating incapacity of the minimum degree of reasoning or control sufficient to prevent the commission of a crime, the way is open not only for a far-reaching frustration of the process of criminal justice, but for the obliteration of the borderlines of criminal law altogether.

Genetic Engineering and the Responsibility of the Individual[53]

Forty years ago, Aldous Huxley, in his *Brave New World*, forecast a human society composed of alpha, beta and gamma types, pre-determined by test-tube selection. Reality is rapidly catching up with this fantasy.[54] In 1959, a leading geneticist and Nobel Prize winner, H. J. Muller, suggested that reproduction should be regulated by the fertilization of stored genes collected from outstanding individuals, and that such genes should be substituted for the female genes in the fertilized ovum (*New York Times*, 2 December 1959). As the same authority suggested shortly after[55] the coordination of

53. For a more comprehensive discussion of the problems surveyed in the following section, see Friedmann, 'Interference with human life: some juris-prudential reflections', 70 *Columbia L. Rev.* 1058 (1970).

54. Just as the political structure of contemporary society is showing some ominous resemblances to the society pictured in George Orwell's *1984*.

55. In a symposium on 'Evolution and man's progress', *Daedalus*, Summer 1961 pp. 432–500.

cultural and biological evolution should control a general extension of artificial insemination to human reproduction. The fertilization of selected female eggs with chosen sperm, subsequently implanted in selected female hosts

would permit the multiple distribution of eggs of a highly selected female into diverse recipient females, and when so desired it would enable the child to be derived on its paternal side from the recipient's husband. Possibly, two techniques involving mature eggs could be combined with deep freezing to allow indefinitely prolonged storage.

Although Professor Muller's belief that, through the control of reproduction by selected genes – from the likes of Beethoven, Lincoln or Einstein – could progress toward a higher intellectual and moral level, was not shared by a majority of the other eminent discussants,[56] the day when the genetic predetermination of human beings will be practicable, is steadily coming nearer. In a symposium held in 1968 (*New York Times*, 27 December 1968), Dr Blackler of Cornell University described the now well-documented experiments in which the nucleus from the skin cell of an adult frog was inserted into an unfertilized frog egg from which the original nucleus had been extracted. This altered egg developed into a normal frog, genetically identical with the frog from which the transplanted nucleus was taken. Dr Blackler perceived no insuperable barrier to the extension of this technique from frogs to mammals and observed that 'Einstein could be rendered in model, while sterile women could bear children, and handicapped children could be born again'. The search into the chemical structure of the gene, which is the determining qualitative factor in the chromosome chain, proceeds all the time.[57] Studies are being pursued to determine to what extent the presence of an extra chromosome (xyy instead of xy) may affect proclivity to criminal behaviour. In February 1970, a British gynaecologist and scientists at Cambridge collaborated in techniques of removing egg cells from a woman's ovary, and fertilizing a human

56. See *Daedulus*, Summer 1961, for the comments of R. S. Morison, pp. 452–3, and Theodosius Dobzhansky, pp. 461–3.

57. In June 1970 a team of University of Wisconsin scientists headed by Dr Gobind Khorana reported that they had succeeded in synthesizing the structure of the DNA molecule that constitutes the yeast gene.

egg outside the body, to be followed by implantation of a fertilised egg in a woman's uterus (*Economist*, 28 February 1970, p. 18).

The methods of genetic manipulation briefly described here represent no more than the most advanced samples of many different ways of influencing the genetic makeup of mankind. Experiments with the isolation of the gene point to the possibility of altering the pattern of the DNA which controls heredity. Professor Edward Tatum has termed these possibilities 'gene deletion, gene insertion and gene surgery' (Taylor, 1968, p. 171).[58]

As these experiments progress and the possibilities of genetic predetermination and standardization become more concrete, our whole concept of individual responsibility may be affected.

As a leading demographer, Professor Kingsley Davis, has observed.

An effective system of eugenic control would involve profound changes in the very web of relations that organizes and expresses the personal lives of moderns. It would overthrow the existing system of emotional rewards and punishments, the present interpretations of reality, the familiar links between the person and social status (Taylor, 1968, p. 181).

Regardless of the variety of legal and social systems that have controlled humanity, the implicit basis of any legal order is the individuality of man. Principles of responsibility may be, and have been, profoundly modified by the conditions of modern urbanization and industrialization. Tort liability is being replaced increasingly by insurance; criminal liability is giving way, at least to some extent, to administrative controls. Legal principles need constant reappraisal in the light of changing social conditions. But the manipulation and indeed the manufacture of human beings according to certain predetermined standards would sweep away the foundations of all

58. Taylor's book is a very helpful survey of the many more or less developed possibilities of genetic engineering. Among the developments which the author considers as technically achievable by 1975 are the following: extensive transplantation of limbs and organs; test-tube fertilization of human eggs; implantation of fertilized eggs in womb; indefinite storage of eggs and spermatozoa; choice of sex of offspring; extensive power to postpone clinical death; mind-modifying drugs; regulation of desire; memory erasure; imperfect artificial placenta; and artificial viruses.

human history. It may become necessary to evolve differential standards of conduct – and, correspondingly – different categories and sanctions of criminality according to genetic types. Although an eminent Australian scientist, Sir Macfarlane Burnet (Taylor, 1968, p. 175), has warned that there are dangers in knowing what should 'not be known', it is far more likely that knowledge which can be turned to somebody's purpose, will be exploited.

Changing Purposes of Punishment

Generally, the philosophy of deterrence still prevails in modern criminology. We continue to be concerned with preventing, by appropriate punitive sanctions, both the individual offender and other members of society from the repetition of crime, or the imitation on the part of others by similar actions. But the contemporary approach to the best way of achieving this general objective has undergone a profound transformation. We are no longer certain that the harshest punishment is necessarily the best way of preventing repetition of the offence. Where we have to concede that the severest possible punishment – execution – will certainly prevent the particular criminal from committing this, or any other, offence again, we are no longer sure that this '*Spezialprävention*' will also have the effect of '*Generalprävention*', i.e. that it will reduce the proportion of capital offences in the body politic. In the continuing controversy about capital punishment, one of the most powerful arguments of those who advocate the abolition of the death penalty is that 'there is no clear evidence . . . that the abolition of capital punishment has led to an increase in the homicide rate, or that its reintroduction has led to a fall' (Report on the Royal Commission on Capital Punishment 1953, section 65).[59]

When, as must be generally accepted in the light of recent thorough investigations, the statistical evidence does not support, for example, capital punishment on the ground of deterrence, the problem comes back to one of basic theory. Here, the older philosophies of retri-

59. See also for a thorough comparative statistical survey, Appendix 6 ('The deterrent value of capital punishment') in the same Report. See also Buxton, 'Murder 1957 to 1968', 33 *Mod. L. Rev.* 302 (1970).

bution – in its various shades (Report, sections 50–61) are increasingly inadequate although they continue to be supported by some eminent theologians, jurists and others.[60] Modern civilized society has, in general, receded more and more from this philosophy of 'an eye for an eye, a tooth for a tooth'. The reason is for some, but only a minority, a revulsion against the arrogation by society of the right to take the life of a human being, a view which could be held consistently only by radical pacifists, and hardly by the great majority who justify killing *en masse* in case of war by order of the state. A more practical reason is the danger of an irretrievable error of justice. Both these arguments apply, of course, only to capital punishment, and not to the theory of punishment in general. What is of far greater importance to the theory of punishment as applicable to all major offences is the progress of social science in a manner parallel to that of modern psychology and psychiatry. We are far from having an exact estimate of the facts which modern urbanization and industrialization, with all the social disruption they entail, have on the rate of crime. We do, however, know beyond reasonable doubt that such factors as congregation of large families and, especially, juveniles in overcrowded slums have a considerable effect on delinquency, as has the diversion of vast numbers of married women in modern industrialized societies from domestic care to paid employment, or the disruption of family ties in estranged families. Individual and social psychology touch each other, when it comes to an appreciation of the effect of social environment or emotional upsets, in family, school, or elsewhere, on the mental balance and health of an individual. The more we understand of the complex web of conditions that go

60. See, for example, the sternly moralistic view expressed by Lord Justice Denning (as he then was) in his evidence before the Commission – contrasting with the same eminent judge's progressive views in regard to the M'Naghten Rules, or the matrimonial relationships, and the function of law in social change in general: 'The punishment inflicted for grave crimes should adequately reflect the revulsion felt by the great majority of citizens for them. It is a mistake to consider the objects of punishment as being deterrent or reformative or preventive and nothing else. . . . The ultimate justification of any punishment is not that it is a deterrent, but that it is the emphatic denunciation by the community of a crime: and from this point of view, there are some murders which, in the present state of public opinion, demand the most emphatic denunciation of all, namely the death penalty.' See also the similar view expressed by the then Archbishop of Canterbury. For a defence of the retributive argument see Hart (1968).

into the makeup of a person, the less can we accept the simple equations of sin and expiation, offence and retribution, and the like. But we are also faced again, as in the more specialized case of the mentally disturbed individual, with the problem of the proper balance.

Generally speaking, the increasing understanding of the social and psychological causes of crime has led to a growing emphasis on *reformation* rather than deterrence in the older sense, as the best way to protect both the individual criminal from himself, and society from the incidence of crime. In practical terms, this has meant the increasing use of corrective and educational measures, either in addition to, or in substitution for, punishment proper. The consideration of such alternatives has gradually spread from specialized categories of offenders to criminal offenders in general.

In the case of persons adjudged insane – whether before trial, at the beginning of the trial (insane on arraignment), as the result of evidence during the trial (special verdict), or after sentence – it is obvious that alternative detention or care must be provided for, in the interest both of the individual and of society. This must be extended, as the categories of these persons widens from the 'insane' in the older sense to others adjudged 'mentally disturbed' or 'mentally deficient'. Various procedures for caring for the mentally ill prisoner are provided for in the English Mental Health Act 1959 (Walker, 1965, pp. 263–94).

A revolution of far greater proportion has, during the last generation, taken place in the treatment of juvenile offenders. Almost universally today, in civilized countries, the juvenile offender (usually a person between the ages of eight and eighteen), who not so long ago used to be subjected to the harshest penalties and thrown together with hardened criminals – is now subjected to a special procedure. The predominant pattern is that of the juvenile court – as introduced, during the last half century in England, Germany, the great majority of the American states and many other countries – a court which differs radically, in procedure and the type of sanctions to be imposed upon the offender, from the ordinary criminal court. Probation and approved schools have become the substitute for imprisonment. A number of modern legal systems have gone further and removed the sanction power altogether from the courts, putting it instead into the hands of the child-welfare authorities.[61] In California the powers of the youth authority have been extended further. This authority now has power to deal with children below the age of juvenile criminality, and to mete out treatment in accordance with the diagnosis of their position.

From the juvenile offender, the substitution of corrective measures for punishment proper has spread to the adult offender. The principal emphasis is on probation for first offenders, as a conditional alternative to punishment.

But emphasis on the need for corrective measures is not confined to the first offender. At the other end of the scale, the recidivist, the habitual offender, is becoming increasingly the object of attention of modern penology. In the case of a first offender, it is felt that corrective measures of an educational and a reformative character will serve to deter him from further offences.[62] This approach follows in the footsteps of the pioneer work of Sheldon and Eleanor Glueck on juvenile delinquency, which has included a social prediction scale for proneness to delinquency.[63]

It is not our purpose to analyse and compare in detail the multitude of educational, corrective and preventive measures that, in a growing number of countries are now applied not only to mentally disturbed persons, juveniles, first offenders, but to all criminals. What emerges as a highly significant and critical fact is the increasing intermingling of the criminal and the administrative process in the modern science

61. Notably the Scandinavian countries and, following the proposal of the American Law Institute in 1940, California, Wisconsin and Minnesota. See also the recent British legislation, Children and Young Persons Act 1969, pt 1; Social Work (Scotland) Act, pt III.

62. The steady progress in scientific measurement of the factors on the basis of which the probability of the commission of further offences by those committed to corrective institutions can be predicted, is shown by the work by Mannheim and Wilkins (1955). From the dossiers of 700 juveniles sentenced to Borstal training, some sixty background factors were obtained, and their relationship to subsequent conduct was measured. From these data, a small number of significant factors were isolated, and from these a prediction table of behaviour for new cases was calculated, which is reported to have proved nearly four times as accurate as the opinion of Borstal governors and housemasters (Gardiner, 'The purposes of criminal punishment', 21 *Mod. L. Rev.* 221, 224 (1958)).

63. See Sheldon and Eleanor Glueck, *Unravelling Juvenile Delinquency*, and the analysis by Thompson in *British Journal of Delinquency*, vol. 3 (1953), p. 289.

and practice of the criminal law. That the criminal offender is no longer seen as an isolated and guilty individual who, at a given moment, is brought before a court, duly sentenced by whatever term appears appropriate to the court within the often fantastically wide range of maximum and minimum penalties and then disappears forever from the sight of the judicial authorities, represents an evolution in the legal thinking on crime from which there can be no retreat. In a properly administered and enlightened modern legal system, the process, in which welfare, administrative and criminal process elements are mixed, starts when the welfare of a child that lacks proper family care and attention, or otherwise shows symptoms that might, in the future, turn him into a criminal, is taken over by the appropriate public authority.[64] It continues when – either despite such measures or in their absence – a juvenile offender comes before a special juvenile court, which increasingly operates as an educational and corrective authority with judicial attributes. From there, adminstrative and welfare authorities take over again, in the shape of the probation officer, child-welfare board, youth authority and of the various official institutions to which the juvenile offender is remanded in lieu of punishment. To these must be added a variety of medical, social and educational experts who enter the process at some stage. Obviously, the old borderlines are becoming less distinct, and it is often uncertain at what stage the criminal process stops and the administrative process begins.

This vital and needed change raises, however, in its turn, some grave problems. In the first place, there must be a degree of coordination between the judicial authorities proper, i.e. the judge and jury, or the judge alone, and the various welfare and administrative authorities, which is still often lacking. This appears to be particularly true of the length of prison sentences, which often bears no relation either to the social usefulness of the sentence imposed, or to the administrative facilities available either in prisons or in other institutions.[65] It is probably still true – as it was certainly not so long

64. See, for example, the English Children Act 1948; Children and Young Persons Act 1969. For a comparison of the Scandinavian and Californian systems see Nyquist (1960).

65. For statistics on the distribution of prison sentences by length see *People in Prison* (Home Office, 1969).

ago – that a majority of the judges have never visited a prison or one of the other institutions now figuring in the punitive process.

Secondly, the distribution of functions between judicial authorities and various administrative and welfare officers emphasizes the need for adequate training and social and professional status of the latter, especially of the probation service, a relatively recent but vitally important institution. The change from a purely repressive to an educative function also emphasizes the need for properly trained prison officers, whose arduous lot must be balanced by adequate recognition in the social and financial scale. This, too, is far from being the case.[66]

Lastly, and perhaps, most important, the blurring of the border-lines between the criminal and the administrative procedure holds not only benefits, but also dangers for the effect on the individual. The administrative process is in its essence discretionary, whereas criminal procedure has, at least in the democratic scheme of values, been surrounded with safeguards against arbitrariness.

As corrective and educational procedures have become inter-mingled with criminal or quasi-criminal processes, so the fear has grown that benevolent but autocratic authority may be able to deprive persons falling under its jurisdiction of liberty, for indefinite periods, without the judicial safeguards attending criminal trial. Criticism has been particularly vociferous in states which, like California, have gone far in the substitution of corrective for criminal procedures in regard to juvenile offenders. The title of an article,[67] is: 'We need not deny justice to our children', while a California judge has written that the juvenile court is 'fast developing into a complete system of Fascism, as dangerous to our institutions as Communism'.[68] Such complaints are based on the vagueness or

66. See, e.g. US National Commission on the Causes and Prevention of Violence, *Law and Order Reconsidered*, ch. 24: 'Problems of corrective systems'. This was tragically underlined by the revolt in New York State's Attica Prison in September 1971 which led to the intervention of state police and the death of forty-three persons, one quarter of them prison guards. Inadequate pay and training of the guards, as well as the physical conditions of this 'corrective institution', were generally held to be major factors in the massacre.

67. Civil Liberties Record of the Greater Philadelphia Branch, A.C.L.U., Feb. 1956.

68. Olney, 'Juvenile courts: abolish them', 13 *California State B.J.* 1, 2 (1938).

elasticity in the procedure of a juvenile court in regard to such essential safeguards as the powers of the police to arrest, the precise formulation of the offence, the right to trial by jury, the right to refuse testimony, the acceptance of hearsay evidence, or the right to counsel.[69] Some of these objections were met in *In re Gault*, which held that a defendant in juvenile proceedings was entitled to, *inter alia*, a right to counsel.[70]

Similar fears have been voiced in regard to the judicial power – introduced in a number of countries (Morris, 1951, ch. 3, ch. 4) – to sentence habitual criminals to 'preventive detention', a procedure varying somewhat from country to country.[71]

The dangers of far-reaching powers of preventive detention are underlined by the Crime Act passed by the US Congress in the summer of 1970, for the District of Washington, but designed to be a model for national legislation. Under the act, a judge may order pre-trial detention up to sixty days for defendants charged with dangerous crimes or crimes of violence, narcotics addicts charged with crimes of violence and defendants who threaten witnesses or jurors. The criterion is 'dangerousness', i.e. the court's view as to the likelihood of the defendant committing a crime of the categories defined in the act, if released on bail. This bill was passed, after bitter debate, and in spite of strong criticisms, which include the following: (1) violation of the constitutional guarantee of a right to bail; (2) violation of the due process clause of the Fifth Amendment, since the arrested person is deprived of his liberty on the mere probability that he will commit a crime; (3) undermining the constitutional presumption of innocence by permitting loss of a defendant's liberty on less than proof of guilt beyond a reasonable doubt. In addition, critics have pointed out that, in view of clear statistical evidence that only 5 per cent of those arrested for dangerous crime are rearrested after release on bail for another crime in the same category, a hundred people will stand the risk of deprivation of their liberty for, at most, five

69. See, for a critical analysis and survey, Paulsen, 'Fairness to juvenile offenders', 41 *Minnesota L. Rev.*, 547 (1956); Allen, 'The borderland of the criminal law', *Social Service Rev.* 32 (1958), p. 107.
70. 387 U.S. 1 (1967).
71. See the symposium, 'The habitual criminal', 13 *McGill L.J.* 533 (1967), especially pp. 652–83 for summaries of eleven statutes.

potentially dangerous persons. Finally, the power to order preventive detention will almost certainly increase social discrimination. It is certain to be applied mainly against poorer, and particularly black, people who, by virtue of their poverty and the slum conditions in which they live, provide the bulk of 'street criminals'.

The bill indicates one of the periodic swings of the pendulum, a readiness to disregard the legal protections of individual liberty, in favour of public safety.

The resolution of this dilemma can hardly be found in sweeping and absolute formulas. Unless we wish to retreat from the entire, laboriously developed process of preventive, educational and corrective methods, either in addition to or in substitution for purely criminal trial and sentence, we cannot seek to wipe out the necessary measure of administrative discretion that must rest in responsible authorities supervising the treatment of the juvenile, the habitual offender, the prisoner sentenced to an indeterminate sentence and the like. Yet, in all too many cases, the 'preventive detention' or the institution to which a juvenile offender is sent, resembles in fact, though not in name, the prison to which it is meant to be an alternative. Certainly, it implies compulsory deprivation of liberty. Such interferences range, however, from the supervisory powers of an officially appointed guardian to the compulsory retention, for an indefinite period, of an offender in a strictly supervised and harsh institution. In regard to the juvenile offender, an opinion of a District of Columbia Court has attempted to draw the borderline in the following terms[72]

Unless the institution is one whose primary concern is the individual's moral and physical well-being, unless its facilities are intended for and adapted to guidance, care, education and training rather than punishment, unless its supervision is that of a guardian, not that of a prison guard or gaoler, it seems clear a commitment to such institution is by reason of conviction of crime and cannot withstand an assault for violation of fundamental Constitutional safeguards (p. 650).

On the even more difficult problem of sorting out the detention aspects from the penal treatment of the habitual offender the authorities appear to be divided. Some consider that, at least until com-

72. *White* v. *Reid*, 125 F.Supp. 647 (D.D.C. 1954).

pletely different institutions are developed, preventive detention cannot be effectively distinguished from prison treatment (Radzino-wicz, 1945, p. 165; Grünhut, 1945, p. 393, but others believe that a genuine differentiation has already been achieved in the Scandinavian countries, and that preventive detention need not be, in effect, a punishment, provided it is administered in the proper spirit (Mann-heim, 1946, p. 213; Morris, 1951, p. 241).

The solution must be sought in further progress in the genuine distinction between penal and educational or corrective institutions in substance rather than in name. The problem of the proper border-line between administrative discretion and individual right is not, after all, confined to this issue, but pervades the whole body of law (see p. 384). The imposition of a new form of criminal procedure on the deliberately elastic welfare procedures of youth authorities, social welfare boards and the like would largely defeat the object for which they were created. On the other hand, there is great merit in the attempt made by the above-mentioned judgement of the District of Columbia Court to draw a genuine distinction between corrective and penal institutions. In the wider sense, this problem borders on the more general one of the new relationship between authority and individual created by the enlarged functions of the modern welfare state. It is, in many ways, easier for the 'negative' State (which confines itself essentially to the minimum functions of defence, police and machinery of justice) to be just to the individual – at the expense of active concern for his social and economic welfare. Such active concern means of necessity interference. On balance, such inter-ference is beneficial; otherwise it would not have been adopted by one State after another during the present century. Nobody seriously wishes to go back to the prison system of the time of Dickens. Instead, we should direct our attention to the working out of the safeguards against the abuse of welfare activities rather than against their substance. This applies to the field of criminology no less than that of administrative discretion in general.

Alternatives to the Criminal Sanction

To those who consider retribution as the principle or exclusive pur-pose of punishment, there can be no alternative to the criminal sanction for offensive and prohibited conduct. But for the adherents of a utilitarian philosophy there are alternatives. In a recent discussion of this question Professor Packer proposed a classification of sanctions into four categories (1968, pp. 23, 205): compensation, regulation, punishment and treatment. Compensation involves the exaction of money or performance to recompense an identifiable beneficiary or class of beneficiaries for damage done or threatened by the actions of another. Regulation embraces a constellation of devices used to bring the impact of public authority directly to bear on private conduct, both before and after the fact. The granting and withdrawal of licences is a prominent example of regulation. Treatment is essentially a diagnostic response. It implies the appraisal of socially condemned conduct as a disease rather than a crime. A widely used form of treatment, as a sanction alternative to punishment, is compulsory civil commitment. This raises the question of how if at all such a measure of deprivation of liberty differs in anything but name from imprisonment. But there are of course many lesser forms of treatment in response to criminal conduct. A contemporary British sociologist (Wootton, 1963) argues in favour of a sentencing policy primarily as a prevention of crime. This means, for example 'that custodial sentences should be indeterminate in respect to the type of institution to which an offender should be committed, and indeed that the rigid division of institutions into the medical and the penal should be obliterated'. Essentially 'decisions as to the treatment of offenders should be common administrative, instead of a judicial, matter' (Wootton, 1963, p. 112). Professor Packer goes less far. For him

the criminal sanction is the best available device we have for dealing with gross and immediate harms and threats of harm. It becomes less useful as the harms become less gross and immediate. It becomes largely inefficacious when it is used to enforce morality rather than to deal with conduct that is generally seen as harmful (1968, p. 365).

The criminal sanction, in other words, is not society's inevitable response to evil, but the most serious of various kinds of remedies.

What Future for Criminal Law?

As a leading criminologist has observed

The study of crime must be brought into a closer connection with psychiatry, psychology and social science. There has been very little change since the nineteenth century in the basic concepts of substantive criminal law, apart from the accretion of what may be described as 'administrative criminality', a product of the growing complexity of modern life and of the new protective and remedial functions of the welfare state. But there has been a sweeping transformation in the penal sphere. A Victorian lawyer would still feel quite at home with our basic offences, but he would be puzzled and bewildered by our methods of punishment and treatment and indeed by our whole attitude (Radzinowicz, 1962, p. 181).

It is, as we have seen, no longer sufficient to concentrate on the alternative purposes and sanctions of criminal law as such. We have to think increasingly of criminal law as only one of a variety of instrumentalities, by which public authority deals with the complex and manifold problems of order in contemporary industrial society. That a criminal sanction – even with the greater variety and flexibility of methods of punishment used today – is but one of a number of devices by which the modern state seeks to exercise authority over private conduct, is the gist of Professor Packer's important book, and particularly of his juxtaposition of compensation, i.e. monetary adjustment, and regulation, i.e. administrative sanctioning, with the sanctions of punishment and treatment – which may be regarded as within the ambit of criminal law proper. In the modern 'positive' state, regulation is a particularly powerful means of dealing out rewards and punishment, outside the purview of criminal law. The granting, refusal, or withdrawal of an occupational or professional licence, or the refusal of security clearance for an individual, which makes him unemployable, are in their moral and economic effect, more powerful sanctions than most punishments. To this we may add another factor not stressed by Professor Packer: The power of quasi-public organizations that enjoy an effective monopoly in their professional or occupational area, to make or break their members by admission to, or exclusion from, membership. A doctor struck from the medical list, a bricklayer excluded from his union may in effect suffer punishment for life. But this occurs entirely outside the ambit of criminal law and the criminal process. It involves the complex relationship between public authority and private or quasi-public institutions, with which we shall deal in another context (see chs.11, 12). While, on the one hand, criminal law and the criminal processes must become increasingly more flexible so as to accommodate a variety of sanctions that are not necessarily punitive in the traditional sense of the word, it is equally necessary to compare the moral, social and economic impact of non-criminal sanctions – including the power of non-public bodies to impose sanctions on their members – with the impact of the criminal sanction.[73]

There must be a much closer coordination of criminal, administrative and civil procedures, with respect to the effect that they have on the status of the individual. While the criminal law proper may well come to occupy a more limited place in the public sanctioning process than it has traditionally done, it is imperative that the technically non-criminal sanctions be subjected to adequate procedural safeguards, so as to protect the basic rights of the individual.

73. For an important study in this direction, see Arens and Lasswell (1961), where the authors rightly maintain that sanction law is wider in scope than the treatment of offenders against prohibitions laid down by the community, and that it includes civil sanctions.

Chapter 7
Family Law

Of all the social groups within the state, the family is at once the most closely knit, the smallest and the most enduring. It has always been recognized by philosophers, jurists and political scientists that the closeness and intimacy of family ties make the relationship between state and family a problem of special importance. To those who regard unconditional devotion to the state as paramount, the family is an obstacle, to be weakened or even destroyed. There was no place for the family in the life of the rulers of Plato's *Republic*. Plato's prescription for the men and women selected to govern the state – put in the mouth of Socrates – is that 'these women should be all of them wives in common of all these men and that no woman should live with any man privately, and that their children, too, should be common, and the parent should not know his own offspring nor the child its parent' (*Republic*, book 5). This is the complete negation of the concept of the family, based on the privacy of relations between husband and wife, and their children.

Because the intimacy of the personal bonds within the family detracts from single-minded devotion to the state, the integrity of the family is an essential part of any code of 'human rights', or of the groups which, like the various religious communities, wish to preserve personal and ethical values against the omnipotence of government.[1] Any philosophy which sees in the state the highest fulfilment of man must devalue the family.

Basic Concepts of the Western Family

The analysis attempted here is that of the western family, a union based on monogamous and – at least in principle – permanent

1. See, e.g. the statement of the Christian view of marriage by the Federal Council of Churches of Christ in America (reprinted in Sayre, 1950, p. 118) or the Encyclical on Christian Marriage (Pope Pius XI, in Sayre, 1950, pp. 132 et seq.).

marriage, with a consequently rigid distinction between the status of legitimate and illegitimate children. While this concept of the family is subject to severe strains and changes within western society itself, it seems to gain ground outside the western world. This is part of the process by which many eastern societies, for many centuries subject to static social and economic conditions, attempt to assimilate their life to western standards. An illustration is the recent Indian statute which has abolished polygamous marriages; even in Moslem states – at least outside the Arab world, as in Pakistan or Indonesia – there is a growing opposition to the exercise of the right to have up to four wives, granted to the husband by the law of the Koran, and to the form of divorce by a simple letter.[2]

In general terms, the basic principles of the western family concept can be summed up briefly: husband and wife, through a solemn and officially sanctioned pact[3] – although the sanction outside Catholic states is no longer necessarily religious – enter into a bond for life, which gives them mutual rights and obligations: material support, sexual fidelity and certain duties in regard to the children's maintenance and education. Sexual or other intimate relations outoutside marriage not only entail legal sanctions for the responsible party itself, but any children born of an illegitimate union suffer from the consequences in their legal status.

Beneath such deceptively facile generalizations, the western concept of family law contains fundamental tensions and conflicts which recent social developments have brought to the surface and intensified. The major problems that have arisen can be summed up in three areas: the husband–wife relationship; the relationships of parents and children; the relationship of the family to the state.

The contemporary crisis of family law results from a variety of factors: changes in social philosophy, which emphasize the freedom of the individual, as against the mainly religiously determined

2. e.g. the strong protests against the second marriages entered into some years ago by a Prime Minister of Pakistan and the President of the Indonesian Republic.

3. The formal sanction is now increasingly civil, i.e. by the authority of the state, rather than the Church, even in many Catholic states, such as France and Italy. How strong the moral authority of Church sanction remains in many communities is shown by the libel action brought (and won) in 1958 in Italy by a civilly married couple against a bishop, who had condemned the lack of religious marriage as sinful and depraved.

indissolubility of the marriage status; the profound transformation in the economic status of the family in modern urbanized society, and, in particular, in the position of married women; modern scientific and medical developments which make birth control and artificial insemination possible; finally, the growing claims of the modern welfare state, which makes new demands on, but also assumes far greater responsibilities towards, the family.[4]

The Indissolubility of the Marriage Tie

The principle that still dominates the marriage laws of the western world is that of the permanency of the marriage union. It is more than a contract, it is a solemn union entered into for life. But behind this broad generalization a deep conflict of philosophies has developed which permeates the controversies about the reform of divorce law.

The basis of the principle of indissolubility is essentially religious; it is the idea of the sacrament of marriage, which is God-made.

The Catholic Church admits that the human will enters into marriage.

For each individual marriage, inasmuch as it is a conjugal union of a particular man and woman, arises only from the free consent of each of the spouses. . . . This freedom however regards only the question whether the contracting parties really wish to enter upon matrimony or to marry this particular person; but the nature of matrimony is entirely independent from the free will of man (Pope Pius XI in Sayre, 1950, p. 133).

From this premise follows the remorseless conclusion that any dissolution of marriage, other than by death, is illegitimate, as contrary to the law of God and nature.[5]

4. See further pp. 284–9. For a survey of the major developments in English law since the Matrimonial Causes Act 1857, see Graveson and Crane (1957), and especially the introductory and concluding chapters, pp. 1, 411 by Graveson; and 'Special family law number', 36 *Mod. L. Rev.*, no. 6, November 1970.

5. However, the ecclesiastical courts have considerably extended grounds of nullity, in particular for impotence and for wilful refusal to consummate the marriage. The latter is really a failure to fulfil a marriage once validly concluded. When the secular courts took over jurisdiction from the ecclesiastical courts, as

The importance of this Catholic doctrine goes far beyond the ecclesiastical sphere. In a considerable number of states it is not only the spiritual, but also the secular law.[6] Implicit in this philosophy is the acceptance of individual unhappiness as part of a status that is ordained by God. 'What therefore God has put together, let not man put asunder' (Matthew, ix, 6). The shadow of St Augustine still hovers over this concept of marriage. For him all human institutions were essentially sinful, and redeemed only by the grace of God. If men and women have chosen wrongly, let them bear their cross, as a duty owed to God.

The opposite approach, which recognizes marriage as dissoluble under certain circumstances, is compounded of different elements. Perhaps the only common factor in the philosophies which oppose the Augustinian and modern Catholic concept of the indissoluble sacrament of marriage is the recognition of matrimony as a human institution, a bond created by the exercise of a free act of will by a man and a woman who are responsible, but fallible, individuals, who may err and blunder. An individualistic philosophy, which certainly plays a large part in modern reform proposals, postulates the individual right to happiness. People should be able to live out their lives as joyfully as is possible, under conditions which enable them to develop their personal capacities and potentialities. This means the right to correct errors, the right to cast off a burden that has become intolerable and may lead to the sapping of vital energies and the moral fibre of the affected parties.[7] In its extreme version the purely individualistic approach to marriage leads to the consent

---

happened in England in 1857, they also took over some of these classifications (for details, see Scott, 'Nullity of marriage in canon law and English law', 1938, 2 *University of Toronto L.J.* 319–43). It is only in its *Report* of 1956 that the British Commission on Marriage and Divorce recommended that wilful refusal to consummate the marriage should be made a ground of divorce rather than nullity. In thirty-six American jurisdictions, impotence now is a statutory ground of divorce. (See Table 3, Appendix II, *Report of the Royal Commission on Marriage and Divorce*, Cmd 9678, HMSO 1956.)

6. Among them are most of the Latin American Republics, Eire, Spain and the Canadian Province of Quebec.

7. The compatibility of this 'existentialist' conception of marriage with Christian ethics and religion has been argued, for example, by Canon Carpenter (*Listener*, 21 August 1958).

theory, the interpretation of marriage as a contract based on revocable mutual agreement.[8]

There is, however, an entirely different justification for the rejection of the indissolubility of marriage, based on social rather than individual grounds. This philosophy considers the family as an intimate social unit, a community in miniature, which can be disrupted by an unhappy marriage to the detriment not only of the life and character of the spouses, but of the children. It recognizes that – as has been clearly demonstrated by the social experience of our

8. According to the report of the British Royal Commission (Table 2, Appendix II), dissolubility of marriage by mutual consent is today openly recognized only in Bulgaria and in Portugal (for non-Catholics). To this may be added since 1968, Soviet law, with some qualifications (see p. 244). The Swedish Marriage Code of 1920 goes a considerable way towards recognition of the dissolubility of marriage by consent. Under this Act, a judicial decree of separation may be granted in cases of 'profound and lasting disruption' due to 'diversity of temperament and opinions or other causes'. Alternatively, two married people can obtain a separation decree if both of them apply jointly. Divorce can be obtained after one year of judicial separation, on application by either spouse if, after the separation decree, they have lived separated for one year. In other words, judicial separation can be obtained by mutual consent at any time, and divorce one year afterwards by unilateral application, where actual separation has taken place. (The author is obliged to Professor Ake Malström of Uppsala University for information on the Swedish law.)

Japanese law, before the modernization effected by the Civil Code of 1898, recognized a unilateral right by the husband to divorce his wife by a simple letter. The Civil Code of 1898 provided for divorce by mutual consent, along with judicial divorce. Where there are children, the parties must accompany their notification to the municipal office with the terms of agreement on custody. If the parties reach no agreement, the family court decides on guardianship and custody, but it has no power to halt the divorce itself. This state of the law has remained unchanged, except that a reform of 1947 has added to the grounds of judicial divorce (unchastity; malicious desertion; absence for three years or more; and severe mental disease) a broad judicial discretion to grant divorce for 'any other grave reason'. The admission of divorce by consent is attributed by Professor Toru Ikuyo, of Nagoya University – to whom I am obliged for this information – to the religious philosophy of the Japanese (Buddhism, Shintoism, Confucianism), which has not condemned divorce as a religious or moral sin. The main progress of the reform of 1898 has been to put the wife, at least in theory, in a position equal to that of her husband. Such equality is still far from being a social reality, although a reform of 1947 provides for a right for either spouse to demand distribution of property in any case of divorce, whether by consent or judgement.

times – disruption of the marriage may be a prime cause of juvenile delinquency and that, short of criminal actions, it may warp the characters and lives of the children. This philosophy is not, of course, incompatible with that of individual self-fulfilment, but its accent is different. Its central concern is the relation of the marriage bond to the family and, through it, the community.

The 'breakdown' principle

Consideration of the family as a social unit, in which the interests, happiness and developments of the children and other members of the household as well as those of the parents have to be considered, tends to militate against the principle of dissolution of marriage by mutual consent of the spouses. On the one hand, availability of divorce through joint application, i.e. by consent of both parties, offers too great a temptation for hasty and ill-considered actions. A marriage may be dissolved as the result of a momentary quarrel, or a temporary difference of opinion, with irrevocable consequences for the whole family. On the other hand, the requirement of consent may permanently bar the dissolution of a marriage that is disrupted beyond redemption, and the maintenance of which only serves to undermine and poison the relations between the various members of the family, and, particularly, between parents and children. Often, one party, for reasons of convention, social status or, sometimes, sheer malice, will continue to refuse his consent to the dissolution of a marriage that only survives in name. These social and human considerations demand an objective criterion other than the subjective agreement of the parties.

A substantial number of modern codifications have, in various forms, adopted the principle of 'breakdown' as the decisive criterion, thus departing both from the principle of fault and the principle of consent. First, the Swiss Civil Code of 1907 (section 142) makes deterioration of marriage a ground of divorce for either side 'if it has gone so deep that the spouses must not be expected to cohabit'. The breakdown principle is, however, blended with the fault theory in so far as deterioration, predominantly due to the fault of one spouse, disables that spouse from being the plaintiff in a divorce action.

A more far-reaching recognition of the breakdown principle was contained in the West German Marriage Act of 1946:

Where the domestic community of the spouses has ceased to exist for three years, and where by virtue of a deep-seated and irretrievable disruption of the matrimonial relationship the restitution of a community of life corresponding to the nature of marriage cannot be expected, either spouse may apply for divorce.

Where the spouse who makes the application has been wholly or overwhelmingly responsible for the disruption, the other spouse may object to the divorce. Such objection is to be disregarded where the maintenance of the marriage is not morally justified [*sittlich gerechtfertigt*] considering a proper estimate of the character of marriage and the total behaviour of both spouses.

The application for divorce is to be refused where the properly understood interests of one or several minor children of the union demand the maintenance of the marriage (*Ehegesetz*, section 48).

In this version, the dominant criterion is the degree to which the marriage ceases to be a relationship which it is worthwhile to maintain. In this estimate, to be made by the court, the moral guilt of one spouse may be balanced by the hopelessness of restoration, which may be due to incompatibility, vast differences of age, or temperament, sexual difficulties, or other causes, but all these factors may, in turn, be offset by the need to maintain the marriage for the sake of minor children. While such a law puts great demands on the wisdom and understanding of a court, it does clearly see marriage as a complex of human and social factors, not as a simple equation of guilt and innocence.

However, the breakdown principle of the 1946 Act was weakened by a revision of 1961, which makes the objection of the other spouse an absolute obstacle to divorce, 'unless the objecting spouse lacks commitment to the marriage and readiness . . . to continue the marriage'. Moreover, the German law courts have tended to reinforce the remaining 'fault' elements in the law and correspondingly weakened the breakdown aspects.[9] In the words of a critic,

the courts have used the right of objection to demolish altogether the principle of breakdown. . . . Alienation between the spouses does not count

9. See, for example, decision of the Supreme Court of 1967 (BGH) reported in NJW, 1967, p. 1080.

any longer. In the perspective of the courts, any reaction within the marriage becomes a decision of will for which the spouses are responsible. There cannot be events for which either of them is not in some degree 'responsible' (*schuldig*) (Simitis, 1969, p. vi).

The far-reaching neutralization of the breakdown principle in recent German judicial developments shows again how judicial and administrative interpretations can turn a generally formulated legislative principle in one direction or another.

Contemporary Soviet law has veered from its original principle of free dissolubility of marriage to an acceptance of the breakdown principle and back to free dissolubility. The Revolutionary Decree of 1917, confirmed in the Family Code of 1926, permitted divorce at the request of one or both of the parties, without need for any reason. Differences between registered marriages and *de facto* marriages were minimized, so much so that in 1929 the Supreme Court regarded two women with whom the deceased had maintained a relationship of factual marriage as both qualified to inherit his estate (Hazard, 1953, p. 247). It was an almost inevitable corollary to this attitude to marriage that the legal differences between persons born in or out of wedlock were for all intents and purposes abolished.

A drastic change occurred, however, with the Law of 1944, which abolished *de facto* marriages and declared registered marriages to be the sole legally recognized form of union between man and woman. Above all, the Law of 1944 radically changed the attitude towards divorce. A trial court was directed to attempt reconciliation before granting a divorce. Notice of the proceedings was ordered to be published in the local newspaper, and fees were drastically increased. If all efforts to reconcile the parties failed, the court was authorized to grant the divorce, if it found it necessary to dissolve the marriage. The law did not spell out the principle on which divorce may be or has to be granted. But the Supreme Court of the USSR in an order of 1949, officially criticized the practice of some courts to accept the desire of the parties for divorce as a directing criterion. The court instructed the lower courts to grant divorce only where there were 'deeply considered and well-founded reasons' and where 'continuation of the marriage would conflict with the principles of Communist morals and could not create the conditions necessary to family law and the rearing of children'.

After many years of widespread protest against the harshness of the 1944 law, the Fundamental Principles of Soviet Family Law, enacted in 1968, and to be implemented by the family codes of the different Soviet Republics, went back to the liberalism of the early period of the Soviet Union. Divorce may now be obtained by simple registration at official registries, where there is mutual agreement and there are no minor children, or where there has been a legal declaration that a spouse is missing and cannot be traced, or has been found to be of unsound mind or an imbecile, or where a spouse has been sentenced to deprivation of liberty for not less than three years because of a criminal offence. In all these cases, divorce may be obtained by court order where the other spouse objects. Divorce may also be obtained by court decree where the court is satisfied that further marital life of the spouses and the preservation of the family have become impossible.

The 1968 reform was the product of a gradual liberalization of Soviet society in the post-war period, following the harshness of the Stalin era. There are now signs of a new orthodoxy in many spheres of Soviet life. It may well be that a new reaction against liberal personal and sex habits, concern about the steadily falling birth rate, and other factors may eventually lead to a new swing of the pendulum.

In the western world, there has been a general though uneven trend towards liberalization of divorce, mainly by the dilution or abandonment of the fault principle. A number of recent reforms in the common-law world have broken with the centuries-old traditions of the common law – largely inspired by Puritan religion and philosophy – which not only restricted divorce to specific grave cases of 'fault' (in particular, adultery) but also tended to impose stricter responsibilities upon the wife than upon the husband. One of the most dramatic changes is that of the English Divorce Reform Act of 1969 which has substituted for all previous specified divorce grounds 'irretrievable breakdown of marriage' as the sole ground for divorce. Evidence of irretrievable breakdown is one of the following five facts:

1. The respondent has committed adultery and the petitioner finds it intolerable to live with the respondent.

2. The respondent has behaved in such a way that the petitioner cannot reasonably be expected to live with the respondent.
3. The respondent has deserted the petitioner for a continuous period of at least two years immediately preceding the presentation of the petition.
4. The parties to the marriage have lived apart for a continuous period of at least two years immediately preceding the presentation of the petition and the respondent consents to a decree being granted.
5. The parties to the marriage have lived apart for a continuous period of at least five years immediately preceding the presentation of the petition.

Australia and Canada have also introduced far-reaching reforms of their divorce laws, although neither of them has abandoned the traditional 'fault' grounds for divorce (notably adultery and cruelty). But both provide in addition for divorce on the ground of breakdown of the marriage. Both under the Canadian Divorce Act of 1968 and the Australian Matrimonial Causes Act 1959–66, separation and living apart for certain specified periods – varying according to certain criteria, from three to five years – are the statutory evidence of breakdown. The Australian Act adds the important qualification that 'there is no reasonable likelihood of cohabitation being resumed'. This may be compared with the, already mentioned, provision of the German Marriage Act of 1946, as amended in 1961, that objection by the other spouse blocks the divorce, and such objection is to be disregarded only if, 'on a correct assessment of the nature of marriage and the entire behaviour of both spouses, the continuation of the marriage is not morally justified'. An interesting comparative study of the two provisions[10] shows that the judicial interpretations of broadly comparable legislative provisions have had totally different results. Using such concepts as '*eheliche Gesinnung*' (feeling for a marriage) or '*Lebensführung*' (conduct of life), the German courts have – fortified by the 1961 revision – reintroduced the fault principle. The Australian courts have, on the other hand, generally implemented the policy of the Act and granted divorces on a much broader base – including, for example, the legitimacy of a desire to remarry, where

10. Turner, 'Divorce: Australian and German "breakdown" provisions compared', 18 *Int. & Comp. L.Q.* 896 (1969).

there are children of the new liaison and the existing marriage has in fact broken down. The author of the comparative survey observes rightly that, in order to prevent such developments

any legislature contemplating the introduction of a 'breakdown' ground for divorce should determine at the outset whether it wishes the innocent respondent to have an absolute veto (as in Switzerland) or the petitioner to have an absolute right to divorce (as in the Scandinavian countries) or to adopt a *via media*. If it decides on the last course, the legislative should state unequivocally the factors which must be taken into account, and the weight to be given to each. It should not leave these vital matters to capricious determination by the judiciary.

Certainly, the greater the latitude given to judicial interpretation by general clauses, the greater the possibility that the judicial interpretations, by courts hostile to the policy of the act, may pervert its objectives.

The liberalization of divorce laws is also gathering momentum in the American jurisdictions. In 1966, the state of New York, which for practically all its history, had recognized only one ground, i.e. adultery, added five more grounds.[11] Three of these are 'fault' grounds: cruel and inhuman treatment, abandonment, confinement to prison for three or more consecutive years after marriage. But in addition there are two 'no fault' grounds, separation, either under a judicial decree of separation – subject to plaintiff's proof of due performance of all terms and conditions of the decree, or a written agreement of separation, one year after execution, and subject to proof of due performance of its terms.

Both California and Texas, in 1969, adopted the breakdown principle. The Texas formulation – which is in addition to the traditional fault grounds – provides for divorce 'without regard to fault if the marriage has become insupportable because of discord or conflict of personalities that destroy the legitimate ends of the marriage relationship and prevents any reasonable expectation of reconciliation'. The California statute, somewhat like the recent British Act, substitutes the 'irremedial breakdown of the marriage' for the earlier grounds.

Generally then, the strong contemporary trend of social philosophy, outside the states governed by Catholic law – is towards greater

11. New York Domestic Relations Law, § 170.

individual freedom and mobility, and the recognition that 'fault' is an inadequate criterion for the many complex factors that make a marriage unbearable and destructive. Even in the Catholic world there are signs of change, as shown by the introduction of a divorce law in Catholic Italy.

Despite these impressive advances of the breakdown principle, a majority of contemporary legal systems – quite apart from those that officially adopt the Catholic philosophy and reject divorce altogether – still adhere to the fault principle. This means that there must be a guilty and an innocent party. Where both parties are guilty, the doctrine of recrimination, generally applied in the American jurisdictions that have not introduced the breakdown principle, demands that the divorce action should be dismissed: 'He who comes to equity must come with clean hands' (Vernier, 1931, vol. 2, para. 78). In some cases, insanity is recognized as a ground for divorce (usually after a specified number of years). This means a limited recognition of the fact that fate, not fault, may destroy marriage.

Breakdown or fault: fact and fiction

It would be highly unrealistic to judge the present state of marriage and divorce by the enumeration of the grounds of divorce as stated in the various legal systems, by statute or jurisprudence. Judicial interpretations have to a large extent condoned or sanctioned practices designed to satisfy the letter of the law, while violating its spirit.

Few areas of legal inquiry point up as dramatically the dangers of letting the tension between legal theory and social reality develop too far.

The strength of the factors undermining the indissolubility of the marriage tie or the strictness of laws which permit divorce only on very few selected grounds, notably adultery of the other party, greatly varies from country to country, and from region to region. On the whole, however, there has been an unquestionable trend towards greater freedom, a trend which is spreading from the western world to other parts, for example, in the areas of Hindu and Muslim cultures, where women are gradually trying to struggle loose from their traditional inferior status.

In the first place, the strength of religious restraints has weakened, though not everywhere to the same degree. They are still obviously powerful in Catholic countries, and in states with a strong Puritan tradition, such as the New England region of the United States. Generally, however, religious restraints appear to be weaker in predominantly Protestant countries where the hold of the Churches on the people is no longer as strong a social force (e.g. in England or in the Scandinavian countries) as in Catholic countries.

But even in Catholic or other traditionally religious communities, such as Italy, some of the Latin-American states, or Quebec, the social facts of modern urbanization, mobility, freedom of movement for women and children, and other social factors are making themselves felt. Above all, the family, outside primitive rural areas, is no longer of necessity held together by physical and economic ties. The livelihood of the family no longer depends predominantly on the common toil of all, and especially of the wife in the house and on the farm. Wives take jobs, exercise professions, conduct business and are now legally free to dispose of inherited property. Children go to work outside or are subjected to increasingly long periods of school and college education which relieves mothers of daily care and custody, at least for the major part of the working day.

These physical and economic changes go together with a philosophy that in most parts of the world comes to regard the woman – including the married woman – increasingly as equal in her right to move about, develop her faculties and manage her affairs. While greater facilities for the dissolution of marriages in theory affect both parties equally, in fact it is the greater freedom of movement of the married woman that produces the greater change.[12] Under the formerly predominant social pattern, the husband's freedom of movement was always relatively greater than that of the wife.

With it all goes the spread of a philosophy – praised by some and condemned by others – which stresses individual self-fulfilment and the realization of personal happiness, as against the stern duty imposed by an unalterable status.

Such challenges cannot, in the long run, be ignored by the law. The types of response varies greatly. As we have seen, few contemporary

12. See the analysis by McGregor (1957, p. 41) of the reasons for the post-war increase in divorce petitions, especially those alleging cruelty 'largely, though not entirely, a husband's offence' (p. 43).

legal systems respond by the free dissolubility of marriage. A growing number of jurisdictions accept the challenge by balancing the continuing social requirement of the stability of marriage against the recognition of major factors that will, openly or otherwise, break up many marriages. But in the states in which the fault principle remains exclusive or predominant, the response of the law must be a more devious one. Theories and concepts remain outwardly unchanged, but their meaning is altered. In this way, the moral principle can be saved. The official conscience, expressing itself in legislative bodies, public platform statements, sermons from the pulpit, and many other ways, can protest that it has not departed from the old and stern morality. Even where, under the pressure of social facts, divorce grounds are enlarged from adultery to 'cruelty', 'violence', 'desertion' and the like, it is still possible to proclaim that the principle of guilt has been preserved.

In fact, however, the reality of the law is transformed, either by processes of elastic interpretation, or by downright fictions reminiscent of the earlier history of the common law.

The first major technique permitting an expansion of divorce is the judicial interpretation of such comprehensive statutory divorce causes as 'cruelty', 'desertion' and 'violence'.

The second technique is acceptance of faked evidence. The result, that parties sufficiently wealthy to afford the cost of litigation, and of the various agreements outside and inside the court, which are necessary for the procedure to be brought to a successful conclusion, can, in effect, obtain divorce by consent, discredits the law. It is reached by fraud, and not infrequently perjury, no less objectionable for having become settled practice. The facade of a semi-puritan ethics is preserved at the cost of sacrificing the integrity of the law and often creating one law for the rich, another for the poor.

Two other reasons of a somewhat different order may be mentioned as adding, at least in some jurisdictions, to the facilitation of divorce without abandonment of the 'fault' theory. The first, welcome as diminishing the gap between the law prevailing for the rich and the poor, is the extension of legal aid in some countries. Among them is, since the Legal Aid and Advice Act of 1948, the United Kingdom. It is quite clear that where legal aid is generally available for people without means, as a matter of right rather than of charity, a vast number of unhappy marriages will be brought before the courts and end in divorce which formerly remained concealed from the public eye, preserved by necessity and poverty.[13]

Finally, in certain federal jurisdictions, particularly in the United States, the divergence of divorce requirements in the different jurisdictions, coupled with the 'full faith and credit' clause of the Constitution, widens the availability of divorce, especially in the age of air transport, as people can evade the law of their home state, and avail themselves of the easier divorce conditions of another state, provided only the divorce thus granted will be recognized.

The remedy: severity or relaxation?

There is some difference of opinion as to the extent to which collusion and other forms of deception have actually undermined the whole edifice of divorce law in the jurisdictions that maintain a theory of restricted divorce grounds based on fault. In those jurisdictions where 'mental cruelty' or 'incompatibility of temperament' as divorce grounds are coupled with easy requirements for the establishment of the local jurisdiction, divorce has become more or less a formality for those who can afford it. The Royal Commission on Marriage and Divorce was almost evenly split on this question. In the view of nine members (*Report*, s. 69, p. 16), cases of 'hotel adultery', while disturbing to the public conscience, are believed to be less frequent than is often supposed. But nine other members went on record with the conviction 'that the law of divorce as it at present exists is indeed weighted in favour of the least scrupulous, the least honourable, and the least sensitive; and that nobody who is ready to provide a ground of divorce, who is careful to avoid any suggestion of connivance or collusion and who has a cooperative spouse has any difficulty in securing a dissolution of the marriage' (p. 23). The latter view has prevailed in the Divorce Reform Act of 1969 which adopts the breakdown principle.

But it is still relevant to study the criticism directed by a social scientist at the report of the Royal Commission. On the basis of

13. McGregor (1957, p. 47) concludes from the statistics published in the annual Reports of the Law Society that 'approximately 45 per cent of the total number of divorce petitions in 1954 were filed by assisted persons'.

detailed statistics, Professor MacGregor (1957) shows that: (a) after an initial post-war rush of divorces the rate of divorce had recently declined; (b) the great majority of divorced couples had remarried; (c) 50 per cent of all divorces occurred amongst marriages which have lasted for more than ten years, and a high proportion of divorces amongst childless couples or those whose children have grown up; (d) a great proportion of the increase in contemporary divorces was due to the availability, since 1950, of legal assistance to the poorer classes, which until then were left to the poor men's device of obtaining separation and maintenance orders from the Magistrates' Courts.

In the light of this analysis – which is confirmed by an American student of the problem[14] – there is, therefore, no evidence that the covert introduction of the breakdown principle has seriously undermined the stability of marriage.

But granted that disagreement is possible on the extent to which the stability of marriage has decreased, there is no serious doubt that deception and fiction have penetrated the divorce law of every country that maintains a theory of strict divorce to such a degree that any complacency with the existing state of affairs is utterly unjustifiable. The question is what conclusions should be drawn from this state of affairs. Is the answer continued or even increased severity of the law? Should modern family law maintain the stern principles of religion and morality which the Puritan forebears imported into the law, trusting that they will educate a laxer generation in the responsibilities of marriage? Or should the law take note of a basic social change, which has reached proportions too great and too universal to be ignored, and adapt the law to the realities of social life by at least reducing, if not eliminating, the tension between fact and theory?

There is, first, the question of values. No conflict arises for the Catholic philosophy, which regards marriage as a sacrament ordained by God, and regards the claim of the individual to full satisfaction of his personal needs as subordinate.[15]

14. Rheinstein, 'The law of divorce and the problem of marriage stability' (1956) 9 *Vanderbilt L. Rev.*, p. 643.

15. Save for the above-mentioned evasion by somewhat extended grounds of nullity of marriage, and the existence of thousands of Catholic marriages which are separate and, in effect, dissolved, except for the legal bond which prevents remarriage. The Anglo-Catholic wing of the Church of England adopts the same

But for all other philosophies, including at least some of the Protestant approaches, which recognize the claim of individual judgement and conscience to a far greater degree than the Catholic philosophy, there is a conflict of values. Sanctity of marriage must be balanced against the often disastrous results of an unhappy marriage for the mental state of the parties, the happiness of the children, and, ultimately, the community.

Overwhelmingly, the western world, even today, rejects the conception of marriage as analogous to an ordinary contract and therefore rejects divorce by mere consent. There is, indeed, considerable justification for the view that the availability of divorce by consent would tempt married couples to magnify temporary disagreement, discomfort or other difficulties into basic failure. There is much experience to show that patience, continuous effort and growing maturity can remedy many situations which, in the agony of the moment, appear beyond repair. It will also often, though certainly not always, be true that the interest of the children will be better served by maintenance of the marriage than by the shock of separation. But the demoralizing effect of daily contact with estranged and embittered parents, who will often embroil the children in their conflicts, may be far more damaging. In any case, the contrast between legal theory and social fact is, today, in many states dangerously wide. Nor is there the slightest evidence in the social or economic moral state of contemporary western society to assume that the maintenance of a strict law would lead to a change in social facts.

Guilt and the duty of maintenance

There is, perhaps, somewhat more justification for making the guilt of a spouse in divorce proceedings a relevant factor in the other spouse's obligation of maintenance. After the dissolution of the marriage, the preservation of the family is no longer a consideration, and the refusal of maintenance for the guilty spouse would – as distinct from maintenance for the children – only affect the individual

---

philosophy as the Church of Rome. On matters of divorce and birth control the Church of England is deeply split. But a resolution passed at the 1958 Lambeth Conference accepted birth control as compatible with Christianity.

involved. However, such differentiation presupposes that 'guilt' is a meaningful, and not, as in so many cases, a purely fictitious, concept.[16] In such circumstances, a discretionary power for the court is the best solution. Such discretionary power is given to the Court in divorce proceedings by the Matrimonial Causes Act 1965, now replaced by the Matrimonial Proceedings and Property Act 1970. In *Porter* v. *Porter*[17] the Court of Appeal made an interim maintenance order against the husband, whose earnings were greatly superior to those of his wife, who had left the matrimonial home, with her twins, who had elected to live with their mother. The wife had committed adultery, but there was evidence of meanness, lack of affection, sexual difficulties and other causes of disruption of the marriage by the husband.

The impact of social change on the application of discretionary principles laid down in 1891, in *Wood* v. *Wood*,[18] was expressed by Sachs L.J.:

The court takes into account the human outlook of the period in which they make their decisions both as regards that important factor 'the conduct of the parties', and also the 'other circumstances' of the particular case. The practice as to discretion has thus naturally varied on this matter as on many others – such as the discretion exercised when granting a decree, where the ambit of the discretion has fundamentally altered in the past twenty-five years. In the exercise of any such discretion the law is a living thing moving with the times and not a creature of dead or moribund ways of thought.[19]

Changing Foundations for the Cohesion of the Family

It is by no means a bad thing that the cohesion of a family should no longer repose essentially on a stern religious doctrine, on economic necessity or on the social and legal supremacy of the husband and father. It may be a sign of maturity that, as it has been said 'of the

16. For an effective criticism of the 'fault' principle in support cases, as applied in the United States, see Paulsen, 'Support rights and duties' (1956) 9 *Vanderbilt L. Rev.* 709, 727.
17. [1969] 1 W.L.R. 1155.
18. [1891] P. 272 (C.A.).
19. [1969] 1 W.L.R., at 1159.

earlier bonds of family, only mutual affection and responsibility for the raising of children are today important, at least in modern western society' (Jacobs and Angell, 1930, pp. 37–8). This change in the foundations of family cohesion does, however, compel a reassessment of the legal remedies for the enforcement of its cohesion or, where necessary, dissolution.

By far the most important factor – entirely neglected in the doctrine of the matrimonial offence, but emerging clearly from the data of modern social statistics: juvenile delinquency, psychological, sociological and ecological studies – is that the relations between husband and wife are not their own exclusive concern, but deeply affect the children. The cost of an unhappy marriage, forcibly maintained by unavailability of legal divorce grounds, or more frequently, by lack of resources to circumvent the law, may be an increase in juvenile delinquency or lesser forms of social maladjustment. It is, therefore, greatly to be welcomed that the Matrimonial Proceedings (Children) Act 1958, now replaced by section 17 of the Matrimonial Proceedings and Property Act 1970, lays greater emphasis on the custody of children in divorce proceedings. No decree nisi (or the corresponding relief in Scotland) is to be made absolute until the court is satisfied, after investigation and report by the court welfare officer, that the arrangements proposed for the care and upbringing of any children under sixteen are the best that can be devised under the circumstances. The court is given wide power to make orders for the future care and upbringing of children under its jurisdiction, for example by the designation of probation officers.

One important corollary to this change of emphasis from the exclusive consideration of the husband–wife relation, and of divorce in particular as a matter of bilateral relation, to the consideration of the family as a social unit, should be a shift from the adversary to the inquisitorial function of the public authority dealing with divorce – be this a court, or an administrative agency.[20] No longer can it be maintained that divorce proceedings are analogous to an action for breach of contract, damages in tort or the recovery of property. A judge, a conciliation board, or any other public official entrusted

20. For a powerful criticism of the inadequacy of the adversary divorce court procedure as a means of eliciting the facts of family life, see Bradway, 'Divorce litigation and the welfare of the family', 9 *Vanderbilt L. Rev.* 665 (1956).

with an equitable arrangement for the care of children cannot possibly rest content with the allegations – contested or uncontested – of the parties in regard to the conduct of the other spouse. If consideration for the welfare of the children has to be a major factor in divorce proceedings, the theory of matrimonial offence is at most one of a number of factors to be considered by the competent public authority. All these factors point to the need for a procedure – less formal, more inquisitorial and less modelled upon adversary litigation than the present divorce procedure. It is reinforced by the – already noticeable – decline in prolonged and expensive divorce litigation following such divorce law reforms as the British Act of 1969.

The principle of an integrated family court, which would deal with the many-sided aspects of family disruption by non-adversary procedures, has, however, been the subject of most intensive study and experimentation in the United States. There are a number of reasons for this difference in approach. The federal structure of the United States, which puts family matters, education and the administration of justice in the hands of fifty different jurisdictions, encourages diversity and experimentation, although it also leads frequently to a bewildering and confusing variety of institutions. The sociological study of legal institutions is taken far more seriously in the United States than in Great Britain. Above all, the United States, and especially many of its major cities, in their mixture of nationalities, races, religions and social classes, creates social problems of disturbing complexity, which are reflected in family life. The need for an integrated treatment by one institution of such matters as juvenile delinquency, support claims between husband and wife or unmarried couples, divorce and other forms of marriage dissolution, custody of children and adoption has been increasingly recognized by all serious students and practitioners to be an urgent necessity. A number of cities, in Ohio and Oregon, have had integrated family courts for a number of years, and in the testimony of one of the outstanding authorities in the field,[21] in these cities 'complaints about overlapping, defective and conflicting jurisdiction, of lack of cooperation, of one court either wilfully or unwittingly undoing what another court has striven to do . . . are almost unheard of'.

21. Judge Paul W. Alexander of Toledo, Ohio, 'The family court of the future', 31 *Journal Amer. Jud. Soc.* 38 (1952).

The city of New York used to be a prominent example of over-lapping jurisdictions and courts, but in 1962 the state established the Family Court of New York, as part of a reorganization of its judiciary.[22] This essentially replaced the Domestic Relations Court of the City of New York and the Children's Court in the remaining counties. It has jurisdiction over substantially all aspects of family life, except actions for separation, annulment and divorce which are constitutionally reserved for the Supreme Court. A similar proposal has been made in 1966 by the Governor's Commission on the Family in California. It proposes a family court where adversary procedures would be minimized and professional counselling would be available to the parties on a voluntary basis. The idea is steadily gaining ground that all aspects of family life, including divorce and separation, are not just another form of litigation, but different aspects of the complex problem of the family, to be dealt with as a social and therapeutic matter rather than in terms of the success or failure of a legal action.

This approach also leads to the increasing recognition of preventive or curative methods, as an alternative to divorce. Marriage coun-selling is becoming increasingly recognized and organized on both the public and the private level as a way of ensuring that marriages are concluded with a proper mutual appreciation of the problems and responsibilities. Reconciliation systems have been incorporated in court procedure in a number of states, e.g. in New York and New Jersey, where reconciliation efforts are mandatory whenever there are minor children of the parties. They consist in a pre-trial con-ference before a reconciliation master designed to make every reason-able effort at reconciliation.[23]

There is almost unanimous agreement on the beneficial effect of these devices in the preparation for marriage and the prevention of unnecessary divorces. The main difficulties are not ones of principle, but of organization. An integrated family court, marriage counselling and reconciliation procedures demand far more well-trained staff than is at present available and legislators are generally willing to provide for. They also require intensive collaboration between lawyers, social

22. New York Family Court Act (McKinney, 1963).
23. For a survey of the New Jersey experiment and those of other states, see the above-mentioned Report of the Joint Legislative Committee on Matrimonial and Family Laws, New York State, 1958.

workers, psychiatrists and others. The need for such collaboration, not only in the field of family law, is one of the challenges put to law and the legal profession in contemporary society. And the provision of the necessary public and private finance is a question of education: of the understanding that the cost of such services is infinitesimal as compared with the material and moral cost to society of juvenile delinquency, broken marriages and uprooted children.

Procreation of Life as the Supreme Goal of Marriage

Although methods of birth control have been known for thousands of years (Himes, 1936), and were certainly practised on an extensive scale by the sophisticated and decaying Roman society of the imperial days, for mankind at large it has only in recent years become a practicable means of controlling the procreation of children. Progress in the science and techniques of birth control have been stimulated not only by the increasing study of the human body and the genetic process; the application, on a large scale, of biological and mechanical contraceptives has been, above all, stimulated by the revolutionary changes in the social conditions of life. Large-scale diseases and famines, until recently more brutal controllers of huge population increases than wars, have been mastered to such an extent that, in countries like India, Pakistan, China and most of the Latin-American states, a net increase of several million births a year swells their already big populations.

In these countries, the spread of birth control on a wide scale, with official encouragement, is becoming increasingly a matter of life and death, of national survival. The already very depressed standard of living of the masses is likely to decline further, unless some alternative is found for the brutal remedies of famine and disease.[24]

24. In Japan, whose population exceeds 100 million, on a small and already fully cultivated and developed island, the official encouragement of birth control in recent years has led to a drastic decline in the birth-rate in a generally educated population. In India, the Government is encouraging birth control clinics, but so far with indifferent success among a still overwhelmingly illiterate peasant population. The Government of Communist China, hitherto addicted to the Communist and totalitarian philosophy of encouraging the maximum number of children on a mixture of strategic grounds and the Marxist faith in unlimited opportunities in a socialist society, has in recent years urged the use of contraceptives on the women of that country.

In the western world, where contraceptive devices have been used on a much wider scale for a considerable time, the availability of an oral pill to be taken by women has immensely increased the general use of contraceptives.

The problem of control over the procreation of life has a social and political, as well as an ethical, aspect. The two are not unconnected, but they start from essentially different premises.

From a social and political perspective, the urgency of radical measures of control over the alarming growth of the world population can no longer be seriously doubted. Recent demographic estimates forecast at least a doubling of the present world population of some 3·5 billion, to 7–7·5 billion by the end of the century. This increase would, of course, continue not at an arithmetical but at an exponential rate. The dangers posed by such a rate of growth to available food resources, housing, urban conglomerations and the – already gravely threatened – ecological balance of the earth are evident. They are greatly increased by the fact that the highest rates of population growth occur in the poorer countries – notably in Asia and Latin America – thus further widening the gap between the minority of the rich and the majority of the poor nations. So great is the growing awareness of the urgency of this problem that more and more governments have come to officially sponsor birth control. This has been done for a number of years – though with little success – by the government of India. Recently, the government of the United States and the president of the World Bank have proclaimed assistance for population control to be among the objectives of development aid. The problem of population control is essentially one of international cooperation, and it is intimately linked with the problem of poverty, and the tensions that ultimately lead to war, on a worldwide scale.

The general public concern with the explosive rate of population growth has led to widespread recommendation of voluntary sterilization. In countries where the use of contraceptive devices is unreliable, because of the poverty, overcrowding and the lack of sophistication of the predominantly rural population – such as India – the government encourages by material incentives voluntary sterilization of families with a certain number of children. There is also growing discussion of the use of tax and welfare laws as a disincentive for large families. Contrary to the, hitherto predominant, tendency to support families by family allowances or tax exemptions, in proportion to the number of children, it is entirely within the range of new legislative policies that such assistance will not extend to children beyond a certain stated number (such as two or three), or that eventually fiscal penalties may be attached to the procreation of children beyond such a number. Even compulsory sterilization – despite the abhorrence produced by its abuse by the Nazi regime – cannot be entirely dismissed, as the social dangers of the population explosion reach ever more alarming proportions.

The social and political aspects of population control do not necessarily coincide with its ethical and religious aspects. An individualistic and liberal philosophy certainly favours individual family planning, as a way by which each family – and particularly the women, who throughout the ages have borne the physical and mental burden of continuous child bearing – can for themselves decide the size and spacing of their families. Modern facilities for education and other aspects of individual development have increased the desire to give better opportunities to fewer children. Sexual desire and fertility are no longer the sole controllers. Birth control is part of man's constant advance in his control over natural processes. In this aspect, it is an aspect of the technological and planned society.

However, individual family planning does not necessarily respond to the social and political necessities of drastically limiting the further rate of population growth. Recent demographic inquiries[25] have shown that the great majority of families – especially in the poorer countries, which have a large peasant population, and where traditionally children are considered as bread winners, would plan for families that would result in an overall world average of more than four children per family. This is far in excess of the rate deemed tolerable by demographic experts, economists and sociologists to prevent the social and political disasters of further population growth. Here social necessity clashes with individual wishes, and sometime, a painful and perhaps brutal choice will have to be made, probably in the direction of compulsory restrictions on population growth.

25. See, in particular, Kingsley Davis, 'Population policy', *Science*, vol. 158 (1967), p. 730.

There are, finally, religious objections to birth control.

The Catholic Church, whose influence upon some four to five hundred million practising Catholics throughout the world is deep, remains the most uncompromising foe of any form of deliberate birth control, other than by the use of the so-called 'rhythm' cycles, i.e. the use by married couples of non-fertile periods for the avoidance of procreation. Even this concession is not unconditional, as we shall see. The reason for this uncompromising attitude has been restated in the discourse given by Pope Pius XII in October 1951, to the Congress of the Italian Catholic Union of Midwives:[26]

Every human being, even the infant in the maternal womb, has the right to life *immediately* from God, not from the parents or any human society or authority. Therefore there is no man, no human authority, no science, no medical, eugenic, social, economic or moral 'indication', which can show or give a valid juridical title for *direct* deliberate disposition concerning an innocent human life.

From this premiss follows the absolute condemnation of sterilization. The deliberate use of sterile periods by the married couple for the prevention of conception is permissible, provided it is not made a condition of marriage, and provided there are serious motives, of an ethical, eugenic, economic or social character that justify the observation of non-fertile periods for a long time.

The distinction thus made is somewhat forced. From an ethical point of view, the deliberate use of the calendar can hardly be judged differently from the use of mechanical contraceptives. If it is immoral to interfere with the God-willed act of sexual union designed to ensure the procreation of children and the conservation of the human race, then any deliberate interference with the natural satisfaction of the sexual impulse between husband and wife must be ethically reprehensible.

Since the pronouncements of Pope Pius XII, the growing use of contraceptive devices, among Catholics as well as non-Catholics, the increasing acceptance of family planning and, above all, the growing awareness of the immense political and social dangers of the accelerating world population explosion, led to the appointment by Pope

26. Pope Pius XII (1951, p. 7).

Paul VI of a highly representative committee of ecclesiastics, which recommended in favour of the reconsideration of Church doctrine on this matter. But, in August 1968, Pope Paul VI issued the encyclical, *Humanae Vitae*, which unconditionally reaffirmed the earlier teaching of the Church. It added little to the above-stated theological arguments of his predecessors, except that it emphasized the dangers of population control being abused by government. It reaffirmed the legitimacy of the use of the rhythm period, as a responsible method of determining the future of the family, but unconditionally condemned the use of artificial contraceptives as an irresponsible incentive to lust and promiscuity, and a perversion of the God-ordained function of marriage.[27]

Humanae Vitae provoked a bitter worldwide debate and the open dissent of many Catholic prelates, theologians and laymen. Even the governments of some of the more strongly Catholic countries, such as Colombia and Puerto Rico, have, with the approval of their churches, begun to introduce family planning and birth control clinics in response to the growing dangers of uncontrolled population growth. It may well be that the uncompromising attitude of *Humanae Vitae* will provide the greatest danger in centuries to the authority of the Church.

The House of Lords, in 1948, expressed a diametrically opposite philosophy when it affirmed the dismissal of a petition for nullity on the ground of a wife's alleged refusal to consummate the marriage, because of insistence on the use by the husband of a contraceptive sheath. Lord Jowitt L.C. adverted to the 'common knowledge' that birth-control clinics existed and that many young people agreed to take contraceptive precautions. 'I take the view that in this legislation Parliament used the word "consummate" as that word is understood in common parlance and in the light of social conditions known to exist. . . .'[28] Later cases[29] have, however, held that refusal by one spouse to have a child where the other desires one may amount to cruelty.

27. For a more detailed discussion of *Humanae Vitae* see Friedmann, 'Interference with human life', 70 *Columbia L. Rev.* 1058 (1970).
28. *Baxter* v. *Baxter* [1948] A.C. 274.
29. *Knott* v. *Knott* [1955] 3 *W.L.R.* 162.

It follows from the general premises of the Catholic Church that sterilization is unconditionally condemned under any circumstances.[30] More surprisingly, it also condemns unconditionally artificial insemination between husband and wife.

To reduce cohabitation and the conjugal act to a pure organic function for the transmission of seed would be converting the home, the sanctuary of the family, into a mere biological laboratory. In Our address of 29 September 1949, to the International Congress of Catholic Doctors, We formally excluded artificial insemination from marriage. In its natural structure, the conjugal act is a personal action, a simultaneous and immediate cooperation on the part of the husband and wife which by the very nature of the agents and the propriety of the act is the expression of the mutual gift which according to Holy Scripture brings about union 'in one flesh only'.[31]

None of the non-Catholic Churches follow the Catholic Church in this condemnation of artificial insemination between husband and wife, though most of them reject insemination by a donor (Williams, 1957, p. 130).

As no possible question of adultery, or any of the many other legal problems created by insemination with the seed of a third donor[32] is involved in cases of artificial insemination between husband and wife, the only justification for its unconditional condemnation by the Catholic Church is the assumption that the natural consummation of the sexual act is more important in the scale of values of the Church than the procreation of children. There seems to be here a strange confusion between nature in the elementary biological sense and nature as an order of reason in which two human beings, endowed with a sense of purpose and conscious love, seek to seal their union by the procreation of a child through artificial insemination, as they cannot achieve it in the usual way. There is surely in such a decision a nobleness of purpose, which should command respect rather than condemnation. While there may be many other objections to the practice of artificial insemination, it seems inconsistent to condemn it – as between husband and wife – on moral grounds.

30. Pope Pius XII (1951, p. 13).
31. Pope Pius XII (1951, p. 20).
32. For the considerable legal literature dealing with these problems, see Williams (1957, p. 129) and Tallin, 34 *Canadian Bar Rev.* 1, 166 (1956).

Legitimacy of Abortion

An even deeper problem is posed by the legitimacy of abortion. Interference with a life created and developing – however remote from a complete human being that lives and acts as a person – is, psychologically and legally, different from acts preventing the creation of life. Again, the Catholic Church has a simple and absolute solution. Its theory is that every human being, including the embryo immediately after the union of the male sperm and the female ovum, has received its right to life from God, not from the parents or any human society or authority, and that, therefore, any interference with this life is a crime against the law of God and nature.[33]

This dogma is based on the conviction that any human being (including the embryo in the womb) which dies unbaptized is incapable of being rescued from sin. With remorseless logic, the Church has deduced from this premiss that the killing of the child in the womb is not even justified in order to save the life of the mother. '. . . the state of grace at the moment of death is absolutely necessary for salvation; without it, no one can attain to supernatural happiness, the beatific vision of God'.[34] Consequently, the life of the infant in the womb must be saved, even if it means certain death for the mother. While the physicians must do everything that modern medicine provides in order to avoid the terrible choice, they have to give preference to the preservation of the innocent life of the unborn infant if there is no other choice. Some slight concession is made by a subtle distinction of intentions which it is extremely difficult to observe in practice: the killing of the embryo may be permitted where it is not the 'direct' consequence of an operation intended to bring about this very result, but only the indirect result of an operation primarily made for other reasons. Thus an operation upon a tubal pregnancy is now apparently permissible, because the killing of the foetus is not direct, but indirect.[35]

As with the distinction made between the use of the calendar and the use of contraceptives, so the permission to use modern medical science to the utmost to avoid the terrible dilemma, seems to under-

33. Pope Pius XII (1951, p. 7).
34. Pope Pius XII (1951, p. 10).
35. Code of Ethical and Religious Directives for Catholic Hospitals cited in Williams (1957, p. 202).

mine the logic of the acceptance of the 'order of nature'. At what point does human interference with the biological processes become 'unnatural'?

There is, between this and the opposing theory – which, in such a situation, gives preference to the life of the mother – a deep conflict of philosophy. The Catholic philosophy accepts the inescapable consequences of an order of things willed by God, and compelling even the greatest human sacrifices for the sake of a higher order of things which demands the saving of the unborn infant, even if the price is the sacrifice of the mother of a large family that will be left unprotected and bereft.

For the opposing philosophy the family is deeply important, but a human and social institution. In this perspective the life of the mother must be more important than the preservation of an embryo.

Most countries now recognize therapeutic abortion. As the preservation of one person's life is not generally recognized in these same systems as justification for the taking of another's,[36] this implies a hierarchy of values opposite to that of the Catholic Church, a recognition that the mother is the centre of the family, a full human being with its responsibilities, rights and burdens, while the embryo is a human being only in a biological but not an intellectual or ethical sense.

The legitimacy of therapeutic abortion is now recognized by legislation in most of the United States (see Williams, 1957, p. 160). The position was universally taken to be the same in England, since the decision in *Bourne's* case,[37] where a famous gynaecologist performed an abortion upon a girl of fourteen who had been raped by a number of soldiers and, consequently, had become pregnant. The decision was influenced by the unusually shocking circumstances of the pregnancy.

As long as the legitimacy of abortion is as strictly and narrowly defined as it still is in most contemporary common-law jurisdictions, interpretation in a concrete case will always remain somewhat uncertain, dependent on the sympathies of judge and jury in the concrete circumstances. Such a state of law is likely to increase, if possible,

36. See *R.* v. *Dudley and Stephens* (1884) 14 Q.B.D. 273; *US* v. *Holmes*, 26 Fed. Case 360 (CCED Pa. 1842).
37. *R.* v. *Bourne* [1939] 1 K.B. 687.

the fantastic discrepancy between prosecutions for abortions and the number of abortions actually performed.[38] Moreover, because of the grave uncertainties of the legal position and the threat to their professional status, or even to their personal liberty in case of an error of interpretation, a very large number of qualified medical practitioners will abstain from performing abortions which they consider necessary and desirable, thus leaving the field to the thousands of unqualified practitioners. These, in order to compensate for the dangers of their clandestine occupation, charge very high fees.

These factors, as well as a widespread shift in public opinion towards individual decision-making in family matters, account for the sweeping legislative reforms enacted in a number of major common law systems, in recent years. This development is all the more remarkable as it follows on decades of passivity. The British Abortion Act of 1967, the recommendations of the American Model Penal Code adopted by about a dozen American states at present, and the more far-reaching abortion law reforms adopted in 1970 in the state of New York, illustrate this new legislative trend. The Model Penal Code[39] permits abortion by a licensed physician

if he believes there is substantial risk that continuance of the pregnancy would gravely impair the physical or mental health of the mother or that the child would be born with grave mental or physical defect, or that the pregnancy resulted from rape, incest or other felonious intercourse. All illicit intercourse with a girl below the age of sixteen shall be deemed felonious for purposes of this subsection.

Two physicians must certify the circumstances which they believe to justify the abortion. Failure to do so gives rise to a presumption that the abortion was unjustified.

The British Act of 1967 substantially adopts the recommendations of the American Model Penal Code. But it goes further in the direction of justification of abortion for reasons of 'social indication'. It provides that, with respect to risk of injury to the health of the pregnant woman, 'account may be taken of the pregnant woman's actual

38. Taking an average of the various semi-official and authoritative estimates made, Williams (1957, p. 210), concludes 'that there is not in England more than one prosecution to every thousand criminal abortions'.
39. Proposed Official Draft, § 230.3 (1962).

or reasonably foreseeable environment'. Where it is 'immediately necessary to save the life or to prevent grave permanent injury to the physical or mental health of the pregnant woman', it is not necessary to establish the facts outlined in the foregoing definition.

The state of New York – as well as a few other American jurisdictions – in 1970 went even further, by making abortion legitimate where there is consent between the pregnant woman and her doctor. This legislative reform – adopted after a bitter and prolonged debate – is all the more remarkable as a substantial and articulate Catholic minority in New York had, until recently, prevented far more modest reforms.

A few American states have thus followed the solution adopted by two of the world's most populous states outside the common-law world. The Soviet Union, together with its many other radical departures in family relations, legalized abortion after the Revolution, until 1936, when the practice was prohibited except for medical and eugenic reasons. At the end of 1955, the legality of abortion – without any restriction, except that the operation has to be performed by qualified persons in hospitals or other health institutions – was restored.

In Japan, where sterilization and abortion were legalized for medical, economic and eugenic reasons in 1948, with the result that well over one million abortions were recorded in 1954, the main reason is unquestionably the threat to Japan's economic existence stemming from the rapid population increase on a small, very densely populated and fully developed island which no longer sees conquest as a means of expansion.

The Model Penal Code is closer to the reforms introduced, first, in Sweden in 1938, and later followed by Denmark and Finland. Apart from medical indication, i.e. serious danger to the life or health of the mother, the ground of abortion recognized in most western countries, and of 'humanitarian' abortion, where the woman has become pregnant through a criminal act such as rape, the Scandinavian laws also permit abortion on account of 'weakness' of the prospective mother, and on certain eugenic grounds (danger of transmission to the offspring through hereditary channels of insanity, mental deficiency or serious physical disease). The administration of these acts is entrusted to medical boards, and it is only on their authorization that pregnancy may be terminated on one of the grounds stated in the law. Simultaneously with this statutory reform, the Scandinavian states have encouraged the setting up of contraceptive clinics, together with their far-reaching social welfare legislation, which includes maternal welfare centres, subsidized housing, far-reaching tax relief for families with children and other measures designed to increase the well-being of families. Although in Sweden, where the experience is longest, the new laws have brought about a very substantial increase in the number of official abortions, there is some controversy as to its effect on illegal abortions.[40]

A modern western legislator must recognize that abortion is a very major social phenomenon in any country, and that the alternative is between giving it some legal outlet or driving it entirely underground.

Beyond danger to life and health, an open recognition of the defence on the grounds given in the Scandinavian laws or the Model Penal Code, for humanitarian or eugenic reasons, should raise no serious problem. Threatened with many other disasters, mankind has no interest in the multiplication of defective children who will be a burden to themselves and to others, nor is there moral justification to compel mothers to have children in the circumstances of *Bourne*'s case.

Abortion for 'social indication' proper will remain a more controversial matter. To this writer it seems that, where a board composed of public officials, social workers and experienced doctors should decide that the continuation of a pregnancy would gravely affect the life of a family, abortion should be permitted. The legitimation of such carefully controlled grounds for abortion, would be likely at least to narrow the glaring discrepancy between the letter of the law and the social reality in every modern country. The criminality of abortion has not proved to be an effective instrument of social control.

Some critics (Williams, 1957, p. 232) reject the criminal sanction as altogether fallacious, since it has involved 'social evils greater than the alleged evil of abortion itself, without, in fact, preventing abortions'. That such is the case, it would be difficult to deny.

40. For a discussion, with reference in particular to Ekblad (1955), see Williams (1957, p. 236). See also Diggory *et al.*, 1970 1 *Lancet* 287; Simms, 1970 *Crim. L. Rev.* 567; Finnis, 1971, *Crim. L. Rev.* 3.

As we have seen, there is today a wide spectrum of legal responses to the problem of abortion, ranging from the near-absolute prohibition of the Catholic Church, and of legal systems inspired by the Catholic Doctrine – to the complete legitimation of abortion by married women in such legally and politically different systems as Japan, New York and the Soviet Union. Between these extremes, a rapidly increasing number of countries are permitting abortion for a variety of medical – and to a certain extent social – reasons.

Equality of Husband and Wife in the Marriage Community

In the present century, the social and economic position of the married woman has changed more drastically than in any previous period of western history. In the predominantly agrarian economy of earlier centuries, the wife played the part of the manager, though not the head, of the household, guarding the children, preparing meals, supervising the staff in the wealthier families, and generally managing the internal economy of the household.[41] In the increasingly industrialized and urbanized society of the nineteenth century, these conditions changed drastically. But the social and legal concepts, framed in earlier centuries, of the supremacy of the husband were preserved and, indeed, to some extent magnified in the Victorian middle-class conception of the patriarchal father, majestically and often pompously ruling the family in his wisdom.

Matrimonial Property Law

The matrimonial law – both of the civil-law codifications of the nineteenth and early twentieth centuries, and of the common-law jurisdictions – reflects this social supremacy of the husband. In the civil-law world, except for the recent statutory reforms in Scandinavia and West Germany, community property systems predominate. Until well into the present century, and to some extent even today, community property means largely that 'husband and wife are one, and

41. Perhaps the most vivid, though poetic, description of a typical rural household of the late eighteenth century is found in the poem *Die Glocke* by Friedrich Schiller.

the husband is the one'. Throughout the nineteenth century, and in some legislations such as that of the Province of Quebec even at the present time, the married woman remains severely limited in her freedom of movement and in the right to dispose of her own property. Community property systems, whether of the full community variety or of the more limited type such as the community of acquests, embody the principle of the supremacy of the husband.[42]

In the common-law jurisdictions, the classical common law as laid down in Blackstone's *Commentaries on the Laws of England* (bk 1, ch. 15; bk 2, ch. 29), enshrines the superiority of the husband. The married woman was incapable of owning, acquiring or disposing of tangible or intangible movable property, as well as of disposing of immovable property (without her husband's consent). A similar position prevailed in Scotland through the *jus mariti*, which made all the wife's movable estate, acquired before or after marriage, the husband's property and gave him the right of administration over her entire estate. Being incapable of acquiring or disposing of property, the married woman was also considered incapable of assuming responsibility for any debts which the law might have imposed upon her. It was only through equity that a gradual change occurred. Originally, it was for the protection of family fortunes against the depredations of extravagant husbands that equity developed the concept of the 'separate property' of the married woman, over which she, herself, was considered capable of disposing, without the concurrence of the husband. Simultaneously, however, equity admitted the 'restraint upon anticipation' by which the family of the wife was enabled to shield the property settled upon a married woman from disposal by her under the influence of her husband. But the equity concept of 'separate property' paved the way in England and, through the adoption of the English common law in the majority of the American common-law jurisdictions, also in the United States for the gradual introduction of the new public policy of equality of husband and wife. In England, a statute of 1882 created a statutory separate estate (all the wife's real and personal

42. See, e.g. for the community of acquest systems prevalent in Louisiana and seven Western states of the United States, the articles by Clark and Morrow in Friedmann (ed.) (1955, pp. 29, 89). On the contemporary law of Quebec, see Turjeon, in Friedmann (1955, p. 139).

property acquired before or after marriage) over which any married woman had free control. The restraint on anticipation was abolished in several stages and, finally, in English legislation of 1949 (Kahn-Freund in Friedmann, 1955, p. 275). By a parallel process, the common-law jurisdictions of the United States[43] have enlarged the equity concept of separate property into a general system of separate ownership and administration, on a basis of equality of the assets of husband and wife (Dean in Friedmann, 1955, p. 315). Thus the modern common-law jurisdictions – in England, the majority of the American states, the common-law provinces of Canada, and in the other units of the Commonwealth which share the common-law tradition – have coupled the notions of equality and separateness. Together with the legal supremacy of the husband, they have abandoned the legal concept of community in the management of the marriage. They have recognized the claim to free mobility and responsibility of the modern married woman by constituting her an equal but separate partner in the marriage household.

At the same time, the civilian systems – responding, though in very unequal measure, to the same social pressures, namely, the gradual transformation of the position of the married woman from domestic inferiority to equal partnership – have attempted to modify the systems of community property so as to give greater legal freedom to the married woman. This process is, however, far from complete. Vestiges of inequality between husband and wife remain in all the legal systems which preserve a community property regime – be it the full community or the community of acquests, or another of the variants of community regimes. It is only in Soviet law, which, in the Family Code of 1926, introduced the community of acquests,[44] that, consistent with the recognition of the full legal equality of the woman,

43. e.g. the Domestic Relations Law of New York, section 50: 'Property, real or personal, now owned by a married woman, or hereafter owned by a married woman at the time of her marriage, or acquired by her as prescribed in this chapter, and the rents, issues, proceeds and profits thereof, shall continue to be her sole and separate property as if she were unmarried, and shall not be subject to her husband's control or disposal nor liable for his debts' (see Dean in Friedmann, 1955, p. 326).

44. i.e. common ownership of all property earned by the spouses during the continuation of the marriage, as distinct from property belonging to the spouses before entering upon marriage – which remains separate property.

the legal status and capacity of the married woman is in no way different from that of the husband or from that of an unmarried woman.[45] 'Marriage creates no limitations upon the capacity of a wife as a legal person' (Hazard in Friedmann, 1955, p. 219). The French Code Civil, which introduced the era of modern statutory community regimes, gave to the husband the most extensive power of administration and disposal over the assets of the community. Though this did not extend to the wife's immovables, the change of emphasis in industrialized society from land to other assets served, if anything, to increase this predominance of the husband.

After decades of pressure for the reform of a legal regime that was increasingly out of step with the contemporary status and activities of the married woman – in France as elsewhere in the western world – the law of July 1965, finally introduced a sweeping change, though it still falls short of complete equality between husband and wife. The new statutory regime is the community of acquests [*communauté des acquêts*]. It is defined in the new article 1401 of the Code as 'the acquisitions made jointly or severally by the spouses during the marriage, and deriving whether from their own industry or from savings out of the fruits and revenues of their separate property'. All assets are presumed to be jointly acquired, in the absence of proof that they are separate property. The latter consists essentially of premarital property as well as property acquired during marriage by way of inheritance, legacy or gift. But it also includes personal items and rights of a personal character. Despite much support in the parliamentary debates for complete equality, the husband is still entrusted with the administration of the communal property, but he requires the wife's consent for most important transactions – such as the sale of immovables or of a business enterprise. Premarital debts of either spouse remain personal and do not bind the community. Another important innovation is that the spouses have freedom to modify all or part of the statutory regime by contract. In particular they may alter the statutory provisions for administration of the common as well as the separate assets. After the 1965 reform, the two basic matrimonial regimes in France that remain are the community

45. The West German *Gleichberechtigungsgesetz* of 1957, like the earlier Scandinavian statutes, which give full equality to husband and wife, have essentially abandoned the community concept (see p. 272).

of acquests – subject to contractual modifications – and the regime of separation of property.

The German Civil Code of 1900 similarly provided for a statutory community of all except certain reserved assets of the wife. The husband had the sole administration as well as the usufruct of all the properties falling into the community. In the eight states of the United States in which community regimes apply, under the influence of French or Spanish antecedents, the prevalent regime is that of the community of acquests, i.e. of property acquired by either spouse after marriage, unless it is specifically reserved by a donor from such a community. But in these systems, too, it is the husband who alone has the power of administration over the community property,[46] except that, in some states, the wife may dispose freely over her own earnings, and that, in some cases, husband and wife must join in real-property transactions (Clark in Friedmann, 1955, p. 101). It is, of course, possible, under any of these legal systems, to exclude the statutory community by marriage contract or to provide for alternative methods of management. However, in family law, the proportion of such arrangements is insignificant. It is on the whole confined to the marriages of propertied people, into which the wife brings a considerable property of her own, or where she runs a separate business. The great majority of family households are run, without settlements or marriage contracts, according to the statutory principles laid down in the law of the land. It is, therefore, the statutory or common-law regime that is of overwhelming practical significance. Except for the USSR, those countries which have introduced full equality of the spouses have done so by abandoning or drastically modifying the traditional community-property system altogether. The basic principle of reform – introduced by the model Swedish Marriage Code of 1920 – which is substantially identical with the laws of Denmark, Finland, Iceland and Norway and whose concepts have, to a large extent, been incorporated in the West German Matrimonial Property Law of 1957 – is that the property of both spouses remains entirely separate during marriage, with full independence and equality on the part of both to administer their property, while, on the dissolution of the marriage, the 'matrimonial

46. For Louisiana, see Morrow in Friedmann (1955, p. 50); for the Western states, see Clark in Friedmann (1955, p. 98).

property', i.e. all property of both spouses other than certain gifts or other property declared separate, is equally divided between the spouses. Thus the community idea applies not during marriage, but only upon its dissolution for the purpose of an equitable settlement (Malmström in Friedmann, 1955, p. 410). This means, in effect, separation of property during marriage. The community idea is preserved only as an accounting procedure on the dissolution of marriage, not as a partnership during marriage.

The importance of the community idea in the management of family affairs is tellingly illustrated by certain recent developments within the common-law jurisdiction, especially in England. As stated before, the emancipation of the married woman in the common-law world has been affected by a coupling of the idea of liberty with absolute separation of goods. In some common-law jurisdictions, notably in the Western Provinces of Canada and some American states in the United States, a certain recognition of the community element is found in the legal acknowledgement of the matrimonial homestead, over which the husband has no power to dispose without the concurrence of his wife, regardless of the formal property rights.[47] Apart from this exception, significant mainly in rural areas,[48] and the introduction of the joint income and property concept into Federal Tax declarations by husband and wife in the United States,[49] the common-law jurisdictions seem to have been content, until recently, with the principle of full separation. But recent developments in England indicate that a factual community of work and property, which controls the overwhelming majority of family households,

47. See, for the relevant Canadian legislation, Auld in Friedmann (1955, p. 259).

48. In a number of other states, certain financial privileges are granted to married women on account of 'homesteads', but here the homestead is merely an accounting item. Moreover, the exemption is usually very low.

49. This is due to the political impossibility of confining the more favourable rate, applicable through the splitting of the joint income of husband and wife on a fifty-fifty basis, to community-property systems. After a number of hasty legislative changes, introducing community property in traditionally common-law jurisdictions, the Federal Tax Law was amended so as to make the income of husband and wife optionally joint throughout the country. After this reform, the common-law states promptly reverted to the common-law system of matrimonial property.

cannot be altogether ignored by the law. In 1953, the Court of Appeal[50] held that where husband and wife have both contributed during marriage to certain acquisitions, such as the purchase of a house, 'and where it is not possible or right to assume some more precise calculation of their shares', the division should be on a fifty-fifty basis, irrespective of the fact that unequal amounts may have been contributed. Here the idea of partnership prevails. The wife contributes through her work to the education of her children and the management of the household as much as the husband who goes out and earns. A long string of decisions, under the leadership of Lord Denning, M.R., continued to develop the idea of 'family assets', using the discretionary power of section 17 of the Married Woman's Property Act 1882, under which '[i]n any question between husband and wife as to . . . the separate property of the wife, [upon application by either party] . . . the judge may make such order . . . as he shall think fit . . .'. In one of the most recent cases,[51] the husband had voluntarily improved his wife's property, and the Court of Appeal, under the Matrimonial Court Rules 1957, awarded the husband a percentage of the proceeds of the house commensurate with the value of the improvements due to his work. In the words of Lord Denning, M.R.: 'In those circumstances, it is not correct to look and see whether there was any bargain in the past, or any expressed intention. A judge can only do what is fair and reasonable in the circumstances.'

But in 1969 the House of Lords in *Pettitt* v. *Pettitt*,[52] after a review of all the relevant cases, in a situation very similar to that of *Appleton*, came down firmly against the whole idea of 'family assets' and a wide interpretation of the discretionary power under the 1882 Act. It denied the husband after divorce a share in the proceeds of a house inherited by his wife, on which he had carried out a number of improvements. While the actual decision may be justifiable, the reasoning is surprising. Absent joint property title or contractual arrangements, the House declared itself unable to alter the interpretation of the 1882 Act 'merely by reason of a change in social outlook since the date of the enactment. . . . We have in this

50. *Rimmer* v. *Rimmer* [1953] 1 Q.B. 63.
51. *Appleton* v. *Appleton* [1965] 1 W.L.R. 25.
52. [1969] 2 All E.R. 385.

country no doctrine of community of goods between spouses and yet by judicial decision were this doctrine of family assets to be accepted some such doctrine would become part of the law of the land' (per Lord Upjohn).

Despite a long string of decisions to the contrary, the profound changes in the relation of husband and wife were dismissed and the ability of courts to develop or adapt existing rules of the 'common law to meet new conditions . . . excluded for matters which directly affect the lives and interests of large sections of the community' (per Lord Reid). Yet the House of Lords has felt able to change established law and interpretations far more radically than that in such recent decisions as *Rookes* v. *Barnard* and *Hedley Bryne* v. *Heller*, discussed elsewhere in this book (see pp. 50–51, 55). Shortly after *Pettitt*, the Court of Appeal reasserted the 'family assets' principle.[53] It held that where a wife had regularly helped her husband in a business that prospered by their joint efforts, without receiving any wages, she was entitled to a half share in the proceeds. Lord Denning M.R. distinguished this type of case from those where one spouse does 'odd jobs' about the house and emphasized that *Pettitt* v. *Pettitt* did not 'affect the many cases where there are no established rights and the court has to do the best it can.' It is doubtful, in the light of the decision of the House of Lords in *Gissing* v. *Gissing*,[54] reaffirming the principles announced in *Pettitt*, whether the Court of Appeal's view of 'family assets' will survive. No mention was made, in any of the judgements in *Pettitt* v. *Pettitt*, of the Matrimonial Homes Act 1967, which gives to a spouse who has no proprietary title the right to occupation of the matrimonial home. Although contrary to earlier proposals, this right ends with the marriage (except under an express court order) and is a *ius in personam*, not an equitable interest,[55] as held in *Bendall* v. *McWhirter*.[56] This adoption

53. *Nixon* v. *Nixon*, [1969] 1 W.L.R. 1676 (C.A.).

54. [1970] 3 W.L.R. 285.

55. It is, however, registrable by an order of the Court. If the spouse is occupying, it is registrable without an order, and binds third parties once registered.

56. In *Bendall* v. *McWhirter* [1952] Q.B. 466, the Court of Appeal sought to create an equitable right for the deserted wife to continue occupation of the marital home. This decision was overruled by the House of Lords in 1964, *National Provincial Bank* v. *Ainsworth* [1965] A.C. 1175.

of a limited kind of 'homestead' principle is a further indication of legislative policy in the direction of family assets. In the overwhelming majority of cases husband and wife make no agreements but pool their work and their assets. Equitable financial adjustments, after separation or divorce, cannot repair the marriage. But their absence can aggravate bitterness and resentment – which, in turn, may affect the children of the marriage.[57]

Basically, the same kind of social transformation has operated in the civilian and common-law jurisdictions of the western world. In the civilian systems, the entrenched power of the husband as 'lord and master', with unilateral powers of management and disposal over the wife's property, is fighting a rearguard battle. The solution had been in part to give both spouses equal powers of management.[58] But in other cases, such as those of Scandinavia and West Germany, it has been found preferable to keep them separate and equal in the actual management of the marriage and reserve the community idea to equitable apportionment. Conversely, the common-law jurisdictions are coming to recognize the *de facto* community of marriage by actual or proposed restrictions on the unilateral power of either spouse to dispose freely of certain matters of joint concern, by protecting the deserted wife in the possession of the matrimonial home against the deserting husband, by protecting the wife, like other dependants, against arbitrary wills by means of a minimum portion. The systematic – and the actual – gap between the two systems is thus diminishing to the extent that they recognize the transformation in the position of the modern married woman.[59]

57. The Law Commission in its *Report on Financial Provision in Matrimonial Proceedings*, specifically underlined the necessity for judicial powers of adjustment of property rights in proceedings ancillary to divorce, nullity or judicial separation. The Matrimonial Proceedings and Property Act 1970 allows the court to take into consideration the wife's contribution in cash or services and to exercise its strengthened powers to settle and transfer property accordingly. For a full discussion of *Pettitt* v. *Pettitt*, see Miller, 'Family assets', 86 *L.Q. Rev.* 98 (1970).

58. The French reform of 1965 goes some way towards equality of management but preserves certain prerogatives for the husband (see p. 271).

59. In 1969, the Ontario Law Reform Commission (Family Law Project) recommended a reform of matrimonial property law very close to that of the German Act of 1957. See Eekelaar, 32 *Mod. L. Rev.* 678 (1969).

Parents and Children

Inevitably, the transformation in the economic and social condition of the modern family has profoundly affected the legal relationships between parents and children. It is naturally least pronounced, or totally absent, in societies which have not yet felt any substantial change in the traditional status of the family, such as many of the contemporary Muslim societies. It is most pronounced in the societies which have more strongly felt the impact of the change in the position of modern women and children, and which are most exposed to the influence of economic, physical and social mobility that characterizes urbanization and industrialization. In the common-law jurisdictions, which have been subjected to gradual evolution, the adaptation is also a gradual and continuing one. In some other legal systems, where there has been a radical social and constitutional change, the transformation is more abrupt.[60]

The transformation of the relationship between parents and children can be summed up under three major headings:

1. The replacement of the more or less absolute powers of the father, based on property rights, by broader moral and legal responsibility towards his children.
2. The translation of the social and legal emancipation of the married woman into a corresponding equality of rights and duties towards the children.
3. The increasing responsibilities of the state and other public authorities for the welfare of children.

In the common-law jurisdictions, a lingering survival of the earlier emphasis on property rights has generally made it necessary to express changes in the legal relationships between parents and children by statutes regulating the functions of the Chancery Courts or their

60. Some modern states, like India, have clearly adopted the principle of the equality of sexes, of equal opportunity for all and of the care, maintenance, and education of children, in accordance with the principles of modern Western societies (see Indian Constitution, Arts. 15, 23, 24, and others). But the translation of these principles into reality, in a society struggling against a centuries-old tradition of caste, sex, and other discriminations, will, of course, take a long time.

modern successors.[61] In a recent Continental statutory reform, however, the West German *Gleichberechtigungsgesetz* of 1957, amending the Civil Code of 1900, the duty of care is formulated as part of the general nexus of relationship between parents and children:

The child stays, as long as it has not come of age, under the parental power of his father and mother.

The father and the mother have . . . by virtue of their parental power the right and the duty to look after the person and the property of the child; the care for his person and property comprises the power of legal representation (s. 1626 BGB as amended).

The care for the person of the child specifically comprises the right and the duty 'to educate, to supervise and to determine his residence' (s. 1631 BGB as amended).

In this modern formulation, the accent is properly shifted from the supervisory functions of guardian courts to the normal relationships of parents and children.

A principal aspect of the duty of care is the duty to support the child. Here again, the common law has only gradually, and by no means unanimously, developed a legal, as distinct from a moral, duty of the parents, 'regardless of any statute, to maintain their legitimate minor children, the obligation being sometimes spoken of as one under the common law, and sometimes as a matter of natural right and justice, and often accepted as a matter of course without the assignment of any reason'.[62] In some American jurisdictions, the obligation of parents to support their minor children is still regarded as a moral, and not a legal, one under the common law.[63] Similarly, it has recently been stated to be the English position that 'the liability of a parent to maintain his or her child arises, not under the common law, but under various statutory provisions' (*Report of the Royal Commission on Marriage and Divorce*, 1956, s. 560).

61. See New York Domestic Relations Law, para. 70, giving the court power to determine, on habeas corpus, for a child detained by a parent, in regard to the custody of the child, 'what is for the best interest of the child, and what will best promote its welfare and happiness and make award accordingly'. See also the English Guardianship of Infants Act of 1925, s. 1. which regulates the powers of custody in similar terms.

62. *Campbell* v. *Campbell* (1942) 200 S.C. 67, 20 S.E. 2nd 237.

63. See the survey in *Porter* v. *Powell*, 79 Iowa 151, 44 N.W. 295 (1890).

Such duty now exists under a variety of statutes.[64] Again, the duty of maintenance is stated comprehensively in the amendment of the German Civil Code by the Statute of 1957:

The spouses are mutually obliged to maintain the family adequately through their work and their assets. . . . The adequate maintenance of the family comprises everything that, considering the circumstances of the spouses, is necessary to meet the costs of the household and to satisfy the personal wants of the spouses and the needs of their common children entitled to maintenance (ss. 1360, 1360a BGB as amended).[65]

Correspondingly, the parent of a minor child is not only empowered to administer his assets, but he is also legally entitled to the services and earnings of the child, until the latter is 'emancipated'.[66] The occurrence of 'emancipation', and the practical significance of this control over property and earnings of the child is, of course, greatly affected by the vastly increased habits and possibilities of minor children of working age – long customary in the working classes, but increasingly practised among the middle classes of the western countries – to take employment, or training, coupled with earnings outside the family. In this they are legally supported by the right, long recognized by the common law, to contract for 'necessaries'. It has been held that 'where . . . the parent in authority permits the child to contract for himself, emancipation in respect of earnings may be implied'.[67] In some cases, the condition under which the parental control over the proceeds of the labour of the child is lost has been formulated by statute. Thus, the Georgia Code, § 74–108, provides that the parental power shall be lost by:

1. Voluntary contract, releasing the right to a third person.
2. Consenting to the adoption of the child by a third person.
3. Failure of the father to provide necessaries for his child, or his abandonment.

64. e.g. the Summary Jurisdiction (Separation and Maintenance) Acts, 1895 to 1949, the Matrimonial Causes Act 1965, c. 72, s. 34, or the National Assistance Act 1948, s. 42, under which the National Assistance Board may take over the liability for maintenance and recover the cost of assistance from the parents.
65. In Scotland, as distinct from England, the common law imposes upon the parents the liability to aliment their children in so far as they are able.
66. *Kehely* v. *Kehely*, 200 Ga. 41, 36 S.E. 2nd, 155 (1946) and the note in Jacobs and Goebel (1961, p. 976).
67. *Bonner* v. *Surman*, 215 Ark. 301, 220 S.W. 2nd, 431 (1949).

4. Consent of the father to the child's receiving the proceeds of his own labour, which consent shall be revocable at any time.

5. Consent to the marriage of the child, who thus assumes inconsistent responsibilities.

6. Cruel treatment of the child.

The restriction and regulation of the once unconditional paternal power over the child has been accompanied by the increasing recognition of the mother's rights and obligations. This is a necessary corollary to the modern emancipation of the married woman, of her recognition as a person equal in status to her husband and contributing fully to the maintenance of the family, whether she goes out to work, in employment, the exercise of a profession, or the conduct of a business, or whether she contributes her share through responsibility for the household. The German Act of 1957 recognizes this evolution by emphasizing the right of every married woman to earn, while emphasizing her primary sphere in the family.[68] Both spouses are under an obligation to collaborate in the professional business of the other spouse in so far as this is usual in the conditions under which the spouses live (section 1356 BGB as amended).

The wife complies with her obligation to contribute to the maintenance of the family by her own work normally through the conduct of the household; she is obliged to engage in gainful work only in so far as the working capacity of the husband and the revenues of the spouses are not sufficient for the maintenance of the family, and in so far as it is not in accordance with the financial circumstances of the spouses that she should use her own capital assets (section 1360 BGB as amended).

While, in the common-law jurisdictions, the primary obligation for maintenance still generally rests with the father,[69] the trend is clearly in the same direction. This finds expression in the generally rather conservative Report of the British Royal Commission

that in England and Scotland the principle that husband and wife are jointly liable for the maintenance of the children should be followed in any matrimonial proceedings in which the question of maintenance of children arises (s. 568).

68. The wife conducts the household in her own responsibility. She is entitled to engage in gainful work (*erwerbstätig*), in so far as this is compatible with her obligations in marriage and in the family.

69. Though not under the National Assistance Act of 1948, c. 29, s. 42.

Again, this only expresses the reality of contemporary conditions in the western world, where

while husband and wife are living together it usually happens that both help to support the children in proportion to their respective means (s. 567).

Where, as in Soviet Russia, the right and the practice of married women to work outside the family is widespread and officially recognized, it is logical that the law should stipulate the duty of mutual support of parents and children.[70] The practice of the Soviet courts and public authorities has emphasized this duty of mutual maintenance (Hazard, 1953, p. 258).

The status of the illegitimate child

The unfortunate, and often tragic, status of the illegitimate child in the great majority of modern western family laws is an outcome of the Christian conception of the monogamous marriage. In polygamous societies, 'children are the *desideratum*; not too great an emphasis is placed on their source'.[71] But it is only the philosophy of original sin and the fall from grace that can justify the continuing discrimination against the illegitimate child. It can hold that to be born out of wedlock is a curse visited on the bastard by a destiny that he must accept, as part of the immutable order of nature, which ordains the monogamous Christian family. As we have seen, this philosophy no longer dominates modern family law outside the strictly Catholic domain. To the consideration that an individual is entitled to be protected in the attainment of his possibilities, as a human being potentially equal to all others, must be added the particular iniquity of punishing the innocent product of a non-marital union. Yet the principle of moral responsibility as a regulator of rights and duties in family law is still abandoned by its upholders when it comes to the illegitimate child. Penalized in social and public life, it is still regarded by all too many as outside the normal fabric of society.

70. RSFSR Code of Laws on Marriage, the Family and Guardianship 1926, sections 42, 48, 49, 50, 54, 55.

71. Robbins and Deak, 'The familial property rights of illegitimate children, a comparative study' (1930) 30 *Columbia L. Rev.* 308; reprinted Sayre (1950, p. 728).

The orthodox view was reaffirmed in 1956 by a majority of the Royal Commission on Marriage and Divorce.

So long as marriage is held to be the voluntary union for life of one man with one woman, that conception is wholly incompatible with the provision that one or other of the parties can, during the subsistence of the marriage, beget by some other person children who may later be legitimated. . . . Any departure from that conception can only be made by ignoring the essential moral principle that a man cannot, during the subsistence of his marriage, beget lawful children by another woman. It is unthinkable that the state should lend its sanction to such a step, for it could not fail to result in a blurring of moral values in the public mind. A powerful deterrent to illicit relationships would be removed, with disastrous results for the status of marriage as at present understood (s. 1180).

What the majority considered as 'unthinkable', became the law of England not many years later. The Family Law Reform Act 1969 Part 2, makes illegitimate children equal to legitimate children with regard to succession in cases of intestacy, the presumed meaning of 'children' in wills, and the meaning of 'dependants' under the Inheritance (Family Provision) Act of 1938. Before then, the Legitimacy Act 1959 had adopted a recommendation of the Royal Commission, to the effect that the child of a void marriage 'shall be treated as a legitimate child of his parents if at the time of the act of intercourse resulting in birth [or at the time of the celebration of the marriage if later] both or either of the parties reasonably believe that the marriage is valid'.

The English reforms correspond to a general trend formulated in 1967 by a sub-committee of the Commission on Human Rights of the United Nations, which says that 'every person, once his filiation has been established, shall have the same legal status as a person born in wedlock'. As in so many fields, the Scandinavian countries have been pioneers in legal reform. In 1915, a Norwegian law established substantial equality for the illegitimate child, by giving him the same legal relationship to his father as to his mother, including the right to bear the father's name, and a claim to maintenance and education by both. The law also puts the responsibility for the search of paternity upon the state rather than on the mother. A subsequent Norwegian law of December 1956 abolished nearly all the remaining legal distinctions between legitimate and illegitimate children. A Swedish law of 1949 and a Danish law of 1960 provide for equal rights of support for illegitimate, as compared with legitimate children.

A number of Latin American countries as well as a few of the jurisdictions of the United States also provide for full equality as between legitimate and illegitimate children.[72] To take but one example, the constitution of Panama provides that 'parents have the same duties to both children born out of wedlock as to all those born in it. All children are equal before the law and have the same hereditary rights in interstate succession.'

The recent reform of illegitimacy law in West Germany is of particular jurisprudential interest.

The German Civil Code of 1900 – which fully reflected nineteenth-century ideas of family law and morality – provided that 'an illegitimate child is not deemed to be related to his father'. Various reform efforts during the Weimar republic did not produce any legislative change. But the provisional constitution of the Federal Republic of Germany [*Grundgesetz*] laid down, in Article VI [5] that

Illegitimate children are to be given by legislation the same conditions for physical and mental development and for acquiring a position in society as legitimate children enjoy.

The federal constitutional court – a post-war institution – laid down in a decision of 1958[73] that this constitutional provision constituted a binding mandate for the legislature, the implementation of which did not lie in its discretion. When another decade passed, without legislative reform, the constitutional court in 1969[74] reaffirmed that the existing law did not comply with Article VI of the *Grundgesetz* and gave the legislature a final deadline to comply with the constitution. In response to this judicial ultimatum, a law was passed in August 1969. Under the new law, the paternity of illegitimate children may be established either by acknowledgement or by a judicial decision. The statutory presumption is that the child was begotten by the man who had intercourse with the mother during the statutory period of conception. The illegitimate child, on proof of

72. For details, see Krause, 'Bastards abroad: foreign approaches to illegitimacy', 15 *Amer. J. Comp. L.* (1967), pp. 726–9.
73. BVerf GE 8, 216.
74. BVerf GE 25, 167.

paternity, can now claim maintenance from the father, according to his means. But it still takes the surname of the mother, although the mother's husband as well as the father of the child can give his surname to the child by declaration before the registrar, provided both child and mother consent. But the illegitimate child under the new law remains under the sole parental power of his mother. The guardianship court has certain supervisory powers. On the illegitimate child's right to succession, the new law compromises between the old position, where the child has no claim whatsoever against the estate of the father, and full equality between legitimate and illegitimate children. An illegitimate child has a 'substitute inheritance claim' [*Erbersatzanspruch*] against the heirs, equal to half the value of the statutory portion which a legitimate intestate heir would be entitled to.

While this legal reform still falls very short of the aim of equality between legitimate and illegitimate children, it does constitute a considerable advance on the law of the civil code. It is not, however, impossible that the constitutional court may regard it as less than a full compliance with the constitution of 1949.[75]

The State and the Family

Every modern state is taking an active and, often, a commanding part in the regulation of family life. Many of these functions are of a judicial or quasi-judicial nature and go back to the traditional role of the courts as guardians of the weak and unprotected. In the history of the common law, these functions originated with the equity jurisdiction of the Chancellor, who became the guardian of persons and properties of infants. Today, the supervisory and protective functions of the Chancery are exercised not only by Chancery divisions or equity courts proper, but also by a multitude of specialized tribunals, such as juvenile courts, family courts, domestic relations courts and the like, as well as by county courts and magistrates' courts.[76] Although adjudication arises, in the form of mainten-

75. For a survey of the new law see Bohndorf, 'The new illegitimacy law in Germany', 19 *Int. & Comp. L.Q.* 299 (1970).
76. See, for example, the various procedures available for applications for adoption orders under the British Adoption Act 1958.

ance or custody actions or disputes about property settlements, overwhelmingly this jurisdiction is of a supervisory and administrative character.[77] It is in that capacity that a court may make 'such order with respect to the property in dispute . . . as he thinks fit'[78] or authorize a deserted wife to continue to reside in the matrimonial home; decide on the custody of children in the case of divorce, give its consent or assistance to the parents in the education of the children,[79] approve or reject an application for an adoption order, appoint tutors or executors, and exercise a multitude of other supervisory activities. The extent of these judicial, quasi-judicial and administrative functions of state courts is an indication of the social importance of the family, and of the responsibility which the state has traditionally felt for the children. But the care which was once concentrated on the protection of property, has now been greatly enlarged, and partly changed in character, in line with the extension of the social-welfare functions of the modern state. In regard to economic subsistence, the primitive beginnings of earlier poor law legislation have been broadened into general schemes of public assistance, such as the British National Assistance Legislation of 1948. It is in regard to the social welfare of the neglected child as a person that the most significant developments have taken place.

The greatly increased role of the state in the life of the family arises from the general pattern of modern state organization.

On the one hand, the number of obligations imposed upon the members of the family has drastically increased compared with even a century ago. Compulsory school education, often including higher education, compulsory health tests, and military service are now standard law in many countries. By establishing the appropriate institutions, the state assumes a large responsibility for the material and spiritual development of the growing child, a responsibility that formerly resided entirely in the parents. Correspondingly, through the provision of education and the maintenance, at the expense of the state, of those serving in the Armed Forces, the state takes over some of the financial responsibilities of the parents. Some countries

77. In German law, this whole sphere of judicial activity is termed *freiwillige Gerichtsbarkeit*.

78. Married Women's Property Act 1882, s. 17.

79. See, for example, section 1631, German Civil Code, as amended in 1957.

have, in recent years, gone further by establishing a state-financed national health service.[80] In these countries, the state regards it as a duty to provide for the health of its citizens, and it thereby takes a great financial burden from the individual family, which it re-distributes among the general taxpayers of the nation.[81]

Every contemporary state, to a greater or lesser extent, further distributes the financial burdens of the family by comprehensive social-insurance schemes. Basic pillars of social insurance are un-employment insurance, health insurance, old-age and retirement pensions, and death benefits in the case of the demise of the insured, usually the breadwinner. While they greatly differ from each other in detail, all these schemes are generally financed by a combination of compulsory contributions by employees and employers, and a contribution from the state out of the general budget (i.e. by the taxpayer). A growing number of states – among them France, Germany, Great Britain and Canada – now grant family allowances as a public contribution to the cost of bringing up children. The alternative method of tax exemptions for dependants is, of course, less beneficial to low-income families which pay little or no tax.

These manifold schemes of social security, public pensions or public assistance are gradually developing a family law that, in many respects, differs from that developed in civil codes or case law. Thus, the tribunals instituted for the purpose of determination of claims under the British National Insurance legislation have held that, for the purpose of calculating the extent to which one member of the family is maintained by any other member, the earnings of all members of a household must be considered as a common family fund, to which some contribute more and others less than the cost of maintaining them.[82] To take another discrepancy between the com-

80. New Zealand, Sweden, the United Kingdom, the USSR.
81. While voluntary group insurance, through Blue Cross schemes and the like, now covers substantial parts of the population in Canada and the United States, it does not cover, at least in the USA, ordinary doctor's or dentist's bills. Moreover, many forms of diseases are excluded from coverage. The burden for the individual family remains very considerable. Why it should be beyond the province of the state to insure a minimum health standard for its people – as asserted by the organized medical profession in both countries – is no more intelligible than opposition to compulsory school education.
82. For details, see Kahn-Freund (1953) 16 *Mod. L. Rev.* 148, 164.

mon law and the public law of family relations, during the last world war, the military authorities regarded a '*de facto* wife' in Great Britain as entitled to dependents' allowance to the same extent as a properly married wife. That this frequent discrepancy between the 'private' family law and the family law of the modern welfare state is not an isolated or national phenomenon, is shown by the following observation made about developments in the United States:

The notable point about this congeries of federal pension plans making payments to surviving spouses is that in administering them the Federal Government does not consider itself bound by the various state rules of law, whether of domestic relations or of matrimonial property. There is thus growing up a vast body of federal family law, largely in the form of administrative rulings, which is independent for the most part of the state rules governing other legal incidents of the lives of the persons concerned. This body of law has not been adequately described or investigated by legal scholars up to this time (Dean, in Friedmann, 1955, p. 361).

Does this growth of an 'administrative' family law, arising from a vast and complex network of modern social-welfare obligations, indicate an undermining of the whole concept of the family? Does it mean that an impersonal bureaucratic machine is gradually replacing the personal responsibility which members of a family, and, in particular a husband and wife, have towards each other?

There are, of course, those who maintain that any social-security scheme undermines the personal sense of responsibility of the husband as provider. This argument is on the same plane as that which regards unemployment insurance as an improper interference of the state in the natural vicissitudes of life. It ignores the fact that the structure of modern industrial society, with the shadow of all-destructive wars hanging over it, has undermined the stability of conditions of employment and the sense of personal security. In no country does social security go so far as to eliminate or even substantially reduce the incentive for the various members of the family, and for the main breadwinner in particular, to improve the standard of living of the family by his work. But in so far as modern social-security provisions ban, for millions of families, the spectre of total misery, in cases of death or disability of the breadwinner, they surely do not loosen or weaken family ties, but, on the contrary, they provide the conditions for a fuller and happier family life by removing at least the worst aspects of total insecurity. This has been amply demonstrated by the remarkable rise of birthrates in most western countries after the last world war, in conditions of stable employment and increased social security.

Contrary to many dire predictions, millions of modern families, to whom contraceptives are known and easily accessible, have preferred the joys and responsibilities of parenthood to the greater material comfort and freedom of movement of childlessness.

The social-security schemes of the modern state recognize the family as an essential unit in it. They seek to strengthen the family, although, in the process, the growing public family law may modify a great deal of the traditional private law of the family. Here, as in other fields, only a combination of public and private responsibilities can create conditions that are in accordance with contemporary social needs.

There is perhaps no more telling illustration of the extent to which the modern state must become involved in the assurance of minimum standards of life for the family, than the plan submitted by the conservative Nixon government to the United States Congress early in 1970. This plan provides for a guaranteed minimum income – supplemented by certain benefits in kind, such as medical aid and food stamps – for families below a certain minimum income standard (see p. 326). This is an open recognition of the social responsibility of government to the people under its jurisdiction, with the family as the basic unit of care.

Looking further into the future, one can predict a steadily increasing involvement of public authority with family matters, reaching not only into the economic but into the more intimate personal domains. As we have seen in the discussion of recent legislative developments with regard to birth control and abortion, the alarming and accelerating rate of increase in the world population, with its attendant dangers to living standards, urban decay and the ecology of the earth, reveals a growing, national and international concern of government with family planning. The pressures are likely to become so intense that increasingly severe financial penalties for families above a certain size, and even compulsory sterilization, cannot be ruled out in the decades to come. The uncontrolled growth of population, accompanied – although with great differences as between one country and another – by progressive industrialization and rising consumer demands, is the single most potent contributor to the pollution of the environment. Scientists and ecologists predict that, in less than a generation, this will reach a state where the survival of mankind is at stake. At this point – and perhaps earlier – the many serious objections to greater compulsive powers assumed by government over the family, in personal as well as economic respects, are likely to be outweighed by the more urgent demands of survival.

Part Three
Economic Power, the State and the Law

Chapter 8
Economic Competition, Regulation and the Public Interest: The Dilemmas of Anti-Trust

Our main concern in this chapter will be with the difficulties and contradictions inherent in the Benthamite idea of free trade as commonly accepted by liberal economic philosophers: that all citizens within a legal community should be given an equal start and an opportunity to trade freely, which, through the pursuit by each trader of his economic advantage, would work out to the common good.

Like a field of runners who start but do not finish together, the field of initially equal free traders soon thins out: favoured by resources, ability, ruthlessness or luck, some competitors will outdistance others. They will accumulate economic power, which will enable them to push others against the wall, devise restrictive schemes which underpin their own stronger position, or, in extreme cases, establish a complete monopoly which extinguishes competition. For the strong or lucky, freedom of trade just means freedom to expand; it means the survival of the fittest and the eventual destruction of the weak. To the others, however, it means the opposite: a duty of the community to restore, as far as possible, conditions of freedom of competition. This means restraint by legislative intervention and, at least to some extent, a denial of the very idea of freedom of trade. For inevitably, any legislature which seeks to establish legal rules preventing the consequences of uninhibited competition, by which the strong may destroy the weak, must establish a legal apparatus, often of great complexity. This is the dilemma of all anti-trust legislation.

The most emphatic defender of anti-trust, as the 'free society's' alternative to socialization, will not pretend that it has restored – or could restore – an economic society of approximately free and equal economic units, even if the full power of the state were applied to that end. In the United States, where anti-trust legislation has been in force for eighty years, concentration of economic power, in a few hundred major corporations, has proceeded steadily. Small groups of these corporations – exercising an oligopoly rather than a monopoly in their field – dominate such vital areas of economic life as steel, aluminium, copper, oil products, petrochemicals, aeroplane and automobile manufacture. This continuing concern with the growth of corporate power and its role in the modern state will be the subject of the following chapter.

The necessity of some kind of legislative and administrative machinery to combat excessive concentrations of economic power, and undue interferences with freedom of trade, is attested by the remarkable spread of anti-trust laws, outside the United States and Canada, its original champions, in the post-war world. Apart from the 'centrally-planned' economies of the socialist world, where the concentration of all economic and productive power in the hands of centrally-directed state enterprises makes the problem of anti-trust – though not of competition – irrelevant, every major industrial country has, since the end of the War, adopted some kind of anti-trust legislation.[1] Perhaps the most remarkable of the many legislative developments in this direction are those of Great Britain and West Germany – both highly industrialized countries with a strong tradition of permissiveness towards restrictive trade practices and economic cartels.[2] It would, of course, be impossible – nor is it the purpose of the present

1. For a comparative survey up to 1956, see Friedmann (1956), and for anti-trust law in the six member states of the European Common Market, see Blake (3 volumes, 1969).

2. England has, of course, had a centuries old doctrine of restraint of trade, a common-law ground of invalidation of contracts. A detailed analysis of the reasons why, in the hands of the British courts, this doctrine has not stood in the way of the most restrictive price production and other cartels, has been given in the 1959 edition of the present book, pp. 222–4, and see Grunfeld and Yamey, in Friedmann (1956, p. 340). The basic philosophy of the courts was that arrangements deemed to be reasonable as between the parties (e.g. price and production cartels, or exclusion of competitors) were also presumed to be reasonable towards the public. On this basis it was, of course, impossible to develop effective anti-trust principles.

chapter – to give even an elementary survey of anti-trust doctrine and jurisprudence in the United States, and other countries that have introduced anti-trust legislation. It is intended rather to discuss some of the basic issues of anti-trust, of the philosophy of economic competition and of the role that state control over the rules of competition can play in contemporary industrial society.

Limits of the Ideology of Competition

The most fundamental question is to what extent economic competition – which means essentially the prevention of monopolies and of restrictive trade practices – is a desirable policy goal – always excluding the alternative of total socialization. In the United States, this question is hardly ever asked. There are a very few advocates of bigness in business as most conducive to economic efficiency and technological progress (Lilienthal, 1953). There are some who acknowledge, generally reluctantly, the need for public enterprise in special and exceptional situations – such as those which led to the establishment of the Tennessee Valley Authority in 1933. But overwhelmingly, the assumption is that maximum competition is good, in so far as it is possible. No distinction is made between basic utilities – such as railroads, electric power and other public transportation systems – and manufacturing industries. There are, of course, a considerable number of governmental corporations, especially on the state level. The New York Port Authority – jointly owned by the states of New York and New Jersey, the Niagara Falls Authority and the Triborough Bridge Authority are among the most important of these public utility enterprises. But anti-trust philosophy continues to be applied to merger propositions of the nation's many ailing and privately-owned railroads, and the generation of electric power, which is divided between a multitude of private and public power companies.

Outside the United States there has long been a basically different approach, which is not affected by the more recent adoption of anti-trust laws. Basic utilities, such as railways, telephone and postal services, electricity, nuclear energy and, in some countries, coal, oil and steel, are considered as public services and operated by nation-wide government enterprises or – as is the case with electricity and some forms of public transport in West Germany – by regional and municipal authorities. This problem is now facing the United States. The absurdity of maintaining a fictitious competition between private railroad systems, which are neither equipped nor willing to continue passenger services essential in the public interest, is gradually giving way to the recognition that public transportation is of vital public concern and must, if necessary, be operated by the Government or other public authorities as a monopoly operation. Certainly, the countries with the most efficient railway services, such as Japan, France, Switzerland, operate them as national public enterprises.

So the first question is the consideration of the limits of competition as a desirable policy goal. What may have been a good philosophy, when the railroads were the principal and prosperous purveyors of transport, may be totally inapplicable to the greatly changed conditions of today. And reduction or absence of competition means almost of necessity governmental control in one of the various forms surveyed in the following chapter.

The borderline between services, utilities – or in some cases, manufactures – that may have to be operated on a national scale in the public interest, and those that are best left to private competitive enterprise, cannot be rigidly or absolutely drawn – as the case of the railways in the United States shows.[3] What can be said with some assurance is that, in the complex industrial societies of our time, with their many threats to the very foundations of civilized co-existence, the range of activities that have to be taken out of the competitive private domain will steadily increase. As late as 1958, Mr Justice Black described the Sherman Act – the basic American anti-trust law – as 'a comprehensive charter of economic liberty' which 'rests on the premise that the unrestrained interaction of competitive forces will yield the best allocation of our economic resources, the lowest prices, the highest quality and the greatest

3. The nationalization of British industries, after the Second World War, was generally guided by a distinction between 'basic' industries – which should be conducted in the public interest, on a non-profit-making, though self-supporting basis, as statutory monopolies – and the other sectors of economic life. See, for example, Schnitthoff, 'The nationalization of basic industries in Great Britain', 16 *Law and Contemp. Problems* 557 (1951). See also Friedmann, 'Forms and functions of public enterprise', *Current Legal Problems 1969*, pp. 79–101.

material progress, while at the same time providing an environment conducive to the preservation of our democratic, political and social institutions'.[4] This unquestioning identification of economic liberty and material progress, with political and social democracy – though probably still approved by most Americans – is more than ripe for reexamination. The great majority of the countries of the world have long accepted the 'mixed economy' as the best overall response to the balance between public interest and private profit-directed enterprise which can be found in contemporary conditions. At a time when so many foundations of the American dream – including the assumptions made by Mr Justice Black – have become questionable, the borderlines of the competitive economy must also be redrawn. This does not mean that public, non-competitive enterprise can remain unchecked.[5]

Basic Concepts and Goals of Anti-Trust

The spread of anti-trust laws throughout the world confirms that, to the extent that the economic system remains in the hands of private enterprise, it must be subjected to the legal controls of anti-trust. The basic concepts of anti-trust have been concisely defined by Professor Milton Handler[6] as 'monopolization, restraint of trade, unfair methods of competition and substantial lessening of competition'. One of these four basic concepts, the outlawing of unfair methods of competition – the major concerns of the United States Federal Trade Commission established by a statute of 1914 – would not be regarded everywhere as a specific anti-trust concept. On the Continent, where anti-trust laws are essentially a post-war phenomenon, laws dealing with unfair competition in business have long been known, and are regarded as a special type of tortious conduct.[7]

4. *Northern Pacific Ry.* v. *United States*, 356 U.S. 1, 4 (1958).
5. See on some of the relevant criteria p. 507 and, in more detail, Friedmann and Garner (1970, pp. 53, 325).
6. Handler, 'Some unresolved problems of anti-trust', 62 *Columbia L. Rev.* 930, at 932 (1962).
7. See e.g. the German Law Against Unfair Competition of 1900, as amended, which to some extent overlaps the provisions of the German Civil Code, section 823. Both cover a broad range of improper interferences with property and other economic interests, including the right to conduct a business enterprise.

The other three concepts listed by Professor Handler would be generally regarded as basic concerns of anti-trust legislation. In the United States the first two are covered by sections 1 and 2 of the Sherman Act of 1890:

Every contract, combination in the form of trust or otherwise, or conspiracy, in restraint of trade or commerce among the several States, or with foreign nations, is hereby declared to be illegal. . . .

Every person who shall monopolize, or attempt to monopolize, or combine or conspire with any other person or persons, to monopolize any part of the trade or commerce among the several states, or with foreign nations, shall be deemed guilty of a misdemeanor.

The third is covered by the Clayton Act of 1914, as amended in 1950. 'Substantial lessening of competion' includes three specific categories: first, acquisitions of stock (and, since 1950, assets); second, tying arrangements; and, third, price discrimination. Generally, these are also the keystones of non-American anti-trust legislation, of which the British Statutes of 1948, 1956 and 1968, dealing with monopolies, restrictive trade practices and mergers, the German Wettbewerbsgesetz of 1957, and the Articles 85 and 86 of the European Economic Community of 1957 are the most important illustrations.

However, to indicate that monopolies, mergers and a vast variety of restrictive trade practices are the subject of anti-trust legislation, leaves room for a very wide spectrum of approaches to these types of interference with the free market economy. Legislative, administrative and judicial approaches to these problems do not only vary greatly as from one country to another, they also fluctuate within one legal system, depending on changes in public opinion, the economic situation of the country, and the philosophy of those entrusted with the application and execution of the legislation. Much the richest case history of policy fluctuations, both on the administrative and the judicial levels, is found in the United States, where the Sherman Act is now eighty years old. But even the much shorter history of the British and German statutes shows significant fluctuations, caused by change of economic priorities as well as of judicial and other key personnel. In the United States, the replacement of one or two of the nine judges of the Supreme Court, which plays the dominant role in the judicial determination of the meaning of the Sherman and Clayton Acts, may mean a basic reversal of direction. Hardly less important are the philosophy of the chairman of the Federal Trade Commission or the Assistant Attorney-General in charge of anti-trust matters in the Department of Justice – both political appointments which change hands not only as between one administration and another, but frequently even within the life span of one administration. But the outlook and personality of the President of the British Restrictive Trade Practices Court – a High Court judge – or the President of the German Federal Cartel Office, which plays a key role in the administration of the anti-trust law, are hardly less crucial to the translation of legislative language into economic and legal practice.

No more can be attempted here than a very general appraisal of the different legal approaches and formulae used in this vital area of legal responses to economic and social change.[8]

Rule of Reason and Public Interest

The most fundamental polarity – at least in theory – in the approach to anti-trust is that between the *per se* rule and the 'rule of reason'.

8. The American anti-trust literature is immense. The most authoritative and systematic survey of the evolution of anti-trust jurisprudence is found, for the period up to 1955, in the *Report of the Attorney-General's National Committee to Study the Anti-trust Laws* (1955), and for the period since 1955, in *Anti-trust Developments 1955–68*, (with a supplement for 1968–9), prepared by the Anti-trust Law Section of the American Bar Association. For regular critical surveys, from the standpoint of an advocate of a flexible application of anti-trust law, see the articles published annually by Milton Handler in American law reviews, notably the following: 'Some unresolved problems of anti-trust,' 62 *Columbia L. Rev.* 930 (1962); 'The polarities of anti-trust', 60 *Northwestern University L. Rev.* 751 (1966): and, most recently, 'Anti-trust: 1969', 55 *Cornell L. Rev.* 161 (1970).

For surveys and critical analysis of the British developments since the 1948 and 1956 legislation, see, Korah (1968); and Yamey and Stevens (1965). For an appraisal of the work of the British Monopolies Commission, see Rowley (1966), and for an analysis of the common law doctrine of contracts in restraint of trade and conspiracy, see Grunfeld and Yamey, chapter on the United Kingdom, in Friedmann (1956). For a recent, thorough analysis of the German law of 1957 including its relation to the anti-trust provisions of the European Economic Community Treaty, see Blake, vol. 3: West Germany (Ebb editor 1969).

The former means that certain restrictive practices are to be considered as illegal, regardless of whether they may be reasonable in the circumstances or not. The latter means that restrictive practices are to be legally condemned only if they are 'unreasonable', or, in the terminology of the British Act of 1956, 'against the public interest'. The rule of reason prevailed for a long period in the history of American anti-trust, ever since the first Standard Oil case[9] laid down as the economic objectives of anti-trust policy the avoidance of arbitrary and unreasonable prices, of limitation of production, and of deterioration of commodities. In the New Deal period under the guidance of Assistant Attorney-General Thurman Arnold, the initiation of a more vigorous enforcement of anti-trust was reflected in increasing judicial affirmations of the *per se* rule. The high-water mark was a decision of the Second Circuit Court of Appeals, rendered by Judge Learned Hand, in 1945, which held that the near-monopoly of the Aluminum Company of America (Alcoa) was to be condemned under section 2 of the Sherman Act, regardless of the intent to obtain a monopoly, or reasonableness of prices, and of other economic or moral factors.[10] Ostensibly the *per se* rule has remained the guiding principle of the Supreme Court ever since. But this is a deceptive criterion since, as we shall see, the judgements of the Court have fluctuated greatly in the interpretation of such key concepts as monopoly, market power, competitive opportunity, and others.

The British approach both in the Monopolies and Restrictive Practices (Inquiry and Control) Act 1948, and in the Restrictive Trade Practices Act 1956 (amended in 1968), broadly corresponds to that of the rule of reason since it makes the 'public interest' the decisive criterion to judge whether monopolisitic operations or restrictive trade agreements are to be legally condemned. The German Statute of 1957 – a most complex and difficult document – takes an intermediate position. Section 1, which is under the title 'Restraints of Competition', declares that 'agreements made for a common purpose by enterprises or associations of enterprises and decisions of associations of enterprises are of no effect in so far as they are likely to influence, by restraining competition, production or market con-

9. *US* v. *Standard Oil Company*, 221 U.S. 1 (1911).
10. *US* v. *Aluminium Co. of America*, 149 F. 2d 416 (2d Cir 1945).

ditions with respect to trade in goods or commercial services.' Chapter 3, which deals with 'market dominating enterprises', empowers the cartel authority to prohibit abuse by market dominating enterprises and declare contracts to be of no effect'. The seemingly absolute prohibition of restrictive trade agreements is, however, greatly mitigated by several statutory exemptions of which the so-called 'rationalization agreements' and 'rationalization cartels' are the most important. A vast number of restrictive practices, including certain rebates, agreements for the promotion of exports, the rationalization of economic processes and organizations through standardization projects, and even price fixing agreements, and other exemptions – the interpretation of which is in the hands of the cartel authority and the regional appeal courts – make the seemingly absolute prohibitions subject to numerous qualifications.

Mergers

With regard to mergers – a subject of increasingly vital importance in an era of increasing concentrations of corporate power – the statutory provisions are more elastic and subject to even wider fluctuations of interpretation. In the Clayton Act, as amended in 1950, the criterion is whether the effect of acquisition of stock or assets 'may be substantially to lessen competition, or to tend to create a monopoly'. The German act, in contrast to its treatment of other competitive activities, deals rather leniently with mergers. The act imposes only a duty to notify the federal cartel office of a combination or concentration of enterprises, if one of the participants has a market share of at least 20 per cent, and certain minimum standards with regard to the total number of employees, and the aggregate annual turnover of the total amount of assets are met.[11]

While in the United States the principal concern is still the danger of excessive concentration of power through mergers – including conglomerate mergers – recent British legislation has actually encouraged mergers under certain circumstances. In 1967 the Industrial Reorganization Corporation was created by statute and provided with certain government funds, with the specific purpose of encouraging

11. For details, see the very lengthy section 23 of the act, reproduced in Blake vol. 3 (Ebb editor 1969), at p. 392.

the amalgamation of firms. The IRC – dissolved in 1971 by the Conservative government – has, in the few years of its existence, vigorously exercised this power, for example, by coupling major investments in the electrical equipment and computer manufacturing industries with amalgamation plans between major firms in that industry. This, of course, would still be rather unthinkable in the United States – although it was pointed out at the beginning of this chapter that in certain public utilities and services of national interest, amalgamation or nationalization may become a major and inescapable policy objective in the near future.

The anti-trust provisions of the EEC Treaty again are rather sweeping in principle. Article 85 (1) prohibits agreements between enterprises, decisions of associations of enterprises, and concerted practices which are liable to affect trade between member states and which are designed to prevent, restrict or distort competition within the common market or which have this effect. But Article 85 (3) permits the authorization of such agreements, decisions or practices if they . . . 'contribute to the improvement of the production or distribution of goods or to the promotion of technical or economic progress . . ., provided such agreements, etc. . . . do not enable such enterprises to eliminate competition in respect of a substantial proportion of the goods concerned'. This has to be coupled with a provision of Article 86, which prohibits 'abuse of a market dominating position'. Although implemented by a relatively strict regulation of the EEC Commission in 1962, neither the practice of the EEC, within the Common Market area, nor the application of the anti-trust provisions of West Germany and the United Kingdom have generally stood in the way of mergers. The stark difference between the European and the American practice in this respect can be easily explained by the difference in the scale of economic concentration. The leading US steel, oil or automobile corporations dwarf in size, capital strength and turnover even the biggest of the European enterprises. Moreover, the leading makers of automobiles or computers and all the major US oil corporations have subsidiaries in Britain and Continental Europe, which they control either entirely or through majority participation in joint ventures. In such circumstances, the legal and business moves initiated in Britain and the Common Market area for greater cooperation or concentration of enterprises are essentially defensive. They are either designed to rationalize, and increase the efficiency of, ailing and overdivided industries – such as shipbuilding in Britain – or to provide more effective competition with the American giants. A completely unified West European community would be comparable, in population, industrial development, technology, and market size to the United States. But the EEC is still far from such a stage, and there have been few outright mergers between parallel industries of the different member states, although significant transnational amalgamations have been authorized in the field of steel-making, photographic equipment and automobile manufacturing.[12]

Illegality *per se*

It is not only the difference of scale but also the much more deeply ingrained belief in anti-trust as the principal response of a competitive capitalistic economy to socialism that makes the American picture so different. In the American practice, at least during the last generation, certain types of restrictive agreements are so clearly illegal that they can be regarded as in the *per se* category. This applies to any concerted measures of exclusion, or imposition of discriminatory conditions on new entrance into a particular business area; market allocations through the imposition of production quotas or the division of markets between potential competitors; fraudulent or collusive tenders; the prevention of the use of patented or unpatented inventions; price fixing; and tying arrangements, i.e. arrangements by which one party will sell his product to another only on the condition that the buyer also purchase a different, tied product or undertake not to purchase it from any other supplier. It was a price-fixing agreement between the major manufacturers of electrical equipment that, in 1960, not only led to the indictment of the leading manufacturers, such as General Electric and Westinghouse, but also to the unprecedented imposition of jail sentences on executives held responsible for the arrangements. In a leading decision,[13] the Supreme Court made it clear that illegality of price fixing

12. A recent example is the acquisition by the Italian giant, Fiat, of a strong minority interest in the French Citroen Company.
13. *US* v. *McKesson & Robbins, Inc.*, 351 U.S. 305 (1956).

does not depend on the showing of its unreasonableness, since it is conclusively presumed to be unreasonable. It makes no difference whether the motives of the participants are good or evil; whether the price fixing is accomplished by express contract or by some more subtle means; whether the participants possess market controls; whether the amount of interstate commerce affected is large or small; or whether the effect of the agreement is to raise or decrease prices.

Monopolization

But, although in many areas, the criteria of anti-competitive, and therefore illegal, behaviour are reasonably certain, major fluctuations of judgement and policy are concealed by the elasticity of certain broad concepts. Foremost among them is the definition of 'monopoly' and 'monopolization'. In the British Monopolies and Restrictive Practices Act – which does not outlaw monopolies absolutely but makes them only the subject of official inquiry – control of 'at least one-third of all goods of that description which are supplied in the United Kingdom or any substantial part thereof', by one or more persons or interconnected bodies corporate subject the situation to investigation as to possible monopoly. In the German Anti-Trust Law of 1957, under the chapter entitled 'Market Dominating Enterprises', a 'concentration of enterprises' must be declared to the cartel authority where the participating enterprises have a share of at least 20 per cent of the market – in addition to other requirements. But in the United States, where the question of monopolization has been an offence under section 2 of the Sherman Act since 1890, and where it presents a vastly greater legal as well as economic problem than in any other country, there is no official definition. It was relatively easy to discern a monopoly in the Alcoa case of 1945, at a time when Alcoa was held to control nearly 90 per cent of the aluminum production of the country. The problem in that case was mainly whether intent to attain such a dominant position was an element of the offence – which was denied. In a later decision,[14] the Supreme Court defined monopoly power as 'the power to control prices or exclude competition'. In a recent case,[15] the Supreme Court

14. *US* v. *I. E. duPont de Nemours & Co.*, 351 U.S. 377 (1956).
15. *US* v. *Grennell Corp.*, 384 U.S. 563 (1966).

singled out two elements as determinative of the offence of monopoly under section 2: (1) the possession of monopoly power in the relevant market; (2) the wilful acquisition or maintenance of that power as distinguished from growth or development as a consequence of a superior product, business acumen or historic accident. But this leaves a wide gyration of differing interpretations as to the definition of the relevant market, the degree of power in the relevant market needed to constitute a monopoly, and the borderline between monopoly positions achieved by a deliberate attempt to squeeze out competitors rather than by 'superior skill, foresight and industry' – a formulation used by Judge Hand in the Alcoa case – or by the normal circumstances of economic competition. How elastic these criteria are is illustrated by the 'Cellophane' decision,[16] where the issue was whether the relevant market was Cellophane – of which du Pont had a 75 per cent share – or all 'flexible packaging material' – of which du Pont had a share of less than 20 per cent. In that case the court held that since Cellophane had competition from other materials and there was 'a very considerable degree of functional interchangeability', there was no legal monopoly. The relevant market was thus defined as being 'composed of products that have reasonable interchangeability for the purposes for which they are produced – price, use and quality is considered'.

There have been equally wide discrepancies as to the size of the market share required to characterize a certain market position as monopolization, or a 'substantial lessening of competition'. In a Supreme Court decision of 1926[17] International Harvester's market share of about 64 per cent was held not to be an offence against the Sherman Act. But a decision of 1961 condemned – under section 7 of the Clayton Act – horizontal mergers which resulted in combined market shares, in shoe sales, of 5 per cent.[18] In some other cases even smaller percentages of the market have sufficed for a judicial condemnation of horizontal accretions or vertical integrations.[19]

16. *US* v. *I. E. du Pont de Nemours & Co.*, 351, U.S. 377 (1956).
17. *US* v. *International Harvester Co.*, 274 U.S. 693 (1927).
18. *Brown Shoe Company* v. *US*, 370 U.S. 294 (1962).
19. See Handler, 'The polarities of anti-trust', 60 *Northwestern U.L. Rev.* 751, 751–5 (1966).

Conspiracy and Parallelism

Under section 1 of the Sherman Act, one of the most puzzling problems is to distinguish between a 'combination' or 'conspiracy' – which are condemned – and parallel actions of several enterprises in the same field, which are dictated by economic conditions and parallel policy decisions. American enterprises have long learned to avoid any normal arrangements which could be classified as conspiracy. Yet the prices fixed from time to time by the leading producers of steel, aluminium, motor cars or oil products are so close to each other that genuine price competition is virtually ruled out. This is possible – or perhaps even inevitable – because prices in major industrial enterprises are today to a large extent dictated by industry-wide collective labour agreements, which determine the cost of labour, and by other administrative costs. But there is also a high degree of solidarity among the leaders of industry in holding a common price front, with only minor variations. Between this type of conduct and 'conscious parallelism' the borderlines are not easy to draw. In a leading decision,[20] the Supreme Court held that evidence of a common and conscious course of action among competitors does not, in the absence of other proof, compel an inference of an unlawful conspiracy, combination or agreement. This certainly saves a great majority of parallel actions from legal prosecution. But the threat of an illegal conspiracy cannot be completely discounted, as shown in a recent decision involving the General Motors Corporation,[21] where the court found a 'classic conspiracy in restraint of trade.' General Motors had elicited and enforced promises from its dealers not to do business with discounters.

The concept of 'trade or commerce among the several states, or with foreign nations', is equally subject to expansive or restrictive interpretations.

The British Act of 1956 formulates a number of 'presumptions as to the public interest', which is the decisive criterion for the approval or disapproval of registrable agreements in restraint of trade. The key term used, in section 21 of the Act for exemption of a restrictive

20. *Theatre Enterprises, Inc.* v. *The Paramount Film Distributing Corp.*, 346 U.S. 537 (1954).

21. *US* v. *General Motors Corp.*, 384 U.S. 127 (1966).

agreement from condemnation as 'contrary to the public interest', is whether the restriction is 'reasonably necessary' or 'reasonably required' for certain defined purposes. This deliberately leaves a wide margin of discretion. In the earlier cases, the Restrictive Practices Court, which decides the issue upon reference by the Registrar, tended to be very strict, particularly in the condemnation of price agreements. In later years, the court, depending on the personality of the presiding judge – and on different approaches to the respective merits of competition and collaboration – has tended to be more lenient and to approve a good many restrictive schemes of the kind described in the German statute as 'rationalization' or 'specialization' or 'structural' cartels. The resulting uncertainty led to a major legislative reform, in the Restrictive Trade Practices Act 1968. This followed upon the establishment of the – now liquidated – Industrial Reorganization Corporation and the Economic Development Committees, all of which, in the words of the President of the Board of Trade, 'are . . . designed to encourage long-run productivity and innovation', and which may therefore 'involve cooperative action between firms and an industry; or . . . a deliberate process of merger and rationalization'. Consequently, under the new act the Board of Trade has assumed the power to exempt restrictive agreements from registration, and thereby from a reference by the Registrar to the Restrictive Practices Court. The criterion is whether the agreement is 'calculated to promote the carrying out of an industrial or commercial project or scheme of substantial importance to the national economy'. Other criteria are the promotion of efficiency, the creation or improvement of capacity, provided that the restrictions are no wider than is reasonably necessary to achieve that object and that 'the agreement is on balance expedient in the national interest'. On the other hand, agreements to exchange information – formerly exempt – have been included among registrable agreements. On the whole, it is likely that the reform of 1968 will reduce the activity and importance of the Restrictive Practices Court and shift the main burden to informal clearance negotiations between the Board of Trade and the business or industry concerned. Such clearances are occasionally obtained in the United States in important transactions, by assurances on the part of the Department of Justice that it will not initiate action against a certain arrangement.[22]

Competition and Cooperation: the Dilemma of Anti-Trust

Despite the many deep divergencies between the economic policies – and consequently the approach to anti-trust law – of different countries, and the vast fluctuations of policy as they have occurred, notably in the paramount champion of anti-trust, the United States, certain broad principles have emerged. Outside the communist world every industrially advanced country is opposed – and has some legal remedy against – the monopolization of an industry by one enterprise. And monopolization does not necessarily mean complete control but a dominant market position. On the other hand, anti-trust law has been neither able nor willing to stop oligopoly, i.e., the domination of a certain industrial or business field by a few leading corporations which, with regard to prices, labour practices and general policy tend to adopt parallel policies and are permitted to do so, as long as the parallelism of their actions does not amount to technical conspiracy or combination. Moreover, in some fields, e.g. the production and refining of oil, the major corporations are driven to cooperate internationally, especially when their opposite numbers are organized as a collective bloc – such as the Organization of Petroleum Exporting Countries (OPEC). In such situations, all countries – whether by specific statutory exemptions, as they are abundant in the German law, or by *ad hoc* clearances as they occur in the United States, or by evaluation of the 'public interest', as in the United Kingdom, will permit or even encourage concerted action.

The basic problem of anti-trust is the definition of the public policy criteria which balance the value of cooperation against the benefits of competition. This is as perennial a problem as it is elusive. Nor can it be answered in absolute terms.

Many years ago the most prominent critic of bigness in business made the following observations in a famous dissenting judgement:

22. A notable example is the Iranian Oil Agreement of 1954, in which the major US oil companies combined with other western oil companies in a complex agreement with the Government of Iran on the production, refining and marketing of Iranian oil, which terminated the serious international crisis provoked by the 1951 nationalization of Anglo-Iranian properties. This was an agreement of great political as well as commercial international importance. Generally, the Department of Justice is reluctant to give advance clearance.

The refusal to permit a multitude of small rivals to cooperate, as they have done here, in order to protect themselves and the public from the chaos and havoc wrought in their trade by ignorance, may result in suppressing competition in the hardwood industry. These keen business rivals, who sought through cooperative exchange of trade information to create conditions under which alone rational competition is possible, produce in the aggregate about one-third of the hardwood lumber of the country. This court held in *United States* v. *United States Steel Corporation*, 251 U.S. 417, that it was not unlawful to vest in a single corporation control of practically the whole shoe-machinery industry. May not these hardwood lumber concerns, frustrated in their efforts to rationalize competition, be led to enter the inviting field of consolidation? And if they do, may not another huge trust with highly centralized control over vast resources, natural, manufacturing and financial, become so powerful as to dominate competitors, wholesalers, retailers, consumers, employees and, in large measure, the community?[23]

On a much wider scale, the benefits and the necessity of defensive collaboration of the relatively small against the very big forms now part of official policy, and are reflected in the anti-trust law of many countries. The so-called 'crisis' and 'rationalization' cartels specifically permitted under certain conditions in the German Act of 1957, and the official sponsoring of mergers for the sake of rationalization and efficiency, by the government-funded Industrial Reorganization Corporation in the United Kingdom,[24] clearly carry out the Brandeis philosophy on a vaster national scale. Economists have long debated the relation of efficiency to bigness. Again this question cannot be answered absolutely, as the capital and technological requirements greatly differ from one industry to another. Obviously, such industries as steel making of the manufacture of electronic computers require major capital investment and scientific and technological foundations that only relatively big enterprises can undertake. Yet the general consensus seems to be that there are limits to the efficiency of bigness, and that beyond a certain point both the bureaucracy of the giant enterprise – which does not differ greatly whether it is

23. Brandeis, J. in *American Column & Lumber Co.* v. *United States*, 257 U.S. 418, at 418–19 (1921).

24. Although the IRC – established by the Labour Government in 1967 – was dissolved by the Conservative Government in 1971, the problem of rationalization, through mergers, e.g. in the shipbuilding industry, remains as acute as ever.

publicly or privately owned – and the lack of spur from competitors have a negative effect (Brennan, 1965, pp. 156–61; Edwards, 1964, pp. 108–21). The result has been – in the majority of major manufacturing fields, the dominance of a limited number of enterprises which engage in limited competition with each other.

The Place of Public Enterprise

However, there are, as we have seen, conditions and fields in which competition cannot be the gospel, where monopoly has to be accepted as an overriding public interest. This inevitably leads to the problem of the place that public enterprise should occupy in a mixed economy which seeks to preserve some private enterprise, some freedom of economic movement and some competition, but is increasingly compelled, by the very complexities of contemporary industrial society, to assume a growing measure of direct responsibility for the minimum conditions of civilized coexistence.

In such a context, it would appear that there are four principal ways in which public enterprise could be fitted into the framework of a decentralized economy.

First, it could take over certain 'basic' industries and utilities, on the assumption that they are a direct and inescapable responsibility of the community and should therefore be operated in the public interest, on a self-supporting but non-profit-making basis, and under public control. In Britain, France and Italy, rail and air transport, the production and distribution of all forms of energy except oil, which is partly publicly and partly privately operated, and, except for France, steel are today operated by separately constituted public corporations, which enjoy a statutory monopoly, or near monopoly.

Second, government enterprise may be needed to fill a vital public need that private enterprise fails to satisfy. A conspicuous example is the American Tennessee Valley Authority, which was established in 1933 to rehabilitate a flood-stricken and destitute region, and to supply it with cheap electric power – a task that the private power industry had conspicuously failed to undertake. On a wider scale, all the developing countries – Latin American, Asian, African – have government-owned development corporations, whose principal task is to finance vital economic development needs, in the absence of sufficient responsible private venture capital.

Third, competition may be spurred by the coexistence of public and private enterprise in given fields – provided that fair rules of competition between the two can be established (see p. 509). Automobile manufacture in France and air transport in Australia and Britain illustrate this kind of limited competition between public and private enterprise.

Fourth, public and private enterprise may cooperate in joint undertakings. At present, Italy, where the major state-owned holding corporations (IRI, ENI) operate hundreds of enterprises in banking, insurance and many types of manufacture jointly with private capital, provides the main illustration. There are also many enterprises with mixed public and private capital in France and Germany, and this form of joint venture is likely to gain increasing significance in the United States to cope with vital urban tasks such as commuter transit systems (see p. 341; Friedmann and Garner, 1970).

The growing flexibility and variation of the types and functions of public enterprise in the mixed economy of today is a reflection of the increasingly intricate mixture of public and private economic activities that characterizes our society. The reality of a partly directed economy has long replaced the private enterprise economy founded upon free trade, free competition and the profit motive. The last of these persists to a far greater extent than the first two, whose disappearance or qualification is disguised by a complex network of government subsidies, protective tariffs, import quotas and regulatory controls. No economy can subsist without the spur of competition, as even the centrally-planned economic systems of the Soviet Union and other communist states have discovered. They have to substitute strict accountability and other sanctions for market competition. But all the other countries have long adopted certain features of the planned economy and a multitude of state controls over the economy. It should therefore be obvious that anti-trust legislation cannot – as the diminishing band of the apostles of unfettered free enterprise pretend – be more than an important but limited weapon in the armory of which the modern state disposes. It can prevent or counter the worst aspects of concentration and abuse of economic power, and induce or protect a modicum of competition. But it cannot re-establish either the conditions or the ideals of the past.

Chapter 9
Corporate Power, the Individual and the State

In this chapter we shall be concerned with some significant aspects of the growth of corporate power and their effect on the legal foundations of modern democracy. The growing aggregate power of the industrial giants, of the labour unions, of the charitable foundations and of certain other organized groups, compels a reassessment of the relation between group power and the modern state, on the one hand, and the freedom of the individual, on the other.

Legal Cloaks of Corporate Power

The sociological and juristic aspects of the problem of group power within the state have largely remained hidden behind accidents of legal form, especially in the Anglo-American system. Here, four legal factors have combined to shield the growth of group power from legal control: first, the ability and the custom of powerful organizations – which do not engage in commercial operations themselves – to remain unincorporated; second, the versatility of the trust device which mitigates to a large extent the clumsiness of the unincorporated society; third, the limitations of equitable remedies which have, to a large extent, prevented the courts from remedying abuses of power by organizations in regard to their members unless 'property' interests were involved; last, an excessive liberality in the interpretation of the 'charitable trust' which has permitted many business undertakings to be clothed in the form of charitable foundations.

To understand the extent to which major social evolutions have been hidden by the combination of a number of technical devices, we must turn back to the brilliant analysis given by Maitland well over half a century ago. In several striking passages he has characterized the social function of the English trust as that of supplying a personalized substitute for the far more comprehensive use of corporate devices in German law.

But there are two achievements of the trust which in social importance and juristic interest seem to eclipse all the rest. The trust has given us a liberal substitute for a law about personified institutions. The trust has given us a liberal supplement for a necessarily meagre law of corporations (Maitland, 1936, pp. 135–6).

[M]any reformers of our 'charities' have deliberately preferred that 'charitable trusts' should be confided, not to corporations, but to 'natural persons'. It is said – and appeal is made to long experience – that men are more conscientious when they are doing acts in their own names than when they are using the name of a corporation (Maitland, 1936, pp. 182–3). But apparently there is a widespread, though not very definite belief, that by placing itself under an incorporating *Gesetz*, however liberal and elastic that *Gesetz* may be, a *Verein* would forfeit some of its liberty, some of its autonomy, and would not be so completely the mistress of its own destiny as it is when it has asked nothing and obtained nothing from the state (Maitland, 1936, p. 207).

Maitland's theme is the contrast between the personalized English concept of trust and the impersonal, 'collectivized', German concept of an association (*Verein*), an incorporated public institution (*Anstalt*), or a private charity (*Stiftung*). The trust has enabled hundreds of important corporate institutions to remain unincorporated because 'the hedge of the trust' made possible a continuity of legal relationships and a stability of property rights which Continental law could not provide without a corporate form. The combination of trust and contract relations has enabled institutions of great social and economic significance, such as the Stock Exchange and the Inns of Court, to remain unincorporated.

None of Maitland's brilliant generalizations would appear to remain unimpaired in the mid-twentieth century. In the first place, the contrast between Continental and Anglo-American legal devices in the field of unincorporated associations and endowments seems to have narrowed considerably; in the second place, unincorporated associations have acquired so many attributes of legal personality that the difference between incorporated and unincorporated bodies, though still important, is no longer fundamental; in the third place, the reluctance of charities and other institutions to incorporate has greatly lessened. The advantages of incorporation are increasingly outweighing the snobbism of aloofness, while in the United States and Canada the heavy taxation demands of the modern welfare state and the tax privileges accorded to all charitable foundations have led to a veritable flood of charities, most of which are incorporated.[1]

The Foundation – Social and Legal Impacts

The foundation is largely an American creation. No doubt the accumulation of vast wealth was one reason for its rise; another – at least in the days when Carnegie, Rockefeller and others perpetuated their names through their now world-famous bequests – was unquestionably a desire of wealthy and successful men to purge their consciences before God and man, and to justify the acquisitive society which had enabled them to accumulate enormous riches by leaving a vast proportion of their wealth for the benefit of mankind (Carnegie, 1895). But in recent years these reasons for the earlier foundations have become less important, and the incorporated foundation or trust has become predominantly a business device, a paramount instrument in the struggle between the demands of the modern welfare state and the wish of the individual entrepreneur to perpetuate his fortune and his name. The greatest and most influential of the foundations (Ford, Rockefeller, Carnegie) are the creations of individuals or families, but the large foundations of the future will increasingly be the creations of corporations. The desires to give and to perpetuate the name of the individual or corporate donor are undoubtedly still important motivations, but the immense growth in the number and size of foundations in recent years[2] suggests that

1. In a recent sample, taken in the United States, 4526 out of 6745 foundations were found to be incorporated (*The Foundation Directory*, 1967). For an analysis of the developments which have, despite the partial approximation of the status of an unincorporated association to that of a corporate legal person and despite the versatility of the trust, led in England to the increasing use of the incorporated charity (company limited by guarantee) (Gower, 1969, pp. 12, 180–81).

2. According to the most recent edition of *The Foundation Directory* (1967) there were some 18,000 active American foundations, of which 6803 either

business considerations play an increasing role. By either bequeathing or giving during his lifetime a proportion of his estate to a permanent institution established for officially recognized charitable purposes, the donor, usually the controller of an industrial or business empire,[3] achieves a number of purposes.[4] In the United States gifts to such organizations are exempt from gift taxes, and bequests to them are deductible for estate-tax purposes. The organizations themselves are normally – though no longer entirely – exempt from income tax, property tax and other taxes. A charitable gift *inter vivos* is an allowable deduction from the taxable income of the donor.[5] The absence of the latter privilege in English law may be one reason why incorporated charities are not so widespread in Britain (apart, of course, from the vastly greater capital wealth of United States business). Otherwise, motivations for the establishment of charitable companies are very similar (Gower, 1969, pp. 12, 180–81). The advantages of transferring both capital and annual income away from the personal estate of a tax-payer in the high-income brackets or away from a corporation are very considerable.[6] But in the age of the managerial revolution and the welfare state, a motive at least equal to that of providing a suitable mechanism for philanthropy and a tax-free reservoir for an otherwise highly taxable income is the

---

possessed assets of at least $200,000 or made grants of at least $10,000. The largest percentage of the 6803 foundations had been created during the periods 1940–49 (1583 or 24 per cent) and 1950–59 (3817 or 57 per cent). There were 236 foundations with assets of $10 million or more; thirteen had assets exceeding $200 million, for a total of $7750 million, or one-third of the assets of all foundations (pp. 9, 11, 16–17).

3. There are, however, also numerous examples of smaller foundations whose main purpose is to secure an income for dependants from a less highly taxed capital fund.

4. See Weaver, *US Philanthropic Foundations* 70–89 (1967); and also an excellent note, 34 *Virginia L. Rev.* 182 (1948).

5. Allowable deductions by individuals to private foundations are limited to 20 per cent of adjusted gross income; the limit is increased to 30 and 50 per cent for certain specifically defined foundations. Allowable deductions by corporations are limited to 5 per cent of taxable income.

6. For detailed calculations see 'How to have your own foundation', *Fortune*, August 1947, pp. 100, 140.

power which the foundation gives to the controller of a business or industry to perpetuate his control.[7]

The Ford Foundation, for example, by far the wealthiest of all, with assets of several billion dollars, has undoubtedly greatly increased the scope of educational and other charitable activities to which foundations have contributed so much in the United States, but it also preserves the bulk of the Ford enterprise in the hands of the family. Originally all its stock in the Ford Motor Company was non-voting stock, and the Ford family retained all the voting stock. This voting stock constituted a very small proportion of the total shares issued, however, and so the foundation received the bulk of the income of the company. In December 1955, a new scheme was devised which enabled the foundation to convert part of its stock into voting shares and to offer these for sale to the public.

The common voting shares sold to the public represent 60 per cent of the total number of votes, with certain restrictions on the right of any one person to hold more than a certain number of shares. The Ford family exchanged its old shares for a new class of non-transferable voting shares representing 40 per cent of the voting power. This arrangement assures continued control of the enterprise to the Ford family, while it enables the Ford Foundation to diversify its holdings.

A detailed analysis of the many methods and purposes for which the modern American foundation is used would greatly exceed the scope of this inquiry. It clearly represents a development strikingly different from the state of affairs which Maitland portrayed. Modern government attempts to counter the accumulation of private wealth and power partly by supervisory regulation and partly by heavy taxation. The controllers of enterprises counter by divesting themselves of assets which they would otherwise pay to the state as income

7. 'It is this peculiar circumstance – *retention of control* – which largely explains the emergence of family foundations as the dominant feature on the foundation scene today. Men who have built successful enterprises and seen the value of their equity swell have sought, naturally, to keep control with the family. They have accordingly established charitable family foundations, minimized their tax, enjoyed the satisfaction of promoting good works, and retained practically all but the dividend benefits of ownership. Such persons, it has been said, actually do not give away their property at all, but only the income thereon – though this is perhaps an overstatement.' Note, 34 *Virginia L. Rev.* 182, 188 (1948).

tax. At the same time they sanctify their name and give public proof of their sense of social responsibility through the establishment of charitable institutions.

The very complexity and size of the enterprises involved makes it necessary to establish these foundations as permanent and, almost invariably, incorporated institutions. They are mostly incorporated as membership or non-profit-making charitable corporations.[8] While they have no capital stock and may not distribute dividends or profits, and while they must hold their funds in trust for the charitable objects defined in the charter, their organization is very much like that of the ordinary business corporation. The charter is the empowering instrument; a board of directors, managers or trustees administers it; and the larger foundations have vast staffs of executive officers, many of them highly paid. Provided its income is destined for charitable purposes, a corporation does not lose its charitable character by conducting a business enterprise.[9]

The Social Impact of Institutionalized Giving

The institutionalization of large-scale giving is a necessary concomitant of the growth of corporate power. The major reasons for the continued growth of the charitable foundation are likely to endure in our time, for they are partly inherent in the structure of modern industrial organization in all but completely socialized states. In the

8. Note, 34 *Virginia L. Rev.* 182, 193–4 (1948); see Latham 'Private charitable foundations, income tax and policy implications', 98 *University of Pennsylvania L. Rev.* 617 (1950). The advantages of incorporation for the American type of foundation have been formulated as follows:

'The advantages of the corporate form are many. In several states exemption of the property of charitable institutions from taxation is limited to incorporated organizations. Also, corporations may generally be created for perpetual duration, thus eliminating questions as to reversion or the difficulties occasioned by death of an individual trustee. Furthermore, where there are restrictions upon the investment of trust funds, they may be found inapplicable to corporations or subject to removal by charter or by-laws. The principal advantage, however, is undoubtedly the insulation of the "trustees" from personal liability' (Note, at 195).

9. A testator devised to a foundation established by his will a ceramics manufacturing business. The income of the foundation was to go to the promotion of the ceramic arts, but a sum actually exceeding its average income was to be paid to the testator's wife for five years. The foundation was held charitable. Edward Orton Jr, 'Ceramic foundation', 9 *T.C.* 533 (1947), 34 *Virginia L. Rev.* 225 (1948).

first place, the incidence of taxation, both income and succession, although fluctuating somewhat with varying economic conditions and government policies, is likely to remain sufficiently heavy to induce both wealthy individuals and corporations to divert as large a proportion of their disposable resources as possible away from the State as revenue collector to channels which they are in a better position to control themselves.[10] Second, in the case of the relatively few but important major industrial enterprises which are still substantially under family control, the foundation is, as already mentioned, the best device to perpetuate the donor's control over the business (see note 7). At the same time, such a giant family foundation is akin to the older foundations of the Carnegie and Rockefeller type in identifying the name of the donor forever with the educational and social improvement of the nation. In the eyes of the average person, the name of Ford today stands not only for a famous automobile but also for an institution that raises university salaries and improves education in India, the name of Rockefeller not only for the founder of an oil empire or a contemporary political leader, but also for major achievements in agricultural and medical research (such as the Mexican wheat strains, which have revolutionized farming yields in India).

The major foundations function as public rather than private institutions. Inevitably they have become one of the major institutional forces of the modern state. In particular, their influence is of increasing importance in the determination of educational policy, the goals of research in all spheres, and the direction of thinking in international affairs.[11] So far the major foundations have maintained the tradition, established by the Rockefeller and Carnegie Foundations, of regarding themselves as trustees of education in a free

10. In this respect the combined effect of the numerous small foundations established by small and medium-sized business firms or wealthy individuals should not be underestimated. In the United States thousands of small firms and affluent individuals establish 'research' foundations with small amounts of capital. Both the initial capital and the annual appropriations, even if they only amount to a few thousand dollars, are diverted from the coffers of the state into a multitude of private or semi-private channels.

11. Thus a number of grants made by the Ford Foundation have undoubtedly a major share in the remarkable increase of cultural and social relations between the United States on the one part and India and the Middle East on the other.

society and have avoided interference with university policy or the attachment of strings to the vast gifts which they make. Senior officers of these foundations are men of integrity and high standards, often coming themselves from an academic background and behaving like civil servants rather than company executives.

However, the major foundations have not been able to stand aside from the growing tensions that have beset American society in the last decade, both internally and internationally. The Ford Foundation in particular, under the direction of its new president, Mr McGeorge Bundy, formerly a leading member of both the Kennedy and the Johnson administrations, has directed many of its major grants towards social objectives and, in particular, elimination of racial inequality and discrimination, in housing, education, voting and other politically sensitive areas. This has provoked the wrath of those sectors of public opinion and the Congress who are, openly or disguisedly, opposed to an energetic integration policy and any basic change in the *status quo*. One effect of this reaction has been the demand for a change in the tax status of the foundations.

The Tax Reform Act of 1969 abolishes the foundations' former total exemption from income tax, but the uniform tax rate of 4 per cent on net investment income is a moderate one, designed to meet the cost which the Internal Revenue must incur in administering the affairs of private foundations. Far more serious are three other changes in the status of foundations. The first restricts their ownership of corporations voting stock, generally to 20 per cent or, where control of the corporation is in another party, to 35 per cent of the voting stock. A time schedule is prescribed for the disposal of existing business holdings. Sanctions for failure to comply consist in taxes, rising from 5 per cent of the value of excess holding to an upper limit of 20 per cent. The second innovation is designed to insure the widest possible distribution of investment by foundations and sets certain limits for the use of its 'unrelated assets', i.e. those not used in the active conduct of the foundation's affairs.

By far the most important and potentially damaging change concerns the definition of 'taxable expenditures'. Previous rules prohibited intervention in political campaigns and any 'substantial' amount of propaganda designed to influence legislation. The new rules set escalating scales of taxes for expenditures which are

The Social Impact of Institutionalized Giving 319

designed: (1) to influence the outcome of a specific election; (2) to influence legislation through attempts to influence the general public (this does not include an examination of broad social and economic problems); (3) to influence legislatures, except when they have officially solicted advice or assistance; (4) to provide grants to non-public charities, unless full disclosure is made; (5) to finance voter registration drives, except in strictly defined circumstances; (6) expenditures for activities that are not within the Internal Revenue definition of charities (i.e. religious, charitable, educational activities).

Evidently, the impact of these new restrictions on the activities of the foundations will largely depend on their administration. Potentially most serious is the limitation listed in the fifth, since this is clearly inspired by the foes of desegregation, who dislike the grants given by the Ford Foundation for the registration of black voters in the South – an objective that would, however, seem to be clearly within the rationale of *Brown* v. *Board of Education* and provisions of the Constitution designed to ensure the equality of all citizens. At the very least, the new rules are likely to restrict the scope of foundations' activities.[12]

Corporate Power and the State

Organized industry and organized labour have, in modern democratic society, become giant and powerful social forces. It is only exceptionally, as in the case of the aluminium industry where until a few years ago one company controlled 90 per cent of the national production,[13] that power is concentrated in a single corporation. More frequently, a small group of major concerns exercises joint dominion over the industry. The nation awaits with bated breath the result of negotiations between the 'Big Three' of the automobile industry – General Motors, Ford and Chrysler – and the United Automobile Workers. Similarly, negotiations between the major steel firms and the United Steel Workers set a pattern not only for in-

12. It might be added that, despite considerable pressures to the contrary, churches of all denominations remain tax exempt. In *Walz* v. *Tax Commission of City of New York* (90 S. Ct 1409 [1970]) the Supreme Court rejected the contention that tax exemption for religious organizations for properties used solely for religious worship was a violation of the First Amendment's prohibition of governmental 'establishment of religion'.

13. *United States* v. *Aluminium Co.*, 148 F. 2d 416, 423 (2d Cir. 1945).

dustrial organization, labour relations and the cost of steel production, but also for the economic life of the nation for years to come. The result of such negotiations has a decisive influence on the volume of production and the price level not only in the industry affected but also in the many ancillary and subsidiary industries; and it has profound effects as well on the general level of wages and national income. A nation-wide social trend is established when General Motors or United States Steel conclude a long-term contract with the appropriate labour union.[14]

To these two great types of organized corporate power in modern industrial democracy must be added other forces that differ in importance from country to country. In the United States, as mentioned, the charitable foundation, a by-product of corporate power, exercises an increasing influence of its own. In a number of European countries, on the other hand, such as Great Britain, Germany or in the Scandinavian states, the consumer exercises a considerable influence through the consumers' cooperatives, organizations which have grown from relatively small non-profit-making cooperative ventures into powerful movements. Like the big industrial corporations, they have become institutionalized; and, in some countries like Great Britain, they exercise a considerable political influence, usually through one of the major political parties.

So decisive is the combined influence of these powerful and tightly organized social groups within the state, that their relationship to the legal and political power of the modern state requires some re-evaluation. During the last few centuries the modern national state has had an increasing tendency to become the Leviathan of which Hobbes wrote, not only the repository of physical and legal restraining power and the protector of the nation against an external enemy, but also the main directive force in the shaping of the economic and social life of the nation. It has gradually absorbed, unified and come to control most of the functions previously exercised by social groups – merchants, landowners, craftsmen's guilds, churches. Are we in the process of another dialectic reversal?

Only a generation ago advocates of 'pluralism', such as Figgis or

14. In recent years the tendency has been to conclude five-year or at least three-year agreements in which the right to strike is suspended for the duration in consideration of a number of benefits, including pensions and social security.

Laski, pleaded for more recognition of the social groups within the state – trade unions, churches and others – in mitigation of the legal and ideological glorification of the state. A generation later, the question must be raised in all seriousness whether the 'over mighty subjects' of our time – the giant corporations, both of a commercial and non-commercial character, the labour unions, the trade associations, farmers' organizations, veterans' legions and some other highly organized groups – have taken over the substance of sovereignty. Has the balance of pressures and counter-pressures between these groups left the legal power of the state as a mere shell? If this is a correct interpretation of the social change of our time, we are witnessing another dialectic process in history: the national sovereign state – having taken over effective legal and political power from the social groups of the previous age – surrenders its power to the new massive social groups of the industrial age.

Before attempting even a tentative assessment of such a generalization, we must clarify the much used, but also much confused, concepts of 'state' and 'sovereignty'. To what extent has the state ever been more than a symbol, more than the machinery developed by the social and economic groupings struggling for supremacy behind the symbols of political sovereignty? On the one side, Marxist theory asserts that the state is no more than the structure erected by the dominant class which moulds the state and its institutions according to its own interests and power. On the other side, Hegelian and Neo-Hegelian doctrine elevate the state into the positive embodiment of the 'absolute spirit', the highest development of human society, the integration of all the human and social forces which have, both logically and historically, developed in the processes of world history.[15] There is no other aspect of Marxist theory which has been as fully refuted in history as the belief in the withering of the state and its coercive machinery. The country which has gone furthest in applying the Marxist theory of the socialization of means of production, Soviet Russia, has politically and legally not only retained the trappings of sovereignty, but reached new heights of concentrated state power. Indeed, there is perhaps no other type of modern state in which the effective power of social groups within the state –

15. For a more detailed account and criticism of the Hegelian philosophy of state and law, see Friedmann (1967, pp. 164–76).

industry, organized labour, cultural groups – has been so completely absorbed into state authority. For in the totalitarian states of Fascist persuasion – Nazi Germany, Mussolini's Italy, Franco's Spain – the real power of the state was, or is, not nearly so concentrated as it would appear. The Nazi state based itself on the integrated co-operation of certain groups which supported its purposes, in particular, the military and the industrialists.[16] The organized labour movement, believed to be hostile, had been destroyed. For a while, the organized political power of the state and the most powerful social groups in the state – the military and organized industry[17] – directed it together towards its doom in the common pursuit of conquest. But it was certainly not a question of one-sided domination. Hegelian ideology, in its nefarious identification of 'the state' with any state as the ideal integration of all human and social forces in society, mainly served as a convenient ideological cloak for the unrestrained glorification of absolute state power. It was put in the service of Nazi philosophy as a justification for the destruction of all institutional obstacles, such as a free labour movement or an independent judiciary.

In democratic societies, which permit and, indeed, depend on a certain play and balance of social forces within the framework of the institutional organizations of state, the picture is less clear. It would be as misleading to regard the modern democratic 'state' merely as a skeleton without flesh, a mere apparatus manipulated by various groups, as it would be to identify the institutional framework of the state and the legal coercive powers which it exercises with the real social power and its distribution in the society. In the normal functioning of a democracy there is a perpetual struggle between various organized social forces striving to translate their particular interests and aims into legislative and administrative action. Clearly, the influence of any particular group is largely dependent on the weight behind it. Such weight can be measured not only in terms of

16. The most brilliant analysis of the social basis of the Nazi state is that of Neumann (1944). See also Fraenkel (1941).

17. In the overwhelmingly Catholic environment of such countries as Italy, Portugal and Spain, the influence of the Church is vital. Apart from its own organization, it operates largely through the other major social groups, such as landowners and industrialists.

numbers of members, but also in terms of financial resources, discipline and organization. In our highly articulate society, public relations have become immensely important. The availability of mass media of communication, such as radio, television and the press, has greatly increased the gap between the influence of the organized articulate pressure group and the mass of unorganized individuals.

There are clearly dangers in this state of affairs. The most powerful, wealthy and highly organized group may succeed in identifying the 'public interest' with its own interests. There are, however, two important counterbalancing and mitigating factors. The first lies, in any normally functioning democracy, in the balance of forces, or, as it has been put by an American economist, in 'countervailing power' (Galbraith, 1952). A highly organized manufacturers' association may be faced by an equally well-organized association of wholesalers or retailers. The once overwhelming power of the owner of the means of production to dictate terms of employment, under the guise of contract, is today checked by the power of the labour unions. Farmers' or consumers' cooperatives may check the power of the traders. However, the degree of organization and the power of these various interest groups are grossly unequal, both inside one particular country and between different countries.

If the legal sovereignty of the modern state were indeed nothing more than the product of the pulls exercised by various social power groups, the 'public interest' or 'national interest' would dissolve itself into an uneasy balance between conflicting pulls. Marxism, at least in its original dogmatic form, accepted this hypothesis and preached the necessity of displacing the identification of the interests of the dominant property-owning middle classes with those of the state by means of a revolution that would identify the interests of the proletariat with those of the state (followed by the Utopia in which the state would eventually wither away because exploitation would no longer occur). Hegelianism, on the other hand, while preaching that 'the state' was the integration and the sublimation of all forces within society, inevitably substituted, in practice, an intensely nationalist and socially conservative state for the abstract and universal ideal. For Hegel the perfect state, the culmination of world history, was, in effect, the autocratic Prussian monarchy of the 1820s. For the Neo-Hegelians it was the Nazi state.

Modern democratic society does not correspond to either of these extremes. We should think of the state not in the Hegelian sense, but as something more than a mere computing machine of conflicting social forces, a 'cash register, ringing up the additions and withdrawals of strength, a mindless balance pointing and marking the weight and distribution of power among the contending groups' (Latham, 1952, p. 37). Clearly, there is a 'reserve function' in the state.[18] Acting through the main branches of government – legislative, executive, judicial – it expresses and articulates, especially in times of crisis, national policies and sentiments which do not normally express themselves in organized pressure groups. Sometimes, this reserve power of the state as expressing the general interest is all but completely paralysed, because of the particular distribution of group pressures within the state. It is regrettable that the direct impact of the unorganized public on state action should seldom occur except under the pressure or threat of war. Faced with the threat of physical extinction, public opinion may impel legislation prohibiting commercially profitable transactions with potential enemies (Berle, 1954, p. 54). It may, and normally does, produce legislation against profiteering in times of scarcity. It tolerates or even demands official price controls. It puts a severe brake on strikes of more than local importance. In times of emergency the 'national interest' may suddenly assume concrete importance in judicial condemnation of the tax dodger[19] who, in times of less stress, is regarded with leniency or even sympathy.[20]

But it is not only the occasional spurt that makes the state something more than the point of balance between contending social forces. The modern state is expected to assume responsibility for an irreducible minimum of welfare functions far exceeding the traditional spheres of state activity: defence, foreign affairs, police and a machinery of justice (see p. 506). In the United States no less than in Great Britain, France, Scandinavia, India or the Soviet

18. This approach, suggested in an earlier version of this chapter, published in 57 *Columbia L. Rev.* 155 (1957), is developed by Miller in 'The constitutional law of the security state', 10 *Stanford L. Rev.*, 610, 645–57 (1958).

19. See the English wartime decisions of *Howard* v. *Inland Revenue Commrs* [1942] 1 K.B. 389, 397; *Latilla* v. *Inland Revenue Commrs* [1943] A.C. 377.

20. See *Levene* v. *Inland Revenue Commrs.* [1928] A.C. 217.

Union, the state is expected to give minimum insurance against such national vicissitudes as unemployment, sickness and accidents suffered in the course of employment. The most conservative Republican Administration in the United States would not be permitted to watch passively – as it still could a generation ago – a major depression. It would be compelled by public opinion to enact a programme of public works and other relief measures designed to stimulate employment. Such a minimum programme entails continuous heavy taxation. The cost of social insurance, whether borne by the taxpayer (as in the case of the British National Health Service) or by a combination of government, employers and employees (as in the case of most other forms of social insurance), burdens the productive machinery of the state. Again, defence expenditure is a major and continuous financial charge on every major democracy. Clearly, each organized group, manufacturers, labourers, retailers, consumers, would improve its own position by having the one or the other of these burdens reduced. But it is not only the balance of forces, it is an irreducible minimum of articulated demands of public opinion at a given time that makes it impossible to reduce basically the minimum responsibilities of the modern state.[21]

21. It is not believed that the analysis of the relationship between state and social groups in modern democracy given above is basically at variance with Earl Latham's brilliant analysis of 'Group conflict and the political process' (1952, ch. 1). Rather, it stresses a different aspect of that relationship. In Professor Latham's analysis, the 'public groups', while endowed with 'officiality', i.e. the power to exercise against all groups and individuals certain powers which they, in turn, may not exercise against the official groups, themselves form a social force, or rather a conglomerate of social forces struggling with each other as well as providing compromises between the conflicting pulls of private social groupings. To that extent, Latham's analysis seems to agree with the theory of the pluralists that the state is, itself, one of a number of social associations, such as churches, corporations and trade unions, with which it has to compete for the allegiance and obedience of the individual. That each of the various groups of officialdom has its own social pull within the fabric of organized democracy is indeed evident from Professor Latham's own analysis of the struggle about the basing point legislation of a few years ago or, again, from the melancholy history of the proposed Missouri Valley Authority, which, despite the obvious need for official action, has been defeated time and again not only by the pressure of the private power lobby, but also by conflicts between various governmental organizations, each jealous of its own prerogatives. What is stressed in the text is that

There is no more telling illustration of the impact of changing demands of social policy on the functions of the state than the programme submitted by the conservative Nixon Administration, in 1970, to the US Congress. The essence of this plan is the provision of a minimum income for poor families. Instead of the vast variety of state and local public welfare schemes, the US Government will, under this plan, provide a minimum income of $1600 for any family of four, and this officially provided minimum income will taper off to zero, in proportion to a scale of income earned by work, by the members of the family. The fact that the suggested minimum level of $1600 is vastly below the so-called poverty line (put at least at $3600, and likely to go up with the accelerating rise in the cost of living)[22] does not detract from the fact that, in the very country that has throughout its history idolized private enterprise and the vast differences of wealth as natural, or even as expressions of divine providence, the state now assumes responsibility for a minimum standard of living. Such a philosophy would, even less than a generation ago, have been condemned by the great majority of Americans as irresponsible 'socialism'.

Recent Analyses of the Function of the Large Corporation

The emergence of the large industrial corporation – depersonalized and institutionalized – as a major social phenomenon and its impact on the legal, economic and social structure of society have, not

---

granted all the conflicting pulls between social groups and within the official family of the state, it becomes at times, though usually only in times of emergency, the articulate expression of something more than a compromise between the various social groups within the state, the articulation of a national public policy. We have tentatively called this the 'reserve function' of the state. This is probably not far removed from the analysis of Kenneth S. Carlston which describes the state as 'the ultimate organization of the national society, since it is characterized by a common acceptance of a certain authority and by the fact that its members identify themselves with it': Carlston (1956, p. 65).

22. It should, however, be noted that the actual benefit provided by the government is somewhat higher, if the value of public housing, food stamps and free medical services provided through Medicaid are added. In 1971, a plan providing somewhat improved benefits were re-submitted to Congress. In August 1971 the plea was postponed for a year as part of a domestic austerity programme.

surprisingly, occupied the attention of American thinkers more than those of any other country. Since the end of the Second World War, several eminent American lawyers, sociologists and economists have attempted to analyse some of the long-term impacts of this new development. They have, again not surprisingly, arrived at very different conclusions. They agree only on one fact: that the big corporation can neither be legislated nor wished out of the fabric of modern industrial society; that it is an inevitable product of society and the minimum demands for mass production, which a world constantly geared for possible war must make on the productive resources of the country. In 1946 Peter Drucker published a study based on an analysis of the General Motors Corporation. Its central theme was that in contemporary American society the large corporation was 'the institution which sets the standard for the way of life and the mode of living of our citizens; which leads, moulds and directs; which determines our perspective on our own society; around which crystallize our social problems and to which we look for their solution' (Drucker, 1946, pp. 6–7). In 1952 two challenging studies were published, one by a lawyer-administrator and the other by an economist. Both studies accepted the permanence and inevitability of 'big business', but arrived at different assessments of the legal and social policy which the community should adopt towards it. David Lilienthal, one-time chairman of the publicly owned Tennessee Valley Authority and later of the Atomic Energy Commission, emphatically came out in defence of big business as the agent of technical as well as social progress (Lilienthal, 1953). He roundly condemned the whole elaborate and cherished edifice of anti-trust legislation as a reactionary curb on the dynamic progress of society, which depended on big business, i.e. the large corporation. The real stimulus to competition he saw not in any artificial attempt to curb bigness or to forbid this or that practice, but in the constant challenge of better and more efficient technological and production processes, stimulated by the increasing competition between different industries and materials, such as wool and synthetic fibres, metal and timber, electricity, coal, natural gas and, eventually, atomic power.[23]

23. This view of competition won an important judicial triumph when a four to three majority of the Supreme Court dismissed a suit brought under sec. 2 of the Sherman Act by the Department of Justice charging du Pont with the

Abuses could, if necessary, be remedied by public administrative controls.

At the same time a Harvard economist, Kenneth Galbraith (1952), surveying the structure of contemporary American capitalism, noticed, like Lilienthal, the curious antinomy between the constant drive towards bigness in industrial organization – reflected in the worship of the big executive, not only in the economic but also in the social scale of values – and the strong, almost axiomatic distrust of bigness in the political life of the nation. Unlike Lilienthal, however, Galbraith did recognize the need for some check on the unmitigated power of bigness. But he saw the check in 'countervailing power', the emergence of powerful, organized economic and social groups, whose respective pulls and interests held those of the other groups in check. The great nation-wide retailers can check price policy abuses on the part of manufacturers. Organized labour counterbalances the massed power of organized business. None of the powerful economic groups within the state could get away with too much without being checked by one of the countervailing forces. On the whole, this analysis not only confirmed that contemporary American democracy was dominated neither by an omnipotent State nor a large number of free individuals, it also implied that the state of affairs was not nearly so dangerous as was often supposed.

Shortly afterwards another – qualified – apologia for the present role of the big corporation was offered by Adolph Berle (1954). Accepting the fact that the two hundred or so largest corporations in the United States had a decisive impact on the economic and social development of the nation, Berle saw the principal restraining factor in the gradual growth of the 'corporate conscience', the increasing transformation of the large corporation from the ruthless and essentially individualistic profit-seeking entrepreneur of the

---

monopolization of interstage commerce in cellophane: *United States* v. *I. E. du Pont de Nemours & Co.*, 351 U.S. 377 (1956). The majority held that, although du Pont controlled 75 per cent of United States cellophane production, and the only other producer had cross-licensing agreements with du Pont, the availability of alternative products such as glassine or wax paper, whose combined sales greatly outstripped cellophane in the 'relevant market', excluded monopolization in the sense of section 2. The minority denied that the alternative products were in any way competitive with cellophane. See also p. 305.

nineteenth century to a social organism conscious of its public functions, its social responsibilities, and of the force of public opinion. These factors compel the large corporations of the present day, for example, to refrain from pushing prices of their products as high as any scarcity might economically allow them (as in the case of the postwar automobile shortage).[24] They also compel the management of the large corporations to refrain from pursuing their own personal advantage in the exercise of their administrative powers.[25] At the same time the large corporations with international interests are often called upon to exercise quasi-diplomatic functions in delicate international situations, as in the case of the Iranian Oil Agreement of 1954. Berle acknowledges, however, that this process of transformation, especially in regard to employment contracts and employment policy, is far from complete (see pp. 366–71). His concluding chapter on 'Corporate Capitalism and the City of God' gives a theological flavour to his thesis that the large corporation is the principal organizational force of modern industrial society, not only in a purely economic or business sense, but as a political institution.[26]

Since the mid 1950s, when the aforementioned studies were published, the problem of the relation of public and private power has been greatly intensified. In several vital spheres, especially in the

24. On the other hand, the rise of automobile prices during a serious depression in 1958 was attributed by many economists to the ability of the Big Three 'to impose administered prices' on the community in 'partial disregard of' the laws of supply and demand. The industry countered by pointing to the inflexibility of labour costs in the age of collective bargaining (see *Administrative Prices, Hearings before the Sub-Committee on Antitrust and Monopoly of the Committee on the Judiciary*, U.S. *Senate*, 85th Congress, Second Session, 1958 (S.Res. 57 and S.Res. 231); *Administered Prices: A Compendium on Public Policy, Subcommittee on Antitrust and Monopoly of the Senate Committee on the Judiciary*, 88th Congress, First Session (1963)).

25. For a striking British counterpart of this philosophy, see the remarks of Lord Citrine, Chairman of the British Electricity Authority, a statutory public monopoly, and a former prominent trade union leader, as reported in *The Economist*, 14 July 1956, p. 149. Industrial statesmanship and the community's insistence on proper disclosure of the operations of huge undertakings – public or private – are, according to Lord Citrine, reasonable guarantees against abuse of power.

26. For a stinging criticism of the apotheosis of the modern corporation, implicit in the oversimplifications of the theories of Galbraith, Lilienthal, and Berle, see Latham in 47 *Papersard Proceedings, Amer. Econ. Soc.* 303 (1957).

defence establishment of the United States, concentration and the influence of economic power of the leading corporations has further increased. On the other hand, the tasks of government, under the combined impact of international defence and economic obligations, of the minimum demands of congested industrialized and urbanized societies, and the rapidly growing dangers of environmental pollution, are steadily increasing. The analyses even of a decade ago are no longer adequate to cope with the problems of the 1970s.

Both Berle and Galbraith have recently published major new studies reflecting their most recent thinking on these issues, while in England Andrew Shonfield's *Modern Capitalism*, deals with the same basic problem: the relation of public and private power.

The most important evolution in Berle's thinking (1969) is his admission that a vastly increased role of the state is inevitable in order to cope with the realities both of the economic power of the modern corporation and of organized labour. In view of the fact that '[p]roduction of all kinds will increasingly be dominated by huge corporate organizations – as the motor car industry is today dominated by three giant corporations', government will become 'increasingly necessary'.

Moreover, 'Socialist' control, that is, direction given and enforced by government, appears to be the single alternative. Ownership has little or nothing to do with it, and may not even be affected. Rather, the task will be to formulate an inventory of desires for those conditions life can afford – if consensus can be had – and devise social controls causing production and distribution to bring them about (Berle, 1969, pp. 257–8).

In view of the fact that more and more economic power will be concentrated not in the 'owners', but in pension trusts, mutual funds and institutional holders of stock, while the owners will increasingly become recipients of interest or dividends 'derived from huge corporate aggregates of which they can have little knowledge and over which they have no influence whatever', there is no alternative to the expansion of the state's role. The need for 'an enhanced social control over economics' is unavoidable, and in Berle's view, it matters little whether it is accomplished 'by statist take-over of property or, with more sophistication, by statist dictation to property holders of what they may or may not do' (1969, pp. 260–61, 262).

While certainly not in disagreement about the need for greatly increased public control over economic activities, Galbraith, (1967) takes a somewhat different approach. In his view, the relation of government authority to private economic power is based on three major factors: first, the increasing transfer of effective power, in the modern industrial state, from individuals to organizations. The effective control of business is increasingly exercised by elite groups which embrace 'all who bring specialized knowledge, talent or experience to group decision-making.' These Galbraith calls the 'technostructure'. The second factor is the increasing displacement of the traditional market system by the management of consumer demand by the producer. This goes together with the increasing manipulation of prices, which contemporary economists call 'administered prices'. Third, and perhaps most important, there is an increasing interpenetration of government and large-scale private business, especially in the realm of defence, which now accounts for at least half of the annual US Government budget – of well over one hundred billion dollars. Galbraith's analysis differs both from the traditional Marxist thesis, in which state power is seen as the main instrument of the controllers of capital, and from the thesis of the defenders of modern capitalism, which regard private enterprise as the best agent of economic progress, only marginally restrained by public power. Galbraith distinguishes between the 'entrepreneurial' corporation – generally a vanishing type in big business – and the 'mature' corporation, i.e. the type represented by General Motors, General Electric or US Steel. The latter does not resist the growth of state control and of the social welfare state because it has formed a close association with the state. The modern, large-scale corporation becomes a major executive arm of the state, and by virtue of this function it controls vital sectors of the governmental establishment.

The mature corporation . . . depends on the state for trained manpower, the regulation of aggregate demand, for stability in wages and prices. All are essential to the planning with which it replaces the market. The state, through military and other technical procurement, underwrites the corporation's largest capital commitments in the area of most advanced technology (1967, p. 308).

Especially in the defence area, the 'technostructure' that controls the mature corporation identifies itself closely with the goals of the armed services, and there is a constant interchange of personnel.

In his recent analysis Andrew Shonfield (1969) also emphasizes the inevitable growth of public power. He argues that the increasingly intimate and complex interrelationship between public power and private interest groups, should be made more explicit and open.

The great enlargement of the sphere of public power does not make that power less sensitive to the pressures of private interests and individuals. On the contrary, the increased range and subtlety of the relationship between the public and the private sectors have made it less feasible to govern effectively by decree. The system will not function unless private organizations give their willing collaboration to the pursuit of public purposes (1969, p. 389).

Shonfield sees the solution in the development of more specific and open safeguards against administrative arbitrariness, partly on the model of the Scandinavian Ombudsman, and partly by an institutional and systematic development of administrative justice, somewhat on the lines of the French system of administrative law.

The Quasi-Public Power of the Large Corporation and the Problem of Legal Control

One paramount conclusion emerges from the various representative analyses that have been sketched out above – and they apply to all industrialized democracies of our time, with differences only of degree rather than substance. The corporate organizations of business and labour have long ceased to be a private phenomenon. That they have a direct and decisive impact on the social, economic and political life of the nation is no longer a matter of argument. It is an undeniable fact of daily experience. The challenge to the contemporary lawyer is to translate the social transformation of these organizations from private associations to public organisms into legal terms. In attempting to do so, we have to recognize that both business and labour currently exercise vast powers. First, they have power over the millions of men and women whose lives they largely control as employees or as members. Second, they exercise power more directly, though not less powerfully, over the unorganized citizens whose lives they largely control through standardized terms of contract, through price policy, through advertising production and the terms and conditions of labour. Last, they exercise control over the organized community, represented by the organs of state, in a multitude of ways: direct lobby pressures, control over the election and policies of the elected representatives of the people, control over the appointment of the judiciary in many states, and far reaching control over the mass media of communication. In this sense 'government' or 'law making' by private groups[27] is today an irreversible fact. But if our previous analysis of the 'reserve function' of the state as the organized expression and instrument of national public opinion, as distinct from a mere parallelogram of group pressures, is correct, a survey of the legal checks, of the 'counter-vailing power', which is or ought to be at the disposal of the organized community, is a paramount task of modern jurisprudence.

Although both big business and big labour currently exercise much quasi-public authority, a 'delegated power of command',[28] they do not do so in identical ways. The power of big business over public life operates essentially in three directions: in the first place, the concentration of disposable capital resources[29] largely determines the direction and tempo of industrial production, technological research, price policy and the standard of consumption (in this, big business is, however, counterchecked by a number of forces, notably collective bargaining with organized labour, the partial dependence on government contracts, and, to some extent, mutual competition); in the second place, the large corporations control the conditions of employment for millions of employees, and they set the tone for the rest of the nation (see pp. 320–21) (in this they are largely counter-checked by the organized bargaining power of labour and by social legislation of various kinds); third, in so far as the large-scale charitable

27. See Jaffé, 'Law making by private groups', 51 *Harvard L. Rev.* 201 (1937); Wirtz, 'Government by private groups', 13 *Louisiana L. Rev.* 440 (1953).

28. A term used by the late Austrian jurist, sociologist and statesman, Karl Renner, in Kahn-Freund (1949).

29. As Professor Berle points out, the giant corporations today increasingly finance themselves out of their own capital assets. They are less and less dependent on investment bankers, although the latter play a decisive role for small businessmen and farmers (1954, p. 35).

foundation with educational and social purposes is increasingly becoming a by-product of the large business corporation, the latter can, to a significant extent, influence educational and cultural policy.

The Role of Organized Labour

Organized labour, on the other hand, has hitherto exercised its influence in two major ways. First, it is steadily increasing its share in the determination of the terms of production, since wages and other terms of collective labour agreements are a major component of the price of products. Second, unions exercise control over those – mainly industrial workers – who are organized in their ranks and generally depend for their livelihood on their union membership (whether or not there is, legally, a 'closed-shop' agreement).[30] Big-scale labour organizations have not hitherto been an important source of investment capital, although there is no reason why they should not become more influential in this field.[31] Nor have the labour unions hitherto exercised a major influence on educational and social policy. Here again, the role played by the trade-union movement in some Continental countries, notably Germany and the

30. In Britain about 40 to 50 per cent of the employed are union members; mostly in the manufacturing, building and construction and transportation. See the Donovan Report, paras. 25–8. The percentage is much lower in the United States (about 25 per cent).

31. In West Germany the powerful central trade union organization has begun to make major industrial investments, for example, in the film industry. In Great Britain, the trade unions held 49 per cent of the shares in the defunct Labour daily, the *Daily Herald*. On the whole, however, the financial (and general) influence of organized labour in press, radio, the film industry and other opinion-making media of communication is remarkably weak. It should, however, be noted that, outside the United States, radio and television are almost everywhere either wholly or in part operated by the government or public corporations. These media of public communications are not, therefore, under the financial control of private entrepreneurs and, indirectly, of the sponsors of programmes. In 1956 the mine owners and the United Mine Workers – which is outside the AFL-CLO organization – set up a joint shipping company to promote export of American coal overseas. This is a remarkable joint capital venture, but one which remains strictly within the traditional objectives of American unions – namely, the promotion of immediate economic interests. That this is now sometimes done by joint action between employers and union is in line with many other current developments.

Scandinavian countries, through workers' colleges and other labour-sponsored educational institutions, has been far more conspicuous. In the United Kingdom, the main direct cultural association of organized labour has been with the Workers' Educational Association, whose influence on the cultural and educational life of the country is limited. Trade unions also exercise a considerable influence on educational policy in a large number of Labour-controlled local government authorities. The very small influence which, by comparison, organized labour has hitherto had in the United States in educational matters is due to several factors. The major reason is probably the almost complete absence – until recently – of ideological motivations in the American labour movement. The older AFL developed from craft unions, devoid of political ideology,[32] and the American labour movement is still dominated by the down-to-earth objective of securing better terms for the members. Under the influence of the newer CIO – now amalgamated with the AFL – political issues are beginning to play a larger part, although it is difficult to imagine a unified policy.[33] By contrast, the European trade unions are closely associated with political movements, notably Marxist and Christian Socialism. This has often led to direct associations with political parties.[34] Another contributing factor is the fact that public education, including college education, is used by a far greater proportion of the population in the United States than in Europe. In Britain and other parts of the Commonwealth, publicly or privately financed scholarships, the establishment of new universities, and other developments are gradually increasing the proportion

32. In so far as the AFL has a political philosophy, it is strongly anti-Socialist. See the manifesto issued by the New York State Association of Electrical Workers-AFL against the Niagara Public Power Bill, *New York Times*, 8 July 1956, § 4, p. E7.

33. cf. the conflicting statements by Meany (AFL) and Reuther (CIO) on the Vietnam war.

34. In Great Britain the Trades Union Congress is the major organizational and financial backbone of the Labour Party. In pre-war Germany, the larger 'Free Trade Unions' were linked with the Social Democratic Party, the smaller 'Christian Unions' with the Catholic Centre Party. Since the last war, the reorganized and unified Trade Union Organization has had no direct links with any party, but the indirect and personal links with the Social Democratic and Christian Parties respectively are strong.

of university students coming from the working class. On the Continent, with the possible exception of Scandinavia and, of course, the Communist countries, the almost exclusive domination of universities by the middle classes is still a marked phenomenon, though changes are gradually occurring.

The problem of public law controls over the large corporate groups therefore arises essentially in three fields: (1) excessive concentration and abuse of economic power; (2) excessive group power over the individual as employee; (3) excessive control over the cultural and educational policy of the nation. The major problem posed by the disciplinary power of organized labour over its members is the degree to which public law can control the actions of legally 'private' organizations.

Legal Remedies for Abuses of Group Power: Total Socialization

That the trend towards corporate bigness was an inevitable and continuing one was on the whole correctly foreseen by Marxist theory. Marxism also devised a theoretically complete solution: the transfer of all means of production into the hands of the community (i.e. the state until it 'withered away'). In application of this doctrine, substantially all industrial assets in the Soviet Union and other Communist states have been transferred from private ownership to that of the state. The Soviet legal system has attempted to counter the danger of excessive concentration and bureaucratization of economic life by constituting the major industries as semi-autonomous state trusts with regional divisions, and by giving the managements considerable, though precarious, autonomy. Accountability is a yardstick by which to measure the efficiency of the state units. Far-reaching political and disciplinary penalties have been added whips, though it is doubtful to what extent they have helped efficiency.

It is, however, difficult to assess the effectiveness of a total socialization of industrial production in a political democracy. In theory, of course, political democracy could be maintained; in practice, the concentration of all economic power in the hands of a managerial public bureaucracy might lead to the undermining of political democracy and freedom. Be that as it may, the democracies both of the common-law and the civil-law worlds have hitherto rejected this solution to the problem of big business, and they show no intention of attempting it in the future.

Public and Private Enterprise in a Mixed Economy

The great majority of nations live under a system that can best be described as 'mixed economy'. This has been defined as indicating 'a situation in which the role of government as owner and regulator has become sufficiently large to cast doubt on the validity of 'capitalist' and 'free enterprise' as appropriate objectives but not sufficiently large to justify the appellation 'socialist' (Mason, 1960, p. 15). In the mixed economy systems, public and private enterprise exist side by side or, in many cases, cooperate in joint public-private corporations. In addition, the state can and does exercise various degrees of control over private enterprise, by the control over rates and tariffs, prescription of modes of employment, and many other devices. In a mixed economy public enterprise serves various purposes. It can be used to respond to nationally felt needs which private enterprise fails, or is financially unable, to satisfy. This motivation for the creation of public corporations naturally plays a much larger part in underdeveloped and capital-poor countries than in industrially more highly developed countries. It accounts for the early emergence of the public corporation in Australia in the 1880s and for the present significance of public enterprise in such countries as India.[35] In the more highly developed countries public enterprise plays only a limited role in the field of manufacture except in war time. It is of considerably greater importance in the field of certain basic services and public utilities. Thus, in the anti-socialist United States, the Tennessee Valley Authority was created on the initiative of President Roosevelt in 1933 to cope with the problem of a chronically flooded, eroded and backward area which badly needed electric power that private enterprise had failed to supply. The result of this eminently

35. In June 1956 a report made for the International Bank for Reconstruction and Development by an economic mission led by Mr Thomas H. McKitterick, Vice-President of one of America's leading banks, acknowledged that economic development in India would, at the present stage, be impossible without a great deal of government enterprise, although the share of private enterprise should be increased.

successful enterprise, which in the course of a decade revitalized an entire region and produced abundant inexpensive electric power, was, among others, to stimulate private enterprise into a new effort and more competitive prices. This can, at best, be one of the constructive functions of public enterprise. Equally successful have been certain public transport enterprises like Air Canada, which has a near-monopoly over air transport in Canada.[36]

The more far-reaching use of the public enterprise in post-war Britain and France is due to a mixture of political and technical motivations. Necessity to save a backward and declining industry of national importance was the predominant motivation for the nationalization of the British coal industry through the National Coal Board. While this agency has not – except for a few years – succeeded in turning the coal industry into a profitable enterprise, it has at least slowed down its decline and effected urgently needed modernization. The nationalization of the electricity and transport utilities in Britain and France, on the other hand, is due in part at least to the political philosophy of the governments which legislated these programmes after the Second World War. The concentration of responsibility for the development of nuclear energy in the hands of the Atomic Energy Authority in Britain is due both to technical reasons and the overwhelming public importance of this matter. In the field of public utilities of national importance, which require nation-wide development and a national policy, there has been little public opposition to such transformation of private into public enterprise.

Generally, and despite widespread criticism of the philosophy as well as the practicality of public enterprise from many quarters, the share of public enterprise in a mixed economy has increased steadily. Thus, in Italy, where state-owned enterprises play a major part in most sectors of the economy, the electric power industry has recently been nationalized, in the form of a state chartered corporation, which is now the third major state-owned complex, after the giant IRI (Instituto per la Riconstruccione Industriale) and ENI (Ente Nazionale Idrocarburi). In Britain, after a succession of nationalizing

36. On the other hand, its parent, Canadian National Railways, is a product of necessity: the amalgamation, in 1919, of a number of bankrupt railway lines which the State had to take over in order to maintain an essential national service.

measures since the last war,[37] the British Steel Corporation now controls the bulk of Britain's steelmaking capacity. In India, most of the banking system has recently been transferred from private to public ownership, which already extended to steel and other basic industries as well as life insurance.

A form of public enterprise that has developed greatly, particularly in the countries that have gained their political independence in the post-war period and suffer from backwardness in economic and social development as well as poverty of private venture capital is the state-owned development corporation. This is designed to finance and stimulate, either singly or in association with local capital or foreign investors, national economic development, usually within the framework of a national economic development plan. In Latin America, development corporations such as the Corporacion de Fomento de Chile, the Nacional Financiera de Mexico, or the Banco de Desinvolvimento de Brasil, have long played a major part in industrial development.

Types of State Enterprise

All over the world, state entrepreneurial activities take one of three legal forms:

1. Departmental government enterprises, with varying degrees of administrative and financial autonomy.
2. Statutory public corporations, i.e. autonomous legal entities which are generally responsible to the competent minister, and through him, to Parliament, but are managed as autonomous or, in principle, self-sufficient entities, according to commercial and business management principles.
3. Commercial companies which outwardly resemble any other private company and are subject to civil and commercial law, but in

37. A contrary trend is apparent in the Conservative Government's reported plan to force the nationalized British industries to 'hive off' their profitable ancillary operations (e.g. chemical products made by the Coal Board or hotels owned by British Rail). Such measures would severely handicap the nationalized industries in comparison with their private competitors and cripple their initiative and commercial viability. At the same time the Conservative Government felt compelled to nationalize the bankrupt Rolls-Royce Company (except for its profitable car division).

which the state or some other public authority – such as a government development corporation – holds a proportion of the shares, varying from complete control to a minority holding.

Generally, the departmental type of state enterprise prevailed in the earlier phase of the mixed economy, when state enterprise was concentrated on public utilities, such as railways, postal services, electric power or forestry. Many of this type of state enterprise still preserve the form of departmental administration,[38] although many of them enjoy a high degree of financial and managerial independence. The public corporation has been the major form in which public utilities and basic industries have been nationalized in the post-war period, particularly in Britain, the Commonwealth and France. The public authorities operating the postal, coal, electricity, gas, steel, atomic energy and air transport industries in Britain are all public corporations, as are many of the parallel public enterprises in France, India and Australia.

But the greatest future is probably in prospect for the mixed company, in which government and private industry jointly operate a particular enterprise. This form of association between public and private enterprise developed after the First World War, mainly in Germany, France and Italy, where the government was compelled to come to the rescue of a large number of financially bankrupt but nationally important enterprises through the acquisition of shares. Although West Germany has, under the impact of the post-war liberal economic market philosophy tended to reduce the number of state holdings or, as in the case of the Volkswagen Company, reduced its majority to a minority share, generally the mixed company has become a permanent pattern of a number of major industrial countries. In Italy, where three giant state holding corporations control vast sectors of the economy, their subsidiary companies – which range from shipbuilding to metallurgy, all forms of mining, petrochemicals, banking and many types of manufacture – generally are mixed public-private companies. In the Anglo-American world, the mixed enterprise was until recently a very exceptional phenomenon. In recent years it has, however, been noticeably on the increase. In Britain, the Labour Government, in 1967, established the

38. e.g. the Swedish Railway and Power Administration, the New Zealand Forestry Administration and the Belgian Régie de Téléphones et Télégrammes.

Industrial Reorganization Corporation (IRC), one of whose functions was to participate with private industry in reconstruction schemes.[39] Perhaps even more significantly, in the United States, a recent and still-hesitant response to the obvious need for greater state involvement in the economy may well be the mixed public-private corporation. In 1970, Congress passed a statute designed to rebuild and reorganize the inter-city railroad transport system, through a corporation in which the government and the privately-owned railroads both participate. Foreign aid, which used to be operated by a government agency, the Agency for International Development, has now been put into the hands of an overseas investment corporation, in which private capital and public capital cooperate. Generally, a mixed public-private corporation is a healthier form of state participation in the economy than the indirect involvement through subsidies, loans and other forms of state aid, which outwardly leave the private character of the assisted enterprise intact but in effect transfer responsibility to the taxpayer and the national economy.

Partnership of Capital and Labour

A very different form of partnership, though also designed to break the excessive predominance of capital ownership and private control over the nation's economic life, is the participation of workers' representatives in the management of corporations. This so-called principle of 'co-determination' (*Mitbestimmungsrecht*) was introduced into the coal and steel industries of West Germany in the course of industrial reconstruction after the Second World War.[40]

39. Although the Conservative Government has liquidated the IRC, which otherwise would have presumably become the government instrumentality for the acquisition of Rolls-Royce's assets (bankrupted and nationalized in 1971), this does not imply repudiation of the concept of mixed public-private enterprise. Thus, a bill introduced in December 1970, proposes to turn the Atomic Energy Authority's fuel division into a separate company, which will be open to investment by private industry up to 49 per cent – *The Economist*, 17 December 1970.

40. For an account, see Fischer, 'Problems arising from co-determination in Western Germany', *Transactions of the Third World Sociological Congress, International Sociological Association*, 204 (1956). See also MacPherson, 'Co-determination: Germany's move toward a new economy', 5 *Ind. & Lab. Rel. Rev.*

The whole principle and its extension to other industries is sponsored by the West German trade-union movement. The underlying idea is that the right of control over enterprises should be shared between the owners of capital, who bear only limited financial risk and otherwise contribute nothing to production, and labour, which contributes the major share of the product. As a result, the supervisory boards (*Aufsichtsrat*)[41] of the firms in the coal and steel industries in West Germany are now composed in equal parts of representatives of the shareholders and of the employees (the workers' representation is divided between direct nominees from the workers concerned and nominees from the central trade-union organization). In the larger corporations each side nominates an equal number. There is also an outside member, the 'odd man', who sometimes, but not always, serves as chairman. He is chosen by agreement of the two groups or, in default of agreement, by an independent agency. There is also a Labour Director (*Arbeitsdirektor*) in the *Vorstand*. While this co-operation seems, generally, to have worked harmoniously, especially in the time of reconstruction of the German economy, it has already become apparent that such partial alteration in the composition of the organs of company control will not produce any basic change in the pattern of industrial management. Workers' nominees soon come to regard themselves as mainly concerned in the progress and efficiency of the enterprise, which is usually dictated by sober realistic and competitive economic conditions. The 'national' or 'workers' interests as a matter of general and distinct policy tend to recede, and what remains is the fact that some of the members of the companies' boards are not elected in the traditional way by the shareholders but come from a different background, and there is a direct line of communication between company and union. Be that as it

---

20 (1951); MacPherson, 'Co-determination in practice', 8 *Ind. & Lab. Rel. Rev.* 499 (1955), and Shuchmann (1957), for a generally positive appraisal of the effect of co-determination on management-worker relations. The statutes governing this matter are of 21 May 1951 (*Bundesgesetzbl.* I, 347) and 7 August 1956 (*Bundesgesetzbl.* I, 707).

41. German company law distinguishes between the managing board (*Vorstand*), which carries out the general administration, and the supervisory council (*Aufsichtsrat*), which exercises general policy supervision. The relative influence and division of functions between the two organs varies considerably.

may, German employers strenuously resist an extension of the *Mitbestimmungsrecht* to other industries, which the German trade unions and the Social Democratic Party demand.

Anglo-American tradition has generally been sceptical of, or downright hostile to, workers' participation in management. Despite the very considerable legal and social differences that exist between the various common-law countries with respect to the status of organized labour, they are all strongly imbued with the tradition of organized labour facing the employers as the opposite party in collective bargaining. This means that the functions of management – representing the shareholders – and of the unions – representing organized labour – are kept separate. In recent years there has, however, been a noticeable change in attitude in Britain, though not so far in the United States, and various proposals for workers' participation in management have been made. The *Report of the Royal Commission on Trade Unions and Employers Associations, 1965–1968* (Donovan Commission)[42] devotes a special chapter to this problem. The Trade-Union Council had submitted proposals to the Commission for securing increased, voluntary, participation by workers in management, firstly at the plant level (shop stewards); secondly, at intermediate, regional or functional levels; and, thirdly, at the top level, where legislation should allow companies, if they wish, to make provision for trade-union representation on boards of directors. The majority of the Commission felt however 'unable to recommend the appointment of "workers' directors" to the boards of companies'. It felt that workers' directors might be exposed to unavoidable conflicts between their duties as directors and as representatives of the workers. They also found it difficult to give 'an equitable definition of the extent to which a workers' director should bear personal responsibility jointly with the other members of the board for their decisions or for any misfeasances on their part.' Finally, they felt that the appointment of a small number of workers' directors, while diverting attention from the urgent task of 'reconstructing company and factory collective bargaining', would not be likely to give workers a significant share in the management of the companies.

42. HMSO Cmd 3623 (1968) ch. 15. For recent discussion of the issue of 'workers' control', see Coates (1968) and Coates and Topham (1970).

Five members of the Commission, however, expressed themselves in favour of the principle of the appointment of workers' directors, and two of these regarded the voluntary principle as insufficient. They recommended that directors be appointed to 'act as guardians of the workers at the stage when companies' policies were being formulated'. Power of appointment should rest with the trade unions concerned. These proposals come close to the position that prevails in West Germany with regard to the coal and steel industry.

In May 1967, the British Steel Corporation invited the Trade-Union Council to participate in top management in the shaping of the policies of Britain's largest nationalized industry. In response, three employees – chosen after consultation with the TUC from within the steel industry – were appointed for a three-year period to each of the four-group-boards of the Corporation. The appointees – who serve on a part-time basis and must not hold any union office during their service, are chosen from all levels of employment. In 1970, the employee directors were allocated to the new Product Division Boards, and their number increased from twelve to fourteen.

Public Regulation of Economic Activities

In economic systems which, in general, reject public enterprise and other forms of economic management by the government on ideological grounds and accept them, at most, in restricted fields such as soil conservation or electric power development or in situations of great emergency, the major check on the excessive power in the hands of private business lies in the use of the supervisory public authority as a regulatory, not as a managing, body. In various vital fields of economic life, federal public authorities in the United States such as the Interstate Commerce Commission, the Federal Trade Commission or the Securities and Exchange Commission, exercise such functions. Thus, the Federal Trade Commission uses such legal means as 'cease and desist orders' to curb all manner of 'unfair competition' which includes the entire field of anti-trust legislation. The role of anti-trust law, in the maintenance of a competitive, private enterprise economy has been analysed in the preceding chapter.

Short of the dogmatic remedy of transferring the entire machinery and means of production of the nation into the hands of the state –

a remedy that, even if politically acceptable, would at best substitute for the power of a small number of giant private corporations the power of an elite bureaucracy – it seems clear that in modern industrial democratic society no single remedy can cope with the problem of private corporate power. There are, on the other hand, as we have seen, a number of various remedies which, singly or in combinations, have modified or can modify the extent as well as the possible abuses of such power. Public enterprise can always be used – and it has been used – to care for vital national developments which are not adequately covered by, or cannot safely be entrusted to, private enterprise. It can also be used to stimulate private enterprise into greater activity, as in the case of rural electrification in the United States. Anti-trust legislation, coupled with some administrative supervision, can remedy the more serious abuses of excessive concentration of economic power, though it can only slow down rather than arrest the continuing process of concentration of industrial production in a relatively small number of big corporations. Social-security legislation and the countervailing process of collective bargaining as well as, more vaguely, the pressure of public opinion on the 'corporate conscience' help to protect those who would otherwise be – and who formerly were – at the mercy of vastly greater economic power than they themselves possessed.

Group Power and the Individual

The impact of group power on the freedom of the individual has dramatically changed, in substance and emphasis, during the present century. Before the turn of the century, the United States and Canada had begun to take the first legislative measures to cope with the rapidly proceeding concentration of monopolistic power, with its double threat to the smaller manufacturer and businessman, who faced extinction or subjection to conditions vitally impairing his freedom of movement, and to the consumer who was inadequately protected against exploitation. The result was a combination of legislative, administrative and judicial measures outlawing some of the most injurious practices in this field, such as price-fixing, tie-in sales, boycotts of newcomers and other restrictions limiting freedom of entry into business.

At the same time, labour unions were still at the beginning of their struggle to restore a modicum of equality of economic power between employers and employees, capital and labour. Today, in most of the industrial democracies of the western world, the problem of recognition of the trade unions as the acknowledged spokesmen of organized labour is no longer so serious (except for women and white-collar workers), although their status and the degree of their actual power varies.[43] In proportion to the status gained by organized labour another problem has arisen: the protection of the individual member of the union against arbitrary penalties, including expulsion, by uncontrollable decisions of the union. This leads us back to the problem raised by Maitland's analysis of the unincorporated association (see p. 313). Is it socially bearable, and jurisprudentially tenable to exempt from legal review associations which control the working life of their members, simply on the ground that the majority of these associations are in form 'clubs', mostly unincorporated and, in regard to their disciplinary powers, classed as 'domestic tribunals' in whose affairs the courts of the State traditionally are reluctant to intervene?[44]

Legal Controls of Labour Unions

As trade unions have progressed from a legally and economically underprivileged status of 'underdogs' to powerful organizations facing employers on an industry-wide or an enterprise basis, as equals, and often exercising a virtual monopoly over the supply and terms of labour in their field, the question of their legal status has increasingly engaged the attention of both legislators and courts in the common-law world.

In the first place, it is possible to judge the activities of labour unions from the standpoint of monopolistic, exclusionary or otherwise restrictive practices, applying, in other words, the standards of anti-monopoly and anti-trust legislation to the practices of collective

43. Recognition is still a serious problem in a 'company town' and in agriculture. In the United States, it took a determined struggle of many years, and a largely successful boycott of 'non-union' table grapes, for grapeworkers to gain recognition and a collective contract from the growers in 1970.

44. This problem was adumbrated in Friedmann (1951, p. 142), and the beginnings of a new trend were noted at p. 46.

labour organizations. Despite some pressures in that direction, the direct application of anti-trust or anti-monopoly legislation to labour has hitherto been excluded not only in the more moderate British and similar types of legislation, but in the far more radical and comprehensive American anti-trust law structure.[45] The major reason for this attitude is an obvious one of principle: labour, despite its important share in the prices of products and the conditions of trade, is not a 'commodity'. The regulation of labour conditions is still predominantly and rightly regarded as a problem of human and social relationships. Within the framework of labour law, recent legislative trends indicate, however, a tendency to restrict or exclude the abuse of monopolistic positions by labour unions in the process of collective bargaining. The basic principle, long established in British and American practice without statutory regulation, and specifically recognized in the United States Wagner Act of 1936, that a labour union representing the majority of the employees in the trade bargains for the unit concerned, remains unimpaired.[46] United States and Canadian legislation has established special public Labour Relations Boards, whose functions include, among others, the certification of a specific union as representing in fact a majority of the employees, and the decision of disputes between rival unions on this question. The United States Labour–Management Relations Act of 1947 (commonly known as the Taft-Hartley Act) has, however, imposed certain further restrictions on union practices, prohibiting 'closed-shop' agreements, and permitting a majority of the employees to vote to rescind the authority of a labour organization to conclude a 'union-shop' agreement.[47]

45. See, for comparative data, Friedmann (1956), p. 329 (Sweden); p. 368 (UK); p. 444 (USA). Anti-trust does, however, apply where labour colludes with employers in exclusionary practices (see Timberg, in Friedmann, 1956, p. 444; ch. 8).

46. The British Nationalization Statutes recognize this position by conferring upon the Boards or Commissions power and the duty 'to seek consultation with any organization appearing to the Commission to be appropriate, with a view to the conclusion between the Commission and that organization of such agreements as appear to the parties to be desirable, . . . for the settlement by negotiation of terms and conditions of employment'. (e.g. Transport Act 1962 (c. 46), § 72.)

47. The distinction between 'closed shop' – which is now prohibited – and 'union shop' – which is normal in most industries requiring skilled labour – is a

Breaking with tradition, and differing from the recommendations of the Donovan Commission,[48] the British Industrial Relations Act 1971, prohibits the closed shop on principle, subject to exceptions known as agency-shop agreements (sections 11–16) and 'approved closed-shop agreements' (sections 17–18). The former permits agreements between employers and registered unions by which a worker can be employed only if he joins the union or makes 'appropriate contributions' to the union, or, if he is a conscientious objector, to an agreed charity. The latter is similar, except that only conscientious objectors are excepted from union membership. While both types of agreements are under close supervision of the Industrial Relations Commission and the new Industrial Court, the 'approved closed-shop agreement' can become effective only if approved by the Court. The employer may have to agree to an agency shop if, on application to the court, and subject to a report by the Commission, a qualified majority of the workers concerned has decided in favour of the agency shop by a ballot. The Act is a complex compromise between the Conservative Government's basic philosophy that every worker shall be free to choose whether to be a member of a union or not (section 5), and the admission that collective bargaining between employers and unions is a basic fact of contemporary industrial democratic society. Generally the new British legislation, which also establishes a legal procedure for the determination of 'bargaining units' and 'sole bargaining agents' (see p. 351) greatly strengthens the official administrative and legal role in labour relations and brings British law much closer to American law.

---

fine one and hardly intelligible to Europeans. A 'closed shop' requires the employer to hire his employees exclusively from the bargaining union (which, in some cases, as in the printing and building trades, combines in effect the functions exercised by trade unions and Handicraft Chambers on the Continent, somewhat like a modern version of the medieval guilds; for it is a bargaining agent as well as the exclusive trainer and judge of the skill required in the particular trade). A 'union-shop' agreement permits the employer to recruit employees anywhere, provided they join the bargaining union within thirty days.

48. Cmnd 3623, para. 602. For a commentary by a member of the Commission, see Kahn-Freund, 'Trade unions, the law and society', 33 *Mod. L. Rev.* (1970), 241, 253–5.

In such strongly unionized countries as Belgium, France, the Netherlands, Norway, Sweden and West Germany, constitutional and other legislative provisions combine with judicial interpretation and the overwhelming opinion of legal writers in the rejection of any legal compulsion to join a particular – or indeed any union – by collective agreement or otherwise. In most of these countries collective agreements may, by administrative order, be extended beyond the parties to an entire industry and thus become official law. In North America the overwhelming emphasis on tough bargaining between strong employers' and labour organizations, and the still powerful distrust by both of state regulation, affords a psychological explanation of this contrast between the American and the Continental approach. In West Germany, the rejection of compulsory unionism is probably part of a constitutional and emotional reaction against the totalitarianism of the Nazi period.[49] There are, however, strong provisions against discrimination by employers based on union membership. The European approach is endorsed in a Report by a Committee of Experts to the 31st Session of the International Labour Organization.

A second major problem is the constitutional or statutory protection of the 'right to work' of the individual against any attempts of a group, in particular of a trade union, to make exclusion of unorganized workers a term of a collective agreement. In Britain the Industrial Relations Act of 1971 gives all employees a right of choice whether or not to belong to a union. But this is subject to the considerable restrictions noted on page 349. The problem has become acute in the United States, where both the Federal and the fifty state constitutions have many explicit provisions on fundamental human rights. Until the advent of the Wagner Act of the 'New Deal' period and other federal and state legislation, giving recognition to the labour unions, and creating statutory obligations for the employer to bargain collectively with representative unions, a constitutional protection of the individual 'right to work' would, in most cases, have been an empty gesture. The vast majority of workers were still struggling for a minimum of economic and social protection through the strengthen-

49. For a comprehensive survey and appraisal of this problem in European labour law, see Lenhoff, 'The problems of compulsory unionism in Europe', 5 *Amer. J. Comp. L.* 18 (1956).

ing of the labour unions, even though in some trades (e.g. printing), unions and collective bargaining had long enjoyed a respected position. But the dramatic advance of the social and legal power of the unions is producing a political reaction against their growing power, particularly in the more conservative states of the South. A series of constitutional and statutory provisions have been enacted purporting to protect the diffident individual against compulsory unionism and collective agreements directly or indirectly making union membership a condition of employment. A representative provision is that of the Nebraska Constitution:

No person shall be denied employment because of membership in or affiliation with, or resignation or expulsion from a labour organization or because of refusal to join or affiliate with a labour organization; nor shall any individual or corporation or association of any kind enter into any contract, written or oral, to exclude persons from employment because of membership in or non-membership in a labour organization (art. 15, para. 13).[50]

Here one of the acute conflicts of public policy and competing social interests, inevitable in a complex democratic society, arises. Since 1936, the United States Congress has made collective bargaining by appropriate employers and labour organizations the cornerstone of its legislative policy. While the Taft-Hartley Act of 1947 has somewhat restricted the coercive powers of the predominant unions, and, correspondingly, strengthened dissenting groups, it has not basically impaired the principle, by which the labour unions – within the procedures laid down in the National Labour Relations Act – are empowered to bargain on behalf of the employees in the unit which they represent, and bargaining with such unions is a statutory duty incumbent on the employers.[51] The philosophy underlying this legislation is that labour unions have been by far the most

50. For a comprehensive survey of state legislation designed to curb 'unfair labor practices' by unions, see generally the *Labor Law Expediter* and the *Labor Relations Reporter*, vol. 4 (State Labor Laws). Twenty states have some form of a right to work law. *Labor Law Expediter*, Union Security and Checkoff, § 28. In November 1958, six states held referenda on constitutional amendments introducing 'right to work' provisions. In all (including the important industrial States of California and Ohio) but one of these (Kansas), the amendment was rejected.

51. The British Industrial Relations Act 1971 – again in departure from

powerful single instrument in the improvement of the social status and the economic lot of the worker, that the organization of modern industrial society recognizes the power, and requires the legal recognition, of groups capable of speaking authoritatively on behalf of employers and employees respectively, whether on a local or nationwide basis, and that the interests of the occasional dissenter – who participates in any case, willingly or otherwise, in the benefits conferred on workers in collective agreements – must be subordinated to this principle of collective bargaining. The Supreme Court of the United States in 1956[52] considered the above-quoted provision of the Nebraska Constitution to be incompatible with the (Federal) Railway Labour Act, which permits 'union-shop' agreements between a carrier and a labour organization, requiring payment of union dues. The court reversed the decision of the Nebraska Supreme Court, which had dismissed the suit brought by organized employees to prohibit the application and enforcement of a 'union-shop' agreement.

The importance of this decision can be assessed only against the social background. It took many decades of bitter struggle to attain the status which labour unions have reached today. Despite some abuses, they have conferred incalculable social and economic benefits on many millions of American workers previously disorganized and underprivileged. Any substantial loophole might reopen the door to company unions or 'yellow-dog' contracts and gradually weaken the position of labour, especially in many states of the South where labour organization is more recent and relatively weaker than in the North-East.[53]

Yet, the problem of threats to individual freedom by union arbitrariness remains.[54] It has led, in the last decade, to some important attempts to impose legal checks on the activities of 'private'

---

tradition – introduces a comparable procedure by defining 'bargaining unit' and 'sole bargaining agent' and putting the settlement of disputes in the hands of, in part the Industrial Relations Commission and in part, the Industrial Court.

52. *Railway Employees Department, A.F. of L.* v. *Hanson*, 351 U.S. 225 (1956).

53. For the different traditions and approaches of Eurpean labour laws, see p. 349.

54. It was foreseen by Brandeis, a strong champion of Labour, in a letter written in 1912 to Lincoln Steffens (quoted from Mason, 1946, p. 303).

associations, in particular of labour unions, *vis-à-vis* their members. It must suffice to mention briefly the most important issues.

We have discussed earlier the anomaly of the characterization as 'private', of associations which exercise an increasingly exclusive – and, to a large extent, legally recognized – control over the livelihood of millions of people. A theory developed for clubs, membership in which confers at most social privileges, has come to be applied to associations, membership in which is a condition for earning one's livelihood. The theory has a twofold root: one ideological, one technical. The ideological motive is respect for freedom of association, and a long standing disinclination of the courts to interfere in domestic quarrels. The technical obstacles to legal control of 'private' associations stem from the fetters put on the courts, especially in the United States, by the 'property' basis of equitable remedies, and the 'contractual' character of membership in an unincorporated association.

British courts have, until recently, adhered to the view that the activities of what are often called 'domestic tribunals' are, with rare exceptions, beyond the control of the courts. A certain amount of supervision is exercised over those bodies which, by law, have statutory jurisdiction over a profession. By controlling the admission, conduct and expulsion of doctors, lawyers, pharmacists, nurses and others, the relevant bodies enjoy a judicial power directly delegated to them by act of state. Consequently, in such cases a prerogative writ will lie to a tribunal, and such writ will occasionally be granted.[55] But a graver and more intractable problem is presented by those bodies which, like non-established churches, employers' organizations, trade associations or labour unions, exercise a *de facto* compulsory control over vast sections of the population while still enjoying the legal privileges of private organizations. Such associations enjoy autonomy in their internal dealings, including the admission and expulsion of members and other disciplinary measures. This is limited however by the so-called principles of 'natural justice', that a fair hearing must be granted and that nobody must be judged in his own cause. Yet, even these modest principles were

55. See *General Medical Council* v. *Spackman* [1943] A.C. 627, where the House of Lords reversed the removal of a doctor from the medical register by the Council on the ground of lack of 'due inquiry'.

seldom applied to private associations. In *MacLean* v. *Worker's Union*,[56] Maugham J. refused to scrutinize the resolution of a union which had expelled the plaintiff. Although the learned judge mentioned the rules of natural justice, he specifically stated that even an unfair or an unjust decision made by a domestic tribunal of this type could not be reviewed, provided it was given 'honestly and in good faith'.

In recent years, British, Canadian and American courts have, however, become increasingly concerned with the facts of union organization.[57] Any labour union of significance has a code of offences and penalties, including the gravest penalty of all, expulsion from the union. Offences cover all kinds of activities deemed injurious to the union, among them opposition to union policies, agitation for rival unions, membership of certain political organizations, arrears in dues and, in some cases, personal moral conduct.

In *Faramus* v. *Film Artistes Association*,[58] the House of Lords reluctantly confirmed the plaintiff's expulsion after many years of active participation, from a closed-shop union, because he had concealed in his application some insignificant offences committed many years ago, and in no way relevant to his union activities. The rules of the Association barred from membership 'any person who has been convicted in a court of law of a criminal offence other than a motoring offence not punishable by imprisonment'. It was held that the plaintiff had never legally become a member. As Professor Kahn-Freund has observed,[59] 'we are all familiar with the story of the active or militant trade unionist whom his employers dismiss for smoking in a forbidden place, which innumerable others had done with impunity'. The same kind of discrimination can be used by

56. [1929] 1 Ch. 602. It should be emphasized again that the widespread lack of impartial procedures and adequate safeguards for disciplined members is not confined to labour unions, but probably general among all kinds of clubs. But, as stated earlier, the public significance of union rules and their impact on the livelihood of their members is vastly greater than that of the normal club.

57. Professor Summers has given a most informative survey of constitutional provisions regarding disciplinary powers in his two articles on 'Disciplinary powers of union', 3 *Ind. Lab. Relations Rev.* 483 (1950); 4 *Ind. Lab. Relations Rev.* 15 (1950).

58. [1964] A.C. 925.

59. 'Trade unions, the law and society', 33 *Mod. L. Rev.* 248 (1970).

union officials against members, and courts would be as powerless to prohibit such concealed kinds of discrimination as they were in *Faramus*. It is not so much the nature of the offences that challenges criticism as it is the procedures by which these offences are determined.[60] The executive officers of the union normally decide whether an offence has been committed, and it is usually the same officers who sit as a disciplinary 'tribunal' on complaints from the members. There is very little, if any, distinction between prosecutor and judge.

In recent years the English Court of Appeal and the House of Lords have attempted, with more than customary boldness, to dispose of the limitations imposed by the law of contract, and the 'private' status of trade unions.

The House of Lords granted damages for breach of contract to a wrongfully expelled member of a union. In *Bonsor* v. *Musicians' Union*[61] the plaintiff, a musician, had for many years been a member of the defendant union. In 1949, when the plaintiff was fifty-two weekly payments of his weekly contributions in arrears, a branch secretary of the union purported to exclude him from membership by virtue of union rules. A few months later the plaintiff asked to be reinstated so as to enable him to obtain employment as a musician. This the branch secretary refused, except on payment of a fine and all arrears. He rejected the plaintiff's offer to pay the sum out of his first week's wages. The plaintiff was therefore unable to obtain employment as a musician. He claimed a declaration that he was wrongfully expelled; that he was entitled to be reinstated as a member, as well as an injunction restraining the union and its officers from treating him as an expelled member, and finally damages or other relief.

In a unanimous decision the House of Lords upheld the dissenting judgement of Denning L.J., in the Court of Appeal, which would

60. It should be stressed that, by virtue of the Taft-Hartley Act 61 Stat. 136 (1947), the economic penalty of expulsion from the union is less severe in the United States than in countries which, like Great Britain, have little legislative regulation in this field. Under s. 8 (*a*) (3), *only* expulsion for refusal to pay dues can result in the loss of a job. Violation of this limitation may entail reinstatement, back-pay, and, generally, *restitutio in integrum*. For indications that English courts will control the substantive content of union rule-books in the name of public policy, see *Edwards* v. *SOGAT* [1970] 3 All E.R. 689 (C.A).
61. [1954] Ch. 479 (C.A.); [1955] 3 W.L.R. 788 (H.L.).

have granted damages. It is difficult to find the common line of reasoning in the judgements of the House.[62] Some judgements sought support mainly in the older decision of the *Taff Vale* case,[63] which had treated an unincorporated but registered union as a *de facto* legal person, capable of being sued in tort. Others preferred to consider an unincorporated trade union as a hybrid, which had certain aspects of a legal person, though not all of them. An unincorporated, but registered, union was capable of being sued in its registered name, despite shifting membership. The House of Lords also disposed of the agency problem. While the membership nexus could, in a sense, be regarded as a contract with the trade union, the latter, in expelling the plaintiff, represented all the members except the plaintiff who, for this purpose, faced the union as an entity. The many nuances of the different judgements are all dominated by the desire of the House of Lords to overcome the technical obstacles created by lack of legal personality.[64]

The Industrial Relations Act of 1971 seeks to regulate some aspects of the relationship between unions and their members and provides for voluntary registration of trade unions, which has the effect of turning them into corporate bodies. Although such registration is voluntary, the advantages conferred by it are considerable. Only registered unions may claim the benefit of the provisions in the Act that limit the monetary damages assessable against trade unions which commit unfair labour practices, and certain tax exemptions, and only registered unions can conclude 'agency-shop' agreements, i.e. agreements whereby a registered trade union represents all the employees in a particular undertaking or establishment or part of it, and is supported by all of them.

62. They have been analysed by D. Lloyd, 'Damages for wrongful expulsion from a trade union', 19 *Mod. L. Rev.* 121 et seq. (1956), and by K. W. Wedderburn, 'The Bonsor affair, a postscript', 20 *Mod. L. Rev.* 105 (1957).

63. *Taff Valley Rly* v. *Amalgamated Society of Railway Servants* [1901] A.C. 426.

64. In Great Britain and the Commonwealth there would probably be strong opposition to any compulsory incorporation of unions, or, indeed, any association. A considerable number of American states have enacted statutes under which the unions are treated as legal entities for certain purposes. See Bureau of National Affairs, *Labor Law Expediter*, Damage Suits, § 4 (LRX 138–9, 1967). For an up-to-date list and text of such laws see *Labor Relations Reporter*, vol. 4 (State Labor Laws).

Another, indirect, attack on certain trade-union activities was made by the House of Lords in 1964, in *Rookes* v. *Barnard*.[65] In this decision, the House of Lords, by some novel interpretations, undermined the legal protections then provided by the Trade Disputes Act 1906 for trade unions (which are normally unincorporated) and trade-union officials against tort actions arising out of their union activities.[66] The key provisions of the Trade Disputes Act which were neutralized by *Rookes*, were section 1, by which an act done in pursuance of an agreement or combination shall 'not be actionable unless the act if done without any such agreement or combination, would be actionable' and section 3, by which an act 'shall not be actionable on the ground only that it induces some other person to break a contract of employment or that it is an interference with the trade, business or employment of some other person.' These provisions are now replaced by the provision on unfair industrial practice in the 1971 Act.

In the case before the House of Lords, the plaintiff had been dismissed from employment with the BOAC, without breach of contract, following a threat by the defendants – acting on behalf of the union – of a strike in breach of a 'no strike' agreement. The House by-passed section 1 by reviving an all but forgotten tort of 'intimidation' as distinct from 'conspiracy', and by holding that the former was not covered by section 1. The decision also neutralized section 3, by holding that the defendants, two fellow employees of the plaintiff and a union organizer who was not an employee of BOAC, could, despite section 3, be held liable for having acted jointly in inducing BOAC employees to break their contract by strike, or in the construction of Lord Devlin, by having been parties to 'a conspiracy to intimidate'.

Rookes v. *Barnard* clearly expresses a reaction to the greatly strengthened status of trade unions, and to the injury they sometimes inflict on the public (i.e. in the cases of transport or dock strikes). *Rookes* was reversed by the Trade Disputes Act 1965, which provided that the protection of the Act of 1906 against actions in tort is not to be lost simply because a person threatens the breach of a contract for employment or threatens that he will procure another person to

65. [1964] A.C. 1129.
66. For a detailed survey of the Trade Disputes Act and its legal history and implications, see the Donovan Report (note 42, §§ 769–951).

break such a contract; and the 1965 Act was in turn – together with the 1906 Act – repealed in 1971.

But neither *Rookes* v. *Barnard*, nor the 1965 Act dealt with another crucial problem of industrial relations in Britain, i.e. the inducement of breaches of contracts other than contracts of employment. In recent years, many situations that have involved the judicial definition of the meaning of a 'trade dispute' – a key term employed in sections 3 and 5 of the Trade Disputes Act 1906 and now repealed by the term 'industrial dispute'[67] – have arisen out of inter-union disputes. They have given rise to two important recent decisions, both giving a restrictive interpretation to the meaning of 'furtherance of a trade dispute', and therefore indirectly restricting the scope of immunities accorded to trade unions and their organizers by the Act of 1906. In *Stratford* v. *Lindley*[68] the House of Lords held that an embargo declared by the Waterman's Union in the handling of barges controlled by a company, one of whose affiliates had concluded an agreement with a rival union, was not in 'furtherance or contemplation of a trade dispute'.[69]

Torquay Hotel Company v. *Cousins*[70] arose out of the attempt of the powerful Transport and General Workers' Union. to prevent the organizing of hotel workers in Torquay by a rival union, the National Union of General and Municipal Workers. The original dispute was between the Transport Union and the Torquay Hotel, which employed workers of the Transport Union but refused to recognize it as having authority to negotiate on their behalf. Consequently, the defendant Union organized the stoppage of fuel oil supplies to the Torquay Hotel. But the subject of the action was an ensuing dispute with the Imperial Hotel, which did not employ members of the Union, but whose manager had said that the hoteliers would have to take concerted action to prevent the kind of action that the Transport Union had taken against the Torquay Hotel. In reaction to these remarks the defendants, the Transport Union, organized a boycott of fuel supplies by Esso to the Imperial Hotel. The Imperial asked for

67. Defined in section 167 of the 1971 Act.

68. [1965] A.C. 269.

69. For a strong criticism of this decision see Wedderburn, '*Stratford* v. *Lindley*' 28 *Mod. L. Rev.* 205 (1965).

70. [1969] 2 W.L.R. 289.

an injunction against the defendant Union, and damages and injunctions against individual Union officials, which would enjoin them from 'blacking' the Imperial Hotel, and from inducing a third party, Esso, to break its fuel oil supply contract. The Court of Appeal dismissed the appeal against the injunction granted by the lower Court restraining the defendants from procuring a breach of contract and from picketing the Hotel, and held that as between the defendant and the Imperial Hotel (as distinct from the Torquay), there was no 'trade dispute'.

The question of the scope of 'trade disputes' and, consequently, of the immunities granted by section 3 of the Trade Disputes Act of 1906 to union officials was a subject of much debate. For the time being this debate has ended with the enactment of sections 96 and 98 on 'unfair industrial practices' in the 1971 Act.[71] But the decisions just mentioned also underline the seriousness of the problem of inter-union disputes, which in recent years have been responsible for some of the most serious work stoppages, e.g. in the motor-car manufacturing and shipbuilding industries. The Donovan Commission referred to this problem as 'multi-unionism', of which it distinguished two types: first, the organization by different unions of the various occupational groups in a factory, e.g. technicians, supervisors, clerks, operatives and craft groups; and second, competition between two or more unions for membership within a given group of workers. The solution of this problem – which has also caused a number of unofficial strikes – is a matter of trade-union organization, and in particular of the relation between the nationwide Trade Unions Council, the individual unions that are

71. A valuable analysis of the tort liability of strikers, based on a comparison of English and Canadian statutory and judicial law up to 1966 is given by I. M. Christie (1967). Professor Christie observes that three Canadian provinces (Ontario, Saskatchewan and British Columbia) have adopted, in part, the principles of the English Trade Disputes Act 1906 (p. 190); Canadian law – unlike, until recently, English law – 'is committed to a policy of regulatory contract and intervention', but 'the activism of the ordinary courts has resulted in a body of tort law that is not in harmony with the statutory framework of industrial relations' (p. 193). This applies particularly to judicial interpretations of acts 'unlawful in themselves' (which the Supreme Court, in *Gagnon* v. *Foundation Maritime Ltd.* [1961] S.C.R. 435 interpreted as including acts 'prohibited by provincial (or federal) labour relations legislation'; and to a wide interpretation of 'inducing breach of contract'.

its members, and the shop stewards and workers in the individual plants.[72] The question of the extent to which a 'pluralistic' organization of workers, in a multitude of unions of very unequal size and importance, is compatible with the requirements of modern industrial democracy and the status of organized labour is one to which we will briefly revert later in this chapter.

Legislative Protection of 'Union Democracy'

In Great Britain, the appointment of the Donovan Commission on Trade Unions and Employers Associations, in 1965, gave further opportunities to study the advisablity of legislative reforms designed to strengthen the protection of the individual union member against union arbitrariness. Generally, the Commission's report, issued in 1968, reaffirms the predominant – though no longer unchallenged – British tradition of regarding the place of organized labour and the management–labour relationship as a matter of social self-regulation rather than legal enforcement.[73] But the Commission made a number of recommendations designed to provide 'safeguards for individuals in relation to trade unions' (ch. 11). One aspect of this complex problem, discrimination on the ground of 'race, colour, religion, sex or national origin', is dealt with in the Race Relations Act of 1968, which is administered by the Race Relations Board. With respect to the delicate question of discrimination in admission to membership – a question that, with a growing influx of non-white labour, has become a considerable problem in Britain, as it has long been in the United States – the Donovan Commission recommended that in the future the rules of trade unions should state who is qualified for admission and should be so framed as to avoid discrimination. It also proposed that applicants should have a right to appeal from the executive committee to the registrar of trade unions, and eventually to an impartial review body, with power to make a declaration that the applicant should become a member, and to award limited monetary compensation for unjustified refusal to admit him. These

72. See now the provisions in sections 44 *et seq.* of the 1971 Act on joint 'negotiating panels' and on the determination of a 'sole bargaining agent'.

73. For the Commission's views on labour participation in management and on the legal enforceability of collective agreements, see pp. 344–5.

proposals were in substance accepted by the Government White Paper *In Place of Strife*,[74] and in a different form some of them were implemented in Part IV of the Industrial Relations Act 1971.

On the second problem – how to protect union members against arbitrary or discriminatory expulsion – we have already mentioned some of the recent judicial attempts to strengthen the legal protection of individuals, and depart from the former, almost total, abstention from interference in the activities of 'domestic tribunals'. The Donovan Commission proposed that, as with refusals to admit, there should be an appeal against expulsion and other disciplinary measures, first to the registrar, and from him to an independent review body which, in cases of 'substantial injustice' could order monetary compensation or, in certain cases, reinstatement. The complainant would, however, have first to exhaust internal union procedures, within certain time limits. This recommendation too was accepted by the Labour Government, and in substance by the 1971 Act enacted under the Conservative Government.

By contrast to the British tradition, the Labour Law of the United States has, since the basic acceptance of collective bargaining in the mid-1930s, been the subject of repeated and comprehensive legislative measures. This applies not only to the statutory and judicial determination of who is entitled to represent the employees in industrial negotiations – under the National Labour Relations Legislation – or to the prohibition of the closed shop by the Taft-Hartley Act of 1947, but it now extends also to the basic rights of individual union members *vis-à-vis* their unions. For many years, the courts have afforded relief, broadly in cases of breach of contract or damage to property interests.[75] In 1959, the subject was comprehensively regulated by the Labour–Management Reporting and Disclosure Act, commonly referred to as the Landrum-Griffin Act.[76]

The act omits to deal with one crucial issue, the right to admission.

74. Cmnd 3888, paras. 114–16.

75. For details, see the basic article of Summers, 'Legal limitations on union discipline', 64 *Harvard L. Rev.* 1049 (1951).

76. For a survey by a leading American authority, see Summers, 'American legislation for union democracy', 25 *Mod L. Rev.* 273 (1962). For a comprehensive review of the various provisions of the act, and their judicial interpretation, after ten years of experience, see Etelson and Smith, 'Union discipline under the Landrum-Griffin Act', 82 *Harvard L. Rev.* 727 (1969).

It is common knowledge that discrimination, particularly against blacks, still prevails in many American unions. But to some extent, the 'Equal Employment Opportunity Commission', established by the Civil Rights Act of 1964, seeks to cope, on an administrative basis, with this kind of discrimination in admission policy. The subject is under constant and heated discussion in the United States, and the US Government has, in a number of cases, made non-discrimination a condition of its own, very considerable patronage powers in the awarding of contracts.

The Landrum-Griffin Act deals with four broad areas: equal rights for all union members; freedoms of speech and assembly; the right to resort to judicial, administrative or legislative process outside the union; and the right to a fair trial in union disciplinary proceedings. The first of these items not only deals with the problem of second-class membership (e.g. membership without voice or vote), but also protects every member in the exercise of his right to participate in union government. The second item protects the right of members to freely criticize union officers and union policy, without incurring sanctions such as expulsion. The third item protects the rights of members to institute actions in any court or administrative agency, to appear as witnesses in official proceedings, or to petition or communicate with any legislative organ. The fourth item lays down certain minimum requirements with regard to disciplinary proceedings (specific charges, a reasonable time to prepare defences, a full and fair hearing).

In the ten years since its enactment, there have been, as reported in a recent comprehensive survey,[77] almost one hundred reported cases, which have given judicial interpretations to such key phrases as 'otherwise disciplined', 'reasonable time', 'full and fair hearing' and 'such relief . . . as may be appropriate'. Courts have in particular been concerned with the definition of the difficult borderlines between legitimate policy actions taken by union management and disciplinary measures against union members that violate his basic rights. It would be impossible – nor is it within the province of this book – to discuss these cases in any detail. The basic question is whether this attempt at broad legislative regulation has been successful. The

77. Etelson and Smith, p. 729.

authors of the most recent analysis[78] are of the opinion that 'the past ten years have seen a satisfactory resolution of most issues', and that 'the courts are steadily moving towards a new and more desirable accommodation between the private institutional needs of labour unions and their public responsibility under our federal labour policy'. Another recent commentator[79] is somewhat more sceptical. He believes that the basic objectives of Congress, in the Acts of 1947 and 1959, to 'create limits on the exercise of union authority without vitiating a labour organization's essential strength', suffer from built-in tensions. 'Each effort to establish a limit can be, and frequently is, challenged as a device to attenuate the vital strength of the union or as an attack upon the very philosophy of collective action. Yet, each effort to preserve some portion of union activity and authority from regulation can be, and frequently is, decried as inadequate regulation.' In Christensen's view, the administrators and courts, entrusted with the interpretation of legislation 'have veered somewhat erratically in accomplishing their task'.

As was observed in the discussion of different legal approaches to collective agreements (see pp. 347–52), the manner and degree of state interference with industrial relations through legal controls is not simply a function of the political antithesis between democracy and totalitarianism. This is further underlined by the different approaches of various contemporary industrial democracies to the problems of admission to, and expulsion from, union membership. Here, as in the legal regulation of collective bargaining, a solidly democratic society as that of Australia differs from both the American and the British approaches. Since, in Australia, the role of the law in the determination and enforcement of the terms of industrial agreements goes much further than in either the United States or Britain, the law must play a correspondingly stronger part in the regulation of trade-union membership. In cases of disputes, of an inter-state character – which is true of almost any important industrial agreement – an award of the Commonwealth Industrial Court ultimately determines the foundations of industrial agreements and thus turns them into official law. This implies strict regulation of the conditions of membership in trade

78. Etelson and Smith, ibid. p. 771.
79. Christensen, 'Union discipline under federal law: institutional dilemmas in an industrial democracy', 43 *New York University L. Rev.* 226, 278 (1968).

unions, since in order to participate in industrial agreements and compulsory arbitration proceedings, the union must be registered as an 'organization'.[80] Under the act, a person employed in connection with an industry must be admitted as a member of an 'organization' and cannot be expelled from it, as long as he complies with its rules. Admission can be refused only where the union proves that the applicant is 'of general bad character' or a member of certain unlawful organizations. The ultimate decision lies with the Commonwealth Industrial Court which can either, on the application of the organization, terminate the membership or, on the application of a member, issue a declaration that the applicant is entitled to membership. The court may also make an order by virtue of which the person concerned becomes or remains a union member.[81]

As Professor Kahn-Freund has pointed out in a penetrating comparison of the rationale of the different legal systems,[82] the Australian approach to the legal regulation of industrial agreements is so different from the American and British approaches that it cannot serve as a model at the present stage. It is equally clear, however, that if and when either of these systems should find itself compelled to take a more direct part in the regulation of the substantive terms of industrial agreements, it would have to strengthen and correspondingly the legal controls over the conditions of union membership.[83]

Trade Unions and the Law – A Reappraisal

The profound transformation in the power and in the economic as well as social status of trade unions, during the last fifty years, cannot but affect their legal status and subject them increasingly to legal controls. Britain has, until recently, prided itself on the *social* rather than the *legal* character of its structure of labour relations. But, prompted by increasingly frequent breakdowns of this process, the frequency of inter-union disputes, the number of unofficial strikes and the breaking of 'no strike' agreements, pressure for legal reform

80. Commonwealth Conciliation and Arbitration Act 1904–1968, sections 63, 132, 172.

81. Commonwealth Conciliation and Arbitration Act, sections 144, 150.

82. 'Trade unions, the law and society', 33 *Mod. L. Rev.* 249 (1970).

83. See also, for comparative studies of methods of dealing with labour disputes Wedderburn and Davies (1969); Aaron (1971).

became increasingly powerful and resulted in the enactment of the 1971 statute. The Donovan Report proposed the registration of the collective agreements of companies of a certain minimum size. One of its principal recommendations, the creation of a Commission on Industrial Relations (CIR), was implemented in 1969 and confirmed in the Industrial Relations Act 1971.

The CIR investigates and reports on industrial relations questions referred to it by the Secretary of State for Employment or in some important cases by the newly created National Industrial Relations Court. These questions include: the organization of employers and members for purposes of collective bargaining; existing procedures re agreements and the need for creating new procedures; the recognition of trade unions; the disclosure of information by employers to their employees and to union officials; facilities for training in industrial relations and in collective bargaining.

The CIR will also give general advice on the reform of industrial relations. It issued its first general report in July 1970. Between May 1969 and May 1970, twenty-five cases had been referred to it, nine of which concerned recognition, and twelve company bargaining procedures. The Commission also recommended legislation to establish statutory machinery to safeguard employees against unfair dismissal and the establishment of 'labour tribunals' with jurisdiction over disputes arising between employers and employees from contracts of employment or from statutory claims they may have against each other as employers and employees. This was to some extent implemented by the Act of 1971. But, in the most controversial part of its report, the Commission refused to recommend that collective agreements should become legally enforceable contracts. It regarded such a change as contrary to the intentions of the parties concerned, and as likely to worsen rather than improve industrial relations.[84]

It is in the approach to collective agreements that the Industrial Relations Act differs importantly from the view of the Donovan Commission – although it agrees substantially with the dissenting view of one member of the Commission, Mr Andrew Shonfield. While the Act stops short of making all collective agreements legally enforceable – as they are in the United States – it establishes

84. Donovan Commission, paras. 458–518.

a presumption that any collective written agreement entered into after a certain date should be held to be a legally binding and enforceable contract unless there is an express written provision to the contrary in the agreement itself. Accordingly, the provision in section 4 of the Trade Union Act of 1871, which precludes the courts from enforcing directly an agreement between the trade-union and an employer's association is repealed. Any action alleging a breach of a legally binding collective agreement is to be heard by the newly established National Industrial Relations Court. This, of course, creates an official enforcement machinery for legally binding collective agreements. But it will still depend largely on prevailing industrial practices, and understandings between employers and trade unions whether collective agreements are to be made legally binding or not. It is with a view to such situations that the Act introduces a complex procedure for the revision of industrial practices, the gist of which is that the already established Industrial Relations Commission may examine existing procedures, which can include the legal enforceability of collective agreements. The ultimate decision rests with the National Industrial Relations Court.

While still respecting the deeply ingrained British tradition of non-enforceability of collective agreements, the new legislation thus goes a considerable distance towards legal enforceability, i.e. in the direction of the law as it prevails in the United States.

Public Authority, Private Power and the Individual – Some Conclusions

The correctness of Shonfield's observations on the blurring of the traditional distinctions between public authority and private power cannot be seriously disputed. This has been a persistent theme throughout this book and, particularly the present chapter. The extension of public power and controls, and the increasingly 'public' role of nominally private organizations that control essential aspects of social life, is an inevitable consequence of the eclipse of *laissez-faire* in the contemporary industrialized and urbanized society. If, even less than a century ago, it was still possible to limit the functions of government to defence, foreign affairs, various police functions, including the formal administration of justice and later elementary education, this is today a distant myth. Yet it is of the very essence of a democratic, as distinct from a totalitarian, society that there should remain a large sphere of group and individual autonomy. It is characteristic of totalitarian systems of all types that they stamp out this autonomy by making group organizations of all kinds – employers', professional and in particular, labour – organs of the state and of centralized power, with only limited delegation of functions. While it is true that in contemporary industrial democracies, corporations, labour unions, professional organizations and other interest groups exercise increasingly important public functions, they must still, in a democratic and capitalistic society, retain a large measure of freedom and autonomy in the organization, and the defence of the interests of their members. In order to exercise influence on the balance of forces in the state, the individual worker or farmer – and to a large extent also the individual doctor, lawyer or journalist – has been compelled to delegate his individual decision-making power to the group that represents him. Once such groups become mere agents of the state, as they do in Fascist and Communist systems, democracy is finished. It is therefore a question of balance, a balance that must be struck differently at different times, and in the light of changing conditions. In 1952, Kenneth Galbraith thought that 'countervailing power' between the different interest groups, with some arbitral role exercised by the state, provided a reasonable balance. In 1967, he came to the conclusion that the power of a small group of leading corporations, especially in the defence industry, had penetrated the public power structure to such an extent that they should be nationalized. Berle has raised the question whether the major corporations should not be subjected to the constitutional guarantees and obligations imposed upon the states (1967, pp. 39– 50). Nationalization is, as we have seen, only one of a number of possible answers to excessive private economic power. Yet, although there are hardly any two countries in the western world that have given identical answers to the problems of corporate power and industrial relations, there has been a universal trend towards a stronger role of the state, through legal controls. In the area of corporate power, the answers range from the nationalization of basic industries to the representation of organized labour in the management of corporations, and, more generally, the drastic strengthening of legal controls over restrictive practices and monopoly power. In the field of labour relations, the answers range from the Australian and New Zealand systems of compulsory arbitration to the Commission on Industrial Relations, recently established in Britain, and the gradually expanding roles of labour courts or industrial tribunals in the determination of labour disputes. In Britain, where the tradition of voluntary self-regulation of industrial disputes is still strong, the Trade Unions Council, in 1969, undertook to play a more active role in the settlement of unconstitutional and unofficial strikes, as an alternative to the imposition of legal sanctions for the breach of industrial agreements. Quite apart from the stronger disposition of the Conservative Government towards legal sanctions, the extension of legal regulation in labour disputes will to a large extent depend upon the success that the TUC may achieve in this endeavour. But certain conclusions emerge clearly from the growing interpenetration of public and private power. First, the rationale of strengthened judicial and statutory controls over labour-union procedures is that they enjoy a monopoly or quasi-monopoly in the supply of labour. This rationale clearly applies to other incorporated associations, which enjoy similar monopoly powers. These include professional associations, e.g. of doctors, lawyers or journalists, whose almost absolute autonomy in matters of registration and licensing may, in some cases, have to be subjected to stronger official controls. They certainly include such institutions as the English Jockey Club,[85] which has a monopoly of issuing trainers' licences, or the Film Artistes Association,[86] which also has a monopoly. These criteria should probably not be applied to purely social organizations, such as golf clubs, which do not directly affect a person's livelihood or freedom of movement but rather his social standing, pleasures or proclivities for 'conspicuous waste'.

Second, the distinctions which, particularly in American law, are

85. See, for preliminary observations, *Russell* v. *Duke of Norfolk* [1949] All E. R. 109 (C.A.) and, directly in point, *Nagle* v. *Fielden* [1966] 2 Q. B. 633 (C.A.). The Stewards of the Jockey Club, which has a complete and unfettered monopoly over horse-racing in Britain, had refused a licence as a trainer of horses to a woman. The Court of Appeal found that her statement of claim disclosed a valid cause of action, basing its decision on public policy (equality of women), the plaintiff's 'right to work', and the duty of the courts to check the capricious exercise of monopolistic power.

86. See *Faramus* v. *Film Artistes Association*, discussed at p. 354.

made between certain 'public' and 'private' services and occupations, with regard to the legitimacy of strikes, are becoming increasingly artificial. Thus, postal workers who, until a statutory reform of 1970, which will put them under an autonomous public organization, have been federal employees – who are forbidden to strike. Early in 1970, the postal employees of New York City and a number of other regions struck in defiance of these provisions, by authority of their local unions, and had much public sympathy, in view of their shockingly low pay. The matter was settled on the federal level by pay increases and a reorganization of the postal services, without legal sanctions. Under the Taylor Law of New York State, teachers and other public employees are forbidden to strike. But the teachers of New York did strike in 1968, and in response obtained a vastly more favourable three-year contract. It is true that the president of the Teachers Union was sent to jail for two weeks. But short sentences, in such circumstances, do not have the effect of normal criminal penalties but, on the contrary, serve to enhance the status of the person affected. The irony of the distinction is underlined by the fact that in the United States such vital public utilities as railroads or telephones are privately operated, therefore not subject to these prohibitions, whereas in most other countries, they are either governmental operations or run by semi-autonomous public enterprises. The solution of this dilemma – which has recently been adopted for the US postal services and may well be applied to the urgently needed reorganization of the railroad system – lies probably in the constitution of basic public services as public corporations (on the British model) which are, in their legal status, detached from the government proper. There is increasing recognition that the collective bargaining process must extend across the artificial distinctions between 'public' and 'non-public' operations and services.

Another area of discrepancy between legal form and social reality is the difference in legal status between the 'employee' or 'servant' and the independent contractor. The economic servitude of the latter often contrasts with his formal legal autonomy – a situation that used to characterize the worker in the early days of the Industrial Revolution, but has been largely remedied where unionism is strong. Many small contractors manufacture parts for the big manufacturers; licensed dealers obtain strictly conditioned 'fran-

chises' from automobile manufacturers. Some of these relationships
come within the purview of anti-trust law. In so far as tie-in clauses,
blacklists or other measures clearly impeding freedom of trade by
exclusionary conditions – either tying an individual to a particular
company or excluding entry for newcomers – unduly impair freedom
of trade, the law provides certain remedies.[87] But their scope is
strictly limited. Where manufacturers exercise a preponderant power,
like the 'Big Three' in the automobile industry or International
Business Machines in the field of automation machines, it is economic
rather than legal conditions that create stark inequality. Anti-trust
law cannot cope with the imposition of minimum capital requirements or the fulfilment of certain minimum quotas of sales as a
condition of the continuation of the franchise. To some extent, of
course, individual dealers can counter this state of affairs by acting
collectively as a group, in the way in which workers act through
unions. In certain fields such a rough restoration of equality has
occurred.[88] But it would appear, for example, from the Congressional investigations made in 1956, that nothing like equality of
bargaining exists between the major corporations and their dealers.[89]

Another, possibly more critical, aspect of the intrusion of public
law into private legal relationships arises from the fact that a considerable proportion of industry, and, in particular, of the large
corporations nowadays work to a very large extent under government contracts. These contracts overwhelmingly relate, directly or
indirectly, to defence requirements. Many of them involve secret
scientific and technological processes with a high security risk. In
so far as all these corporations enter into contracts with the Defence

87. For a survey, see Timberg, in Friedmann (1956, p. 425).

88. For example, in the relations between newspaper proprietors and newspaper vendors. See the English case of *Sorrell* v. *Smith* [1925] A.C. 700.

89. This lack of equality increases greatly, of course, in times of economic
depression, somewhat comparably to, but probably less so than in, the relations
between employers and labour. The large unions are usually now able to accumulate in times of prosperity large reserves which enable them to hold out in major
disputes until either the companies feel the strain as much as the unions or
national interests become so strongly involved that public authority intervenes
with a compromise settlement. But such retailers as automobile dealers or the
usual middle- or small-type business man have seldom reserves large enough
remotely to equal the vast capital reserves of large corporations, which can tide
them over periods of crisis.

Department – and few of the large manufacturers today do not – they come under the security regulations of the Department of Defence, which are incorporated in the terms of the contract.[90] To that extent the private corporations are in fact, though not in name, agents of the government. The security officers of the Defence Department or, in certain situations, the Congressional Committee, may investigate the personnel of any of these plants. The officers may demand the dismissal of certain employees as bad security risks. While these employees are in this respect 'public' employees, they do not enjoy any of the modest safeguards of public employees against arbitrary dismissal. As far as the individual employee is concerned, he might conceivably find protection in the terms of a collective labour agreement. But they do not normally touch these matters. A joint arbitration machinery in cases of security dismissals disputed by a member might afford some relief. Generally, the unions show little inclination to intervene in the protection of the individual who is, rightly or wrongly, suspected of Communist affiliations. While no official stigma attaches to the determination of a private relationship, it may affect the individual's employability as severely as the loss of union membership (which it may, incidentally, entail). As shown in official statutes, employers sometimes anticipate public inquiry by terminating an employment that may conceivably come under questioning. Although the effect of unemployability is graver than punishment for all but major criminal offences, dismissal is not, of course, in any sense classified as criminal law so that the protection of criminal procedure is absent. The 'right to work' may be destroyed without any legal process or remedy.

It is of the essence of a pluralistic and non-totalitarian society that it cannot give a single answer – that of total state control – to the problem of abuses and excesses of private group power. Instead, the survey attempted in this chapter has shown a variety of responses,

90. The Report of the Special Committee on the Federal Loyalty Security Programme, set up by the Association of the Bar of the City of New York (Dodd, Mead & Co., New York, 1956) reports the number of private employees covered by the Defense Department's Industrial Security Programme as nearly three million. This is based on official testimony. To these must be added over 800,000 long-shoremen and seamen, who, under the Port Security Programme – a survival of the Second World War security operations – have been subjected to security clearance (p. 115).

which are deeply influenced by specific political and social situations, and the differences of legal and social traditions. There can be no uniformity of response. Yet, it is equally clear that certain hard facts common to all contemporary industrial societies will more and more push back the variety of social and historical traditions. In the field of corporate power, such different analysts as Berle, Galbraith and Shonfield agree on the need for a stronger role of public law. In the field of labour relations, as staunch a defender of the social traditions of British labour relations as Otto Kahn-Freund has said that 'the role of the law is growing in the regulation of labour relations and of conditions of employment in Britain' (1968, p. 79).

Increasingly, the common problems of urban conglomerations, of industrial concentration, and of the pollution of the elements transcend national and historical differences, The responses of the law, in this as in other fields, will therefore tend to resemble each other more closely than in the past. As we shall see in the chapters dealing with the contemporary international scene, some of the most vital responses can only be found on an international scale.

Part Four
The Growing Role of Public Law

Chapter 10
The Growth of Administration and the Evolution of Public Law

The Growth of the Administrative Function

The growth of public administration has been a universal phenomenon of contemporary society, although both speed and manner of its development have varied greatly from country to country. A minimum of administration is, of course, inherent in the very notion of government. The most ardent advocates of *laissez-faire* policy concede to government the minimum functions of defence, administration of justice and police. But, regardless of political philosophy, the needs of an increasingly complex society have forced upon one country after another a multiplicity of additional functions: to the protection of elementary standards of health and safety, both for the public in general and employees – which accounted for the first major growth of public services in nineteenth-century England – were rapidly added a vast number of additional social services, from elementary measures of public assistance to the highly diversified social-security systems of the mid-twentieth century; the supervision of public utilities, labour relations and many other economic and social processes intimately affecting the public interest. In times of war or emergency, a multitude of controls over supply and distribution of essential commodities and products further enlarges the functions of government.

Beyond the irreducible minimum imposed by external conditions, the type and direction of the administrative function is influenced by the political and economic system of the country. In socialized states – as shown by the Soviet Union and its affiliated systems – the state takes over the managerial as well as the regulatory function. The conduct of major economic enterprises becomes an administrative function: contracts of supply between the state-owned corporations producing commodities and manufactured goods are at once civil and administrative transactions. Managers and other personnel are not only in the civil relationship of servants to masters, but also in the disciplinary relationship of public officials to their superiors.

At the next level, the mixed economies which today characterize the political and economic systems of many states – such as France, Great Britain, Italy, India, Japan, as well as many of the smaller states, both of Western Europe and Asia – have a combination of managerial and regulatory administrative functions. Certain industries and public utilities are operated by the state itself – either through government departments, e.g. the Swedish railways, or with increasing frequency through semi-autonomous public corporations, responsible to government, but equipped with more or less far-reaching managerial autonomy (see pp. 340–41). At the same time, the bulk of industry and business, which remains in private ownership, is subject to varying degrees of public supervision and regulations, while another set of public authorities administers the various social services.

In the United States, too, the managerial aspect of the administrative process is not unknown, although, perhaps due to ideological inhibitions, astonishingly little attention is paid by the highly developed science of administrative law to this aspect of public activity. The main emphasis, however, has been on the regulatory function of administration. The establishment of a series of permanent regulatory federal agencies[1] testifies to the fact that even the most strongly private-enterprise and capitalist-minded contemporary state cannot leave its economic system to the free play of economic forces. It cannot watch passively strong enterprises squeezing out the weak, with the consumer being helpless against exploitation by monopolies and unregulated public utilities. Under such conditions, 'the general statutory or common law which administers itself through the moral conscience of the citizen is no longer enough to deal with the vast machinery of power and abuses which economic

1. Such as the Interstate Commerce Commission established in 1887, followed in the present century by the Federal Trade Commission, the Federal Communications Commission, the Security and Exchange Commission, the Civil Aeronautics Board, and the National Labor Relations Board, not to speak of the many non-permanent wartime agencies.

control can become if unfettered from the ties of public interest'. On the other hand, public ownership, adopted, wholly or in part, in so many other countries, is overwhelmingly rejected by American public opinion 'as the complete pattern of our economy and final destiny of our whole lives'.[2] Between the opposites of unregulated economic enterprise and total public ownership lies public regulation, 'the answer to the challenge which public ownership and operation of all economic enterprise presents' (McEntire in Gellhorn and Byse, 1954).

In a highly industrialized and dynamic society like that of the United States, which is complicated by the existence of fifty state governments, side by side with the Federal Government, such regulation means, however, a vast and complicated mechanism of administration. In a sense, the contemporary United States is the administrative state *par excellence*, if administration is taken in the traditional sense of the public supervision and control of private and official activities.

The Need for a System of Public Law

In an absolutist state, whether of the feudal, the monarchical, the Communist or the Fascist pattern, the dichotomy of public and private law makes no sense, even though, in modern systems of this kind, it may be maintained as a matter of form. Ultimately, all law dissolves into administrative discretion. Such was the conclusion drawn for Communist society by the once influential Soviet legal philosopher Pashukanis, who maintained that in a Communist state there was no room for law at all, since all law became administration directed by the demands of public utility (Hazard, 1951, p. 120; Friedmann, 1967, pp. 370–71). The same thought was expressed in more conventional terms by Lenin when he wrote that 'for us everything in the field of economy bears the character of public law and not of private law. . . . Hence we should broaden the application of state intervention into "private-law" relation-

2. Both these quotations are from a thoughtful address by Richard B. McEntire, Commissioner, Securities and Exchange Commission, 1946–53 given before the National Association of Securities administrators in 1947, and reprinted in Gellhorn and Byse (1954, pp. 8–9).

ships' (letter to Kwskii quoted by Yudir in Hazard, 1951, p. 292).

From very different premises, the idea of a dichotomy of public and private law, with the former representing a system of norms regulating the legal relations between public authority and the individual, has been opposed by three major legal thinkers of the western world, vastly though they differ from each other in background and philosophy.

The French legal philosopher and constitutional lawyer, Léon Duguit, opposed the dualism of public and private law in the name of 'social solidarity', which demanded that all, governors and governed alike, were subject to the same principle of service to the community. From the standpoint of a hierarchy of legal norms in a system of 'pure science of law', Hans Kelsen opposes the division of public and private law, as being contrary to the 'step by step' unfolding of legal norms from the ultimate *Grundnorm* to the individual decisions of administrative authorities and private parties alike. Coupled with this, however, is a consideration of political theory, which sees in the development of administrative law an entrenchment of public authority in a position of superiority and arbitrariness as against the private citizen.

Neither of these two influential legal theorists has prevented the continuous growth of highly developed systems of administrative law in the civil-law jurisdictions, buttressed by a complete hierarchy of administrative courts (see p. 423). Far more influential has been the opposition of the English jurist Dicey to any system of *droit administratif* in England, as being contrary to the spirit and tradition of the common law.

For Dicey[3] (Wade, 1959, ch. 4) the 'rule of law' has three aspects: first, no man is punishable except for 'a distinct breach of law established in the ordinary legal manner before the ordinary courts of the land', and therefore the rule of law is not consistent with arbitrary 'or even wide discretionary authority on the part of the government'. In the second place, the rule of law means equal subjection of all classes to the ordinary law of the land as administered by the ordinary law courts, and therefore a rejection of so-called administrative justice applied by special tribunals on the Continental

3. See also F. R. Lawson, 'Dicey revisited', 7 *Political Studies* (1959), 109, 207.

model. The third aspect of Dicey's rule of law means in essence a historic generalization: in English law, private individual rights derive from court precedents rather than from constitutional codes. This quite clearly applies only to Britain itself and would have no application to a state which, like Australia, is governed by a written constitution, or Canada, which, since 1960, has had a Bill of Rights, let alone to the United States, whose constitution embodies a comprehensive catalogue of individual rights.

It is no exaggeration to say that the views of this eminent jurist played a considerable part in delaying the growth, not of administration, but of administrative law in the common-law world, for several decades. Yet, almost simultaneously with the publication of the first edition of Dicey's *Law of the Constitution*, in 1885, his great contemporary, Maitland, clearly saw the growth of administrative law in England, the growing importance of 'the subordinate Government of England' (1887, p. 415).[4]

That Dicey ignored the then prominent privileges and immunities of the Crown, that he completely misunderstood the French *droit administratif* which, far from protecting governmental arbitrariness, had already gone far – and has since gone further – in the legal protection of the citizen against such arbitrariness, has been pointed out by many contemporary critics of Dicey's theory (Jennings, 1959; Robson, 1951; Wade, 1959; Allen, 1967; Hamson, 1954). For an understanding of the essential conditions of a system of administrative law, it is perhaps more important to point out the basic fallacy in Dicey's juxtaposition of two principles: one expresses the need for restraint of the arbitrary power of government; the other says that there must be 'equal subjection of all classes' to 'the ordinary courts'. Even within the formulation of these two principles, Dicey makes some questionable assumptions. The equation of 'arbitrary' with 'wide discretionary' power of government is one that few students of the modern administrative process would accept without severe reservations. Again, the identification of 'ordinary' courts with the courts developed in the common-law tradition assumes *a priori* that no differently constituted courts, including courts of the eminence,

4. For a recent discussion of the need for a system of public law in the UK, see Mitchell, 'The state of public law in the United Kingdom', 15 *Int. & Comp. L.Q.* 133 (1966).

expertise, and judicial independence of the French *Conseil d'État*, can be considered as genuine courts.[5]

The deeper fallacy of Dicey's assumptions lies in his contention that the rule of law demands full equality in every respect between government and subjects or citizens. But it is inherent in the very notion of government that it cannot in all respects be equal to the governed, because it has to govern. In a multitude of ways, government must be left to interfere, without legal sanctions, in the lives and interests of citizens, where private persons could not be allowed to do so with impunity. To some extent, the range of these immunities is expressed in the 'prerogatives' of the Crown, or in the equivalent French concept of *'actes de Gouvernement'*. Declarations of war, or other military interventions, diplomatic relations including the recognition of governments, may or may not be subject to legislative control, but they cannot form the subject of individual actions, even though incalculable damage may be inflicted on millions of individuals as a result of irresponsible action by the executive. No action may be brought for loss of life, limb or property, as the result of foreign policy decisions, although most states, in and after the last World War, enacted certain legislation compensating citizens for war damage. The refusal of Anglo-American courts to examine or question the recognition of foreign states or governments is another indication of this basic distinction between government and citizens. It goes, however, beyond the international sphere. Where the borderline between governmental freedom and legal responsibility has to be drawn, is the key problem of administrative law. But we can only begin to understand it after having accepted, unlike Dicey, that inequalities between government and citizens are inherent in the very nature of political society.

Although the struggle against a system of administrative justice had its counterparts on the Continent,[6] Continental jurisprudence, following the French model, has long established full-fledged systems of administrative justice, which have come to be recognized as bulwarks against arbitrary administrative power, and not, as contended

5. For a criticism of this narrow conception of 'ordinary' courts, see Jennings (1959, pp. 312–13).

6. See the famous controversy in Germany between Baehr (1864), who wanted to subject all public law to civil law and procedure, and von Gneist (1868), who advocated a system of administrative justice.

by Dicey or Kelsen, as legitimized oppressions of the individual.[7]

In the common-law world, there has been a belated and hesitant, but now increasingly accepted, development of a system and science of administrative law.[8] In England a Parliamentary Commissioner for Administration has been created and the Law Commission has begun to study the need for a system of administrative law. The definition of the sphere of administrative law has, however, especially in the United States, tended to remain narrowly confined to procedural methods and safeguards.[9] This distinguishes the American science and doctrine of administrative law – and to a far lesser extent, that of English administrative law – from the Continental conception of administrative law. As even a cursory survey of any of the leading texts (Waline, 1963; Forsthoff, 1958) will show, the discussion of remedies and procedures against administrative authorities, and the system of administrative justice, occupies only one, and not the major, part of administrative law. For the greater part, Continental administrative law is concerned with such matters of substance as public-law contracts, domains and principles of public ownership, principles of legal responsibility on the part of government and other public authorities.[10] By contrast, in the common-law world,

7. Among many other examples, we might mention, from the judicial practice of the *Conseil d'État*, the doctrine of *imprévision*, from which, unlike the jurisprudence of the Supreme Civil Court, the *Cour de Cassation* has developed a system of compensation in public contracts, where the equilibrium of the contract has been disturbed by certain outside events (see further pp. 400–401), or the decision in the *affaire Barel* (RDP 1954, 509), which quashed the exclusion, by the Minister, from admission to the Concours of the *École Nationale de l'Administration* of candidates suspected of Communist sympathies. No less significant is the retention and strengthening of the system of administrative justice in West Germany, after the Second World War, as a means of restoring the rule of law. This was done under the guidance of British and American Military Government authorities.

8. See, for the United States, the treatises by Davis (1958, 1959) or Gellhorn and Byse (1970); for England, Griffith and Street (1967); for Australia, Benjafield and Whitmore (1970).

9. See Davis, (1959, p. 1): 'Administrative law, as the term is used, is limited to law concerning powers and procedures, and does not include the enormous mass of substantive law produced by the agencies.' This limitation is accepted by all the leading case-books.

10. Discussion of such matters can be found, incidentally, in the corresponding American works, e.g. in the discussion of the scope of government immunities.

many of the vital problems of public law have to be culled from scattered decisions, standard conditions of government contracts and other materials found in the case-books and textbooks on contract, tort, or property, which, in turn, largely fail to analyse the public-law problems as such. Because such limitations greatly impede the understanding of the essential characteristics of public law, a – necessarily cursory – survey of some of the substantive as well as of the procedural problems of administrative law will be attempted, on a comparative basis, in this chapter.

Separation of Powers and Administrative Law

In 1881 the Supreme Court declared in *Kilbourne* v. *Thompson*[11] that all powers of government are divided into executive, legislative and judicial, and that it is 'essential to the successful working of this system that the persons entrusted with power in any one of these branches shall not be permitted to encroach upon the power confided to the others, but that each shall by the law of its creation be limited to the exercise of the powers appropriate to its own department and no other . . .'.

The antithesis to this deceptively simple conception of government[12] was stated by Woodrow Wilson in 1908.

The trouble with the theory is that government is not a machine, but a living thing. . . . No living thing can have its organs offset against each other as checks, and live. On the contrary, its life is dependent upon their quick cooperation, their ready response to the commands of instinct or intelligence, their amicable community of purpose. Government is not a body of blind forces; it is a body of men, with highly differentiated functions no doubt, in our modern day of specialization, but with a common task and purpose. Their cooperation is indispensable, their warfare fatal (1908, p. 56).

In the late-twentieth century, it is commonplace that a strict doctrine of separation of powers is not only a theoretical absurdity

11. 103 U.S. 168 (1881).

12. It should not, perhaps, be taken too seriously. Madison, one of the principal architects of the Constitution, displays a far more realistic understanding of the interplay of the different branches of government, in his analysis of Montesquieu and the British Constitution (*The Federalist*, Letter no. 47).

and a practical impossiblity, but that it has not been embodied, in anything like the strictness presumed by the Supreme Court in the above-quoted decision, in any contemporary constitution. The constitutional system of the United States has been recently characterized by one American scholar as one of checks and balances rather than separation of powers (Davis, 1959, para. 1.09), while another has stressed that not separation of powers, but judicial supremacy is a characteristic feature of the American Constitution.[13] Yet another analysis[14] detects, on the contrary, a decline of the relative power of both judiciary and legislature, 'accompanied by a corresponding growth of relative power in the executive . . . branch of government'. Clearly, all these analyses emphasize different aspects of a complex and constantly shifting system of checks and balances.[15] Whichever aspect is emphasized, it is evident that separation of powers can be only relative, not absolute. The executive must appoint judges, unless the legislature or the electorate do so. Executive and legislature must cooperate in the enactment of laws, although the forms of doing so differ in various democracies. In Great Britain, which formed the model for Montesquieu's theory of the separation of powers, the principle has never been even theoretically enshrined. The executive is formed by the majority party in the House of Commons, which thus both controls the Government and is, in turn, under its direction. The Lord Chancellor combines the functions of the highest judge, a member of the Cabinet, and the presiding officer of the Upper Legislative Chamber. The vitality and importance of the doctrine of the separation of powers lies not in any rigid separation of functions, but in a working hypothesis, i.e. in the basic differentiation of the three functions of law-making, administration and adjudication. By far the most important aspect of separation of powers is judicial independence from administrative direction, and that is perhaps the only aspect of the doctrine on which all democracies concur.

13. Parker, 'The historic basis of administrative law: separation of powers and judicial supremacy', 12 *Rutgers L. Rev.* (1958), pp. 449 et seq.
14. Miller, 'The constitutional law of the "security state",' 10 *Stanford L. Rev.* 620, 639 (1958).
15. cf. Frankfurter J. in *Youngstown Sheet & Tube Co.* v. *Sawyer*, 343 U.S. 579 (1952).

As we have seen, the process of law-finding is a constant and painful adjustment of conflicting values. So is the problem of adjustment between private economic power and public interest. Nor are public and private interests always clearly distinct. The regulatory authority sometimes becomes too closely identified with the interest and outlook of the regulated industry.[16] The exercise of public functions may, deliberately or by stealth, slide into the hands of private groups, such as employers' associations or trade unions.

The problem of the relations between public authority and the citizen (private or corporate) cannot be solved in terms of conceptual absolutes. Nor can it be solved simply by the elaboration of procedural safeguards. Whether and to what extent such safeguards have to be provided, must in large measure depend on the fundamental adjustment of the relations between public power and private rights.

The Limits of Administrative Discretion

Once we have conceded that government must govern, and that it cannot, therefore, be in all respects on a footing of equality with the citizen, the formula stated by Dicey that government must not have 'arbitrary' or even 'wide discretionary' powers becomes mere question begging, as do the limitless variations of this formula used in Bar Association speeches, on public platforms, and the like. For what is 'arbitrary' and where, consequently, the limits of the discretion have to be drawn, depends on the scale of human values as it is enshrined in the contemporary legal system. It should be evident that this has, in many respects, greatly altered during the present century. As the basis, there remains, in all civilized systems, the protection – though not unqualified and subject to due process – of life, liberty and property. Administrative processes are seldom concerned with the protection of life, except in connection with the execution of capital sentences. But they are deeply and seriously concerned with the protection of liberty and property. However, instead of devoting all our attention to the minute details of safeguards, we should, perhaps, do a little rethinking on the meaning of

16. See Jaffé, 'The effective limits of the administrative process: a revaluation', 67 *Harvard L. Rev.* 1105 (1954).

such basic values as liberty and property in the legal and social context of contemporary society. At a time of international tensions and apprehensions about Communist subversion, the very same people who, a generation ago, condemned the growth of the administrative process as an intolerable encroachment on separation of functions and the rule of law are today disposed to leave almost unlimited powers to administrative discretion in the domain of national security, deportation, immigration, and other matters vitally concerning the liberty, freedom of movement, and employability of the citizen at large, of aliens, or of more limited groups of the population. Conversely, those who favoured wide administrative discretion in the era of economic and social reform, now condemn administrative latitude, especially in the area of human rights. Professor Gellhorn has drawn up an impressive catalogue of administrative powers which have been allowed to grow with little or no legal check (1956, p. 14). These include press and book censorship, the various 'loyalty' procedures, the issue of passports and others. Again, if liberty is a value to be protected, unless there is a clear statutory command to the contrary, such decisions as *Liversidge* v. *Anderson*,[17] where the power of the Home Secretary to detain aliens where he 'has reasonable cause to believe' was interpreted by the majority of the House of Lords as equivalent to: 'where the Home Secretary thinks that he has . . . cause to believe', are open to serious objections.

The right to earn a living, according to one's capabilities and training, may be regarded either as an aspect of liberty (to develop one's personality) or as an aspect of property, if property, as it must, is no longer defined as a compound of tangible, real and personal assets, but the totality of all rights and interests capable of legal protection which have an economic value. Whatever its characterization, the right to earn a living[18] has barely been articulated as an essential value to be protected in the administrative process, although its protection is for the ordinary citizen, the 'common man', perhaps a matter of greater practical importance than any of the traditionally

17. [1942] A.C. 206.
18. See de Smith (1968, p. 511): 'In recent years the courts have been readily persuaded to declare the illegality of undue restraints imposed on freedom to engage in a trade or occupation.' See also the dicta of Lord Denning M.R. in *Nagle* v. *Fielden* [1966] 1 All. E.R. 689.

articulated values. If this is a value worthy of protection in contemporary democracy, the unchecked power of Congressional committees, government departments or even private employers,[19] to deprive persons of their livelihood and employability in the field of their training and skill, is truly 'arbitrary' power. So is the delegation, by indirection, of the power to deprive a person of employment in his trade to labour unions which effectively control employment in a particular industry (see pp. 359–64).

From the same angle, the steady – and largely unnoticed because scattered – growth of licensing powers over a multitude of professional and commercial activities, not by public authority, but by interested groups, is a serious interference with the right to earn a living (Gellhorn, 1956, ch. 3) unless checked by constitutional tests or public supervision.

While liberty and property should thus be interpreted not in the light of conditions and ideas prevalent a century ago, but of those of the late twentieth century, the right of property is subject to reinterpretation in other respects. In the light of official legal policy, as embodied not only in the Sherman Anti-trust Act, the statutory powers of the Federal Trade Commission, and ancillary legislation in the United States, but also more recently in the anti-trust laws of England, Germany and other states (Friedmann, 1956; Blake, 1969), the protection of property certainly must find its limitation in the concentration of excessive economic power. Again, the statutory acknowledgement of legal values, such as soil conservation or the husbanding of agricultural resources or of water resources, does mean a different adjustment of values, and, therefore, a different conception of 'arbitrary' than would have been the case a century ago.

Continental textbooks on administrative law, while hardly sufficiently elaborate on the subject, stress certain elementary *Rechtsgrundsätze* (Forsthoff, 1958, p. 67) or *principes généraux du droit* (Waline, 1963, § 762–75) which must guide administrative decision. First among these basic principles stands that of equality. This, of course, is general, not without ambiguity and subject to

19. For a survey, see the Report on the Federal Loyalty-Security Programme, prepared under the chairmanship of Professor Elliott Cheatham for the Association of the Bar of the City of New York (1956) and Brown (1958).

many qualifications. Yet, it is of great practical significance, often insufficiently appreciated in the discussion of problems of administrative law. Procedurally, the principle of equality means non-discrimination in the treatment of persons or groups entitled to equal consideration, e.g. in the awarding of building licences, trading permits or admission to educational establishments (Waline, 1963, § 763, § 790). It must be based on comparable standards; there must be no discrimination between equals, whether based on personal vindictiveness, pecuniary interests, or political prejudices not sanctioned by the law. All such actions are aspects of abuse of power (*détournement de pouvoir*).

A consideration of basic principles governing administrative law would not, of course, by itself, solve a multitude of problems which, as stated before, depend on a delicate balance of conflicting interests and values. It would, however, give a firmer background, and a greater sense of direction to many decisions of administrative agencies, administrative tribunals and ordinary courts, which today seem to vacillate all too often between general platitudes and pure empiricism.

But even if we attain such sense of direction in the basic principles of administrative law, in the great majority of cases an administrative body exercises powers given to it by statute in good faith, without discrimination, for a public purpose. It is in these cases that the problem of the limits of administrative discretion emerges in all its complexity.

Despite the vast differences in the organization of administrative services, and in the structure and scope of legal remedies against administrative action, this problem presents itself, basically in similar terms, to any system – civil law or common law – which attempts to balance the necessary freedom of governmental decision-making with the protection of basic individual rights.

The general common-law approach was put tersely in a lecture by an eminent British judge:

Broadly speaking, the courts will investigate and give relief in respect of acts of the executive which are shown to be bad in law or to have been done without or in excess of authority, or in bad faith, or because of irrelevant or extraneous considerations; but they will not revise decisions lawfully taken or interfere by substituting one view of the merits for another (MacDermott, 1957, p. 81).

More recently, a leading British treatise has described the limits of administrative discretion as follows:

Discretionary powers must be exercised for the purposes for which they were granted, relevant considerations must be taken into account and irrelevant considerations disregarded; they must be exercised in good faith and not arbitrarily or capriciously. If the repository of the power fails to comply with these requirements, it acts *ultra vires* (de Smith, 1968, p. 89).

In the United States, where the main emphasis is on the scope of review from a multitude of administrative agencies constituted by statute, a similar principle is expressed with a different emphasis in a judgement of the Supreme Court:

Our duty is at an end when we find that the action of the Commission was based on findings supported by evidence, and was made pursuant to authority granted by Congress.[20]

After a much longer preoccupation with organized administrative justice and in the light of many hundreds of authoritative decisions on the problem, contemporary Continental authorities on administrative law have given up any attempts to define the limit of administrative discretion in more than a very few broad formulas. While a leading modern French textbook (Waline, 1963, § 741) enumerates five major limits of discretionary power (lack of competence, fault of form, violation of the law, incorrect motivation and, most important and vaguest of all, failure to act 'in the public interest'), modern German doctrine is content with three (Jellinek, 1931, p. 37; Forsthoff, 1958, p. 87): first, error about the existence or limits of the exercise of discretion, or their conscious violation; second, error about legitimate motives, or their deliberate neglect; third, faults in the appreciation of the relevant facts.

From these broad formulations we gain little more than the insight that there are certain limits to the freedom of administrative action. But under what circumstances a particular administrative action has been 'improperly motivated', or neglected to be guided by the 'public interest', cannot be ascertained from general formulas. To be sure, the multiplicity of administrative contacts with individual interests is infinite, and it increases steadily as the activities of governments and other public authorities spread out, horizontally and

20. *National Broadcasting Co.* v. *United States*, 319 U.S. 190, 224 (1963).

vertically. Regulatory and supervisory activities range from the control of sanitary standards, in houses and factories, of the uses of land, the control of floods, dykes, forests, to the public supervision, by way of arbitration or active regulation, of labour conditions. On the other hand, governments, municipal authorities and public corporations make long-term contracts for supplies and services, and they operate a large number of public utilities and, in some cases, industries. With the multiplicity of functions, the possibilities of friction between public and private interests increase. It is not surprising that the growing flood of decisions on the proper limits of administrative discretion, by semi-judicial agencies, ordinary courts or administrative tribunals, should be full of contradictions and inconsistencies, that more and more we have to look to the courts' experience and good sense in the delicate adjustment of conflicting values and interests in the individual case at hand.

A very recent French survey (Long, Weil and Braibant, 1969, p. 23) shows that there is considerable fluctuation in the extent to which the *Conseil d'État* goes into the motives and circumstances of administrative actions to determine whether there has been *détournement de pouvoir*. The decision is simple enough where there has been a manifest abuse of public powers for private purposes. Thus, in a recent decision,[21] the Conseil invalidated the decision of a prefect who expropriated a private property for the sole purpose of housing there a private equestrian club. But generally the situation is less clear. The learned authors note that between 1910 and 1940 the *Conseil d'État* tended to go into a detailed study of the administrative records to determine whether the powers had been properly exercised, but that since then it has retreated from that position and confined itself to censoring 'acts inspired by considerations entirely alien to the public interest'. The authors note that, paradoxically, the use of the remedy of *détournement de pouvoir* has declined at the very time when 'the extension of the activities of the state and the powers of public authorities, and the prerogatives entrusted to economic services and professional institutions would have justified an enlargement of its reach' (p. 26).

Similar fluctuations are, as we shall see, observable in the common-law world. It is not the general principles as much as their application

21. C.E., 4 March 1964, *Dame veuve Borderie*, Rec. 157.

in detail that is largely determined by changing judicial attitudes towards the borderline between non-interference with administrative discretion that a government must be accorded to exercise its policy-making functions and the need to protect the individual from arbitrary interferences by public authority.

First, it is accepted in the theory and practice of all states that certain major policy functions of government, especially in the international sphere, cannot be subject to judicial control. The most articulate discussion of the scope of this immunity has been in French law, around the concept of '*actes de gouvernement*' (Trotabas, 1925, p. 342; Waline, 1963, § 357). The scope of this once wide exemption has been greatly curtailed in recent times, but it still includes *actes diplomatiques*. While there is some controversy on the exact scope of this immunity of governmental action in international affairs (Waline, 1963, § 360), it would seem to correspond to the scope of governmental prerogative conceded by the common-law courts to the actions of government in international affairs. A well-known English illustration is the *Amphitrite* case,[22] where, during the First World War, a Swedish ship was seized by the British Government, despite an undertaking given by the British Legation at Stockholm that, by carrying a cargo of at least 60 per cent approved goods, the ship would be released. In rejecting the claim for damages Rowlatt J. held that an 'intention to act in a particular way in a certain event' could not be made binding on the government (at p. 503; see also Keir and Lawson, 1967, pp. 344–6; Mitchell, 1954, p. 28).

To the exemptions concerning government actions essentially in the sphere of international relations French practice and doctrine add a certain, not very precisely defined, category of actions concerning 'public security' (Street, 1953, p. 73). This has been steadily narrowed down from its formerly very wide scope, and now appears to be confined to actions dealing with very major disturbances, such as war, states of siege, but probably no longer anti-flood or anti-epidemic measures. There is less and less disposition to grant the executive a blank cheque, in the form of emergency powers, unless they are clearly defined by statute. In recent United States practice a certain parallel to this development may be seen in the *Steel Seizure*

22. *Rederiaktiebolaget Amphitrite* v. *The King* [1921] 3 K.B. 500.

cases,[23] where the Supreme Court refused to legalize a presidential executive order directing the Secretary of Commerce to seize the steel industry on behalf of the Government (during a prolonged strike), alleged to be inherent in the functions of the President as the Supreme Executive. In Great Britain the last World War produced a far-reaching substitution of statutory emergency legislation for common-law prerogative power. The majority of the House of Lords, over the vigorous dissent of Lord Atkin, construed the Home Secretary's emergency power to detail aliens 'which he had reasonable cause to suspect . . .' as being a decision to be taken in his own discretion, and not therefore reviewable.[24]

The second category of governmental exemptions from legal responsibility is far more important in the everyday practice of administration. It concerns what is variously called the 'planning' or 'policy-making' decisions of governments and other public authorities. In its law-making, planning or policy decisions, government must not be hampered by contractual or tort liabilities. In the former sphere this means that either a commitment given to a private individual cannot be construed as contractual or that the contract will be superseded by superior considerations of public policy.

It has long been held by the Court of Claims that the United States when sued as a contractor cannot be held liable for an obstruction to the performance of the particular contract resulting from its public and general acts as a sovereign.[25]

In *Ransom and Luck* v. *Surbiton B. C.*[26] a local authority had, under the then effective Town and Country Planning Act, given permission for interim development to land owners, subject to certain conditions laid down in agreements between the owners and the local authority. After the war, acting under a new Town and Country Planning Act, the Minister included the area in the so-called Greater London Plan and withheld permission for further development, although the plaintiffs had already laid out some money for the construction of sewers. The Court of Appeal held that the Planning Authority could not bargain away its statutory powers of planning

23. *Youngstown Sheet & Tube Co.* v. *Sawyer* 343 U.S. 579 (1952).
24. *Liversidge* v. *Anderson* [1942] A.C. 206.
25. *Horowitz* v. *US* (1924) 267 U.S. 458.
26. [1949] 1 Ch. 180.

conferred on it by a statute in the public interest. Consequently, the agreements into which the authority had entered were not construed as being contractual and, in any case, subject to the overriding purpose of the statute as a whole. Another decision of the Court of Appeal, a few years later,[27] held that the City of London Corporation could not impair its powers of regulation as a health authority by a private contract, and that, therefore, the exercise of these powers rendered the further performance of the contract impossible, without attaching to the public authority any liability for breach of contract.

In the sphere of tort the problem has become acute in the interpretation of the 'discretionary' exemption from tort liability in the United States Federal Torts Claims Act[28] by a confusing trilogy of decisions. In *Dalehite* v. *United States*[29] the Supreme Court held the US Government not liable for a disastrous explosion in Texas City caused by the negligence of various government agencies and officials in planning, manufacturing, storing, and fighting the explosion of fertilizer-grade ammonium nitrate used as part of a foreign-aid programme. Some years later the Court held the Government liable for damages resulting from failure of a lighthouse light, due to negligent maintenance of the light by the coast-guard.[30] More recently, the Court again held the Government liable for negligence in the fighting of a forest fire by the US Forest Service.[31]

One aspect of the reasoning in the *Dalehite* decision is of basic importance to the present discussion. The Supreme Court refused to hold the Government liable for negligence in the manufacture of the explosive materials on the ground that 'the decisions held culpable were all responsibly made at a planning rather than operational

27. *William Cory & Son, Ltd* v. *City of London Corp*. [1951] 2 K.B. 476.
28. 'Any claim based upon an act or omission of an employee of the Government, exercising due care in the execution of a statute or regulation, whether or not such statute or regulation be valid, or based upon the exercise or performance or the failure to exercise or perform a discretionary function or duty on the part of a federal agency or an employee of the Government; whether or not the discretion involved be abused is withheld from jurisdiction of the courts'. (28 U.S.C. § 2680 (a)).
29. 346 U.S. 15 (1953).
30. *Indian Towing Co.* v. *US*, 350 U.S. 61 (1955).
31. *Rayonnier* v. *US*, 352 U.S. 315 (1957).

level and involved considerations more or less important to the practicability of the Government's fertilizer programme'.[32]

In the view of a leading American authority on administrative law,[33] 'the concept of "a planning rather than operational level" is important and may be destined to become a landmark in law development'.

From this antithesis of 'planning' and 'operational' activities we can draw certain conclusions which should help to clarify the often extremely confusing interpretations by both British and American courts.

The sound kernel of the 'planning' exemption not only for federal and state governments but also for other public authorities, such as municipal corporations, catchment boards and others, is that they must have freedom to exercise a choice entrusted to them for the execution of their functions, and not be hampered by subsequent court judgements on the wisdom of such decision. Without such freedom of movement any effective administration would be paralysed. If, for example, a public authority, limited in its budget and personnel, has been given a discretion to repair breaches in dykes,[34] to undertake a lighthouse service[35] or to fix wages of municipal employees 'as they think fit',[36] it is certainly not for any court to substitute its own judgement *ex post* on the policy considerations governing the exercise of this discretion. Against this principle English courts appear to have sinned more frequently than American courts. The high-water mark is still the decision of the House of Lords in *Roberts* v. *Hopwood*, where a London local authority had exercised its statutory power 'to fix wages as they think fit' by granting a minimum wage to all employees, without distinction of sex. The House of Lords confirmed the surcharge imposed by the District Auditor on the councillors. It rejected the very conception of a basic minimum wage for all employees as not being a reward for labour.[37]

32. 346 U.S., p. 42.
33. K. C. Davis, 'Tort liability of governmental units', 40 *Minnesota L. Rev.* 751, 785 (1955).
34. *East Suffolk Catchment Board* v. *Kent* [1941] A.C. 74.
35. *Indian Towing Co.* v. *US*, 350 U.S. 61 (1955).
36. *Roberts* v. *Hopwood* [1925] A.C. 578.
37. The House was apparently unaware that at the time, as now, the basic wage had already become the corner-stone of Australian industrial law.

It also considered the weekly minimum wage of £4 as grossly extravagant. Lord Atkinson said that the council 'allowed themselves to be guided in preference by some eccentric principles of Socialist philanthropy, or by a feminist ambition to secure the equality of the sexes in the matter of wages in the world of labour'.[38] In order to translate this outburst of political prejudice into legal reasoning the House had to interpolate the word 'reasonably' into the text of the statute, contrary to all canons of statutory construction.[39]

There was reason to hope that the *Roberts* v. *Hopwood* approach had given way to a wider conception of the relations between administrative discretion and judicial supervision.[40] But a later decision of the Court of Appeal[41] is reminiscent of the *Roberts* attitude. The Birmingham Corporation was authorized by statute to maintain and operate its transport undertaking and to 'charge such fares as it thought fit', subject to certain conditions with which the corporation had complied. With the consent of the licensing authority, it decided to provide free travelling facilities at certain hours for a limited class of aged men and women, to be financed out of the general rate fund. The Court of Appeal held this action to be *ultra vires*, with the following reasoning:

We think it clearly implicit in the legislation, that while it was left to the defendants to decide what fares should be charged within any prescribed statutory maxima for the time being in force, the undertaking was to be run as a business venture, or, in other words, that fares fixed by the defendants at their discretion, in accordance with ordinary business principles, were to be charged.

Just as the House of Lords in the earlier case had read the word 'reasonably' into the unqualified discretion granted by statute, so the Court of Appeal in the later case read 'ordinary business prin-

38. [1925] A.C., at 594.

39. This, in contemporary Britain, rather exceptional exhibition may be compared to the long line of decisions in which the Supreme Court of the United States, for many decades, interpreted the 'due-process' clauses of the Constitution so as to invalidate social legislation – Federal and state – which regulated conditions of labour by minimum wages, maximum hours, etc.

40. See, e.g. the wartime decision in *Re Decision of Walker* [1944] 1 K.B. 644, and the postwar decision of the Court of Appeal in *Associated Provincial Picture Houses, Ltd* v. *Wednesbury Corp.* [1948] 1 K.B. 223.

41. *Prescott* v. *Birmingham Corp.* [1954] 3 W.L.R. 990 (C.A.).

ciples' into the statutory power to charge fares as the local authority, with the consent of the licensing authority thought fit. It would be difficult to find any guidance in the court's judgement on the meaning of 'ordinary business principles' and, in particular, on the point at which differential fares would cease to be permissible as 'giving away rights of free travel'.[42]

More recent decisions of the House of Lords and of other British courts appear to confirm a tendency to review the statutory discretions granted to public authorities – including ministers. Thus, in *Padfield* v. *Minister of Agriculture*,[43] the House of Lords confirmed an order of mandamus issued by the Divisional Court, ordering the Minister to appoint a committee of investigation under the Agriculture Act 1958, to review a regional price scheme laid down by the Milk Marketing Board. The House of Lords held that the Minister's discretion under the Act was reviewable where the effect of its decision was to frustrate the policy of the Act.[44] And in *Anisminic* v. *Foreign Compensation Commission*[45] a decision of the Foreign Compensation Commission was held to be a nullity for excess of jurisdiction because it was based on issues irrelevant to the claim involved. The above-mentioned decisions of the House of Lords and the Court of Appeal may have been attempts to grant something like a regular appeal against decisions of administrative authorities. This is, of course, due to the fact that there is as yet no full-fledged system of administrative justice, as it has long been developed on the Continent, following the French model (see p. 432). It is, however, far better to develop a proper system of administrative justice, i.e. a hierarchy of review tribunals than to

42. See, among other criticisms, Benjafield, 'Statutory discretions', 2 *Sydney L. Rev.* (1956), p. 7.

43. [1968] A.C. 997.

44. This approach has been compared to the famous decision of the French *Conseil d'État* in the *Affaire Barel* (C.E. 28 May 1954, Rec. 308), which compelled the French Minister of the Interior to disclose the evidence for the exclusion of certain candidates – suspected of Communist sympathies – from admission to the Concours of the *Ecole Nationale de l'Administration*, and the Minister's decision was subsequently annulled. It is, however, easier to appreciate judicial review of administrative actions that discriminate against individuals and therefore violate basic principles of equality before the law, than judicial interference with economic and social policy decisions.

45. [1969] 1 All E.R. 208, 2 W.L.R. 163 (H.L.).

interfere with administrative policy, often by the distortion of clear statutory language. This, in effect, tends to substitute the court's policy views for those of the planning or other administrative authority.

If the courts have thus, on more than one occasion, confused administrative action and discretion by policy interferences, they have on the other hand, been often remarkably, though confusedly, liberal in the protection of public authorities from legal liability, where no such immunity should or need be granted.

The principle of equality which, as we have seen, is a cornerstone of administrative justice, demands that public authorities be held liable for interference with legitimate interests of citizens, unless such liability would impede the overriding needs of public service. Where, in other words, public authorities engage in transactions with private citizens through contractual commitments, or where they interfere with their interests through tortious conduct, they should be held liable unless principles of superior validity prevent it. Such a view does emphatically not mean an acceptance of the dichotomy of 'governmental' and 'proprietary' or 'non-governmental' functions. That such a distinction is both bad in principle and incapable of practical application will be shown later in this section (see pp. 417–19). It is the above-mentioned distinction between the 'planning' and the 'operational' level which furnishes a guide. Many decisions, both in the British and the American jurisdictions, have entirely failed to make a distinction between: (1) the exercise of an administrative discretion as such which, as discussed earlier, should not be reviewable, and (2) the manner of carrying out an administrative decision after the discretion has been exercised. The latter should be subject to general principles of legal liability. For this reason the argument of the Supreme Court in the *Dalehite* opinion was unsound, in so far as it denied liability for negligence in firefighting by public employees. The phrase that the Federal Torts Claims Act 'did not change the normal rule that an alleged failure or carelessness of public firemen does not create private actionable rights' begs the question.[46] This reasoning was entirely, and rightly, abandoned in the two later decisions of the Court, which held the coast-guard liable for negligent

46. See Davis, 'Tort liability of governmental units', 40 *Minnesota L. Rev.*, 786 (1955); Fleming James, 'The Federal Tort Claims Act and the "discretionary function" ', 10 *University of Florida L. Rev.* 187 (1957).

maintenance of a lighthouse service which they need or need not have undertaken in the first place, and held the United States Forest Service liable for negligence in the fighting of fires once they had undertaken the responsibility of doing so.

The correct test was formulated by Lord Greene M.R., in a judgement by the English Court of Appeal on the question whether local authorities, absolved during the last war from their normal duty to light streets and simultaneously equipped with power to build air-raid shelters, were absolved from legal responsibility for accidents happening in the blackout to pedestrians, cyclists and motorists.[47]

The question, therefore, in any given case appears to resolve itself into this – does the statute, on its true construction, in authorizing the act in question, exclude the duty of taking care in its performance?

The true view, in my opinion, is that the duty to take reasonable care to prevent danger to the public is present throughout: that so long as the streets are properly lit the duty is *ipso facto* performed: but that when the street lighting is suspended, either as the result of lighting restrictions or (in cases where street lighting is optional) as the result of the local authority's decision to extinguish the street lamps or as the result of a breakdown in the lighting system it becomes the duty of the local authority to take such steps to safeguard the public by special danger lights or otherwise, as in the circumstances of the case are reasonably possible.[48]

This decision makes a clear distinction between the planning or policy level – where discretion must be unhampered, unless the statute imposes a clear duty to act – and the operational level – where the duties of care and the standards to be demanded of public authority must, in the public interest, be equal to those demanded of private citizens.

The consistent application of this distinction would eliminate many unjust decisions based on a wrong theory: it would obviate the need to resort to spurious distinctions such as that between 'governmental' and 'non-governmental' activities; it would, at the same time, preserve the inequalities between government and governed, where they are justified by the necessities of public service.

47. *Fisher* v. *Ruislip U.D.C.* [1945] K.B. 584.

48. This analysis is in accord with the suggestion made by the present author shortly before the decision of the Court of Appeal; see Friedmann, 'Statutory powers and legal duties of local authorities', 8 *Mod. L. Rev.* 31, 48 (1945).

Chapter 11
Government Liability, Administrative Discretion and the Individual

Some Lessons from the Continent

In the major countries of continental Europe the progress of the *Rechtsstaat* idea, combined with the all but universal recognition of a separate system of administrative law and jurisdiction, promoted the principle of governmental legal responsibility at a time when the common-law jurisdictions were still firmly caught in the web of feudal government immunities. On the one hand, the *Rechtsstaat* principle demanded that governments and other public authorities should, as far as possible, be held liable on a basis comparable with that of private law. On the other hand, the gradual elaboration of the distinctive principles of administrative law led to the early recognition of inherent differences in the position of public authorities and private individuals, especially through the development of the *contrat administratif* in French jurisprudence, but also through the development of distinctive principles of governmental liability outside contract.

Liability in contract

The *Blanco* case of 1873,[1] which held that damages against the central administration were within the exclusive jurisdiction of the administrative courts, set the *Conseil d'État* free to develop its own judge-made body of rules of administrative liability. One of its most important creations was the development of legal characteristics of administrative transactions. Public authorities are now held in French law to be able to engage in transactions, either on a private-law basis (*gestions privées*) – in which case they are subject to civil

1. Dall. Pér. 1873, 3, 17.

jurisdiction and the principles of private law – or by way of a public-law contract, a *contrat administratif*, which is compounded of elements of contract and inequalities held to be inherent in the concept of public service. A public authority may, for example, contract for the services of radio performers or the supply of uniforms, or the purchase of paving stones in the form of a civil or an administrative contract. Normally, but not necessarily, the contracting for the execution of typical public-service functions, such as water supply or electricity grids, or sanitary services will indicate an administrative contract. In the summary formulation of an English comparative study on the subject:

What is necessary is, it seems, to contemplate the whole surroundings, the parties, the nature of the administrative organization with which the contract is made, the nature of the service, and the terms of the contract itself and the conditions on which it is made. In the last resort it seems that it is the terms of the contract which will decide the issue, provided that they are operative terms. The test may sound uncertain but probably the appearance is more uncertain than the reality, and in the ordinary cases there will be little doubt. In borderline cases doubt will remain whatever test is chosen (Mitchell, 1954, pp. 167, 179–80).[2]

It may suffice to add to this summary a reference to two decisions of the *Conseil d'État* on this subject.[3] Where the administration had contracted with a private individual for the food supplies to a repatriation centre for foreign refugees the contract was held to be an administrative one – whether or not it contained terms specifically derogating from the provisions of civil law,[4] since the contract had, for its direct object, the execution of a public service, namely, the repatriation of foreign refugees. On the other hand, a contract between the state and a transport company for the handling of customs, transit and transport of certain merchandise was held not to be a *marché de fourniture*, and therefore a *contrat administratif*, but a contract of private law. The reasoning was, first, that the contract did not contain any *clause exorbitante du droit*, i.e. that it was formulated in the manner of a private contract, and, second, that, although

2. See also Street (1953), and for a French analysis Waline (1963, § 136–8).
3. *Affaire époux Bertin*, D. 1956, 433; *Affaire Soc. française de Transports Gondrand frères, C.E.* 20 *avril–11 mai 1956*, both with note by de Laubadère.
4. The so-called *clause exorbitante du droit commun*.

concluded for the purpose of a public service, the object of the contract was not the very execution by a private party of the public service. The notion of *service public* was the decisive criterion in a holding that the loading of a ship to ensure supplies in time of war was an administrative contract.[5] On the other hand, a number of recent decisions[6] have held that contracts concluded between public services of an industrial and commercial character with their users are always private-law contracts, regardless of the form in which they are concluded. The fundamental characteristic of a *contrat administratif* is the recognition of certain unilateral powers of control by the administration in the public interest. The demands of the public service empower the administrative authority to carry out continuous supervision over the execution of the contract. To ensure this continuity of execution the administration has certain unilateral powers: to suspend, vary or rescind the contract, to transfer it to another party, or to take it over itself (*mise en régie*) (Mitchell, 1954, p. 184). Not only does the administrative authority have the right to interfere unilaterally in the contract; it has the duty to do so, because it is responsible for the public service. Hence, consumers or other interested parties may bring an action to compel the administration to exercise its powers and sue for damages for its refusal to do so (a kind of mandamus).[7] Moreover, the contract is always subject to the changing needs of the public service, '*suivant les besoins sociaux, économiques du moment*'.[8] Thus, a long-term concession for street lighting by gas may be converted into a demand for lighting by electricity if this is required by modern technical developments and public needs.[9] If the contractor is unable to fulfil the changed conditions the contract may be terminated or transferred to another contractor. However, the contractor is entitled to a full indemnity in any case of variation. The private party has '*ce que l'on appelle l'équilibre financier de son contrat*' (Waline, 1963, § 1037). This means not only an indemnity for the interference other than for fault

5. *Compagnie Havraise de Navigation à Vapeur*, Rec. 490, 13 July 1961.
6. See an enumeration and annotation in Long, Weil and Braibant (1969, p. 436).
7. See, for example, *Affaire Storch*, S. 1907, III, 33.
8. Conclusion de M. Corneille in *Soc. Déclarage de Poissy*, S. 1924, III, 2.
9. *Soc. Le centre électrique*, D. 1932, III, 60.

on the part of the contractor, with the contract by the administrative authority; it means also – by one of the most famous pieces of judicial law-making evolved in any modern system – an equitable adjustment of the remuneration contractually agreed upon, if the equilibrium of the contract has been upset by economic causes beyond the control of the parties, and the increasing burden on the contractor, caused thereby, was not foreseeable at the time of the conclusion of the contract. This is the theory of *imprévision* first established by the *Conseil d'État* in the *Gaz de Bordeaux* case in 1916,[10] and since then steadily developed through the vicissitudes of inflation, war, shortages of materials, and the other major economic disturbances that have characterized European history since the First World War (Waline, 1963, § 979).

The elasticity of the contract, the restrictions on *pacta sunt servanda*, are not, therefore, entirely a unilateral matter. If the public authority has many prerogatives and unilateral powers which would be improper in a private contract, the private contractor enjoys, on the other hand, the recognition of variability of terms in his favour, where the circumstances so demand.[11]

The *contrat administratif* is, in fact, dominated by the principles of the continuity of the public service, from which flows the concept of the relation between authority and contractor as one of cooperation. The contractor is an instrumentality for the execution of public services and functions. As such, he may incur graver risks than the private contractor, because in undertaking the supply of a long-term service or commodity he subjects himself to the above-mentioned variations or vicissitudes demanded by the public interest. On the other hand, it is in the interest of the public that the contractor should be enabled to supply the contracted goods or services satisfactorily; that he should not go bankrupt; that he should be able to pay his workmen adequately; and that he should be in a position to purchase the essential raw materials. Hence, the theory of *imprévision* – now usually replaced by specific terms of adjustment

10. S. 1916, III, 17.

11. It has been noted by the advocates of the French *droit administratif* that the *Cour de Cassation*, the highest French civil court, has never recognized anything equivalent to *imprévision*, or, indeed, any form of frustration of contract as developed by Continental courts in other countries (see Mitchell, 1954, p. 190).

in the conditions which form the basis of the contracts – and the concept of the administrative contract as basically different from the civil-law contract, not indeed in all respects – for in the absence of a public code of contract there is, of course, reference to many provisions of the civil law – but in some essential respects.

While the concept of a distinctive public-law contract is also well known in Belgium, Italy[12] and some Latin-American countries influenced by French law, it is far less developed in Germany, where the emphasis is still on the unilateral character of the '*Verwaltungsakt*'. Thus, the granting of concessions and licences – a typical illustration of the *contrat administratif* – is generally regarded as a unilateral administrative act. However, arrangements for the use of public utilities (such as electricity or telephones) may be concluded in the form of a '*Vertrag*', an agreement between the public authority and the individual. The main field of application of the public-law contract in the German system is the regulation of relations between the numerous persons of public law, such as regional, municipal, or functional authorities which abound in the German administrative system, contrasting with the centralization of French administration (Forsthoff, 1958, p. 253; Langrod, p. 354). The *öffentlichrechtliche Vertrag* does not, like the *contrat administratif*, blend administrative and contractual elements in the relations between public authority and the citizen. It is characterized by the coordination of the parties, which are administrative authorities (Forsthoff, p. 221).

It has been rightly observed (Langrod, p. 362) that there is far more similarity to the French conception in modern Anglo-American legal developments, although the disinclination to recognize the dualism of private and public law still prevents, especially in England, clear recognition and elaboration of the concept of public or administrative contract (Street, 1953, p. 81; Mitchell, 1954).

In American law there is growing recognition of the 'government contract' as a distinct category.[13] Now that liability and action-

12. See the comparative studies by Langrod, 'Administrative contracts', 4 *Amer. J. of Comp. Law* (1955), 325, 347, and by Imboden (1959, 9–37), which detects a gradual growth of the administrative contract in German post-war practice.

13. See, for example, Cherne (1941); the chapter 'Government contracts' in Williston (1957, ch. 60); the Symposium on Various Aspects of Government Contracts in the *George Washington L. Rev.*, vols. 24, 25, 26 (1956–8)

ability of governments in contract have at last been widely recognized in the major common-law jurisdictions,[14] the legal analysis of government contracts is a matter of growing importance.

The admission that English legal practice and theory is hardly yet aware of government contracts as a category distinct from private contracts does not mean that there is not, in fact, such a category. But this branch of the law is hidden in standard conditions of governments, where the real 'living law' of today is to be found.[14] From these standard conditions, the individual contractor is no more able to depart in his bid for government contracts than an individual insurer can modify the standard terms of insurance contracts, or the passenger of an ocean liner or an aeroplane can modify the conditions of transportation. Much of the law of the *droit administratif* will be found in these standard terms: the continuing power of the government officer to give directions as to the carrying out of the work; the unilateral power of the government authority to require alterations in the work done under the contract, subject to adjustment of the contract price; repayment of liquidated damages in the event of default; and, most important of all, the liberty of the Government to terminate the contract at any time by notice in writing, subject to compensation for work done. In fact, the terms of compensation for the contract in the event of termination by the Government are more favourable to the Government than those elaborated by the French courts. The default clause of the Standard Building Contract, used by local authorities in Britain, provides that, given certain stated conditions of default, the public employer may

---

and the articles by Miller, 'Government contracts and social control', 41 *Virginia L. Rev.* 27 (1955); Pasley, 'The interpretation of government contracts', 25 *Fordham L. Rev.* 211 (1956).

14. For the United States, see the Tucker Act of 1887; for the United Kingdom, see section 1 of the Crown Proceedings Act 1947; and for the Commonwealth, see the brief survey in Street (1953, p. 6). Since then the Canadian Crown Liability Act 1952–3 (*Statutes of Canada*, ch. 30, s. 3), and the Petition of Rights Act (RSC. 1952, ch. 158), have made the Federal Government in Canada generally liable in contract and tort.

15. See, for example, General Conditions of Government Contracts for Building and Civil Engineering Works, form CCC/Wks 1 (1959). See also Turpin, 'Government contracts: a study of methods of contracting', 31 *Mod. L. Rev.* 241 (1968).

determine the employment of the contractor by registered notice.

Although it has frequently been said that government contracts are governed by general principles of contract law,[16] recent students of the subject have pointed out the distinctive features of the government contract in terms that show the similarity of problems and solutions imposed by the functions of modern government on systems as fundamentally different as French and American law.

To begin with, a government contract is a contract of adhesion, that is to say, a contract with standard terms and conditions, prepared by one party and offered to the other on a take-it-or-leave-it basis. The consensual element is reduced to a minimum. . . . Obviously, principles of general contract law, based on theories of freedom of contract, can have little application to such a clause.

Also, a government contract is apt to differ markedly from a private contract in the very feature which lies at the heart of the traditional contract relationship: the concept of a voluntary assumption of risk, agreed to by parties dealing at arm's length. Many government contracts are nothing of the sort. Between the two extremes of the simple purchase order and the cost-reimbursement-no-fee research contract is every variety of pricing and risk-taking arrangement. . . . Hanging over all government contracts and sub-contractors is the prospect of renegotiation to recapture excessive profits. In short, while the risk element is still present (the Government does not insure contractors against loss), the simple bargain-exchange of the typical private contract has been transformed into something much more complicated. Risk of loss and prospect of profit have become interwoven into a whole complex of tangled relationships, which only the lawyer and cost-accountant can fully understand.[17]

Federal contracts in the United States used to contain provisions that the decision of the federal contracting agent would be final as to disputes over questions of fact,[18] or, in some cases, as to questions of law as well.[19] Such clauses have recently been outlawed by statute which provides that final decisions by the administrative authority to the contract on questions of law are no longer permitted, and that

16. e.g. *Reading Steel Casting Co.* v. *US*, 268 U.S. 186 (1925) and some of the opinions in the *Bethlehem Steel Case*, 315 U.S. 289.

17. Pasley, 'The non-discrimination clause in government contracts', 43 *Virginia L. Rev.* 846 (1957).

18. *US* v. *Wunderlich*, 342 U.S. 98 (1951).

19. *US* v. *Moorman*, 338 U.S. 457 (1950).

findings of fact can be set aside whenever 'fraudulent or capricious or arbitrary or so grossly erroneous as necessarily to imply bad faith, or . . . not supported by substantial evidence'.[20] Apart from the outlawing of this particularly obnoxious form of inequality, there is no doubt that, despite a general statement that the contractual relations between the United States and contractors are governed by rules of law applicable to contracts between individuals,[21] 'there are so many exceptions to this generalization . . . that government-contract law is often treated as a special field of its own'.[22] This applies, for example, to the necessarily different and stricter rules about agency and authority to contract on behalf of the government; or to the problems created by governmental action which causes impossibility of performance. Here, the dual capacity of one of the contracting parties, as a government taking action binding on all its citizens, and as a party to an individual contract between itself and a private person, becomes relevant. Such problems, known in French jurisprudence as '*le fait du prince*', are no less relevant in common-law jurisdictions, for the dual position of public authority is the same. Nor is the answer to the problem any different. In the United States the general rule is that the Government is said to act in its sovereign capacity whenever its acts are public and general in their application, so that they are not considered as directed against the other con-tracting party alone, and therefore entail no sanction for breach of contract. Although it has been suggested that, where the Government, for reasons of general public policy, creates conditions that make the performance of the contract impossible, it should be held liable to pay the fair value of the benefits received in quasi contract,[23] this does not affect the basic fact that government contracts are not just another species of private contracts.

The fact that the common law recognizes in theory only one type of contract has, however, another consequence: in the legal systems that know both private and public-law contracts a commitment

20. 41 U.S.C. § 321. See the Note on 'Remedies against the United States', 70 *Harvard L. Rev.* (1957), p. 887. The difficulties of distinguishing between questions of fact and law have, in the light of recent court practice, been analysed by Pasley, 'The interpretation of government contracts', 25 *Fordham L. Rev.* 219–22 (1956).
21. *Lynch* v. *US*, 292 U.S. 571, 579 (1934).
22. 70 *Harvard L. Rev.*, p. 884.
23. See 70 *Harvard L. Rev.*, p. 886.

given by a public authority to a private party, under conditions which make it justifiable to assume a legal commitment, can be allocated to the sphere of either private or public-law contract. The remedies for the other party are, as we have seen, not identical, but they are substantial in either case, and, in some respects, the position of the private party in the *contrat administratif* is more favourable than that of a party to a private contract.

In the common law, however, the alternative is between contract according to the common law or no legal tie at all. Hence, common-law courts often find themselves in the difficult position of having to hold public authorities, especially state governments or municipal authorities, in circumstances where no standard conditions apply, either liable for contract under common-law rules, or not held by any contractual commitment at all.

Reference has already been made to the *Amphitrite* case, which may, however, be justified as dealing with the freedom of government in matters of international policy, especially in wartime. A contrary tendency, to make governments liable for promises made by the authorized officers to individuals, was encouraged by the decision of Denning J. (as he then was) in *Robertson* v. *Minister of Pensions*.[24] The Minister of Pensions attempted to revoke the acceptance by the War Office of liability to pay a disability pension to an officer injured in the war, partly on the ground that it amounted to a fetter on the future executive action of the Crown. In his judgement, Denning J. sought to liken the formal promise of a government authority to an individual to a contractual commitment not revocable by unilateral Crown action. Reference has also been made to the decision of the Court of Appeal, which found that the Minister of Town and Country Planning could not be hampered in the exercise of his planning functions by the existence of a previous contractual commitment of a local authority, although, alternatively, the court suggested that that commitment had not been of a contractual nature at all. On the other hand, in another post-war case,[25] a local education authority which, on the outbreak of the last war, had

24. [1949] 1 K.B. 227. This decision was criticized in *Howell* v. *Falmouth Boat Construction Co*. [1951] A.C. 837, at 845, 849.
25. *Turberville* v. *West Ham Corp*. [1950] 2 K.B. 203.

promised employees joining the forces certain pay increments which they would have received in the ordinary way, was held by the Court of Appeal to have 'entered into a contract voluntarily, and when they made payments under such a contract, they did so in pursuance of the contract, and not in the execution of any public duty'. However, another decision of the same court denied that a local authority could be hampered in the exercise of its public-health functions by contractual ties.[26] Unquestionably, many of these decisions were prompted by individual considerations of equity and fairness. Nevertheless, the situation remains confused, and the state of the authorities most uncertain.[27] While the *contrat administratif*, as developed by the Conseil d'État, has many features which cannot be easily detached from the peculiar structure and traditions of the French legal system, the case for open recognition, and appropriate regulation, of contracts between government and other public authorities on the one part, and private individuals on the other is overwhelming.[28] The Renegotiation Acts in the United States, which were the reaction to situations created by wartime contracts of the *Bethlehem Steel* case type (see p. 127), underline the necessity to regard the contracts made between government and private parties in a mixed economy, often in fields of defence and other matters of vital public interest, as cooperative efforts subject to certain legal rules – like partnerships and other social compacts – rather than as contracts subject to rules shaped centuries ago for entirely different conditions and social systems.

Some of the constitutional and other legal problems of contracts to which governments are parties (such as authorization by Congress or the necessity of parliamentary approval for expenditure (Mitchell,

26. *William Cory & Son Ltd* v. *City of London Corp.* [1951] 2 K.B. 476.

27. Professor Street, after a lucid comparative discussion of government liability in England, the United States, and France, criticizes the French jurisprudence for 'the lack of precision consequent upon a denial of the binding force of precedent' (1953, p. 77). Whatever the weaknesses and uncertainties of French jurisprudence, it can hardly exceed that of the corresponding jurisprudences of the common-law countries. Indeed, elsewhere in his book, Professor Street concedes that the main objection to the present English system is the lack of certainty (p. 104).

28. cf Street, 1953, p. 104; Note in 70 *Harvard L. Rev.*, p. 886.

1954, p. 68)) can probably be avoided where a semi-autonomous government corporation can take the place of government departments.[29]

The legal status of the public servant

Brief reference should be made to the complex problem of the legal status of the public servant. In this field, too, the insufficient elaboration of public-law relationships as being distinctly legal in character, but different from civil-law relationships, has created, and still continues to cause, in the common-law jurisdictions, an unsatisfactory mixture of lingering feudal concepts, public-law concepts and civil-law concepts.[30]

Generally, it may be a fair summary of many conflicting and uncertain decisions to say that, both in Britain and the United States, a civil servant, well below the level of policy-making or other senior officers, may be dismissed at pleasure, as an exercise of what, in Britain, is still the prerogative of the Crown, and in the United States, the general executive power of the President.[31] The relatively few subsequent decisions dealing with this point seem to be inconclusive in both systems.[32] Much uncertainty prevails on the point to what extent central governments as well as other public authorities may exclude the power of arbitrary dismissal by contract, although in Britain at least, statutory authorities (i.e. in particular

29. On the position of the government corporation (public corporation in English terminology), see further pp. 419–22.

30. For a discussion of the conditions governing the appointment and removal of federal officials in the United States, see Gellhorn and Byse (1970, pp. 97–102); for comparative surveys of the position in Great Britain and the United States, with brief observations on the comparative French position, see Griffith and Street (1967, pp. 270–74); also Street (1953, p. 111).

31. The leading cases are, for Britain, *Dunn* v. *R*. [1896] 1 Q.B. 116; and for the United States, *Myers* v. *US*, 272 U.S. 52 (1926). But in *Wiener* v. *US* (357 U.S. 349 (1955)), the Supreme Court denied the President's power to remove at will a member of an adjudicatory commission.

32. See, for Britain, the contradictory dicta in *Reilly* v. *R*. [1934] A.C. 179 (Lord Atkin); *Rodwell* v. *Thomas* [1944] K.B. 602; and *Robertson* v. *Minister of Pensions* [1949] 1 K.B. 231. For the United States, see *Morgan* v. *TVA*, 115 F. 2nd 990 (C.A.6, 1940), cert., denied, 312 U.S. 701; *Wiener* v. *US*, 357 U.S. 349 (1958).

local authorities) do not share the privileged position of the Crown (Griffith and Street, 1967, pp. 270–2). On the other hand, it appears to be established in the US but not in Britain, that a public servant may sue for accrued pay, a question obviously different in principle from the question of dismissibility.[33]

It should be added that the actual position of public servants, especially in regard to pay, pensions, etc., is now largely regulated by statute, and in practice more secure than would appear from the general legal rules governing civil servants in the common-law systems.[34] The problem of dismissibility at will remains, however, one of great significance, not only in theory, but also of practical importance in times of public nervousness and preoccupation with security and loyalty considerations.[35] Again, the position is dramatically different in the Continental jurisdictions, long schooled in the dichotomy of civil and administrative law. It may be that the very elaborate structure of *Beamtenrecht*, characteristic of the German legal system,[36] is to some extent due to the high status of the *Beamte* in that country. But the principle of statutory regulation of the status rights, and duties of the civil servant is also implemented in France.[37] The statutory regulations in both countries amount to a complete code defining the obligations and rights of the public servant.

33. *Fisk* v. *Jefferson Police Jury* (1885) 116 U.S. 131; *O'Leary* v. *US*, 77 Ct Cl. 635 (1933); contrast *Lucas and High Commissioner for India* [1943] P. 68, and the critical article by D. W. Logan, 'A civil servant and his pay' in 61 *L.Q. Rev.* (1945), pp. 240 et seq.

34. However, there is a growing army of temporary public servants in a variety of government programmes, often dependent on shifting policies (e.g. in the field of foreign information services and broadcasting) and the whims of appropriation committees.

35. See, for example, the decision of the United States Supreme Court in *Bailey* v. *Richardson* 341 U.S. 918 (1951), affirming by an evenly divided vote the majority judgement of the lower court that a civil servant could not claim that she had been denied due process in a loyalty order proceeding, because she had no legally protectable interest to which the due process could apply.

36. See the *Bundesbeamtengesetz* of 1953 in conjunction with the *Bundes-disziplinarordnung* of 1952, and the express constitutional provision, both in the Weimar Constitution and the Bonn Constitution, that no statute must exclude the ability of a civil servant to sue for his pay in the ordinary civil courts.

37. See the Law of 19 October 1946.

For Dicey, the principle that the government servant was personally liable for wrongs committed in the exercise of his public functions – coupled with the then prevailing immunity of the Crown from any corresponding liability – was a vindication of the principle of equality before the law.

With us every official, from the Prime Minister down to a constable or a collector of taxes, is under the same responsibility for every act done without legal justification as any citizen (1939, p. 193).

Today, the very opposite philosophy may be said to predominate among the students of this problem.[38] The scope, as well as the delicacy of the multitudinous functions of public service that affect private interests, is seen to be demanding freedom of action unhampered by fears of personal liability, which could, in many cases, ruin the individual officer concerned, and thus would lead to a general attitude of excessive caution and passivity, detrimental to the public interest. In fact, the whole doctrine of the common law has long ceased to have much vitality, mainly by the exemption, either through traditional 'prerogatives' of the Crown, or, more frequently in recent times, through the scope of discretionary powers granted to public officials by the relevant statutes (Davis, 1959, pp. 469–70, 479; Gellhorn and Byse, 1970, pp. 290–321). A case like *Miller* v. *Horton*,[39] where a public-health officer vested with statutory authority to destroy diseased animals was held liable for the destruction of the plaintiff's horse which he wrongly believed to be infected with the disease, is difficult to imagine today. But, of course, the extension of the personal immunity of public officers makes all the more urgent the problem of the corresponding extension of governmental responsibility.

The problem of state liability for tortious actions – and, to a considerable extent, for interferences with private interests beyond the realm not only of fault, but of tort altogether – has long ceased to be a major juristic problem in Continental jurisdictions, although a number of new problems has arisen through the very recognition of

38. See, for example, Jennings, 'Tort liability of administrative officers', 21 *Minnesota L. Rev.* 263 (1937); Davis (1959, pp. 469–80); Schwartz (1954, p. 250).
39. 152 Mass. 540 (1891).

state liability. Contemporary French law is based on the distinction between *faute de service* and *faute personnelle*. The public official is personally liable for a wrong committed by him *hors de l'exercise de ses fonctions* (Waline, 1963, § 1366). This is construed fairly widely, for personal fault includes not only such action clearly 'outside the scope of employment' as the use of a government motor-car for personal business,[40] but also any act characterized as malicious or grossly negligent, e.g. commitment, in error, of persons to a mental instead of an ordinary hospital, or a hospital for prostitutes (Waline, 1963, § 1369–70). The public official is thus not personally immune from liability, even for acts which might be construed by Anglo-American courts as being, however objectionably, committed in the exercise of public functions. Personal liability is, in French jurisprudence, in a sense a penalty for such actions as are so clearly unworthy of public office as not to be properly attributable.[41] But in the overwhelming majority of cases, including even most cases of excess of statutory power (Waline, 1963, § 1372), the personal liability of the individual official – before the ordinary civil courts – is replaced by the liability of the state before the administrative courts.[42]

The development in German law has been somewhat similar, under parallel and partly overlapping provisions of the German Civil Code[43] and of both the Weimar Constitution and the Bonn *Grundgesetz* of 1949 (art. 34). Under these provisions, the state is liable to a third party for any delictual conduct of a public official in the exercise of a public function, and in violation of an official duty owed to a third party. In the case of negligent conduct, state liability is, in principle, subsidiary, although this direct liability of the official plays no greater part in modern conditions than it does in the Anglo-American jurisdictions by virtue of the discretionary statutory exemptions. Contrary to French law, however, all actions against the state,

40. e.g. *Affaire Pastor*, C.E. 28 November 1947.

41. For this and other reasons, the leading modern textbook (Waline, 1963) rejects the terminology of '*faute de service*' and '*faute personnelle*', for which the concept of '*faute détachable de l'exercice des fonctions*' is substituted (§ 1365).

42. Attribution of the whole field of state liability for damages to private individuals to the administrative courts goes back to the decision of the Cour des Conflits in the *Pelletier* case of 1873.

43. Art. 839 BGB.

arising from liability for violation of duty to a private party, must be brought before the civil, not the administrative, courts.[44]

The precise delimitation between acts committed in exercise of a public function for service, and those not connected with such service, with an intermediate category, in French law, of 'service-connected' torts, have, of course, been the subject of innumerable decisions and controversies. This, however, is not a criticism against the principle and the distinction as such – which only illustrates the basic difficulty of applying any general definition to concrete cases.[45] The principle that responsibility for illegal interference with the protected interests of the citizen is primarily a responsibility of the public authority in whose service the officer stands rather than of the individual concerned, is firmly and irrevocably established in the Continental jurisdictions, even though they differ on the allocation of these matters to civil or administrative courts.

The recognition of state liability has, in fact, gone far beyond the traditional fault liability. This is, in part, due to the evolution of the law of tort itself, which, particularly in France, by a creative interpretation of article 1384 C.C., has adapted the principles prevalent at the beginning of the nineteenth century to the vastly more complex conditions of the industrialized society of the second half of the twentieth century.

However, it is still the prevalent view that, in the sphere of the private law of tort, fault should remain the rule, since it is concerned with the problem of adjustment of a burden between two private parties and that it is still generally a proper principle that, as between two innocent parties, the burden should lie where it falls.[46] But in the field of public-law responsibility, the position is different. As it has been stated in a leading French treatise, [47] damage to private persons arises often from actions taken in the public interest, deliberately. The prejudice caused to the private party is, in such cases, a kind of

44. See article 839 BGB.

45. For an illuminating comparative survey, see Schwartz (1954, ch. 9) and regarding the present state of the French law, in particular, p. 276.

46. The extension of modern tort liability is, in fact, largely derived from the widening of the notion of responsibility, which makes the transition between presumed fault, and actions or omissions apt to cause damage without 'fault' a fluid one.

47. H. and L. Mazeaud, *Traité de la responsabilité* (4th edn), no. 353.

public charge, which, in accordance with the principle of equality, should not accidentally rest with the one or small number of persons affected by the public measure, but be redistributed among the members of the community, through the responsibility for compensation attached to the public authority.[48] Accordingly, state responsibility under French law has been extended not only to *responsabilité du fait des choses*, i.e. to responsibility for damages arising from dangerous operations,[49] or to movable and immovable objects for which the state ought to assume responsibility, because they are under its control (notably motor-cars) – for these are extensions parallel to those of the civil law by the jurisprudence of the civil courts – or for *risques professionels* – a kind of workmen's compensation principle in public law – but also for what is called the *risque social* (Waline, 1963) i.e. for public disorders of varying magnitude. In a similar vein, the principle of liability for dangerous activities has, in the field of public law, been extended to the consequences of general measures justified by public necessity – such as ammunition depots[50] – but apt by their very existence to cause damage to various sections of the public field. In commenting on developments since *Regnault-Desroziers*, the most recent survey of administrative jurisprudence (Long, Weil and Braibant, 1969, pp. 153–6) observes that *responsabilité sans faute* is today extensive, as shown by a decision of the *Conseil d'État* in 1968, which held the state responsible for the 'special and abnormal' risks caused to a child of a pregnant teacher by contagious disease.[51] Nevertheless, the liability of public authorities is still based on the fault principle. Thus, the *Conseil d'État* has refused to extend the risk theory to harm caused by voluntary vaccination.[52]

Since the Second World War, the jurisdictions of the British

48. The Mazeaud theory is quoted with evident approval by Waline (1963, §§ 1530–33).

49. *Cie. du gaz de Lyon*, 1919, and subsequent decisions quoted in Waline (1963, § 1462).

50. *L'arrêt Regnault-Desroziers*, S., 1919.3.25, note Hauriou; D., 1920.3.1, note Appleton; *R.D.P.*, 1919.239, concl. Corneille, note Jèze.

51. C.E., 6 November 1968, *Ministre de l'Education nationale c. Dame Saulze*, *Rev. admin.* 1969, p. 174, note Chaudet.

52. C.E., 7 March 1958, *Secrétaire d'Etat à la santé publique c. Dejous*, Rec. 153.

Commonwealth[53] have, at last, abolished the privileges which had originated in feudal English doctrine of the immunity of the sovereign. Such doctrine rested basically on an identification of the person of the sovereign with the state; this has never been explicitly abandoned in Britain, where the Government is still exercising its functions in the name of His or Her Majesty. The King as a person is today entirely different from the King as the nominal head of government. The theory of the immunity of the sovereign had, in fact, become a theory that 'government can do no wrong'. The British Crown Proceedings Act of 1947 states: 'the Crown shall be subject to all those liabilities in tort to which, if it were a private person of full age and capacity, it would be subject in respect of torts committed by its servants or agents'.[54] It is furthermore liable for breach of duties of an employer to an employee and for breach of the duties attaching at common law to the ownership, occupation, possession or control of property. While some difficulties have arisen from the definition of 'agent or servant',[55] the British Act, and those modelled on it in the Commonwealth, can be fairly said to have established government liability in tort on a basis of equality between governors and governed, in so far as the position of government is not inherently different (as, for example, in the substitution of an authorizing order for a writ of execution against the Crown). In particular, the British Act is free from the qualifications which, as will be seen, greatly restrict the scope of the liability of government in the US Federal Tort Claims Act. In so far, for example, as tort liability is, in contemporary English law, strict and not fault liability, government liability will be the same.

However, as an eminent British judge has pointed out (Mac-Dermott, 1957, p. 108), the very fact that government liability in tort has been hitched on to private-tort liability, has prevented the courts from 'settling the general nature of the duties owed by the executive to the subject outside the realm of contract'. A subsection provides that no action shall lie against the Crown in respect of torts com-

53. The Commonwealth of Australia had established the principle of tort liability in the federal sphere as early as 1903.
54. Section 2.
55. Some of these relate to the relation of the semi-autonomous public corporation to the Government (see further p. 421).

mitted by its servants or agents, 'unless the act or omission would apart from the provisions of this Act, have given rise to this cause of action in tort against that servant or agent or his estate'. This means, according to Lord MacDermott, 'that a plaintiff has to show that, apart from the Act, his loss was due to the negligence of some official of a Ministry who would have been *personally* liable if he had been sued'. There may, however, be cases in which the government should be held responsible to a private person, even though the official acting for it would not have been so liable, e.g. where a Ministry negligently delays the issue of a trading licence (MacDermott, 1957, p. 108).[56] In other words, there may be public-law duties which find no parallel in the private law of tort. This underlines again the need for the common law to develop a public law, of tort as of contract, not as a mere appendix to the private law.

It is one of the great ironies of legal history that British immigrants who left the country in protest against autocracy and oppression, took with them, not only the great principles of the common law, but also those aspects of the common law which were expressions of absolutism and feudalism. After early hesitations,[57] United States courts wholeheartedly embraced the doctrine of sovereign immunity during the nineteenth century, and this doctrine survives to the present day in a majority of the state jurisdictions, while it has been curtailed, though not abolished, in the federal sphere. Meanwhile, England, whence the doctrine came, has abolished it.

Not only did the American courts introduce the doctrine of sovereign immunity into the republican setting of the United States but they extended it to municipal corporations, as subdivisions of states, at a time when the decision of Blackburn J. in *Mersey Docks and Harbour Board Trustees* v. *Gibbs*[58] denied its application to statutory authorities. In this manner, public authorities other than organs of the general government of the country were subjected to the ordinary liabilities of the common law. But not so in the United States.

56. See also *Dorset Yacht Co. Ltd* v. *Home Office* [1970] 2 W.L.R. 1140 (H.L.), which held the Home Office liable for the negligence of three borstal officers in allowing the escape of seven borstal trainees, during which they caused significant damage to sailing vessels used in the escape.

57. e.g., *Chisholm* v. *Ga.*, 2 U.S. 419 (1793).

58. (1866) L.R. 1 H.L. 93.

Today, the Federal Tort Claims Act of 1946 recognizes government liability in principle, but subject to certain exceptions. Of these, the exceptions for claims arising out of wilful torts,[59] for acts or omissions 'based upon the exercise or performance or the failure to exercise or perform a discretionary function or duty on the part of a federal agency or an employee of the Government', and the limitation of liability to claims based on 'negligent or wrongful' acts or omissions, which follows from the limitation of the clause conferring jurisdiction upon the district courts for claims against the United States,[60] are the most important. Of these exceptions, the one limiting tort liability to 'fault' seems unreasonable, in view of the extension of general liability in tort far beyond the fault principle. It is in contrast to the above-mentioned Continental trends towards state liability for dangerous operations and, beyond that, for risk situations created by state action. Nor has this limitation of federal tort liability any parallel in the British corresponding legislation. Without it, the action in *Dalehite* (see p. 392) would probably have succeeded. The main difficulty of the 'discretionary' exception is its vagueness, and the consequent uncertainties and vacillations in judicial interpretation, which we have discussed earlier. If, however, as has been suggested here in accordance with the views of Professor Davis,[61] it is interpreted as separating the planning from the operational level, it is a good and, indeed, an inevitable limitation which must be accepted in every legal system.

Government immunities are still strongly entrenched in most of the fifty state jurisdictions. The most recent surveys[62] show that, to date, only twenty-two out of fifty states have abrogated some aspects of governmental immunity. Often this has been limited to municipal corporations, i.e. statutory authorities which in Britain were denied the privileges of government immunity over a century ago. In a number of states, the initiative for the elimination of government immunities has come from the judiciary, but in some cases the legislature intervened to restore the former position. Thus, in 1959,

59. See in detail 28 U.S.C., § 2680(*a*).
60. See 28 U.S.C. § 1346.
61. 40 *Minnesota L. Rev.*, pp. 785, 789.
62. Harper and James (1956, supp. 1968, §§ 29.1, 29.11); van Alstyne, 'Government tort liability: a decade of change', 1966 *University of Illinois L. Forum* 919.

the Supreme Court of Illinois, in a convincingly reasoned decision held – prospectively, i.e. without application to the case before it – that local authorities should no longer be exempt from liability for negligence, e.g. where children riding in a school bus had been injured by negligence of the driver.[63] The Illinois Legislature promptly intervened to restore the immunity doctrine, but some years later (1965) passed another statute that accepted the reasoning and principles of Molitor. The Supreme Court of California, in 1961, went even further by overruling the old immunity doctrine retroactively[64] and set in motion an inquiry that led to a legislative reform in 1963.

Some attempts have been made to limit immunities to 'governmental' as distinct from 'proprietary' activities. It is hardly necessary to add to the many criticisms of the logical fallacy and practical absurdity of the distinction between 'governmental' and 'non-governmental' functions. Such justification as there exists for it derives from extra-legal considerations: the desire to protect the impecunious small authority from liability.[65] But, as has been stated before, the remedy for such a state of affairs should be administrative and budgetary reorganization, not the shifting of the burden to the helpless victims of particular accidents. In 1955, a majority of the Supreme Court justices described the distinction as a 'quagmire that has long plagued the law of municipal corporations'.[66] The quagmire is well illustrated by one of hundreds of decisions,[67] where the plaintiff had been injured when her hand struck a barbed wire fence while in a swimming pool owned and operated by the City of Richmond. After a careful survey of the cases which have, for example, held the operation of hospitals or the regulation of streets, maintenance of police forces and the removal of garbage to be governmental functions, while the operation of a wharf and the conducting of public utilities, such as gaslight and sewage systems, is 'proprietary', the court finally held the swimming-pool operation to

63. *Molitor* v. *Kaneland Community Unit District No. 302*, 18 Ill. 2nd 11, 163 N.E. 2nd 89 (1959).

64. *Muskopf* v. *Corning Hospital District*, 395 P. 2nd 457 (Cal. 1961).

65. This is comparable to the desire to protect charitable medical institutions from liability by the now equally discredited distinction of 'administrative' and 'medical' functions.

66. *Indian Towing Co.* v. *US*, 350 U.S. 61, 65 (1955).

67. *Hoogart* v. *City of Richmond*, 172 Va. 145, 200 S.E. 610 (1939).

be 'proprietary', because it could best be compared to the furnishing of water for domestic purposes. Yet, the municipal swimming pool is obviously designed for the promotion of public health and recreation.

The distinction is misconceived, and other than arbitrary answers to the question whether a particular activity belongs to the one or the other category are impossible, because the test artificially divides and truncates the ubiquitous functions of public authority which, today, extend to a multitude of businesslike operations that are nevertheless conducted for the general welfare.

Meanwhile, the situation is mitigated by a number of practical devices.[68] The most important ways by which the theoretical severity of government immunity is mitigated in practice are the following:

1. In many cases – such as the Texas City explosion, which was the subject of the *Dalehite* case – private laws are passed granting compensation and assuming liability, often irrespective of fault.[69]

2. A vast number of claims sounding in tort are settled by administrative machinery, through government departments, such as the departments for the Army, the Interior and the Postmaster-General.

3. Employees who are held personally liable, are frequently indemnified by the authority in whose service they are.

4. It is sometimes possible to bring a claim for wrongful injury not under the heading of tort, but under that of 'taking of property', which is subject to just compensation.[70]

5. Many of the public authorities take out liability insurance, the terms of which often specifically exclude the defence of sovereign immunity.[71]

68. See Gellhorn and Lauer, 'Congressional settlement of tort claims against the United States', 55 *Columbia L. Rev.* 1 (1955); Gellhorn and Lauer, 'Federal liability for personal property damage', 29 *New York University L. Rev.* 1325 (1954); Davis, 'Tort liability of governmental units', 40 *Minnesota L. Rev.* 751, 757 (1955).

69. During the 82nd Congress (1951–3), for example, 123 tort claims were recognized by statutory settlement. Gellhorn and Lauer, 29 *New York University L. Rev.*, p. 1330.

70. A well-known example is *US* v. *Causby*, 328 U.S. 256 (1946), where the owner of a chicken farm recovered damages from the United States for the injury done to his property, i.e. to the airspace immediately above his land, by very low flying, considered as 'an invasion of the surface'.

71. Liability insurance is, in most cases, the best answer to the argument that liability and tort would burden smaller authorities to an undue and unforeseeable extent.

Granted all these concessions and mitigations of the harshness of an antiquated principle, the legal situation remains unsatisfactory. The various exceptions depend upon legislative or administrative action, by a multitude of federal, state and municipal authorities. Compensation is not a matter of law, but of concession. Moreover, a bad legal theory is perpetuated, obscuring an understanding of the greatly changed functions and methods of modern government and entailing the retention of basically misconceived legal criteria, such as the distinction between 'governmental' and 'proprietary' functions.

Legal status of government enterprise

The steady multiplication of government functions of all kinds, as well as the increasing complexity of carrying out such modern government functions as the operation of vast public utilities, and, in some cases, industries, the provision of hospital and many other social services, or the administration of government loans to business, has, during the present century, led to the development of a new type of public institution, designed to overcome the antithesis of government and business, as it still survives in the judicial distinction between 'governmental' and 'proprietary' or 'business' activities of public authorities. Hence, the public corporation,[72] an institution 'clothed with the power of governments but possessed of the flexibility and initiative of a private enterprise',[73] has, since the end of the First World War, become a familiar device for the organization of public enterprises and services, in many different countries and legal systems.[74]

It co-exists with departmental government enterprises and

72. The term 'public corporation', used in the countries of the British Commonwealth, where this institution has been developed to great theoretical and practical significance, is used here, rather than the usual American term: 'government corporation'. As will be seen, the difference in terminology reflects to some extent a difference in legal theory.

73. President Roosevelt's message to Congress in 1933 recommending the formation of the TVA.

74. For comparative surveys of the role and legal status of the public corporation see Friedmann (1954); Hanson (1963); Hanson (1955); Friedmann and Garner (1970).

commercial companies in which the government holds controlling interest. A survey of these different types of public enterprises has been given in an earlier chapter (see pp. 340–42).

The legal form of public enterprise affects its legal status and liabilities. While departmental enterprises share the legal status and responsibilities of the government department to which they belong and state participations in commercial companies are governed by commercial law, the legal responsibilities of public corporations have become a subject of divergent practices and controversy. In Continental systems, which have the theoretical and jurisdictional duality between private and administrative law and jurisdiction, the main difficulties are caused by the growing artificiality of the distinction between *gestion privée* (civil courts) and *gestion publique* (administrative courts) with respect to public corporations, whose purpose is the carrying out of public purposes in the forms of commercial organization and transactions. The understandably great difficulties and chanciness of characterisation of a transaction as public or private, at a time when both the basic functions and the methods of state economic activity are quite different from the period of *laissez-faire* and the night-watchman state, have been analysed by recent writers (Mitchell, 1954, p. 167; Martin-Pannetier, 1966, pp. 39, 155). On the other hand, allocation of a transaction to private or administrative law does not entail the alternative between liability or legal immunity of the public corporation. The Continental systems have, under the guidance of the French *Conseil d'État*, developed elaborate and tough principles of legal liability, for government and other public authorities, especially through the *Contrat Administratif* (Waline, 1963, § 136–8; Mitchell, 1954, p. 167). The common-law world, on the other hand, still has no clear duality of systems and jurisdictions.[75] If the status of a public enterprise and its transactions are classified as being within the prerogatives of government, the 'shield of the Crown' applies. This is not now as serious as it was in the days of Dicey. Post-war British and Commonwealth legislation has generally abolished the government immunities in contract and tort, as a deliberate corollary to the expansion of state activities. Moreover, the British public corporations are fully liable, in contract,

75. On the *de facto* development of a public-law contract, see Mitchell (1954) and pp. 401–8.

tort and taxes. But important patches of the old doctrine remain. There are still 'Acts of State'. The Crown still has preferred creditor status and still benefits from the presumption that the Crown is not deemed to be bound by statute unless the contrary is specifically stipulated. And British courts still stubbornly, and almost alone in international practice, adhere to the absolute immunity of governments in international transactions, instead of adopting the distinction between commercial and non-commercial state activities accepted almost everywhere else.[76] The doctrine of the 'shield of the Crown' which necessitates a futile distinction between actions of public corporations that are and are not 'emanations of the Crown'[77] is not yet dead and buried, as it should be. But the realization that the public purposes of a public corporation should not imply legal immunity of privileges is gaining ground. In *Tamlin* v. *Hannaford*[78] the Court of Appeal (*per* Denning L.J.) stated that the British Transport Commission is 'in the eyes of the law . . . answerable as fully as any other person or corporation. . . . It is, of course, a public authority and its purposes, no doubt, are public purposes, but it is not a government department nor do its powers fall within the province of government.' It should follow from the very *raison d'être* of the public corporation – the organization of commercial state activities through separate, commercially managed and accountable legal persons – that they should be legally separated from the Crown.

It is in the United States that the combination of the failure to develop an adequate theory of public enterprise with the partial survival of government immunities has led to confusion as to the extent to which government corporations of a commercial character should be regarded as identical with the government, a question that arises mainly in the context of foreign government immunities before American courts. Some, but not all, extend government immunities to commercial government corporations, although unlike Britain the US has tentatively adopted the theory of restricted government

76. See *Baccus S.R.L.* v. *Servicio Nacional del Trigo*, [1957] 1 Q.B. 438, and pp. 479–82.

77. For criticism, see Sawer in Friedmann (1954, p. 38); Williams (1948, ch. 2); Friedmann, 'The shield of the crown', 29 *Australian L. J.* 275 (1950).

78. [1950] 1 K.B. 18. And see, for a more recent Australian decision in the same sense, *Professional Engineers' Case*, 107 C.L.R. 208 (1959).

immunity.[79] Internally, the regrettable refusal of American administrative lawyers to develop a theory of public enterprise has contributed to such unfortunate results as the exemption of revenue-earning public enterprises, like the TVA – which makes payments 'in lieu of taxes' – from income tax. An adequate theory of government enterprise, reflecting the functions of government in a mixed economy, remains an urgent task.

79. For conflicting decisions, see, e.g. *US* v. *Deutsches Kalisyndikat*, 3 F. 2d 199 (1929) and *Re Investigation of World Arrangements*, 13 F.R.D. 280 (1952). The 1965 *Restatement of the Foreign Relations Law of the United States* extends the immunity of governments to government corporations. This is in line with post-war US legislation reducing government corporations to departmental operations tightly controlled by the Budget Bureau and Congress. For general critiques, see Wedderburn, 'Sovereign immunities of foreign public corporations', 6 *Int. & Comp. L.Q.* (1957), p. 290; Friedmann, in Friedmann and Garner (1970, pp. 322–5).

Chapter 12
The Problem of Administrative Remedies and Procedures

Where administrative justice is recognized as an equal and autonomous branch of judicial administration, designed to regulate the legal relations between public authority and citizen, the problem of remedies against administrative authorities is relatively simple.

French and German Approaches

In France the general administrative remedy is a petition filed by the person seeking review with the appropriate administrative court, and containing a summary statement of the facts, the grounds on which relief is sought, and the nature of the relief that is sought. This remedy is characterized by the utmost absence of technicalities (Schwartz, 1954, p. 120). Although the *Conseil d'État* requires an individual interest for any petitioner to have *locus standi*, this has been construed very liberally, so that, for example, any consumer of a product affected by administrative action is entitled to petition for review. Delays and complexities arise mainly from the difficulty, in some cases, of deciding whether the civil or the administrative tribunals are competent, a matter over which the *Tribunal des Conflits* has ultimate jurisdiction, and on which delays may be protracted.

Perhaps even more significant are recent developments in Germany, where administrative law has been, and to a lesser extent still is, within the competence of the individual *Länder*. In most of these, notably in Prussia, administrative remedies were enumerative. Under the impact of Allied Military Government, which, in this field at least, wisely saw the value of the system of administrative justice and did not attempt to substitute common-law principles, the availability of the remedy has been greatly strengthened, so that now the so-called *Generalklausel* applies throughout Western Germany. The

Generalklausel gives anyone who claims to be injured in his rights by public power a right to legal redress (article 19, para. 4, *Gerichtsverfassungsgesetz*). The challenge is by petition, either for nullification (*Anfechtungsklage*), declaration (*Feststellungsklage*), or – and this is a significant innovation – for performance of an administrative act (*Vornahmeklage*) (Forsthoff, 1958, § 28).

Like France, Germany has no *actio popularis*, but any injury to a legitimate interest suffices, and the remedy is widely available.

There is thus no doubt that in the leading Continental systems there are, at the disposal of the aggrieved individual, simple and comprehensive remedies which may lead to the annulment of the challenged act, to a declaration of rights, to compensation,[1] or, under the post-war German reform, to a kind of equivalent of mandamus.[2]

Remedies in the Common-Law Systems

By contrast, the development of administrative-law remedies in the common-law sphere proceeded piecemeal from a variety of historical antecedents and, until well into the present century, without any recognition of the character and needs of administrative justice as a separate legal discipline.

An eminent American authority has both characterized and castigated the prevailing common-law system in no uncertain terms:

For no practical reason, the remedies are plural. A cardinal principle, now and then erratically ignored, denies one method of review when another is adequate. The lines are moved about through discussions of such concepts as judicial, non-judicial, discretionary and ministerial. These concepts are acutely unfortunate not only because they defy definition but because of the complete folly of using any concepts whatever to divide one remedy from another. [. . .]

The cure is easy. Establish a single, simple form of proceeding for all review of administrative action. Call it 'petition for review'. Get rid of

1. Which, in France, is, since the *Blanco* decision, handled by the administrative courts, but in Germany by the civil courts (see pp. 398, 411).
2. How far the injunction can be used in administrative proceedings is doubtful. Legal opinion in Germany is divided, since a number of writers argue that the preliminary injunction (*einstweilige Verfügung*) is not appropriate to administrative proceedings (see Forsthoff, 1958, p. 505).

extraordinary remedies as means of review. Focus attention then on the problems having significance – whether, when and how much to review (Davis, 1959, pp. 443, 444).

The cure prayed for by the learned author is, in fact, the law in Continental jurisdictions, such as those of France and Germany. While there is little sign of any response, in either the British or the American jurisdictions, to a simple uniform review procedure as a substitute for the multiplicity of present remedies, there are signs of tendencies to widen the scope of the administrative appeal.

Whether the revocation of a cab-driver's licence by a police commissioner,[3] or the exercise of disciplinary authority by a chief fire officer over a fireman,[4] or the granting of a licence for the Sunday opening of a cinema,[5] or the approval of a limited-dividend housing project by a state agency,[6] or the granting, modification, reversal or revocation of countless other licences, is 'administrative','judicial'or 'quasi-judicial' in character remains uncertain and controversial.[7]

The considerable but uncertain stretching of prerogative remedies, originally designed to cure excesses of jurisdiction, into some kind of appeal against decisions of administrative bodies has been aided by the use of various concepts designed to review the substance of the challenged decision.

First, the courts, in the examination of 'excess of power', have often gone into the so-called 'jurisdictional facts'. Following the lead given by Lord Esher, M.R. in *R.* v. *Commissioners for Special Purposes of the Income Tax*,[8] the action of an inferior 'court or tribunal or body' which has wrongly interpreted the facts constituting its jurisdiction (such as the definition of a 'park', 'an employee' or

3. *R.* v. *Metropolitan Police Commissioner* [1953] 1 W.L.R. 1150.

4. *Ex poste Fry* [1954] 1 W.L.R. 730.

5. *R.* v. *L. C. C., ex poste Entertainments Protection Association* [1931] 2 K.B. 215.

6. *Mount Hope Development Corpn* v. *James*, 258 N.Y. 510; 180 N.E. 252 (1932).

7. For a discussion of this subject, see, among innumerable other discussions, Davis (1959, chs. 23, 24) (U.S.); Griffith and Street (1967, pp. 144–8, 186–91, 242–3) (UK); Davis, 'Forms of proceeding', 44 *Illinois L. Rev.* 565 (1949); de Smith, 'Wrongs and remedies in administrative law', 15 *Mod. L. Rev.* (1952), 189; Wade, 'Courts and the administrative process', 63 *L.Q. Rev.* 164 (1947); Carrow, 'Types of judicial relief from administrative action', 58 *Columbia L. Rev.* (1958), p. 1; Benjafield, 'Statutory discretions', 2 *Sydney L. Rev.* (1956), p. 1.

8. (1888) 21 Q.B.D. 313.

'fitness for human habitation') has acted in excess of jurisdiction, so that the superior court can reconstrue these concepts.[9]

Second, the courts review so-called 'procedural defects', i.e. proceedings before the lower body alleged to constitute a 'denial of justice', e.g. by insufficient opportunity for the aggrieved to be heard, failure to give due notice of an impending decision, etc.[10]

Third, there is the so-called 'error of law on the face of the record' which, in an English leading case, has been extended to bodies that are not courts of record.[11] Where, upon the face of the record, it appears that the determination of the inferior tribunal is wrong in law, certiorari will be granted. Apart from documents which record the determination, documents which initiate the proceeding and the pleadings are also now included. The efficacy of such a remedy has been increased by the Tribunals and Inquiries Act 1958, section 12, which imposes the duty to supply reasons for a decision when requested on a large number of statutory tribunals and on Ministers notifying decisions after the holding of a statutory inquiry.

Fourth, in the United States the so-called 'substantial-evidence' rule enables a superior court to review findings of administrative bodies to determine whether they are supported by 'such relevant evidence as a reasonable mind might accept as adequate to support a conclusion. . . .'[12] But, on the whole, this review power has been exercised with considerable restraint.[13]

Lastly, there is the power of the superior courts to review adminis-

9. See *Harmon* v. *Brucker*, 358 U.S. 579 (1958). See also *Anisminic* v. *Foreign Compensation Commission* [1969] 1 All E.R. 208, 2 W.L.R. 163 (H.L.), see p. 395.

10. A duty to observe 'natural justice', e.g. notice of the charges and an opportunity to be heard, may arise by implication in any case involving the exercise of a power, whether characterized as 'judicial', 'quasi-judicial', or otherwise, that determines the rights of an individual, see *Ridge* v. *Baldwin*, [1964] A.C. 40, noted at 26 *Mod. L. Rev.* 543 (1963). For a discussion of the scope of 'natural justice', see de Smith (1968), pp. 135–230 (the right to a hearing) and pp. 231–63 (interest and bias).

11. *R.* v. *Northumberland Compensation Appeal Tribunal, ex p. Shaw* [1952] 1 Q.B. 338.

12. Hughes C.J. in *Consolidated Edison Co.* v. *N.L.R.B.*, 305 U.S. 197 (1938).

13. See decisions collected in Gellhorn and Byse (1970, pp. 334–61). But see *Harmon* v. *Brucker*, 358 U.S. 579 (1958) for a stronger exercise of review powers by the Supreme Court over a decision by military authority endowed with statutory finality.

trative decisions for 'abuse of discretion' or for being 'unreasonable'. This is the corner-stone of judicial review of administrative decisions, even in Continental systems (*détournement de pouvoir*). But this test can be and has been used at times to substitute the reviewing courts' own opinions and prejudices for those of the administrative body (see pp. 393–6).

Injunction and Declaratory Judgement as Administrative Remedies

In recent years two more 'ordinary' remedies have been added to this array of 'extraordinary' remedies: the injunction and the declaratory judgement. In the United States the injunction has, at least in the federal sphere, taken the place of certiorari, which was declared to be inapplicable to the review of administrative orders[14] but remains an important appellate remedy in the state jurisdictions.[15] In England the Attorney-General must be joined as the party applying for an injunction to the motion of a private individual, unless some private right of the plaintiff is interfered with or unless he suffers damage peculiar to himself from the interference with a public right (Griffith and Street, 1967, p. 250; de Smith, 1968, pp. 466, 472). But the remedy has become increasingly popular, for example, in judgements restraining trade unions and other 'domestic tribunals' from unlawfully expelling members.[16]

The declaratory judgement is the most ubiquitous, but perhaps the most generally useful, of the remedies now available in proceedings against administrative authorities. A good example is a decision of the English Court of Appeal.[17] The plaintiffs, a number of registered dock-workers, had been dismissed by the board manager, to whom the London Dock Labour Board had purported to delegate certain statutory disciplinary functions. They asked for a declaratory judgement that the delegation of power had been *ultra vires* and invalid. The Court of Appeal granted the declaratory judgement to the effect that there was no such power, and it also pointed out that certiorari could not have been obtained in this case because the plaintiffs did not know the facts. 'In certiorari there is no discovery, whereas in an

14. *Degge* v. *Hitchcock*, 229 U.S. 162 (1913).
15. See Carrow, 58 *Columbia L. Rev.* p. 2.
16. See de Smith (1968, pp. 489–90).
17. *Barnard* v. *National Dock Labour Board* [1953] 2 Q.B. 18.

action for a declaration it can be had.'[18] In the United States the declaratory judgement has been used in a number of cases where it was important for the petitioner to have a doubtful legal situation clarified, such as the obligation to obtain certain licences.

Finally, there are a considerable number of statutory appeals, usually on points of law or on a case stated from certain administrative bodies to a court of law.[19] In the United States this applies particularly to the federal sphere; statutory appeals are less frequent on the state and local levels. These statutory appeals bring administrative remedies much nearer to the ordinary appeal procedure, and they are steadily gaining in importance as legislative regulation of administrative procedures increases.

While the details of this complex subject-matter must be studied in the voluminous literature on this subject, the brief survey attempted here shows clearly that the pressure towards a widening scope of review against administrative decisions has been irresistible in the common-law jurisdictions, but that the methods of accomplishing it in part have led to an immensely complicated and confusing structure, still falling far short of a simple general remedy against wrongful administrative decisions.

The systematization and unification of the principles governing the review of administrative actions can be attempted either by the granting of a general right of reviewability of administrative decisions to the 'aggrieved' party; or by a reform of the machinery of justice, e.g. by the establishment of a general appeal court from administrative decisions; or by a combination of these two methods. To some extent the United States Administrative Procedure Act of 1946 chooses the first of these alternative methods, while the Report of the British Committee on Administrative Tribunals and Inquiries[20] concentrates on the second problem.

18. ibid, at p. 43, per Denning L.J. However, declaratory relief will not be granted where, as in *Punton* v. *Ministry of Pensions and National Insurance* (No. 2) [1964] 1 W.L.R. 226, the decision had been made within the Commissioner's jurisdiction and there was no means whereby it could be revoked or benefits paid. The appropriate remedy would be an order of certiorari to quash the error on record.

19. For a survey of the various forms of appeal in Australia see Benjafield and Whitmore (1971).

20. HMSO (1957), Cmnd 218.

However, the reservation of statutory exceptions from the right of review as well as of discretionary decisions, coupled with the uncertainty of the meaning of 'affected' or 'aggrieved', makes the scope of this apparent reform very uncertain.[21] The uncertainty of the state of the law is illustrated by a number of decisions arising from the dismissal of public employees on 'loyalty' grounds. In a strong criticism of observations on standing made by Frankfurter J. in *Adler* v. *Board of Education*,[22] where the action by a group of parents, teachers and taxpayers, alleging the unconstitutionality of a New York statute authorizing the dismissal of teachers suspected of 'advocating the overthrow of government' by virtue of membership of certain listed organizations, was dismissed, Professor Davis has formulated the following general principle of standing in matters of reviewability:

One whose interests are *in fact* subjected to or imminently threatened with substantial injury from governmental action satisfies the requirements of standing and ripeness to challenge the legality of that action unless for reasons of substantive policy the interests are undeserving of legal protection.[23]

Community Interests as 'Grievances'

The question remains what the substantive content is of such general concepts as 'interest', 'substantial injury' or 'abuse of discretion'. The meaning of such words is profoundly affected by changes in social values and public opinion. In this respect, there have been important judicial developments in the United States during the last few years. They reflect major, and yet unfinished, transformations in public thinking.[24] Broad identification of 'interest' or 'grievance' with certain economic and particularly property interests as the principal criterion of standing and ripeness

21. See the trenchant criticism by Davis (1959, p. 400).
22. 342 U.S. 485 (1952).
23. 'Standing, ripeness and civil liberties: a critique of *Adler* v. *Board of Education*', 38 *A.B.A.J.*, 924 et seq. (1952). As an example of an interest 'undeserving of legal protection', Professor Davis gives the interest of a business in freedom from new competition.
24. For the following survey, I am greatly indebted to an unpublished essay by Thomas E. Maloney, 'The new standing applied to eminent domain', prepared under the supervision of Professor Walter Gellhorn at the Columbia University Law School.

to challenge the legality of a public action is giving way to broader social criteria. Individuals and groups of citizens are, in a growing number of cases, held entitled to bring actions and challenge administrative decisions as representatives of environmental and other social interests. This is a development of potentially enormous significance. In 1951, Justice Frankfurter, in his concurring opinion in *Joint Anti-Fascist Refugee Committee* v. *McGrath*[25] had observed that a 'case or controversy', as used in Article III of the Constitution, presupposed that the plaintiff possesses 'adverse personal interest', in conflict with that of the defendant. And the Administrative Procedure Act of 1946 makes judicial review available to any 'person suffering legal wrong because of any agency action, or adversely affected or aggrieved by such action within the meaning of any relevant statute' (Section 10(a)). The change from a narrow definition of personal interest or grievance to the broader public perspective is illustrated by the landmark decision in *Scenic Hudson Preservation Conference* v. *FPC*.[26] Here an unincorporated association, formed by several non-profit conservation groups to press their opposition to a project approved by the Federal Power Commission, which authorized Consolidated Edison of New York to construct a pump storage hydro-electric plant on the scenic Storm King Mountain, was given standing to attack the FPC in court. The court held that the relevant statute had commanded the FPC to plan hydro-electric development in a way that would, among other criteria, further 'recreational purposes'. The court further held that 'a statute may create new interests or rights and thus give standing to one who would otherwise be barred by the lack of a "case or controversy".' No personal economic interest was required. Persons or groups who have exhibited a special interest in the aesthetic and recreational aspects of power development must therefore be held to be included in the class of 'aggrieved' parties. Another broadening of 'standing' occurred in a case where members of a television station's audience intervened in a broadcast licence renewal proceeding before the Federal Communication Commission.[27] The Court held, in an

25. 341 U.S. 123 (1951).
26. 345 F. 2d 608 (2nd Cir. 1965), cert. denied, 384 U.S. 941 (1966).
27. *Office of Communication of United Church of Christ* v. *F.C.C.*, 359 F. 2d 994 (D.C. Cir. 1966).

opinion delivered by then Judge Burger – now the Chief Justice of the United States – that the listening public had standing to intervene in protection of the public interest, even though the FCC, a public, regulatory agency, had been designated by law to serve the same purpose, i.e. the protection of the public interest. 'Intervention on behalf of the public is not allowed to press private interests but only to vindicate the broad public interest relating to a licensee's performance of the public trust inherent in every licence.'[28]

Building on the *Scenic Hudson* case, a Federal Court held in 1967[29] that two civic associations and a non-profit association concerned with community problems had standing to challenge the location of a proposed interstate highway. And in a most recent decision[30] the Second Circuit Court of Appeals held that failure on the part of the Corps of Engineers to obtain the consent of Congress and the approval of the Secretary of Transportation as required by the Rivers and Harbors Act of 1899, for the erection of a dyke and a causeway constituted a breach of a non-discretionary duty, which a non-incorporated association of citizens residing near the proposed road, and a national conservation organization, had a right to challenge, as representatives of the public interest in protecting the environment.

The aforementioned decisions are perhaps no more than straws in the wind and leave many questions open. Moreover, state courts still vary greatly in their approach to the problems of standing. But the trend is unmistakable and underlines a theme that has been stressed time and again in the present book: that the borderlines between public and private interest – and correspondingly between public and private law – are shifting, because the congested industrialized societies of our time have reached a stage where there is no longer unlimited scope for the pursuit of private interest, on the theory that private enterprise and the pursuit of private gain, in a competitive economy, is of necessity the best promotion of the national interest.

28. *ibid.* at 1006.
29. *Road Review League, Town of Bedford* v. *Boyd*, 270 F. Supp. 650 (S.D.N.Y. 1967).
30. *Citizens' Committee for the Hudson Valley* v. *Volpe*, 425 F. 2d 97 (2d Cir. 1970).

The range of remedies, on behalf of the public interest, against both public authorities and private enterprises, must be drastically widened, in a society that must discipline itself in order to survive.

How far does the organization of administrative justice in some of the principal Continental legal systems meet this need?

Administrative Justice: Some Comparative Observations

In the Continental systems, built upon a dichotomy of civil and administrative law, full-fledged hierarchies of administrative courts, equal in status to the 'ordinary' courts, but staffed with judges who combine legal qualifications with administrative experience, provide a separate and – subject to occasional conflicts of jurisdiction, to be settled by a Conflicts Tribunal – self-contained structure of administrative justice. Post-war reforms in both countries have made the French and West German systems rather similar in this respect. In France, the reform of 1953 has relieved the *Conseil d'Etat* of the increasingly unmanageable burden of being, in all major matters, a court of first, as well as of last, instance, and has instituted, as courts of first instance, twenty-four '*tribunaux administratifs*', staffed with a president and from three to four counsellors. Their competence extends to the overwhelming majority of administrative litigation. The *Conseil d'Etat*, principal architect of the French *droit administratif*, since the reforms of 1953 generally acts as appeal court against the decisions of the administrative tribunals (Waline, 1963, § 234).

Similarly, in West Germany, since the post-war reforms, administrative disputes are in first instance decided by administrative tribunals, now – though not formerly – completely separate from the administrative authorities whose decisions are challenged. An appeal (on facts and law) lies to the administrative appeal courts (*Verwaltungsgerichtshöfe*) of the different states, from which, in certain matters of fundamental importance, a revision (on points of law) lies to the newly established federal administrative court (*Bundesverwaltungsgericht*) (Forsthoff, 1958, § 28). The administrative courts of first instance are usually staffed by a combination of professional judges and lay assessors, while the appeal courts and the supreme administrative court are entirely staffed with professional judges.[31]

It should be added that, particularly in Germany, there has been a tendency to create separate court structures for an increasing number of special subjects: such as tax law, labour law and cartel law, while constitutional disputes also go to a special court, the Supreme Constitutional Court for the Federal Republic. But in all these cases hierarchies of courts have been established, which are equal in status and prestige to the ordinary courts.

In the common-law world a proliferation of administrative tribunals of all kinds has resulted from the prolonged delay in recognizing the need for a discipline and system of administrative justice, although the multiplication of the administrative functions is shared by the common-law world with the civil-law world. Neither American nor British reforms have attempted to substitute for the multiplicity of specialized administrative tribunals any uniform structure of administrative courts of first instance. Instead, attempts have been made to introduce minimum standards applicable to all administrative actions and agencies. In this respect the principal provisions of the Federal Administrative Procedure Act 1946, prescribe: (a) minimum standards of public information, on the organization, procedure and rule-making by administrative agencies; (b) minimum standards on hearings in every case of administrative adjudication; (c) separation of functions of hearing officers and reviewing bodies.[32]

In a similar vein the British (Franks) Committee on Administrative Tribunals and Inquiries (1957) recommended, as basic in all administrative proceedings, the principles of 'fairness, openness, impartiality'. To that end the Committee made various recommendations to ensure fair procedure before, at, and after the hearing before an administrative tribunal. This includes requirements of publicity, fair notice, the issue of reasoned decisions and other matters which may fairly be compared to the standards of the US legislation.

31. Except for Rheinland-Pfalz where the court of second instance consists of three professional judges and two lay assessors.
32. 'An employee or agent engaged in the performance of investigative or prosecuting functions for any agency in any case may not, in that or a factually related case, participate or advise in the decision, recommended decision, or agency review pursuant to section 8 except as witness or counsel in public proceedings.' (§ 5(c), 60 Stat. 239, as amended, 5.U.S.C. § 554 (d)).

The Committee's recommendations go some way towards the systematization of judicial procedure in administrative matters and even the recognition of a separate hierarchy of administrative tribunals.

Having acknowledged that, despite various criticisms, the 'method of decision by tribunals' has worked 'on the whole reasonably well' (para. 403), the Committee recommends that there should be an appeal on fact, law, and merits from an administrative tribunal of first instance to an appellate administrative tribunal, except in three specified cases, where the tribunal of first instance was considered as exceptionally strong and well qualified.[33] In many cases such an appeal would take the place of the present appeal to the competent Minister, i.e. the superior departmental authority, a procedure which the Committee firmly rejects.

On the question of a further appeal, the Committee's recommendation that, in addition to the prerogative remedies, a statutory right of appeal on points of law or on a case stated by the tribunal, to the High Court (more specifically the Divisional Court of the Queen's Bench Division) should be created, has been substantially accepted by the Tribunals and Inquiries Act 1958.[34] This, for the present, disposes of the question of a general administrative appeal tribunal, to which the Committee gave some consideration but which it rejected, reasoning, first that 'appeals would thus lie from an expert tribunal to a comparatively inexpert body', and second,

that the establishment of a general appellate body would seem inevitably to involve a departure from the principle whereby all adjudicating bodies in this country, whether designated as inferior courts or as tribunals, are in matters of jurisdiction subject to the control of the superior courts. This unifying control has been so long established and is of such fundamental importance in our legal system that the onus of proof must lie clearly upon the advocates of change.

Third, the Committee deprecates the likely evolution of 'two

33. i.e. the National Insurance Commissioner, the Industrial Injuries Commissioner and the National Assistance Appeal Tribunal.

34. This Act also establishes a Council on Tribunals to keep under review the constitution, working and procedure of administrative tribunals. It also tightens up the methods of appointment and qualifications of the chairman of administrative tribunals, so as to promote greater uniformity of standards.

systems of law . . . with all the evils attendant on this dichotomy' (§§ 121–6).

Two common-law scholars who have studied the working of the French administrative-law system, and who, in most respects, regard it as providing better protection for the citizen than present-day common law, nevertheless agree with the rejection of a separate administrative appeal court. Professor Schwartz (1954, p. 73)[35] rejects the duality mainly because of the possibility of conflicts of jurisdiction between administrative and civil courts, and the consequent prolongation of a dispute which, in certain cases, might take many years. Considering his previous praise of the standing, quality, and spirit of independence of the *Conseil d'Etat*, this seems a remarkably narrow ground to choose. Professor Hamson concludes an admiring account of the role and working of the *Conseil d'Etat*, and of its highly beneficial work in the restraint of administrative arbitrariness, due in large part to the administrative expertise of its members, with a rather curt rejection of the dual structure for the common-law world. 'A tribunal independent of and parallel to the high court would introduce a duality into our jurisdiction which we could not easily tolerate' (1954, p. 213).

This reasoning is no more convincing than that of the Franks Committee. It appears to be based on several fallacies.

First, there is in all these arguments a total absence of doubt in the expertise and ability of the 'ordinary' judges to deal with matters of administrative law, and to pave the way for its further development – as the highest administrative courts on the Continent have done. This assumption is all the more surprising as the multitude of present-day administrative tribunals have sprung from the very absence of such ability. A British authority on administrative law, who also has first-hand experience of administrative tribunals (Street, 1968, p. 5), had recently confirmed that the 'ordinary' judges are generally without administrative experience, are steeped in the individualistic tradition of the common law, and tend to disregard the social element in a problem. This observation is, however, less true for the United States, where lawyers have a more diversified

35. For an apparent change of view, see the same author's proposal for the creation of an Administrative Court of the United States to exercise the functions now exercised by the six Commissions (Schwartz, 1959).

background than in Britain. Unless there is a drastic change in the training and experience of lawyers from whom the judges are recruited, it is a matter of sheer accident if some of them, through wartime government service, or some other public mission, have acquired experience of the administrative process.[36] Nor is it an answer that the High Court should function as the highest appeal court only on 'points of law'. The whole discussion of this chapter has shown how deeply, though indirectly, even the present-day prerogative jurisdiction of the ordinary courts in matters of administrative law goes into questions of fact. It seems contradictory to praise the achievements of the *Conseil d'Etat* and of similar bodies in other countries, largely because of their combination of full judicial independence with intimate acquaintance of the processes of administration, and then to reject any similar system for the common-law jurisdictions, although the administrative and social problems with which they are faced are basically the same as in the civil-law jurisdictions. And why, in the light of the experience of the Continental highest administrative appeal courts, such a court in England – or the United States – should be a 'relatively inexpert' body is difficult to grasp. What is needed is experience in, and understanding of, the nature of the administrative process and of the basic problems of the relation between governors and governed. Whether such a highest administrative court should be constituted inside or outside the organization of the superior courts of the common law is a relatively subordinate question. The latter solution would preserve something of the mystical 'unity' of the common law, but such a special division with the High Court would certainly make sense only if it were staffed with judges trained in the processes of administration and more than casually acquainted with the problems of administrative law.

This leads us to the final and probably the most basic fallacy in the reasoning of the Committee (as of many others). As the discussion of this chapter has shown on almost every page, there *are*, in fact, two systems of law in existence, and the dichotomy, 'evil' or otherwise, has been with us for some time. The only difference

36. cf. the observations of Professor Robson 'Administrative justice and injustice: a commentary on the Franks Report', *Public Law*, Spring 1958, pp. 12–32.

between the civil-law and the common-law jurisdictions is that the former openly recognize administrative law as a discipline of its own, with its characteristic problems and solutions, whereas the latter continue to live with the fiction that there is only one system of law, the common law, with administrative sideshoots sprouting from the stem here and there. The result is, as we have seen, that there is a widespread lack of proper appreciation of characteristic public-law problems and institutions, such as the nature of government contracts, the status of the public corporation, the statutory immunities of public authorities, and many more. The recognition of the duality of the legal system as an inevitable corollary to the development of modern government – is a basic problem which the common-law world can continue to ignore or belittle only at the cost of failing to develop a healthy balance between the needs of administration in the modern welfare state and the essential rights of the citizen.

Public Power and the Individual: Some New Approaches

The foregoing observations have, it is hoped, shown that a broadening – and in the common-law world a systemization – of administrative justice is essential. But this may no longer be sufficient to cope with the multiple ways in which the individual, in a society characterized by the increasing concentration of power in the hands of both public authorities and the public-private 'technostructure' (see p. 332) finds himself more and more the object of decisions and pressures beyond his control. The centralization of data affecting all aspects of a person's life and work in computerized 'data banks' and their indiscriminate use by government agencies as well as by banks and other private institutions that can make or break an individual and his family, is an indication of the shape of things to come. Is the individual helpless against this proliferation of uncontrolled public or private power? In June 1970, the Court of Appeals for the District of Columbia indicated that he was not, by remanding the following case for trial and 'more complete factual development'.[37] A Maryland man had been arrested in California in 1965 on suspicion of burglary. When the police found no basis for charging him with a crime, he was released, but a record of his detention, with fingerprints, was retained in the FBI criminal files. The person concerned brought

37. *Menard* v. *Mitchell*, 430 F. 2d 486 (D.C. Cir. 1970).

action to have the record purged from the FBI files, on the ground that the record was misleading and could be interpreted as a 'criminal record'. Whether, following the remanding by the Court of Appeal, an order for removal will be made, remains to be seen. But there can be no doubt that the centralization as well as the uncontrolled use of computerized data, by government agencies, private employers, credit institutions and others, presents a potential interference with a person's privacy and status, which can lead ominously close to the society of Big Brother, depicted in George Orwell's *1984*, unless stringent legal safeguards are provided. The hierarchy of administrative justice, as developed in France and other Continental systems, has itself become a full-fledged and complex system of judicial administration, where years may elapse between a complaint and the ultimate decision. Moreover, as we have seen, legal remedies in the process of administrative justice are, on the whole, limited to strictly defined abuses of administrative discretion.

The Ombudsman

It is the widespread feeling that many injustices and grievances remain outside the purview of the administrative legal process that has, in recent years, led to the growing adoption of an institution first introduced in Sweden in 1809, and now known the world over under its original Swedish title, 'Ombudsman'.[38] After more than a century of quiescence, similar institutions were created in the other Scandinavian countries, and, more recently, in some common-law systems. In the countries that have been the principal architects of fully-fledged systems of administrative justice, such as France, prevailing opinion is still that this makes additional institutions for the protection of the rights of the individual unnecessary. But it is by no means certain that even countries with highly developed systems of administrative justice will not be compelled to adopt procedures that, in a manner modelled upon the ombudsman, will supplement administrative justice by less formal non-judicial or quasi-judicial methods.

The most authoritative comparative study of the subject (Gellhorn, 1966) surveys institutions described by the author as 'citizens' pro-

38. The full title of the office created by the Swedish Constitution of 1809 is 'Ritsdageus Justitieombudsman'.

tectors' in nine countries. These include the four Scandinavian countries, as well as Japan and three systems with a socialist structure of government, Yugoslavia, Poland and the Soviet Union.[39] The first common-law country to introduce an ombudsman was New Zealand in 1962. In 1967, the United Kingdom established the office of a Parliamentary Commissioner for Administration (Parliamentary Commissioner Act 1967), with considerably more limited functions than those of the New Zealand ombudsman. Three Canadian provinces also have ombudsmen. Since then, largely owing to the work of Professor Gellhorn and other advocates of new ways to protect the citizen against administrative arbitrariness, this institution has found increasing interest in the United States. Two American states – Hawaii and Nebraska – have enacted statutes that adopt the ombudsman institution; a number of local governments – counties and cities – have introduced the system in one form or another; and discussion concerning its extension into other states continues.

Space permits only the briefest and most general description of this institution, its functions and purposes.

Whatever the merits and inadequacies of both the Continental and the common-law type of administrative justice may be, a number of countries of both systems – socialist as well as capitalist – have found it necessary to empower readily accessible, professionally qualified, wholly detached critics to inquire objectively into asserted administrative shortcomings. Institutionalizing the giving of expert criticism, accomplished by each of the countries in its own way, has distinctly contributed to strengthened public administration (Gellhorn, 1966, p. 422).

The common feature is the institution of a high-level public official, independent of the civil service, whose main business it is to receive and to inquire into complaints brought by individuals or organizations, with a minimum of formality and cost. But the ombudsman[40]

39. It should be noted that the political and economic system of Yugoslavia now differs decisively from the centrally planned systems of Poland, the Soviet Union and other countries of Eastern Europe.

40. Although only the Scandinavian countries and New Zealand use the term officially, this word is used here for shorthand. In the Soviet Union and Poland the function of holding inspection of, and inquiry into, sections of public authority, is exercised by the procurators. In Yugoslavia, the corresponding organ is the Bureau of Petitions and Proposals.

can also conduct inquiries on his own, without receiving any complaint, where his concern about official actions is aroused by other means, e.g. by a newspaper article. The functions of the British Parliamentary Commissioner are more limited, since he may undertake an investigation only when a complaint is referred to him by a member of the House of Commons – a limitation that has been widely criticized. In some of the countries concerned, for example, in New Zealand, the ombudsman cannot act upon a complaint concerning administrative action that is subject to judicial review.

The ombudsman is typically empowered to examine official files, demand reports by officials, and summon any person concerned with the matter under investigation for interviewing. In three of the Scandinavian countries he is directed to make periodic inspections of government establishments, a function somewhat parallel to that of the procurators in the Soviet Union and Poland, who exercise general supervision over government activities.

Typically, the ombudsman acts by way of informal inquiries and seeks to obtain the redressing of a grievance he considers to be justified by negotiation with the authority concerned. The extent to which he succeeds is, of course, dependent upon his general official and personal prestige which has uniformly been high.

The kind of inquiries initiated by the ombudsman cover a very wide range. Thus, the Danish ombudsman – a law professor – regularly inspects places of detention where he confers with persons in custody. But he also took up a widespread newspaper discussion of the way in which the Royal Veterinary and Agricultural College had treated a thesis (Gellhorn, 1966, p. 18). And he has successfully proposed procedural and organizational improvements in the determination of tax matters, a study undertaken after a single taxpayer had complained about an extraordinary delay in obtaining a ruling. The impressive activities of the New Zealand ombudsman have included improvement in hospital administration, improved tax treatment of widowed, divorced or unmarried breadwinners who must engage housekeepers, reforms in the practical administration of social security benefits, and revisions in the salary reclassification of a teacher who felt aggrieved by the application of the relevant legislation (Gellhorn, 1966, p. 122).

The characteristic aspects of the institution of the ombudsman, and his activities, is that he is not so much concerned with general legislative or administrative principles, as with specific individual grievances, often arising from a legally correct but, in the circumstances, inequitable application of laws and regulations. As the few given examples illustrate, the matters taken up by the ombudsman are quite often of less than world shaking importance, but not only are they of profound importance to the individual affected, they also sometimes lead to significant legislative or administrative reforms.

The basic importance of the institution of the ombudsman and its equivalents is that, in a society where the individual is increasingly overwhelmed by the impersonal machinery of public authority, a direct link is reestablished between public power and the citizen. It is not a substitute for administrative justice. But neither does a well developed system of administrative law make it unnecessary.

Part Five
The Changing Scope of International Law

Chapter 13
National Sovereignty and World Order in the Nuclear Age

National Sovereignty and the United Nations

After the disasters of the First World War – which shook the physical and moral foundations of the prosperous and relatively pacific western-dominated world of pre-1914 – there was a widespread belief that the destructiveness of modern war and the growing proximity and interdependence of nations was bound to lead the world out of the age of national sovereignty and of the national state as the ultimate repository of legal and political power. The alternative vision of universal world order began to take practical shape in the Covenant of the League of Nations. But this was widely seen only as the beginning of further developments, which would ultimately produce a world federation or even a world state. The inter-war period witnessed dozens of blueprints, setting forth in detail the constitution of such supra-national bodies. Meanwhile, the League of Nations, cautiously constructed on the principle of unanimity of decisions by national sovereigns, struggled to work out the procedures which would turn it into an effective organization for the outlawing and suppression of aggressive war, by a combination of the processes of peaceful settlement and – economic or military – sanctions provided in Articles 11, 15 and 16 of the Covenant. After many years of doubt and failure, these efforts very nearly triumphed when Mussolini's Italy committed an act of unprovoked and naked aggression against Abyssinia, challenging, without adequate military and economic resources, the combined economic and military power of the League members, who had then the sympathy of the United States, not itself a member of the League. It was not the constitutional weaknesses of the League that led to its tragic failure at that historic moment – for the procedures of condemning an act of aggression and imposing the necessary sanctions were developed quickly, and with amazing smoothness, both in the League Council and in the League Assembly – but the combination of political weakness, lack of leadership and economic interests, particularly in Great Britain and France. The collapse of the League as an effective instrument of international policing against aggression gave the final push to the new Nazi imperialism, which had visions of world order based on one-sided domination.

After the Second World War, an even more deeply shaken and disorganized world approached the problem of world order, as it seemed, more soberly and realistically. The United Nations Charter made a limited gesture in the direction of world law supremacy over national supremacy, by empowering the General Assembly to make recommendations by simple, or in important matters, by a two-thirds majority. But as the recommendations of the Assembly have, in the theory of the Charter, no binding effect, the concession to the majority principle is a limited one. The executive authority was placed by the UN Charter in the hands of the Security Council, whose effectiveness depends, by virtue of the veto power of any one of them, on the collaboration of the five permanent members of the Council in the supervision and enforcement of peace and security throughout the world. Provided that a majority of the members of the Security Council, including the five permanent members, agree on a particular course of action, all the members of the United Nations are bound and, to that extent, they have renounced the sovereignty of national decision. But as the veto principle applies to the enforcement of any decisions against one of the permanent members of the Security Council, the national sovereignty of the 'Big Five' effectively limits the majority principle and thereby the supremacy of international law over national sovereignty.

So much for the theory of the United Nations Charter. In practice, the persistence of the tension between the Soviet Union on the one hand, and the other permanent members on the other hand, has paralysed the Security Council as an effective instrument of world order, while it has, to a limited extent, strengthened the authority of the General Assembly and given its recommendations in some cases a moral force stronger than that of a mere recommendation. The relative strengthening of the General Assembly has occurred simultaneously with the creation and admission to the United Nations of many new states. As, in the General Assembly, each member has one vote, the collective influence of the small states has risen to unprecedented dimensions – ironically at a time when effective military and economic power has come to be more than ever concentrated in the hands of a very few super-states. Whereas, in the former, less organized, international society, a new state had to make its place in the family of nations slowly, by a gradual process of recognition, diplomatic relations and its effective role in international affairs, today new states obtain international status and an equal vote, almost immediately after their creation, through their admission to the United Nations. However weak and poor, the new state must establish the apparatus and symbols of sovereignty – diplomatic representation, a government, a civil service and at least token armed forces. The irony of the situation is heightened by the fact that one of the world's most important states – Germany – is kept outside the United Nations, as a result of the tensions between the Soviet *bloc* and the West. The conception of the UN Charter, which was to restrain the theoretical legal principle of the equality of all states by an effective predominance, by rights and responsibilities, of the major Powers, has thus become rather distorted, at least in so far as the United Nations still effectively reflects the actual balance of forces in the world. The price of this increasing gap between political reality and legal form may be a continuous decline in the effectiveness of the United Nations as an international organization of peace, security and order.

The most effective contribution made by the United Nations – through the Secretary-General and the General Assembly – was the role it played in the solution of the Suez Canal crisis of 1956, by the constitution of the United Nations' emergency force (UNEF), which guarded the Gaza Strip separating Egypt and Israel and kept the peace in that area, until President Nasser forced its withdrawal immediately preceding the Six-Day War of 1967. The role of the United Nations in the 1956 crisis was greaty facilitated by the fact that its two most powerful members, the United States and the Soviet Union, jointly backed the resolution demanding the withdrawal of the British, French and Israeli forces, concurrent with the establishment of the United Nations policing force.

The second major police action of the United Nations – initially sponsored both by the Security Council and the General Assembly – i.e. its role in the Congo crisis of 1960–61 – was also at first facilitated by the concurrence of the two super powers. Consequently, however, the USSR withdrew its support, which made it impossible for the Security Council to act and left further initiatives to the General Assembly. United Nations action in that crisis consisted in the sending of a mixed international police force (ONUC) to cope with an internal civil-war situation, which, in the opinion of the Secretary-General, threatened to lead to grave international implications. The effect of UN intervention was eventually to liquidate the attempted secession of Katanga and to restore the political unity of the Congo Republic.[1]

But – apart from a continuing police function exercised in Cyprus by a United Nations force, designed to prevent the recurrence of hostilities between the Greek and Turkish groups on that island – the Congo operation is likely to remain the last of the United Nations' major police actions. After the termination of the Congo action, the International Court of Justice, in an advisory opinion[2] held that the expenses of the operation were incurred by an action within the competence of the General Assembly and therefore to be borne by all the members in accordance with Article 17 of the UN Charter. But both France and the Soviet Union – notwithstanding the adoption of the opinion by the General Assembly – refused to pay their share. This makes the organization and financing of similar operations unlikely if not impossible, unless at least all the major members of the United Nations concur.

The triumph of national sovereignty is thus, to some extent, illusory. A price has to be paid for the increasing divergence between legal and political sovereignty. The United Nations General Assembly as a forum of world opinion is used by the major Powers to the extent that they wish to support their claims and positions in international controversies by an appeal to the organized voice of the

1. For an analysis of this operation and its various legal implications, see Schachter, 'The relation of law, politics and action in the United Nations, [1963] *Recueil des Cours* 166.
2. *Certain Expenses of the United Nations*, [1962] I.C.J. Rep. 151.

smaller nations of the world, and these are usually – like the big Powers – divided into contending *blocs*.

In the most dangerous conflicts of recent years, the United Nations has either been unable to intervene effectively, or it has not been concerned at all. The secession of Biafra from the Federal Republic of Nigeria – which, early in 1970, ended in defeat for Biafra and its reabsorption in the Federation – was no less dangerous internationally than the attempted secession of Katanga from the Congo Republic. The major powers, though not directly militarily engaged, were divided. Britain and the USSR supported the Federation, while France and some of the African states supported Biafra. Yet the United Nations – unquestionably because of the aftermath of the Congo affair – never sought to intervene in that conflict. In the continuing war between Israel and its Arab neighbours, the United Nations has intervened, through the appointment of a Swedish mediator who has tried to bring the warring parties to the negotiating table. In the cease-fire initiated by the US in the summer of 1970, the UN serves as a forum where the UN mediator can meet the representatives of the warring states.[3] The outside influence that really matters on both sides is the political and material support of the major powers. While the USSR and, to a more limited extent, France have increasingly supported the Arab states and particularly Egypt, with arms and advisors, the USA has supplied arms to Israel and has pledged to increase such support if the balance of power should be upset in favour of the Arab states. The confrontation is increasingly dangerous, and may ultimately lead to a direct clash between the United States and the Soviet Union. It is very unlikely that the United Nations will be able to intervene effectively in this, probably the most dangerous of all the international conflicts of the post-war era.

In the other major conflict area of this time, Indochina, the

3. Since the Six-Day War of 1967, Israel relies, however, less and less upon the United Nations' machinery, partly because it does not wish to implement a Security Council resolution asking the restoration of the pre-war frontiers unless a surrender of all or part of the occupied territories is coupled with direct peace negotiations between Israel and the Arab States, and partly because in the Security Council the Arab States and its political supporters now enjoy a commanding majority.

United Nations has proved equally powerless. The Geneva Accords of 1954, involving Vietnam, Cambodia and Laos, and the Laos agreement of 1962 were concluded between the powers directly concerned. Although the US intervened – at first through advisers and military supplies – and later with increasingly massive military forces, it did not seek to obtain UN action until the end of 1966, without success. The principal opponent, North Vietnam, is not a member of the United Nations. Neither is Communist China, one of its two principal supporters, while the other, the USSR, has shown no inclination whatsoever to invoke United Nations action.

Thus, after a brief period of active intervention in some of the major international crises, the General Assembly of the United Nations is following the Security Council into paralysis in the field of international security. Whereas the Security Council remains, in most cases, powerless because of the division between the major powers, the General Assembly is rendered increasingly impotent by the swelling number of its members – whose nominal equality and articulateness in the resolutions of the General Assembly cannot be a substitute for effective power.

It would, however, be dangerously superficial to dismiss the proliferation of national sovereignties as a mere *fata morgana*, a fictitious application of the principle of equality of nations in international law, hiding the reality of world power and world order. In the voting procedures of the United Nations, the triumph of national sovereignties, measured in numbers, may be largely deceptive. But, it is buttressed by the stalemate between the major Powers, which, in their world-wide battle for influence and position, must pay high regard to the individual or collective voice of smaller States. Disregard of the claims of any Arab or Muslim state, however small by itself, may inflame the entire world of Islam and, incidentally, threaten oil supplies. A cavalier treatment of the territorial waters claims of any one Latin-American state may affect the entire Latin American world. Alienation of one of the new states of South-East Asia may swing one of several of them from a pro-western or a neutral position to increasing alignment with the Communist world.

Both the Arab states and Israel can, by the recklessness of their actions, draw the major powers into a conflict which they do not seek.

The tension and continuing manoeuvring for position between the big Powers, has worked in support of claims of national sovereignty, especially of the smaller states, mainly in two respects: first, nationalist tensions and the stalemate in the battle between the major Powers have combined to produce a spate of partitions of states once united. In a few cases, the pressure has come mainly from within, an expression of religious, racial or other factors tending to create a new state. In the post-war period, this has been the main cause of the partition of British India between the Republic of India and the Republic of Pakistan. In the latter, only the common Muslim religion links two almost equal parts, separated from each other geographically, traditionally and economically.[4] Religious and national sentiment have carved the state of Israel out of Palestine. Piecemeal liberation from colonial control has created a large number of new Arab states, but it is the stalemate of the cold war, and no genuine force of nationalism that has produced the separate states of West and East Germany, of North and South Korea, of North and South Vietnam. But the longer the stalemate goes on, the more do the originally artificial new landmarks of sovereignty tend to become permanent. The new state creates its symbols, its machinery and traditions. Divergent political, economic and educational systems in course of time widen the gulf, and a new act of force is needed to restore former or create new unities.

The new partitions and sovereignties create many problems of international law. The division of the waters of the Indus system between India and Pakistan, and of the River Jordan between Israel and the hostile neighbouring Arab states, has highlighted the unsolved problems of the allocation of water rights between various riparian states. The – technically quite feasible – solution of these problems is made infinitely more difficult by the antagonism between the rival partitioned states. In the case of the Indus River, after years of tension and increasing bitterness between India and Pakistan, a World Bank initiative led to the Indus Basin Development Fund Agreement of September 1960 which, with the World Bank as manager, established an international aid-giving consortium, whose

4. In 1971 the overwhelming support given by East Pakistanis to far-reaching regional autonomy led to military intervention by the essentially West Pakistan army, and a continuing occupation marked by great brutality.

contributions to the fund have enabled Pakistan to construct an irrigation system in compensation for the loss of the use of the Indus tributaries. This is a costly substitute for the sharing of water resources in a formerly unified country. But it is immensely preferable to the continued partition of the River Jordan into sections owned by the various riparian states that are at war with each other.

Expanding National Claims to the Sea

The second, and in this case world-wide, extension of national legal claims, at the expense of long-established international legal freedoms, is a continuing spread of national territorial claims over the once-free sea. The traditionally prevalent three-mile limit for territorial waters is today virtually abandoned even by powers with strong maritime interests and traditions (Great Britain, Japan, the United States). A number of states, big and small, such as the Soviet Union, Canada, Communist China, Iceland, have long claimed a twelve-mile limit. The effectiveness of this inroad upon the freedom of the seas is considerably increased by the decision of the International Court of Justice, in the *Anglo-Norwegian Fisheries* case[5] – adopted by Article 4 of the Geneva Convention on the Territorial Sea and the Contiguous Zone, of April 1958 – that 'in localities where the coastline is deeply indented and cut into, or if there is a fringe of islands along the coast in its immediate vicinity, the method of straight base lines joining appropriate points may be employed in drawing the base line from which the breadth of the territorial sea is measured'. This has been used, for example, by the Republic of Indonesia to draw the base line along the entire group of the archipelago of islands, thus enclosing a formerly open part of the sea as national waters.

A far more dangerous erosion of international legal rights and freedoms, through expanding national claims, has been the evolution of the doctrine of the continental shelf. Although the concept of the continental shelf has been known to geographers since the nineteenth century, as a legal doctrine it is little more than a quarter of a century old. It was the so-called Truman Proclamation of 28 September 1945

5. [1951] I.C.J. Rep. 116.

that launched it, by proclaiming that 'the exercise of jurisdiction over the natural resources of the sub-soil and seabed of the continental shelf by the contiguous nations is reasonable and just . . . since the continental shelf may be regarded as an extension of the land mass of the coastal nation and thus naturally pertinent to it'. The proclamation stated that the United States 'regards the natural resources of the sub-soil and seabed of the continental shelf beneath the high seas but contiguous to the coast of the United States as appertaining to the United States, subject to its jurisdiction and control'.

During the subsequent decade, every nation that had a continental shelf, i.e. a continuation of the land mass along the seabed, adopted the Truman doctrine. So rapid was the universal acceptance that a little more than a decade later, in 1958, the Geneva Convention on the Continental Shelf, ratified by nearly forty states and in force since June 1964, confirmed the acceptance of the Continental Shelf Doctrine as a general principle of international law. But even the states which, like West Germany, did not ratify the Geneva Convention, have claimed jurisdiction over the continental shelf. The International Court of Justice, in its judgement in the *North Sea Continental Shelf*[6] case of February 1969, dealing with a dispute about the respective continental-shelf boundaries between West Germany on the one side and Denmark and the Netherlands on the other side, confirmed the existence of an *ipso jure* right of the coastal state to the continental shelf.

The Truman Proclamation, without giving any horizontal limitation, at least limited the vertical extension of the continental shelf to a maximum depth of 200 metres. But the Geneva Convention, by a modification of that limit which may have seemed innocuous at the time but has turned out to be the key to an almost limitless expansion of national claims, allowed an extension of the depth beyond the limit of 200 metres 'to where the depth of the superjacent waters admits of the exploitation of the natural resources of the said areas'. The rapid technological progress of underwater exploration and exploitation of seabed resources, including stationary oceanbed laboratories, submerged vessels, the laying of pipes along the ocean bed and other means of making exploitation of seabed resources

6. [1969] I.C.J. Rep. 3.

possible at ever greater depths, has led to ever expanding claims. Under the pressure of oil and other industrial interests, the concept of the 'continental shelf' is gradually being replaced by that of the 'continental margin'.[7]

Although the substitution of such terms as 'continental slope' or 'continental margin' is a blatant perversion of the term 'continental shelf' as used in the Geneva Convention and in all the discussions leading to it, licences are in effect granted for exploration and exploitation of resources in that wider area, in the hope that a *fait accompli* will prevail over any possible future international legal restrictions. An historic speech by the Maltese Ambassador to the United Nations, Arvid Pardo, on 1 November 1967, warning against the continuing erosion of the freedom of the seas and proposing an international authority to control the uses of the ocean bottom 'beyond the limits of national jurisdiction', led to the appointment of a special United Nations committee and certain resolutions affirming the freedom of the seas. But the lack of any internationally authoritative definition of the 'limits of national jurisdiction' leads to ever widening encroachments on the international status of the ocean bed. And despite theoretical protestations of the freedom of the seas, it is evident that the rapidly growing number of artificial structures and seabed installations, with all the attendant dangers of water pollution, will increasingly encroach upon the freedom of navigation and the freedom of fisheries.[8]

Some coastal states – such as Chile and Peru – have steeply

7. See, for example, the debate in the US Senate, 16 April 1970, *Congressional Record* S5933. For support of the contention that 'continental shelf' includes the 'continental slope', and possibly also the 'continental rise', see R. Y. Jennings, 'The limits of continental shelf jurisdiction: some possible implications of the North Sea case judgement', 18 *Int. & Comp. L.Q.* 28 (1969).

8. The American branch of the International Law Association in 1968 demanded a vertical limit of 2500 metres, which would comprise more than a fifth of the ocean floor. But other claims prefer not to stipulate any depth limit whatsoever. In May 1970, the US Government declared itself in favour of an international treaty limiting the continental shelf to a depth of 200 metres and placing the seabed beyond the shelf under international control, but giving 'trusteeship' over an intermediate zone to the limit of the continental margin to the coastal states. Subsequently, the US submitted a draft convention spelling out these principles to the UN Seabed Committee. No agreement was reached in the Committee's sessions of 1970 and 1971.

descending coastlines. They – and a growing number of Latin-American states, including some which have good continental shelves – have proclaimed a 200-mile zone as territorial waters. This means an open and massive encroachment upon the freedom of the seas, but the maritime nations that claim major areas of the ocean bottom for exclusive exploitation are in a very weak position to resist such claims. And one of the most stalwart champions of international law, Canada, in April 1970, proclaimed exclusive jurisdiction in matters of pollution control over an area of a hundred miles, while at the same time modifying its acceptance of the jurisdiction of the International Court of Jurisdiction, so as to exclude any international adjudication of this claim.

The nations are in effect well on the way towards a division of the oceans into national zones of exploitation and control, although they may stop short of an open appropriation of the various portions of the oceans as such. It is an incidental consequence that this expansion of the claims of maritime nations further disadvantages the twenty-nine landlocked nations of the world – most of which are also poor countries.

The erosion of the freedom of the seas – probably the single most important achievement of the law of nations as it has developed since the days of Grotius – occurs at a time when long-range missiles can cross the oceans within minutes, and when the worldwide dangers of the pollution of air and water, and the threat to the survival of marine life have become overwhelming international concerns. The need for international sharing and policing of the resources of the earth has never been more urgent. But the weakness of the United Nations is only the single most visible symbol of the unwillingness of the great majority of the nation states to limit short-term national claims and sectional interests for the sake of the long-term future of mankind.

Regional Groupings and Universal International Law

For all the deep political rivalries and fissures of the post-war world, the legal organization of mankind, on a universal basis, has made some advance. It is, however, significant that real progress has been almost entirely confined to the fields in which the vital interests and standards of nations diverge little. Thus the World Health Organization has been empowered and been able to get certain international sanitary standards and procedures adopted among its near-universal membership; the International Civil Aviation Organization has enacted a navigation code which is used not only by the large number of its member states, but also by non-members, such as the Soviet Union,[9] as they come to take a significant part in international commercial aviation. On the other hand, the International Labour Organization has been able to make only very limited progress in the adoption, by way of multilateral conventions, of labour standards in all but a few fields, even though its advisory influence has been considerable. For the common regulation of labour conditions in matters of wages, working hours, holidays, employment of women and children, labour organization comes up against vastly divergent national economic and social standards. The most important institutional progress in universal international organizations has been attained in the field of international development aid and monetary regulation. Both the World Bank (IBRD) and the International Monetary Fund (IMF) are financially autonomous, since their original capital was supplied by capital subscriptions of the member states. Both organizations have developed highly expert staffs of international civil servants, who are in charge of the complex operations that are the province of the World Bank's development loan activities and the International Monetary Fund's supervision of international monetary exchanges and parities. They are assisted by full-time resident executive directors representing the various member states, singly or in groups. The governing boards normally meet only once a year. These organizations, in which the supranational elements prevail over the national decision-making power, indicate perhaps a pattern of things to come – provided that mankind recognizes in time the overwhelming urgency of the common needs and tasks, which today remain divided among some 130 national 'sovereignties'.[10]

Because a common law in matters affecting constitutional, social,

9. In 1971 the Soviet Union joined the ICAO.
10. The series of unilateral currency parity changes following the US announcement of dollar inconvertibility into gold and a 10 per cent surcharge on imports in August 1971, may, however, indicate a weakening of the role of the IMF (and of the GATT).

economic and personal life demands a degree of common interests and values that, unhappily, does not at present unite the nations at large, some of the most important developments in international law have occurred through regional or functional groupings, some of them antagonistic to each other. Such groupings arise from a variety of motives. The North Atlantic Treaty Organization (NATO) and the Warsaw Pact bring together, in military alliances that entail varying degrees of integration of military command, coordination of defence production and joint policy bodies, the states that face each other in the European theatre of the cold war. The various European regional organizations which partly supplement and partly overlap each other, such as the Organization for Economic Cooperation and Development (OECD) and the Council of Europe, have arisen from the recognition of joint interests and values, which the preservation of old national sovereignties and rivalries would increasingly have imperilled. Significantly, much the most important development in this direction, the European Economic Community, has occurred among mature European states, which have long histories of national sovereignty, and bitter memories of the destructiveness of the exercise of military, political and economic sovereignty in our time. Much more dimly, similar tendencies begin to take shape among other groups of states, linked by common ties of geography, religion, political aspirations or economic interests, but as yet too much enmeshed in their recently won political or economic sovereignty to see it in all its limitations. The nearest approach to the partial integration achieved by the European Economic Community is the Central American Common Market, formed by the five small republics of central America. But it has been hindered by political tensions, especially the hostility between Honduras and San Salvador. Free-trade associations have been formed between a larger number of Latin American states as well as by Britain and six other states of northern and western Europe, outside the European Economic Community. There are incipient signs of a measure of economic integration in Africa and Asia, symbolized by the constitution of the African and Asian Development Banks – designed to foster regional economic development. But all these are as yet modest beginnings, overshadowed by national rivalries in the economic as well as in the political sphere.

The Development of International Law on Three Levels

International law is today developing on three different levels, and it is only by seeing them in perspective that we can hope to ascertain the trend of international society.

On the first level, international law is still based and, in certain respects as shown, continues to expand on the basis of national sovereignty and legal equality of nations.[11] But the growing discrepancy between the extravagant claims based on the national sovereignty of a rapidly increasing number of states, only a small minority of which have the minimum attributes of political, military, economic – as distinct from legal – sovereignty, heightened by the strategic exigencies of the cold war, is leading to a second level of regional or functional groupings of states. Such groupings may well be the most fertile and intensive source of international legal development in the fields reaching below the surface of social and human relationships. Thirdly, universal international law, as represented by the United Nations, its special agencies and international conventions on specific subjects, of a universal or near-universal character, is expanding slowly in those fields where common interests and necessity are not deeply affected by divergent interests and standards. This is particularly the case in the areas of communications, transport and health.

The interrelation of these three levels of international law requires further elaboration.

Much the most definite developments in the direction of closer legal integration between like-minded states are today presented by the Communist *bloc* directed by the Soviet Union, and by the more halting efforts of groups of West European nations to form closer legal units.

Without any need to abandon the formal symbols of national sovereignty – which, indeed, is a vital weapon in the arsenal of the Communist ideology of 'coexistence' – the policies and systems of Communist nations can be easily coordinated because of the similarity of their structure. Their political organization, centred in a strong executive, operating throughout the monolithic party organization which controls all spheres of public and social life, is almost

11. As expressed in the wishful formula of 'sovereign equality', employed in the Preamble to, and various other provisions of, the United Nations Charter.

identical in all the Communist states. Where they threaten to diverge, they are coerced into conformity, as was Czechoslovakia in 1968. This facilitates, in inter-state relations, the formation of a trading *bloc*. All external trade is centred in national agencies which form part of the national economic plan and can trade with the other Communist states on a basis of barter for specific items guided by economic development plans.

Far more interesting as well as difficult are the corresponding efforts recently made by democratic nations of western Europe and the North Atlantic region.

The widest of these, NATO, is also the most loosely organized. It has no separate legal personality; it is essentially still a multilateral alliance, although one that, contrary to the traditional alliances, has permanent headquarters and coordination at the command level, and, to a limited extent, on the operational level. A permanent Secretariat, headed by a Secretary-General, and a permanent Council of Delegates, supplemented periodically by meetings of Foreign Ministers, reinforces this structure, however. In the long run, the fate of NATO depends on the success of, so far inconclusive, efforts to coordinate the various national defence organisms and, in particular, the allocation and production of vital defence items. The theoretically most challenging provision of the Treaty is Article 2,[12] which so far has remained an aspiration, and it is doubtful whether it will ever surmount the obstacles presented by national economic policies as well as by other more active regional economic groupings.

The Council of Europe also is a loose organization without separate personality, expressing the common aspirations of western Europe in the wider sense rather than an integrated organization. It is devoid of executive power and the deliberations of its Assembly often have an air of impotence and futility. Yet, it has to its credit some significant achievements, such as the initiative in the creation of the European Payments Union. By far its most important achievements

12. 'The Parties will contribute toward the further development of peaceful and friendly international relations by strengthening their free institutions, by bringing about a better understanding of the principles upon which these institutions are founded, and by promoting conditions of stability and well-being. They will seek to eliminate conflict in their international economic policies and will encourage economic collaboration between any or all of them.'

in the legal field are the Conventions on Human Rights, concluded in 1949 and 1952. For these Conventions have established, within the framework of the Council, both a Commission equipped with inquiry and quasi-judicial functions, and the European Court of Human Rights,[13] to which the member states and, where the particular state has agreed, also groups and individuals within the state, may appeal for redress against infractions of human rights.[14] In other words, a supra-national authority is here empowered to call to justice states for the infringement of rights that are generally still considered as a cherished preserve of national sovereignty. Such a partial transfer of national power to a supra-national authority is possible only among states which, for all differences of tradition and political philosophy, share a minimum of common standards and traditions in the relation of state and individual.

Perhaps the most important experiment in the partial transfer of national powers and privileges to a supranational authority is the European Economic Community, which was established in 1957, and which is now gradually integrating the earlier two communities, i.e. the European Coal and Steel Community, established in 1952, and the – largely ineffective – Atomic Energy Community. A supranational element in the Community is the Commission – which has now absorbed the executive authorities of the earlier two communities – but which, unlike the High Authority of the Coal and Steel Community, has only recommendatory, not decision-making, powers. The effective power rests with the Council of Ministers, who represent their respective countries, and thus the competing national sovereignties. The Assembly – formed not yet by direct election but by the political parties of the member countries – has a theoretical power

13. The European Convention for the Protection of Human Rights and Fundamental Freedoms, 213 *UNTS* 221, became effective on 3 September 1953. By 31 December 1967, eleven states had accepted the competence of the Commission to receive petitions from individuals and the compulsory jurisdiction of the Court ([1967] *Yearbook European Convention of Human Rights* 52–3 (1969)). See Weil (1963); Greenberg and Shalit, 'New horizons for human rights: the European convention, court and commission for human rights', 63 *Columbia L. Rev.* 1384 (1963).

14. These are defined in the Convention and include the usual freedoms of person, expression, assembly, equality and fairness in the administration of justice, and peaceful enjoyment of possessions, subject to law.

to dismiss the executive, but is essentially a debating forum that has no effective control over the policy decisions of the other organs of the Community or over its budget. A more effective supranational organ is the European Court of Justice, before which not only governments but also the industries and business enterprises concerned may appear as plaintiffs or defendants. It is a very busy court, and it has done much to make the obligations of the Community treaties immune against repeated attempts by the various member states to erode them. But, on the whole, the supranational elements, even in this most advanced type of regional organization, are still weak; and the principal decision-making powers rest with the member states as such.

The partial integration of national sovereignties, in regional or functional groupings, presents new problems for a universal international order. The establishment of a Customs Union between the six west European states, through the Economic Community, creates tensions with the wider and looser OECD Organization, as well as with the even wider General Agreement on Tariffs and Trade (GATT). Whether the eventual effect of these partial and more closely knit international organizations on universal world order will be beneficial or otherwise is as yet an open question. But it is a situation which cannot be altered by mere technical improvements of organization and coordination. It is quite possible that the international or supra-national associations, now developing monolithically in the Communist world and, more experimentally, in different parts of the western world, will remain or even grow in mutual antagonism, that they will establish a minimum of mutual contacts, beyond the necessities of diplomatic relations, or that they will even go to war with each other. But the political and social forces in the world today are such that it is these competing orders which are the chief agents in the development of 'cooperative international law', and that some of them may become federal or even unitary states. Certainly, it is not possible to evade this problem by elaborate constitutional blue-prints of world organizations (Clark and Sohn, 1966). The proposal, for example, to divide the members of a reformed General Assembly of the United Nations into seven groups, from those over 140 million to those under 0·5 million, with correspondingly staggered representation, as the pre-condition of giving such an Assembly legislative power in matters related to the maintenance of peace, is more realistic than one which would maintain the equality of vote for all. But it ignores the vital question whether the rapidly increasing number of states will be prepared to entrust legislative powers to such an Assembly, merging all their deep-seated differences and conflicts of values and interests. Creative imagination and scholarship are indeed needed to articulate nascent trends and ideas, to fire the imagination of the indifferent and the hesitant, and to devise legal procedures concretizing new principles and ideas. But to elaborate detailed constitutional procedures unrelated to the basic political realities of a period is an exercise in draftsmanship rather than a contribution to the overwhelming problems of our time.

The only serious justification for any hope that the deeply divided and antagonistic nations and power *blocs* of the world may merge their powers and purposes in a universal organization equipped with more than debating functions, lies in the overwhelming threat of contemporary technological and scientific developments to the security and, indeed, to the survival of mankind. The rapidly growing – and world-wide – threat to the human environment and the very elements of life, air and water, the destructive capacity of the H-bomb, the development of inter-continental missiles, the landings on the moon and the exploration of outer space, are held by some to be an almost irresistible impelling force towards a far more advanced world order than that represented by the present world Organization (Clark and Sohn, 1966, pp. xliii–lii).

There can be few who would not ardently desire that this prediction come true, but many who will doubt that fear of untold misery and extinction, even if mutually administered to all the major powers and perhaps all mankind, will, by itself, bring about the surrender of vital sovereign powers to a body in which no one nation can hope to attain control. Perhaps another, unimaginably destructive world war will teach the lesson, though mankind, after such a war, is more likely to find itself reduced to a level of primitive and disorganized existence rather than engaged in the elaboration of world constitutions. Meanwhile, the evidence seems overwhelming that the admittedly unparalleled destructive power of modern weapons will, at best, induce the contending *blocs* to remain at arm's length and to develop for this purpose such legal relations and contacts as are required for the maintenance of a live and let live co-existence. This is a very different thing from the gradual integration of principles and institutions, as it is being attempted by the nations of western Europe. It is possible that the desire to minimize serious and possibly mortal conflicts between the rival groups of powers will lead to some agreement on partly or wholly neutralized zones of 'disengagement', and to a measure of joint or international control over the maintenance of the state of balance. It is conceivable that the almost fantastic progress of the means of transport and communication will at last bring home to the nations of the world the anachronisms of national sovereignty. In the Antarctic region, some at least of the many different nations that have established outposts and sent scientific expeditions have so far refrained from claiming sovereignty over certain parts of the region, while they are far from agreeing on any form of international ownership or control. National sovereignty over outer space has been renounced by a treaty of 1967, sponsored by the UK, the US and the USSR.

The fate of the Treaty on Non-proliferation of Nuclear Weapons – also co-sponsored by the United States, the Soviet Union and Britain – is still uncertain, since not only France and Communist China are non-participants, but a considerable number of other nations are reluctant to ratify a treaty which would perpetuate the supremacy of the two super powers. The growing reluctance of such countries as India or Japan to accede to this treaty is a reflection of decreased confidence in the authority of the United Nations and collective security.

It is essential that, in the field of coexistence – i.e. of the minimum conditions of international order – there should be the widest possible participation of states. This makes the need to bring Communist China fully into the legal community of nations imperative and requires the detachment of recognition of governments from the ideological considerations that have dominated in particular US policy since the end of the war. On the level of the international law of cooperation, there are also certain worldwide concerns. Global communications, pollution of the air, the seas and the other international waters, the exploitation of the ocean-bed resources, and general environment problems all call for universal cooperation.

The sphere of worldwide concerns is not static. From year to year, worldwide coordination of measures to stem the continuing population explosion and the growing gap between the minority of rich and a great majority of poor nations calls for an increasing range of international development assistance. But many of the international cooperative concerns – e.g. in the fields of human rights, of integration of labour and social security standards, of economic, cultural and educational cooperation, presuppose a measure of common standards and values that confines progress in these areas to regional collaboration, or to other forms of association of states and international groups which share values on a scale not attainable at this time on a worldwide level.

Chapter 14
The Broadening Scope of International Law

New Dimensions of International Law

As has been shown in the foregoing chapter, the growing inter-dependence of mankind has not so far significantly shaken the legal and political structure of international society. The national sovereign state remains the principal legal form of political organization and by far the most important focus of emotional loyalties. To be stateless for any individual means not only to be bereft of the right to live in a particular country and to be devoid of state protection in a hostile world. It also means being an international outcast. As we have seen, the attempts made to overcome the divisive and destructive consequences of a world divided into some 130 national states, by a transfer of certain powers over peace and war to an international authority, have failed twice. The disasters of the First World War did not suffice to sustain the League of Nations. The even greater catastrophes of the Second World War proved insufficient to sustain the authority of the United Nations against the proliferation of new and old nationalisms, and the social, political and economic divisions of the post-war world.

But at the same time the stark realities of the contemporary world are pressing against the ramparts of the national state and the symbols of national sovereignty. Politically, the world is still divided – indeed more so than ever, since the number of national units has more than doubled since the end of the last world war. But in its physical and social reality, the world is a unit. Jets and supersonic aeroplanes are turning the airspace above the national territories into an increasingly complex and dense net of traffic lanes. The fact that, unlike the seas, the air forms part of the national territory and jurisdiction below it, greatly complicates international regulation, but does not make it any less necessary. The growing intensity of the use of the air – and of outer space above the atmosphere – in turn increases the need for international collaboration in meteorological information. The advent, since the end of the last world war, of a large number of new states – most of them former colonies or protectorates of the western Powers – has created irresistible pressures for permanent organizations of development aid, in response to the inescapable need to bridge, for political as well as humanitarian reasons, the stark gap between the rich and developed nation states and the rest. This has produced a whole network of international organizations, on the universal, regional and national levels. The World Bank and its affiliates, the regional development banks, and the national aid agencies represent new types of functional international organizations. In the United Nations Conference for Trade and Development (UNCTAD), the developed and the developing countries form institutionally distinct groups. At the same time, the problems of international trade affect, on the one hand, the relations between the developed countries, i.e. the conflict between nationalist pressures for protective tariffs, import quotas and other restrictions, and the international benefits of free trade. The General Agreement on Tariffs and Trade (GATT) expresses a compromise between these conflicting tendencies. On the other hand, the problem of trade is also a problem of development, since the dependence of the less developed countries on the export of staple products and primary commodities – which generally have been in overproduction, and since the end of the Korean War, in a stage of price depression – increases the economic gap between the under-developed countries and the industrially developed countries, whose export income has steadily increased. International trade movements are closely linked with international monetary stability, which is the main concern of the International Monetary Fund. The recent creation of 'special drawing rights', i.e. of additional credits available to the member states, in proportion to their foreign exchange quotas, is a direct response to the need for increased international trade. Trade conditions are in turn closely linked with international standards of labour and social services.

These, and many other new international concerns, have been reflected in the progressive creation of an entirely new area of international legal relations, which we might call the vertical, as distinct from the horizontal, dimension of international law. International law, like municipal law, is increasingly concerned with the development and regulation of international collaboration in spheres formerly outside the field of international law. While textbooks and casebooks on international law still predominantly emphasize the traditional fields of inter-state relations, i.e. the various aspects of international diplomacy conducted on a more or less formal level between governments, the vital concern of international law, as of international politics, has in recent years been increasingly with international economic and social organization, and with problems of human welfare.

But as the rate as well as the direction of the advance of law into a widening field of social and human relationships varies from state to state, universality becomes more difficult to attain. The chief makers of international law in the nineteenth century were broadly agreed on the scope of law, and with it, on the function of the state. Governments were generally held entitled and assumed to be responsible for what was then conceived to be the scope of external affairs: the control of armed forces and of diplomatic relations. They were furthermore assumed to be responsible for the administration of justice and the maintenance of internal order. From this followed certain rules of international state responsibility predicated on the assumption of certain general minimum standards of justice, i.e. a reasonably independent judiciary, and a certain minimum of protection of the individual against arbitrary state action. The sphere of international law corresponded broadly to this implicit assumption of the scope of government functions held among the chief makers and exponents of international law.

The relatively few international agreements or conventions on matters outside the sphere of traditional diplomacy were concerned with certain services and communications on which little more than technical agreement had to be obtained, and in regard to which differences of state organization were not relevant (as in the field of postal services or copyright protection).

Both in volume and scope, the area of international institutions and agreements has greatly widened. International law is today actively and continuously concerned with such divergent and vital matters as human rights and crimes against peace and humanity, international control of nuclear energy, trade organization, international labour standards, satellite communications, transport control or health regulation. This is not to say that in all or any of these fields international law prevails. But there is no doubt today that they are its legitimate concern.

As international law moves today on so many levels, it would be surprising indeed if the traditional principles of inter-state relations developed in previous centuries were adequate to cope with the vastly more divergent subject-matters of international law of the present day.

International legal rules remain basically unimpaired so far as they concern the minimum international attributes of state sovereignty. Such matters as the position of states in international relations (personality, rank, dignity, independence, self-preservation, intervention and the limits of jurisdiction over foreigners); legal rules relating to the limits of territorial sovereignty on land, sea and air; the problems relating to the freedom of the seas; and the numerous rules relating to state representation, diplomatic immunities, etc., are not greatly affected by the social change of which we have spoken. They relate either to the elements of statehood or to the universally acknowledged responsibilities of the state in matters of defence and foreign affairs.[1]

New Subjects of International Law

Not only has the scope of international law widened from the traditional fields of inter-state diplomatic relations to a variety of international economic and social transactions; there is also an increasing multiplicity of agents of international law. Governments as such appear in different capacities and functions – not only as 'sovereign', but also as lenders, borrowers and partners in international business enterprises and suppliers of goods.

1. This does not, of course, imply any judgement on the effectiveness of these rules. Recent controversies over the Continental shelf, for example, show how much disagreement on the physical extent of national sovereignty, and the limitations imposed by the principle of freedom of the seas. But the disagreements arise from conflicts of national interests, not of social organization.

Governments often act internationally through public corporations, which have certain private-law aspects and should legally be clearly distinguished from the government, or through private-law companies in which they hold a controlling or substantial interest.[2]

Although the states remain by far the most important – and the only *full* – subjects of international law, since they alone have all the attributes of territorial and jurisdictional sovereignties, and a full apparatus of government, for which they can act and be represented internationally, they are no longer the *only* subjects of international law. A major new type of international legal person is the public international corporation, the main institutional instrumentality of the new international law of cooperation. It is through public international organizations – equipped with more or less functional and financial autonomy – that the states carry out the various cooperative activities which are increasingly becoming a condition of survival of the contemporary world. There is a great variety of these public international agencies, with regard to functions, powers and legal status. On a worldwide level, most of them have been constituted as specialized agencies of the United Nations. These range from the, operationally and financially, autonomous agencies such as the World Bank and the International Monetary Fund, to the predominant type of advisory or research bodies, in the fields of labour, health, food and agriculture, education and communications. Many other organizations of this type have been established on a regional basis – such as the various regional development banks or the European Communities. There are also mixed public-private bodies such as the Intelsat, an international consortium for satellite communications, in which the principal shareholder is a private – though publicly supervised – US corporation (Comsat), while the other parties are represented through government postal or telecommunications agencies.

It is now generally recognized that international personality must attach to public international organizations, and many of the constitutive treaties specifically confer legal personality upon the agencies constituted by these treaties. Although functional international organizations, not being states, cannot claim the full attributes of

2. e.g. the British Government in the British Petroleum Company or the French Government in the Compagnie Française des Pétroles.

national sovereignty, their increasing role in the international legal processes is now universally recognized. As the Rapporteur for the last of the International Law Commission's drafts on the law of treaties stated:

the number of international agreements concluded by international organizations in their own names, both with States and with each other, and registered as such with the Secretariat of the United Nations, is now very large, so that inclusion in the general definition of 'international agreements' for the purposes of the present articles seems really to be essential.[3]

Whether public international organizations are to be considered as having the capacity of being parties to 'treaties', was left open by the Commission, and the subsequent Vienna Convention on Treaties. But whether they be called 'treaties' or 'quasi-treaties', the steadily increasing number and range of international agreements concluded by public international organizations is an inevitable reflection of their growing role in the functional collaboration between nations, in a vast variety of matters – ranging from international development loans to communications and international measures to curb pollution.

International Economic Development Law and the Role of Private Corporations

The most important new field of international law that has emerged in the post-war world, is that best described as 'international economic development law'. This comprises the complex of international economic transactions, in which governments, public international organizations and private corporations participate, as parties to bilateral, or multilateral transactions designed to promote the economic and general development of the less developed countries. Of course, international transactions concerning the exploitation of natural resources, have existed for a long time. But the purpose as well as the legal character of these 'concession agreements' is essentially different from that of the post-war economic development agreement. The former is a purely commercial transaction governed

3. [1962] 2 *Ybk I.L.C.*, at p. 32.

by private law. Concessions were granted, in return for the payment of a – usually low – licence fee or royalty, which left it entirely to the concessionaire to decide whether and in what manner to exploit the concession. Overwhelmingly, concessions were obtained by the industrial companies of the developed countries, either in the colonies of the western world or in the countries of Latin America which, while politically independent, generally were not in a position of equal economic bargaining power *vis-à-vis* the American or European corporations.

A series of nationalization measures of the last thirty years – beginning with the Mexican land expropriations of the late 1930s, and including such events as the 1951 nationalization of the Anglo-Iranian Oil properties in Iran, the nationalization of the Dutch tobacco plantations in Indonesia, the nationalization of the Suez Canal owned by the Suez Canal Company, the more recent partial nationalizations of foreign-owned copper mines and other mineral properties in the Congo, Chile, Guyana and Zambia, and the nationalization of banking in several African countries, are all part of the reaction against, and the transformation of this kind of international relationship.

The new type of economic development agreement must be regarded as essentially pertaining to the sphere of public international law, although its parties are usually the government of a developing country on the one side, and a private corporation, or a consortium on the other side – quite often with the participation of a national or an international public lending agency. These transactions, such as the Iranian Oil Agreement of 1954, between the Government of Iran and seven major western oil companies, the Lamco Iron Ore Venture of 1960, beteeen the Government of Liberia and various foreign consortia, or the recent agreements between the governments of Nigeria and Zambia, converting the full ownership of the foreign companies into minority holdings in joint ventures with the governments – generally form part of a national economic development plan. They are often based on national investment laws, which lay down the conditions of foreign investments. Invariably they impose definite obligations upon the foreign investors, including the training of local labour, managerial and scientific personnel, definite production goals, and a complex of economic and social obligations such as roads, harbours, hospitals, schools and other social facilities. The public-law character of these agreements is underlined by the frequent inclusion of arbitration clauses. The arbitration tribunals usually consist of three members, a neutral chairman – often an international law professor – and the other two appointed by the parties. The tribunals are often directed to apply 'the general principles of law recognized among civilized nations' (e.g. in the Iranian Oil Agreement) or to apply 'principles of good faith and good will' (as in the Sapphire-NIOC arbitration) – which amounts to very much the same thing. The institutionalization, and the essentially public-law character of the international economic development agreement has been underlined by the World Bank sponsored Convention for the Settlement of Investment Disputes between states and nationals of other states, of 1965, which established an international centre for the settlement of investment disputes. The convention provides for conciliation and arbitration procedures.

It is an inevitable consequence of this mixture of public and private participants and objectives in contemporary international transactions that not only is there an increased intermingling between public and private law but also that private corporations must now be regarded as – in a limited but important sense – participants in the development of public international law. This is in accordance with the analysis of such outstanding contemporary writers as Phillip C. Jessup who in 1956 observed that 'The use of transnational law would supply a large storehouse of rules on which to draw, and it would be unnecessary to worry whether public or private law applies in certain cases'[4] (1956, p. 51) and of Myres McDougal who, in his Hague lectures of 1953, stressed a need for a contemporary study of international law that would include international government, government organizations, private associations and private corporations.

The Legal Character of International State Transactions

The widening and diversification of international transactions is no less important for the legal characterization of international state

4. McDougal, 'International law, power and policy: a contemporary conception', 82 Hague *Recueil des Cours* (1953), p. 137.

transactions. The traditional doctrine is that governments entering into international commercial transactions and, in particular, governments seeking foreign loans, can never be deemed to have submitted to a law other than their own, because to hold otherwise would derogate from their sovereignty. This doctrine, which, in its most radical form, sponsored by Latin America, regards state loans as diplomatic acts rather than legal transactions, received a rather fatal blow from the decision of the House of Lords in the *Bond-holders'* case[5] and in simultaneous decisions of the Supreme Courts of Sweden and Norway. All these cases arose in connection with the Joint Resolution of the United States Congress (1933) which had declared any provision requiring payment in gold or in a particular kind of coin or currency to be contrary to public policy. The above-mentioned judgements all denied that the fact that a state was a party to a transaction precluded it from submitting to a foreign law, in this case, the law of the United States:

It cannot be disputed that a government may expressly agree to be bound by a foreign law. It seems to me equally indisputable that without any expressed intention the inference that a government so intended may be necessarily inferred from the circumstances; as where a government enters into a contract in a foreign country for the purchase of land situated in that country in the terms appropriate only to the law of that country; or enters into a contract of affreightment with the owners of a foreign ship on the terms expressed in a foreign bill of lading; or employs in a foreign country labour in circumstances to which labour laws would apply.[6]

The significance of the admission that sovereign states entering into financial or commercial transactions may drop the mantle of sovereignty and participate in agreements either governed by the private law of another state, or by some specially drawn-up provisions that may contain elements blended of public and private law, will survive the occasion that caused the new departure. This does not mean that this type of transaction is 'non-sovereign' or 'non-governmental'. The basic social fact, of which international, like municipal, law must take account, is that:

5. *R.* v. *The International Trustee for the Protection of Bondholders Aktien-gesellschaft*, [1937] A.C. 500.
6. [1937] A.C. 500, 531 (per Lord Atkin).

The lines of demarcation between the political and economic activities of the State have become blurred and it is in this borderland that State trading flourishes.[7]

Governments may borrow money from foreign private institutions, as in the above-mentioned cases; or they may subscribe shares in international public institutions which, in turn, make loans to other governments or private enterprises. Such loans may have to be backed by government guarantees (as in the case of loans made by the International Bank for Reconstruction and Development), or they may be given on a commercial basis (as in the case of the International Finance Corporation, an affiliate of the IBRD). The public lender may acquire bonds (portfolio investment) or equity shares. Governments that need the investment of capital and skill from abroad may go into partnership with foreign private enterprises through joint companies in which they retain a majority, and the foreign interest acquire a minority holding (as in the case of the reconstituted copper mining operations of Chile and Zambia, where the governments hold 51 per cent and the foreign investor 49 per cent);[8] or through a concession agreement between the government and a group of foreign companies (as in the case of the Iranian Oil Consortium of 1954); or a government may make a loan to an international public entity for a mixture of economic and political reasons (e.g. the 1954 loan of $100,000,000 by the US Government to the European Coal and Steel Community). Public international institutions and governments may engage in a joint loan to another government (as in the case of the Indus Basin Development Fund). Governments have become increasingly engaged in international economic transactions and enterprises in a variety of ways. Neither politically nor technically has the ancient assumption that a government, when consenting to borrow money from abroad, does so with the condescending gesture of a sovereign, kept much of its validity. At present, most of the relevant transactions are *sui generis*. Certain standard forms are developing very much like the standard contracts of private law. Arbitration clauses often avoid the awkward problem of the submission of the borrowing state to a foreign municipal law

7. Fawcett, 'Legal aspects of state trading', 25 *Brit. Ybk Int. Law* 35 (1948).

8. In Chile, the left-wing Allerde government, in 1971, took over the remaining foreign copper interests, on terms not agreed at the time of writing.

and jurisdiction. In the absence of specific provisions, the usual tests of private international law will decide the proper law and competent jurisdiction, and the above-mentioned difficulties of deciding by the form of transaction or by the status of the parties recur in this connexion. In a basic article on the subject, Dr Mann has not only suggested that the intention of the parties should be the guiding test for the ascertainment of the 'proper law' of the transaction, but also that these international contracts should be internationalized, in the sense that generally acknowledged international contract rules, perhaps the specific application of the general principles of law recognized among civilized nations in this sphere, should be applied.[9]

The Impact of State Trading on International Legal Obligations

If the transition from the 'night-watchman' state to one actively moulding the economic and social life of the nation proceeded everywhere to the same degree and at the same pace, the equilibrium of international law would not be greatly disturbed. While the substance of mutual obligations might be affected, it would be essentially the same for all states, and the reciprocity of international obligations, which is essential to the functioning of international law in a society of sovereign states, would not be impaired. However, the change in the functions and philosophies of government is not universal. At the very least there are vital differences of emphasis. This is most marked in the sphere of international trade. Such legal rules and standards as have developed in this field presuppose that trade is conducted by private enterprise, while the state exercises at most certain police functions, notably in the regulation of exports and imports, through customs, tariffs, quotas, quality tests and the like.

While, in the course of the present century, this presumption of a family of nations trading freely, through private enterprise, guided only by economic considerations of cost price and profit, has been increasingly eroded under the impact of nationalist policies, the forms of private trade have been retained in a majority of states. The political scientist or the economist may well hold that, for

9. See Mann, 'The law governing state contracts', 21 *Brit. Ybk Int. Law* 11–33 (1944).

example, the apostle of free enterprise, the United States, has, through a powerful arsenal of legislative and administrative measures, greatly departed from the concept of free international trade.[10] In this arsenal are tariffs or quotas, the direction of trade in certain goods to certain countries, the granting of subsidies to agricultural products, the compulsory use of American shipping for waterborne trade or bilateral deals in surplus commodities. But in legal theory international trade in the United States remains private. In many states, on the other hand, notably in the whole of the Communist bloc, the state as such is, either directly or through a wholly government-controlled corporation, the actual manager and operator of trading corporations. International trading organizations and mechanisms in such states are instruments of economic planning. They are also, to a far larger extent than in the more or less liberal economic systems that survive, agents of state policy. For example, the granting of long-term credits, at very low rates of interest, by state-owned Soviet credit institutions to the governments of under-developed countries may or may not be justified in the long run by economic considerations. Certainly, the terms of the loans made are determined by considerations of state policy. The relatively liberal states may counter – and they may, indeed, be compelled to do so by the exigencies of international politics – by using their own state instrumentalities, such as government-owned export-import banks, for the corresponding granting of low-interest loans at deliberately uneconomic rates. But they can do so only at the expense of their free-trade philosophy, and by the sacrifice of the principles of commercial and economic philosophy which their private industries and commercial financial institutions wish to maintain.

For an international economy which is at least basically directed by private enterprise and free-trade ideals, the most important single instrument of legal support for an expansion of international trade has been the 'most-favoured-nation' clause. As formulated in the General Agreement on Tariffs and Trade (article I), this means that 'any advantage, privilege or immunity granted by a contracting

10. See, for a critical survey of these measures and of their impact on international trade, Miller, 'Foreign trade and the security state', 7 *Journal of Public Law* 37 (1958). And, for a survey of British state-trading agencies, see Fawcett, 'Legal aspects of state trading', 25 *Brit. Ybk Int. L.* 34 (1948).

party to a product originating in or destined for any other country . . . should be immediately and unconditionally accorded to similar products originating in or destined for the territories of all other contracting parties' (see Seyid Muhammad, 1958, ch. 5, Dam, 1970).

The 'most-favoured-nation' clause does not as such lead to a direct increase of trade between two or more states. But, by guaranteeing equality of treatment to rival commercial states in the markets of a third state, and by thus eliminating discriminatory measures, especially through tariffs and customs duties, the clause serves to expand international trade under free market conditions. Any concession, any advantage granted, under free enterprise conditions by one state to another would open the doors to the enterprises able to compete commercially of any other state benefiting from the clause.

The duty of the government under the clause is, in free trade conditions, essentially one of abstention. The obligation is not to put obstacles in the way of trade flowing between private parties. But a state which conducts its own trade, through the government itself or through state-controlled corporations, buys and sells, lends or borrows, supplies or hires services, as part of an official economic policy. It tends to operate by way of specific agreements, which implement this policy: by barter deals, by special loan or technical assistance agreements, by bulk purchases or sales. Hence, the 'most-favoured-nation' clause cannot have the same meaning for a state-trading state as it has for a differently organized state. Thus the first commercial agreement between the USSR and the USA of 11 July 1935, accorded most-favoured-nation treatment (except for purchase of coal) to the USSR in the American markets, but the USSR instead of a reciprocal obligation, was asked to commit itself to purchase in the United States commodities of a specified value within a given period.[11]

In the words of a commentator:

The [most-favoured-nation] clause cannot operate to encourage expansion of trade by opening markets on a non-discriminatory basis to low-cost producers because factors other than cost and tariffs influence the decisions of state-trading buyers. In short, the most-favoured-nation clause has proved itself to be no longer a sufficient desideratum for private-enterprise

11. cf. Domke and Hazard, 'State trading and most-favored-nation clause', 52 *A.J.I.L.* (1958), pp. 55, 57.

states in their commercial relations with state-trading states to constitute a *quid pro quo* for important tariff concessions by private-enterprise states.[12]

Yet, the state-trading nations of the Soviet bloc have been insistent on the use of the most-favoured-nation clause, for example, in a Soviet proposal to include an unconditional most-favoured-nation clause in an all-European Agreement of Economic Cooperation.[13] They have explained this desire as an expression of the principle of sovereign equality in the relations of nations, as a symbol of the principle of non-discrimination rather than an instrument of active expansion of trade.[14] But after the unsuccessful experiments of the inter-war period it is unlikely that a general agreement on these lines, between state-trading nations and the others, will be possible. General trade agreements, such as GATT, based on the most-favoured-nation clause are likely to remain limited to states that share at least a minimum of common organization and principles in the conduct of trade. Even in the relations between these states serious rifts have already occurred, because some of the parties depart more heavily than others from the principle of free trade and equality of opportunity (for example, through the granting of special subsidies to agriculture). In an insecure and tense world, preoccupied with cold-war strategy and defence considerations, the tendency is, in many ways, more strongly towards state trading than towards free trade. Moreover, the concern of underdeveloped countries for economic growth has led to the nationalization of import–export trade. As for the relations between 'private traders' and 'state traders' – at least those state-trading nations that are politically divided from the private-trade nations – international economic relations are likely to develop, if at all, on the basis of *quid pro quo*.[15] Any retention of the most-favoured-nation clause in relations between

12. Hazard, 'Commercial discrimination and international law', 52 *A.J.I.L.* 495 (1958).

13. Economic Commission for Europe, *UN Doc. E/ECE/*270, 12 March 1957.

14. See the arguments as reported by Hazard, 52 *A.J.I.L.*, p. 495.

15. Although the Finnish-Soviet Treaty of 1947 contains the most-favoured-nation clause, the really important provision is that 'the Governments of the Contracting Parties will from time to time enter into negotiations for the purpose of concluding agreements defining the size and character of mutual delivery of commodities . . .' (Art. 1).

state-trading nations and others has political rather than economic significance. It emphasizes the principle of equality of opportunity.[16] But the actual trade relations between such states will be governed by specific agreements for the purchase and sale of fixed quantities of goods (Seyid Muhammad, 1958, p. 240). Trade agreements concluded in recent years between the new states of Africa and such essentially private enterprise countries as Japan bear this out. The principal objective of these trade agreements is to ensure an approximate equilibrium between exports and imports. It is only within these overall objectives that limited freedom of trade is permitted. Schedules of categories of goods for export and import are laid down (Verbit, 1969).

The difficulties of maintaining an equilibrium of rights and obligations, or even a comparable meaning of concepts, such as 'commercial and financial considerations'[17] or 'most-favoured-nation treatment' between states of basically different economic organization are likely to lead to an intensification of trade relations between more compact groups of states linked by common interests and principles. The counterpart to the Communist trading bloc, whose members all regard trade as an adjunct of state policy, is not so much GATT as the evolving European Economic Community.

Government Immunities in International Transactions

It is a necessary corollary of the extension of government activities in international commerce that the immunities from foreign jurisdiction granted by traditional international law to governments should no longer be applied to commercial transactions – whether the state acts directly through a government agency, or through the intermediary of a semi-autonomous government corporation. The need for such a restriction is in fact now recognized in the great majority of states – with the notable exception of the British courts, which – despite doubts voiced in some decisions[18] continue to maintain the

16. Schwarzenberger, 'The most-favoured-national standard in British state practice', 22 *Brit. Ybk Int. L.* 96, 113 (1945); Wilson (1953, p. 246).

17. British-Soviet Commercial Agreement of 1930.

18. See, e.g. *Lord Denning* in *Rahimtoola* v. *Nizam of Hyderabad*, [1958] A.C. 379, [1957] 3 All E.R. 441.

principle of absolute immunity for governments.[19] The United States adopted the principle of restricted immunity in 1952, in the so-called Tate Letter,[20] although a decision of 1955[21] limited the practical effect of the principle by refusing the establishment of New York jurisdiction through the seizure of the assets held by the Republic of Korea, the defendant, in a New York bank. But in 1961 the State Department, in another case declared that 'Where under international law a foreign government is not immune from suit, attachment of its property for the purpose of obtaining jurisdiction is not prohibited.'[22]

However, the United States, like a majority of foreign states, still refuses to execute a judgement against the property of a foreign sovereign.

The restriction of government immunity has been rationalized in two different ways. The first approach, now adopted by most Continental countries, substitutes for the doctrine of absolute state immunity that of qualified immunity. Foreign states, under this doctrine, may or may not be immune from jurisdiction, according to the kind of activity in which they are engaged. Following the leadership of the Belgian and Italian courts which have since been followed by the courts of France and many other Continental countries, a distinction, familiar in Continental administrative law (see p. 398), between acts *jure imperii* and acts *jure gestionis* has been applied to this branch of international law.[23] The difficulty is how to find a reasonably precise distinction between acts of the one and the other kind, in view of the many diverse ways in which governments may engage in economic and commercial activities. For this reason neither the functional test (Does the state act in its sovereign capacity?) nor the test of the form of the transaction is satisfactory.

19. See, e.g. *Baccus S.R.L.* v. *Servicio Nacional del Trigo* [1957] 1 Q.B. 438 (C.A.).

20. 26 *Dept. of State Bull.* 984 (1952).

21. *New York and Cuba Mail S.S. Company* v. *Republic of Korea*, 132 F. Sup. 684 (S.D.N.Y. 1955).

22. Letter from Legal Advisor to Attorney-General, quoted in *Stephen* v. *Zivnostenska Banka, National Corp.*, 222 N.Y.S. 2d 128, 134 (1961).

23. For surveys of the state of the doctrine and the alternative criteria, see Lauterpacht in 28 *Brit. Ybk Int. Law* 250–72 (1951), and Schmitthoff, 'Sovereign immunity in international trade', 7 *Int. & Comp. Law Quarterly* 452 (1958).

Any government activity may fulfil 'sovereign' purposes.[24] But many government departments obtain their purchases and supplies in the form of commercial contracts.

The second approach, which makes the nature of the transaction the criterion, was adopted in the Brussels Convention of 1926. Under the convention, seagoing ships (with their cargoes) operated or owned by governments for commercial purposes are in time of peace subject to the same rules as those applicable to private vessels, cargoes and equipment, and do not enjoy the immunities of government property.[25]

While this pragmatic distinction between commercial and non-commercial activities avoids the fallacious criterion of sovereignty, it leaves other doubts and difficulties unsolved. It is implicit in the doctrine that the states will continue to enjoy the traditional immunities in regard to such activities as have traditionally been held to be their proper sphere. This is not because commercial activities should be regarded as 'non-sovereign', but because any distinction between privileged and non-privileged government activities must separate out the hard core of an *irreducible minimum of government activities*. While economic activities may, in contemporary society, be undertaken by private enterprise, governments or mixed undertakings, certain activities are universally recognized to be necessarily governmental in the practice of nations. These minimum spheres include, undoubtedly, military and foreign affairs, the administration of justice, and the activities inevitably related to them. Here the difficulties of the other tests recur, at least to a limited extent. Military operations may include purchases, service contracts and licence agreements. The conduct of foreign affairs may include broadcasting contracts or the purchase of land. These problems are parallel to the difficulties of distinguishing between *gestion publique* and *gestion privée*, in the administrative law of France and other countries, as a criterion for the allocation of jurisdiction to either the administrative or the civil courts (see p. 358). But no theoretical test or principle

24. cf. *The Pesaro*, 271 U.S. 562 (1926), where the Supreme Court declared: 'We know of no international usage which regards the maintenance and advancement of economic welfare of the people in time of peace as any less a public purpose than the maintenance and training of a naval force.'

25. See 176 *L.N.T.S.* 199.

can avoid the complexities of the concrete decision. The distinction between commercial and non-commercial activities of a state is, in contemporary conditions, a sound and necessary one, even if it is difficult to apply in certain individual cases.

International Minimum Standards of Justice

Generally speaking, the citizens of any country residing abroad are subject to the laws of their state of residence. They are thus, in most respects, subject to the combination of legislative, administrative and judicial standards of the country of residence. But international law has long imposed certain limitations upon the absoluteness of that territorial sovereignty of the national state. The state of the nationality of the alien,[26] claiming on his behalf, has been held entitled to assert a certain minimum of rights in the name of international law. The type of claim that arises in this field – damages for injury to life, liberty or property caused by legislative, administrative or judicial actions of the defendant state – is, more than most parts of international law, a matter for litigation. Hence it is not surprising that in this branch of international law international courts and arbitral tribunals have been responsible for the main development of such principles as exist. Despite the voluminous number of judicial precedents, and the extraordinarily large number of monographs and articles written on the subject, much uncertainty remains.[27] This is not surprising, for the question of what may be regarded as a 'minimum standard' of international justice as reflected in the treatment of aliens[28] is intimately connected with the

26. For a recent discussion of the principles governing the 'nationality' of a multinational corporation for purposes of bringing an international claim, see *Case Concerning the Barcelona Traction, Light and Power Company, Limited*, (*2nd Phase*), [1970] I.C.J. Reports, which denied standing to the state of the great majority of shareholders of the injured corporation and held that only the state of incorporation could bring the claim.

27. For a general survey of the most important case collections and literature, see among others, Bishop (1971, ch. 9); Friedmann, Lissitzyn and Pugh (1969, pp. 745–869).

28. The term is used, for example, by Borchard, 'The minimum standard of the treatment of aliens', 38 *Michigan L. Rev.* 445 (1940); Freeman (1938, p. 497); Roth (1949).

prevailing political philosophy and practice of states. It is not the general subject of state responsibility for international delinquencies, but only the question to what extent major shifts in political and social philosophy may have affected the international minimum standards that will occupy us here.

The problem of minimum standards of protection for individuals is not, of course, confined to international law. It arises in any municipal legal system, either articulately through the embodiment of certain basic rights in a constitution – as in the United States Constitution – or implicitly in standards evolved over the centuries by the courts – as in English law. But international minimum standards are obviously more difficult to ascertain, and more liable to modifications, because only such standards as are prevalent and firmly adhered to among the majority of states that form the family of nations can be deemed to be incorporated in international law.

The most sensitive aspects of 'international minimum standards of justice' crystallize around two major areas: On the one hand, there is the problem of 'due process', a complex of procedural safeguards designed to protect the individual against arbitrariness in the dealings of a foreign state with his life, liberty or property. On the other hand, there is the question whether there are any limits that international law may properly impose – or can, at least, in the present state of international society, be deemed to have imposed – upon the liberty of any one state to interfere with the life, liberty and property of an alien in the course of a general legislative change.

To some extent the approach to both these questions depends upon one's basic legal philosophy. Those who believe in a minimum of inalienable natural rights will be more disposed to regard the departure from such rights by any one state as a violation of basic legal principles. Those who, like the present writer, believe that there are no transcendental and immutable natural-law principles detached from specific political and ethical beliefs – however widely these may be accepted among nations – will reject this approach (Friedmann, 1967, pp. 95–155, 356–9). However, the practical differences between these two approaches should not be exaggerated, at least in the realm of international law. Even the most enthusiastic supporters of natural-law philosophy must concede wide liberty of action to the 'sovereign' states which, with all the variety of their political philosophies, administrative standards and degrees of development, compose the family of some one hundred and thirty nations. On the other hand, the most determined positivists will not deny that 'general principles of law recognized by civilized nations' constitute a proper source of law, not only for the International Court of Justice,[29] but for the ascertainment of international minimum standards at any given time. It is only on this question, how far, at a time of great turbulence of clashes of political philosophies, and of much social experimentation, such international minimum standards still exist, that some observations will be offered.

Nationalization and expropriation

The basic position is concisely formulated in a statement made by Elihu Root in 1910:

There is a standard of justice, very simple, very fundamental, and of such general acceptance by all civilized countries as to form a part of the international law of the world. The condition upon which any country is entitled to measure the justice due from it to an alien by the justice which it accords to its own citizens is that its system of law and administration shall conform to this general standard. If any country's system of law and administration does not conform to that standard, although the people of the country may be content or compelled to live under it, no other country can be compelled to accept it as furnishing a satisfactory measure of treatment to its citizens. . . .[30]

But the contention that a state may be held legally responsible for any discrepancy between its own legal standards, if applied to nationals and foreigners alike, and any international minimum standards for the benefit of any aliens resident within its jurisdiction, is challenged in the Convention on Rights and Duties of States adopted by the Seventh Pan American Conference at Montevideo in 1933:

The jurisdiction of states within the limits of national territory applies to all the inhabitants.

Nationals and foreigners are under the same protection of the law and

29. See Art. 38, para. 3, of its Statute.
30. Elihu Root, 'The basis of protection to citizens residing abroad', *Proceedings, American Society of International Law* (1910), p. 16, at pp. 20–22).

the national authorities and the foreigners may not claim rights other or more extensive than those of the nationals.[31]

The controversy between the states that maintain an international minimum standard for aliens, even if this means preferred treatment over nationals, and those states that do not go beyond the acknowledgement of equality between nationals and aliens, is unlikely ever to be resolved. The first group will generally consist of the capital-exporting states, interested in the protection of their foreign investments and the commercial activities of their citizens abroad. The latter will consist of the capital-importing states in a relatively primitive stage of economic development. The number of these states – formerly concentrated in Latin America – has, in the last generation, vastly increased, not only with a series of social revolutions that have swept over eastern Europe, but through the political emancipation of a number of Asian and African countries which wish to be unimpeded in the manner of their economic and social planning. These countries are to a large extent the same that are still emotionally influenced by resentment against former political and economic domination by certain western Powers. In practice, however, this attitude is mitigated by their need to give reasonable protection to foreign capital and enterprise, whose participation, though not domination, the under-developed countries need. On the other hand, even the Communist countries seek increased commercial relations with the west.

It is believed that a solution must be sought on the basis of certain principles 'generally recognized by civilized nations'.

The first of these principles is that generally international law – as distinct from specific regional or bilateral arrangements – cannot interfere with the freedom of political and social experimentation – a legitimate and cherished aspect of national sovereignty on which present-day international law is based. No state or individual can therefore challenge any legal measures of another state that interfere with property, however sweepingly, provided only such legal measures are of general application in the country and do not single out aliens for discriminatory treatment. A necessary proviso is that such seemingly general measures do not disguise a deliberate

31. *A.J.I.L. Supp.* 75 (1934).

discrimination against aliens. This can be ascertained only against the specific circumstances of the case. A state is therefore under an obligation to pay compensation for the taking of individual properties of aliens when nationals are not similarly treated.[32] On the other hand, the liberty of a state to expropriate the property of aliens in the course of a general measure affecting nationals and aliens alike is no longer seriously challenged by most authors. Indeed, it is specifically acknowledged by the United States Government in its discussion with Mexico of 1938. There is not a single state today which, by means of an entire or partial nationalization of industries, by police-power or 'eminent domain', restrictions on the acquisition and use of property, or by taxation and a multitude of other instruments of the modern welfare state, does not, to a larger or smaller extent, interfere with private property.

On the second and consequent question whether, in the case of a general expropriation, international law can demand compensation for foreigners, even if it means preferred treatment of aliens, opinions are deeply divided.[33]

It has already been pointed out that on the general principle the 'have' and the 'have-not' nations are bound to remain divided. At the very least, it must be admitted that the assumption that nationalization without compensation is generally held to be a violation of international law is no longer valid. Here, as in so many other fields, beliefs once universally held now deeply divide the nations according to political development and economic circumstances. This division was acknowledged by the US Supreme Court in the much debated *Sabbatino* case,[34] where it held, eight to one, that the nationalization

32. See the *de Sabla Claim* (*US* v. *Panama*), Hunt's *Report*, 379, 447 (1933); also the note by Bishop (1971, pp. 851–99; Fatooros (1962, pp. 249–51).

33. For opposing viewpoints, see, among many others, Fachiri, 'Expropriation in international law', 6 *Brit. Ybk Int. L.* 159 (1925), in favour of the compensation principle; on the other hand, Fischer Williams, 'International law and the property of aliens', 9 *Brit. Ybk Int. L.*, 1 (1928), against any duty of compensation in the case of general legislative measures; and, for a general survey, Roth (1949), and Friedmann; (1953); see further p. 487. The majority of writers consider expropriation without compensation as an international delinquency. An intermediate view is taken by Lauterpacht, in the 8th edition of Oppenheim, vol. 1, p. 352, where 'the granting of partial compensation' is advocated. See also White (1961) and Schwarzenberger (1969).

34. *Banco National de Cuba* v. *Sabatino*, 376 U.S. 398 (1964).

(on terms approaching confiscation) of US-owned sugar enterprises by Cuba had to be recognized as an Act of State by US courts, even if the action violated international law. One reason for the decision – which was subsequently overruled by Congress, in the so-called Hickenlooper Amendment – was 'the basic divergence between the national interests of capital importing and capital exporting nations and between the social ideologies of those countries that favour state control of a considerable portion of the means of production and those that adhere to a free enterprise system'. Nor does the International Declaration of Human Rights of 1948, which may be said to be representative of universally held opinions, take us any further. Article 17, paragraph 2, says that 'No one shall be arbitrarily deprived of his property.' But the word 'arbitrarily' is, of course, subject to different interpretations, and the states claiming the right to expropriate without compensation in the course of a general legislative reform affecting nationals and foreigners alike will claim with strong reason that this is not an 'arbitrary' measure.

It seems more profitable to single out certain situations in which general principles of law recognized among civilized nations clearly demand compensation for the taking of alien property.[35]

The first category derives from the principle of *pacta sunt servanda*. Where a state, by international treaty, or by special contractual arrangements or concessions with foreign individuals or companies, has undertaken to protect them against expropriation or other forms of interference with property, a breach of such undertaking will be clearly an international delinquency. This is so regardless of the international constitutional position of the offending state. A distinction must be drawn between municipal power and international obligation.[36] A national parliament may have power to

35. For a principle of law to be regarded as 'generally' recognized, it is not necessary to show that it should be *universally* accepted. 'If any real meaning is to be given to the words "general" or "universal" and the like, the correct test would seem to be that an international judge before taking over a principle from private law must satisfy himself that it is recognized in substance by all the main systems of law, and that in applying it he will not be doing violence to the fundamental concepts of any of those systems.' Gutteridge (1949, p. 65).

36. It is an established principle of the international law of treaties that changes in the government – as distinct from changes in the international status – of one of the parties can have no influence on the binding force of treaties (see McNair 1961,

amend legislation that has incorporated promises in regard to the sanctity of foreign property. The enactment of such amending legislation in breach of an international commitment nevertheless constitutes an international delinquency.

Secondly, the principle of unjust enrichment should now be held to be a general principle of law recognized by civilized nations.[37] Where, as for example in the *Lena Goldfields* case,[38] a foreign company at the specific request of a foreign government has invested capital, work and technical skill in the development of mines, the expropriation of such property without compensation constitutes an unjust enrichment by the expropriating government at the expense of the alien.

But the principle of unjust enrichment works both ways. It also furnishes criteria by which a developing country, which nationalizes foreign investments or – as in the case of recent measures taken by Chile, the Congo Republic and Zambia – converts a wholly foreign-owned enterprise into one in which the foreign partner retains a minority holding, may reduce the amount of compensation due. As applied to public international law, the principle of unjust enrichment should serve to balance the benefits and losses of the parties,

---

ch. 41; Oppenheim-Lauterpacht, 1955, 925). The rationale is that internal political decisions – whether of an administrative or a legislative character – cannot affect international obligations once validly entered in accordance with constitutional process.

37. There has been surprisingly little discussion on this principle in the literature of public international law (see, however, Schwarzenberger, 1957, vol. 1, pp. 577–9; Friedmann, 1964, p. 206). That the principle of unjust enrichment is one generally recognized, though with many differences in detail, in both the common and civil-law systems, can no longer be doubted. It is specifically embodied, for example, in the German, Swiss, Italian, Spanish and Russian Civil Codes, while the French courts have developed similar principles. The principle of restitution is now sufficiently firmly established in American law to justify a separate *Restatement on Restitution*. In English law, the various actions for money had and received *quantum meruit*, constructive trust, etc., constitute the elements of a principle of unjust enrichment (cf. Lord Wright, *Legal Essays and Addresses*, chs. 1 and 2). For a comparative analysis of the principle of unjust enrichment, see, among others, Dawson (1951); Friedmann, 'The principle of unjust enrichment', 16 *Canadian Bar. Rev.* (1938), pp. 243, 365 et seq.; (1967, pp. 552–3); David and Gutteridge, 'The doctrine of unjust enrichment', 5 *Cambridge L.J.* 204 et seq.; O'Connell, 'Unjust enrichment', 5 *Amer. J. Comp. Law* 2 et seq. (1956).

38. *Annual Digest* (1929–30), Case No. 1.

in the light of contemporary concepts of equity as expressed for example in the UN resolution of December 1962, on Permanent Sovereignty over Natural Resources. In many cases of colonial or quasi-colonial investments, the investors, by virtue of their great economic superiority, and often under the political and military protection of their governments, secured concessions for their exploitation of minerals or other natural resources on terms starkly diverging from those of commercial transactions between equals. Vast tracts of lands were acquired at nominal rates, and native – often indented – labour employed at conditions far below those of a free labour market. On the other hand the investors often developed land or unexploited resources into prosperous and profitable growing concerns, which the newly independent countries have taken over. The principle of unjust enrichment would require the balancing between the undue benefits conferred upon the foreign investor, and the gain conferred upon the national economy by the development of unused resources. Although most international lawyers of the western world maintain the principle of 'vested rights', i.e. of 'prompt, full and adequate' compensation, including damages for lost profit, post-war practice has gone a considerable way towards a compromise, which can be rationalized by the principle of unjust enrichment. The settlements reached in such controversial situations as the nationalization of the Suez Canal, the Dutch Tobacco Plantations in Indonesia, or the partial nationalization of the mineral resources in various Latin American and African countries, reflect a recognition of this balance between the claims of the foreign investors and the legitimate interests of the developing countries in the control over their resources, on terms that do not burden them with crushing obligations incurred at a time when they had no control over their destinies.

Thirdly, there is the principle of estoppel.[39] Where, for example, a state invites, by prospectus or general advertisement, foreign capital to invest in the development of certain utilities or industries, and foreign entrepreneurs have responded to this invitation, an expropriation without compensation clearly justifies the application of the

39. See, in particular, Lauterpacht (1927, p. 203); Cheng (1953, p. 141); Schwarzenberger, 'The fundamental principles of law', 87 *Hague Recueil* (1955), p. 312; MacGibbon, 'Estoppel in international law', 7 *I.C.L.Q.* (1958), p. 468.

principles of estoppel or *venire contra factum proprium*. The government must be held estopped from acting contrary to reasonable expectations that it has itself created.

If to these categories is added the above-mentioned case of discriminatory treatment of aliens, a large number of situations in which compensation can fairly be expected can be met consistently with general principles of international law and equity, and without adopting the conflicting philosophies and interests of either the 'have' or the 'have-not' countries.

The solemn public affirmation of certain principles of conduct has a moral as well as a practical sanction, and it is on these that international law mainly rests. Any state that wishes to keep in good standing with international credit institutions such as the World Bank, will hesitate long before showing contempt for promises freely given to foreign investors.

A legally somewhat stronger instrument of protection is the bilateral or multilateral treaty, which binds states as such.

The United States has concluded a series of bilateral Treaties of Friendship and Commerce, which contain the following typical clause:

Property of nationals and companies of either Party shall not be taken within the territories of the other Party except for a public purpose, nor shall it be taken without the prompt payment of just compensation. Such compensation shall be in an effectively realizable form and shall represent the full equivalent of the property taken; and adequate provision shall have been made at or prior to the time of taking for the determination and payment thereof.[40]

Further typical clauses provide against discrimination in the matter of expropriations and sequestrations and beyond expropriation proper, and include a general injunction against 'unreasonable or discriminatory' impairments of vested interests.

Such treaties are no protection against bad faith or revolutionary upheavals, which may sweep the arbitration clauses overboard, together with the substance of the treaty. But neither do internal

40. Treaty between the USA and Japan, 1953, art. VI, para 3. On the whole subject, see Walker, 'Treaties for the encouragement and protection of foreign investment', 4 *Amer. J. Comp. Law* (1956), p. 229.

constitutions offer absolute protection against revolution or disobedience, as the struggle over desegregation in the United States, or the suspension of the Weimar Constitution by the Hitler government show.

But they do represent express and articulate commitments which impose restraints on the parties as long as observance of international standards does not cease altogether.

There is far less prospect at the present stage for a multilateral convention for the protection of foreign property and investment as it has been proposed, for example by the OECD.[41] Such a convention must either comprise a majority of capital-importing as well as of capital-exporting states, or it is worthless. But while states of the former group, such as India or Mexico, may enter into *ad hoc* arrangements departing from their general principles, the gap between the interests as well as the political systems and social philosophies of the two groups of states is too fundamental to permit formal agreement on the sacrosanctity of private property. The price of any multilateral convention would be vagueness, and a host of reservations in cases of 'national interest', public emergencies, 'economic necessity' and the like.

The less spectacular methods described earlier are likely to be more effective in the slow and painful evolution of principles of international law commensurate with the economic interdependence of nations.

Due Process. A far more absolute stand can be taken on the 'due-process' problem. It is true that there are considerable divergences in the civil and criminal procedure as between the common-law and the civil-law countries. It is also true that totalitarian countries, of both the Fascist and the Communist persuasion, have often deviated drastically from standards of administration of justice commonly assumed among civilized nations. Judges selected by political standards, arrest without judicial safeguards, conviction without proper trial, unlimited powers of a secret police responsible to no one except the government, extrajudicial methods of deprivation of personal

41. *Draft Convention on the Protection of Property* (Organization for Economic Cooperation and Development 1957).

liberty, procedures of the modern police state – these and a host of other matters are only too familiar. But this is not comparable to the movement for greater legal freedom in regard to interference with property and economic interests – a reflection of general developments in the structure of modern industrial society. With the partial exception of Nazi Germany, totalitarian states have not openly acknowledged or defended arbitrary procedures. They often conflict with their own professed protestations, and international law can clearly take them at their word. The Soviet Constitution of 1936 proclaims the independence of justice (article 112), the inviolability of the person (article 127) and the inviolability of the homes of citizens (article 128). The Universal Declaration of Human Rights – from which the five Communist members abstained, but did not dissent – specifically states (in Articles 9–11) that no one shall be subjected to arbitrary arrest or detention, that everyone is entitled to fair and public hearings by an independent and impartial tribunal, and that everyone charged with a penal offence has the right to be presumed innocent until proved guilty in a public trial provided with proper safeguards for the defence.

From all this it follows that we can still regard a minimum set of safeguards of proper procedure as a general principle of law recognized among civilized nations, and as one which any state can claim on behalf of its nationals abroad.[42]

42. These minimum standards of 'due process', on which judicial precedent and literature are voluminous, have been summarized by Professor Orfield in 12 *University of Pittsburgh L. Rev.* 35, 41–4 (1950) in eleven principles embodying the elements of a fair trial.

Part Six
The Function of Law in Contemporary Society

Chapter 15
The Rule of Law, the Individual and the Welfare State

State, Group and Individual

Each of the foregoing chapters has been concerned with some aspects of the tension between the claims of the individual, the claims of a group with which the individual is linked by ties of choice or necessity, and the claims of the state. Which of these is supreme in contemporary society? Has the state, a modern Leviathan, absorbed the individual in his service, determining not only the conditions of his material existence, but of his thoughts and emotions? Or is he enchained by the group to which he is linked, by tradition or necessity, such as the Catholic Church – more demanding in its control over the lives and actions of its members than any other religious authority; the industrial corporation by which he is employed; the labour union to which he must belong, in law or in fact, if he wishes to exercise his skill; the semi-official guild which controls the conditions of admission to a profession? Or has the individual, on the contrary, begun to be truly emancipated, free at last from the shackles of status, from the taboos of caste class or race distinctions, freer above all than at any other time in history from the enslaving effects of poverty and ignorance?

It is possible to support any of these contentions with powerful arguments.

That the state today exercises a degree of control over the individual far exceeding, in scope and intensity, that of any other period in history, has been apparent throughout our discussion of the major legal institutions of the contemporary world. It has taken over many responsibilities formerly confined to the family, or it has added new duties which take the individual out of the family nexus: responsibility for education, obligations of national service, family allowances; in the field of personal family relations, the enlargement of divorce and nullity grounds, the liberalization of abortion laws, adoption and other new state-regulated institutions profoundly affect the conditions of family life. The state has taken over vast responsibilities in the field of employment: statutory minimum standards of wages and of conditions of work: unemployment insurance and old-age pensions; workmen's compensation or industrial insurance; and the official protection of collective labour agreements.

The state has everywhere imposed far-reaching restrictions upon the use of private property, culminating in various degrees of power to expropriate for public purposes and, in many cases, the public ownership and operation of basic industries.

In the field of contract, public policy restricts the freedom of the parties by various illegality tests, designed to protect certain basic freedoms: of worship, association, labour, trade and others, and by shielding, to some extent, the weaker party from the more obvious effects of inequality of bargaining. The growing concern with the environment is bound to lead to further public-law restrictions on freedom of property and contract.

Where trade remains in private hands, a complex supervisory apparatus regulates the conditions of fair trade, by a multitude of statutory provisions and institutional controls, from compulsory tariffs of hire-purchase transactions to the elaborate apparatus of anti-trust laws, restrictions on mergers, monopolies and conditions of trade.

To some extent, similar functions are exercised by the criminal law which, by means of so-called public-welfare offences, assures compliance with certain minimum standards of trade and business.

To many it will appear, however, that, at least in contemporary western society outside the Communist sphere, the group to which the individual is immediately beholden controls his life more directly, and more powerfully, than the more distant state.

While, on the whole, religious controls have greatly weakened in modern society, the Catholic Church still has a commanding influence over the personal life of its followers, especially in such matters as divorce and birth control. The great majority of people, dependent for their livelihood on gainful employment, are subject to the dual discipline of their employer and of the collective organization – professional body, trade association or labour union – which in large measure controls the conditions under which they may work, and often enjoys monopolistic power. At the same time, every member of the community is, as citizen and consumer, subject to the conditions imposed by the standardized contract terms of the group in control of the particular activity: transport, insurance, rent, supplies of basic materials.

To a considerable extent, the power of one group is checked by the countervailing power of another: that of the corporation by that of the labour union, that of the big manufacturer by that of the big retailer, that of the dominating producers of one commodity by the competition of other materials. But the consumer is generally unorganized and helpless, except for the minimum protection afforded to him by the state, e.g. through supervision of public utilities or the protection, as yet very halting, of the individual employee or worker against the arbitrary power of the corporation or the union.

Again, certain important activities are controlled in some communities by the state, in others by a private group. This is particularly true of the sensitive and, for the long-term future of humanity, probably decisive, sphere of the activities of the mind: schools, universities, public press, radio and television. Here, the freedom of the mind and the ability of the individual to develop to his fullest potential are perilously poised between the dangers of total state control over the instrumentalities of modern education and communications and the dangers of private group control, dominated by commercial interests and the political philosophy of big business.

Clearly, the balance between these conflicting claims, pressures and values is differently struck in different communities. Where either the state – controlled by a small group of policy-makers – or a private group equipped with overwhelming resources is wholly or overwhelmingly in control, the individual is crushed and freedom is either extinguished or emptied of its meaning. Either the direct thought-control of the totalitarian state – Communist or Fascist – or the more subtle thought-control of political or commercial television and other media in the democracies, may lead modern mankind towards 1984.

The law can do much to ensure a fair balance between the

conflicting demands and pressures. It can, as we have seen, devise safeguards for the protection of the individual, both against arbitrary executive power and against the unchecked power of private groups, so that it can help to ensure a fair balance between conflicting groups within the state. It can help or hinder a particular trend. But in the strong battle of social forces on which our future depends, the law is but one of many moulding elements. Although, as we have seen in the introductory chapter, the law is today a much more active agent in social evolution than in former times, it is still an instrument of order, bearing the imprint of the forces that shape our society.

Freedom and status

In legal terms, some of the major issues of our time can be formulated in terms of the antithesis of status and freedom. Maine's celebrated dictum that, in progressive societies, the move has been from status to contract, has long been modified by events which have surrounded the freedom of modern man with new status conditions. This expresses itself not only in the field of contract – Maine's symbol of the emancipation of the individual – but in many other fields of law. The institutionalization of contract, through compulsory terms, standardized conditions, collective bargaining and other developments, has been analysed in an earlier chapter (see chapter 4). The result is a new kind of status, for the worker who must accept the conditions set for him by groups of employers and labour officials, while the consumer must eat, dwell or travel on terms prescribed for him by standardized contracts. Similar developments can be traced in the field of tort liability and, to some extent, in criminal law. The theory corresponding to Main's contract dictum would show a movement from liability and responsibility for acts as such, to liability for actions or omissions for which a morally fully responsible individual would answer because he has exercised freedom of choice. Yet, we have seen that tort liability is increasingly moving away from the fault principle – which, itself, has lost the moral connotation of former centuries – and that, to an ever-increasing extent, status-like insurance is substituted for the individual responsibility flowing from the tortious act. In some degree, the growth of the statutory offence – often detached from *mens rea* –

shows a parallel development in criminal law. The growth of the new status versus individual freedom means that legal liability again results more and more from a given position – as employer, land owner, consumer, worker – rather than from the exercise of the free will by an independent individual.

Yet this is not the status of medieval law. For the new status, while limiting this often theoretical freedom of decision of the individual – a freedom that led to the degradations, the slums, the miseries of the many, compared with the wealth and power of a very few – has at the same time released new energies and given new opportunities. The worker who is dependent on whatever his employer and union may work out for him between them has, at the same time, far greater opportunities of education and intellectual development. The law ensures for him minimum standards of work, housing and compensation, which free him from the incessant toil of the feudal peasant and the early industrial worker. In modern democracies the law has gradually, though often against tremendous obstacles, diminished or removed the status barriers that kept people relentlessly within their class, race or religion. In particular – and here we see the main principle still working itself out in a kind of delayed action effect – the woman now enjoys a legal freedom of movement, which is still far from full equality with that of men, but which she has never enjoyed before in the history of western civilization.

And where modern industrial and urbanized man has surrendered his legal freedom – as he has largely in labour relations or as a member of the armed forces or civil service, or as a consumer – he has done so – at least to some extent – less by a necessity inherited from generation to generation, than by choice, for in a world where the average person is perilously poised between an abundant life and total destruction, the craving for security has largely displaced the craving for freedom. It is not only the worker who increasingly prefers a civil-service-like security to the individual freedom to come and go as he likes, but in the days of the large corporation, of the salaried executive replacing the old-style entrepreneur, the desire for security and stability of employment has largely displaced the adventurousness and uncertainties of early capitalism. The mythology of 'free enterprise' survives, especially in the annual speeches of the presidents of manufacturers' and employers' associations. The ideology of 'free enterprise' is usually more articulate when it is a question of opposing taxation or union demands than when it comes to a call for state action for higher protective tariffs against competitive imports. It is not from higher taxes – which may, or at least should, in part finance better schools – but from the dulling of the minds through mass-produced slogans and entertainment that the danger of a new 'status' society arises, a society more enslaved than feudal Europe, because it has the memory and the techniques of freedom, because it is articulate in a way than an inner élite of skilful and ruthless manipulators can exploit to consolidate their own dominion, while keeping the masses in a state of dumb passivity, hovering between contentment and the threat of annihilation.

The welfare state and the rule of law

The scientific significance of the vast volume of discussion – and otherwise – about the meaning of the 'rule of law' is of modest proportions.

In a purely formal sense, the rule of law means no more than organized public power. In that sense, any system of norms based on a hierarchy of orders, even the organized mass murders of the Nazi regime, qualify as law.[1] As the 'science of law' is understood by positivist theories – the rule of law means the rule of organization. Such a concept is as unassailable as it is empty.

It is on the rule of law in its ideological sense, as implying the yardstick by which to measure 'good' against 'bad' law that the discussion has centred.[2] The difficulty, however, is that to give to the 'rule of law' concept a universally acceptable ideological content

1. cf. Goodhart, 'The rule of law and absolute sovereignty', 106 *University of Pennsylvania L. Rev.* 943 et seq. (1958) who distinguishes 'rule by law which can be the most efficient instrument in the enforcement of tyrannical rule' from 'rule under the law which is the essential foundation of liberty'. See also the present writer's earlier discussion (1948) and (1951, ch. 13). This distinction is ignored, and the present writer's position incorrectly stated, by Fuller (1969, p. 107).

2. See for an example, the colloquium on 'The rule of law as understood in the west', held in September 1957 at the University of Chicago under the sponsorship of the International Association of Legal Science and the International Committee of Comparative Law. For a general survey, see Marsh, 'Defining the rule of law', 'Freedom and legislative power', *Listener*, 28 May, 4 June 1959.

is as difficult as to achieve the same for 'natural law'. In fact, the two concepts converge. Just as natural-law philosophy covers the whole spectrum from revolutionary to ultra-conservative ideologies, so the 'rule of law' means to one the absolute integrity of private property, to another the maintenance of private enterprise, free from state control and official regulation, and to another the preservation of the 'right to work' against the power of the unions to determine conditions of labour. To some, the rule of law means a minimum of administrative power, even if it entails the sacrifice of good government, whereas to others it means, on the contrary, assurance by the state to all of minimum standards of living and security.

Is it possible to extract, from the welter of extravagant and conflicting claims, any minimum content that is generally acceptable? Such an attempt must, of course, base itself on values and standards acceptable to contemporary society, not on conditions of the past. For this reason, as we already noted in an earlier chapter (see p. 378), Dicey's formulation of the rule of law is no longer acceptable, since it equates the rule of law with the absence not only of arbitrary, but even of 'wide discretionary' power.[3]

The weaknesses of Dicey's conception are magnified in the modern reformulation of the rule of law by Hayek, which: (a) identifies the rule of law with the economic and political philosophy of *laissez-faire*, and (b) is predicated on the fixity of legal rules, and the corresponding absence of judicial discretion.[4]

Other than in a purely formal sense, we cannot formulate any content for the 'rule of law' which would be equally applicable to

3. The following reformulation of Dicey's ideas as applicable to the modern welfare state eliminates the equation of arbitrary and wide discretionary power: 'There are, I believe, ideas of universal validity reflected in Dicey's "three meanings" of the rule of law. . . . (1) in a decent society it is unthinkable that government, or any officer of government, possesses arbitrary power over the person or the interests of the individual; (2) all members of society, private persons and government officials alike, must be equally responsible before the law; and (3) effective judicial remedies are more important than abstract constitutional declarations in securing the rights of the individual against encroachment by the State' (Harry W. Jones, 'The rule of law and the welfare state', in 58 *Columbia L. Rev.* 149 (1958)).

4. For a more detailed criticism of Hayek's concept of the rule of law, see Friedmann (1951, ch. 13); also, Jones, 'The rule of law and the welfare state', p. 143.

Democratic, Fascist, Communist, Socialist and Catholic states.[5] The problem is narrowed down if we seek to establish a meaning for the rule of law in modern democratic society, but even here we shall have to differentiate between various types of democracies. Thus, the common-law tradition emphasizes the need for a unitary system of judicial control as an essential safeguard of individual liberties against administrative arbitrariness, while the Continental systems regard the full-fledged hierarchy of administrative courts as a more secure safeguard against abuse of public power.

But the differences within the common-law family are no less important, especially as between the British and the American models of a 'government under law'. Any attempt to formulate a concept of the rule of law acceptable to modern democratic ideas must seek to find a common denominator.[6]

A democratic ideal of justice must rest on the three foundations of equality, liberty and ultimate control of government by the people. It is, however, far from easy to give these concepts a specific content. Democracy is certainly based on the ideal of equality, but no democratic state has seriously attempted to translate this ideal into the absolute equality of all. There are numerous inevitable inequalities of function and status, between adults and infants, between sane persons and insane, between civilians and military, between private citizens and officials. We can still not formulate the

5. A notable attempt to formulate minimum requirements for a legal system based on the 'inner morality' of law, but distinct from the traditional natural law philosophy, is that of Professor Lon Fuller (1964; rev. edn, 1969). Fuller regards the following eight principles, which constitute a kind of 'procedural natural law', as essential to any legal system: (1) generality; (2) promulgation; (3) prospective legal operation, i.e. generally prohibition of retroactive laws; (4) intelligibility and clarity; (5) avoidance of contradictions; (6) avoidance of impossible demands; (7) constancy of the law through time, i.e. avoidance of frequent changes; (8) congruence between official action and declared rule.

Among the many critics of this approach, see H. L. A. Hart, Book Review 78 *Harvard L. Rev.* 1284 (1965), who describes Fuller's eight principles as 'essentially principles of good craftsmanship'. Also see Friedmann (1967 at p. 18). For Fuller's reply to his critics, see (1969, ch. 5).

6. For an important attempt to analyse the meaning of the rule of law, and especially the tension between economic liberties and public interest in contemporary American law, see Hale (1952). For a briefer analysis of contemporary British developments, see Lord Denning (1949).

principle of equality in more specific terms than Aristotle who said that justice meant the equal treatment of those who are equal before the law. We can give to this apparent tautology a more concrete meaning by saying that a democratic ideal of justice demands that inequalities shall be inequalities of function and service but shall not be derived from distinctions based on race, religion, or other personal attributes. In a society governed by international law we should add that inequalities must not be based on nationality. But in a society still dominated by national sovereignty this is no more than a pious aspiration.

The meaning of 'liberty' is hardly more easy to define. In terms of a democratic ideal of justice, liberty means certain rights of personal freedom which must be secure from interference by government. They include legal protection from arbitrary arrest, freedom of opinion and association, of contract, labour and many others. Briefly, they may be subsumed under the two broad categories of the freedom of the person and the freedom of the mind. But there is perhaps only one legal and constitutional maxim of general validity which can be deduced from this principle: that in so far as an individual is granted specific rights they should be secure from arbitrary interference.

This means that a judiciary as independent from interference by the executive as is possible, given the interlocking of state functions and the human factor in the judicial function, is an essential of the democratic ideal of justice. But it is impossible to lay down a generally accepted rule either as to the substance of these rights or as to the manner of their protection. The Declaration of Rights, adopted in 1948 by the United Nations, is vastly different from the Bill of Rights embodied in the American Constitution. The Australian Constitution contains no individual rights other than the guarantee of religious freedom and perhaps – though this is still very much open to doubt – a protection of the individual from the restriction of free inter-state trade by state regulation (section 92). British law knows of no guarantees of individual rights other than the limited guarantees of personal freedom in the Bill of Rights of 1688 and the Habeas Corpus Acts. Some additional protection for individuals is provided by the procedures established under the European Convention on Human Rights and Fundamental

Freedoms. In one type of democracy, a written constitution, which it is normally very difficult to alter, formulates and at the same time petrifies the meaning of the rule of law in a manner binding upon legislative and executive alike. Under these systems, a law court acquires the decisive function of an authoritative interpreter of the meaning of the rule of law, within the framework of the constitution. This conception of 'government under law', classically represented by the United States legal system, commends itself especially to federal democracies (though not to all of them) and the post-war Constitutions of West Germany and India have placed a court in a comparable position of ultimate arbiter, both of individual rights guaranteed in the Constitution, and of the respective rights and powers of federation and states. Although the Canadian Bill of Rights (1960) is, in form, an ordinary statute, the Supreme Court of Canada, in the *Drybone* case (see p. 59) treated it as 'higher law', which invalidates any legislative provision incompatible with it (such as discrimination against Indians). The only difference between this type of constitutional guarantee and that of the aforementioned federal constitutions is that the Canadian Bill of Rights can, in theory, be amended or abrogated by ordinary statute. It is difficult to exaggerate the difference between this system of ultimate judicial control, which gives way to political control only in the rare cases of constitutional amendment, and the purely political control of constitutional power which prevails in countries such as Great Britain.[7] There the rule of law leaves Parliament as the supreme law-giver, and the judge has the much more limited function of interpreting statutes, in so far as they come before him. If his interpretation differs too much from that of prevailing public opinion, a simple statute will alter the law. The difference between these two types of democratic systems is far more fundamental than that between English and Continental ideals of justice which Dicey exaggerated so much.[8]

Lastly, the principle of control by the people means that law must

7. See, for an interesting brief comparative appreciation, Hamson, '*La Notion de l'égalité dans les pays occidentaux*', *Revue internationale de droit comparé*, January–March 1958, p. 54.

8. The French Constitution of 1958 gives to the *Conseil Constitutionnel* the power (and duty) to rule on the constitutionality of laws and regulations before their promulgation (Article 61).

ultimately be the responsibility of the elected representatives of the people. This is, indeed, a vital principle but it can say little about the technique by which the modern legislator can discharge this function.

A more serious and universal danger to the principles of representative democracy arises from the decline of active civic participation – a product of the explosive increase of numbers, of urbanization and of the dulling impact of modern mass media of communication. Some democracies – e.g. Australia – seek to solve the problem of apathy by statutory compulsion to vote. But even such a system – which many other democracies reject as basically undemocratic – cannot create an active sense of participation, beyond the occasional process of voting. On the national level, only a few small democracies, notably Switzerland, have been able to preserve something of a direct participation of the average citizen in national processes. The large democracies of today must seek to maintain or revive the average citizen's sense of responsibility and participation by a variety of devices: education in public and international affairs, which, of course, is meaningful only where freedom of press and other media of opinion is vigorously maintained; the decentralization of functions in the body politic, which enables the citizen to participate actively in the affairs of his local community (covering such vital fields as education, health, town planning and the like), of his church, his trade union or the various social services. None of these devices can counter the basic facts of our society, which tend to separate the elected representatives of the people more and more from the electors, because of numbers, distances and the complexities of the modern machinery of government. It is all the more important that the law should be rigorous and vigilant in its watch over abuses, e.g. in assuring freedom from pressure in elections, in the standards of integrity imposed upon members of legislative bodies no less than those of the executive and the judiciary. By such preventive and curative devices, the law can help to maintain or restore the principles of control by the people – and the means by which it attempts to do so must vary from country to country and from one situation to another. The basic safeguard of this aspect of the 'rule of law' lies, however, in extra-legal elements: only a society whose members are imbued with their personal sense of responsibility can profit from legal safeguards.

The expansion of government functions and the rule of law[9]

No contemporary analysis of the rule of law can ignore the vast expansion of government functions which has occurred as a result both of the growing complexity of modern life, and of the minimum postulates of social justice which are now part of the established public philosophy in all civilized countries.

Five different state functions call for analysis. They result from the activities of the state: first, as Protector; secondly, as Provider; thirdly, as Entrepreneur; fourthly, as Economic Controller; fifthly, as Arbitrator.

The state acts first as a protector. This is its traditional function, and classical liberal thought regards it as the only legitimate function of the state. Older British and American decisions reflect this conception in describing defence, foreign affairs, police and the administration of justice as the legitimate functions of the state.[10] To this may be added a limited taxing power confined to the efficient discharge of these functions. These are the traditional spheres of state sovereignty, and consequently, it is in this field that the inequalities which detract from the rule of law in Dicey's sense are most evident, though Dicey consistently attempted to belittle them for the sake of his principle. The immunities and privileges of the Crown, in regard to litigation, taxing, submission to statutes and other fields, are survivals of feudal sovereignty; the special law and jurisdiction for military forces are an aspect of the defence power. The important prerogatives of the executive lie in the fields of foreign affairs and defence. The emergency defence powers of the executive in time of danger, the so-called acts of state, and other prerogatives which are above judicial scrutiny are all detractions from the principle of equality. They are bearable only as long as state functions are limited. As the activities of the state extend in the direction of industrial and commercial enterprise and of social services, the whole field of these privileges and immunities requires redefinition and limitation; otherwise it would gradually engulf a growing portion of the whole field of law (see pp. 413–19).

9. See further Friedmann (1971, chs. 2–4).
10. cf. *Ohio* v. *Helvering*, 292 U.S. 360 (1934); *Coomber* v. *Berks Justices* (1883) 9 App. Cas. 61.

But four further and increasingly important functions of the modern state now look for adequate legal analysis. The first of these is the function of the state as provider. Legally it expresses itself in two different ways. Many important social services are discharged through the imposition of compulsory duties and conditions on private relationships. A multitude of statutory duties affects both public and private law; their infringement leads to fines, as well as to remedies at the suit of persons protected by the statute. There is a parallel expansion of common-law duties of employers towards employees through the assimilation of new principles of public policy by the law courts.[11] At the same time, social minimum standards are enforced through compulsory conditions in contract. Service contracts are subject to many such compulsory terms. The Truck Acts invalidate provisions for payment in kind to defined categories of servants. Repatriation Acts compel the reinstatement of ex-servicemen. Agriculture Acts lay down compulsory terms of agricultural tenancies in the interests of agricultural efficiency. Employment contracts are subject to compulsory insurance terms.

The discharge of social-service functions also requires a multitude of active administrative and managerial functions by government departments or independent public authorities. Public and private law are intermingled. Catchment boards, regional hospital boards, repatriation commissions, forest commissions, discharge administrative functions of a social-service character. In doing so, they must make contracts, buy and sell large quantities of equipment and other goods, engage and dismiss staff, and undertake altogether a multitude of activities regulated by the law of property, tort and contract. The main legal problem here is the adjustment of administrative discretion and private-law obligations. The discussion of this problem has shown the need to bring the legal duties of public authorities into line with the general law, except where this would impair the fulfilment of overriding public duties (see p. 396).

Next, the modern state acts as entrepreneur. It increasingly engages in the conduct of industrial and commercial activities. It does so either directly, through the state ownership of ships or railways or – increasingly – through independent corporate authorities, such as

11. See, in particular, *Wilsons & Clyde Coal Co.* v. *English* [1938] A.C. 57.

coal boards, transport commissions, atomic energy authorities or state trading and development corporations. Sometimes, the state simply acquires a controlling interest in a company. The legal form of the enterprise, which is, from a sociological and economic point of view, a matter of accident, should not determine legal rights and liabilities. While the Crown must be made fully liable in tort and in contract, commercial and industrial activities should as a rule be carried on by incorporated public authorities. The Crown will always enjoy certain privileges, for example, freedom from certain taxes; but the incorporated public authority should be subject to the same rights and liabilities as any other legal person. It should be liable for taxes, rates and other charges and be bound by general statutes. This is the legal position of the nationalized industries in Britain.

Subjection to ordinary legal liabilities need not prevent the fulfilment of economic, social and other planning functions. Both government departments and separate public authorities operate in the service of public interests or national plans, to which the legal principle of security of transactions must be adjusted. As we have seen, the break clauses in government contracts safeguard the power of the government to terminate contracts which have lost their purpose, such as war supplies, subject to fair compensation and indemnification. This is no worse, and in some cases compares favourably with the standard terms contractually imposed by private industries on the other party. But the government should not be judge in its own cause. Disputes arising from such contracts should be justiciable, whether before the ordinary courts, an arbitration court, or an administrative tribunal.

In a mixed economy public enterprise operates side by side with private enterprise. In Australia, for example, a decision of the High Court[12] has confirmed the constitutional power of the Commonwealth to establish a government-operated interstate airline, but has denied it the power to operate an inter-state airlines monopoly. As a result, a government-controlled airline operates side by side with private airlines.

In many cases, public and private enterprises coexist in the same field, as a result of partial or *ad hoc* nationalizations. Thus, in France, the largest motor-car manufacturer, Renault, is a state enterprise,

12. *Australian National Airways* v. *Commonwealth* (1946) 71 C.L.R. 29.

nationalized after the Second World War. The other motor-car manufacturers remain in private hands. In India, the new steel mills constructed by British, German and Soviet contractors are, in accordance with the Indian Constitution, state-owned. But a sizeable sector of the steel industry remains in the hands of the giant private concern, TATA.

There are also indirect forms of competition between private and public enterprise, where alternative products or services compete for the same market. Thus, in Britain coal, electricity, gas and atomic energy are operated by government-owned corporations, while the production and refining of oil remains in private hands.[13]

Does the rule of law demand that the government should dispense its favours equally among its own instrumentality and the private operators? Is there anything objectionable, for example, in the government giving all air-mail contracts to the government enterprise or ordering civil servants to use no other air transport? It seems that to hold so would be an impossible legal fetter on policy decisions in a democratic community. The establishment of public enterprises is the result of a parliamentary decision and subject to parliamentary control. It is a perfectly legitimate objective for the government of the day to encourage a form of enterprise which it regards as preferable to private enterprise, within the limits set by a constitution or other positive legal restrictions. It would be absurd to expect a Labour Government to allocate contracts equally among its own enterprise and private competitors if this is contrary to its avowed policy, and in the play of political forces it will be for any alternative government to reverse this policy if it wishes. For the sake of continuity, a wise government will act with moderation either way; but this is a matter of policy, not of law.

The dual role of the state which both enters into the field of government and industrial commercial management and, at the same time, acts as the general controller over the allocation of economic resources for the nation, leads, however, to a further and more subtle

13. Although the British Government holds a 48·9 (formerly 51·6) per cent interest in the voting stock of British Petroleum, it has traditionally abstained from any interference in the management of this enterprise, which is, in effect, conducted like a private enterprise. On the plans of the Conservative Government to denationalize ancillary activities of the nationalized industries see p. 340.

problem. The state as economic controller allocates scarce resources among different industries and for different purposes. Economic necessity may reinforce social policy. In a social democracy like modern Britain after the war or India at the present time, essential industries are favoured as against luxury industries, exports at the expense of home consumption. This means not only the allocation of essential materials and foreign exchange according to a priorities plan, but also sometimes the direction of labour. In this capacity, the state can exercise a twofold vital influence which is not immediately apparent in individual legal transactions, but which regulates them by remote control. A state can thwart certain industries and encourage others. But it can also exercise a vital influence on the scope of individual liberties. Steel or coal are purely economic commodities; paper is not only an economic commodity which costs money, but also the material basis without which intellectual freedom is bound to wither. Again, the direction of labour threatens one of the most vital aspects of personal freedom, the right to choose one's job. It is true that both freedom of opinion and freedom of labour are severely restricted by existing social and economic conditions, by newspaper or broadcasting monopolies, economic compulsion, and other factors. But the threat is no less great if it comes from the state itself. The problem does not exist in a totalitarian planned economy, where any protection of individual freedoms is at best conditional and where such rights of private property and enterprise as remain are clearly subject to overriding state necessities. But it is acute in a planned economy of the democratic type which regards certain individual freedoms as essential and recognizes the existence of a private economic sector along with public enterprise.

The power of the government of the day to throttle criticism by its policy in allocating paper or broadcasting licences, or to curtail freedom of personal movement by direction of labour, certainly raises one of the gravest problems in modern planned democracy. Under the American Constitution, such action might result in complex legal controversies, about the interpretation of the Bill of Rights of the Constitution, in particular the First, Fifth and Fourteenth Amendments. In Great Britain, this is a matter of purely political decision, for Parliament and public opinion. The vigilance of Parliament and public opinion may, in special cases, justify the setting up of representative commissions to investigate problems of urgent concern.[14] But, ultimately, it is the alertness and strength of conviction of a community on which the prevention of destruction of liberties by such eroding processes depends.

Finally, the state functions as arbiter between different groups in society. The term 'collectivist' state is often used loosely. A social-service state need not be collectivist. It can be a parental or dictatorial state, dispensing social welfare among the citizens while forbidding them to engage in any autonomous collectivist association, like Nazi Germany or Fascist Italy or Franco's Spain. On the other hand, the state may take complete responsibility for all group activities going on within its borders, while regarding their quasi-autonomous organization as convenient and necessary from an administrative and managerial point of view. This is the position in Soviet Russia where the managements of state-operated industries face trade unions. But the trade unions are not genuinely autonomous collective organizations. They represent group interests, within a well-defined national plan, and subject to overriding state policy ensured by the one-party system, political pressure and the many other sanctions at the disposal of the totalitarian state. In the modern democratic society, group associations are still permitted to develop freely in principle and to adjust their relations by mutual agreement, that is in the sphere of private law. This purely passive function of the state is proving increasingly insufficient. As the moral and legal authority of employers' associations and trade unions increases, their agreements become more and more a matter of national concern. The vast majority of states are now in a condition of more or less permanent economic crisis. They cannot afford a prolonged standstill of production, or a rise of prices, profits and wages which paralyses the economic capacity of the nation. Hence the state must intervene, by wage boards, conciliation commissioners, compulsory awards, arbitration courts and other means designed to ensure industrial peace as well as a certain amount of public influence on the formation of prices and wages. It is almost impossible to reconcile a compulsory national wage policy with the recognition of full freedom of organized groups and the consequent right of unimpeded collective

14. Such as discrimination in the allocation of paper, extent of newspaper monopolies, abuses of patents, and so forth.

bargaining. The most desirable solution is voluntary agreement and persuasion, but this leaves the legal dilemma unsolved. Freedom of association must include the freedom not to associate. It is true that, increasingly, agreements made between the major employers' and employees' associations are applied to the whole industry so that even non-members join in the benefits of such agreements. Graver, however, than this situation would be the recognition of a general principle of compulsory union membership as a condition of employment. This would transform democratic industrial society into that of the corporate state. The practical difference is small, for the trend is towards powerful unions which hardly need coercion. The freedom of the occasional dissenter makes a difference of principle out of proportion to its economic significance.

In short, the state as arbiter in a democratic society has three tasks: the maintenance of a rough balance between contending organized groups and the usually unorganized consumer; the protection of the individual freedom of association; and the safeguarding of overriding state interests.

Chapter 16
The Changing Role of Law in the Interdependent Society

The guiding theme of this book has been the interaction of social and legal change, and emphasis on the increasingly active role that the law plays as an agent of social change. The law – through legislative or administrative responses to new social conditions and ideas, as well as through judicial re-interpretations of constitutions, statutes or precedents – increasingly not only articulates but sets the course for major social changes. Nevertheless, we are still apt to consider the law, in all its branches, as a separate function and discipline, as a way in which a great variety of social relations are formulated and systematized.

Should the society of the seventies take a somewhat different view of the role of law – and of the function of the lawyer? The reason for asking this question is not only the constantly accelerating rate of social change – which necessitates the continuous reappraisal of legal responses. It is also the growing interconnectedness and inter-dependence of the different aspects of social development, which demand an ever closer interaction of technological, economic, social, environmental and legal decisions.

This cannot be dismissed as a merely quantitative change, an acceleration in the tempo of legal response to social evolution. It is true that centuries ago social change was slow enough to make custom the principal source of law. A law could develop its response to social change over decades or even centuries. Even in the earlier stages of the industrial revolution, a major change, such as the invention of the steam engine, or the advent of electricity as a source of light and power, would be gradual enough to make legal responses valid for a generation. But today the tempo of social change has accelerated to a point where today's assumptions may not be valid even a few years from now. The taming of nuclear energy, both for war and peaceful uses, the invention of the computer, the advent of the supersonic jet plane, are among the technological changes that tend to alter many bases of social life within years. The rapidly growing urbanization – most pronounced in the most highly developed countries – is leading to giant metropolitan entities such as the emerging 'megalopolis' from Boston to Washington. The population shift to the cities and the industrialization of agriculture produce major changes in the composition and habits of the population, in the ecology of the land, in transportation, education and many other aspects of social life.

The law is one of many responses to such changes. In certain respects it is the most important, since it represents the authority of the state, and its sanctioning power. The legal response to a given social or technological problem is therefore in itself a major social action which may aggravate a given problem – or alleviate and help to solve it. In any system there is an inevitable time lag between social change and legal response. In theory at least the problems are relatively smaller in a totalitarian society, where both legislature and judiciary are essentially arms of government. They are more complicated in democratic and pluralistic societies, and most complex in federal democracies where the divisions of functions and legal powers between the federal and the state components of the federation tend to make swift and unified responses to urgent social needs much more difficult.

But to a large extent, the problems of the technologically sophisticated, highly urbanized, functionally interdependent society transcend differences of political ideology and organization. The pollution of air and water by industrial and urban conglomerations transcends the ideological differences between communism and democracy. So do the choices between the development of highways and railways. This choice in turn profoundly affects such important segments of contemporary industrial society as automobile manufacturing. This often deeply influences social habits, and the proportion between urban and rural communities. These correlations and actions can be extended indefinitely. It may suffice to give three illustrations of the kind of forward planning required in contemporary industrial society, and of the role of law in this process.

In 1963, the Buchanan Committee issued its report on traffic in towns in Britain. The terms of reference of the committee were 'to study the long-term development of road and traffic in urban areas and their influence on the environment'. The report begins with a general factual estimate of the expected increase in the number of motor vehicles in Britain during the next few decades. It then outlines some of the effects of such an increase on various aspects of social life. This implies an analysis of various quantitative and qualitative interactions of the different variables relevant to the situation – including types of traffic, accessibility of buildings, the functions of streets in towns and their multipurpose uses (traffic, trade, personal intercourse, etc.). The report also had to make certain assumptions as to the choice of values likely to be made by Englishmen during the period under review.[1] At some point, traffic intensity and air pollution produced by such traffic – will make a value choice inevitable between preference for the conveniences of motor traffic and preservation of the basic amenities of life. Eventually, the intensity of traffic may be such that – as is already happening in various parts of the world – immobility will nullify the conveniences of cars. In short, there are implicit in this complex and interconnected appraisal judgements of fact and judgements of value which interact.[2]

A second illustration may be based on the recent order, issued by the Federal Water Pollution Authority (see p. 200) to all industries using Lake Michigan not to discharge any water at a temperature higher than one degree above the current temperature of the lake. This legal injunction was the expression of the new concern about environment and ecology. But it involves the study and appraisal of a complex web of questions: technological feasibility of water cooling; the cost of an adequate cooling process, and its effect on the price of the product or service concerned; the impact of any possible price increase on the profitability of the enterprise and unemployment in

1. For a more recent illustration of this approach, see the Roskill Commission's Report (1970) on the siting of the third London Airport, and in particular the criteria adopted there for evaluating 'social amenity'.

2. Sir Geoffrey Vickers, in his pioneer study (1965), distinguishes between reality judgements, value judgements and instrumental judgements. A combination of these three types of judgements is involved in the process of 'appreciation' which is the final policy judgement. See also the same author (1968, especially ch. 8: 'The multi-valued choice').

the region; the relative values to be placed on the economic, the social, the aesthetic, aspects of preservation of the natural lake temperature, as against the values of greater production consumption and employment; the possible impact of a migration of industry from the region to other areas. These and many other problems have to be assessed factually, and their relative weight to be appraised in the light of current public policies. Further complications arise where authority does not reside in the Federation but in one of the fifty states or in a local authority. In this latter case, choices of alternative locations are available to the industry or utility affected, which are excluded where the jurisdiction is federal.

In the first of the above-quoted examples, certain legal and administrative measures – such as certain orders issued by the Minister of Town and Country Planning or the Board of Education – can be one of many aspects of an eventual implementation of the Buchanan Report. In the second example, the legal injunction is the starting point, setting in motion a complex sequence of reactions. In either case, the substance and form of the law plays an important part. It should by now be apparent that the legal solution cannot be considered as a separate problem of legislative drafting or of distribution of legal powers. It must be an integral aspect of the process of 'appreciation'. To put it differently, there cannot be an – often prolonged – time interval between the engineering, environmental, economic, sociological and legal aspects of the situation. They must be integrated and coordinated with each other. The interrelation of the various elements must be tested by what the American pragmatic philosopher John Dewey has called the 'logic of inquiry'. Certain solutions will have to be worked out tentatively – e.g. the effect of certain fines, levies or prohibitions on the industrial production and unemployment pattern of the region – and they will have to be rejected for another solution, if the cost is considered too high. The computer, which reduces the time to work out complex multiple equations to a minute fraction of the time needed formerly, makes such 'systems analysis' possible. It does not and cannot, however, replace the appreciative judgement, the weight to be given to the various factors, i.e. the choice of values. The computer is able to work out the quantitative effects of certain pollution charges on the cost of production and its impact on employment, but it cannot decide what comparative value is to be attached to the preservation or restoration of amenities, or to the balance between urban and rural life.[3]

A third illustration of the role of law as an element in a complex process of systems analysis is the legal status of the ocean bed – a question discussed in an earlier chapter (see p. 452). As a result of the growing colonization of the ocean bed due to the feasibility of ocean bed mining, profound changes are occurring in the legal control over the oceans – which cover seven-tenths of the earth's surface. The broad legal alternatives are: first, as a minimum, exclusive exploitation rights of the coastal states over a strictly defined continental shelf; second, the expansion of exclusive claims by coastal states to the edge of the continental margin, which covers 23 per cent of the oceans, and includes the overwhelming majority of the seas' exploitable minerals and biological resources; third, the virtual division of the oceans among the major coastal powers; fourth, the establishment of an international ocean-bed regime, with varying degrees of operational or regulatory control over the utilization of the oceans, outside limited areas of national jurisdiction.

Each of these alternatives has to be tested in correlation to, among others, the following factors:

1. Its impact on the balance of military power.
2. Its effect on the distribution of wealth among the nations, with all its attendant political and social consequences.
3. The impact of any of the alternative solutions on the manner and

3. Economists are familiar with 'cost-benefit analysis'. This has been defined in a modern textbook (Due, 1968, p. 62) as: 'as a systematic examination of the benefits and costs of a particular governmental programme setting out the factors that should enter into the evaluation of the desirability of the programme and frequently analysing several alternatives for the attainment of the objective. Cost-benefit analysis is designed to determine whether or not a particular programme or proposal is justified, to ascertain an optimal alternative for the attainment of the desired goals, and to rank other alternatives. In contrast to usual evaluations, cost-benefit analysis seeks to take both a long-range view of benefits and costs and a broad view, considering so far as possible, all benefits and costs, direct and indirect, rather than merely the direct obvious benefits alone.' The integrated analysis suggested in the text is a broadened version of this approach, in so far as it considers legal and other non-economic factors together with the long-range economic aspects.

the extent of the exploitation of living and mineral resources of the seas.

4. The effect of the alternative solutions on international shipping and fisheries.

5. The degree of pollution likely to be produced by any of the alternative solutions.

Behind these quantitative, mathematical and statistical analyses, there is an ultimate value choice: between a world of competing national sovereignties, dominated by a few super powers that will more than ever combine military, economic and technological supremacy, and a world order that considers mankind as a whole, and the resources of the seas as its common heritage.

The Changing Role of the Lawyer

If our analysis of the changing role of law in the society of the 1970s is correct, it means a corresponding reappraisal of the lawyer's function. The lawyer has, of course, always contributed to the legal implementation of social change. As a legislative draftsman, as a member of Parliament, of law revision commissions, of other bodies concerned with the reappraisal of major social problems, the lawyer has always played a major part in the continuous process of legislative adjustment. In recent years, lawyers have prominently participated in such important policy reappraisals as the British Royal Commissions concerned with the reform of trade-union law, capital punishment and divorce, or the various American commissions concerned with the causes of violence and crime, the reform of the welfare system or the reorganization of foreign aid. In these activities, the lawyer has taken his place along with representatives of other professions and sections of the community. More specifically, the lawyer has contributed, as judge, scholar or advocate, to the many-sided processes of adaptation of the law to social change, through academic studies,[4] or through judicial interpretations which, at times – as notably in the last fifteen years of the US Supreme Court – have had a profound impact on the social fabric of the country.

4. To take but one example, it is academic scholars who have played a predominant part in the proposals for a reform of the present system of automobile insurance (see ch. 5).

Predominantly, however, the lawyer in the western world has been a defender of the established order and of vested interests. Since, in a society dominated by commerce and industry, the individual and corporate owners of property and of business enterprises have been the lawyer's principal clients, his role has been generally more important in the realm of private rather than of public law. It is private law that has – particularly in the common-law world – been until recently the most important part of the legal system.

At a time of rising threats to personal liberties, at a time when intolerance and the growing powers of government increase the danger of interference with freedom of opinion, of information and of discussion, as well as administrative encroachments of private interests, the lawyer's function as a defender of individual rights and interests will continue to be important. This will be particularly significant in the protection of 'due process' in the relationship between public authority and private interests.

Nevertheless, in two vital respects, the lawyer's role will have to shift from his predominant preoccupation with the defence of private interests. One is a need to participate more and more actively in the steadily growing role of public law, which reflects the increasing involvement of government with the widening spectrum of economic and social life. The reasons for this have been analysed earlier. It is noteworthy that in recent decades, a growing proportion of the best graduates from American law schools have chosen to work in government departments and agencies – particularly under administrations that have regarded themselves as responsible for the implementation of vital changes in society – in international organizations and in the growing number of agencies concerned with the socially underprivileged. Many parts of public law are as yet insufficiently developed. In a previous chapter, attention has been drawn to the complexities of the Government's regulatory and entrepreneurial role in a mixed economy. Almost certainly, this sphere of public and mixed public–private enterprise will grow, notably in the United States, where it has hitherto played a limited role and where the status and function of public enterprise have been almost totally neglected by the lawyer.

This second change of emphasis in the lawyer's orientation is an inevitable reflection of the changing role of the law as it has been briefly portrayed in a preceding section. The lawyer must consider himself increasingly as part of a team, involved in the long-term planning processes in which systems analysis will require the integration of the lawyer's skills with those of the economist, the social worker, the scientist, the engineer, the industrial manager. In a sense, the concept of 'general counsel', familiar in the structure both of American business corporations and of some government agencies, points towards the role that the lawyer will have to play in the future. Just as a contemporary architect is less concerned with the building of individual houses and structures than with the coordination and overall planning of various types of community projects, so the lawyer will have to see himself more and more as a participant in a community planning process. While this may be a relatively less prominent role than in the past, it is socially perhaps a more vital one. It will not preclude the particular function of the lawyer as a guardian of justice, especially in the relations between public authority and private interests. There are many occasions on which it will be the lawyer's function to act as a brake on the zeal of politicians and social reformers who will tend to ride roughshod over interests that may stand in their way. This situation has frequently occurred, particularly in the post-war history of the developing countries, which on gaining independence, have been impatient to transform their static and tradition-bound societies into developing and industrialized societies. The tendency has often been to use legislative sovereign power to dispose of private, national and foreign interests. In the realm of international law, the adjustment between the developing country's interest in national control over its resources and development, and the interests of foreign investors, has been a particularly critical area (see p. 484). But if the developing countries have often shown insufficient concern with the legitimate interests of foreign investors, and scant recognition of the contribution made by them to the development of indigenous resources, the majority of western lawyers have been equally lacking in understanding of the legitimate needs of the developing countries, and insensitive to the reaction against many decades of often unscrupulous exploitation of their resources. They have tended to cling to a strict theory of vested interest, of 'prompt, full and adequate' compensation for foreign investments, regardless of their origin and operation, and they have thus contributed to the widening of the gap between the developed and the less developed world (see p. 486).

In this, as in many other fields, it is incumbent upon the contemporary lawyer to look beyond the narrow legalistic defence of a specific interest, to the wider social, economic and political implications of a problem. This applies in the international as well as in the internal domain. The active and enlightened role of the lawyer in the complex process of social engineering is an indispensible and vital aspect of mankind's increasingly urgent and precarious struggle for civilized survival.

The Role of the State in the Overcrowded Society

In the years ahead, the active intervention of government in the economic and social affairs of nations is certain to increase greatly. This is a matter of necessity rather than of ideology. The most industrialized, urbanized and congested nations will be in need of the strongest and most ubiquitous forms of government control. The rate of change, and the corresponding transformation of the general political ideology, is likely to be most dramatic in countries which, like the United States, have grown and prospered under the ideology of private enterprise, but now face the problems of industrialization, urbanization and pollution of environment on a larger scale than any other country. It has become apparent with dramatic suddenness that, at the present, more or less uncontrolled, rate of industrial and urban development, the major rivers and lakes of the country will become – as many of them already are – incapable of sustaining marine life and unusable for humans. By-products of a gasoline operated motor car and of the generation of electricity, notably carbon and sulphur compounds, are poisoning the air. At the same time, the enormous increase in the production of carbon dioxide is affecting photosynthesis and the temperature of the earth (through its effect on the atmosphere and the radiation of sun rays). Mercury and other industrial by-products are making fish unfit for human consumption. It is now apparent that the use of DDT and other pesticides has profoundly affected the ecology and the balance of plant and animal life in many parts of the world. At the same time, the most industrialized nations also produce the greatest amount of non-organic materials, such as discarded motor cars and other metal waste, plastic containers for beverages and other consumer products, glass bottles, mountains of paper and the like. While the worldwide growth of the population will remain virtually unchecked for the next few decades – even assuming more radical changes in the rate of reproduction than occur or are planned at this time – the effects will not be even as between one country and another. In the countries where the birth rate is the highest, such as India or Latin America, the population explosion affects the already depressed standards of living and congestion in urban slums. But it is in the wealthiest countries, with the highest standards of living, such as the United States, that the relatively greatest contribution to pollution of environment will be made. It has been estimated that each baby born in the United States contributes many times the amount of potential pollution of a baby born in India.

While some of the problems of the overcrowded society are national, many of them are international and can only be solved on a worldwide scale. Neither the air nor the oceans have national physical – as distinct from legal – boundaries. Supersonic air transport and nuclear radiation have worldwide effects. The growing exploitation of the ocean bed, especially through offshore oil drilling, increasingly affects, as we have seen, the freedom of the seas and creates worldwide problems of water pollution and destruction of marine life.

The effects on legal priorities and the coercive role of the state – though as yet only dimly perceived – are likely to be shattering. The minimum demands of human survival will necessitate a far-reaching reordering of priorities and a correspondingly increased coercive role of the state. Thus, the almost universal legal policy of providing family allowances, tax exemptions and other financial benefits for children may have to give way to disincentives and even penalties. As is already the case in India, sterilization, for both males and females, will increasingly have to be officially sponsored. Eventually, even compulsory sterilization beyond a certain number of children may become inevitable.

In the economic sphere, there may have to be a reversal of the basic philosophy of the industrial society – capitalist and socialist alike. The unquestioned goal has been the unlimited increase of production. But it may well become necessary to restrict the production of certain commodities, and especially of non-essential consumer goods, for the sake of survival. At least this is likely to be the case, unless methods of production – and of corresponding industrial waste and pollution – are drastically altered. In so far as increases in the cost of production are a sufficient incentive towards the abatement of industrial waste and pollution, fines or levies may suffice. But it may be that even more drastic prohibitions will be required, nothing less than a change in the rhythm of life in a society that is on the way towards self-strangulation. Public law, controls by way of statutory prohibitions, administrative regulations, fines and levies, and the imposition of much more far-reaching restrictions on freedom of property and contract than already occur, are a virtual certainty in the years to come – provided mankind preserves its instinct for survival.

The same factors are also likely to increase the direct participation of government in a variety of economic activities. Thus, in the United States, the progressive congestion of the highways, the air pollution caused by the motor car, and the threat to many communities posed by the continuing expansion of the highway system, is producing increasing pressure for a revival of an adequate public transportation system. Since the privately-owned railroad systems are either unwilling or unable to undertake and finance the necessary rehabilitation – after decades of neglect – the participation of public authorities – federal, state and municipal – appears to be inevitable. In the New York area, the Metropolitan Transit Authority, designed to coordinate public transportation has taken over the operation of the commuter systems, with most of the finance provided by the State and the City of New York. In 1971, a mixed public–private corporation was established, with some financial support by the US government, to take over and reorganize what remains of long-distance passenger rail transport.

Neither the drastic increase of public regulatory controls – administrative, penal and civil – nor an increase of direct state participation in public utilities and other activities of public concern is a panacea. The increasingly complex interlocking of controls – especially in a system where the constitutional and administrative powers are divided between federation states and local authorities – may make a vast bureaucracy even less manageable. The participation of government does not necessarily improve management, although it does put the responsibility and the resources of the state behind the enterprise. Yet, there seems to be no alternative to the vastly increased role of government, both as regulator and as entrepreneur. It is simply a further and inevitable stage in the growing role of the state in the management of a society that can no longer be left to the free play of forces without catastrophic consequences.

Conclusions

Our individual ideals of the rule of law may correspond to the enlightened rationalism of the eighteenth-century aristocracy, to nineteenth-century Manchester middle-class Liberalism, to the value system of the Catholic Church, or to the centrally directed economy of a Socialist state. But a meaningful definition of the rule of law must be based on the realities of contemporary society, and this means that we must recognize the irreducible minimum functions of modern government, as well as the ubiquitous strength of group power. This still leaves plenty of choice between different ideas. A meaningful formulation of the rule of law for a contemporary democracy can only set the sights. It cannot be spelt out in terms of nineteenth-century ideals, of the philosophy of the Founding Fathers, of a Bentham or a Dicey. The basic value remains the same: the fullest possible provision by the community of the conditions that enable the individual to develop into a morally and intellectually responsible person. But the means by which this goal is to be attained cannot but be deeply influenced by the social conditions in which we live. The ideal of social welfare, i.e. of the responsibility of the community for minimum standards of living and protection against the major vicissitudes that would leave the individual – except the fortunate few – destitute and degraded, provided only with the theoretical freedoms of contract, property and trade, is now almost universally accepted. But welfare and work, without responsibility, can lead to the completely regimented and conditioned society. The rule of law in democracy must, therefore, safeguard the elementary rights of participation in the process of government. It must devise adequate protection against the abuse of both public and private power. How the balance is to be struck must, to a large extent, depend on the changing conditions of society. Today the elementary standards of living are, more than at any previous period, protected by social-security laws and the recognition of collective bargaining as the predominant instrument of regulation of labour conditions. Emphasis is therefore shifting to safeguards against administrative arbitrariness, the legal immunities of public authority, the excessive concentration of corporate power and abuses of union power over the individual. No less important are efforts designed to preserve effective, as distinct from nominal, freedom of opinion, and measures to preserve or restore the minimum possibilities of civic participation in public affairs without which democracy must wither. In all these fields the law has a vital part to play.

That the content of the rule of law cannot be determined for all time and all circumstances is a matter not for lament but for rejoicing. It would be tragic if the law were so petrified as to be unable to respond to the unending challenge of evolutionary or revolutionary changes in society. To the lawyer, this challenge means that he cannot be content to be a craftsman. His technical knowledge will supply the tools but it is his sense of responsibility for the society in which he lives that must inspire him to be jurist as well as lawyer.

References

Page

39   ADAMS, J. L. (1970), 'Civil disobedience: its occasions and limits in political and legal obligation', *Nomos*, vol. 12, p. 294.

255   ALEXANDER, P. W. (1958), 'The family court and the future', 31 *J. Amer. Jud. Soc.* 38.

58, 379   ALLEN, C. K. (1967), *Law in the Making*, Oxford University Press, 7th edn.

230   ALLEN, F. A. (1958), 'The borderland of the criminal law: problems of socializing criminal justice', 32 *Social Science Rev.* 107, 2 June.

167, 416   ALSTYNE, A. van (1966), 'Government tort liability: a decade of change', *University of Illinois L. Forum* 919.

299   AMERICAN BAR ASSOCIATION, ANTI-TRUST LAW SECTION (1968, supp. 1971), *Anti-Trust Developments*, 1955–68, American Bar Association.

203, 206, 207, 210, 216–17, 265, 266–7   AMERICAN LAW INSTITUTE (1962), *Model Penal Code (Proposed Official Draft)*, American Law Institute.

422   AMERICAN LAW INSTITUTE (1965), *Restatement of the Foreign Relations Law of the United States*, American Law Institute.

27   ANDERSON, J. N. D. (1956), 'Law reform in the Middle East', *International Affairs*, vol. 32, p. 43.

235   ARENS, R., and LASSWELL, H. D. (1961), *In Defense of Public Order; The Emerging Field of Sanction Law*, Colombia University Press.

370   ASSOCIATION OF THE BAR OF THE CITY OF NEW YORK (1956), *Report of the Special Committee on the Federal Loyalty Security Program*, Dodd, Mead.

380   BAEHR, R. (1864), *Der Rechtsstaat*.

179   BARRY, D. D. (1967), 'The motor car in Soviet criminal and civil law', 16 *Int. & Comp. L.Q.* 56.

97, 105   BASTIAN, D. (1950), 'La propriété commercials en droit francais', *Travaux de l'Association Henri Capitant*, vol. 6.

62   BEASLEY, F. R. (1951), 'Australia's Communist Party Dissolution Act', 28 *Canadian Bar Rev*. 490.

186   BENGTSSON, B. (1970), 'Personal injury boards in Sweden', 18 *Amer. J. Comp. Law* 108.

395, 425   BENJAFIELD, D. G. (1956), 'Statutory discretions', 2 *Sydney L. Rev.* 1.

381, 428   BENJAFIELD, D. G., and WHITMORE, H. (1971), *Australian Administrative Law*, Law Book Co. Ltd, 4th edn.

325, 329, 334   BERLE, A. A. (1954), *The Twentieth-Century Capitalist Revolution*, Harcourt, Brace & World.

367   BERLE, A. A. (1967), *The Three Faces of Power*, Harcourt, Brace & World.

331–2   BERLE, A. A. (1969), *Power*, Harcourt, Brace & World.

101, 102   BERLE, A. A., and MEANS, G. C. (1968), *The Modern Corporation and Private Property*, Harcourt, Brace & World.

140, 141   BERMAN, H. J. (1947), 'Commercial contracts in Soviet law', 35 *California L. Rev.* 191.

140, 141, 142, 157   BERMAN, H. J. (1963), *Justice in the USSR*, Harvard University Press.

196   BERMAN, H. J. (1966), *Soviet Criminal Law and Procedure: The RSFSR Codes 186–91*, Harvard University Press.

70, 71, 72   BICKEL, A. M. (1970), *The Supreme Court and the Idea of Progress*, Harper & Row.

482, 486   BISHOP, W. W. (1971), *Cases and Materials on International Law*, Little, Brown, 2nd edn.

269   BLACKSTONE, W. (1922), *Commentaries on the Laws of England*, Bisel.

294, 299, 301, 386   BLAKE, H. M. (ed.) (1969), *Business Regulation in the Common Market Nations*, McGraw-Hill.

175–6   BLUM, W. J., and KALVEN, H. Jr (1965), *Public Perspectives on a Public Law Problem: Auto Compensation Plans*, Little, Brown.

48   BOHLEN, F. H. (1926), *Studies in the Law of Tort*, Bobbs, Merrill.

284   BOHNDORF, M. T. (1970), 'The new illigitimacy law in Germany', 19 *Int. & Comp. L.Q.* 299.

482   BORCHARD, E. M. (1940), 'The minimum standard of the treatment of aliens', 38 *Michigan L. Rev.* 445.

254   BRADWAY, J. B. (1956), 'Divorce litigation and the welfare of the family', 9 *Vanderbilt L. Rev.*, 665.

89   BREITEL, C. D. (1959), 'The courts and lawmaking', in M. G. Paulsen (ed.), *Legal Institutions Today and Tomorrow*, Columbia University Press.

310   BRENNAN, M. J. (1965), *The Theory of Economic Statics*, Prentice-Hall.

386   BROWN, R. S. (1958), *Loyalty and Security: Employment Tests in the United States*, Yale University Press.

157   BUCKLAND, W. W. (1944), 'The nature of contractual obligation', 8 *Cambridge L.J.* 247.

224   BUXTON, R. J. (1970), 'Murder 1957–1968', 33 *Mod. L. Rev.* 302.

159   CAHN, E. N. (1949), *The Sense of Injustice*, New York University Press.

176   CALBRESI, G. (1965), 'Fault accident and the wonderful world of Blum and Kalven', 75 *Yale L.J.* 216.

46–7   CARDOZO, B. N. (1921), *The Nature of Judicial Process*, Yale University Press.

327   CARLSTON, K. S. (1956), *Law and Structure of Social Action*, Stevens.

314   CARNEGIE, A. (1895), *Share the Wealth*.

425, 427   CARROW, M. M. (1958), 'Types of judicial relief from administrative action', 58 *Columbia L. Rev.* 1.

87, 489   CHENG, B. (1953), *General Principles of Law as Applied by International Courts and Tribunals*, Stevens.

402   CHERNE, L. M. (1941), *Government Contract Problems*, Research Institute of America.

95   CHESHIRE, G. C. (1967), *The Modern Law of Real Property*, Butterworths, 10th edn.

124, 128   CHESHIRE, G. C., and FIFOOT, C. H. S. (1969), *The Law of Contract*, Butterworths.

363   CHRISTENSEN, T. G. S. (1968), 'Union discipline under federal law: institutional dilemmas in an industrial democracy', 43 *New York University L. Rev.* 226.

359   CHRISTIE, I. M. (1967), *The Liability of Strikes in the Law of Tort*, Queen's University Industrial Relations Center.

152   CLARK, G. DE N. (1970), 'Letter to editor', 33 *Mod. L. Rev.* 117.

461   CLARK, G., and SOHN, L. B. (1966), *World Peace through World Law*, Harvard University Press.

344   COATES, K. (ed.) (1968), *Can the Workers Run Industry?*, Institute for Workers' Control.

344   COATES, K., and TOPHAM, A. (eds.) (1970), *Workers' Control*, Institute for Workers' Control.

121, 131, 140, 157   COHEN, M. R. (1933), *Law and the Social Order*, Harcourt, Brace & World.

176   CONRAD, A. F. (1964), *Automobile Accident Costs and Payments: Studies in the Economics of Injury Reparation*, University of Michigan Press.

176   CONRAD, A. F. (1964), 'The economic treatment of automobile injuries', 63 *Michigan L. Rev.* 279.

136   COOPER, W. M., and WOOD, J. C. (1966), *Outlines in Industrial Law*, Butterworths.

38   COX, A. (1968), 'Civil rights, the constitution and the courts', 40 *New York State Bar J.* 161.

154   COX, A. (1958), 'Collective-bargaining agreements', 57 *Michigan L. Rev.* 1.

153   COX, A., and DUNLOP, J. T. (1950), 'Regulations of collective bargaining by the National Labor Relations Board', 63 *Harvard L. Rev.* 389.

477   DAM, K. W. (1970), *The GATT: Law and International Economic Organization*, University of Chicago Press.

488   DAVID, R. J. A., and GUTTERIDGE, H. C. (1934), 'The doctrine of unjust enrichment', 5 *Cambridge L.J.* 204.

259   DAVIS, K. C. (1967), 'Population policy', 158 *Science* 730.

381   DAVIS, K. C. (1958), *Administrative Law Treatise*, West Publishing.

381, 383, 410, 425, 429   DAVIS, K. C. (1959), *Administrative Law Text*, West Publishing.

425   DAVIS, K. C. (1949), 'Forms of proceeding', 44 *Illinois L. Rev.* 565.

393, 396, 416, 418   DAVIS, K. C. (1955), 'Tort liability of governmental units', 40 *Minnesota L. Rev.* 751.

429   DAVIS, K. C. (1952), 'Standing, ripeness and civil liberties: a critique of *Adler* v. *Board of Education*', 38 *A.B.A.J.* 924.

488   DAWSON, J. P. (1951), *Unjust Enrichment*, Little, Brown.

502   DENNING, LORD (1949), *Freedom under the Law*, Stevens.

193	DEVLIN, P. (1965), *The Enforcement of Morals*, Oxford University Press.
19, 46, 124	DICEY, A. V. (1914), *Law and Public Opinion in England during the Nineteenth Century*, Macmillan, 2nd edn.
379, 410	DICEY, A. V. (1939), *Law of the Constitution*, Macmillan, 9th edn.
107	DICKENS, B. M. (1970), 'Discretions in local authority prosecutions', *Crim. L. Rev.* 618.
125	DODD, E. M. (1943), 'From maximum wages to minimum wages: six centuries of regulation of employment contracts', 73 *Columbia L. Rev.* 643
477	DOMIE, M., and HAZARD, J. N. (1958), 'State trading and most-favored action clause', 52 *AJIL* 55.
138	DRAKE, C. D. (1968), *Labour Law*, Sweet & Maxwell.
328	DRUCKER, P. (1946), *Concept of the Corporation*, John Day Co.
517	DUE, J. F. (1968), *Government Finance: Economics of the Public Sector*, R. D. Irwin.
129	DWORKIN, R. (1962), '*Store decisis* in the House of Lords', 25 *Mod. L. Rev.* 163.
193	DWORKIN, R. (1966), 'Lord Devlin and the enforcement of morals', 75 *Yale L.J.* 986.
42	DWORKIN, R. (1968), 'On not prosecuting civil disobedience', *New York Review of Books*, 6 June.
42	DWORKIN, R. (1970), 'Taking rights seriously', *New York Review of Books*, 17 December.
135	EASTWOOD, R. A., and WORTLEY, B. A. (1938), 'Administrative law and the teaching of the law of contract', *J. Soc. Pub. Teachers L.* 23.
310	EDWARDS, C. D. (1964), *Maintaining Competition*, McGraw-Hill, rev. edn.
204, 205	EDWARDS, J. L. T. (1955), Mens Rea *in Statutory Offences*, St Martins, Macmillan.
276	EEKELAAR, J. M. (1969), 'Ontario Law Reform Commission: family law project, property subjects', 32 *Mod. L. Rev.* 678.
165	EHRENZWEIG, A. A. (1951), *Negligence without Fault*, University of California Press.
174	EHRENZWEIG, A. A. (1954), '*Full Aid*' Insurance for the Traffic Victim: A Voluntary Compensation Plan*, University of California Press.
20	EHRLICH, E. (1936), *Fundamental Principles of the Sociology of Law*, Harvard University Press.

267   EKBLAD, M. (1955), *Induced Abortion on Psychiatric Grounds*, Einar Munksgaard Forlag.

168   ESMEIN, Q. (1953), 'Liability in French law for damages caused by motor vehicle accidents', 2 *Amer. J. Comp. L.* 156.

361, 362   ETELSON, J. I., and SMITH, F. N. (1969), 'Union discipline under the Landrum-Griffin Act', 82 *Harvard L. Rev.* 727.

786   FACHIRI, A. Q. (1925), 'Expropriation in international law', 6 *Brit. Ybk Int. Law*, 159.

39   FALK, R. A. (1968 and 1969), *The Vietnam War and International Law*, Princeton University Press.

486   FATOUROS, A. A. (1962), *Government Guarantees to Foreign Investors*, Columbia University Press.

474, 476   FAWCETT, J. E. S. (1948), 'Legal aspects of state trading', 25 *Brit. Ybk Int. Law* 35.

267   FINNIS, J. M. (1971), 'Abortion act: what has changed?', *Crim. L. Rev.* 3.

342   FISCHER, G. (1956), 'Problems arising from workers' co-determination in the Federal German Republic (Western Germany)', *Transactions of the Third World Congress of Sociology*, International Sociological Association.

165   FLEMING, J. G. (1967), 'The role of negligence in modern tort law', 53 *Virginia L. Rev.* 815.

221   FLUGEL, J. C. (1945), *Man, Morals and Society*, International University Press.

381, 386, 388, 402, 424, 432   FORSTHOFF, E. (1958), *Lehrbuch des Verwalltungsrechts*, Allegmainer Teil.

42   FORTAS, A. (1968), *Concerning Dissent and Civil Disobedience*, New American Library.

315   FORTUNE (1947), 'How to have your own foundation', *Fortune*, August, pp. 100.

482   FREEMAN, A. V. (1938), *The International Responsibility of State for the Denial of Justice*, Longman.

486   FRIEDMAN, S. (1953), *Expropriation in International Law*, Stevens.

500   FRIEDMANN, W. (1948), *The Planned States and the Rule of Law*, Melbourne University Press.

140, 212, 347, 500, 501   FRIEDMANN, W. (1951), *Law and Social Change in Contemporary Britain*, Stevens, rev. edn.

488   FRIEDMANN, W. (1938), 'The principle of unjust enrichment', 16 *Canadian Bar Rev.* 243, 365.

104   FRIEDMANN, W. (1943), 'Social security and some recent developments in the common law', 21 *Canadian Bar Rev.* 369.

397   FRIEDMANN, W. (1945), 'Statutory powers and legal duties of local authorities', 8 *Modern L. Rev.* 31.

58   FRIEDMANN, W. (1948), 'Statute law and its interpretation in the modern state', 26 *Canadian Bar Rev.* 1277.

421   FRIEDMANN, W. (1950), 'The shield of the crown', 29 *Australian L.J.* 275.

419, 421   FRIEDMANN, W. (ed.) (1954), *The Public Corporation*, Carswell.

269, 270, 271, 272, 273, 287   FRIEDMANN, W. (ed.) (1955), *Matrimonial Property Law*, Carswell.

199   FRIEDMANN, W. (1955), 'Monopoly, reasonableness and public interests in the Canadian anti-combines law', 33 *Canadian Bar Rev.* 133.

199, 294, 299, 370, 378, 386   FRIEDMANN, W. (ed.) (1956), *Anti-Trust Laws: A Comparative Symposium*, Stevens.

126   FRIEDMANN, W. (1956), 'Property, freedom, security and the supreme court of the United States', 19 *Mod. L. Rev.* 461.

325   FRIEDMANN, W. (1957), 'Corporate power, government by private groups and the law', 57 *Columbia L. Rev.* 155.

74   FRIEDMANN, W. (1960), 'Legal philosophy and judicial law making', 61 *Columbia L. Rev.* 841; reprinted in *Essays on Jurisprudence from the Columbia Law Review*, 1963.

488   FRIEDMANN, W. (1964), *The Changing Structure of International Law*, Stevens.

19, 41, 49, 52, 56, 93, 129, 201, 207, 322, 327, 483, 502   FRIEDMANN, W. (1967), *Legal Theory*, Stevens, 5th edn.

296   FRIEDMANN, W. (1969), 'Forms and functions of public enterprise', *Current Legal Problems*, pp. 79–101.

135, 297, 311, 419, 422   FRIEDMANN, W., and GARNER, J. F. (eds.) (1970), *Government Enterprise*, Stevens.

221, 261   FRIEDMANN, W. (1970), 'Interference with human life: some jurisprudential reflections', 70 *Columbia L. Rev.* 1058.

482   FRIEDMANN, W., LISSITZYN, O. J., and PUGH, R. C. (1969), *Cases and Materials on International Law*, West Publishing.

506 FRIEDMANN, W. (1971), *The State and the Rule of Law in a Mixed Economy*, Stevens.

35 FREUND, P. A. (1949), *On Understanding the Supreme Court*, Little, Brown.

125 FULLER, L. L. (1947), *Basic Contract Law*, West Publishing Co.

53 FULLER, L. L. (1958), 'Positivism and fidelity to law: a reply to Professor Hart', 71 *Harvard L. Rev.* 630.

500, 502 FULLER, L. L. (1969), *The Morality of Law*, Yale University Press, rev. edn.

143, 332, 367 GALBRAITH, J. K. (1967), *The New Industrial State*, Houghton Mifflin.

324, 329, 367 GALBRAITH, J. K. (1952), *American Capitalism; the Concept of Countervailing Power*, Houghton Mifflin.

227 GARDINER, G. (1958), 'The purposes of criminal punishment', 21 *Mod. L. Rev.* 221.

95 GARNER, J. F. (1967), 'Land Commission Act 1967', 30 *Mod. L. Rev.* 303.

207 GAUSEWITZ, A. L. (1937), 'Criminal law: reclassification of certain offences as civil instead of criminal', 12 *Wisconsin L. Rev.* 365.

385, 86 GELLHORN, W. (1956), *Individual Freedom and Governmental Restraints*, Louisiana State University Press.

439, 440 GELLHORN, W. (1966), *Ombudsmen and Others*, Harvard University Press.

377, 381, 408, 410, 426 GELLHORN, W., and BYSE, C. (1957; 1970) *Cases and Comments on Administrative Law*, Foundation Press, 3rd and 5th edn.

418 GELLHORN, W. and LAUER, L. (1955), 'Congressional settlement of tort claims against the United States', 55 *Columbia L. Rev.* 1.

418 GELLHORN, W. and LAUER, L. 'Federal liability for personal property damage', 29 *New York U.L. Rev.* 1325.

45 GÉMY, F. (1899), *Methode d'interpretation et sources en droit privé positif*, A. Chevalier Manescq & Cie.

224 GIBSON, E., and KLEIN, S. (1961), *Murder 1957 to 1968*, Home Office Research Unit, HMSO.

215 GLUECK, S. (1928), 'Psychiatry and the criminal law', 12 *Mental Hygiene* 575.

227 GLUECK, S., and GLUECK, E. (1950), *Unraveling Juvenile Delinquency*, Harvard Law School.

300	GNEIST, R. VON (1872), *Der Rechtsstaat*, Springer.
500	GOODHART, A. L. (1958), 'The rule of law and absolute sovereignty', 106 *U. Pennsylvania Law Rev.* 943.
52	GOODHART, A. L. (1959), 'The ratio decidendi of a case', 22 *Mod. L. Rev.* 117.
314, 315	GOWER, L. C. B. (1969), *The Principles of Modern Company Law*, Stevens, 3rd edn.
238	GRAVESON, R. H., and CRANE, F. R. (eds.) (1957), *A Century of Family Law*, Sweet & Maxwell
164, 179	GRAY, W. (1965), 'Soviet tort law: the new principles annotated', in W. R. Lafave (ed.), *Law in Soviet Society*, University of Illinois Press.
42	GREENAWALT, K. (1970), 'A contextual approach to disobedience', *Nomos*, vol. 12, Atherton Press.
460	GREENBERG, J., and SHALIT, A. R. (1963), 'New horizons for human rights: the European convention, court and commission for human rights', 63 *Columbia L. Rev.* 1384.
174, 175	GREEN, L. (1958), *Traffic Victims: Tort Law and Insurance*, Northwestern University Press.
381, 408, 409, 425, 427	GRIFFITH, J. A. G., and STREET, H. (1967), *Principles of Administrative Law*, Pitman.
231	GRÜNHUT, M. (1948), *Penal Reform: A Comparative Study*, Oxford University Press.
105	GSOVSKI, V. (1948), *Soviet Civil Law*, Stevens.
103, 104	GUTTERIDGE, H. C. (1933), 'Abuse of rights', 5 *Cambridge L.J.* 22.
487	GUTTERIDGE, H. C. (1949), *Comparative Law*, Cambridge University Press.
23	GUINS, G. K. (1954), *Soviet Law and Soviet Society*, M. Nijhoff.
125	HALE, R. L. (1943), 'Bargaining duress and economic liberty', 43 *Columbia L. Rev.* 603.
502	HALE, R. L. (1952), *Freedom Through Law*, Columbia University Press.
81	HALL, L. (1935), 'Strict and liberal construction of penal statutes', 78 *Harvard L. Rev.*, 748.
202, 204, 205, 206	HALL, J. (1947), *General Principles of Criminal Law*, Bobbs Merrill (2nd edn, 1960).
379, 435	HAMSON, C. J. (1954), *Executive Discretion and Judicial Control*, Stevens.

534 References

504	HAMSON, C. J. (1958), 'La notion de l'egalité dans les pays occidentaux', *Revue international de droit compare*, January–March, p. 54.
65, 66, 68, 69, 70	HAND, L. (1958), *The Bill of Rights*, Atheneum.
297, 299	HANDLER, M. (1962), 'Some unresolved problems of anti-trust', 62 *Columbia L. Rev.* 930.
299, 305	HANDLER, M. (1966), 'The polarities of anti-trust', 60 *Northwestern University L. Rev.* 751.
299	HANDLER, M. (1970), 'Anti-trust: 1969', 55 *Connell L. Rev.* 161.
135, 419	HANSON, A. H. (ed.) (1955), *Public Enterprise*, Routledge & Kegan Paul.
419	HANSON, A. H. (ed.) (1963), *Nationalization: A Book of Readings*, University of Toronto Press.
96	HARGREAVES, A. D. (1956), 'Modern real property', 19 *Mod. L. Rev.* 14.
167, 180, 181, 182, 183	HARPER, F. V., and JAMES, F. (1956), *The Law of Torts*, Little, Brown.
178	HARRIS, D. R. (1958) 'Compensation for accidents', 102 *Solicitor's J.* 729, 749, 765, 783.
79, 193	HART, H. L. A. (1963), *Law, Liberty and Morality*, Oxford University Press.
502	HART, H. L. A. (1965), Book Review, 78 *Harvard L. Rev.* 1284.
53	HART, H. L. A. (1958), 'Positivism and the separation of law and morals', 71 *Harvard L. Rev.* 593.
225	HART, H. L. A. (1968), *Punishment and Responsibility*, Oxford University Press.
205	HART, H. M. (1958), 'The aims of the criminal law', 23 *Law and Contemp. Problems* 422.
72	HART, H. M. (1959), 'Foreword: the five charts of the justices', 73 *Harvard L. Rev.* 84.
478	HAZARD, J. W. (1958), 'Commercial discrimination and international law', 52 *AJIL* 495.
377, 378	HAZARD, J. N. (ed.) (1951), *Soviet Legal Philosophy*, Harvard University Press.
23, 187, 243, 281	HAZARD, J. N. (1953), *Law and Social Change in the USSR*, Carswell.
23, 76, 106, 140, 142, 164, 179, 187, 196	HAZARD, J. N. (1969), *Communists and their Law*, University of Chicago Press.
106	HAZARD, J. N., SHAPIRO, I., and MAGGS, P. B. (1969), *The Soviet Legal System*, Oceana Publications.

156, 157   HAZARD, J. N., and WEISBERG, M. L. (1950), *Cases and Readings on Soviet Law*, Columbia University Press.

185   HELLNER, J. (1970), 'Damage for personal injury and the victim's private insurance', 18 *Amer. J. Comp. Law* 126.

184   HELLNER, J. (1962) 'Tort liability and liability insurance', 6 *Scandinavian Studies in Law*, 129.

193   HENKIN, L. (1963), 'Morals and the constitution: the sin of obscenity', 63 *Columbia L. Rev.* 391.

257   HIMES, N. E. (1936), *Medical History of Contraception*.

157, 161, 190   HOLMES, O. W. (1881), *The Common Law*, Little, Brown.

228   HOME OFFICE (1969), *People in Prison*, HMSO.

361   HOME OFFICE (1969), *In Place of Strife: A Policy for Industrial Relations*, Cmnd 3888, HMSO.

95, 118   HORDING, A. L. (1958), 'Free man versus his government', *Southern Methodist Studies in Jurisprudence*, vol. 5, Southern Methodist University Press.

38   HUGHES, G. (1968), 'Civil disobedience and the political question doctrine', 43 *New York University L. Rev.* 1.

402   IMBODEN, M. (1959), *Der Verwaltungsrechliche Vertrag*, Helbing & Lichtenhohn.

187   IONASCO, T. (1970), 'The fault requirement and the contract liability of socialist organizations', 18 *Amer. J. Comp. Law* 31.

178   ISON, T. G. (1967), *The Morensic Lottery*, Staples Press.

254   JACOBS, A. C., and ANGELL, R. C. (1930), *A Research in Family Law*, Columbia University School of Law.

279   JACOBS, A. C., and GOEBEL, J. (1961), *Cases and Other Materials on Domestic Relations*, 3rd edn, Foundation Press.

384   JAFFE, L. L. (1954), 'The effective limits of the administrative process: a revaluation', 67 *Harvard L. Rev.* 1105.

334   JAFFE, L. L. (1937), 'Law making by private groups', 51 *Harvard L. Rev.* 201.

396   JAMES, F. (1957), 'The Federal Tort Claims Act and the 'discretionary function'', 10 *University of Florida* L. Rev. 187.

536 References

182   JAMES, F. (1952), 'Social insurance and tort
               liability', 27 *New York University L. Rev.* 552.
388   JELLINEK, W. (1931), *Verwaltungsrecht*, Springer.
410   JENNINGS, E. G. (1937), 'Tort liability of
               administrating officers', 21 *Minnesota L. Rev.* 263.
454   JENNINGS, R. Y. (1969), 'The limits of
               continental shelf jurisdiction: some possible
               implications of the North Sea case judgement',
               18 *Int. & Comp. L.Q.* 28.
379, 380   JENNINGS, W. I. (1959), *The Law and the
               Constitution*, University of London Press, 5th edn.
472   JESSUP, P. C. (1956), *Transactional Law*,
               Yale University Press; Oxford University Press.
40   JONES, H. W. (1969), *The Efficacy of Law*,
               Northwestern University Press.
501   JONES, H. W. (1958), 'The rule of law and the
               welfare state', 58 *Columbia L. Rev.* 149.
152   KAHN-FREUND, O. (1943), 'Collective agreements
               under war legislation', 6 *Mod. L. Rev.* 112.
137   KAHN-FREUND, O. (1948), 'Legislation
               through adjudication: the legal aspect of fair
               wages clauses and recognized conditions', 11
               Mod. L. Rev. 269, 429.
137   KAHN-FREUND, O. (1949) 'Minimum wage
               legislation in Great Britain', 97 *Pennsylvania L.
               Rev.* 778.
95, 99, 115, 334   KAHN-FREUND, O. (1949), Introduction to
               K. Renner, *The Institutions of Private Laws and
               Their Social Functions*, Routledge & Kegan Paul.
286   KAHN-FREUND, O. (1953), 'Inconsistencies and
               injustices in the law of husband and wife', 16
               Mod L. Rev. 178.
135, 138   KAHN-FREUND, O. (1965), *The Law of Carriage
               by Inland Transport*, Stevens.
138, 148, 171 KAHN-FREUND, O. (1968), *Labour Law: Old
               Traditions and New Developments*, Clark, Irwin.
138   KAHN-FREUND, O. (1965), *Labour Relations
               and the Law: A Comparative Study*, Stevens.
349, 354, 364 KAHN-FREUND, O. (1970) 'Trade unions, the law
               and society', 33 *Mod. L. Rev.* 241.
168, 173, 174, 175   KEETON, R. E., and O'CONNELL, J. (1965),
               Basic Protection for the Traffic Victim, Dow Jones,
               Irvin.
390   KEIR, D. L., and LAWSON, F. H. (1967), *Cases on
               Constitutional Law*, Oxford University Press.

125, 130 KESSLER, F. (1943), 'Contracts of adhesion', 43
Columbia L. Rev. 629.

125, 127 KESSLER, F., and SHARP, M. P. (1953),
Contracts: Cases and Materials, Prentice-Hall.

27 KHADDURI, M., and LIEBESNY, H. J. (1955),
Law in the Middle East, Middle East Institute.

173 KLINE and PEARSON, (1951),
The Problem of the Uninsured Motorist.

299 KOREH, V. (1968), *Monopolies and Restrictive
Practices*, Stevens.

283 KRAUSE, H. Q. (1967), 'Bastards abroad:
foreign approaches to illegitimacy', 15
Amer. J. Comp. L. 726.

98 KRUSE, F. V. (1950), *The Community of the Future*,
Oxford University Press.

70 KURLAND, P. 'Equal in origin and equal in title
to the legislative and executive branches of the
government', 78 *Harvard L. Rev.* 143.

187 LAPTER, W. W. (1954) *Le Système des Contrats
Economiques dans le Republique Democratique
Allemande.*

402 LANGLOD, G. (1955), 'Administrative contracts',
4 *Amer. J. Comp. L.*, 325.

171 LARSON, A. (1954), 'Changing concepts in
workmen's compensation', 14 *N.A.C.C.A.L.J.* 23.

330 LATHAM, E. (1957), 'Anthropomorphic
corporations, elites, and monopoly' 47 *Papers and
Proceedings*, *Amer. Econ. Soc.* 303.

317 LATHAM, F. C. (1950), 'Private charitable
foundations, income tax and policy implications',
98 *U. Pennsylvania L. Rev.*, 617.

789 LAUTERPACHT, H. (1927), *Private Law Sources
and Analogies of International Law*, Longman.

480 LAUDERPACHT, H. (1951), 'The problem of
jurisdictional immunities of foreign states', 28
Brit. Ybk Int. Law, 250.

85, 87 LAUTERPACHT, H. (1958), *The Development of
International Law by the International Court*,
Stevens.

378 LAWSON, F. R. 'Dicey revisited', 7 *Political
Studies* 109, 207.

167 LEFLAR, R. A., and KANTOZOWICZ, B. E.
(1954), 'Tort liability of the States', 29
N. Y. University L. Rev., 1363.

162, 165 LEFLAR, R. A. (1952), 'Negligence in income only',
27 *N. Y. University L. Rev.*, 564.

538 References

350   LENHOFF, A. (1956) 'The problems of compulsory unionism in Europe', 5 *Amer. J. Comp. L.* 18.

135   LENHOFF, A. (1943), 'The scope of compulsory contract proper', 73 *Columbia L. Rev.* 586.

295, 328   LILIENTHAL, D. (1953), *Big Business: A New Era*, Harper & Row.

130   LLEWELLYN, K. (1939), 'Book review', 52 *Harvard L. Rev.* 700.

130   LLEWELLYN, K. (1931), 'What price contract?', 40 *Yale L.J.* 704.

356   LLOYD, D. (1956), 'Damages for wrongful expulsion from a trade union', 19 *Mod. L. Rev.* 121.

123   LLOYD, D. (1953), *Public Policy*, Athlone.

142   LOEBAR, D. A. (1965), 'Plan and contract performance in Soviet law', in W. R. Lafave (ed.), *Law in the Soviet Society*, Illinois University Press.

409   LOGAN, D. W. (1945), 'A civil servant and his pay', 61 *L.Q. Rev.* 240.

389, 400, 413   LONG, M., WEIL, P., and BRAIBANT, G. (eds.) (1969), *Les grands Arrets de la Jurisprudence Administrative*, 5th edn.

387, 414, 415   MACDERMOTT, J. C. (1957), *Protection from Power under English Law*, Stevens.

472   McDOUGAL, M. (1953), 'International law, power and policy: a contemporary conception', 82 *Recueil des Cours* 187.

489   MACGIBBON, I. C. (1958), 'Estoppel in international law', 7 *Int. & Comp. L.Q.* 768.

248, 250, 251   McGREGOR, O. R. (1957), *Divorce in England*.

342   MACPHERSON, W. H. (1951), 'Co-administration: Germany's move toward a new economy', 5 *Ind. & Lab. Rel. Rev.* 20.

343   MACPHERSON, W. H. (1955), 'Co-determination in practice', 8 *Ind. & Lab. Rel. Rev.* 499.

487   MCNAIR, A. D. (1961), *The Law of Treaties*, Oxford University Press.

312-13   MAITLAND, F. W. (1936), 'The unicorporate body' and 'Trust and cooperation', in *Selected Essays*, Cambridge University Press.

475   MANN, F. A. (1944), 'The law governing state contracts', 21 *Brit. Ybk Int. Law* 11.

232   MANNHEIM, H. (1946), *Criminal Justice and Social Reconstruction*, Oxford University Press.

227   MANNHEIM, H., and WILKINS, L. T. (1955),
       Prediction Methods in Relation to Borstal Training,
       HMSO.
500   MARSH, N. (1959), 'Defining the rule of law',
       Listener, 28 May.
420   MARTIN-PANNETIER, A. (1966), *Element
       d'analyse comparative des etablissements publics
       en droit français et en droit anglais*, Pinchon;
       Durand-Auzias.
352   MASON, A. T. (1946), *Brandeis: A Free Man's Life*,
       Viking Press.
126   MASON, A. T. (1955), *Security through Freedom:
       American Political Thought and Practice*,
       Cornell University Press.
412   MAZEAND, H., and MAZEAND, L. (1947),
       *Traité theorique et pratique de la responsabilité
       civile et contractuelle*, Librairie du Recueil Sirey,
       4th edn.
168   MEHREN, A. VON (1967), *The Civil Law System*,
       Little Brown.
208, 209, 214   MICHAEL, J., and WESCHLER, H. (1940,
       supp. 1956), *Criminal Law and Its Administration*,
       Foundation Press.
325, 383   MILLER, A. S. (1958), 'The constitutional law of
       the "security state"', 10 *Stanford L. Rev.* 610.
476   MILLER, A. S. (1958), 'Foreign trade and the
       security state', 7 *J. Public Law* 37.
403   MILLER, A. S. (1955), 'Government contracts
       and social control', 41 *Virginia L. Rev.* 27.
140   MILLER, A. S. (1955), 'Government contracts and
       social control: a preliminary inquiry', 41
       Virginia L. Rev. 56.
226   MILLER, J. G. (1970), 'Family assets', 86 *L.Q.
       Rev.* 98.
181   MINISTRY OF HEALTH (1942),
       *Social Insurance and Allied Service:
       Report by Sir William Beveridge*, Cmd 6404,
       HMSO.
390, 399, 400, 401, 402, 408,   MITCHELL, J. D. B. (1954), *The Contracts of
420   Public Authorities: A Comparative Study*,
       University of London.
379   MITCHELL, J. D. B. (1966), 'The state of public
       law in the United Kingdom', 15 *Int. & Comp. L.Q.*
       133.
52   MONTROSE, J. L. (1957), 'Ratio decidendi and
       the House of Lords', 20 *Mod. L. Rev.* 124.

97   MORIN, G. (1950), 'Le sens et l'evolution contemporaine du droit de propriete' 2 *Etudes Ripert* 7; in *Le droit privé français au milieu du XXe siècle:* études offertes à Georges Ripert, tome 2.

174   MORRIS, C., and PAUL, J. C. N. (1962), 'The financial impact of automobile accidents' 110 *University of Pennsylvania L. Rev.* 913.

230, 232   MORRIS, N. (1951), *The Habitual Criminal*, Harvard University Press.

323   NEUMANN, F. N. (1944), *Behemorth: The Structure and Practice of National Socialism*, Oxford University Press.

315, 316, 317   NOTE (1948), 'The use of charitable foundations for avoidance of taxes', 34 *Virginia L. Rev.* 182.

180   NOTE (1949), 'The mitigating effect of damages on social welfare programs', 63 *Harvard L. Rev.* 333.

132   NOTE (1950), 'Contract clauses in fine clauses', 63 *Harvard L. Rev.* 504.

405, 407   NOTE (1957), 'Remedies against the United States', 70 *Harvard L. Rev.*

405, 407   NOTE (1957), 'Remedies against the United States and its officials', 70 *Harvard L. Rev.* 827.

228   NYQUIST, O. (1960), *Juvenile Justice*, Almquist & Wiksells.

488   O'CONNELL, D. P. (1956), 'Unjust enrichment', 5 *Amer. J. Comp. Law* 2.

491   OECD (1957), *Draft Convention on the Protection of Property*.

229   OLNEY, J. (1938), 'Juvenile courts: abolish them', 13 *California State B.J.* 1.

486, 488   OPPENHEIM, L. F. L., and LAUTERPACHT, H. (1958), *International Law*, Longman.

492   ONFIELD, L. B. (1950), 'What constitutes fair criminal procedure under municipal and international law?', 12 *University of Pittsburg L. Rev.* 35.

192, 232–3, 234   PACKER, H. L. (1968), *The Limits on Criminal Sanction*, Stanford University Press.

383   PARKER, R. (1958), 'The historic basis of administrative law: separation of powers and judicial supremacy', 12 *Rutgers L. Rev.* 449.

94	PASHKOV, A. I. (1956), 'Radical changes in property in the USSR in the twentieth century', *Transactions of the Third World Congress of Sociology*, International Sociological Association.
403, 405	PASLEY, R. S. (1956), 'The interpretation of government contracts', 25 *Fordham L. Rev.* 211.
404	PASLEY, R. S. (1957), 'The non-discrimination clause in government contracts', 43 *Virginia L. Rev.* 837.
121, 157	PATON, G. W. (1951), *A Textbook of Jurisprudence*, Oxford University Press, 2nd edn.
52	PATON, G. W., and SAWER, G. (1947), 'Ratio decidendi and *obiter dictum* in appelate courts', 63 *L.Q. Rev.* 461.
230	PAULSEN, M. (1956), 'Fairness to juvenile offenders', 41 *Minnesota L. Rev.* 547.
253	PAULSEN, M. (1956), 'Support rights and duties', 9 *Vanderbilt L. Rev.* 709.
149	PELLING, H. (1968), 'Trade unions, workers and the law', in *Popular Politics and Society in Late Victorian Britain*, Macmillan.
207	PERKINS, R. M. (1952), 'The civil offense', 100 *University of Pennsylvania L. Rev.* 832.
113	PLAGER, S. J. (1970), *New Approaches in the Law of Property*, Foundation Press.
123	PLANIOL, M. (1937), *Traité elementaire de droit civil*, Librairie générale de droit et de jurisprudence, Paris.
261	POPE PAUL VI (1968), *Humanae Vitae*, Paulist Press.
260, 262, 263	POPE PIUS XII (1951), *Moral Questions Affecting Married Life: The Apostolate of the Midwife*, Paulist Press.
81	POUND, R. (1908), 'Common law and legislation', 21 *Harvard L. Rev.* 383.
162	POUND, R. (1954), 'The rule of the will in law', 68 *Harvard L. Rev.* 1.
121	POUND, R. (1957), *Introduction to the Philosophy of Law*, Harvard University Press.
130	PRAUSNITZ, O. (1937), *Standardization of Commercial Contracts in English and Continental Law*, Sweet & Maxwell.
104, 105, 164, 167	PROSSER, W. L. (1964), *Handbook of the Law of Torts*, West Publishing, rev. edn.
234	RADZINOWICZ, L. (1962), *In Search of Criminology*, Heinemann.

221	RADZINOWICZ, L. (1945), 'The persistent offender', in P. H. Winfield (ed.), *Modern Approaches to Criminal Law*, Macmillan.
260, 262, 263	REIWALD, P. (1950), *Society and its Criminals*, International Universities Press.
173	*Report by the Committee of Study Compensation for Automobile Accidents* (1932), Columbia University Council for Research in Social Sciences.
201	*Report of the Committee on Homosexual Offences and Prostitution* (1957), Cmnd 747, HMSO.
256	*Report of the Joint Legislative Committee on Matrimonial and Family Law* (1958), New York State.
112	*Report of the President's Water Resources Policy Commission: Water Resources Law* (1958).
213, 214, 215, 217, 219, 224, 225	*Report of the Royal Commission for Capital Punishment, 1949–53*, Cmnd 8932, HMSO.
50, 239, 240, 250, 278, 280, 282	*Report of the Royal Commission on Marriage and Divorce*, Cmnd 9678, HMSO.
150–53, 335, 344–5, 349 357, 359–60, 364–5	*Report of the Royal Commission on Trade Unions and Employers Associations, 1965–8* (1968) (Donovan Commission), Cmnd 3623, HMSO.
251	RHEINSTEIN, M. (1956), 'The law of divorce and the problem of marriage stability', 9 *Vanderbilt L. Rev.* 633.
170	RIESENFELD, S. A. (1954), 'Contemporary trends in compensation for industrial accidents here and abroad', 42 *California L. Rev.* 531.
68	RIBBLE, F. D. G. (1957), 'Look at the policy making powers of the Supreme Court and the position of the individual', 14 *Washington and Lee L. Rev.* 167.
281	ROBBINS, H. H., and DEAK, F. (1930), 'The familial property rights of illegitimate children: a comprehensive study', 30 *Columbia L. Rev.* 308.
436	ROBSON, W. A. (1958), *Public Law*, Stevens.
97	RIPERT, G. (1955), *Les Forces Creatrices du Droit*, Librairie générale de droit et de jurisprudence, Paris.
379	ROBSON, W. A. (1951), *Justice and Administrative Law*, Stevens.
784	ROOF, E. (1910), 'The basis of protection to citizens residing abroad', *Proceedings Amer. Soc. Int. Law* 16.

482, 486	ROTH, A. H. (1949), *The Minimum Standard of International Law Applied to Aliens*, A. W. Sijthoff.
299	ROWLEY, C. K. (1966), *The British Monopolies Commission*, Allen & Unwin.
214	RUSSELL SAGE FOUNDATION (1967), *The Foundation Directory*, Foundation Liberty Center.
128	SALMOND, J. W. (1969), *Salmond on the Law of Torts*, Sweet & Maxwell, 15th edn.
109	SAVATIER, R. (1952), *Les Metamorphoses Economiques et Sociales du Droit civil d'aujourd'hui*, Dalloz, 2nd edn.
202	SAYRE, F. B. (1933), 'Public welfare offenses', 33 *Columbia L. Rev.* 55.
236, 238, 281	SAYRE, P. (ed.) (1950), *Selected Essays on Family Law*, Assoc. of Amer. L. Schools.
448	SCHACHTER, O. (1963), 'The relation of law, politics and action in the United Nations', *Recueil des Cours* 166.
480	SCHMITTHOFF, C. M. (1958), 'Sovereign immunity in international trade', 7 *Int. & Comp. L.Q.*, 452.
296	SCHMITTHOFF, C. M. (1951), 'The rationalization of basic industries in Great Britain', 16 *Law and Contemp Problems*, 557.
331, 333, 366	SCHONFIELD, A. (1969), *Modern Capitalism: The Changing Balance of Public and Private Power*, Oxford University Press.
343	SHUCHMANN, A. (1957), *Codetermination: Labor's Middle Way in Germany*, Public Affairs Press.
126	SCHWARTZ, B. (1950), 'The changing role of the United States Supreme Court', 28 *Canadian Bar Rev.* 78.
410, 412, 423, 435	SCHWARTZ, B. (1954), *French Administrative Law and the Common Law*, World, New York University Press.
85, 87, 488	SCHWARZENBERGER, G. (1957), *International Law*, Stevens, 3rd edn.
486	SCHWARZENBERGER, G. (1969), *Foreign Investment and International Law*, Praeger.
489	SCHWARZENBERGER, G. (1955), 'The fundamental principles of law', 87 Hague *Recueil des Cours*, 312.
479	SCHWARZENBERGER, G. 'The most-favoured action standard in British state practice', 22 *Brit. Ybk Int. Law*, 96.

544 References

202	SCHWENK, E. H. (1943), 'The administrative crime, its creation and punishment by administrative agencies', 42 *Michigan L. Rev.* 51.
239	SCOTT, W. L. (1938), 'Nullity of marriage in canon law and English law', 2 *University of Toronto L.J.*, 319.
162	SEAVEY, W. A. (1951), 'Candler *v.* Crane, Christmas & Co.', 67 *L.Q. Rev.* 466.
152	SELWYN, N. (1969), 'Collective agreements and the law', 32 *Mod. L. Rev.* 377.
477, 479	SEYID MUHAMMED, V. A. (1958) *The Legal Framework of World Trade*, Stevens.
154	SHULMAN, H. (1955), 'Reason, contract and law in labour relations', 68 *Harvard L. Rev.* 999.
243	SIMITIS, A. (1969), *Recht und sozialer Wandel*
267	SIMMS, M. (1970), 'Abortion law reform: how the controversy changed', *Crim. L. Rev.* 567.
219	SIMON, R. J. (1967), *The Jury and the Defence of Insanity*, Little, Brown.
52	SIMPSON, A. W. B. (1957), 'The ratio decidendi of a case', 20 *Mod. L. Rev.* 413.
52	SIMPSON, A. W. B. (1958), 'The ratio decidendi of a case', 21 *Mod. L. Rev.* 155.
165	SINHA, S. PRAKASH (1969), 'The problem of application of the fault principle to automobile accidents', 14 *Villanova L. Rev.* 386.
144, 146	SMIT, H. (1958), 'Frustration of contract', 58 *Columbia L. Rev.* 287.
107	SMITH, M., and PEARSON, A. (1969), 'The value of strict liability', *Crim. L. Rev.* 5.
425	SMITH, S. DE (1952), 'Wrongs and remedies in administrative process', 15 *Mod. L. Rev.* 189.
385, 388, 426, 427	SMITH S. DE (1968), *Judicial Review of Administratisve Action*, Stevens, 2nd edn.
486	SOVUTTAS, T. E. (1922), 'Work of the commercial courts', 1 *Cambridge L.J.* 6.
164	STALYBASS, W. T. S. (1929), 'Dangerous things and the non-natural user of land', 3 *Cambridge L.J.* 376.
192, 214	STEPHEN, F. (1883), *History of the Criminal Law in England*.
201	STRAWSON, P. F. (1961), 'Social morality and individual ideal', 37 *Philosophy* 1.
390, 399, 402, 407, 408	STREET, H. (1953), *Governmental Liability: A Comparative Study*, Cambridge University Press.

435   STREET, H. (1968), *Justice in the Welfare State*, Stevers.

178   STREET, H., and ELLIOTT, D. W. (1968), *Road Accidents*, Penguin.

52   STONE, J. (1946), *Province and the Function of Law*, Associated General Publications.

330   SUBCOMMITTEE ON ANTI-TRUST AND MONOPOLY OF THE SENATE COMMITTEE ON THE JUDICIARY (1958), *Administrative Prices: Hearings on S. Res. 57 and S. Res. 231*, 85th Congress 2nd Session; (1963), *Administered Prices: A Compendium on Public Policy*, 88th Congress, 1st Session.

354   SUMMERS, C. (1950), 'Disciplinary powers of unions', 3 *Jud. Lab. Relation Rev.* 483; 4 *id.* 15.

361   SUMMERS, C. W. (1962), 'American legislation for union democracy', 25 *Mod. L. Rev.* 273.

361   SUMMERS, C. W. (1951), 'Legal limitations on union discipline', 64 *Harvard L. Rev.* 1049.

156   SYKES, E. I. (1964), 'Labor arbitration in Australia', 13 *Amer. J. Comp. L.* 214.

221, 222   SYMPOSIUM (1961) 'Evolution and man's progress', *Daedalus* (Summer).

238   SYMPOSIUM (1970), 'Family law', 36 *Mod. L. Rev.*

230   SYMPOSIUM (1967), 'The habitual criminal', 13 *McGill L.J.* 533.

402   SYMPOSIUM (1956–8), 'Various aspects of government contracts', *George Washington L. Rev.* vols. 24, 25, 26.

158   SZLADIFS, C. (1955), 'The concept of specific performance in civil law', 4 *Amer. J. Comp. Law* 208.

262   TALLIN, G. P. R. (1956), 'Artificial insemination', 34 *Canadian Bar Rev.*, 1, 166.

106   TAY, A. E. (1968), 'The law of inheritance and the new Russian civil code of 1964', 17 *Int. & Comp. L.Q.* 472.

223, 224   TAYLOR, G. R. (1968), *The Biological Time-Bomb*, New American Library.

39   TAYLOR, T. (1970), *Nuremberg 2nd Vietnam: An American Tragedy*, Quadrangle Books.

153   TELLER, L. (1940), *The Law Governing Labor Disputes and Collective Bargaining*, Baker, Voorhis.

227   THOMPSON, R. E. (1953) 'Research and methodology: a validation of Glueck social prediction scale for proneness to delinquency', 3 *British Journal of Delinquency*, 289.

156   THOMPSON, D. C. (1948), 'Voluntary collective agreements in Australia and New Zealand'. 1 *University of Western Australian L. Rev.* 80.

54   TRAYNOR, R. (1959), 'Courts and lawmaking', in M. Paulsen (ed.), *Legal Institutions Today and Tomorrow*, Columbia University Press.

74   TRAYNOR, R. (1962), 'La rude vita, la dolce giustizia: or hard cases can make good law', 29 *University of Chicago L. Rev.* 223.

390   TROTABAS, L. (1925), 'Les actes de gouvernement en matière diplomatiques', in *Revue Critique de Legislation et de Jurisprudence*, R. Pichon.

179   TUNC, A. (1965), 'Current legal developments: France – tortius liability', 17 *Int. & Comp. L.Q.* 1041.

179   TUNC, A. (1967), 'Un bilan provisoire', *Droit Social*, no. 2, February.

245   TURNER, J. N. (1969), 'Divorce: Australian and German "breakdown" provisions compared', 18 *Int. & Comp. L.Q.* 896.

703   TURPIN, C. C. (1968), 'Government contracts: a study of methods of contracting', 31 *Mod. L. Rev.* 241.

229   US NATIONAL COMMISSION ON CAUSES AND PREVENTION OF VIOLENCE (1969), *Law and Order Reconsidered*, US Govt Printing Office.

184   USSING, H. (1952), 'The Scandinavian law of torts', 1 *Amer. J. Comp. L.*, 359.

479   VERBIT, G. P. (1969), *Trade Agreements for Developing Countries*, Columbia University Press.

247   VERNIER, C. G. (1931), *American Family Law*, Oxford University Press.

515   VICKERS, G. (1965), *The Art of Judgement: A Study of Policy-Making*, Basic Books.

515   VICKERS, G. (1968), *Value Systems and Social Progress*, Basic Books.

425   WADE, E. C. S. (1947), 'Courts and the administrating process', 63 *L.Q. Rev.* 164.

378, 379	WADE, E. C. S. (1957), *Dicey's Law of the Constitution*, Macmillan.
381, 386, 387, 388, 390, 399, 400, 401, 413, 420, 432	WALINE, M. (1963), *Droit Administratif*, 9th edn (Paris) Editions Sirey.
490	WALKER, H. (1956), 'Treaties for the encouragement and protection of foreign investment', 7 *Amer. J. Comp. Law*, 229.
226	WALKER, N. (1965), *Crime and Punishment in Britain*, Edinburgh University Press.
217	WALKER, N. (1967), *Crime and Insanity in England*, Edinburgh University Press.
199	WALTON, C. C., and CLEVELAND, F. W. (1964), *Corporations on Trial: the Electric Cases*, Wadsworth Publishing Co.
42, 43	WASSERSTROM, R. A. (1963), 'The obligation to obey the law', 10 *University of California Los Angeles L. Rev.* 780.
315	WEAVER, W. (1967), *U.S. Philanthropic Foundation*, Harper & Row.
191	WECHSLER, H. (1955) 'The criteria of criminal responsibility', 22 *University of Chicago L. Rev.*, 374.
217	WECHSLER, H. (1968), 'Codification of criminal law in the United States: the Model Penal Code', 68 *Columbia L. Rev.* 1425.
70, 72	WECHSLER, H. (1961), *Principles, Politics and Fundamental Law*, Harvard University Press.
356	WEDDERBURN, K. W. (1957), 'The bonson affair: a postscript', 20 *Mod. L. Rev.* 105.
422	WEDDERBURN, K. W. (1957), 'Sovereign immunities of foreign public corporation', 6 *Int. & Comp. L.Q.* 290
358	WEDDERBURN, K. W. (1965), Stratford *v.* Lindley', 28 *Mod. L. Rev.* 205.
152	WEDDERBURN, K. W. (1971), *The Worker and the Law*, Penguin, rev. edn.
460	WEIL, G. L. (1963), *The European Convention on Human Rights*, A. W. Sijthoff.
208	WELSH, R. S. (1946), 'Criminal liability of corporations', 62 *L.Q. Rev.* 345.
81	WHITE, J. B. (1934) *Criminal Law in Action*, Holston House, Sears.
506	WHITE, G. (1961), *The Nationalization of Foreign Property*, Stevers.

48   WIGMORE, J. H. (1894), 'Responsibility for
              torticus acts', 7 *Harvard L. Rev.* 441.
486   WILLIAMS, F. (1928), 'International law and the
              property of aliens', 9 *Brit. Ybk Int. Law* 1.
421   WILLIAMS, G. L. (1948), *Crown Proceedings*,
              Stevens.
191   WILLIAMS, G. L. (1955), 'The definition of
              crime', in *Current Legal Problems*, Stevens.
111   WILLIAMS, H. R. (1956), 'The continuing
              evolution of the land', in *Transactions of the
              Third World Congress of Sociology*, v 1, 2.
201, 262, 263, 264, 265, 267   WILLIAMS, G. L. (1957), *The Sanctity of Life and
              the Criminal Law*, Knopf.
77, 83, 202, 205, 208, 212   WILLIAMS, G. L. (1961), *Criminal Law*, Stevens.
58   WILLIS, J. (1938), 'Statute interpretation in a
              nutshell', 16 *Canadian Bar Rev.* 1.
402   WILLISTON, SAMUEL (1957–1970),
              A Treatise on the Law of Contracts (3rd edn)
              H. E. Walker, Jaeger, Rochester N.Y., Balker,
              Voorlis & Co., and the Lawyers Cooperative
              Publishing Co.
479   WILSON, R. R. (1953), *The International Law
              Standard in Treaties of the United States*,
              Harvard University Press.
382   WILSON, W. (1927), *Constitutional Government
              in the United States*, Columbia University Press.
334   WIRTZ, W. W. (1953), 'Government by private
              groups', 13 *Louisiana L. Rev.* 440.
233   WOOTTON, B. (1963), *Crime and the Criminal
              Law: Reflections of a Magistrate and Social
              Scientist*, Stevens.
299   YAMEY, B. S., and STEVENS, R. B. (1965),
              *The Restrictive Practices Court: A Study of the
              Judicial Progress and Economic Policy*,
              Weidenfeld & Nicolson.
144   ZEPOS, P. J. (1948), 'Frustration of contract in
              comparative law and the new Greek code of 1946',
              11 *Mod. L. Rev.* 36.
202   ZIFF, H. L. 'Recent abortion law reforms', 60
              J. Crim. L. 3.
42   ZINN, H. (1968), *Disobedience and Democracy:
              Nine Fallacies on Law and Order*, Random House.

Table of Cases

Table of Statutes

United Kingdom

Select Bibliography

Chapter One: The Interactions of Legal and Social Change

Dicey, A. V., *Law and Public Opinion in England during the Nineteenth Century* Macmillan, 2nd edn, 1914.

Ehrlich, E., *Fundamental Principles of the Sociology of the Law* (English translation 1936), Harvard University Press.

Friedman, L. M., and Macaulay, S. (eds.), *Law and the Behavioral Sciences*, Bobbs-Merrill, 1969.

Hazard, J. N., *Communists and Their Law*, University of Chicago Press, 1969.

Hazard, J. N., *Law and Social Change in the USSR*, Carswell, 1953.

Hepple, B., *Race, Jobs and the Law in Britain*, Penguin, 2nd edn, 1970.

Hurst, J. W., *Law and Social Process in United States History*, University of Michigan Law School, 1960.

Sawer, G., *Law in Society*, Oxford University Press, 1960.

Scarman, L., *Law Reform*, Fernwell, 1969.

Stone, J., *Social Dimensions of Law and Justice*, ch. 15, Stanford University Press, 1966.

Strawson, P. F., 'Social morality and individual ideals', 37 *Philosophy* 1, 1961.

Chapter Two: The Courts and The Evolution of Law

Bickel, A. M., *The Supreme Court and the Idea of Progress*, Harper & Row, 1970.

Breitel, C. D., 'The courts and lawmaking', in M. Paulsen (ed.), *Legal Institutions Today and Tomorrow*, Columbia University Press, 1959.

Cardozo, B. N., *The Nature of the Judicial Process*, Yale University Press, 1921.

Friedmann, W., 'Legal philosophy and judicial lawmaking', 61 *Columbia L. Rev.* 841, 1961, reprinted in *Essays on Jurisprudence from the Columbia Law Review* 101 (1963).

Friedmann, W., *Legal Theory*, pp. 436–555, Stevens, 5th edn, 1967.

Hall, J. I., 'Strict or liberal construction of penal statutes', 48 *Harvard L. Rev.* 748, 1935.

Hand, L., *The Bill of Rights*, Atheneum, 1958.

Hart, H. M., 'Foreword: the time chart of the justices', 73 *Harvard L. Rev.* 84, 1959.

Hart, H. L. A., 'Positivism and the separation of law and morals', 71 *Harvard L. Rev.* 593, 1958.

Hart, H. L. A., *Law, Liberty and Morality*, Stanford University Press, 1963.

Goodhart, A. L., 'The ratio decidendi of a case', 22 *Mod. L. Rev.* 117, 1959.

Kurland, P., 'Foreword: equal in origin and equal in title to the legislative and executive branches of the government', 78 *Harvard L. Rev.*, 1964.

Lauterpacht, H., *The Development of International Law by the International Court*, Stevens, 1958.

Montrose, J. L., 'The ratio decidendi of a case', 20 *Mod. L. Rev.* 587, 1957.

Paton, G. W., and Sawer, G., 'Ratio decidendi and obiter dictum in appellate courts', 63 *L.Q. Rev.* 461, 1967.

Paulsen, M. (ed.), *Legal Institutions Today and Tomorrow*, Columbia University Press, 1959.

Schwarzenberger, G., *International Law*, Stevens, 3rd edn, 1957, vol. 1.

Simpson, A. W. B., 'The ratio decidendi of a case', 20 *Mod. L. Rev.* 413, 1957 · 21 *Mod. L. Rev.* 155, 1958.

Stone, J., *Social Dimensions of Law and Justice*, Stanford University Press, 1966, ch. 14.

Wechsler, H., *Principles, Politics and Fundamental Law*, Harvard University Press, 1961.

Chapter Three: Changing Concepts of Property

Bastian, D., 'La propriété commerciale en droit français', 6 *Travaux de l'Association Henri Capitant* 76, 1950.

Berle, A. A., and Means, G. C., *The Modern Corporation and Private Property*, Harcourt, Brace & World, 1932, rev. edn, 1968.

Harding, A. L., 'Free man versus his government', 5 *Southern Methodist Studies in Jurisprudence* 81, Southern Methodist University Press, 1949.

Hargreaves, M. O., 'Modern real property', 19 *Mod. L. Rev.* 14, 1956.

Hazard, J. N., *Communists and Their Law*, pp. 145–222, University of Chicago Press, 1969.

Kahn-Freund, O., 'Introduction' to K. Renner, *The Institutions of Private Law and their Social Function*, Routledge & Kegan Paul, 1949.

Morin, G., 'Le Sens et l'Evolution Contemporaire du droit de propriété', *Etudes Ripert*, vol. 2, p. 3, Librairie de général de droit et de jurisprudence, 1950.

Plager, S. J., *New Approaches in the Law of Property*, Foundation Press, 1970.

Ripert, G., *Les forces créatrices du droit*, Librarie général de droit et de jurisprudence, 1955.

Savatier, R., *Les métamorphoses économiques et sociales du droit civil d'aujourd'hui*, Dalloz, 2nd edn, 1952.

Chapter Four: The Changing Function of Contract

Berman, H. J., *Justice in the USSR*, Harvard University Press, rev. edn, 1963.

Cohen, M. R., *Law and the Social Order* pp. 69–111, Harcourt, Brace & World, 1933.

Hazard, J. N., *Law and Social Change in the USSR*, pp. 48–56, Carswell, 1953.

Hazard, J. N., *Communists and Their Law*, pp. 311–41, University of Chicago Press, 1969.

Kahn-Freund, O. (ed.) *Labour Relations and the Law: A Comparative Study*, pp. 1–124, Stevens, 1965.

Kessler, F., 'Contracts of adhesion', 43 *Columbia L. Rev.* 629, 1943.

Loeber, D. A., 'Plan and contract performance in Soviet law', in W. R. Lafave (ed.) *Law in the Soviet Society*, University of Illinois Press, 1965.

Mitchell, J. D. B., *The Contracts of Public Authorities*, *A Comparative Study*, University of London, 1954.

Paton, G. U., *Textbook of Jurisprudence*, §80, 3rd edn by D. Derham, Oxford University Press, 1964.

Pound, R., *Introduction to the Philosophy of Law*, ch. 6, Yale University Press, rev. edn, 1954.

Report of the Royal Commission on Trade Unions and Employers' Associations, 1965–8 Cmnd 3623, 1968.

Selwyn, N., 'Collective agreements and the law', 32 *Mod. L. Rev.* 377, 1969.

Shulman, H., 'Reason, contract and law in labour relations', 68 *Harvard L. Rev.* 999, 1955.

Smit, H., 'Frustration of contract', 58 *Columbia L. Rev.* 287, 1958.

Symposium, 'Compulsory contracts in theory and practice', 43 *Columbia L. Rev.* 565, 1943.

Turpin, C. C., 'Government contracts: a study of methods of contracting', 31 *Mod. L. Rev.* 241, 1968.

Chapter Five: Tort, Insurance and Social Responsibility

Barry, D. D., 'The motor car in Soviet criminal and civil law', 16 *Int'l & Comp. L.Q.* 56, 1967.

Bengston, B., 'Personal injury boards in Sweden', 18 *Am. J. Comp. L.* 108, 1970.

Blum, W. J., and Klaven, H. J., *Public Perspectives on a Private Law Problem: Auto Compensation Plans*, Little, Brown, 1965.

Conrad, A. F., *Automobile Accident Costs and Payments: Studies in the Economics of Injury Reparation*, University of Michigan Press, 1964.

Calabresi, G., 'Fault, accident, and the wonderful world of Blum and Klaven', 75 *Yale L.J.* 216, 1965.

Ehrenzweig, A. A., *Negligence without Fault*, University of California Press, 1951.

Ehrenzweig, A. A., *'Full Aid' Insurance for the Traffic Victim: A Voluntary Compensation Plan*, University of California Press, 1954.

Elliott, D. W., and Street, H., *Road Accidents*, Penguin, 1968.

Esmein, P., 'Liability in French law for damages caused by motor vehicle accidents,' 2 *Amer. J. Comp. L.* 156, 1953.

Fleming, J. G., 'The role of negligence in modern tort law', 53 *Virginia L. Rev.* 815, 1967.

Gray, W., 'Soviet tort law: the new principles annotated', in W. R. Lafave (ed.), *Law in the Soviet Society*, p. 180, University of Illinois Press, 1965.

Green, L., *Traffic Victims: Tort Law and Insurance*, Northwestern University Press, 1958.

Harper, F. V., and James, F., *The Law of Torts*, §§ 25.19–25.23, Little, Brown, 1956, Supp. 1968.

Hazard, J. N., *Communists and Their Law*, pp. 381–416, University of Chicago Press, 1969.

Hellner, J., 'Tort liability and liability insurance', 6 *Scandinavian Studies in Law* 129, 1962.

Hellner, J., 'Damages for personal injury and the victim's private insurance', 18 *Amer. J. Comp. L.* 126, 1970.

Ionasco, T., 'The fault requirement and the contract liability of socialist organizations', 18 *Amer. J. Comp. L.* 31, 1970.

Keeton, R. E., and O'Connell, J., *After Cars Crash: The Need for Legal and Insurance Reform*, Dow-Jones, Irwin, 1967.

Keeton, R. E., and O'Connell, J., *Basic Protection for the Traffic Victim: A Blueprint for Reforming Automobile Insurance*, Little, Brown, 1966.

Leflar, R. A., 'Negligence in name only', 27 *New York University L. Rev.* 564, 1952.

Leflar, R. A., and Kantrowicz, B. E., 'Tort liability of the states', 29 *New York University L. Rev.* 1363, 1954.

Morris, C., and Paul, J. C. N., 'The financial impact of automobile accidents', 110 *University of Pennsylvania L. Rev.*, 913, 1962.

Report by the Committee to Study Compensation for Automobile Accidents, Columbia University Council for Research in the Social Sciences, 1932.

Salmond, J. W., *Salmond on the Law of Torts*, Sweet & Maxwell, 15th edn, 1969.

Sinha, S. P., 'The problem of the application of the fault principle to automobile accidents', 14 *Villanova L. Rev.* 386, 1969.

Tunc, A., 'Current legal developments: France – tortious liability', 14 *Int'l & Comp. L.Q.* 1041, 1965.

Ussing, H., 'The Scandinavian law of torts', 1 *Amer. J. Comp. L.* 359, 1952.

Weyers, H.-L., *Unfallschäden*, Athenäum Verlag, 1971.

Zweigert, K., and Kötz, H. *Einführung in die Rechtsvergleichung*, J. C. B. Mohr & Paul Siebeck, pp. 368–407, 1969.

Chapter Six: Criminal Law in a Changing World

Arens, R., and Lasswell, H. D., *In Defense of Public Order: The Emerging Field of Sanction Law*, Columbia University Press, 1961.

Devlin, P., *The Enforcement of Morals*, Oxford University Press, 1965.

Edwards, J. L. J., *Mens Rea in Statutory Offenses*, Macmillan, 1955.

Flügel, J. C., *Man, Morals and Society*, International Universities Press, 1945.

Gardiner, G., 'The purposes of criminal punishment', 21 *Mod. L. Rev.* 117, 221, 1958.

Goldstein, A., *The Insanity Defence*, Yale University Press, 1967.

Hall, J., *General Principles of Criminal Law*, Bobbs Merill, 1947; 2nd edn, 1960.

Hart, H. L. A., *Punishment and Responsibility*, Oxford University Press, 1969.
Hart, H. L. A., *Law, Liberty and Morality*, Stanford University Press, 1963.
Hart, H. M., 'The aims of the criminal law', 23 *Law & Contemporary Problems* 422, 1958.
Hazard, J. N., *Communists and Their Law*, pp. 417–79, University of Chicago Press, 1969.
Henkin, L., 'Morals and the constitution: the sin of obscenity', 63 *Columbia L. Rev.* 391, 1963.
Morris, N., *The Habitual Criminal*, Harvard University Press, 1951.
Packer, H. L., *The Limits of the Criminal Sanction*, Stanford University Press, 1968.
Paulsen, H., 'Fairness to juvenile offenders', 41 *Minnesota L. Rev.* 547, 1956.
Radzinowicz, L., *In Search of Criminology*, Heinemann, 1962.
Reiwald, P., *Society and Its Criminals*, International Universities Press, 1950.
Report of the Royal Commission on Capital Punishment, 1949–53, Cmnd 8932, 1953.
St John-Stevas, N., *Life, Death and the Law*, Indiana University Press, 1961.
Ten, C. L., 'Crime and immorality', 32 *Mod. L. Rev.* 648, 1969.
Wechsler, H., 'The criteria of criminal responsibility', 22 *University of Chicago L. Rev.* 374, 1955.
Wechsler, H., 'Codification of criminal law in the United States: the model penal code', 68 *Columbia L. Rev.* 1425, 1968.
Williams, G. L., *Sanctity of Life and the Criminal Law*, Knopf, 1957.
Williams, G. L., *Criminal Law*, Stevens, 1961.
Wootton, B., *Crime and the Criminal Law: Reflections of a Magistrate and Social Scientist*, Stevens, 1963.

Chapter Seven: Family Law

Berman, H. J., *Justice in the USSR*, pp. 330–44, Harvard University Press, rev. edn, 1963.
Bohndorf, M. T., 'The new illegitimacy law in Germany', 19 *Int'l & Comp. L.Q.* 299, 1970.
Friedmann, W. (ed.), *Matrimonial Property Law*, Carswell, 1955.
Harper, F. V., *Problems of the Family*, Bobbs Merrill, 1952.
Graveson, R. H., and Crane, F. R. (eds.), *A Century of Family Law*, Sweet & Maxwell, 1957.
Hazard, J. N., *Communists and Their Law*, pp. 269–309, University of Chicago Press, 1969.
Krause, H. D., 'Bastards abroad: foreign approaches to illegitimacy', 15 *Amer. J. Comp. L.* 726, 1967.
Hazard, J. N., *Law and Social Change in the USSR*, pp. 245–73, Carswell, 1953.
McGregor, O. R., *Divorce in England*, Heinemann, 1957.
Jacobs, A. C., and Angell, R. C., *A Research in Family Law*, Columbia University School of Law, 1930.

Miller, J. G., 'Family assets', 86 *L.Q. Rev.* 98, 1970.
Paulsen, M. G., 'Support rights and duties', 9 *Vanderbilt L. Rev.* 709, 1956.
Report of the Royal Commission on Marriage and Divorce, Cmnd 9678, 1956.
Rheinstein, M., 'The law of divorce and the problem of marriage stability', 9 *Vanderbilt L. Rev.* 633, 1956.
Sayre, P. (ed.), *Selected Essays on Family Law*, Foundation Press, 1950.
Schlesinger, R., *The Family in the USSR*, Harvard University Press, 1949.
Scott, W. L., 'Nullity of marriage in canon law and English law', 2 *University of Toronto L.J.* 319, 1938.
Turner, J. N., 'Divorce: Australian and German 'breakdown' provisions compared', 18 *Int'l & Comp. L.Q.* 896, 1969.
Vernier, C. G., *American Family Laws* (1931), Stanford University Press; Oxford University Press.
Williams, G. L., *The Sanctity of Life and the Criminal Law*, Knopf, 1957.

Chapter Eight: Economic Competition, Regulation and the Public Interest: the Dilemmas of Anti-Trust

American Bar Association, Anti-Trust Section, *Anti-Trust Developments 1955–1968*, 1968.
Blake, H. M. (ed.), *Business Regulation in the Common Market Nations*, McGraw-Hill, 1969.
Edwards, C. D., *Maintaining Competition*, McGraw-Hill, rev. edn, 1964.
Friedmann, W. (ed.), *Anti-Trust Laws: A Comparative Symposium*, Stevens, 1956.
Friedmann, W., *The State and the Rule of Law in a Mixed Economy*, Stevens, 1971.
Handler, M., 'Some unresolved problems of anti-trust', 62 *Columbia L. Rev.* 938, 1962.
Handler, M., 'The polarities of anti-trust', 60 *Northwestern University L. Rev.* 751, 1966.
Korah, V., *Monopolies and Restrictive Practices*, Stevens, 1968.
Lilienthal, D., *Big Business: A New Era*, Harper & Row, 1953.
Report of the Attorney General's National Committee to Study the Anti-Trust Laws, American Bar Association, 1955.
Rowley, C. K., *The British Monopolies Commission*, Allen & Unwin, 1966.
Stevens, R. B., and Yamey, B. S., *The Restrictive Practices Court: A Study of the Judicial Process and Economic Policy*, Weidenfeld & Nicolson, 1965.

Chapter Nine: Corporate Power, the Individual and the State

Berle, A. A., *The Twentieth-Century Capitalist Revolution*, Harcourt, Brace & World, 1954.
Berle, A. A., *Power*, Harcourt, Brace & World, 1969.
Berle, A. A., and Means, G. C., *The Modern Corporation and Private Property*, Harcourt, Brace & World, 1932; rev. edn, 1968.
Christensen, T. G. S., 'Union discipline under federal law: institutional dilemmas in an industrial democracy', 43 *New York University L. Rev.* 227, 1968.

Carlston, K. S., *Law and Structures of Social Action*, Stevens, 1956.

Drucker, P., *The Concept of the Corporation*, John Day, 1946.

Economist Intelligence Unit, *Growth and Spread of Multinational Companies*, 1969.

Eells, R. S. F., *The Government of Corporations*, Free Press, 1962.

Etelson, J. I., and Smith, F. N. Jr., 'Union discipline under the Landrum-Griffin act', 82 *Harvard L. Rev.* 727, 1969.

Friedmann, W., and Garner, J. F. (eds.), *Government Enterprise*, Stevens, 1970.

Galbraith, J. K., *American Capitalism: The Concept of Countervailing Power*, Houghton Mifflin, 1952.

Galbraith, J. K., *The New Industrial State*, Houghton Mifflin, 1967.

Glicsberg, R., 'New law threatens private foundations', 32 *J. Taxation* 156, 1970.

Gower, L. C. B., *Modern Company Law*, 3rd edn; Gower, Park, Weaver & Wedderburn, 1969; p. 57 *et seq*. 'The future of company law in a mixed economy'.

Kahn-Freund, O., 'Trade unions, the law and society', 33 *Mod. L. Rev.* 241, 1970.

Kahn-Freund, O., *Labour Law: Old Traditions and New Developments*, Clarke, Irwin, 1968.

Latham, E., *The Group Basis of Politics*, Cornell University Press, 1952.

Lenhoff, A., 'The problems of compulsory unionism in Europe', 5 *Amer. J. Comp. L.* 18, 1956.

Lilienthal, D., *Big Business: A New Era*, Harper & Row, 1952.

Mason, E. S., *The Corporation in Modern Society*, Harvard University Press, 1960.

Christie, I. M., *The Liability of Strikers in the Law of Tort*, Queens University Industrial Relations Center, 1967.

Pelling, H., 'Trade unions, workers and the law', in *Popular Politics and Society in Late Victorian Britain*, Macmillan, 1968.

Report of the Royal Commission on Trade Unions and Employers' Associations, 1965–8.

Renner, K. *The Intsitutions of Private Law and their Social Functions*, Routledge & Kegan Paul, 1949

Ruder, D. S., 'Public Obligations of Private Corporations', 114 *University of Pennsylvania L. Rev.* 209, 1965.

Shonfield A., *Modern Capitalism*, Oxford University Press, 1969.

Summers, C. W., 'American legislation for union democracy', 25 *Mod. L. Rev.* 373, 1963.

Selznick, P., *Law, Society and Industrial Justice*, Russell Sage Foundation 1969.

Vagts, D. F., 'The multi-national enterprise: a new challenge for international law', 83 *Harvard L. Rev.* 739, 1970.

Walton, C. C., *Corporate Social Responsibilities*, Wadsworth, 1967.

Weaver, W., *US Philanthropic Foundations*, Harper & Row, 1967.

Wedderburn, K. W., *The Worker and the Law*, Penguin, 2nd edn, 1971.

Chapter Ten: The Growth of Administration and the Evolution of Public Law

Benjafield, D. G., and Whitmore, H., *Principles of Australian Administrative Law*, Law Book Co. Ltd, 4th edn, 1971.

Davis, K., *Administrative Law Treatise*, West Publishing, 4 vols., 1958.
Davis, K. C., *Discretionary Justice: A Preliminary Inquiry*, Louisiana State University Press, 1969.
Gellhorn, W., *Individual Freedom and Government Restraints*, Louisiana State University Press, 1956.
Griffith, J. A. G., and Street, H., *Principles of Administrative Law*, Pitman, 4th edn, 1967.
Lawson, H., 'Dicey revisited', 7 *Political Studies* 109, 207, 1959.
Long, M. T., Weil, P., and Braibant, G., *Les Grands Arrêts de la Jurisprudence Administrative*, Sirey, 5th edn, 1969.
Mitchell, J. D. B., *The Contracts of Public Authorities; A Comparative Study*, University of London, 1954.
Parker, R., 'The historic basis of administrative law: separation of powers and judicial supremacy', 12 *Rutgers L. Rev.* 449, 1958.
de Smith, S., *Judicial Review of Administrative Action*, Stevens, 2nd edn, 1968.
Street, H., *Governmental Liability; A Comparative Survey*, Cambridge University Press, 1953.
Waline, M., *Droit administratif*, Editions Sirey, 9th edn, 1963.

Chapter Eleven: Government Liability, Administrative Discretion and the Individual

van Alstyne, A., 'Governmental tort liability: a decade of change', *University of Illinois L. Forum* 919, 1966.
Davis, K., 'Tort liability of governmental units', 40 *Minnesota L. Rev.* 751, 1955.
Davis, K, *Administrative Law Treatise*, West Publishing, 4 vols., 1958.
Friedmann, W., and Garner, J. F. (eds.) *Government Enterprise*, Stevens, 1970.
Imbodon, M., *Der verwaltungsrechtliche Vertrag*, Helbing & Lichtenhohn, 1959.
Harper, F. V., and James, F., *The Law of Torts* § 29.1–29.15, Little, Brown, 1956, Supp., 1968.
Langrod, G., 'Administrative contracts', 4 *Amer. J. Comp. Law* 325, 1955.
Leflar, R. A., and Kantgrowicz, B. E., 'Tort liability of the states', 29 *New York University L. Rev.* 1363, 1954.
Long, M., Weil, P., and Braibant, G., *Les Grands Arrêts de la Jurisprudence Administrative*, Sirey, 5th edn, 1969.
Mitchell, J. D. B., *The Contracts of Public Authorities; A Comparative Study*, University of London, 1954.
Street, H., *Governmental Liability; A Comparative Study*, Cambridge University Press, 1953.
Waline, M., *Droit Administratif*, Editions Sirey, 9th edn, 1963.
Wedderburn, K. W., 'Sovereign immunities of foreign public corporations', 6 *Int'l & Comp. L.Q.* 290, 1957.
Williams, G. L., *Crown Proceedings*, Stevens, 1948.

Chapter Twelve: The Problem of Administrative Remedies and Procedures

Benjafield, D. G., and Whitmore, H., *Principles of Australian Administrative Law*, Law Book Co. Ltd., 4th edn, 1971.

Davis, K., *Administrative Law Text*, West Publishing, 1959.

Friedmann, W., *The State and the Rule of Law in the Mixed Economy*, Stevens, 1971.

Gellhorn, W., *Ombudsmen and Others*, Harvard University Press, 1966.

Griffith, J. A. G., and Street, H., *Principles of Administrative Law*, Pitman, 4th edn, 1967.

Hamson, C. J., *Executive Discretion and Judicial Control*, Stevens, 1954.

Schwartz, B., *French Administrative Law and the Common Law World*, New York University Press, 1954.

Street, H., *Justice in the Welfare State*, Stevens, 1968.

Chapter Thirteen: National Sovereignty and World Order in the Nuclear Age

Clark, G., and Sohn, L. B., *World Peace through World Law*, Harvard University Press, 3rd rev edn, 1966.

Falk, R. A., *Legal Order in a Violent World*, Princeton University Press, 1968.

Falk, R. A., and Mendlovitz, S., *The Strategy of World Order*, World Law Fund, 4 vols., 1966.

Greenberg, J., and Shalit, A. R., 'New horizons for human rights: the European convention, court and commission for human rights', 63 *Columbia L. Rev.* 1384, 1963.

McDougal, M. S., and Associates, *Studies in World Public Order*, Yale University Press, 1960.

McDougal, M. S., and Feliciano, F. P., *Law and Minimum World Public Order*, Yale University Press, 1961.

Schachter, O., 'The relation of law, politics and actions in the United Nations', 1 *Recueil des Cours* 166, 1963.

Stone, J., *Legal Controls of International Conflict*, Holt, Rinehart & Winston, 1954.

Weil, G. L., *The European Convention on Human Rights*, A. W. Sijthoff, 1963.

Chapter Fourteen: The Broadening Scope of International Law

Fatouros, A. A., *Government Guarantees to Foreign Investors*, Columbia University Press, 1962.

Fawcett, J. E. S., 'Legal aspects of state trading', 25 *Brit. Ybk Int'l L.* 35, 1948.

Friedman, S., *Expropriation in International Law*, Stevens, 1953.

Friedmann, W., *The Changing Structure of International Law*, Stevens, 1964.

Jenks, C. W., *The Common Law of Mankind*, Praeger, Stevens, 1958.

Jessup, P. C., *Transnational Law*, Yale University Press; Oxford University Press, 1956.

Mann, F. A., 'The law governing state contracts', 21 *Brit. Ybk Int'l L.* 11, 33, 1944.

Mann, F. A., 'Reflections on a commercial law of nations', 33 *Brit. Ybk Int'l L.* 20, 1957.

McDougal, M. S., 'International law, power, and policy: a contemporary conception', 82 *Recueil des Cours* 137, 1953.

Roth, A. H., *The Minimum Standard of International Law Applied to Aliens*, A. W. Sijthoff, 1949.

Reuter, P., *Institutions Internationales*, Presses Universitaires de France, 5th edn, 1967.

Röling, B. V. A., *International Law in an Expanded World*, Djanbaton, 1960.

Schwarzenberger, G., 'The principles and standards of international economic law', 117 *Recueil des Cours* 7, 1966.

Seyid Muhammad, V., *The Legal Framework of World Trade*, Stevens, 1958.

Verbit, G. P., *Trade Agreements for Developing Countries*, Columbia University Press, 1969.

Chapter Fifteen: The Rule of Law, the Individual and the Welfare State

Denning, A. T., *Freedom under the Law*, Stevens, 1949.

Friedmann, W., *Legal Theory*, pp. 422–9, Stevens, 5th edn, 1967.

Friedmann, W., *The State and the Rule of Law in the Mixed Economy*, Stevens, 1971.

Fuller, L. L., *The Morality of Law*, Yale University Press, rev. edn, 1969.

Goodhart, A. L., 'The rule of law and absolute sovereignty', 106 *University of Pennsylvania L. Rev.* 943, 1958.

Hale, R. L., *Freedom through Law*, Columbia University Press, 1952.

Hayek, F. A. von, *The Road to Serfdom*, University of Chicago Press, 1944.

Hayek, F. A. von, *The Constitution of Liberty*, University of Chicago Press, 1960.

Jones, H. A., 'The rule of law and the welfare state', 58 *Columbia L. Rev.* 143, 1958.

Marsh, A., 'Defining the rule of law, *Listener*, 28 May 1959; 'Freedom and legislative power', *Listener*, 4 June 1959.

Reich, C., 'The law of the planned society', 75 *Yale L.J.* 1227, 1966.

Index

For general Readings see also the details of the Table of Contents. Only those authors and judges whose views are quoted or discussed are listed. For a full bibliography see the list of references.

Herbert, A. P., 26

Hewart, Lord Chief Justice, 79

Holmes, O. W., 157, 161, 190

Homosexual offences and prostitution, Committee on, 193, 194, 201

Homosexuality, 200–201

House of Lords, 49, 50, 51, 55, 60, 66, 78, 79, 103, 167

Humanae Vitae (papal encyclical), 261–2

Human Rights, 59 (Canada), 68–74 (US), 503–4

Illegitimacy, 281–4

Immunity, Governmental, 29, 165–7, 415–18, 479–80

India, 26, 31, 35, 340

Individual freedom
group power and, 346–7, 366–72
labour unions, and, 347–64
public power and, 437–8
status, contrast with, 498–500

Individual responsibility, 221–4, 503

International Court of Justice, 84–7, 484

Indus Basin Development Fund, 451–2

Industrial accident insurance, 169

Industrial development, 99–102, 129, 130–32, 162, 164

Industrial Relations Commission (UK), 151, 364

Industrial Reorganization Corporation, 301–2, 307, 309, 341–2

Industrial tribunals, 149

Injunction in administrative law, 427

Institutionalized giving, 317–20

Insurance
automobile accidents, 171–3
industrial accident insurance, 169–71
reform proposals, 173–7
social insurance, 169–71, 178, 179, 181–7
tort liability, relation to, 158–9, 180–87

International Bank for Reconstruction and Development, 456

International Civil Aviation Organization, 456

International Court of Justice, 448, 452, 453, 455

International economic development law, 470–72

International Labour Organization (ILO), 456

International law
communist theories of, 458–9
compensation *see* Minimum standards of justice
continental shelf, 452–5
discrimination against aliens, 486
due process, 491–2
economic development and, 470–75
equality of states, 446–7
estoppel, 489–90
expropriation, 484–91
freedom of the seas, 452–5
friendship and commerce treaties (US), 490–91
general principles of law, 484, 487–90
government immunities, 479–82
human welfare and, 466–8
international rivers, 451
judicial law-making and, 84–7
League of Nations, 445–6
minimum standards of justice, 482–4
most-favoured-nation clause, 476–8
national sovereignty and, 445–64
nationalization, of foreign interests *see* Expropriation
pacta sunt servanda, 487–8
private corporations and, 470–72
regional groupings, 455–7
scope of, 458–64, 465–70
state responsibility *see* Minimum standards of justice
state trading, 472–9
subjects of, 468–70
territorial waters, 450, 452–5
United Nations *see* United Nations
unjust enrichment, 488–9

International Law Commission, 470